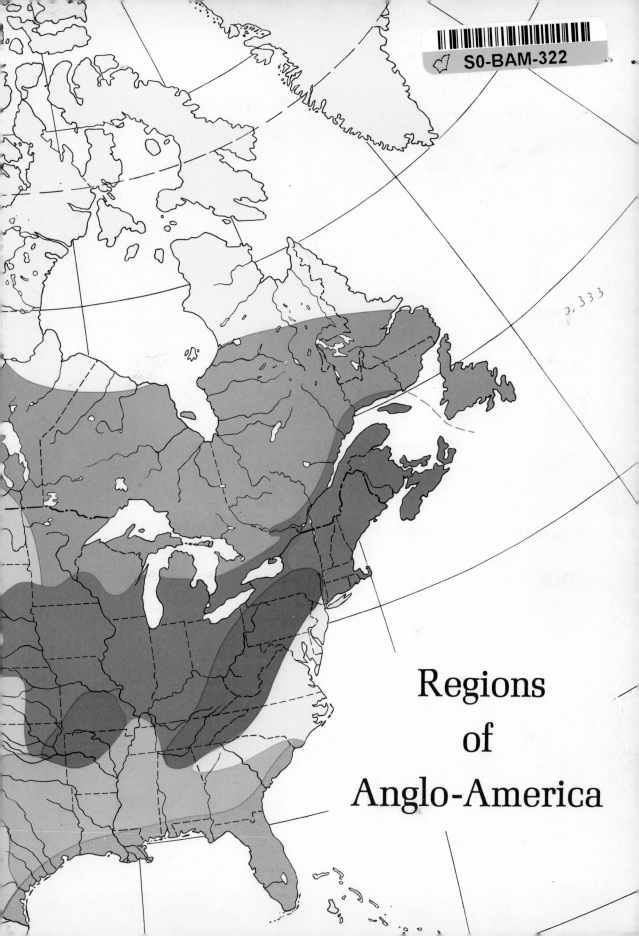

p. 333

Regions
of
Anglo-America

917
W58r   63207

egional

Geography

glo-America

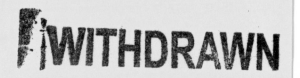

C. Langdon White • Edwin J. Foscue • Tom L. McKnight

Professor Emeritus
Stanford University
Professor, San Jose State College

Professor Emeritus
Department of Geography
Southern Methodist University

Associate Professor of Geography
University of California
Los Angeles

PRENTICE-HALL, INC., ENGLEWOOD CLIFFS, N. J.

Regional

Geography

of Anglo-America

third edition

Current printing (last digit):

13 12 11 10 9 8 7 6

REGIONAL GEOGRAPHY OF
ANGLO-AMERICA, 3rd ed.

C. Langdon White, Edwin J. Foscue,
Tom L. McKnight

© 1943, 1954, 1964 BY PRENTICE-HALL, INC.
ENGLEWOOD CLIFFS, N. J.

PRENTICE-HALL INTERNATIONAL, INC., *London*
PRENTICE-HALL OF AUSTRALIA, PTY., LTD., *Sydney*
PRENTICE-HALL OF CANADA, LTD., *Toronto*
PRENTICE-HALL FRANCE, S.A.R.L., *Paris*
PRENTICE-HALL OF JAPAN, INC., *Tokyo*
PRENTICE-HALL DE MEXICO, S.A., *Mexico City*

Library of Congress Catalog Card No. 64-10071
PRINTED IN THE UNITED STATES OF AMERICA [C]

Preface

Regions are formed by man as he adjusts himself to his natural environment rather than by arbitrary survey lines resulting from historical settlement and the various acts of legislatures. Canada and the United States are not compact, single economic units, but each consists of numerous parts having their own economies based upon distinctive natural environments. Few generalizations are applicable to the whole of the United States or Canada. Since regions vary in such natural elements as location, climate, landforms, soils, water, minerals, fauna and flora, man tends to think and react differently in each region in dealing with such factors.

Geographical contiguity and similarity of economic and defense problems have created a sense of interdependence between Canada and the United States. Moreover, American movies, telecommunications, magazines, mechanical devices, and the friendship resulting from movement back and forth across the border, have created a strong community of interest between the two peoples.

The reader of this volume will see how a people took possession of the land and how the land took possession of a people. He will become aware of the fact that the population is by no means evenly distributed through this living space, and the geographical factors are largely responsible for the uneven distribution.

The flowering of civilization in Anglo-America is partly a reflection of the degree to which man has levied tribute against the natural resources. From the Atlantic to the Pacific and from the Arctic to the Gulf, the white man has been a destroyer. Pioneers could not think about the distant future; but the day of the pioneer is past. Today no more good virgin land, well-located or potentially productive, stands ready for the plow. There are no new frontiers. The future standard of living of Anglo-Americans depends upon how well they use the land they already have. It is for this reason that conservation of natural resources is discussed repeatedly throughout the book.

Canada and the United States have a common heritage and have been moving toward similar goals. Geographical factors and the rapidly changing technology of modern warfare have developed a common war and defense strategy. It is clear that mutual endeavor and good faith based on an understanding of the problems of the two countries would augur for success in the struggle for enduring peace and prosperity.

This book is not a simple compendium of facts. Wherever possible, facts are shown by maps or photographs, since most human knowledge is gained through the eye, and the language of pictures and maps is universal.

The textual material has been used in the classroom many times by the authors. Frequently a significant question or comment by a keen student has been incorporated. So have many ideas of professors who have used the book. The authors have traveled widely over the continent and have carried on field investigations in many of the regions.

Agreement has been lacking among geographers on suitable names for the various regions of Anglo-America. Accordingly, a number of Anglo-America's leading geographers were consulted, and the titles used here are those suggested by the largest number of persons.

The major changes in the third edition include:

(1) updating of all, and rewriting of much, of the text;
(2) redrawing of all the maps;
(3) the use of many photographs; and
(4) the inclusion of the Hawaiian Islands as a region of Anglo-America.

The attention of the student is called to the appendices, which, although located at the end of the text, contain information of both physical features and human occupance that is introductory in nature.

Acknowledgements

In writing this book, the authors have leaned heavily upon many geographers and colleagues in the closely related natural and social sciences. They have benefited also from the labors of numerous government employees who have collected statistical material, carried on surveys, and made maps. They have drawn especially upon articles in the professional geographical journals. Accordingly, the number to whom they are grateful is so large that only a general acknowledgement is possible. When quotations are used, the sources are cited in appropriate footnotes. The authors wish especially to express thanks to those colleagues who have commented critically upon specific chapters. They were consulted because they live within a given region or have made that region their special field of research and are, therefore, especially familiar with it. The authors wish to make clear, however, that these critics are not responsible for any mistakes in fact or philosophy. They are: S. Earl Brown, Ohio State University; G. Loyd Collier, Mississippi Southern University; Arthur H. Doerr, University of Oklahoma; Albert G. Farley, University of British Columbia; Louis Gentilcore, McMaster University; James P. Latham, Bowling Green State University; Stanley Ross, Arizona State University; Charles B. Varney, University of Florida; and William H. Wallace, University of New Hampshire.

The authors also wish to thank Marylee McKnight, who devoted many months of her time to problems connected with this volume, and William Mitchell, who skillfully prepared the maps for this third edition.

Stanford, California
Dallas, Texas
Los Angeles, California
January 8, 1964

C. Langdon White
Edwin J. Foscue
Tom L. McKnight

Table of Contents

Maps,
Illustrations,
and Tables

Tables

Regional
Geography
of Anglo-America

chapter one

Anglo-America
and
Its Regions

The Western Hemisphere usually is divided, on a geographical basis, into North America and South America. A division on the basis of cultural and economic contrasts, however, breaks the Hemisphere into Anglo-America (Figure 1-1) and Latin America.

Anglo-America comprises the United States, Canada, and Greenland.[1] Superficially, Canada and the United States appear to be compact economic units, and in our everyday practice we assume that they are sufficiently uniform throughout to make generalizations that can apply to the two nations as wholes. Close study and inspection, however, reveal that such a practice is not justifiable. Generalizations about the

[1] Quebec and Greenland are insular concentrations of French and Danish nationalities and Hawaii contains strong elements of Polynesian and Oriental culture in the otherwise (except for Indians and Eskimos) predominantly English continent.

1

whole of either nation force a vast number of unlike units into the same category. Actually these countries are mosaics composed of a large number of dissimilar pieces. Geographers call these pieces *regions*.

It is well known that people vary, in speech, customs, etc., from region to region. There is, however, no agreement as to why this is so. One school attributes this variation to the natural environment, asserting that the differences remain despite the mobility and fluidity of the people. Thus streams and counterstreams of migrants have flowed, sometimes mingling, from one end of Anglo-America to the other. Yet, this school maintains that despite these migrations and the great levelers of mass media, Americans and Canadians are not homogeneous peoples. The Southerner, Middle

Westerner, New Englander, Great Plainsman, Westerner, and Newfoundlander all have their individual manners and customs. This school asserts that so long as the various parts of Anglo-America differ markedly in climate and soils, water supply and minerals, flora and fauna, geographical location and landforms, just so long will man behave differently in adjusting himself to these factors.

The other school does not deny the importance of the natural environment, but insists that the physical quality of the land is not equally significant for all men at all times; rather, the physical land, or resource base, must be re-evaluated in each region and at each historical period in terms of the attitudes, objectives, and technical abilities of the settlers. According to this school the resulting variation in the occupance of different regions is more closely related to culture than to nature. In short, this school believes that so long as the land remains relatively changeless, man, the active agent, determines how the land will affect his use of it. The natural environment is passive.[2]

Thus both schools utilize regions for geographical study, and the spokesmen of both schools are eminent geographers.

These differences in development will be noted later in the chapters on specific regions. Compare, for example, the Great Plains Region with any other in Anglo-America. Small, unrelated groups of settlers entered the Great Plains and, without an understanding of the climate, began adjusting themselves to this new kind of natural environment. They had to unlearn much of what they formerly knew about farming; they even had to develop and use different tools. Today the region is politically unstable; the people have a gambler's

Figure 1-1. The Americas — Anglo and Latin.

[2] Preston E. James, "Toward a Further Understanding of the Regional Concept," *Annals of the Association of American Geographers*, Vol. 42 (September 1952), pp. 220-21.

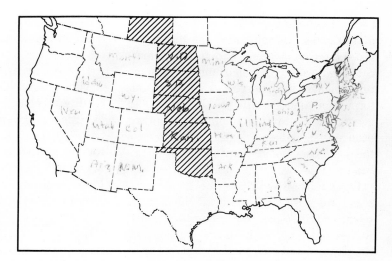

Figure 1-2. The states and provinces losing population during the years 1930–1940 — the decade of the "black blizzards."

psychology because of their constant conflict with the vagaries of nature (wind, rain or lack of it, hail, blizzards, dust storms, and insect pests). When their crops and livestock do well, the farmers reinvest their profits; but when things go badly, they call upon their government for help or migrate in large numbers, as they did during the days of the "Dust Bowl" (Figure 1-2). This region has accordingly witnessed a long pageant of political movements and events. Actually there is nothing wrong with the Great Plains folks; their tribulations stem from the fact that the people have geared their human geography to the good years and not to the bad, nor even to the average ones. The one thing with which these people have been equipped has been a superabundance of hope—hope particularly for the following year's rainfall. In order to fulfill these hopes and bring stability to this region, the governments of both countries supply crop-planting and many other kinds of advice and assistance.

The United States and Canada are unions composed of many units, each with its own peculiar and distinctive economy, an economy based upon its own sources of wealth, each dominated by self-interest and competing with every other unit.

This book will treat Anglo-America by regions, with broad sweeps of the brush, because it is hoped that this treatment will bring readers to a fuller appreciation of regionalism, a vital concept to those who seek a better understanding of the world around them. Nation-wide businesses, for example, usually employ regional systems. Montgomery Ward and Company and Sears, Roebuck and Company maintain mail-order houses in various cities, each serving an assigned region. Federal Reserve Districts, Army Corps Areas, wholesale trade areas, and many other sorts of regional breakdowns have been devised by businessmen and other administrators as a means of coping with the varied problems and opportunities that they face in operations that cover such extensive areas as the United States and/or Canada. By working with large units, regional geography can make a real contribution to understanding national life. This method of approach provides the best opening to an understanding of Anglo-America's fundamental achievement, for people live and work together as units of a geographical region far more than they do as citizens of a state or province. The Federal Reserve Act of 1913, which divided the United States into 12 Federal Reserve Districts, the boundaries of which sometimes divide states, has reinforced the thesis that state lines are often inadequate demarcators of viable economic units. For some time scholars have perceived a lack of uniformity in American life and attitudes, and geographers, historians, political scientists, economists, and sociologists all recognize the significance of regions and of regionalism.

Geography, which links the data of the social sciences with those of the natural sciences, is a logical discipline for dealing with regions. It sees in the region not only the physical and biological, the social, political, and economic factors but it synthesizes them. In short, it considers the region in its totality—not merely as things that are there, but all the processes and relationships now operating and those that will presumably occur in the future. As J. Russell Smith once said, "The geographer is like the builder of a house who takes brick, stone, sand, cement, nails, wire, lath, boards, shingles, and glass —the products of many industries—and builds them into a symmetrical structure which is not any one of the many things that have entered into it, but is instead a house for the occupancy of man."

Region and *section* are used synonymously by some social scientists. *Section,* as a historical term, was made famous in the essays of Frederick Jackson Turner. The sociologists Odum and Moore speak of the divisive power of self-seeking "sections" and the integrating power of coordinated "regions" fabricated into a united whole.[3]

Among geographers, sectionalism is inseparably associated with politics, emotionalism, and sentiment; therefore, as currently used, it adds only confusion to the geographer's study of areal differentiation. Re-

gionalism, on the other hand, provides the motif for economic organization.

The Geographical Region

The geographical region includes the totality of place and people in association. Whittlesey, James, and others use the term *compage* as an areal concept based on the totality of the human occupance. It is defined without reference to the physical or biotic regions with which it might profitably be compared. Preston James says:

> I would draw surface regions, climatic regions, vegetation regions, and "compages," and then compare their area spread, never expecting them to coincide. In fact, if they did, I would suspect something to be wrong because of the nature of regions.[4]

Every region has a core area of personality and individuality, in which the regional characteristics are best exemplified. The core possesses two distinct qualities which may be blurred in the periphery:

a. It differs noticeably from neighboring core areas.

b. It exists as a recognizable and coherent segment of space defined by the criteria whereby it is selected.

Beyond the core lies a marginal area. Regional boundaries are usually not lines but rather transitional zones that partake of the character of adjoining regions or cores. The width may vary from a few feet to many miles. Thus the field geographer making his reconnaissance survey seldom knows when he leaves one region and enters another. At some point, of course, he passes from one to the other, but the human eye cannot usually perceive it at the moment of change. The distinguishing features of one region melt gradually into those of the neighboring region, save along a mountain range, along the shore of a large body of water, or at the border of a desert.

---

[3] H. W. Odum and H. E. Moore, *American Regionalism: A Cultural-Historical Approach to National Integration* (New York: Holt, Rinehart, & Winston, Inc., 1938).

[4] Preston E. James, personal communication.

Regionalism is something felt by the people who occupy the unit—a kind of collective consciousness. No region in Anglo-America corresponds exactly to state, provincial, or physical boundaries.

While most geographers agree that regional geography is the heart of their subject—that it is even the final goal of the discipline—they nonetheless admit that there is one glaring weakness: the statistics (quantitative data concerning the functions and functioning of communities) produced by the various data-collecting organizations are applicable only to statistical regions and very seldom indeed do the boundaries of geographical and statistical regions coincide. This is unfortunate, for the data should have a more specific meaning for the classes of problems with which they are concerned. The fact that the boundaries of states, counties, townships, and other civil divisions are often nonfunctional has fostered an attitude that the data collected for these units are seriously deficient for research use. To ameliorate this situation, various refined statistical units, such as urbanized areas, standard metropolitan statistical areas, state economic areas, industrial areas, and labor market areas have been designated. These new divisions are intended to represent the fundamental physical structure of the United States economy.

In many respects they might be considered synonymous with geographical regions; certainly in most instances their cores are identical. If geographers will try to see eye-to-eye with the groups working on these "economic regions," the difficult problem of fitting statistics to regions might be well on the way to solution.[5]

Geographical regions obviously occur at different levels of subdivision. In this text

[5] Students interested in the "economic regions" should consult Donald J. Bogue and Calvin L. Beale, *Economic Areas of the United States* (New York: Free Press of Glencoe, Inc., 1961).

the region sometimes is comprised of several minor areas called subregions.

Determination of Regions

The geographical region has already been defined. Dividing a continent into regions is a matter of "scientific generalizing" and is not, as someone once remarked, "merely a pedagogical device to facilitate the presentation of geographical material to classes of students," although it may admittedly serve this latter purpose.

One recognizes a region by noting the intimate association existing between peoples of like interest and the area they occupy. Similarity of interest may and often does indicate a similarity of natural environmental conditions. In the American Manufacturing Belt, especially the part west of the Appalachians, a large segment of the population thinks and talks in terms of iron and steel and the many products derived from them; in fact, iron and steel are called the "barometer of industry," because nearly all manufacturing enterprises depend upon them in some way. East of the mountains, though iron and steel are still important, manufacturing includes nearly the whole gamut of fabricated products. In the Agricultural Interior to the west, however, the people are vitally interested in corn, oats, tobacco, fruit, hay, hogs, and beef and dairy cattle as the economic barometers of life. In either region, the natural environment is a factor in the popular interests.

The Cultural Landscape in Regional Analysis

Geographers deal with both natural and cultural landscapes. Everyone who has traveled, even if only slightly, has noted that the natural landscape changes from one part of the country to another. When two greatly unlike areas are neighbors, the geographer may separate them on his map by a line, thereby recognizing them as separate natural regions. Similarly, he may study the cultural or man-made landscape, and resolve it into separate cultural regions.

Whenever man comes into any area, he promptly modifies its natural landscape, "not in a haphazard way but according to the culture system which he brings with him. . . . Culture is the agent, the natural area is the medium, the cultural landscape the result." [6] He cuts down the forest, plows under the native grass, raises domesticated animals, erects houses and buildings, builds fences, constructs roads, railroads, telephone and telegraph lines, digs canals, builds bridges, and tunnels under mountains. All this constitutes the "cultural landscape."

Geography, however, consists of more than the mere distribution of men and things in the landscape. The distribution of races or climates or landforms by themselves is never geography. Rather it is ethnology, climatology, and geology or geomorphology. Such distributions become geographi-

[6] Isaiah Bowman, *Geography in Relation to the Social Sciences* (New York: Charles Scribner's Sons, 1934), pp. 149-50.

cally significant only as they function in the mutual relationship of mankind to natural environment, as these relations are themselves recorded in the landscape (Figure 1-3).

Are Regions Fixed?

In several of the disciplines closely related to geography, the regional systems are fixed by nature; climatic, pedologic, physiographic, and vegetation regions are all based on static or almost static natural boundaries. Geographical regions, however, are not fixed; instead of having hard and fast boundary lines, they have ever-changing ones. When man pushes wheat culture farther north in Canada or farther west in Kansas, or when he grows cotton farther north and west in Texas or Oklahoma, he is responsible for changes in geographical regions, because raising wheat or cotton may be of such significance in the regional totality that a shifting of cultivation limits requires a similar shifting of regional boundaries.

Figure 1-3. Indian corn — showing man's close adjustment to the rainfall regime. Note the large hills widely spaced in each direction. The soil is sandy and the surface layers are dry in spring so that deep planting is necessary in order to place the seed in contact with moist soil. (Courtesy of Soil Conservation Service.)

Sequent Occupance

Sequent occupance is a concept supporting the principle that the significance of the physical environment changes as the attitudes, objectives, and technical abilities of the people living in it change. It is a succession of different modes and patterns of man's penetration and use of the landscape.

One studies sequent occupance by studying the man-land relationship in a particular region within a period during which the culture of the people remains essentially unchanged. With any change, such as the opening of new land to fur trappers or the advent of steam transportation, a new period of sequent occupance begins.

The Goal of Regional Geography

We have seen that Anglo-America is a fabric of regions. As we go from chapter to chapter we will see that it is the functioning of these interrelated areas that gives us our balance between regional and national life through specialization on one hand and integration on the other. Regional study is useful in social science research and in governmental regional planning, because it provides the most useful framework within which to organize the use of resources. Regional inventories can determine what resources are available, and regional plans can provide for their wisest use.

Every region offers to its people a certain range of possibilities. The actual use made of these possibilities, however, depends to a very great extent upon the economic, social, and cultural heritage of the people. In other words, such additional factors as ideals, psychology, and inherited intellectual habits—all derived from the inhabitants of a region—function along with the natural environment.

As each of the following chapters is considered in its turn, the reader will see that there is a mutual relationship (cultural,

psychological, and economic) between the people of the region and the conditions of the natural environment. He will also get a broad picture of the current conditions of life in the different parts of the continent. Finally, he will have ample opportunity to judge the proposition that the division of Anglo-America into geographical regions provides the most meaningful way to understand the whole.

Regions of Anglo-America

In this book Anglo-America is divided into sixteen regions. The criteria chosen for making the regional divisions are both multiple and varied. In some cases physical considerations have been dominant and in others cultural factors have been more important. But in all instances the broad regions defined reflect as accurately as possible the basic features of homogeneity inherent in the various parts of Anglo-America at the present time. In general, the principal criteria used in determining regional boundaries are the socioeconomic conditions currently characteristic, which, of course, often have been decisively influenced by the physical environment and/or historical development. The regions, as shown in Figure 1-4, are as follows:

1. The American Manufacturing Region
2. Northeastern Anglo-America
3. The Atlantic Coastal Plain and the Piedmont
4. The Appalachians and the Ozarks
5. The Cotton Belt
6. The Humid Subtropical Coast
7. The Agricultural Interior
8. The Northern Continental Forest
9. The Great Plains
10. The Rocky Mountains
11. Intermontane Basins and Plateaus
12. The Subtropical Pacific Coast
13. The Hawaiian Islands
14. The North Pacific Coast
15. The Yukon-Kuskokwim Basins
16. The Tundra

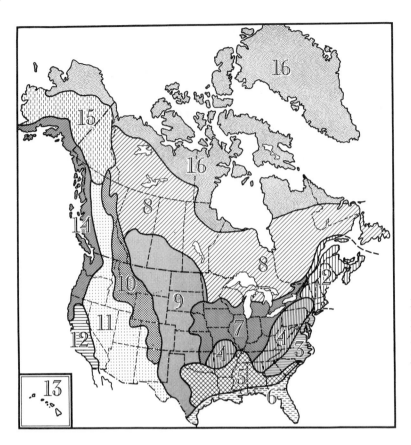

Figure 1-4. Geographic regions of Anglo-America. The numbers on the map correspond to the numbers of the regions listed on page 7. Note that region 1, *The American Manufacturing Region,* is omitted from the map. For details concerning this region see figures 3-1 and 3-2, pages 33 and 34.

Selected Bibliography

Davidson, Donald, "Where Regionalism and Sectionalism Meet," *Social Forces,* Vol. 13, October 1934, pp. 23-31.

Hesseltine, William B., "Regions, Classes and Sections in American History," *Journal of Land and Public Utility Economics,* Vol. 20, 1944, pp. 35-44.

James, Preston, "Toward a Further Understanding of the Regional Concept," *Annals of the Association of American Geographers,* Vol. 42, September 1952, pp. 195-222.

Jensen, Merrill, *Regionalism in America.* Madison: University of Wisconsin Press, 1952.

Mumford, L., "Regionalism and Irregionalism," *Sociological Review,* October 1927, April 1928.

Odum, H. W., "Regionalism vs. Sectionalism in the South's Place in the National Economy," *Social Forces,* Vol. 12, March 1934, pp. 338-354.

Platt, Robert S., "Field Approach to Regions," *Annals of the Association of American Geographers,* Vol 25, 1935, pp. 153-174.

"Regionalism in the United States," *Current History,* Vol. 40, May 1961, pp. 257-297.

Roach, H. G., "Sectionalism in Congress, 1870-1890," *American Political Science Review,* Vol. 19, August 1925, pp. 500-526.

Selected General Bibliography on Canada and the United States

Alexandersson, Gunnar, *The Industrial Structure of American Cities.* Lincoln: University of Nebraska Press, 1956.

Atwood, Wallace W., *The Physiographic Provinces of North America.* New York: Ginn and Company, 1940.

Bogue, Donald J., and Calvin L. Beale, *Economic Areas of the United States.* New York: The Free Press of Glencoe, Inc., 1961.

Brown, Ralph H., *Historical Geography of the United States*. New York: Harcourt, Brace & World, Inc., 1948.

Bureau of Commercial Fisheries, *Fishery Statistics of the United States*. Washington: U.S. Government Printing Office, annual.

Bureau of Mines, *Mineral Facts and Problems*. Washington: U.S. Government Printing Office, 1960.

Bureau of Mines, *Mineral Yearbook*. Washington: U.S. Government Printing Office, 3 vols., annual.

Calef, Wesley C., and Howard J. Nelson, "Distribution of Negro Population in the United States," *Geographical Review*, Vol. 46, January 1956, pp. 82-97.

Dominion Bureau of Statistics, *Canada*. Ottawa: Queen's Printer and Controller of Stationery, annual.

Dominion Bureau of Statistics, *Canada Year Book*. Ottawa: Queen's Printer and Controller of Stationery, annual.

Forest Service, *Timber Resources for America's Future*. Washington: U.S. Government Printing Office, 1958.

Hart, J. Fraser, "The Changing Distribution of the American Negro," *Annals of the Association of American Geographers*, Vol. 50, September 1960, pp. 242-266.

Haystead, Ladd, and Gilbert C. Fite, *The Agricultural Regions of the United States*. Norman: University of Oklahoma Press, 1958.

Higbee, Edward, *American Agriculture: Geography, Resources, Conservation*. New York: John Wiley and Sons, Inc., 1958.

Hills, Theodore L., "Canada," *Focus*, Vol. 9, January 1959.

Klove, Robert C., "The Growing Population of the United States," *Journal of Geography*, Vol. 60, May 1961, pp. 203-213.

Marschner, F. J., *Land Use and Its Patterns in the United States*. Washington: U.S. Government Printing Office, 1959.

Olmstead, Clarence W., "American Orchard and Vineyard Regions," *Economic Geography*, Vol. 32, July 1956, pp. 189-236.

Paterson, J., *North America*. London: Oxford University Press, 1960.

Putnam, Donald F., "Pedogeography of Canada," *Geographical Bulletin*, Vol. 1, 1951, pp. 57-85.

————, Benoit Brouillette, Donald P. Kerr, and J. Lewis Robinson, *Canadian Regions*. New York: Thomas Y. Crowell Company, 1952.

————, and Donald P. Kerr, *A Regional Geography of Canada*. Toronto: J. M. Dent & Sons, 1956.

Riley, C. M., *Our Mineral Resources*. New York: John Wiley & Sons, Inc., 1959.

Shaw, Earl B., *Anglo-America: A Regional Geography*. New York: John Wiley & Sons, Inc., 1959.

Stewart, George R., *U.S. 40: Cross Section of the United States of America*. New York: Houghton Mifflin Co., 1953.

Visher, S. S., *Climatic Atlas of the United States*. Cambridge: Harvard University Press, 1954.

Wright, Alfred J., *United States and Canada: A Regional Geography*. New York: Appleton-Century-Crofts, Inc., 1956.

Zelinsky, Wilbur, "Changes in the Geographic Patterns of Rural Population in the United States 1790-1960," *Geographical Review*, Vol. 52, October 1962, pp. 492-524.

chapter two

The City[1]
and Industrial
Geography

The great city is not new. Ancient Carthage, Alexandria, and Rome all had populations of half a million or more. But they were political creations of great empires; the majority of modern cities are the product of economic-geographic conditions. Prior to the era of steam, few cities had

[1] Viewed *geographically* a city is an area of the earth that is in sharp contrast in appearance, attitudes, and functions to its rural surroundings. The core is its distinguishing characteristic—the quality that gives it personality; its actual boundaries often are difficult to determine. Cities differ one from another much as do people, although in Anglo-American cities the differences in both appearance and function are often more subtle than overt. Nevertheless, it is a truism that cities are important because of the functions that they per-

form. Most cities are more or less multifunctional, but often a single function is predominant. Commercial functions are the most common, but industrial, mining, recreational, political, residential, transportational, educational, and other functions may be particularly noteworthy in some instances.

THE CITY AND INDUSTRIAL GEOGRAPHY

populations of more than 100,000, and it is doubtful whether any city, even such renowned ones as Rome, Nanking, and Peking, ever attained populations of as much as one million. It was not until significant social and economic changes were wrought by the Industrial Revolution that the modern city became possible. On the other hand, the *wholesale growth* of cities is quite recent, because the strategic quality of a place is measurable solely in terms of transportation and communication, and these have experienced major improvements only in modern times. So long as transport facilities were backward, large numbers of people could not be confined to a small area and at the same time be fed and clothed. Thus at the time of the first census, in 1790, the United States was 75 per cent rural.

The principal difference between urban growth in the Old World and in the United States and Canada is the slow evolution of cities in the former and their rapid growth in the latter. In the Old World they grew over a period of centuries from town economies to their present urban caste. In the New World they started as wilderness communities on the outskirts of civilization, bridging the gap from primitive agriculturalism to mature urbanism in little more than a century. Thus Anglo-American cities have almost no past; nearly all have grown up in response to the same influences and they are among themselves far more homogeneous than European cities. There are, of course, variations among them, but these variations are slight indeed. The major influence in the growth of modern United States and Canadian cities has been manufacturing.

Historical Development of Anglo-American Cities

Colonial Period to 1865 In early colonial days small cities sprang up along the Atlantic Seaboard, mostly in what are now New England and the Middle Atlantic States in the United States, and in the Maritime Provinces and Lower St. Lawrence Valley in Canada. This was natural because these areas were nearest England and France, particularly the former, whence came capital goods and many consumer goods. Merchandising establishments were, accordingly, more advantageously located in port cities from which goods could be more readily distributed to interior settlements. Here, too, were the favored locations for assembling raw materials for export and for performing what little processing was necessary prior to shipment abroad. Boston, Philadelphia, New York, Montreal, and several other Atlantic cities throve, and, as the United States and Canada grew, the cities increased in importance.

This was less true in the Colonial South, where life centered around the plantation, rather than the town, as in New England. The local isolation and the economic self-sufficiency of the plantation were antagonistic to the development of towns. Thus, nearly all Southern settlements were located on navigable streams, and each planter owned a wharf accessible to the small shipping of that day; in fact one of the strongest reasons for the planter selecting his land as he did was to have it front on a water highway.

With independence the new nation (the United States) started its career without a single city as large as 50,000 inhabitants; and it was not until 1820 that it had a city of more than 100,000 persons, and not until 1880 that it recorded one in the million class.

From the close of the Revolutionary War until 1823, American industry suffered from economic chills and fevers. Although the war of 1812 temporarily stimulated manufacturing, it was not until after 1823 that it really boomed. The mechanization of spinning and weaving set the pace. Influences were at work drawing farm youths to the cities; such migration was particularly rapid following the Civil War.

The large port cities, especially, grew in size with the building of canals, roads, and railroads. Each began to develop its own railroad and push it westward toward Chicago. Boston alone of the major American ports was forced to content itself with connecting lines; its Boston and Albany Railway never got beyond the Hudson River. There was very little railway development at this time in Maritime Canada. The Grand Trunk Railway, built after 1850 from Chicago through Toronto and Montreal, reached the Atlantic in the United States at Portland, Maine. Hence, Canada had few large Atlantic port cities.

The Period from 1865 to 1914: Era of Great Urban Growth in Anglo-America. As the United States and Canada grew, the coastal cities, particularly in the former, became more and more important. At first manufacturing catered only to local markets; ultimately, however, it served national markets. The Civil War marked a definite turning point in manufacturing in America. The geographical division of labor, a basis for present-day regionalism, was beginning to become apparent by the end of the Civil War period. Then followed a quarter century of accelerated westward movement, rapid population increase, heavy immigration, and accelerated growth of urban centers. Cities found their functions multiplying as the growth of manufacturing became pronounced. Yet, as late as 1890 the economy in Anglo-America was still dominantly agricultural, still highly dependent on trade with Europe.

1914-1930 During this period revolutionary things were happening. The continuous mechanization of farms resulted in a great population movement from farms, hamlets, and villages to cities. Manufacturing was concentrating more and more in cities dur-

ing the early part of this period, but was moving away from the congested central parts of cities during the latter part of the period.

The automobile industry was winning its position as an important new enterprise that not only was soon to become the nation's largest single industry in the value of its product, but also was to become responsible for the explosion of cities and the birth of suburbs.

The techniques of mass production came into their own at this time, embracing particularly such industries as steel, paper, cement, glass, automobiles, and chemicals. And, accompanying mass production, came movements toward standardization, industrial research, and industrial management. Manufacturers turned their attention likewise to marketing techniques, particularly the popularization of installment selling. A stream of new products made their appearance—plastics, radio, and sound movies. Industry became more highly mechanized because labor was comparatively scarce. This scarcity was largely caused by the restriction of immigration in 1924. A wave of industrial consolidations also characterized this period.

1930-1960 By 1930, however, there were more urban than rural people in the United States, and by 1960, 70 per cent of the 183,285,009 people in the nation resided in urban territory and only 30 per cent in rural territory.[2]

By the middle of the twentieth century approximately 20 per cent of the world's population lived in cities of 20,000 or more inhabitants, while the comparable figure for Anglo-America was 42 per cent, the highest proportion of any populous portion of the

2 Bureau of the Census, *United States Census of Population, 1960,* Final Report PC (1)-1A, "United States Summary" (Washington: Government Printing Office, 1961), p. XIV. The 1961 census of Canada showed an urban population of 70 per cent of the total of 18,238,247 population.

globe.[3] Thus the agglomeration of urban population on this continent is not only of recent vintage and sizeable magnitude, but also has occurred at a remarkably rapid rate.

This shift in population from rural to urban areas has resulted in significant occupational changes in the nation; in short, in a little more than a century the United States has been transformed from a rural frontier settlement into a full-fledged industrial society. This change has greatly affected our civilization—our way of living and our ways of making a living. It is obvious that urbanization has become the outstanding feature of life today in much of Anglo-America.

Factors Stimulating the Founding, Growth, and Maintenance of Cities

Cities come into existence to serve the demands of regions, but their actual sites are determined by geographical conditions. In short, cities do not spontaneously come into existence without the operation of causal factors. They are thus the product of locations possessing a strategic quality. If we think in terms of the American Manufacturing Region (see Chapter 3), 50 of its 400-odd cities are situated on the shores of the Atlantic Ocean and the southern Great Lakes; not less than 210 are situated on rivers of considerable size, and 30 on canals either used or abandoned. Altogether more than three-quarters were originally located and grew up near waterways. Only 70 of the 400 have no such situation, and nearly all of these owe their development to their important sites beside railroads. Even the railroads did not differentiate the business of the river and lake cities, for at first they were conceived as supplements to

[3] Kingsley Davis, "The Origin and Growth of Urbanization in the World," *American Journal of Sociology*, Vol. 60 (March 1955), p. 434.

water trade routes and were built to connect river towns with each other.

Important cities grew up especially at bulk-breaking points at the heads of navigation where goods and passengers had to shift from water to rail transport at a waterfall, a rapid, or a gradual shallowing in the stream beyond which boats could not go. The exact town site was often determined by the local terrain—a terrace, a convenient ferriage, a navigable tributary stream—or even by some historical accident, such as the wording of a charter or an agreement made with the Indians. With the growth of manufacturing, many large water-consuming industries arose in cities having good supplies of industrial water.

The Nature of Cities

Cities as Functional Entities To use an expression of the late Professor J. Paul Goode, all of the *great* cities were born great. To be sure man helps make them what they are, but without their favorable endowment, man alone could not make them great; their importance "rests on factors far beyond man's puny story." All are located at a unique place so that the urban functions serve the articulated area. It may be said that such cities are of three kinds: (1) those performing comprehensive services for the tributary area; (2) those performing bulk-breaking services along transport routes; and (3) those engaged in special functions, such as mining, manufacturing, and commerce. Most cities, of course, represent a combination of the three. Modern mechanization, transportation, and interdependence enable much of the economic activity of mankind to be centered in cities.

All cities greatly influence the areas in which they are located but all, too, are helpless without the rural lands that sustain them. For every city workman and every member of his family, some four acres of reasonably productive land must be farmed to enable him and his family to maintain the American standard of living. Assuming an average of three dependents per man, a factory employing 1,000 men is thus drawing on an agricultural area of 16,000 acres. Back of Cleveland, Ohio, there must be some 3½ million acres in production. The American machine-tending farmer now produces 500 times more food than he eats. City folks are dependent every day for many necessities besides food, and all are supplied at a price—a price that seems to go up with the size of the city.

But just as the city cannot exist without the country, neither can the country prosper without the city, for some settlements, for example, Des Moines, Dallas, and Salt Lake City, exist to supply the needs of the surrounding and distant country. In fact, this is true of nearly all Anglo-American cities outside the American Manufacturing Region.

Cities also relieve the population pressure of the rural areas when they can no longer afford to keep their surplus sons and daughters.

The Typical American City Viewed from an airplane, a typical American city appears as a sprawling mass of structures of varying size, shape, and construction, crisscrossed by a checkerboard street pattern which here and there assumes irregularities (Figure 2-1). The blocks into which the city is divided seem to lack any organic grouping into units. The general impression is one of stereotyped monotony. Internal structure is repeated so often that broad generalizations seem valid, especially if confined to cities of similar size, function, and regional setting. Within the city the

Figure 2-1. Salt Lake City is a representative, medium-sized American city. Its downtown business district is characterized by a rectangular street pattern, vertical growth, and lack of trees. The surrounding residential areas are masked by numerous trees. Utah's state capitol is seen on the rising ground to the left. (Photo courtesy Salt Lake City Chamber of Commerce.)

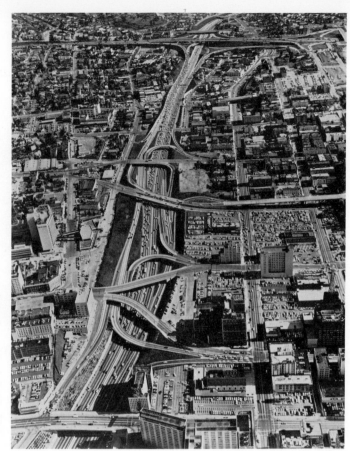

Figure 2-2. Los Angeles contains the most complete and complex system of freeways in Anglo-America. Shown here is a section of the Harbor Freeway near the central business district. At the top of the photograph is "The Stack," the city's famous four-level interchange. Another facet of urban Anglo-America's traffic problem is demonstrated by the large amount of space devoted to off-street parking lots. (Photo courtesy Los Angeles Chamber of Commerce.)

several portions are utilized for different functions. Heavy manufacturing gravitates to the flat lands somewhat removed from the city center, for it requires much space; if the area is a plain, this is no serious problem, but if it is hill country or mountain terrain, a valley must be utilized. Commerce, too, keeps to the flat land. The location of heavy industry will also be oriented with respect both to railways and highways and to the water front if the city is a port. The downtown business district normally occupies an area near, but slightly removed from, the original town site, and it is likely to be surrounded by an area of miscellaneous manufacturing, wholesaling, and storage buildings, blighted districts, and one or more brave attempts at urban renewal. Adjacent to this belt are the tenements and workingmen's homes, beyond them the apartment houses, and finally the

sprawling residential suburbs, marked by detached single-family dwellings with small yards and dotted with dispersed suburban shopping centers where increasing amounts of the city's retail and service business is carried on. Cemeteries are located on the better-drained land. Here and there are parks; some may be in the most highly congested areas and on the most expensive land; others may be well out from the core. Increasingly large amounts of land are required for transportation, particularly for automobiles. Multilaned, controlled-access trafficways (variously called freeways, expressways, or thruways) are laid, scar-like, in direct lines across the metropolis from one complicated interchange to another (Figure 2-2) in marked contrast to the right-angled pattern of the older traffic-clogged thoroughfares with their linear borders of one-block-wide commercial zones. Off-street

15

Figure 2-3. An upper class residential neighborhood in Kansas City. (Photo courtesy of the Chamber of Commerce of Kansas City.)

parking facilities, another result of the ubiquitous motor car, occupy vast acreages of the commercial core as well as the suburban shopping centers. On the periphery of the urbanized zone the suburb changes to farm land. At especially favorable sites, partly obscured by woods, nestle imposing mansions and country clubs (Figure 2-3). In detail, of course, each city is unique.

Ills of the Large City The big city everywhere is the object of criticism by thoughtful people. These critics insist that all cities are ailing and are not good places in which to live. They point to the smog, crowding, strain on family life, snarled traffic, segregation of minorities, juvenile delinquency, and impersonality.

Moreover, as cities become larger, the cost of living rises and workers' real wages decline. The cities accordingly are hotbeds of labor strife.

The lack of control over city growth has led to extreme congestion, the debasement of housing standards because of space shortage, increasing distance between home and place of employment, and incurable dead-

locks in traffic. Every large city has acres of slum areas threatening law enforcement, health, and the tax base. Many of the cities of Anglo-America have surpassed their optimum size.

The Skyscraper—Adjustment to Congestion The skyscraper is a visible symbol of congestion and high land values. If building cannot spread outward, it has to spread upward or the city ceases to grow. No city has had to adapt itself to the skyscraper as has New York, for on Manhattan Island, space is acutely restricted (Figure 2-4). In most cities lateral expansion is almost unlimited. Fortunately, Manhattan is almost entirely solid rock and hence provides the foundations for the skyscrapers which make New York's jagged skyline one of man's most awe-inspiring constructions.

Although the skyscraper permits many more people to live and work in a restricted area, it also adds to traffic confusion, for most American cities grew so fast that little conscious thought was given to form, function, or the satisfactions they should provide. Their streets were designed for smaller

Figure 2-4. New York City, looking toward the north. Brooklyn is in the foreground, with Manhattan Island in the right-center. The Bronx appears in the upper right. The Hudson River flows north to south and is joined by the East River at the southern tip of Manhattan. New Jersey is on the west side of the Hudson. Manhattan Island contains the greatest concentration of skyscrapers in the world. (Photo courtesy of Port of New York Authority.)

cities, lower buildings, and fewer people and hence cannot carry the traffic load without friction and delays. Traffic slows to a snail's pace in the very places where speed and promptness are most desired. Nowhere has the traffic dilemma been more vividly presented than in an article in *Fortune*, where the reader suffers with one truck driver as he maneuvers, frets, and battles to cover 4 miles and make 35 deliveries in 8 hours.[4]

The Future of Cities

Growth and Growing Pains One of the major unresolved problems of our age is

[4] "A Day in New York's Traffic Jungle," *Fortune*, October 1946, pp. 112-114.

what to do about the big city. In spite of the fact that urban people in both the United States and Canada have a markedly lower birth rate than do rural dwellers, a pronounced net migration to cities for many decades has resulted in increased population concentrations in urban areas. The most recent census data (1960 in the U.S., 1961 in Canada) show that approximately 40 per cent of the total population of Anglo-America resides in the 50 largest urbanized areas, ranging in size from New York City's 14,114,927 to Hartford's 381,619 (Figure 2-5). This is the largest proportion in history. Whatever the cause, it is obvious that the metropolis attracts people.

But growth results in growing pains, and such massive migrations to the city present

Figure 2-5. The 50 largest urbanized areas in Anglo-America. (Based on 1960 United States census and 1961 census of Canada.)

staggering problems to the city planner and administrator. First and foremost is the problem of urban sprawl. Metropolitan growth is most pronounced around the urban fringe; indeed, the central city frequently suffers a net population loss.[5] As the urbanized area expands in all directions, the provision of necessities such as water, sewerage, paved streets, utilities, refuse collection, police and fire protection, schools, and parks becomes a continuing

headache, particularly when more than one municipal governing body is involved.[6] And as the "flight to the suburbs" continues, it is generally accompanied by a degeneration of much of the core of the city, resulting in intensified slums, loss of merchandising revenue, and a decline in the tax base.

As the metropolitan area expands, local transportation becomes more complicated. As many more cars drive many more miles on only a few more streets (relatively speaking), traffic congestion becomes intense, the journey to work lengthens, and parking facilities become inadequate. The big city

[5] Twelve of the 20 largest cities in the United States actually experienced a population decline "within the city limits" between 1950 and 1960, but all of them showed a significant increase in the total metropolitan population, due to suburban growth.

[6] Metropolitan Los Angeles, the epitome of urban sprawl, includes more than 80 municipalities.

must maintain constant vigilance to keep from choking.

The maintenance of enough good domestic water also challenges the "exploding" metropolis. In subhumid regions cities must sometimes reach out dozens or hundreds of miles [7] to pipe in adequate water, and even such humid-land cities as New York and Boston have to extend lines farther and farther to tap satisfactory watersheds.

Where humans congregate, the delicate problem of pollution is accelerated. Rare indeed is the stream in any urban area that is not heavily infiltrated by inadequately treated liquid waste from home and factory. The shocking condition of American waterways has caused some civic groups to wage stringent clean-up campaigns, with emphasis on adequate sewerage treatment. The result has been heartening improvements in such infamous rivers as the Ohio and Philadelphia's Schuylkill [8]—improvements which show that this problem can be solved in other areas. More recently the menace of atmospheric pollution has arisen. The highly (and justifiably) publicized smog of Los Angeles is the most striking instance, but "smust" in Phoenix, "smaze" in Denver, and smoke in Montreal are further examples of an undiminishing phenomenon in most large cities. Industrial vapors and burning refuse contribute, but automobile exhaust fumes are generally believed to be the major cause. The air pollution problem will undoubtedly get worse before it gets better.

City Planning   To combat the burgeoning problems of the expanding cities, most large municipal governments are relying more and more on the professional city planner, who must synthesize the contri-

butions of architect, engineer, economist, geographer, sociologist, statistician, and other specialists with the hard-headed realities of municipal financial resources.

Questions and Prospects   Whatever the ills of the big city, urbanization is a pronounced reality in Anglo-America. The metropolitan growth rate shows no sign of slackening. What does this portend for the future? Will there be a tendency to develop political city-states, as in ancient Athens and Sparta? Will urban agglomeration continue until there is a single "Megalopolis" extending along the Atlantic seaboard from southern Maine to northern Virginia,[9] with other massive conurbations developing around the southern and western sides of Lake Erie, around the southern end of Lake Michigan, along two hundred miles of southern California coastline, and elsewhere to a lesser extent? Is there any maximum size to which cities will grow?

The modern urbanite apparently believes that cities can be pleasant places in which to live and is attempting to combine the better aspects of both urban and rural living by settling in the suburban fringes (Figure 2-6). The movement is stimulated by the desire to get more fresh air and sunshine, lower taxes, cheaper land, and better parking accommodations, and still be relatively near the business, cultural, and recreational opportunities of the city center. The principal drawback to the scheme is the time and trouble involved in traveling between home and city.

An important technique for revitalizing the city as a pleasant place to live is urban renewal—the demolition of blighted sections near the central business district and their replacement with tall, self-contained residential and commercial buildings where apartment dwellers can be surrounded by

---

[7] Los Angeles, for example, obtains more than half of its municipal water supply from two extensive pipelines, one 200 miles and the other 300 miles in length.

[8] *The Wall Street Journal,* January 16, 1959.

[9] See Jean Gottmann, "Megalopolis, or the Urbanization of the Northeastern Seaboard," *Economic Geography,* Vol. 33 (July 1957), pp. 189-200.

Figure 2-6. A new subdivision in Dallas. Suburban living is relatively inexpensive in most Anglo-American cities because of mass production building techniques. (Photo courtesy Dallas Chamber of Commerce.)

lawns and shrubs and yet be quite near "downtown" (Figure 2-7).

The pattern of urban development in the future is obscure, but Anglo-Americans like the city's amenities and will endure considerable discomfort to attain them. Gottmann's epic study of the urbanized northeastern coastal plain emphasizes both sides of the coin, the bad:

> . . . it is true that the air is not clean any more, the noise is disturbing day and night, the water is not as pure as one would wish,

and transportation at times becomes a nightmare.

and the good:

> . . . statistics demonstrate that in Megalopolis the population is on the average healthier, the consumption of goods higher, and the opportunity for advancement greater than in any other region of comparable extent.[10]

Cities and Manufacturing

Most of Anglo-America's manufacturing is carried on in cities. At first manufacturing was a home enterprise and, therefore, an unimportant factor in urbanization. But very soon—by the close of the eighteenth century—the fabrication of cotton and

[10] Jean Gottmann, *Megalopolis: The Urbanized Northeastern Seaboard of the United States* (New York: Twentieth Century Fund, 1960).

Figure 2-7. A new apartment project in Newark, New Jersey. Built as an urban renewal project in a large area that had been cleared of slums, the building is only a ten-minute walk from the center of the city. The building has more than 400 apartment units of varying sizes. (Photo courtesy Public Service Electric and Gas Company of Newark.)

woolen textiles and shoes was introduced into New England. Thus began the factory system, the concentration of factory workers, and the birth of the industrial city.

The economic history of both Canada and the United States shows conclusively that manufacturing and urbanism go hand in hand and that manufacturing has been the dominant influence in the growth of the majority of their cities, because growing factories and mills employ vast numbers of people. Because they also require a great variety of materials and services, industries grow up in the large urban areas, where these are most available.

Once the experimental period is past and commercial production has begun, manufacturing goes through two stages: (1) pronounced and increasing concentration in a given area during industrial youth, and (2) a redistribution or decentralization away from that area during maturity.

Concentration When many units of the same industry are located in a given city, the industry is said to be *concentrated* there. The success of the initial plant generally indicates that the original location was a satisfactory one.

Concentration occurs when industry is young and growing rapidly, for there are certain advantages in having plants located together that fabricate the same kind of products. Among these advantages are the following: the principal market may be there or at least nearby; a pool of varied labor is assured; power, raw materials, and capital (local bankers understand the industry well) are all available; service industries are present (machine repair and machine construction); and municipal and other ordinances are apt to favor the industry. This has been the case in the development of New England's shoe, textile, and brass industries, of Richmond's cigarette industry, and of Akron's rubber industry. In these cases, the biggest single advantage

was the low cost of manufacturing, whereas the biggest disadvantage, once the entire country became the market, was the high cost of distribution.

Inertia Despite the trend towards decentralization, a strong force tends to keep manufacturing in a given place once it has become thoroughly established. This is frequently described as the "inertia of invested capital."

Decentralization When industries reach technical maturity, they appear to find less advantage in the region or city than when they were young. Contributing to decentralization are:

1. Shifts in population
2. Wide distribution of electrical power
3. Sharply rising freight costs
4. Widespread development of hard-surface roads and the ease of moving raw materials by truck
5. Mobility of labor
6. Fluidity of capital
7. High cost of living in congested areas
8. Inequalities of the tax burden
9. Standardization of industrial processes
10. Cramped and inefficient plants and sites
11. Changed financial status
12. Elimination of the basing-point system in some industries
13. Closer and more satisfactory relations between management and labor in smaller places
14. Greater danger from air attack (in the event of war)
15. The popularity of the assembly plant.

The Assembly Plant As the population shifts in the United States, many industries set up assembly plants in expanding market areas. Such an arrangement keeps primary manufacturing near the raw materials, and assembling the final product near the new market centers improves labor and markets and reduces transport. The automotive has been foremost among industries moving to expanding market areas. As heavy and competitive a product as the automobile cannot be produced in one central area and be sold nationally for long. This has been possible until recently only because the automobile was a new thing that everyone wanted and hence consumers were willing to pay freight charges from Detroit. Although the Southern Michigan Automotive Subregion is still the automotive center of Anglo-America, assembly plants in other places are steadily becoming more vital to the industry.

Is Industry Really Abandoning the City? With so many factors encouraging decentralization, is industry actually abandoning the cities—the former centers of concentration? The answer appears to be no: much of what is called decentralization is really recentralization or diffusion, that is, industries are moving only to the outskirts and hinterlands of the large cities. (Figure 2-8) Thus they achieve more appropriate locations as part of an even larger centralized pattern, the metropolitan area.[11] In most

[11] See Donald Kerr and Jacob Spelt, "Manufacturing in Suburban Toronto," *Canadian Geographer*, No. 12 (1958), pp. 11-19.

instances the industries maintain close ties between the moved plants and the central cities.

Cities and Diversified Industry Some cities have predominantly one industry: Lynn—shoes, Akron—rubber, Youngstown—steel, Wichita—aircraft, and Flint—automobiles. Dependence upon a single industry has meant suffering during depressions for the entire city as well as for the people of nearby farms and of the communities that supply parts. Actually, comparatively few, if any, modern large Anglo-American cities are wholly dependent upon a single industry, but the condition of even a dominant industry can affect the life of the entire community. Thus Detroit's growing automotive industry flourished with reckless abandon prior to 1929, but after this date it encountered the toughest kind of depression problems, and many people moved out of the city during the 1930's.

Some cities are more diversified in their industrial enterprises. Thus Cleveland, Buf-

Figure 2-8. Suburbanization of industry, as illustrated by Texas Instruments Incorporated's 350-acre plant near Dallas. As with many new factory locations, this site is characterized by extensive parking acreage and ready access to an expressway. (Photo courtesy of Texas Instruments Incorporated.)

falo, and Chicago have different "atmospheres" from Detroit, Akron, or Youngstown. Cleveland is primarily an iron and steel and metalworking center, with emphasis on precision parts for automobiles, airplanes, household appliances, and industrial equipment. It makes a large proportion of the parts used by the big automotive companies. It does not go into the "deepest valleys"—it does not suffer quite so much—during severe depressions as does the single-industry city.

The Geography of Manufacturing

We have seen that cities and manufacturing are almost inseparable. Only in a few parts of Anglo-America—the Appalachian Piedmont, the Ohio Valley, the "hydroelectric" valleys of southern Quebec, and the Gulf Coast of Texas and Louisiana—are significant amounts of manufacturing found in nonurbanized areas. Much the greater part of all our manufacturing takes place in cities. This does not result from mere chance; there are good reasons for it. Finding an appropriate site for a plant is a scientific business requiring the application of economics and geography. A well-located factory has access to markets, materials, power, and labor, which form an unshakable base upon which executives may make plans with confidence. Competition forces manufacturers to pay careful attention to costs and the location of the plant. Costs are all-important because an industry dies if its costs of production become too high. In fact, the basic reason for spatial differentiation in the location of manufacturing is spatial differentiation in costs of manufactural operations.

It should be noted, however, that cost factors are not invariably the sole basis for plant location. Indeed, there are at least three types of noneconomic factors that sometimes play significant roles in determining where factories will be built. These will be discussed in a later section.

Time changes all and a good factory location today can be a bad one tomorrow. The technique of industrial location is dynamic, not static.

Economic Location Factors Early manufacturers in the United States did not choose the sites for their industries so deliberately as they do today. For the most part early industries sprang up in the home town of some individual who had sufficient capital to start a factory. The market was local. Transportation was poorly developed, and raw materials had to be procured near the plant. The better-situated of these enterprises prospered, but many of those badly located lost money, withered, and finally disappeared.

Thus manufacturing as much as agriculture is influenced by favorable or unfavorable natural environmental conditions. It is not reasonable that the great iron and steel industry of Anglo-America, in which billions of dollars are invested, should have become established in its present locations through chance or human whim; yet the industrial changes in Anglo-America have been so rapid that some of the steel plants are now in bad locations. This is one of the cases where subsequent changes have occurred that were unforeseen when the plants were started. Industrial location factors are both complex and numerous.[12]

PROXIMITY TO MARKET According to many authorities, the market is the most vital location factor in manufacturing. Nearly all manufacturers need to be alert to the location of their market, but some *must* locate near the market, such as:

(1) Those who make products that are bulkier than the raw materials; for example, agricultural implements, pianos, boxes, barrels, and assembled automobiles——

(2) Those who make perishable products —ice, ice cream, and soft bakery goods——

[12] See, for example, Leonard C. Yaseen, *Plant Location*, rev. ed. (New York: American Research Council, 1960).

Figure 2-9. Making charcoal, the fuel for reducing iron ore, in the early days. The sticks were stacked on end in a pile, turf and loose earth were placed over them, leaving a small chimney in the center, and then the pile was lighted. The charring took 3 to 10 days. (Courtesy of American Iron and Steel Institute.)

(3) Those who require a quick sale of their products—newspapers and some magazines.

Generally speaking, proximity to markets depends directly on the transportation rate for the finished product.

PROXIMITY TO PRODUCTION MATERIALS Certain types of manufacturing have to be near the source of raw materials and purchased parts, especially those using perishable commodities and those using commodities which lose weight or bulk in the manufacturing process. Canning, cheese-making, and sugar-milling are examples of the first, since their raw materials cannot be shipped far without spoilage. Cement-making and

smelting of ores are good examples of the second type.

PROXIMITY TO POWER Before the era of electricity and its transmission, industrial machines had to be near a source of stationary power. The first iron furnaces were erected in the heart of a forest—the source of charcoal (Figure 2-9); when the timber was mined out, the furnace, which was a simple and relatively inexpensive structure (Figure 2-10), was abandoned and a new one constructed elsewhere on a tract of virgin timber. Another example is New England's widely scattered pioneer textile mills, which squatted beside almost every accessible waterfall. Water power was in-

Figure 2-10. Early American furnace. The preferred location of early furnaces was on a stream next to a hillside. Note covered bridge to charging platform, water wheel, blast pipe to tuyere, and cast house at right. (Courtesy of United States Steel News.)

disputably the first basic physical factor in establishing cotton processing in New England. Still another example is the aluminum-smelting industry, which is a voracious consumer of electric power, using 20 times as much per ton as the iron and steel industry. Demanding cheap power, the aluminum industry has frequently gone into areas rich in hydroelectric power but remote from large urban markets. Later it tapped the rich storehouse of natural gas in the Southwest and more recently the extensive thermal electric (coal) resources of the Ohio Valley.

The wider distribution of electric power has no doubt helped make many industries more foot-loose, for wherever a power line runs, there manufacturing and labor can make their home if other location factors are favorable.

PROXIMITY TO RESERVOIRS OF MANPOWER AND SKILLS When an industry is young and its problems unfamiliar, it tends to be concentrated in those few places which provide the basic skills. Local concentration thus encourages those skilled in a particular industry to live in the concentrated area. Certainly Akron and New York City had a larger source of labor, skilled and experienced in the fabrication of rubber goods and garments, than any rival locations. This advantage tends to perpetuate the concentration of plants engaged in the same industry. With the passage of time, however, the enterprise and its main center mature, the general labor supply becomes more skilled, and the plants become more automated. Dispersion of the industry then takes place.

Labor normally constitutes a factory's largest item of expense, and wage-cutting is quickly reflected in the profit account. Hence cities where labor is militant and highly organized tend to lose ground. Labor organizations have been a dominant factor in the decentralization of industry.

Further, labor has become highly mobile. Today more than 30 million men, women, and children live in states other than those in which they were born. Nearly 15 million civilians were migrants during the three years 1942-1944 and probably 5 million cross state lines every year in search of work. Almost half of California's population, for example, was born in other states. Even so, labor is not completely foot-loose. Skilled workers, for instance, tend to be less mobile on the average than unskilled ones.

SIGNIFICANCE OF TRANSPORTATION Every outstanding transportation center is also a major manufacturing center (Figure 2-11). Most modern industries are located well within the "zone of minimum transportation costs." Ports are particularly favored as industrial centers because they serve as functional connections between land and water transport routes, and therefore as "bulk-breaking" points in the shipment of goods. If the goods must be handled in the port, it is only logical to process or fabricate them there as well.

INDUSTRIAL WATER SUPPLY Water is so critical in many industries that it merits consideration as a major location factor,[13] particularly for industries making iron and steel, rubber, chemicals, and pulp and paper.

Nearly three billion gallons of water are used daily by the American iron and steel industry alone. Thirty tons are required to produce a single ton of pig iron. From 250,000 to 400,000 gallons are used in producing one ton of rayon. The total consumed by American industry is estimated at 35 billion gallons per day—about one-seventh of the total water consumption of the nation. Quality is as important as quantity in many industries. Textile mills should have clean, soft water, and mills engaged

[13] Gilbert F. White, "Industrial Water Use: A Review," *Geographical Review*, Vol. 50 (July 1960), pp. 412-30.

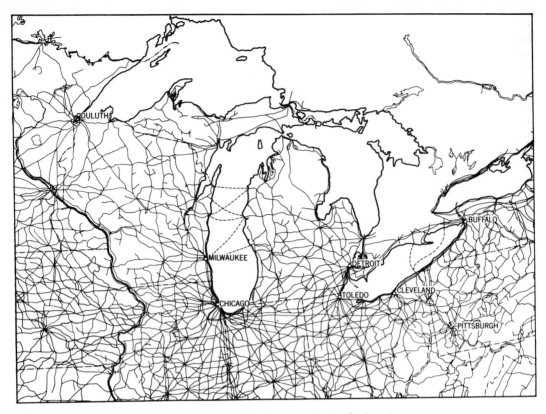

Figure 2-11. Chicago, the most important railroad center in Anglo-America, and probably in the world, is the hub of a bafflingly intricate maze of railway lines and facilities. (Map drawn by David Dahle.)

in bleaching and dyeing need water of exceptional purity.

Most manufacturing districts have adequate water, but some are better off than others. Thus the iron and steel industries of Buffalo and Gary which use water from Lake Erie and Lake Michigan are better off than that of Fontana, which depends on wells.

The West has recently discovered how important water is. Industrialization is hampered in parts of the area because of limited supply and/or poor quality of its water. In spite of the numerous real advantages for industrial development in such rising centers as Denver, Albuquerque, and Phoenix, no large water-using firm would seek out (or be sought by) these cities as a location for a new factory.

CAPITAL Capital is so mobile that it becomes available in almost any location where satisfactory financial returns from manufacturing are assured. In some industries, however, the amount needed is so great that only powerful corporations can afford to build plants. In the late 1940's, New England tried desperately to acquire an iron and steel industry of her own, but all the major companies refused to locate there. Apparently New Englanders themselves have been either unable or unwilling to raise the necessary capital. To construct an integrated, well-balanced plant, including blast furnaces, coke ovens, open hearths, and rolling mills, costs nearly 500 million dollars. Industries such as canning, meat packing, flour milling, and shoe and furniture manufacturing, on the other hand, may require little capital; hence this factor is not always a major one in the location of a plant. Even so, capital can serve as a locational factor, dependent upon its relative availability, the relative conservatism of local financial institutions, and the adjacency required by lenders for observing the firm's operation.

LAND AND CONSTRUCTED FACILITIES Not infrequently an old, well-established company, which started with what it considered to be an abundance of room, suddenly finds itself cramped. Unable or unwilling to purchase additional land at high prices, it often migrates. In Pittsburgh, some of the steel companies, hedged in by rivers, steep hills, railroads, or neighboring plants, moved as far as 40 miles down the Ohio River to have plenty of room on low-cost land.

In what was probably the largest industrial moving job in the history of the United States, the Chance Vought Division of United Aircraft Company moved all its facilities and 1,300 employees to Texas in 1948-49, partly because its Connecticut site was too cramped. The provision of adequate room for expansion can be a major consideration for any company that is contemplating a heavy investment in a new location. Many large corporations have a rule of thumb to follow—purchase five times as much land as is needed initially.

Constructed facilities are sometimes an important inducement. For example, disposal of surplus government defense plants by the War Assets Administration in the late 1940's attracted many firms to localities they might otherwise have ignored. And very few aircraft plants are successfully located unless an airfield is already available (Figure 2-12).

TAXATION Tax policies vary widely from

Figure 2-12. All large aircraft plants require extensive areas of flat land around the factory buildings to provide for parking lots, take-off and landing runways, and aprons for outdoor maintenance and storage. This is the Boeing plant in Seattle. (Photo courtesy of Boeing Airplane Company.)

state to state and from city to city. In order to secure lower taxes as well as more favorable conditions, Henry Ford, whose original factory was in Detroit, moved to the then small village of Highland Park.

In the closely competitive business world of today, with precise cost-accounting procedures, anticipated production costs often may be essentially identical at two or more potential factory sites. Under such conditions a difference of just a few mills in local tax rates may influence the choice.

COST OF LIVING   High cost of living makes high wages imperative. Accordingly, many industries have been moving from large cities to suburbs, small cities, towns, and villages, for labor is invariably cheaper in the smaller places. The cost of living presses hard upon city workers, the general cost of living—food, fuel, rent, and amusements—sometimes being as much as 50 per cent higher than in smaller communities.[14]

DISPOSAL OF WASTE   A large proportion of American industries empty their solid and liquid waste into streams. In fact, this is a major reason why many industrial plants were located on rivers. When streams are inadequate, they fail to attract manufacturing plants. With increasing industrialization, stream pollution has become a major problem in many places. When only one or two small plants turn their wastes into a river, there may be no deleterious effects, but when 50 or 100 large industries do so, then the stream may become a dead, vile thing—a scourge to all those living within its basin. Most industrial wastes are acid and many of them are highly poisonous. In some instances, all fish are killed for scores of miles along a stream course. In some areas pollution has become so serious

that it has alienated the inhabitants from the companies. The most progressive concerns are alert to public opinion and are of their own accord fighting stream pollution. In fact some cities and states, through regulatory agencies, now have laws and sanitary regulations against stream pollution.

FINANCIAL INDUCEMENTS   Although most firms tend to choose their factory locations on a more or less logical basis, unaffected by external influence, a significant minority of locational choices are determined by direct or indirect subsidy from a state or local governing body or booster organization. Some inducements consist of free or inexpensive land or buildings; others comprise tax concessions or outright grants of capital.

Such subsidy often proves to be advantageous for both parties, though this is not always the case. Financial inducements play a large part in factory location in certain states, as Arkansas, whereas in others, as Arizona, this practice is forbidden by law.

Noneconomic Location Factors   In a capitalistic economy the profit motive tends to be the most important consideration in determining where a factory will be situated. However, under certain conditions economic considerations are relegated to a secondary role, and the choice is made on the basis of other factors. Two of these are of utmost significance.

THE HUMAN FACTOR   Difficult indeed is it to dissociate certain men from their industries and their cities. Man cannot succeed if the environmental factors do not favor a given industry, but often a given environment would not be used for a manufactural enterprise were it not for the vision, imagination, and determination of some man. Henry Ford might not have built his great automobile empire had he gone to Bismarck, North Dakota, instead of Detroit. The following list is typically representative but by no means complete:

[14] The big-city dweller is by force of environment dependent daily upon a thousand others for everything—food, heat, transit. He is supplied by middlemen at a price—a price that seems to increase with the size of the city.

Figure 2-13. An aluminum extrusion plant in an unusual location. This Reynolds Metal Company facility is located in Phoenix, where it was built as a part of the wartime decentralization policy. (Photo courtesy of Southern Pacific Company.)

Andrew Carnegie	steel—Pittsburgh
H. C. Frick	coking coal, steel—Pittsburgh
Henry Ford	automobiles—Detroit
B. F. Goodrich	rubber—Akron
Cyrus McCormick	agricultural implements—Chicago
Ambrose Swasey	machine tools, telescopes—Cleveland
E. D. Libbey	glass—Toledo
David Buick	automobiles—Flint
R. E. Olds	automobiles—Lansing
J. A. Dagyr	shoes—Lynn
John Deere	steel plow—Moline
Samuel Slater	cotton textiles—Pawtucket
Gustavus F. Swift	meat—Chicago
P. D. Armour	meat—Chicago

In each case the industry was originated in large part by the personal whim of an individual, but the location proved to be economically sound in the long run.

In a surprising number of instances the chief initial location factor cited by industrialists is the bare fact that the company's founder lived in a certain town and liked it, so when he decided to begin manufacturing, he never really gave serious consideration to locating his plant anywhere else.

This is a factor of universal importance, though its significance varies from industry to industry and from locality to locality. And it affects more small factories than large ones. But its influence is rising, particularly in areas of benign climate, where amenities are attractive to both management and labor, as in Florida and Arizona.[15]

STRATEGIC CONSIDERATIONS From 1940 to about 1955 the governments of Canada and the United States made major efforts to decentralize defense industries for strategic purposes—to minimize bomb and missile targets and to shun coastal locations. A relatively small number of factories was affected, but most of these were large and significant. The effect of these policies is still noticeable on the industrial map, even though decentralization is no longer being particularly emphasized. A large aluminum refinery at Phoenix (Figure 2-13), major aircraft plants at Wichita, Ft. Worth, Dallas, Tulsa, and Atlanta, a missile factory at Den-

[15] A 1959 study showed that personal choice was the principal location factor for 57 per cent of the factories in Arizona. See Tom L. McKnight, *Manufacturing in Arizona* (Berkeley: University of California Publications in Geography, 1962).

ver, and many other examples, attest to the continued impress of the strategic decentralization policy on the contemporary distribution of factories.

General Location and Specific Site In giving thought to industrial location, the company considers the *general location* and the *specific site*. The general area is selected usually on the basis of lowest costs of assembly of raw materials and sale of the fabricated product in the market. Thus, for example, the Lower Great Lakes Area has been considered the best general location in Anglo-America for the manufacture of iron and steel. This does not, however, mean that *any* and *every* place in this large area is satisfactory. Within it are great local differences; this introduces the problem of specific locality, which is concerned mostly with site factors. Some of these are physical, others social and political.

As an example, when "Big Steel" finally decided to establish major production facilities west of the Pittsburgh-Cleveland district, they chose metropolitan Chicago because of its position advantages. However, in selecting a specific site for plant construction, it was decided that the suburban area of Gary, Indiana, had the most favorable site factors. The *position* advantages of the Chicago area and the *site* advantages of Gary are listed below:

Position factors (general location)
1. Location in midst of a tremendous steel market.
2. Easy access to all raw materials.
3. A crossroads position, where the cheapest direct route between the coal and the iron ore is crossed by the important Atlantic Seaboard-Chicago rail routes.
4. Proximity to Chicago, enabling management to transact business there conveniently.
5. Stimulating climate because of moderating influence of lake.
6. Densely populated surrounding general area, hence availability of a large and efficient labor supply.

Site factors (specific site)
1. Fairly level and uniform topography.
2. Location at extreme end of water route on Lake Michigan, an advantage over Milwaukee or even Chicago.
3. Adjacent lake with an almost unlimited water supply.
4. Unproductive soil, priced lower than first-class agricultural land.
5. Lower taxes than in a metropolis.
6. Less stringent laws in Indiana than in Illinois.

Proper and Improper Location: The Scientific Survey Meat-packing plants are located in Omaha, flour mills in Buffalo, blast furnaces and steel mills in Gary and Pittsburgh, automobile plants in Detroit, and clothing establishments in New York City. These are, in each case, excellent locations.

Every industrialist is vitally interested in having his plant well situated. He must scrutinize each possible locus and compare production costs in all parts of the country. If a poor choice is made, the company pays for its error in high freight costs, labor troubles, inefficiency, and poor access and service to market. The industrialist then may consider relocation, which always involves risks and uncertainties. Never should a move be undertaken without careful analysis of all advantages and disadvantages.

The analysis of industrial location is a relatively new field. Trained personnel apply requisite position and site criteria to a number of potential locations and then compare their advantages.

A foreign rubber-tire manufacturing company, contemplating spending a million dollars on a new plant in the United States, knew it should locate somewhere in the American Manufacturing Region. A careful survey was made of some 20 cities—all possible locations. Each was graded for the specific requisites of the tire industry. Buffalo, with more points of advantage than any other city, got the plant. Some of the considerations which led to this choice were: (1) There are fourteen lines of railroad operating into Buffalo. (2) The city is within easy access of power, fuel, and markets. (3) New York City, the nation's largest rubber-importing port, is within easy access. (4) Buffalo enjoys stable business conditions, and its growth has been steady and normal over a period of years, free from the booms and mushroom growth of many other cities. (5) More than 200 acres of land were available on the Niagara River, making it possible to take advantage of any future development in water transportation. (6) The river was a constant source of cold water, a necessity for rubber-processing.

Thus industry has learned that in countries of large size, varied resources, markets, and people, it is not profitable to locate factories just anywhere. There is a proper location for every industrial plant.

Selected Bibliography

Bartholomew, Harland, *Land Uses in American Cities.* Cambridge: Harvard University Press, 1955.

Berry, Brian J. L., and William L. Garrison, "Cities and Freeways," *Landscape,* Vol. 10, Spring 1961, pp. 20-24.

Burck, Gilbert, "How to Unchoke Our Cities," *Fortune,* May 1961, p. 118, *et seq.*

Gaffney, M. Mason, "Urban Expansion—Will It Ever Stop?" *Land, The 1958 Yearbook of Agriculture.* Washington: U.S. Government Printing Office, pp. 503-522.

Gottmann, Jean, "Revolution in Land Use," *Landscape,* Vol. 10, Winter 1958-59, pp. 15-21.

Harris, Chauncy D., "A Functional Classification of Cities in the United States," *The Geographical Review,* Vol. 33, 1943, pp. 89-99.

——— "Suburbs," *American Journal of Sociology,* Vol. 49, July 1943, pp. 1-13.

Hoyt, Homer, "Classification and Significant Characteristics of Shopping Centers," *Appraisal Journal,* April 1958, pp. 214-222.

Kitagawa, Evelyn M., and Donald J. Bogue, "Suburbanization of Manufacturing Activity Within Standard Metropolitan Areas," *Studies in Population Distribution,* No. 9, 1955.

Klove, Robert C., "The Definition of Standard Metropolitan Areas," *Economic Geography,* Vol. 28, April 1952, pp. 95-104.

Murphy, Raymond E., and J. E. Vance, Jr., "Delimiting the C.B.D.," *Economic Geography,* Vol. 30, July 1954, pp. 189-222.

Nelson, Howard J., "A Service Classification of American Cities," *Economic Geography,* Vol. 31, July 1955, pp. 189-210.

Shindman, B., "An Optimum Size for Cities," *Canadian Geographer,* No. 5, 1955, pp. 85-88.

Siddall, William R., "Wholesale-Retail Trade Ratios as Indices of Urban Centrality," *Economic Geography,* Vol. 37, April 1961, pp. 124-132.

Wissink, G. A., *American Cities in Perspective, with Special Reference to the Development of Their Fringe Areas.* Assen, the Netherlands: Royal Vangorcum, Ltd., 1962.

chapter three

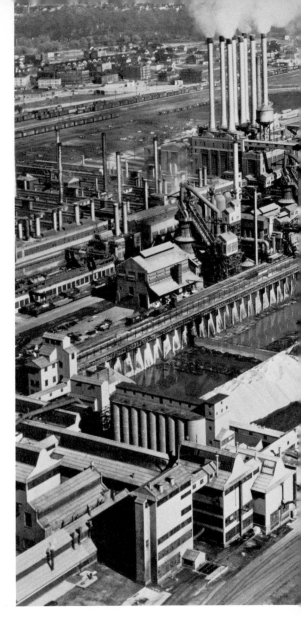

The American Manufacturing Region

The American Manufacturing Region is the great industrial workshop of Anglo-America. It is located mostly in northeastern United States but includes also parts of the provinces of Ontario and Quebec. A map showing the distribution of urbanized areas, which indirectly portrays reservoirs of labor and the degree of industrialization, emphasizes the fact that manufacturing in Anglo-America has, for the most part, tended to concentrate in and near big cities. Urban agglomerations here, therefore, are predominantly industrial.

Within the roughly shaped parallelogram that describes the boundaries of this region is found approximately 63 per cent of the factory production of the United States and 73 per cent of that of Canada. Included are 18 of the 25 largest industrial cities of the United States and 7 of the 10 largest in Canada.

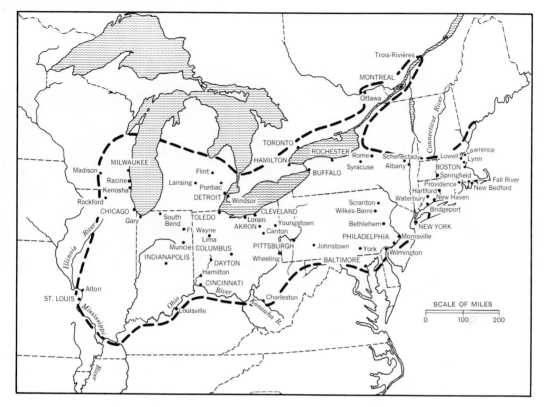

Figure 3-1. The American Manufacturing Region. An urban region of diversified industries.

The Region

The American Manufacturing Region is characterized by many areas of high manufacturing activity. Its dominant traits are urban interest and mode of life—themselves results of transport advantages and proximity to raw materials, power, labor, and markets. Actually the region consists of an insular concentration of industrial intensity in a sea of agriculture and dairying (Figure 3-1). There is no *total land* occupation by industrial plants, cities, and towns comparable with what is to be seen in the Agricultural Interior with its even pattern of *farms, fields, pastures, and villages*. Farm land or pastures or wooded hills or mountains separate the various urban industrial centers one from another.

Thus manufacturing causes an intensive but spotty utilization of the land within any region dominated by it, in contrast to agriculture, which uses broad acres and covers them with a continuous pattern of farms. Within a given industrial area then, much less land is actually occupied by factories and mills than is generally supposed. In even so highly an industrialized area as that engaged in making steel between Cleveland, Youngstown, and Pittsburgh, the so-called "Ruhr of America," only a relatively small part of the land is used industrially. However, it is useful to recognize that much of the matrix of residential, commercial, and transportational land use in urban areas is likely to be in direct relationship with the functional requirements of a manufacturing economy. In its space requirements, manufacturing is extremely modest, whereas in its space utilization it is dynamic.

In some places long rows of industrial

33

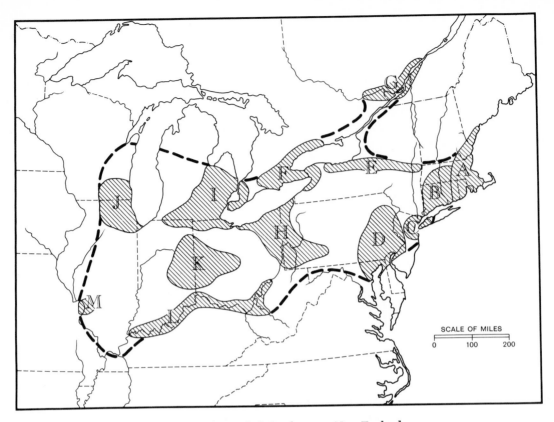

Figure 3-2. Principal manufacturing districts: (A) Southeastern New England; (B) Southwestern New England; (C) Metropolitan New York; (D) Philadelphia-Baltimore District; (E) Central New York; (F) Niagara Frontier; (G) Middle St. Lawrence District; (H) Pittsburgh-Cleveland District; (I) Southern Michigan Automotive District; (J) Chicago-Milwaukee District; (K) Inland Ohio–Indiana District; (L) Middle Ohio Valley; (M) St. Louis District.

cities are to be found along major transportation routes. One major route runs from New York up the Hudson River to Albany and west to Buffalo. Here it breaks into two branches, one going north of Lake Erie through Canada to Detroit and Chicago, the other south of Lake Erie through Cleveland and Toledo to Chicago. At Chicago routes fan out, though major stems extend northward to Milwaukee and southwestward to St. Louis (Figure 2-11). "Fall line" and coastwise routes extending from Baltimore to southern Maine early stimulated the growth of industry, making their tributary areas the original home of the American factory.

Manufacturing Districts

Though manufacturing has put its stamp on the American Manufacturing Region, actual industrial production is spotty; in short, there are large areas of meager manufactural component among numerous hives of industry. The belt is, therefore, divided into districts (Figure 3-2). Even though within the districts much of the land is not used for manufacturing, these divisions are useful to show manufactural use of the land.

Basis for Mapping Amount of Manufacturing No one factor suffices as an absolute measuring stick for amount of manufacturing. Several factors have been used by different individuals. Sten De Geer, in the pioneer study, based his analysis on the number of wage earners in towns of more than 10,000 population.[1] Two weaknesses characterized this study: (1) manufacturing is not limited to cities of 10,000 or more persons, and (2) the study reflected the general distribution of population, since his wage earners were not all factory workers. Richard Hartshorne decided that possibly 10 per cent of the total population of any city might be engaged in manufacturing. He then took a figure of 500 workers in non-local industries as his minimum figure for an industrial city worthy of a place on his map.[2] Helen Strong, convinced that Hartshorne overemphasized concentration, included *all* manufacturing in her study. Her density of manufacturing was based on machine horsepower.[3] Alfred J. Wright proposed that value added by manufacture be accepted as the criterion for the distribution and relative importance of manufacturing areas. Like De Geer he used cities with populations of 10,000 and more and like Strong insisted that *all* industries be included.[4] Clarence F. Jones believed that the county rather than the city of 10,000 or more persons should be employed as the basic areal unit.[5] Chauncy Harris classified industrial cities functionally on the basis of employment in manufacturing.[6]

More recently, John Alexander has prepared an exhaustive analysis of all possible single-factor measures for which statistics are normally collected. His study shows that the resultant pattern will be essentially the same (in the United States) whether the measurer plots total employment in manufacturing, wage earners in manufacturing, value added by manufacturing, or wages and salaries paid to factory workers.[7] In addition to the absolute amount of manufacturing in an area, it is also important to know something of its relative significance to the local economy. This can be measured in a variety of ways, generally using proportional ratios, as shown by John Thompson.[8]

The authors of this book have consulted maps made by all these methods in preparing their classification, but the most important criterion utilized has been the regionalist's "feel" of the area. The district boundaries as drawn are believed to enclose areas in which the industrial components have certain major elements of unity, and thus differ from adjacent districts.

Principal Districts of the American Manufacturing Region

Southeastern New England

The American industrial era had its beginning in this area's early cotton mills with a factory system that was established before the Civil War. New England had the largest supply of potential factory workers (native-born, and European immigrants) and the greatest amounts of investment capital.

[1] Sten De Geer, "The American Manufacturing Belt," *Geografiska Annaler,* Vol. 9 (1927), pp. 235-359.

[2] Richard Hartshorne, "A New Map of the Manufacturing Belt of North America," *Economic Geography,* Vol. 12 (1936), pp. 45-53.

[3] Helen Strong, "Regions of Manufacturing Intensity in the United States," *Annals of the Association of American Geographers,* Vol. 27 (1937), pp. 23-47.

[4] Alfred J. Wright "Manufacturing Districts of the United States," *Economic Geography,* Vol. 14 (1938), pp. 195-200.

[5] Clarence F. Jones, "Areal Distribution of Manufacturing in the United States," *Economic Geography,* Vol. 14 (1938), pp. 217-22.

[6] Chauncy D. Harris, "A Functional Classification of Cities in the United States," *Geographical Review,* Vol. 33 (1943), pp. 86-99.

[7] John W. Alexander and James Lindberg, "Measurements of Manufacturing: Coefficients of Correlation," *Journal of Regional Science,* Vol. 3 (Summer, 1961), pp. 71-81.

[8] John Thompson, "A New Method for Measuring Manufacturing," *Annals of the Association of American Geographers,* Vol. 45 (December 1955), pp. 416-36.

Included within this subregion are the industrial parts of Maine, New Hampshire, eastern Massachusetts, eastern Connecticut, and Rhode Island. Boston obviously is the dominant center and Providence is of strong secondary importance. Other industrial towns of note include Worcester, New Bedford, Fall River, Lawrence, Manchester, and Lowell.

This is an area of diversified light industry. Formerly some type of manufacturing was characteristic of almost every village. Today most of the small mills are abandoned, but this district will not become one of ghost cities, for in spite of certain competitive weaknesses, it offers attractive conditions for the types of manufacturing that specialize in high-grade products that utilize skilled labor and are made from nonbulky or imported raw materials.

The Textile Industry: Cotton New England was long the center of the nation's cotton textile industry, and cotton-making still is important in every one of its states save Vermont. However, 75 per cent of all cotton textile workers and 90 per cent of the mills are in the two states, Rhode Island and Massachuetts. In fact Bristol County, Massachusetts, and Providence County, Rhode Island, have one half of New England's total active spindles. Here are the famous cotton-mill cities of Fall River, New Bedford, Pawtucket, and Woonsocket.

Among the early advantages of New England for the manufacture of cotton textiles were: (1) damp air, which is essential to prevent twisting and snarling during spinning (in dry air frictional electricity causes the yarn to snarl and twist) and reduces breakage in weaving; (2) excellent water-power facilities; (3) clean, soft water; (4) skilled labor; and (5) location in a major market area.

However, New England has yielded supremacy to the South in the manufacture of coarse and medium goods. It has lost scores of plants and millions of spindles. The decline, which has been precipitous since 1920, resulted from several conditions. (1) In comparison to the South, the plants were not kept as modern and efficient, (2) labor was costlier and unions were stronger, (3) taxes were higher, and (4) electric power was more expensive.

Despite New England's decline in textile manufacture, there are still more than 40,000 cotton-textile workers in the district.

The Textile Industry: Wool The woolen industry prospered longer. In the early days it had local wool in addition to water power, clear, soft water, skilled labor, and an appreciable nearby market. Boston is the great wool-importing port of the nation, handling about half of all the fiber used in the country.

Rapid decline engulfed New England's woolen textile industry in the late 1940's, essentially cutting production in half within the space of four years. Even so, it is still a significant type of manufacturing in Rhode Island, southeastern Massachusetts, and the Merrimack Valley (Figure 3-3).

Generally speaking, the textile industry of the United States has been in poor economic health for years. It is the only major type of manufacturing that has suffered an absolute decrease in production since World War II (approximately 10 per cent between 1947 and 1960). In southeastern New England the decrease during the same period was on the order of 40 per cent. And this is doubly significant because of the lofty position textiles had in the New England economy—19 per cent of all manufacturing in 1947 in comparison with 9 per cent in 1960.

The Shoe Industry New England is a major producer of leather goods, especially shoes. Eastern Massachusetts possesses the greatest concentration of plants, though adjoining parts of New Hampshire and Maine are important too. The chief locative factor

Figure 3-3A. A textile mill in Exeter, New Hampshire. Typical of the older mills, it has a riverside location. (Photo courtesy State of New Hampshire, Division of Economic Development.)

is skilled labor. But access to leather and other materials and proximity to markets are important. Brockton, Haverhill, and Lynn are dominantly shoe towns—the first two concentrating on men's shoes, and the last on women's shoes.

New England cannot, however, indefinitely retain supremacy over other areas having large local markets and better access to raw materials. So long as shoemaking depended upon skilled labor, New England dominated by virtue of its early start. However, mechanization, the system of leasing machinery, high labor costs, high rents, high taxes, and difficulties with unions all have fostered decentralization. Movement

Figure 3-3B. A former woolen mill that has been subdivided and is now used by several companies, including manufacturers of costume jewelry, coated paper, jewelry plating, boxes for the jewelry trade, and Christmas tree ornaments. It is located in North Providence, R.I. (Photo courtesy Rhode Island Development Council.)

out of this district has been largely into the Middle West, though not to the exclusion of the Middle Atlantic States, the South, and the Pacific Coast. New York, Ohio, Illinois, and Wisconsin all have become important in shoe manufacturing—a response to the westward migration of the center of population and hence of the market.

Leading Industrial Centers Metropolitan *Boston* vies with Pittsburgh as the sixth largest industrial city in Anglo-America. Its industrial structure is well diversified, although the textile industry is virtually absent. It is a major producer of machinery (particularly electrical machinery), as well as apparel and leather goods. The *Providence* area (including *Pawtucket, Fall River,* and *New Bedford*) is noted for textiles (declining), jewelry and silverware (slowly growing), and apparel (rapidly growing). The other important industrial area of the district is the *Merrimack Valley* (*Haverhill, Lawrence, Lowell, Nashua, Manchester*), whose economy is under great strain due to the decline of its two dominant industries, textiles and leather.

Southwestern New England

This district includes those parts of Massachusetts and Connecticut from the Connecticut Valley westward. Cities are dotted along the Connecticut Valley and additional important industrial centers lie in the smaller valleys of the Berkshire Hills and along the north shore of Long Island Sound. The principal places of industrial significance are *Hartford, Springfield-Holyoke, Bridgeport, New Haven, Waterbury,* and *New Britain.* In this district factories specialize in diversified light products requiring high mechanical skill—machinery, tools, hardware, firearms, plastics, electrical goods, electronics equipment, precision instruments, watches, and clocks. These are all products of high value and small bulk, which require little raw material and power and can easily stand transport charges to distant markets (Figure 3-4).

Southwestern New England has adjusted much better than Southeastern New England to the economic facts of life. The flight of textiles has not resulted in nearly so many abandoned factories; rather, other types of

Figure 3-4. A metal-working plant in Springfield, Massachusetts. A great variety of factories producing metallic items is found in Southwestern New England; often the factories occupy old buildings on long-established premises. (Photo courtesy Springfield Chamber of Commerce.)

industry were attracted to utilize the cadre
of trained workers and the available buildings.

The growth in electrical machinery production has been steady, partly due to the
research and product-development facilities
of the district.[9] Aircraft engine and propeller manufacture are significant in Connecticut, even though airframe assembly is
accomplished in other parts of the country.
Hardware and other light metal goods are
produced in quantity in several cities.

On the basis of the proportion of the
labor force employed in manufacturing (44
per cent), Connecticut is the most highly
industrialized state in the nation.[10] This exemplifies the great dependence of New
England upon manufacturing. Despite textile problems, the postwar years generally
have been prosperous, although there have
been several lingering pockets of relatively
high unemployment.

Metropolitan New York

The Metropolitan New York District,
which comprises the small, concentrated
area of New York City and its industrial
suburbs, is one of superlatives. It is Anglo-
America's most populous and cosmopolitan
district and its most intense mixing-bowl. It
has the best harbor and is the largest port,
and it leads the world in commerce, manufacturing, and finance. It also dictates the
nation's styles and attracts the greatest number of tourists.

This district is located at the mouth of
the navigable Hudson River on a well-protected deep-sea harbor and at the focus of
major land and sea routes. By value it handles approximately one half of the nation's
commerce. Its harbor consists of 7 bays, 4

[9] R. C. Estall, "Changing Industrial Patterns of
New England," *Geography*, Vol. 46 (April 1961),
p. 127.
[10] Comparable figures for Massachusetts, Rhode
Island, and New Hampshire are 36 per cent, 42
per cent, and 43 per cent, respectively.

rivers, 4 estuaries, and 42 different channels. The Hudson River scours out the
mouth of the bay, keeping the channel deep.
The direct water frontage is 771 miles, almost half of which has been developed.
Most of the channels are deep enough to
accommodate the largest ships afloat. The
channel leading to the Atlantic is direct.
The tidal range is so small that ships may
come and go at almost any time. The rush
of the tides from the sound to the ocean
and back, however, is cursed by seamen
because of the tricky whirlpool of Hell
Gate, where two tides and a river meet and
currents move back and forth with a velocity as great as six miles per hour. Staten
Island and the bar of Sandy Hook afford
fine protection from storms. Ice never blocks
the harbor, though fog occasionally holds
up traffic.

New York is the only Atlantic port with
an easy route through the Appalachians—
the Hudson-Mohawk Depression. The Erie
Canal (now the New York State Barge
Canal) more than any other single factor
contributed to New York's greatness as a
port, for it made all the country between
the Great Lakes and the Ohio River and
between the Mississippi River and the Atlantic Ocean tributary to the Atlantic Seaboard and especially to New York City. The
New York Central Railroad, following the
route of the Erie Canal, brought the steel
rail from the Middle West to downtown
Manhattan. Other railroads have established
marine and rail termini on the west side of
the Hudson, and they maintain large fleets
of lighters, barges, and tugboats, to transfer
cargoes across the river and the harbor.

Congestion   The great amount of water,
while advantageous to commerce, is a barrier to traffic between Manhattan and the
rest of the New York area. For decades attempts have been made to mitigate the
traffic congestion in and about the city. New
York's subways, busses, and taxis handle

more than three billion passengers annually.

Because Manhattan occupies only a small area and because its own inhabitants, as well as thousands of daily commuters from the suburbs, require transportation, an elaborate subway system has been built, while above ground is operated an extensive bus system. Long vehicular tunnels have been constructed; great suspension and steel-arch bridges have been built across the rivers. Passenger trains enter Manhattan via tubes under the Hudson and East rivers. Local movement of goods over the area's water barriers is expensive; a ton of freight could move 200 to 600 miles by rail for what it costs to send it by lighter across New York Harbor.

Population   The white population of New York in 1626, the year Manhattan passed from the Indians, was less than 200. In 1960 the population of New York City had reached a total of 7,781,984. If we add to this the population of the urbanized area, the total is 14,114,927. The greater part of this population is concentrated in Manhattan and Long Island and in the peninsulas of the Bronx and Bayonne.

New York's foreign-born population, representing every part of the globe, is extraordinarily high. More than one-half of the foreign-born whites have come from eastern and southeastern Europe and less than one-third from northwestern Europe.

Commerce   New York, the greatest port in the world, has a ship entering and a ship leaving every ten minutes of the daylight hours. Possibly 400 ships line its docks daily.

The Hudson River, including the New Jersey side, handles more than half the port's business based on value, and yet it occupies only about ten miles out of a total of 771 for the entire port. The imports include chiefly fuel oil and gas, crude oil, raw sugar, fruits, coffee, flaxseed, raw natural rubber, gypsum, and paper; the principal exports

are iron and steel scrap, refined petroleum products, automobiles and parts, wheat and flour, and livestock feeds.

Statisticians estimate that one out of every ten persons gainfully employed in the New York district earns his living directly or indirectly from shipping or kindred enterprises.

Finance   New York City has become the financial center of the world, having replaced London following the First World War. Because New York is the financial center of the United States, many national concerns have selected it for their headquarters. This is true, for example, of big oil, steel, and automobile companies whose actual manufacturing operations are carried on elsewhere.

Manufacturing   New York's greatness depends more upon commerce than upon industry, more upon its great rail-end piers in Jersey City and its berths for enormous liners on lower Manhattan than upon its factories. Nonetheless, it is the nation's, and the world's, leading industrial center.

Unlike Chicago, Pittsburgh, and Cleveland, the factories of the New York area do not make heavy products such as pig iron and steel. However, they manufacture significant amounts of most other types of products. With more than 1,800,000 industrial workers, Metropolitan New York has in excess of 10 per cent of the nation's factories.

The Garment Industry   The garment industry is decidedly dominant in the district. Only four Anglo-American cities have more employees in all manufacturing combined than are employed in New York in this single industry (375,000). Moreover, the garment factories largely are concentrated in an area of 200 acres in central Manhattan. And yet they are so inconspicuous as to pass unnoticed by the casual visitor.

The typical clothing plant occupies part of an upper floor of a 10-to-20-story building between Twenty-Fifth and Forty-Second Streets and Sixth and Ninth Avenues. It has 30 to 50 employees, nine-tenths of them female. Probably no part of the city is so congested as the garment center; the streets are clogged, and overcrowding increases factory overhead. The higher cost of housing here is reflected in higher wages —the differential between the Midwest and New York City ranging from 15 to 25 per cent. New York promises to remain the capital of the garment industry, however, so long as it can maintain itself as the style and buying center of the United States. The importance of the city in both the garment and textile industries is indicated by the fact that New York is also the foremost cotton-textile market in the world.

About three-fourths of the nation's women's clothing and one-third of the men's wear are made in New York City.

New York's advantages for making garments. If New York overwhelmingly dominates the garment industry, it must enjoy advantages over competing cities. Foremost among these advantages are:

(1) The clothing industry is a *city industry,* for cities supply it with both *market* and *labor.* In a big city materials can be transferred quickly to different contractors and suppliers in various stages of production so that quick style changes can be met.

(2) The trade accepts New York City as the national clothing market. Buyers accordingly congregate from all parts of the nation to compare prices and goods of competing sellers.

(3) *Any item* needed by the industry is quickly available.

(4) The trade got an early start in New York City.

Other Industries New York is also the printing and publishing leader of Anglo-America. The principal book and magazine publishers have offices in Manhattan.

The district is a major producer of ma-chinery, chemicals, processed foods, transportation equipment, and fabricated metals. Apart from the dominance of apparel production and the virtual absence of primary metal output, New York's industrial structure is well diversified.

Factories are distributed widely over the metropolitan area, but there are three broad locational groupings. Garment factories, printing shops, publishing plants, and a variety of food processors are found mostly on Manhattan Island. Heavy and nuisance industries (petroleum refineries, shipyards, foundries, chemical plants) are concentrated on the reclaimed marshes of the New Jersey waterfront. Long Island is the site for many miscellaneous industries.

Philadelphia-Baltimore District

The Philadelphia-Baltimore District comprises the eastern third of Pennsylvania, adjacent portions of New Jersey and Delaware, and Maryland as far south as Baltimore. No other subregion shows such a combination of heavy and light manufacturing—everything from iron and steel to silk. Its factories turn out about 10 per cent of the nation's fabricated goods. Though Philadelphia is the hub, much business and trade, especially in the Lehigh Valley, flows to New York City. Baltimore, southeasternmost point of this district as well as of the entire American Manufacturing Region, is noted for both commerce and manufacturing. Industrial development in this district is almost as old as that of New England.

Iron and Steel This district has long been important as a major producer of iron and steel, and is benefiting from much new construction. Bethlehem Steel Corporation's plants at Sparrows Point, Maryland, and elsewhere are of long standing, but the United States Steel Corporation's mill at Morrisville, Pennsylvania, is new. The location of this new plant on navigable water, which is a trend away from the traditional location on or near the Lower Great Lakes, results primarily from four circumstances:

(1) The presence of the big market along the seaboard—one of the largest in the world.

(2) The decline in reserves of high-grade ore in the Lake Superior District, and growing dependence for ore upon Chile, Venezuela, Canada, Brazil, Liberia, and Peru.

(3) Proximity to inexpensive coal shipped from West Virginia to Hampton Roads by rail and then by coastal vessel to the major mills.

(4) The abolition of the basing-point system in selling iron and steel, which made it unprofitable for Pittsburgh, Youngstown, Buffalo, Cleveland, and the Midwestern centers to compete with a center nearer the big Atlantic Seaboard market from Boston to Baltimore.[11]

MORRISVILLE, PENNSYLVANIA At Morrisville, the Delaware River makes a big bend, the stream changing direction. Here on a 3,800 acre tract of land, the United States

[11] In the steel industry, the customer pays the freight charges on the product from the mill. If the customer's plant is close to the steel mill, his charges are small; if far away, they will be high —a decisive handicap in competition.

Steel Corporation has constructed at a cost of more than 450 million dollars the Fairless Works, an integrated plant spreading over 2,000 acres, employing 6,000 workers, and adding 2,700,000 ingot tons to the nation's annual steel capacity. The additional 1,800 acres are insurance for expansion should that become necessary. Never before has so complete a plant been constructed all at once. The project, which was on the drawing boards for 4,000 hours of engineering time, is one of the best examples in Anglo-America of the purposeful location of industry.

The raw materials come from widely separated and distant sources: iron ore from Cerro Bolivar in Venezuela, coal from Pennsylvania and West Virginia, and limestone from Pennsylvania.

SPARROWS POINT, MARYLAND The world's largest steel mill was located here after a careful engineering study had indicated that Sparrows Point was the most desirable site on the Atlantic Seaboard (Figure 3-5). Though all of the raw materials come from some distance (limestone from Pennsylvania, coal from the Virginias, and iron ore from Chile and Venezuela), Sparrows Point

Figure 3-5. Aerial view of the world's largest steel plant, at Sparrows Point, Maryland. The ore dock at the right can berth three ships at one time. At left center is the shipyard, which serves as an important user of steel. (Photo courtesy Bethlehem Steel Company.)

has probably the lowest pig-iron manufacturing costs outside of Birmingham. Expansion of Sparrows Point's steel capacity during the 1950's actually represented a larger tonnage than the building of the Fairless mill at Morrisville.[12] As a result, Baltimore is the fourth largest iron and steel producer in the Western Hemisphere.

Shipbuilding   Except in wartime when the Pacific Coast and the Gulf Coast assume major importance, the area under consideration—Delaware River and Bay, Chesapeake Bay and the New York area—build about three-fifths of our tonnage.

The Delaware River, with yards at Philadelphia, Camden, Chester, and Wilmington, is the most important river for shipbuilding in Anglo-America and hence merits the appellation "the American Clyde." Nature endowed the Delaware more generously for this industry, however, than she did the Clyde. If America does not approach Scotland in importance in shipbuilding, it is for economic rather than geographic reasons (it costs about twice as much to build ships here as there). Great shipyards also have grown up at Sparrows Point, where they are closely integrated with steel production.

Chemicals   That portion of the Delaware Valley between Philadelphia and Wilmington contains a notable assortment of chemical plants, particularly those associated with E. I. Du Pont de Nemours and Company. These factories, producing a variety of items ranging from refrigerants to explosives, are highly mechanized. Relatively few production workers are required, with the result that more than three-quarters of the employees are in administrative and research capacities.

There is also a significant concentration

of petroleum refineries around Marcus Hook, Pennsylvania, on the Delaware. These are market-oriented plants that receive their crude oil via inexpensive sea transportation.

Other Manufactures   *Philadelphia* is the most diversified manufacturing city in the United States, with a remarkably even balance to its industrial structure. *Baltimore* depends upon steel, shipbuilding, and missiles. The smaller centers, *Bethlehem, Allentown, Scranton, Wilkes-Barre, Wilmington, Reading, Morrisville, Lancaster,* and *York* generally emphasize only one or two types of products.

Apparel manufacture is important in most cities of the district, often utilizing "parasite" labor.[13] Electrical machinery, printing and publishing, textiles, and food processing (particularly vegetable canning in Baltimore and Camden) are also notable.

Central New York

The Mohawk Valley and the Ontario Plain occupy the great water-level route from Troy to Buffalo and are traversed by the main line of the New York Central Railroad, the New York State Barge Canal, U.S. Highway 20, and the New York State Thruway. The route through the Mohawk Valley is almost as level as the Ontario Plain. This results from the fact that during glacial times (when the mouth of the St. Lawrence was choked by a glacier) the outlet for much of the Great Lakes watershed was by this route.

The district contains many cities. The first arose in response to the stimulus of the Erie Canal, built in 1825; the later ones arose near a series of short railroads that paralleled the river and canal. Later these lines

[12] Gunnar Alexandersson, "Changes in the Location Pattern of the Anglo-American Steel Industry; 1948-1959," *Economic Geography,* Vol. 37 (April 1961), p. 105.

[13] This term refers to the wives of steel workers, coal miners, and the like who take relatively low-paying jobs in their local communities to supplement the family income, which may be under stress because of decelerated steel or coal output.

were consolidated and the area became one of the major traffic arteries of Anglo-America. Factories sprang up all along the route. Each city tends to specialize in several products, and nearly every conceivable product is manufactured somewhere in the area. Thus *Rochester* makes cameras, electrical machinery, optical goods, and men's clothing; *Rome,* copper and brass; *Syracuse,* machinery and alkalies; *Schenectady,* electrical equipment and locomotives; *Cohoes,* knit goods. Like the output of Southwestern New England, nearly all of these products require skill. Few districts are so well located as this one with respect to (1) efficient and economical transportation facilities; (2) raw materials (brought easily and economically by railway, truck, or barge); (3) power—both hydroelectric and coal; (4) dense population, which assures an abundance of skilled labor; and (5) large markets. This district, however, lacks a capital of its own, and therefore lies within the orbit of New York City.

The Niagara Frontier

This subregion lies between Lake Ontario and Lake Erie in western New York and adjacent Ontario. It is complicated by the international boundary which, as a result of the tariff, plays a vital role in causing manufacturing to be more important on the Canadian side than it would be otherwise.

The power from Niagara Falls is widely used on both sides of the border and has played an important part in the development of chemical, metallurgical, and other industries. Because of the international border there are two industrial capitals—Buffalo on the American side and Toronto on the Canadian.

Iron and Steel At Lackawanna, a part of metropolitan Buffalo, is one of America's greatest iron and steel industries. The Lackawanna Iron and Steel Company moved here from a location it had occupied at

Scranton for 60 years. Like other Lower Lake cities, Buffalo is an economical meeting place for coal, iron ore, and fluxing limestone. Its blast furnaces and coke ovens are so placed on a ship canal that lake carriers deliver the raw materials economically directly to the stacks. This district is able to ship steel to eastern markets by barge, lake freighter, railway, and truck. Buffalo mills deliver steel to New York City at lower cost than any competitors west of the Appalachians. Besides the huge Lackawanna plant, there are several smaller ones.

The Canadian portion of this district, the nation's outstanding in iron and steel fabrication, shows little promise of ever becoming a second Pittsburgh, Chicago, or even Youngstown, for its raw materials are too widely separated for economical assembly. Her coal lies far from the iron ore and the blast furnaces, except at Sydney, Nova Scotia, which is outside this region. Canada, accordingly, imports about as much coal from the United States as she mines. A growing market and considerable tariff protection, however, assure the nation a place of importance, and Canada now ranks among the top ten countries in output of steel.

More than one-half of Canada's steel production is from the mills in Hamilton, which ranks as the eleventh largest steel center in Anglo-America (metropolitan Buffalo is sixth). Basic raw materials mostly are imported from the United States, coal from Pennsylvania and West Virginia and the bulk of the iron ore from the Lake Superior iron ranges. The industry is oriented toward the markets of eastern Canada and is in a good position to serve the larger cities by rail and waterway.

Flour Milling Buffalo vies with Kansas City as the world's leading flour-milling center (Figure 3-6). This is a reversal of the trend of early days when mills grew up in the wheat-growing regions, as in Roch-

Figure 3-6. Flour mills and elevators in Buffalo. (Fitzgerald Air Photo; Courtesy Buffalo Chamber of Commerce.)

ester and Kansas City, or on the market sides of them, as in Minneapolis. Buffalo's mills reap the advantages of cheap water transportation on the Great Lakes, nearness to the large consuming markets of the East, low power costs, excellent transportation facilities for the product in all directions by canal, railway, and highway, and the milling-in-bond privilege.[14] There are relatively few employees in the industry, as it is highly mechanized.

Other Manufacturing The automotive industry is well established in the Niagara Frontier, with many parts factories and a few assembly plants in Toronto, Hamilton, and Buffalo. Electrochemical and electro-

[14] The milling-in-bond privilege is one that is offered by the United States government to any place that can economically make use of it. Unless a city is in the line of transportation followed by Canadian grain, it cannot economically make use of the privilege. The mill has to pay the salaries of government inspectors, and the plan can be operated only on a large scale. The milling of flour in bond simply means that the wheat is milled in transit and that the flour is bound for foreign markets. Flour that is milled in bond cannot be sold in the United States.

metallurgical facilities have been established on both sides of the border to utilize Niagara Falls power. Fabricated metals (especially in Buffalo) and agricultural machinery (particularly in Toronto) are productions also of note.

Industrial Centers The two large centers, *Buffalo* and *Toronto*, have approximately equal numbers of factories and manufactured employees, sufficient to rank them thirteenth and fourteenth among the largest industrial cities of Anglo-America. *Hamilton* is only one-third as large as either, and yet ranks as the third largest Canadian industrial center.

Middle St. Lawrence District

This district is somewhat separated from the rest of the region, but logically can be considered a part of the American Manufacturing Region. It is one of Canada's two leading industrial districts, the other being the Niagara Frontier. Most of the nation's manufacturing cities and all of its major ones are located in these two districts. Located along the St. Lawrence and the lower

Ottawa and St. Maurice Rivers, this district comprises the industrial heart of the St. Lawrence Valley.

Half the total trade of Canada passes through it, and many exports and imports are processed or manufactured there. An abundance of cheap hydroelectric power, a plentiful supply of intelligent labor at a reasonable price differential, plenty of clear, cold industrial water, good transport facilities, ample room for the establishment of new and for the expansion of old industrial plants, and a rapidly growing market have made the area more interested in manufacturing than in agriculture or shipping.

The area's principal factories are engaged in the manufacture of aluminum, lumber, pulp and paper, flour, textiles, shoes, sugar, chemicals, oil, railway and electrical equipment, farm implements, aircraft, and cement. Many of these industries, of course, could not exist if it were not for the tariff on products made south of the border. Only the cement industry needs coal and this is delivered cheaply by boat.

Pulp and Paper   Canada leads the world in the production of pulp and produces much paper also. Altogether the nation has more than 100 pulp and paper mills widely scattered, but the string of water-driven mills lining the southern edge of the forest along the lower St. Lawrence is most noteworthy and we are concerned with it here.

The pulp and paper industry, the principal manufacturing enterprise in the nation, has a larger capital investment than any other in Canada and is first in employment, in wages paid, in export values, and in the net value of production. Moreover, it provides the principal and ofttimes the only industrial activity in many towns. Yet in spite of its importance, the industry utilizes less than 20 per cent of the annual forest consumption—considerably less than that used for fuelwood. The pulp and paper industry has been one of the major reasons

for the huge development of water power in Canada; in fact cheap power is the major locative factor, for in order to produce a ton of newsprint 60 to 80 H.P. daily are required. The cost of transportation is equally important in the location of pulp mills. Since it is cheaper to transport the newsprint than the semi-finished material, the industry tends to cling to the source of supply of the raw material—the forest.

Canada much prefers to export newsprint than logs, for it is six times more valuable. The further the pulpwood is processed, the more revenue the provinces and the national government obtain and the more employment the people find in the Canadian forest industries.

The greatest concentration of pulp and paper mills is at the confluence of the St. Maurice and St. Lawrence Rivers, in the twin cities of *Trois-Rivières* (Figure 3-7) and *Cap-de-la-Madeleine*. Most logs are floated down the rivers to the mills in large booms, but some are barged or trucked in. Enormous grappling machines aid in unloading and sorting the logs, and in guiding them into the mills. Dozens of other mills are found in the district, especially at *Montreal* and *Ottawa-Hull*.

Aluminum   The aluminum industry, like that of pulp and paper, is dependent upon an *abundance of cheap power.* No other electrometallurgical operation consumes so much electricity. To make 1 ton of aluminum requires electrical energy equivalent to that of 16 tons of coal; this amount produces 18 tons of newsprint. Moreover, power comprises a higher percentage of the total manufacturing cost than in any other industry—16 per cent as compared with an average of 3 per cent for all industries. The aluminum industry then is a huge consumer of power and of necessity seeks out cheap electricity. The Canadian Shield, and its southern fringe, with its riches of water power, has enabled Canada to rank among

Figure 3-7. Pulp and paper mills at Trois Rivières. The St. Maurice River flows into the picture from the left and joins the St. Lawrence just to the right of the island. The pulp logs are stored in huge piles between the mills and the river. (Photo courtesy Canadian International Paper Company and Canadian Pulp and Paper Association.)

the first three world producers of aluminum despite the fact that all the raw materials must be imported.

Canada's principal reduction works are located on the Saguenay River, north of this district, and at Kitimat in British Columbia. Within the Lower St. Lawrence district there are two centers of note, Shawinigan Falls and Beauharnois.

Canada's first reduction plant was built by a United States firm at Shawinigan Falls on the St. Maurice River in 1899. It was enlarged considerably during World War II, at which time the Beauharnois plant, on the St. Lawrence River southwest of Montreal, was constructed.

As in the Saguenay Valley, the raw materials are assembled by water transport. The bauxite comes from Jamaica and British Guiana, cryolite is brought from Greenland, and fluorspar from Newfoundland.

Other Manufacturing Most other manufacturing in the district is in metropolitan Montreal, which is Canada's largest industrial center and ranks about eleventh in Anglo-America. The city is situated on an archipelago of islands in the St. Lawrence River (Figure 3-8), with the steep slopes of Mount Royal presenting an effective transportation barrier in the center of the city. The principal area of heavy industries is in the suburb of Montreal East, which, curiously enough, is north of the city. Montreal's major industrial products are machinery, railway equipment, aircraft, clothing, textiles, and food and tobacco products.

Figure 3-8. The business district of Montreal. The St. Lawrence River flows in the background. (Photo courtesy National Film Board, Ottawa.)

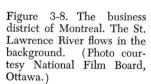

Montreal is Canada's leading port, in spite of being icebound for four or five months each year.

The Pittsburgh-Cleveland District

The Pittsburgh-Cleveland district is the continent's outstanding producer of iron and steel. It also is a leading producer of metal products in their secondary and tertiary stages—fabricated metal and machinery. Some other industries (as rubber and glass products) are important, but predominantly this is a district of metalworking.

Iron and Steel This area supplies southeastern Michigan and most of Ohio and eastern Indiana with the raw and semi-finished steel used in secondary industries.

The area is strategically located for heavy industry, since it lies between Lake Erie on the north, over whose waters move millions of tons of iron ore and limestone, and the productive Northern Appalachian coal field on the south. Here, too, is one of Anglo-America's leading markets for iron and steel.

In Europe most of the prosperous steel centers are locationally oriented to coal or ore, but in Anglo-America market is the more compelling factor. The center of balance of the American steel market is gradually shifting westward, and the Pittsburgh-Cleveland district is feeling the pinch of competition from the Chicago-Gary mills, which are better situated with respect to the Midwestern market, and from the Atlantic tidewater mills, which are better located for the East Coast market.

In the United States iron ore usually moves toward the coal fields, the main reason being the presence in or near the coal fields of general manufacturing districts (the largest markets for most steel products). The problem of fluxing stone is less important than that of ore and coal because limestone is widely distributed. Two states,

Pennsylvania and Michigan, supply more than half of the country's metallurgical stone.

So long as Lake Superior ores are in general use, the bulk of the American iron and steel industry will be located on or near the Lower Great Lakes, and the Pittsburgh-Cleveland area will occupy a prominent place. It is pointed out in other chapters that high-quality "Lake" ore is diminishing and that several new plants have already been constructed on the Atlantic Coast for utilization of Canadian, African, and Latin American ores. On the other hand, the big steel companies have made investments of hundreds of millions of dollars for getting iron economically from taconite.

In the Pittsburgh-Cleveland District are 6 of the 15 largest steel producing cities in the United States: *Pittsburgh* (2nd), *Youngstown* (3rd), *Steubenville-Weirton* (7th), *Cleveland* (8th), *Lorain* (14th), and *Canton-Massillon* (15th). Typically the mills are of medium size, are several years or even decades old, may suffer from congestion and lack of space, and are nearly always located beside a river or stream. These valley sites provide water for cooling, flat land for building, and access to transportation facilities (Figure 3-9).

The Rubber Industry The rubber industry and *Akron* have long been synonymous. Rubber *made* Akron. In 1917-1918 it, together with nearby Barberton, employed 70,000 persons in its rubber factories and was probably the most highly specialized city in the nation. This city along with its suburbs still is the world's leading rubber-manufacturing center, with about one-fourth of the total United States rubber output.

Akron's first rubber factory was established in 1870—the result of sheer accident. B. F. Goodrich, dissatisfied with his business prospects at the close of Civil War,

Figure 3-9. The "Golden Triangle" of Pittsburgh. The central business district occupies a peninsula of land between the Allegheny River (on the left) and the Monongahela River (on the right); these rivers unite at this location to form the Ohio River. The point of land projecting into the rivers was a blighted slum area until the 1950's, when the slums were dismantled and replaced with modern office buildings, parking lots, and city parks. The principal steel-making area is up the Monongahela and off the picture to the right. (Photo courtesy Chamber of Commerce of Greater Pittsburgh.)

engaged in the oil business. Being unsuccessful, he went to New York and dealt in real estate. In his dealings he came into possession of a rubber factory at Hastings-on-Hudson. Handicapped by lack of funds, he was encouraged to go to Akron by a friend who lent him money. His small factory there became the nucleus of the great Akron rubber industry.

Concentration of rubber manufacturing was a good thing during the industry's infancy, for buyers and sellers could get together conveniently. Akron was also a central spot for skilled labor. Now that the industry is mature, however, such concentration is no longer desirable. Mills have sprung up in Alabama, California, Maryland, Mississippi, New England, New York, and Texas, as well as in foreign countries.

This decentralization is in large measure the outgrowth of serious strikes. As labor unions became increasingly powerful, the cost of labor soared and Akron's cost of production became high—the highest in the country. The companies then introduced more and more labor-saving machinery. To make such a change harmoniously is difficult and more strikes resulted. Decentralization away from Akron followed. Another decentralizing factor has been the need for more economical distribution of the finished product.

The Clay-Products Industry This industry, whose products include brick, china ware, clay refractories, porcelain, terra cotta, tile, pottery, and vitrified sewer pipe, is especially important in the Upper Ohio Valley of Pennsylvania and Ohio. The high

49

degree of concentration, despite the fact that clays are widely distributed throughout Anglo-America, indicates that the raw material as a factor of location is less important than fuel and access to large markets and skilled labor. The Ohio River area is especially well located with respect to fuel—both coal and natural gas.

The stoneware industry is centered at East Liverpool, the continent's leader in pottery fabrication. It procures kaolin from Georgia, Florida, and South Carolina; feldspar from Maine; ball clay from Kentucky and Tennessee; and flint from Illinois and Pennsylvania. The industry making clay refractories (heat-resisting products) is located principally in the Allegheny Plateau of Pennsylvania, where the fire clay is interlayered with bituminous coal. This clay is procured underground rather than from surface pits. Clay refractories are in demand by the nearby iron and steel industry.

Because of America's high tariff on imported china, the Havilands, after much research on American clays, selected New Castle, Pennsylvania, on the Shenango River, as the site for their United States factory.

The Glass Industry   For 5,000 years glassmaking was a handicraft because the workers had to be highly skilled. About 1908, machines began to perform the operations and, except in the nonstandardized and small-volume business, glassmaking has become a mechanized industry. Glass is made by fusing sodium sulphate, calcium carbonate (pure limestone), and quartz sand. From 60 to 70 per cent of all the glass sand used in the country, and certainly the best in quality, comes from Illinois, Pennsylvania, and West Virginia.

Charcoal, the first fuel used, was later displaced by coal, and coal in turn by natural gas. At first glassmaking was concentrated east of the Appalachians, but the adoption of the new fuels resulted in western Pennsylvania, southeastern Ohio, and northern West Virginia becoming the chief centers. Natural gas is the ideal fuel because it is clean and inexpensive and produces very high and uniform temperatures. An immense amount of heat must be available to melt the raw materials. Glass sand and other materials invariably travel to where cheap fuel is located. Natural gas is thus the major factor contributing to the location of this manufacturing enterprise, though nearness to market is also important. So fragile and bulky a product naturally takes high freight rates.

Machine Tools   The machine-tool industry came into being as a separate entity about 1870, when industrialists were widely adopting mass-production methods. New England had been the source of most of America's machine tools. As manufacturing migrated westward, it had to have metal-cutting machines, and New England's factories were too far away to supply them. The first plant in Ohio was established in Cincinnati shortly after the Civil War. Cleveland, which today ranks next to Cincinnati in production of machine tools, did not get started until the early 1880's. The principal locational factors in this industry are availability of highly skilled labor, proximity to markets, and availability of raw materials. Machine-tool plants producing parts used in the assembly of other machine tools are usually located in or near the regions producing the final product. Most of the factories in the United States are located in the American Manufacturing Region, and the Pittsburgh-Cleveland District ranks very high.

Machinery   Various other types of machinery, both nonelectrical and electrical, are produced in the district. Cleveland is particularly noted for the former, and Pittsburgh for the latter (especially heavy equipment, such as turbines, generators, and transformers).

The Southern Michigan Automotive District

The automobile-manufacturing district, which includes, besides the metropolitan areas of *Detroit* and *Windsor,* the "inner" and "outer" rings of cities (Figure 3-10), contains the heart of the world's automotive industry. This industry dominates this district much more than steel dominates the Pittsburgh-Cleveland District.

Included in the semisuburban inner ring are *Pontiac, Ann Arbor, Ypsilanti,* and *Monroe.* Included in the outer ring are ten cities definitely in the orbit of Detroit's great industry—*Port Huron, Bay City, Saginaw, Flint, Owosso, Lansing, Jackson, Adrian, Toledo,* and *South Bend.*

The Automotive Industry

The automotive industry has made Detroit the most heavily industrialized major city in Anglo-America.[15] Within Detroit are more than 40 major automotive-parts factories, and almost a dozen assembly plants.

The making of motor vehicles is not, however, a single industry, for the automobile is an assembled product. The materials going into its parts are legion. Nearly every steel part is made of *alloy steels.* These are

[15] Approximately 43 per cent of Detroit's total employees work in factories. Comparable figures for other metropolises are Cleveland, 40 per cent; Philadelphia and Pittsburgh, 37 per cent each; Chicago, 36 per cent; Los Angeles, 33 per cent; New York, 31 per cent; and Boston, 28 per cent.

Figure 3-10. The Southern Michigan Automotive District. Although Detroit is the focus, neighboring cities and towns in Michigan, Indiana, Ohio, and Ontario produce many of the bodies and parts.

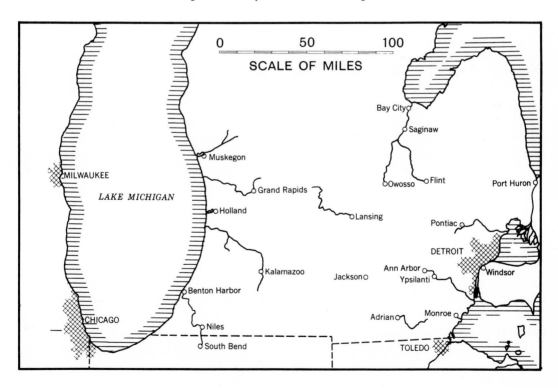

made by adding precise quantities of one or more of the ferro-alloys to the heated steel in the furnace to impart specific qualities—additional hardness, greater toughness, increased elasticity, and resistance to stain and to rust. Thus axles, requiring toughness and shock-resistance, must be made from different steel than that used in the spring and engine block. Several nonferrous metals are utilized—aluminum, lead, copper, tin, and zinc—for electrical devices, pistons, and other vital parts. Glass, upholstery, rubber tires, paint, and a host of other products must be purchased. In no industry is there so much subcontracting.

Throughout southeastern Michigan and adjacent parts of Ohio and Indiana there are dozens of cities, towns, and even villages that are functionally tied to Detroit because they have one or several factories that produce items for the automotive industry. Many of these outlying centers are even more dependent on this single industry than is Detroit. Flint is the prime example. Not only is it the most industrialized small city in Anglo-America (nearly 60 per cent of its labor force works in factories), but it is the second largest automobile-producing city on the continent and the most specialized manufacturing center in the nation (90 per cent of its manufacturing is for the automotive industry).

Detroit became the first great automobile center "by the accident of being the hub of a circle within which were located the pioneers of the industry." [16] Ford developed an automobile cheap enough for almost every family; he adapted the assembly line to the industry; and he introduced standardization and interchangeable parts to the industry, thereby making mass production possible. Ford was not the innovator, however, of modern mass production, despite

the fact that most engineers and production men believe he was.[17] The credit for this achievement goes to Eli Whitney.[18] Moreover, Ford raised the necessary capital among local bankers rather than on Wall Street. He and the alert local capitalists are largely responsible for the rise of automobile manufacturing in Michigan.

Geographic and economic conditions have justified the selection of Detroit as the automotive center. The industry had to be strategically located with respect to steel. In the American Manufacturing Region is concentrated 87 per cent of the finished-steel-producing capacity of the United States. Besides having locally made steel, Detroit's automotive industry has easy access to the steel mills at South Chicago, Gary, Cleveland, Lorain, and Buffalo. If Cleveland's pioneer inventors—Stearns, Winton, and Gaeth—had gone in for mass production of inexpensive cars, and if Ford had done just the reverse, in all probability Cleveland and not Detroit would be the hub of the automotive industry today. And if Ford had started tinkering with clocks in Bismarck, North Dakota, and had remained there permanently, his fame would have been local and short-lived—"the visionary who didn't make good."

However, the automobile industry has been decentralizing toward both coasts, to Canada, and overseas. Thus it has been following the twin principles of modern relocation: first, regional plants; and second, production in well-balanced communities where labor efficiency is high.

The automotive industry is dominated by three large corporations that together supply nine-tenths of the automobiles in Anglo-America and that are among the world's

[16] John A. Piquet, "The Factor of Plant Location in Automobile Production," *Industrial Management,* Vol. 68 (November 1924), p. 297.

[17] Roger Burlingame, *Backgrounds of Power: The Human Story of Mass Production* (New York: Charles Scribner's Sons, 1949).
[18] Jeanette Mirsky and Allan Nevins, *The World of Eli Whitney* (New York: The Macmillan Co., 1952).

leading industrial corporations in size and organizational complexity. Largest of the three is General Motors Corporation, which, with its subsidiaries, contributes more than half the total production; second and third largest are the Ford Motor Company (Figure 3-11) and the Chrysler Corporation.

The Canadian motor-vehicle industry, which is mainly centered at Windsor and Oshawa in Ontario, is this province's most important industry. As in the United States, however, factories in many widely scattered cities and towns provide the innumerable parts. Some of these devote so large a part of their total industrial output to the automobile that they may justifiably be termed "automobile cities."

Windsor is the "Detroit of Canada," as well as one of the outstanding automotive centers of the entire British Commonwealth. It has several advantages for automobile manufacture. (1) It is separated from Detroit by the international boundary; if there were no boundary Windsor would be a suburb of Detroit instead of a city with more than 100,000 inhabitants. (2) It is just across the river from Detroit, and parts of all kinds can be assembled easily and cheaply. (3) It is close to the branch factories in Canada of the big American companies. (4) About 60 per cent of Canada's people live in the two provinces of Ontario and Quebec; this means that most of the Canadian market is easily accessible. (Windsor is not so strategically located to market, however, as Toronto.)

Figure 3-11. A portion of Ford's River Rouge complex at Dearborn, a suburb of Detroit. Shown here are ore boat slips, raw material storage bins, coke ovens, open hearth furnaces, and rolling mills. In addition to this steel center, the company manufactures automobiles on adjacent land. (Photo courtesy Educational Affairs Department, Ford Motor Company.)

The Chemical Industry   So important is the automotive industry in this area that it overshadows the manufacture of chemicals which is also an impressive enterprise. Most of the chemical plants, drawing upon huge deposits of salt which underlie Detroit, are located down the Detroit River from the Rouge and just beyond the northern edge of the city.

Agricultural Implements   Canada's agricultural implement industry is important in this district. When implements were made largely from wood, it was natural that their manufacture should have taken place in the lowlands where such hardwoods as oak and maple were available. Due to the early start here, the industry has remained even though iron and steel implements have replaced those made from wood, the prairie was opened up to agriculture, and farm implements acquire bulk in the process of manufacture. To save freight costs in shipping, of course, the implements are "knocked down" and reassembled near the market. In addition to the huge market for farm machinery in the Prairie Provinces, a large demand is also near at hand in Ontario and Quebec. Finally this area is well located for exporting, the importance of which is indicated by the fact that about one-third of the total Canadian output is shipped abroad.

Iron and Steel   Though Detroit is the largest steel-consuming center in the United States and though it enjoys every advantage of other Lower Lake cities for the economical assembly of raw materials at the blast furnaces with resulting low manufacturing costs, the city produces only one-fourth as much steel as Chicago or one-third as much as Pittsburgh. Even so, it ranks just behind Baltimore as the fifth largest steel maker in Anglo-America.

Only two conditions may prevent Detroit from becoming the great iron and steel center that its economic and geographic conditions would seem to guarantee it: (1)

security requirements and consequent dispersion of most industry and (2) the increasing decentralization of the automotive industry itself.

The Chicago-Milwaukee District

The Chicago-Milwaukee District occupies the western and southwestern shores of Lake Michigan from Gary to Wauwatosa and includes satellite towns and cities extending a short distance inland. Heavy industry predominates. The fountainhead of all manufacturing is thus the great primary iron and steel industry at the southern end of Lake Michigan, from which fan out in all directions, though mostly to the west and north, the many industries that utilize steel. The type of product made varies with the distance from the steel mills: heavy products obviously are fabricated close by, lighter articles farther away. This district, then, may well be considered to be the western outpost of both the primary and the secondary iron and steel industries of the continent.

Other major industrial enterprises produce electrical machinery, farm equipment, railway rolling stock, automobiles, apparel, oil, and beer. Food processing and printing and publishing are also notable.

Most manufacturing in Wisconsin and Illinois is confined to this district. *Chicago* is the second largest industrial center in the continent, and *Milwaukee* ranks twelfth. Smaller centers of note include *Rockford, Joliet, Racine,* and *Kenosha.*

Iron and Steel   Chicago-Gary, comprising one of the outstanding manufacturing areas of the world, is strategically located for making iron and steel, for iron ore and limestone can be brought directly to the blast furnaces by lake carrier, and coal is not far distant in central and southern Illinois, though most coking fuel is brought from West Virginia and Kentucky, by rail or by the combination of rail and lake carrier. This district has the best balance between production and consumption of any iron and steel area in the United States. Its output of steel is greater than that of the entire United Kingdom, and almost as much as that of West Germany.[19]

Gary is one of the outstanding examples of a thoughtfully planned industrial location. For 60 years its metallurgical industry has been built up step by step. In 1905 the United States Steel Corporation needed a new plant to serve the rapidly growing Midwestern market. What is now Gary was then an area of sand dunes and swamps. Its intermediate location between the Northern Appalachian coal fields and the Lake Superior iron-ore deposits enables this area to assemble these two raw materials economically, and limestone is available in Indiana and Michigan. Gary's location with respect to markets is unsurpassed (see Chapter 2).

Further expansion of steel making to the east around the southern tip of Lake Michigan is projected. A major conflict of interests has developed between industrialists who want to use the sandy lake margin for factories and conservationists who would prefer to have the area reserved for recreational purposes.

Agricultural Implements   Though the American agricultural implement industry had its inception along the Eastern Seaboard, it migrated westward with the population via New York, Pennsylvania, and Ohio. Illinois ultimately became the leading state and today turns out approximately one-half the country's production. Chicago is the outstanding center, and Milwaukee has considerable production also. Since agricultural implements are bulky, this industry locates as near as possible to the farmers who use them.

[19] Alexandersson, "Changes in the Location Pattern of the Anglo-American Steel Industry," p. 101.

Machinery   In addition to farm machinery, the district produces many other types of mechanical devices. Not only is machinery production Chicago's leading industry, but the city is Anglo-America's largest machinery producer. Communications equipment (telephone, radio, television) is outstanding, but the quantity and variety of total machinery output is unequalled.

Petroleum Refining   The Whiting-South Chicago industrial district, lying within the Chicago Metropolitan Area, is one of the three largest petroleum refining and storage centers in the American Manufacturing Region. Whiting represents the *market-oriented* refinery location—today the most important of the basic types of location. More than two-thirds of the refineries in the United States are located with respect to concentrated markets, either in coastal areas or at strategic interior points. Whiting is well situated to serve the Midwestern market.

Many products are procured in the distillation process. Hence it is more profitable to refine oil near the market for these products than to ship them from refineries in or near oil fields and far from large consuming areas. Crude oil can be moved to inland refineries today by pipeline at very low cost.

Oil refining as now carried on is more of a chemical industry than a processing operation. The industry, to be profitable, must be conducted on a steady basis of operation and on a large scale.

Meat Packing   Prior to the development of big cities, slaughtering was a local enterprise. The first real concentration of slaughtering and meat packing took place at Cincinnati, which predominated so long as its tributary area led in the production of livestock; but after cattle raising developed farther west, meat packing followed. The basic characteristic of the meat-packing industry is that about two-thirds of the livestock of the United States are raised west of the Mississippi River, whereas about two-thirds of the people live east of it. This separation of production and consumption means that livestock or meat or both must move considerable distances.

Meat packing in recent years has been migrating still farther west into areas where range animals are sent for winter fattening, a response to the proximity of grazing lands, feedlots, and rapid transportation. This is an effort to avoid heavy freight charges on the waste material (actually by-products rather than waste) forming a large part of the weight of each animal and to prevent the animals from losing weight enroute to slaughtering centers. The refrigerator car, which was developed about 1880, has enabled the industry to overcome the handicap of geographical location. Since only 70 to 75 per cent of a hog is pork and only 50 to 60 per cent of a steer is beef, transportation costs are reduced when slaughtering houses are located near grazing and fattening areas.

Although still an important meat-packing center, Chicago no longer dominates the industry as it did before 1955. Its large, old packing plants, located in the congested Stockyards district, were expensive to operate and to modernize. Also, other manufacturers competed for labor in terms of wage rates. As a result, three of the "Big Four" packers terminated their Chicago operations. Omaha is now the leading beef-packing city, and Omaha, South St. Paul, and East St. Louis all slaughter more hogs than does Chicago.

The Industries of the Rock Valley On the fringe of the district is the Rock Valley of southern Wisconsin and northern Illinois. The leading products of the valley are metal goods, machinery, hardware, machine tools, and automotive equipment, although some furniture, textiles, and foods are also manufactured.

The cities which contribute most to production—Rockford, Beloit, Madison, Janes-

ville, Sterling, and Freeport—constitute the core of the area.

Considering the Valley's prominence industrially, it is surprising to note the paucity of local raw materials, absence of an important local source of coal and hydroelectric power, lack of a substantial encircling market, and merely average transport facilities.

The big advantages are imaginative and inventive management, a labor supply with disposition and talents for manufacturing, location near enough to Eastern markets to prevent prohibitive transport costs, early start (the factories were built to supply the local market and were based upon local water power and local timber resources) and the advantages inherent in small cities. Wages are slightly lower than those paid for the same work by Eastern competitors. The first of these factors is indisputably the most important; nearly half of the native factories can be traced directly to local inventions.

Inland Ohio-Indiana District

This district is situated between the Great Lakes and the Ohio River; thus, it can draw on both for transportation, but suffers in cost by being adjacent to neither. It lies between the coal fields to the east and the productive farm lands to the west. Its industries are diversified—machine tools, cash registers, refrigerators, soaps, meat, tobacco, iron and steel, beer, shoes, radios, and clothing. The most intensely industrialized part is the Miami Valley from Springfield to Hamilton. Indianapolis is the major center in the western part; Dayton and Columbus, in the eastern.

Miami Valley Within the valley are several cities with a long industrial history and considerable production today. They early supplied commodities for use in the prosperous farming hinterland, but the real stimulus to manufacturing was the building

Figure 3-12. The main offices and factory of the National Cash Register Company in Dayton. (Photo courtesy the National Cash Register Company.)

of the Miami and Erie Canal in the 1820's. Three stages distinguished the industrial evolution of the Miami Valley: (1) the days of the early river and canal, when mostly quasi-manufactured goods from the farms— flour, meat, leather, and wool—moved down the Ohio and Mississippi Rivers to Southern markets; (2) the railroad period when the manufactured products—agricultural implements, tobacco, soap, paper, and machinery —moved to national markets; and (3) the present period of specialized products—iron and steel, machine tools, all kinds of machinery, radios, aircraft, automatic and calculating machines—also moved to national markets.

This area is unique in that it lacks raw materials and power. It is strongly individualized by the high value of its manufactures, an emphasis upon precision machinery, and a widely ramified market. This area has become a reservoir of skilled labor.

Dayton is the largest industrial center in the valley. It specializes in machinery production, particularly refrigerators, cash registers (Figure 3-12), accounting equipment, and machine tools. *Hamilton* is famed for its output of paper and paper-making machinery, as well as pig iron; *Middletown* has a large primary steel industry; and *Springfield* is a diversified machinery center.

Other Industrial Cities Elsewhere in the district manufacturing complexes are found only in isolated cities. Indianapolis and Columbus, the two largest, are landlocked localities that have prospered because of an early start at the crossing of surface transportation routes. *Indianapolis* is a diversified industrial center, with an emphasis on metalworking factories. Food processing, especially meat packing and flour milling, are also important. *Columbus* is not primarily an industrial city, but its factories have prospered because of its central location, its skilled labor force, and the strong impetus given to local metalworking firms by the establishment of a large aircraft factory during World War II. Smaller industrial

57

cities in the district include *Fort Wayne,* *Muncie,* and *Lima.*

Middle Ohio Valley

One of the more dynamic manufacturing districts in the world extends for 500 miles along the valley of the Ohio River. The district benefits by its river location, but cheap water transportation is only one of the factors that has attracted many large industrial enterprises in the last few years.

The availability of large, reliable supplies of coal from nearby mines is an important consideration. The seasonal vagaries of hydroelectricity have caused many industrialists to consider coal again as a power source, and the Ohio Valley has a plentiful supply. In addition, the valley earlier had an abundance of land, at reasonable prices, although now flat land is more expensive. And in general there is a greater surplus of suitable labor in and near the district than in any comparable portion of Anglo-America.

Older Centers The four older, established industrial centers of the district have shared in the new boom. (1) *Cincinnati,* largest city in the valley, has added electrical equipment to the machine tools, auto parts, and aircraft engines that were its previous stock in trade. (2) *Louisville* is famous for its distilleries, cigarette factories, and chemical plants, but its principal recent growth has been in machinery production, which is dominated by General Electric's Appliance Park, a 1,000-acre complex of diversified household-appliance manufacture (Figure 3-13). (3) The three neighboring cities of *Huntington* (W.Va.), *Ashland* (Kentucky), and *Ironton* (Ohio) have expanded their metallurgical and

Figure 3-13. General Electric's Appliance Park in Louisville. This is the world's largest household appliance manufacturing center, with 10,000 employees. (Photo courtesy General Electric Company.)

chemical production. (4) The Kanawha Valley of West Virginia, both upstream and downstream from *Charleston,* has long been noted for its output of a variety of chemicals (Figure 3-14). The availability of good local coal, natural gas, and brine has attracted a variety of plants to riverside locations along the only good artery of transportation through the hill country.

Other Recent Developments Many of the most spectacular industrial developments in this district have taken place away from the older centers, often in the splendid isolation of a completely rural setting some distance from any urban settlement. The lure of "firm" power has been sufficient to attract the three newest aluminum refineries in the country. Chemical and glass plants have proliferated considerably.

In the early 1960's the boom continues. Some problems are becoming clearer, however. The 46 dams on the Ohio River are several decades old, and their locks are not big or fast enough to move the barge traffic with dispatch at peak times. Cross-river traffic flow is also slow; there are few bridges, so that ferries must be used. Water pollution (in spite of the good work of the Ohio River Valley Water Sanitation Compact) and a growing scarcity of flat land may slow the pace of expansion, but new plant investment is measured in billions of dollars, an indication that expansion will continue. Construction has begun according to a master plan that calls for the reduction of the number of dams and locks on the river by 60 per cent, which will result in longer pools and considerable saving of time for the carriers.

St. Louis District

The St. Louis District lies mostly in Missouri but partly in Illinois. The largest urban center between Chicago and the Pacific Coast, *St. Louis* is a commercial and trans-

Figure 3-14. Charleston and the Kanawha River. This is the heart of "Chemical Valley." (Photo courtesy Charleston Chamber of Commerce.)

portation hub and one of the ten leading industrial centers in Anglo-America. It exerts strong influence in the Middle Mississippi Basin. Its industrial structure is more diversified than that of any other city except Philadelphia. The largest of its industries, transportation equipment, represents less than 10 per cent of the total product.

Despite its importance in manufacturing, St. Louis is essentially a commercial city. Its strategic location on the high west bank of the Mississippi River, a short distance below the mouth of the Missouri, has enabled St. Louis since early days to dominate much of the river trade. The city later became an outstanding railway center and today as such ranks second only to Chicago.

The metropolitan district, which includes East St. Louis, Alton, Belleville, and Granite City, contributes heavily to the nation's total output of shoes, automobiles, beer, meat, electrical equipment, airplane engines and accessories, chemicals, drugs, furs, glass, refined petroleum, and iron and steel. About 75 per cent of the factories and plants are in the city and its Missouri suburbs; the remaining 25 per cent are on the Illinois side of the river.

Transportation

In a region where manufacturing is predominant, cities numerous, and population dense, transportation must be superior. The American Manufacturing Region has an unsurpassed network of railways, highways, airways, and waterways that bind it together and link it with other regions.

Ocean Transportation Brief reference must suffice for this topic since New York, Baltimore, Philadelphia, and Boston have already been treated and it was seen that as port cities they all excel. All are connected with the far corners of the earth and all have ready access to the food, industrial raw materials, and markets of interior Anglo-America.

The Great Lakes The Great Lakes comprise the most valuable system of inland waterways in the world. For 1,700 miles

they extend in an east-west direction, connecting the Central Northwest, a rich source of raw materials, with the fuel, industries, and markets of the East. Few barriers to navigation now exist between Duluth and Montreal. The lakes seldom experience severe storms, but they are closed by ice normally from December to May. The shores of the lakes are dotted with great industrial and commercial cities.

Most of the traffic consists of bulky products—iron ore, coal, wheat, and limestone. These are handled economically by specially designed boats capable of carrying enormous cargoes. Speedy loading and unloading facilities have been installed at the ports.

Transportation on the Great Lakes was dramatically augmented in 1959 by the completion of the St. Lawrence Seaway, a $1,000,000,000 joint Canadian-United States navigation and power project. The Great Lakes had been open to ocean-going traffic ever since the construction of the Welland Canal, but only for small vessels. With the

Figure 3-15. A St. Lawrence Seaway scene. Dams and a dredging operation near Cornwall, Ontario. (Photo courtesy National Film Board, Ottawa.)

completion of the Seaway, there is a channel at least 27 feet deep all the way to the western end of Lake Superior.

Most Seaway construction was undertaken along the St. Lawrence River between Montreal and Lake Ontario. Canals and locks were built to bypass rapids and dams in this stretch of the river (Figure 3-15). The Welland and Sault St. Marie canals were also deepened as ancillary features of the project.

The net result (aside from the tremendous amount of hydroelectricity that can now be generated) is that medium-sized ocean-going vessels can now penetrate the Great Lakes as far as Chicago or Duluth. In spite of considerably increased ship movements, many problems have developed, and the Seaway's backers have been somewhat disappointed by the results of the first few years' traffic. It seems likely that a period of readjustment will be necessary before the full potential of the Seaway is realized.

The basic pattern of movement on the Lakes has not been altered. The Seaway is essentially an iron ore and grain waterway, with these two commodities accounting for two-thirds of the bulk carried. Canadian ore is brought up the Seaway from Sept Îles and American ore is taken down the Lakes from the Lake Superior deposits. Both United States and Canadian grain (primarily wheat) is carried down the Lakes and out the Seaway for export overseas.

In its first years of operation, the Seaway has been most important as a route for trade within Canada, for trade between Canada and the United States, and for export of grain from both countries. Many improvements have been made in port facilities on both sides of the border, especially in Chicago. In early operations Toronto is the port that has benefited most from Seaway construction, but the benefits undoubtedly will be shared more widely as the long-range traffic pattern begins to be revealed.

The cost has been high, but commerce has been and will be augmented, and industry in many parts of the American Manufacturing Region will be stimulated.

Rivers Rivers were the great highways of colonial days, having been used whenever possible in preference to the hard and slow overland routes. Their chief advantages as highways were low cost and convenience. Many a stream that now seems too small or shallow to have served was very extensively used, and many a settlement would have died out had there been no stream over which to float products to market. All large western communities in the period 1800 to 1850 were located on the Ohio or the Mississippi.

The Detroit (a link in the Great Lakes system), Monongahela, Ohio, Kanawha, Hudson, Mississippi, and Illinois are the principal rivers of the American Manufacturing Region, and most important are the first three.

THE DETROIT RIVER The Detroit River, which drains Lake St. Clair into Lake Erie, is 28 miles long and one-half mile to three miles wide. A shoal that formerly blocked its entrance from Lake St. Clair has been cut through. About three-fourths of the tonnage moving down the lakes passes through the Detroit River and this is more than the total tonnage moving through the Suez and Panama Canals.

THE MONONGAHELA RIVER The Monongahela, a deeply entrenched river, is unique in two respects: (1) it is the most used in Anglo-America, and (2) it is one of the few important streams flowing northward. Its valley is a land of chemical works and coke plants, of glass-works and steel mills—and of coal.

The Monongahela was the first river in the United States to be improved for navigation, because it was essential for transport of coal when Pittsburgh was the world's leading iron and steel center, and it was rendered unreliable by annual droughts and floods. Today it is navigable from Fairmont, West Virginia, to its mouth at Pittsburgh.

Pittsburgh's principal competitive advantage in the iron and steel industry is the low-cost barge transportation of coking coal from river tipples to by-product coking plants without transshipment.

THE OHIO RIVER   The channel of the Ohio River was not navigable during the droughts of late summer until the federal government established a permanent nine-foot stage with a system of four dozen dams which back the water into a succession of pools deep enough for navigation. Locks permit boats to get around the dams.

The Ohio accordingly has become one of the continent's leading carriers of freight. Thousands of commodious barges, shackled in tows, are propelled over the river at all seasons, except for several days in spring when the water is too high or in winter when ice is objectionable. The tonnage is several times greater now than it was at the height of the steamboat period. Ninety-five per cent of the total freight consists of bulky products—coal, coke, ore, sand and gravel, stone, grain, pig iron, and steel. Increasing quantities of gasoline are being shipped. Most of the traffic is in the hands of contract and private carriers.

Canals   Space forbids adequate treatment of the fascinating and romantic subject of canals. Though most of them proved inadequate, particularly because they were closed by ice for several months each year, they did, nevertheless, play a vital role during the decades when people depended primarily upon inland water transportation. Canals were built to connect natural waterways.

THE WELLAND CANAL   Most important in this region is the Welland Canal, built to avoid Niagara Falls and connecting Port Colborne on Lake Erie with Port Weller on Lake Ontario. Built in 1829, it was a tortuous ditch with 25 locks. Nevertheless, it did a tremendous business and during the boom grain year of 1928 handled 131,-531,000 bushels. Unfortunately, the large lake carriers, which constitute about 90 per cent of the ships on the lakes, could not navigate the canal; cargoes had to be unloaded at Port Colborne, the Canadian terminal harbor 25 miles west of Buffalo, and placed aboard smaller ships. These required about 16 hours to make the canal trip, against 8 hours today. The greater economy and efficiency attained by larger lake vessels led to a desire to enlarge the canal; the work was begun in 1913 and completed in 1931. The new Welland Canal can handle any ship on the lakes. Whereas the old canal had 25 locks, the new one has but 7. Though 30 miles long, it has few curves and no bad ones.

NEW YORK STATE BARGE (ERIE) CANAL This canal, which connects Lake Erie with the Hudson River, was opened in 1825. It follows the only practical route through the Appalachian barrier—the Mohawk Gap and the Ontario Plain. Freight rates between Buffalo and New York immediately dropped from $100 to $5 per ton and the transit time was shortened from 20 to 8 days. The Erie Canal, probably more than any other single factor, made New York City the greatest port on the Atlantic Coast. Traffic from the interior poured into New York Harbor. The Erie was financially successful, and it was the busiest inland waterway in the world for many years.

In 1875, however, it was surpassed by the railway. Tolls were abolished in 1883, but this was only a temporary solution. By 1895 the tonnage fell to 3.5 million as against 19 million for its competing railroad. The solution appeared to be a larger canal. Its construction was undertaken and it was completed in 1918—the New York State Barge Canal. It followed the route of its predecessor most of the way. It is 353 miles long from Buffalo to Waterford (near Troy) on the Hudson. But little traffic was generated. It is used only by self-propelled vessels or tows propelled by them. Traffic has been increasing in recent years but only slowly.

THE ILLINOIS AND MICHIGAN CANAL   As early as 1673 the explorers Joliet and Marquette spoke of the advantages of a canal that would connect the Illinois and Des Plaines Rivers with the Chicago River. Construction on the Illinois and Michigan Canal was not begun until 1836, however, and it was not open for traffic until 1848. The waterway was 6 feet deep, 48 feet wide, and 97 miles long. Fed in part by Chicago River water, it also aided in solving Chicago's sewage problem, which had been critical, since no current could carry the waste away from the dead end of Lake Michigan. In 1871 Chicago deepened the summit level of this canal in order to reduce the pollution of the lake. In 1911 the Chicago Drainage Canal, which paralleled its predecessor to Joliet, was opened. Since it had a depth of 21 feet, it soon drew away all through traffic from the old canal.

In the 1920's the Lakes-to-Gulf Waterway, of which the Illinois-Michigan Canal is a part, was further improved, and the canal is now nine feet deep and a barge waterway from Lake Michigan to the Illinois River. Traffic is definitely increasing.

THE CHESAPEAKE AND DELAWARE CANAL   The Chesapeake and Delaware Canal, connecting the Delaware River on the east with an arm of Chesapeake Bay on the west, is 19 miles long and 27 feet deep. It was completed in 1829, providing an all-water route from Philadelphia to Baltimore. Tideless and toll-free, it constitutes an important link in the Intra-coastal Waterway, which has been owned and operated by the United States government since 1919. Accommodating all but the very largest ocean-going vessels, it shortens the water route from Baltimore to Philadelphia by 316 miles.

Railroads   Though the United States has but seven per cent of the world's population and seven per cent of its area, it has nearly one-third of the railroad mileage. Most cities in the United States developed simultaneously with railroads; 73 per cent of all rail traffic terminates in urban areas. As early as the 1850's, far-seeing men felt certain that the West would be developed by railroads rather than by rivers and canals. By 1860 railroads had triumphed over inland waterways, and since then port rivalries have been expressed in the competition of the railroads serving them.

The American Manufacturing Region has a real rail web—the most important in the United States. Its railways carry more than half the passengers and tonnage handled by all American railroads. This volume of traffic is attributable to the fact that so large a part of the total population dwells in the Manufacturing Region that most of the products of the farm, the mine, and the factory must be consumed there. Most of the lines run east and west. In this region no one, be he an inhabitant of a city, town, village, hamlet, or farm, is more than a few miles from a railway.

Highways   The roads of the colonies were little more than cleared paths and were made mostly for local traffic. Toll roads were built by private companies between 1790 and 1840. The federal government began construction on the National Road in 1811, opening it in 1817. Since then, this nation, but more particularly the American Manufacturing Region, has been spider-webbed with roads, because hard-surface highways and heavy traffic are synonymous with dense population and high productivity.

Without automobiles and motor trucks speeding over the roads day and night, urban dwellers would experience difficulty in securing food. Motor trucks benefit from low capacities and high speed and can, therefore, provide frequent shipments at low cost. They also have a distinct advantage over railroads in short hauls, and are competing successfully with railroads on intermediate and even long hauls. Most major rail lines have organized piggyback operations (hauling loaded trailers on flat cars) in order to win back some of their lost business. Trucks have been a potent factor in decentralizing industry.

Unfortunately the highway system in this region is glutted with bottlenecks, especially in and around cities. Bypasses, parkways, freeways, and turnpikes are, however, relieving some of the congestion.

Various states in the American Manufacturing Region have built toll turnpikes as important arteries in their highway transportation systems. The principal ones are: (1) a network of toll roads in southern New England; (2) five toll highways radiating out of New York City into Connecticut, New York, and New Jersey; (3) a continuous toll road from New York City to Chicago, crossing parts of five states; and (4) a series of short turnpikes radiating out of, or bypassing, Chicago.

Toll roads, however, are no longer being planned because of the extensive national interstate highway system that is under construction in the United States (planned extent, 42,000 miles; estimated cost, $41,-000,000,000; planned completion, 1975). All of the large, and most of the medium-sized, cities in the nation will be connected by this system, normally with a four-lane, divided, controlled-access type of highway. A large portion of the new roadway system is located in the American Manufacturing Region.

Pipelines   Petroleum, when first discovered, was transported in barrels by wagons, and somewhat later by railroads. As production skyrocketed, a new method of get-

ting petroleum to market had to be found. The pipeline resulted. Pipeline routes are chosen with great care—often with the aid of aerial surveys. Sharp valleys, ridges, and rivers are avoided whenever possible, and even soil, climate, and vegetation are considered. The routes usually go directly to their destinations except when skirting urban centers.

The American Manufacturing Region has attracted many of the trunk pipelines from the Mid-Continent and other oil-producing areas to refining and marketing centers on the Great Lakes, the Mississippi River, and the Atlantic Seaboard of both Canada and the United States.

Formerly only crude oil was shipped, but now considerable quantities of oil products move by pipeline.

Natural gas production began in 1820, when the first well drilled explicitly to produce gas was completed at Fredonia, New York. Today natural gas provides nearly one-third of all the energy consumed in the nation, gaining at the expense of both coal and petroleum. Few businesses have boomed in recent years as has that of production and transportation of natural gas. Much of this expansion must be attributed to the increasing use of long-distance transmission lines. Today the United States has nearly 500,000 miles of natural gas pipelines; several of the individual lines exceed 1,500 miles in length. Many of these pipelines extend from the South into the American Manufacturing Region.

Air Transportation   The great size of the United States and Canada, along with the demand for speedy transportation, stimulated the rapid growth of airways, particularly after 1930. Most of the traffic is passenger but the amount of air freight is increasing.

Airline routes of the United States and Canada are confined to fairly well-defined lines of travel, since they connect leading cities and depend upon ground aids. The natural environment of the region over which planes fly has much influence on weather conditions and hence on safety. Especially is this true of mountains and of areas affected by fog, heavy rain and snow, thunderstorms, surface winds, and upper winds.

The Outlook

It has been pointed out that the American Manufacturing Region contains a disproportionate share of Anglo-America's population, metropolitan areas, cities, manufacturing plants, and wealth. It is essentially a region of industrial cities and towns.

This region's future undoubtedly will continue its present trend, a prediction that seems to be well substantiated by the fact that during the 1950's most of the industrial growth of the two nations occurred in this Region. This is contrary to the public notion that most of the new industry has sprung up in the South and Far West in the United States.

The American Manufacturing Region is a region of great cities. Cities will continue to grow, the suburbs will continue to grow even faster, and the nation's population will become increasingly urban. Continued mechanization of farms will release more and more young people from the land, and a large percentage of them will gravitate to the urban areas where there are more opportunities. Thus, farms and farm villages function as "seed bags" of our cities.

For some time a form of decentralization known as diffusion has been going on in the United States. This is a movement out of the centers of metropolitan areas to their peripheries. Decentralization and diffusion have been going on for some years but only when companies could be sure it was to their economic advantage.

The internal functional pattern of cities in this region will probably continue to change, but slowly. Rail-side sites are still important for factories, but increasingly the industrialist will seek out suburban locations near arterial streets (particularly expressways or freeways) that will provide rapid automobile access for his employees. As suburbs expand, the city centers will either decay with economic blight or be rejuvenated by costly urban renewal projects. The ease of internal transportation may determine the speed of economic growth or decay for given cities.

Within the American Manufacturing Region certain districts will prosper more than others. Chicago should strengthen its position because of market and transportation advantages; Detroit's steel industry is likely to expand in order better to satisfy the local market; metropolitan Toronto seems favored by growing markets and increased Seaway traffic; the Ohio Valley's coal-triggered boom should continue for some time.

Over-all, the region is blessed with many advantages. There will be setbacks and erratic advances, but generally the future is bright for the world's largest and most productive industrial region.

Selected Bibliography

"A Decade of Manufacturing in Western Pennsylvania," *Monthly Business Review*, Federal Reserve Bank of Cleveland, March 1959, pp. 2-5.

Alexander, John W., "Location of Manufacturing: Methods of Measurement," *Annals of the Association of American Geographers*, Vol. 48, March 1958, pp. 20-26.

Alexandersson, Gunnar, "Changes in the Location Pattern of the Anglo-American Steel Industry: 1948-1959," *Economic Geography*, Vol. 37, April 1961, pp. 95-114.

Barton, Thomas Frank, "The Sewer or Waste Disposal Use of the Ohio River," *Journal of Geography*, Vol. 59, October 1960, pp. 326-336.

Carlson, Fred A., "Traffic on the Ohio River System," *Journal of Geography,* Vol. 59, November 1960, pp. 357-361.

Estall, R. C., "Changing Industrial Patterns of New England," *Geography,* Vol. 46, April 1961, pp. 120-138.

Hills, Theo L., "The St. Lawrence Seaway," *Focus,* Vol. 11, December 1960.

Kenyon, James B., *Industrial Localization and Metropolitan Growth,* Research Paper No. 67, Department of Geography, University of Chicago. Chicago: University of Chicago Press, 1960.

Kerr, Donald, "The Geography of the Canadian Iron and Steel Industry," *Economic Geography,* Vol. 35, April 1959, pp. 151-162.

Kerr, Donald, and Jacob Spelt, "Manufacturing in Downtown Toronto," *Geographical Bulletin,* No. 10, 1957, pp. 5-22.

————, "Manufacturing in Suburban Toronto," *Canadian Geographer,* No. 12, 1958, pp. 11-19.

Langlois, Claude, "Problems of Urban Growth in Montreal," *Canadian Geographer,* Vol. 5, Autumn 1961, pp. 1-11.

Libera, Charles J., "1975: A Target for Highways," *Monthly Review,* Federal Reserve Bank of Minneapolis, July 1961, pp. 1-6.

Lounsbury, John F., "Industrial Development in the Ohio Valley," *Journal of Geography,* Vol. 60, September 1961, pp. 253-262.

Mayer, Harold M., "Prospects and Problems of the Port of Chicago," *Economic Geography,* Vol. 31, April 1955, pp. 95-125.

Megee, Mary, "The American Bottoms: the Vacant Land and the Areal Image," *Professional Geographer,* Vol. 13, November 1961, pp. 5-9.

Montreal Research Council, *The Impact of the St. Lawrence Seaway on the Montreal Area.* Montreal: 1958.

"New England Continues as Leading Shoe Center," *New England Business Review,* Federal Reserve Bank of Boston, February 1958, pp. 1-4.

Pearson, Norman, "Conurbation Canada," *The Canadian Geographer,* Vol. 5, Winter 1961, pp. 10-17.

Reinemann, Martin W., "The Pattern and Distribution of Manufacturing in the Chicago Area," *Economic Geography,* Vol. 36, April 1960, pp. 139-144.

Rodgers, Allan, "Industrial Inertia—A Major Factor in the Location of the Steel Industry in the United States," *The Geographical Review,* Vol. 42, January 1952, pp. 56-66.

Smith, Richard Austin, "The Boiling Ohio," *Fortune,* June 1956, pp. 109ff.

Spelt, J., *The Urban Development in South-Central Ontario.* Assen, Netherlands: Van Gorcum and Company, 1955.

"The St. Lawrence Stairway to the Sea," *Business Review,* Federal Reserve Bank of Philadelphia, September 1960, pp. 2-12.

"Voltage Valley," *Fortune,* June 1956, pp. 115-122.

Wallace, William H., "Merrimack Valley Manufacturing: Past and Present," *Economic Geography,* Vol. 37, October 1961, pp. 284-308.

chapter four

Northeastern
Anglo-America

Northeastern Anglo-America is a region that lies partly in the United States and partly in Canada, and it serves as an excellent illustration of a geographical region which is not limited by political boundaries. The region consists of several parts that differ from each other in physical appearance as well as in economic responses, but when considered as a whole show considerable regional unity. Here in one way or another the majority of the people are influenced by the sea. Whether they are engaged in fishing, lumbering, pulp and papermaking, shipping wheat, mining coal, quarrying building stones, growing apples, or raising dairy cattle or foxes, their outlook is generally seaward.

To many regionalists the inhabitants of all six New England states are New Englanders: "Americans of the older stocks think of the words 'New England' as connoting not only a region but a group of traditions, institutions, and ways of living and of thinking." [1] In fact, much work has been done that would in a way justify New England as being considered a region.[2] The difficulty here, however, comes in drawing a boundary between the highlands of Vermont and the Adirondack Mountains of New York, or of separating either the Canadian

Maritime Provinces or the St. Lawrence Lowlands from the coastal areas or the highlands of New England. For that reason the authors feel that the entire Northeast should constitute one region (Figure 4-1), and that at least four subregions should be recognized. These subregions are: (1) Coastal New England, including the lowlands to the south and the coast to the immediate northeast through Maine, but not including the large industrial centers discussed previously in Chapter 3; (2) the Northeastern Uplands, including the Adirondack Mountains; (3) the Coastal Lowlands of the Maritime Provinces of Canada; and (4) the Lower St. Lawrence Valley.

[1] American Geographical Society, *New England's Prospect: 1933*, Special Publication No. 16 (New York: 1933), p. 459.
[2] National Resources Committee, *Regional Planning, Part III—New England* (Washington: Government Printing Office, 1936); and Council of Economic Advisers, Committee on the New England Economy, *The New England Economy: A Report to the President* (Washington: Government Printing Office, 1951).

Figure 4-1. Northeastern Anglo-America. A region of fisheries, forests and forest products, quarrying and mining, dairying and specialized farming, commerce, and resorts.

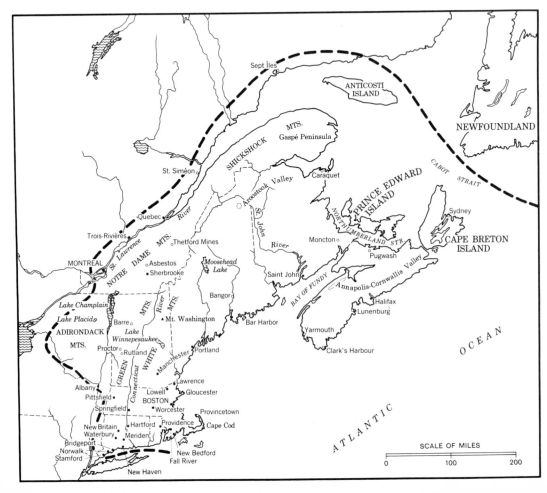

Physiographically, the provinces of the United States extend into Canada, and no marked differences appear in the way of life of the two peoples except in French Canada. The fact that each country, at the more important points of interchange, has resources which the other lacks has served to bring each country's railroads to important objectives beyond its border. It also helps to explain why Canada's railroads have been projected into the United States as a means of reaching strategic points—especially ports that are open to navigation during the winter.

The Physical Setting

Northeastern Anglo-America occupies North America's indented coastal ribbon from New York to and including the north bank of the St. Lawrence River. It comprises the littoral of Connecticut, Rhode Island, Massachusetts, New Hampshire, Maine, and New Brunswick, all of Nova Scotia, Prince Edward Island, and that part of Quebec on both sides of the river as far south as the city of Quebec. It also includes the Adirondack Mountains, the Green Mountains, the Berkshire Hills and Taconic Mountains, the White Mountains, and the Notre Dame and Shickshock Mountains, and several lowland areas such as the Aroostook Valley, the Lake Champlain Lowland, and the Connecticut Valley.

Surface Features The coastal area consists primarily of low rounded hills and valleys. Most of the region is traversed by fast-flowing streams and much of it is dotted with small lakes. The coastal area has been slightly submerged; accordingly, ocean waters have invaded the lower valleys, giving rise to bays or estuaries. Often branch bays extend up the side valleys. The coast is characterized by innumerable good harbors. Superficially, the coasts of Maine and Nova Scotia appear to be fjorded, but they are probably drowned normal river valleys and have been but little modified by ice action. The restricted and indented nature of much of the coast line has given rise to some of the greatest tidal fluctuations to be found anywhere.

The Lower St. Lawrence Valley, which extends from the Isle d'Orleans to the constriction in the river between Pointe des Monts and Cap Chat, is bounded by steep cliffs which, in places, rise abruptly from the river bank. The escarpment is 1,500 to 2,000 feet high on the north side, and on the south side opposite Quebec it is 1,000 feet, rising to 3,000 feet as it nears the Gaspé Peninsula. Coastal terraces mantled with marine soils provide the more important sites for settlement. The Lower St. Lawrence is really an arm of the Atlantic, for the submergence of the region has enabled ocean waters to penetrate tidally as far as Montreal. Below the Isle d'Orleans the river expands into a broad stream 10 to 20 miles wide.

All mountains of the upland area are geologically old and have been worn down by erosional agents (Figure 4-2). The Taconics, which border the western side of the Berkshires, are among the oldest in Anglo-America. The Green Mountains of Vermont have rounded summits—the result of the great ice sheet which overrode ridges and valleys alike. The highest summits are less than 4,500 feet above sea level. The White Mountains are higher and bolder, particularly in the Presidential Range of central New Hampshire, where Mount Washington rises to an elevation of 6,293 feet. Northeastward the mountains become more rounded and less conspicuous, although their summits remain at an elevation of nearly 5,000 feet.

The mountains of eastern Canada are lower and more rounded, having been subdued through long periods of erosion. Their general elevation is slightly more than 2,000

Figure 4-2. The highlands of New England are characterized by running water, exposed bedrock, and thick forests. This scene is on the Swift River in New Hampshire. (Photo by Dick Smith; courtesy State of New Hampshire, Division of Economic Development.)

feet above sea level. The Adirondacks, geologically an extension of the Laurentian Uplands, are also considered a part of this region because of the similarity of the activities of the inhabitants. Although an older upland mass, the Adirondacks underwent changes at the time of the Appalachian mountain-building movement, which caused a doming of the upper surface. Furthermore, they were eroded profoundly during glacial times. While not so high as the White Mountains, the Adirondacks cover more area.

The entire upland is composed of igneous and metamorphic rocks—granites, schists, gneisses, marbles, and slates—so valuable that this has become the leading source of building stones on the continent.

The stream courses of the upland area were altered by glaciation. Many water bodies, such as Lake Placid, Lake Winnipesaukee,[3] and Moosehead Lake, characterize the region. They have been of inestimable value in the development of the tourist industry.

The Aroostook Valley, occupying the upper part of the St. John River drainage, is the result of stream erosion in softer rocks.[4] The Lake Champlain Lowland and the Connecticut Valley were eroded severely by tongues of ice that moved southward between the Green Mountains and the Adirondacks, and between the Green Mountains and the White Mountains.[5]

Climate Climatically the region is not a unit. The littoral area differs from the uplands, from the Lower St. Lawrence Valley, and also from Maritime Quebec.

Nearly every part of the littoral area lies within 35 miles of the ocean and hence is greatly influenced by it. Along the coast of Maine, New Brunswick, and Nova Scotia, the marine influence results in a milder and more equable climate than would be expected in these latitudes. Nova Scotia's mean January temperature is about the same as that of central New York, despite being two to five degrees of latitude farther north. Winters, though long and cold, are not severe for the latitude. Temperatures, however, may fall below zero, and snow covers the ground throughout most of the winter. Spring surrenders reluctantly to

[3] There are on record 132 different ways of spelling this name. *Sixth Report of the United States Geographic Board* (Washington: Government Printing Office, 1933), p. 822.

[4] N. M. Fenneman, *Physiography of Eastern United States* (New York: McGraw-Hill Book Co., 1938), p. 367.

[5] Wallace W. Atwood, *The Physiographic Provinces of North America* (Boston: Ginn & Co., 1940), pp. 220-21.

summer because of the presence of ice in the Gulf of St. Lawrence and because of the Labrador Current. Summers are cool—temperatures of 90 degrees being extremely rare. The growing season varies from 100 to 160 days in Nova Scotia.

Except in northern New Brunswick, the precipitation of 40 to 55 inches is well distributed throughout the year. Summer fogs characterize the coasts of New England, New Brunswick, and Nova Scotia when southeast winds from the warm Gulf Stream blow across the cold waters between the Gulf of Maine and Newfoundland.

Maritime Quebec, the area comprising the Gaspé Peninsula and Anticosti Island, does not have a true maritime climate. Winters are long (November through April) but not severe for the latitude. Because of its proximity to the sea, its summers are not hot. The precipitation of about 30 inches is considerably less than in the littoral area; moreover, it varies from year to year. Though well distributed, the rainfall is greater in summer. Fierce gales are common in winter and are by no means unknown during the season of navigation.

The Lower St. Lawrence Valley has cold, long winters, though periods of mild weather are not uncommon. The river is closed to navigation normally from December to April. Summers are short and warm but the days are long. The growing season averages 135 days at Quebec. The precipitation of 35 to 42 inches is not heavy but is evenly distributed throughout the year. As would be expected, the snowfall is heavy. It remains on the ground all winter, for little of it thaws. Winter surrenders to spring, and summer to winter, with great rapidity.

The upland area lies within the humid continental climatic region, with the Atlantic Ocean exerting little influence. The growing season is short, averaging less than 120 days. Summers are cool and winters extremely cold, temperatures dropping at times to 30 degrees below zero. The abundant precipitation is evenly distributed throughout the year, but in winter most of it falls as snow. This seeming handicap has been turned to economic advantage by the commercial development of winter sports.

Natural Vegetation   It is extremely difficult to get an accurate word-picture of the forest in its primitive state. Probably nine-tenths of the land included in this region was once covered with trees. About the only treeless parts were the dunes, marshes, meadows, bogs, and some mountain summits (if ice-scoured or exposed to wind).

The composition of the forest was closely adjusted to land forms, soil, and climate. There was a great variety of species and a great difference in the ages and sizes of the trees. Between the pine forest of the valleys and the spruce forest of the mountains was a belt of hardwoods—maple, yellow birch, and beech—with occasional sprinklings of pine, hemlock, spruce, ash, and paper birch.

Coastal New Hampshire and most of coastal Maine contained white pine, spruce, hemlock, red oak, and white ash. White pine was the outstanding tree. Attaining a height of 240 feet and a diameter of 6 feet at the butt, it dwarfed even the tall spruce. It was sometimes called the "masting pine" because the larger trees were marked with the Royal Arrow and reserved for masts for the Royal Navy. Maine still is called the "Pine Tree State."

All of the upland area except the highest mountains was originally clothed in a dense forest. The higher slopes had the typical fir, hemlock, and spruce of the northern forest; the lower ones had white pine and mixed hardwoods. As men cut the more accessible timber for lumber and firewood and later cleared much of the land for farms, the primeval forests began to disappear. Rapid cutting, followed by forest fires, ruined much of the natural beauty of the upland, accelerated stream run-off, and caused floods and soil erosion. But natural regeneration and some artificial reforestation have healed many of the woodland scars, and there have been established several state forest preserves as well as the Green Mountain and the White Mountain national forests.

Soils The soils are extremely varied, partly because of differences in the parent rock and partly because of widespread glaciation. Most of the farm land is on the sedimentaries. All the mature soils are pedalfers: gray-brown podzolic soils predominate in coastal New Hampshire and Maine, while podzols prevail in New Brunswick, Nova Scotia, and the Lower St. Lawrence Valley. (The student is referred to Appendix A for brief background reading on soils and other physical elements of geography.) In addition, there are large areas covered with hydromorphic, or poorly drained, soils. The gray-brown soils which develop under a forest cover (chiefly deciduous) are less leached and less acidic than the podzols and are among the better pedalfers.[6] They are low in lime and need continuous fertilization.

The podzols, on the other hand, comprise the light gray soils characteristic of climates with cool, moist summers and cold, long winters. Here the natural vegetation is coniferous forest, huckleberry, and fern—plants adapted to acid soils. Because of the acidity, this region has few good agricultural areas.

The uplands have thin soils which belong almost exclusively to the podzol group. The forests (largely coniferous) and the heavy year-round precipitation have together pro-

duced leached, acid soils of low productivity.

Settlement and Early Development

Northeastern Anglo-America was not settled by immigrants from a single country; the earliest settlers in the Maritime Provinces and Quebec were French, while those in New England were English.

The New England Segment The first important settlement in what is now New England was founded at Plymouth in 1620. All the early colonies, including those before and immediately after the landing of the Pilgrims were planted on the seaboard. The coast was, then, the first American frontier. Its settlements were bounded by untamed hills on the west and by the stormy Atlantic on the east. Its shore-dwelling pioneers, beckoned alike by the soil and the sea, obeyed both, and their adjustments to the two environments laid the foundations for the land life and sea life of the nation.

As population became denser in maritime New England and Canada, the more venturesome settlers, seeking new lands, trekked farther into the wilderness. As long as the French controlled the St. Lawrence Lowlands, the Indians of the upland remained entrenched in this so-called "neutral ground," thus restricting white settlements to the seaboard. In the Adirondacks hostile Iroquois kept the English confined to the Hudson and Mohawk valleys until the close of the Revolutionary War. After the conquest of Canada by the British, pioneers from the older parts of New England penetrated the upland, feeling that at last the power of the Indian had been broken. By the 1760's most of the lower valleys in New Hampshire and Vermont were occupied. Only forested slopes were therefore available to "newcomers"—slopes that never should have been cleared. Agriculture was of the subsistence type.

[6] For soil terminology, see *Soils and Man, Yearbook of Agriculture, 1938* (Washington: Government Printing Office, 1938); and *Soil, the 1957 Yearbook of Agriculture* (Washington: Government Printing Office, 1957).

In New England ... the colonial pattern of agriculture continued dominant until the second decade of the nineteenth century. Cultivation was extensive and exploitative, tools clumsy, systematic crop rotation and fertilizers generally absent, livestock neglected, and orchards and woodlands badly managed. ... For the most part tools and clothing were made in the farm home.[7]

The clearing of the forest for farms led to an early development of logging and lumbering, which could be carried on in winter when farm work was not feasible. The logs, dragged on the snow to frozen streams, were floated to mills in the spring when the ice melted, thus providing a supplemental source of income for the pioneers, which continued to be important until the latter part of the nineteenth century.

Between 1800 and 1810 Merino sheep, imported from Spain, greatly improved the domestic flocks and gave a new industry to the upland farmer. Raising wool sheep became a leading activity for the next three decades, and was especially profitable during the 1830's. By 1840, Eastern wool growers owned 60 per cent of the country's sheep. The New England industry was confined almost exclusively to Vermont and the hills of western Massachusetts and Connecticut.

Because of remoteness and a more severe winter climate, the Canadian section of the Northeastern Uplands has remained largely a wilderness.

Maritime Canada The first permanent settlement in North America north of Florida was at Port Royal on the Bay of Fundy. Here the French found salt marshes which needed no clearing. This environment was attractive to men from the mouth of the Loire, whose forbears for generations had reclaimed and dyked somewhat similar land. These French called their new home Acadie (Acadia), and the Acadians converted the river marshes into productive farm land which characterized the cultivated area almost exclusively for a century.[8]

The French population grew rapidly after the Treaty of Utrecht in 1713. Louisburg was fortified to guard the mouth of the St. Lawrence and the fishing fleet.

> Except during very brief intervals, they received little continuous aid or protection from their mother country. They were truly a self-made people, and by the opening of the eighteenth century they were native to Acadie. They conquered it to provide themselves with sustenance. They were almost independent of the outside world. They knew little of and cared less for its problems and its politics. The only strong tie connecting them with Europe was their religion, kept alive and real by priests.[9]

Acadia thus became a backwater off the main stream of Anglo-American life.

The Acadians remained here until the outbreak of hostilities between the British and French preceding the Seven Years' War. Then more than 6,000 of them were rounded up and banished; they were scattered from Massachusetts to South Carolina. Some fled into the forests of what are now New Brunswick, Prince Edward Island, and Quebec; some made their way to Quebec City, the Ohio Valley, and even to Louisiana; others joined the French in St. Pierre, Miquelon, and the West Indies. Many starved. The reason most commonly given for their expulsion was the fear on the part of England that so heavy a concentration of French in this part of the continent was a menace to English safety.

---

[7] Everett E. Edwards, "American Agriculture— The First 300 Years," *1940 Yearbook of Agriculture* (Washington: Government Printing Office, 1940), p. 205.

[8] J. B. Brebner, *New England's Outpost: Acadia Before the Conquest of Canada* (New York: Columbia University Press, 1927), p. 37.

[9] Brebner, *New England's Outpost,* p. 38.

This destruction and dispersal continued for eight years, ending in 1763. Then individuals and groups began to trickle back, and, though denied their old properties, they found abodes here and there in what are now called the "Maritime Provinces."

The first appreciable number of British to settle in the Maritimes arrived in 1749 at the site now occupied by Halifax. Shortly afterward 2,000 Germans founded Lunenburg. Highlanders, who were to make Nova Scotia a Scottish province, did not arrive until 1828; then they came by thousands. Although the largest group of British Loyalists arrived after the close of the Revolutionary War, many came prior to 1776.

The Lower St. Lawrence Valley The French colonized the Lower St. Lawrence Valley, occupying first the land along the river. As early as 1675 nearly all the ancestors of the present inhabitants had reached Canada. They practiced subsistence farming on terraces. Because of isolation, a culture became established that was picturesque in its retarded development and less affected than any other group in Anglo-America by ideas and customs from the outside.

The Present Inhabitants

The international boundary between the Canadian and United States portions of the region does not mean what it would in Europe, for there is much contact across the border between the English-speaking peoples. There is a great difference, however, between these people and the French Canadians.

The New Englanders The original white settlers, of English stock, remained dominant until about 1840. For two and one-half centuries "during the period of poverty and struggle, the Yankees increased, beat down the forest, won the fields, sailed the seas, and went forth to populate Western commonwealths." [10] To them work was a virtue, idleness a sin.

The Yankees no longer dominate New England numerically, save in the rather isolated agricultural areas of the highland interior where there is a large proportion of old people. Yankee stock still contributes most of the bank directors, business executives, and college and university presidents —officials "not elected by popular vote."

The Inhabitants of Atlantic Canada
The Maritime Areas are not densely settled and the number of cities is small. The population is about equally divided between English and French, though other nationalities are represented. About one-fifth are descendants of the Acadians.

This area has lost heavily through emigration to New England and to the Canadian Prairie Provinces. The rural population is less uniform than that of New England, because large blocks of immigrants settled together in groups. Thus most of northern New Brunswick is French, south-central Nova Scotia is predominantly German, western Nova Scotia is English, eastern Nova Scotia, eastern New Brunswick and Prince Edward Island are Scottish.

The French Canadians The Lower St. Lawrence Valley is inhabited almost entirely by French Canadians,[11] who have one of the highest birth rates in North America. They have overpopulated their lands. Pressure of population has encouraged emigration to the United States and to the more western parts of Canada, as well as within French Canada itself. In order to stem the tide of migration and keep the people attached to the soil of the Province, the Roman Catholic Church and the Quebec Government are cooperating. They are creating

10 J. Russell Smith and M. Ogden Phillips, *North America* (New York: Harcourt, Brace & Co., 1940), p. 113.
11 In Quebec as a whole, more than 80 per cent of the people are of French origin and nearly 90 per cent are Roman Catholic.

a new Quebec in the Abitibi District in the western part of the Province (outside this region), where many farmers and miners have settled. The present generation is less conservative than most Americans picture it. Many of the young people especially are no longer attracted to the soil, feeling it will not provide them with an adequate livelihood.

The Decline of Agriculture

Farming naturally was the first occupation of the colonists in the Maritime Provinces, the Lower St. Lawrence Valley, and New England. It was on a small scale and with few exceptions on infertile soils. Moreover, the cool, cloudy summers and the long, cold winters retarded the development of a thriving agriculture.

New England Those who originally settled New England arrived at the worst possible time for farming—the beginning of winter. At first they lived largely on corn and beans, which they obtained from the Indians. When they began their farming operations, they found that European cereals did not thrive. They accordingly grew more and more Indian corn, a pioneer crop with many advantages, including excellent keeping qualities and utility for food and feed. Not for some years were the Pilgrims successful in growing European cereals. Farming was very hard; it meant battling ceaselessly with the earth. A man had to spend a month removing stones from a single acre before he could plant his crops in it.

The rugged topography and the infertile soils necessitated small farms. It was impossible to accumulate capital in a small-farm economy—a circumstance that led New Englanders to turn to other occupations, especially fishing and trading.

In the early part of the nineteenth century, the level, more fertile, and more accessible lands of the Upper Mississippi and Ohio River valleys began to compete seriously with the stony hillside farms of New England. The Erie Canal, opened in 1825, brought a steadily increasing quantity of foodstuffs and wool to Eastern markets. The building of railroads west of the Appalachians opened up still larger farm areas in the Middle West. Meanwhile, because of its inability to meet this competition, the sheep industry declined. Besides, high wages in the mills of southern New England or the possibility of greater profits on new lands in the West attracted the more energetic farmers, resulting in a widespread exodus of young people. Only the more conservative preferred to remain on the hillside farms (Figure 4-3).

The peak in rural population and agricultural development occurred early in the 1800's. A large percentage of the land was

Figure 4-3. Throughout most of New England the farms are located on hillsides. This farmstead is near Cornville, Maine. (Photo courtesy of Maine Department of Economic Development.)

then farmed. Most of the farms were abandoned later, however, and today there is abundant evidence of this in terms of irregular stone walls that used to bound fields but now merely border plots of tangled and forested wilderness. Also, the large shade trees that were planted along many country lanes are now almost indistinguishable from the natural forest that has grown up.

So long as they were able to supplement their income by working in the woods in winter, the farmers could remain; but after they had cleared the forest, they had either to leave or to tolerate a lower standard of living because their small farms were definitely submarginal.

In describing the deserted town of Lyme, New Hampshire, James W. Goldthwait wrote:

> ... for almost a century deserted farms in New Hampshire have been growing up to blueberry pasture, woodland, and forest. The sturdy population that was once evenly distributed over thousands of square miles of the stony upland has slowly and steadily moved down from the hilltops, emigrating to distant places or lingering yet awhile in the valleys. Large tracts of land have been abandoned or have become the summer homes and playgrounds of well-to-do vacation seekers from the cities. ... The eastern half of this (Lyme) township is deserted country, with scarcely an occupied house and very few traveled roads . . .[12]

Between 1920 and 1930, two-thirds of Vermont's and half of New Hampshire's townships lost population. Since 1940, however, this tendency toward depopulation has decreased in the rural areas, and the total population of the two states actually increased by nearly 10 per cent between 1950 and 1960.

The Maritime Provinces Agriculture began in the Maritimes in the seventeenth century when, by dyking, the Acadians re-

claimed the tidal marshes along the Bay of Fundy. Before their expulsion in 1755, some 10,000 Acadians were supported comfortably in Nova Scotia. It is estimated that they had put 100,000 acres of land into pasture, orchard, and garden. They got as many as 20 bushels of wheat to the acre, made their orchards of apples, pears, plums, and cherries yield remarkably well, grew luxuriant small fruits, and pastured their cattle in natural meadows.

Because much of Nova Scotia, New Brunswick, and Prince Edward Island is characterized by low rounded mountain ranges, lakes, swamps, and forests, arable land always has been restricted. Most of New Brunswick still is in forest. Nova Scotia, though more favored, is not well endowed for agriculture; scarcely one-third of its area is occupied as farm land. Its productive areas are confined primarily to the western coastal belt, the Atlantic Coast being an upland of crystalline rocks. The first successful farming colony was in the meadows around Port Royal—now Annapolis. Subsequent settlement was along the more extensive marshlands about Minas Basin, Cobequid Bay, and at the head of Chignecto Bay.

The Lower St. Lawrence Valley The French Canadians in this area began as farmers. Settlement was in the form of large estates (*seigneuries*); that of Beaupre, for instance, was 48 miles long and 18 miles deep—the long side paralleling the river. The land was rented by the *seigneur* to vassals. The peasant holdings were laid out perpendicular to the river bank in narrow strips 2,600 yards long and 260 yards wide. Thus each holding had access to the river highway, which for a long time was the only thoroughfare, while the narrow width promoted continuous settlement. The houses and outbuildings were built close together for miles and gave the impression of continuous villages. The same system was used

---

[12] James W. Goldthwait, "A Town That Has Gone Downhill," *Geographical Review,* Vol. 17 (October 1927), p. 527.

Figure 4-4. The land ownership pattern of most Quebec farmland is in long, narrow, rectangular strips. The narrow dimension of these strips fronts on a river or a roadway (as above), insuring each farmer of access to transportation routes. In the foreground of this photo is the village of St. Barnabe, with its typically conspicuous Roman Catholic church. (Photograph by George Hunter.)

with respect to roads, for it was easier to keep a single road clear of winter snow (Figure 4-4). As time passed, holdings were subdivided. The long lots extended back into the forest and, besides giving each family access to the river, gave it property in each of the different zones—arable, grazing, and forest. The land devoted to pasturage increased with the clearing of the forest. The crops, with the exception of wheat, were mostly hardy ones, the same as those grown today. The agricultural technique was primitive; in the eighteenth century the two-field system was used, with alternation of wheat and fallow.

Present-Day Agriculture

Today agriculture throughout Northeastern Anglo-America continues on a small scale.

New England In coastal Maine and New Hampshire, Indian corn was the staple crop, and it continued to be so until large-scale agriculture was developed in the Middle West. Faced with this competition and realizing that rough land surface discouraged extensive use of machinery in growing corn and wheat, the New England farmer turned to specialized crops—tree fruits, berries, vegetables, and dairy and poultry products.

Hay was and still is an important crop. It had great cash value when lumbering was at its height and large numbers of horses were used. But, when pulp cutting replaced logging and lumbering, and machinery replaced horses, the market for hay was reduced. It continues to be important, however, because of dairying, and the New England farmer receives a greater return

77

per unit of labor by producing hay than do farmers in any other parts of the United States.[13]

Most of the crops of this area are grown for consumption in nearby urban areas, although potatoes and cranberries are marketed nationally. The concentration of a large population in the nearby American Manufacturing Region affords an important market for perishable foodstuffs. Dairying is the principal farm activity in New England, and due to excellent transport facilities the emphasis is on whole-milk production.

In southern Maine dairying has an adjunct, the important sweet-corn canning industry. The business of canning corn began here. The stalks and even the factory wastes —husks, shanks, silks, and cobs—are used for manure and silage. And throughout New England there are huge poultry houses that illustrate a rapidly growing facet of agriculture, the production of chickens and turkeys and their eggs.

The most significant aspect of the New England poultry industry is the raising of broilers (young, tender-meated chickens weighing about three pounds), to some extent in Connecticut, but particularly in Maine. The Maine operations, concentrated in Waldo County, are relatively costly in comparison to their competitors in the southern states. However, quality control is much closer due to highly integrated production procedures, with the result that Maine birds command premium prices on the New York market.

In the uplands of New England agriculture has continued to decline in importance except in areas such as the Lake Champlain Lowland and Aroostook County, which specialize in dairying or potato growing.

[13] Ruben W. Hecht and Glen T. Barton, *Gains in Productivity of Farm Labor* (Washington: Government Printing Office, 1950), p. 38.

The Maritime Provinces In Nova Scotia the cultivated land lies mostly in the northern lowland, the granitic interior and the Atlantic Coast tending to discourage settlement. Seventy-five per cent of the land is still in forest. The dyked lands of Old Acadia, made famous by Longfellow in *Evangeline*, still are fertile, easily cultivated, and productive. Farm crops are primarily those that mature in a short growing season—forage crops, potatoes, vegetables, and small fruits. The commercial production of apples is important also in the Annapolis-Cornwallis Valley. Nevertheless, the sea has influenced Nova Scotia's economic life more than has the land.

In New Brunswick the area in farms is about equal to that in Nova Scotia, but the area in field crops is nearly twice as great. That the province is not outstanding agriculturally seems proved by the fact that forest still covers nine-tenths of the land. An exception is the Saint John River Valley, which is farmed almost as intensively as the Connecticut Valley, although the crop possibilities are more limited. The upper part of the valley is a major potato-growing area. Pasture is less important here than in Nova Scotia. Dairying is favored in southern New Brunswick by heavy summer precipitation and proximity to urban markets. Farming in New Brunswick is characterized by small and fragmented areas of fertile soil, a large proportion of part-time farmers, and a fifty-year history of farm abandonment.

Prince Edward Island, with about two-thirds of its inhabitants engaged in farming, sustains a prosperous agriculture. Its situation is generally suitable for farm production and nonagricultural resources are virtually absent, so that this island, possibly more than any other political unit in Anglo-America, is almost completely dependent on agriculture. Over-all the countryside is a delight to the eye, with alternation of field and woodlot, unbelievably green cultivated land, neat farmsteads, and a frequent view of water. The principal commercial crop is potatoes. The island enjoys an international reputation for certified seed potatoes. When the soil becomes exhausted, mussel mud, consisting of the decay of oyster, clam, and mussel shells, is dug up from the bays and river mouths (though not within 200 yards of live oyster beds) and is spread over the land.

The Lower St. Lawrence Valley Farming continues as the principal occupation of most of the French Canadians in this area. On the north shore, the crops consist of hardy small grains, hay, vegetables, and tobacco for home consumption. Except near Quebec City, where milk, butter, and vegetables are produced for the urban market, cheese has long been the chief "money crop."

Farming practically terminates east of St. Simeon. On the south shore, where there is more lowland and the climate is somewhat milder than on the opposite shore, potatoes constitute the chief crop. Dairying is important, too, partly because it enables the farmer to work in winter in a climate where he would otherwise be idle. Winter feeding and housing, however, are costly.

The average farm is about 150 acres in size, and in the shape of a long, narrow rectangle, with the narrow axis parallel to the road. The wooden house (usually unpainted, with high dormers and an extensive veranda) with its kitchen garden faces the road. Cordwood generally is stacked beside the house, and in the rear are other farm buildings—garage, chicken house, woodshed, piggery, two-story barn with an inclined ramp leading to the upper level, one or two silos, and a machinery shed.

The land is divided into four or five parts on which hay and pasture crops alternate in rotation with hoed crops (potatoes, silage corn, mangels, and swedes) and with grain (coats and mixed grains). The pasture is often maintained apart from the rotation on a piece of land divided into several parcels which are ploughed up in turn following a four-year cycle.[14]

The typical field is bordered by a rail fence and contains a long linear "centerpiece" of stones that have been gathered and stacked by the farmer over many years. At the far end of the farm is the woodlot and the sugarbush (maple trees). The significant farm animals are dairy cattle (principally Holsteins or Ayrshires); in addition there may be poultry, sheep, or hogs.

In general, however, these Atlantic areas of Canada maintain the poorest and least economic units in Canadian agriculture. Farming on an essentially subsistence level is characteristic of the south and southeastern coasts of Nova Scotia, much of Cape Breton Island, central and northeastern New Brunswick, and the Gaspé Peninsula;[15] this is true of no other large area of Anglo-America.

Agricultural Specialization: Crop-Specialty Areas

Cape Cod and Cranberries Southeastern Massachusetts and Cape Cod lead the nation in cranberry output, accounting for more than that from all the rest of the country combined. Other producing areas include the coastal lands of New Jersey, the bog lands of Wisconsin, and the wet coastal areas of Oregon and Washington. Cape Cod first grew cranberries in 1810 but did not begin commercial production until 40 years later. This area, with hundreds of ponds, marshes, and swamps of glacial

[14] René Trepanier, "Modern Trends in Agriculture: a Glance at Rural Quebec," *Canadian Geographical Journal*, Vol. 58 (June 1959), p. 170.
[15] Royal Commission on Canada's Economic Prospects, *Final Report* (Ottawa: Queen's Printer, 1958), p. 149.

origin, grows its cranberries exclusively in bogs. These, averaging about an acre in size, have the necessary acid soils.

The growers clear the bogland and spread over it a layer of coarse sand about four inches thick, to prevent the growth of weeds. Once the crop is planted, the growers watch the weather reports with great care. If frost is forecast, they flood the bogs to protect the crop.

Harvesting begins early in September and continues through October. Mechanical pickers are used to some extent but are not favored because their weight crushes and destroys many of the valuable berries. Most harvesting is done by laborers using wooden-toothed scoops (Figure 4-5). Since thousands of the berries fall to the ground under the vines, a freshly harvested bog is usually flooded and the loose cranberries floated to the surface. This fruit is used mainly for canning. Each acre yields between 25 and 40 barrels of fruit.

Washington County and Blueberries Washington and Hancock counties along the eastern coast of Maine are in an area of leached, acid, podzolic soils called "blueberry barrens." These counties produce most

of the nation's blueberries, and can about nine-tenths of the total pack. When the tree cover is removed, low-growing blueberry bushes take possession of the ground. To keep down brush and tree growth, the land is fired every two or three years.

Aroostook County and Potatoes Northeastern Maine produces about one-eighth of the total potato crop of the United States (Figure 4-6). The area lies in a narrow belt from one to three townships wide along the northeastern border of the state. It has a short growing season and an easily cultivated silty loam glacial soil. Large-scale enterprises and highly mechanized production methods have built up a sizable industry in this remote corner of the United States.

The crop is grown both for seed potatoes and for food. Seed potatoes are especially in demand by the truck-farming areas of the Atlantic Seaboard and the southern states, while for food purposes Aroostook potatoes supply the markets of almost all states east of the Mississippi River. Although commercial production in this area began in the 1870's, it did not become important until after the completion of the first railroad in 1895.

Figure 4-5. Harvesting cranberries in a Cape Cod bog. Pickers move on their knees through a bog in a "duck line," combing the bright red berries off the low-lying vines. (USDA photo.)

***The Lake Champlain Lowland and
Dairying*** Throughout its early agricultural
development, the Lake Champlain Lowland and tributary valley areas produced
wheat, oats, and other small grains. But
western competition forced much of the
area to abandon the growing of cereals. The
mild, moist summers, however, were highly
conducive to the growing of forage crops.
This lowland, in spite of its cold winters,
provides an excellent environment for the
dairy cow. With the coming of railroads and
good motor highways, the area became connected with the large urban markets of New
York and Boston, and developed into one
of the major dairy regions of the country.
While it has to compete with dairy regions
to the west, nearby markets for fluid milk
(which is 85 per cent water and hence is
expensive to transport) gave it a decided
advantage. The Champlain Lowland occupies the center of the great overlapping
milksheds (areas from which cities draw
their fluid milk) of New York and Boston.
Vermont, dominating the major part of the
Lake Champlain Lowland, ranks first among
the states in per capita production of milk.

The agriculture and agricultural practices
of the pioneer have vanished, except in the
most remote localities. In the valleys and
on the lower slopes of hillsides, the dairy
cow is supreme. Fields of oats and hay occupy the fertile bottom lands, while apple
orchards cover many hillsides. The newer
and more scientifically located orchards occupy northward-facing slopes where blossoming is retarded until the danger of frost
is passed.

The Connecticut Valley and Tobacco
The lower central part of the Connecticut
Valley is a leading tobacco-growing area.
In recent years emphasis has shifted from
cigar-binder types to the more valuable
Sumatran wrapper varieties.

Binder types, as the name implies, are
used mainly for binding the fillers into the

Figure 4-6. Aroostook Valley potatoes.
(Photo courtesy of Maine Department
of Economic Development.)

forms of cigars. Good-burning qualities,
aroma, and elasticity characterize binders
of high quality. Sumatra tobacco is grown
for wrappers, the best wrappers being thin,
smooth, and fine in texture. In order to obtain such qualities, protection is needed
against the sun and extremes of weather,
and hence Sumatra tobacco is grown under
shade at considerable expense. A permanent
framework is erected over which open-mesh
cloth is tacked, enclosing large fields (Figure 4-7). The plants are set in rows and
cultivation is carried on in the fields under
the cover. The cloth overhead and on all
sides diffuses the direct rays of the sun,
minimizes wind movements, and affords
some protection from overnight changes in
temperature. Much of this type of tobacco
is produced by large corporations under
the most modern scientific methods. Because
tobacco is grown on the same land continuously, liberal applications of commercial fertilizer (more than one and one-half tons

Figure 4-7. Shade-grown tobacco in the Connecticut Valley. (Photo courtesy of Connecticut Development Commission.)

per acre) must be used to insure satisfactory yields.

In addition to tobacco, the Connecticut Valley grows onions and other vegetables, and produces some hay. Dairying is also important, especially in the north.

The Annapolis-Cornwallis Valley and Apples A large proportion of Canada's leading fruit crop, the apple, is produced in the Annapolis-Cornwallis Valley, the only area of outstanding commercial agriculture in Nova Scotia. This fairly level valley, 80 miles long and 10 to 15 miles wide, is sheltered from northwest winds and fogs by North Mountain, which lies along the Bay of Fundy. Paralleling the valley on the other side is South Mountain. The valley trends in a general west-east direction from Digby to Windsor. This area, first settled by the French, is characterized by farms which are narrow strips of 20 to 120 acres, having meadow and hay land in the bottom, orchard land midway, and pasture and

woodland above. By growing their trees on slopes the farmers benefit both from well-drained soils and from air drainage. The latter especially is significant since there is danger to fruit trees from late spring frost. Although apples are still the main crop, their production has decreased because of a steady decline in shipments to the British market since World War II. Hay and potatoes are also grown, and there has recently been a significant increase in specialty production, particularly poultry and beef cattle.

Lumbering

Northeastern Anglo-America, the continent's pioneer logging region, possessed an almost incomparable forest of tall, straight conifers and valuable hardwoods. Perhaps nine-tenths of the region was forest-covered. For 200 years or more after the landing of the Pilgrims in 1620, the settlers continued uninterruptedly the removal of trees. At first they had reverence for the forest, since it supplied their fuel, game, and the timber for their homes; but it also harbored their enemies—Indians and wild beasts. Moreover, their agriculture had to be of the self-sufficing type. To make room for their crops they had to clear away the trees, hence, there grew up in their minds a hostility to the forest; they did not consider its destruction reprehensible.

Some commercial forestry began almost with the first settlements. A power sawmill was established on the Piscatagua River in 1636, and forest products were among the earliest exports. Eventually logging became a big business. The straightest and tallest trees were felled and river-driven downstream to shipbuilding plants. The coast of Maine was pre-eminent in this industry. Bangor, on the Penobscot River, became the outstanding cènter specializing in the making and shipping of lumber. It had its own locally built fleet which carried lumber into far corners of the earth and brought back exotic products. Moreover, its loggers invented the snubber for handling sleds of logs on steep slopes, the log-branding ax, and the peavey,[16] "the greatest lumber invention since the saw." North of Bangor were two and one-half million acres of virgin timber in a solid block owned by a single individual. So impressed was the young Thoreau when, in 1846, he saw this now historic lumber town, that he wrote:

> There stands the City of Bangor like a star on the edge of night, still hewing at the forest of which it is built, already, overflowing with the luxuries and refinements of Europe and sending its vessels to Spain, to England, and to the West Indies for its groceries—and yet only a few axmen have gone up-river into the howling wilderness that feeds it.[17]

The heyday of forest industries in New England is long since past. There is still considerable woodland, but much of the good timber is inaccessible and much of the accessible timber is of poor quality. Even so, a moderate amount of sawtimber is cut each year, Maine ranking 15th, New Hampshire 23rd, and Vermont 25th among the states in annual lumber production. Pulpwood production is more significant; in most years only Washington and Georgia yield more than Maine. The principal commercial timber species in New England are spruce, balsam fir, white pine, yellow birch, and sugar maple.

Logging was and still is a winter activity. Cutting began in autumn and usually terminated around the first of January. As soon as the snow became deep and the ground frozen, tens of thousands of logs were hauled over iced roads by horse-drawn sleds to streams, which in late spring and summer carried the logs to sawmills. The end of each log was marked with the brand of its owner.

Logging and lumbering have been important also in the Canadian portion of Northeastern Anglo-America, especially in New Brunswick, where all other economic activities have been secondary. Trading in lumber in the Maritimes began as early as 1650. Mariners returning to Europe took cargoes of masts, spars, and ship timbers.

The entire upland area, with the exception of the highest peaks, was covered originally with a dense forest. At first the land-hungry settlers considered the forest an enemy in the same sense that they did the Indian. But with the Atlantic Seaboard's increasing demand for timber for structural purposes and for shipbuilding, these same farmers soon found it profitable to cut logs in winter when they could not farm. In some places in the region this supplemental income surpassed that from farming.

New Brunswick, with 80 per cent of its area in productive forest, is an important producer of lumber, fuelwood, and pulpwood. Major mills are located at Fredericton, Saint John, Bathurst, Dalhousie, and Campbellton. Nova Scotia is three-quarters forested, mostly in private ownership, and contains some six hundred sawmills as well as four large pulp mills. The woodlands of Prince Edward Island are in small, individually owned woodlots, but annual pulpwood exports are considerable. Quebec, of course, is an outstanding producer of both lumber and pulp, but most of it originates outside this region.

Fishing

The first shore-dwelling settlers obeyed both the call of the land and the call of the sea. But the hard land environment yielded little more than subsistence farming, whereas the sea was rich in fish. The fish caught here in colonial days paid for

---

[16] A pointed iron lever fitted with a movable hook and used for handling logs.

[17] As quoted in S. H. Holbrook, "Historic Lumber Towns—No. I, Bangor, Maine," *American Forests*, Vol. 44 (February 1938), p. 69.

imports of sugar and molasses. Cane sugar, brought back in payment for fish, was the basis for the refining and distilling industries; cacao, the basis for the confectionery industries; hides, for the shoe factories; and gold and silver, for the southern New England jewelry industries. Also, the extensive New England brass industry started with a market for ship chandlery. All of these have been significant in New England's regional economic life.[18] Fish was the first export from the New World. From Newfoundland to Cape Cod lie the Grand Banks—one of the richest fishing areas in the world (Figure 4-8). These banks were frequented by

Scandinavian, Portuguese, Dutch, English, and French fishermen before the period of colonization in America. As early as 1504 Breton and Norman fishermen—men born to the sea—were catching cod in the western North Atlantic, and by 1577 France had 150 vessels, Spain 100, Portugal 50, and England 15, fishing for cod on the banks.[19]

Banks are shallows in the ocean at or near the outer margin of the continental shelf. Occasionally they reach the surface, though ordinarily they lie about 200 feet below it. Banks are invaluable for fishing for two reasons. Their very shallowness makes fishing convenient. And their waters

[18] Edward A. Ackerman, *New England's Fishing Industry* (Chicago: University of Chicago Press, 1941), p. 3.

[19] R. H. Fiedler, "Fisheries of North America," *Geographical Review,* Vol. 30 (April 1940), p. 201.

Figure 4-8. Emptying nets in a sardine weir. The nets are set in a circular pattern with the top of the nets near the surface at high tide. Small boats enter the weir and gather the fish at low tide, taking them to dump in the holds of the larger boats, visible outside the weir. This area on the southeast coast of New Brunswick has some of the highest tides in the world. (Photo courtesy of New Brunswick Travel Bureau.)

are rich in fish because the sun's rays penetrate to an adequate depth for the abundant growth of algae, the primary food in the food chain of fish. Only a small number of species can tolerate the cold water of the Grand Banks; the uniformity of catch aids the fishermen in selling to a single merchant. The Grand Banks also lie near the densely populated, highly industrialized eastern seaboard of the United States—a great market for fish.

Fishing is further aided by the fact that the entire coast is dotted with sheltered harbors, bays, and coves from which fishermen can operate with comparative ease and safety. The fisheries fall into two distinct divisions: (1) coastal or inshore, and (2) deep-sea—demersal (bottom) and pelagic (surface).

Coastal Fishing Coastal fishing is done usually within five miles of shore in small, swift motor boats carrying two or three men. The catch is brought into port each day. However, some "draggers" (inshore otter trawlers) from 30 to 50 tons in size may stay away from port as long as 48 hours. The fish caught are primarily cod, haddock, mackerel, and herring. Some of these are ground fish (cod and haddock) and some are surface fish (mackerel and herring). Pollock, cusk, hake, and flounder also are important. Herring are used for bait. The bulk of the catch, after gutting and washing, is kept fresh in ice-packed chambers.

Deep-sea Fishing For banks or deep-sea fishing, large vessels are used in the deeper waters over the 70,000 square miles of the Grand Banks, where bottom fish such as cod, cusk, flounder, and haddock are sought. Both schooners and trawlers are used, but schooner fleets are rapidly disappearing. Off New England the efficient otter trawler catches as many fish as all other kinds of gear combined.

Trawlers permit exploitation of distant fishing grounds, are quite safe and seaworthy in even the roughest weather, operate throughout the year, and are speedy in delivering their cargo. They tow along the bottom a huge bag-shaped net, called an otter trawl, which, as it is drawn over the ocean floor, envelops the fish. Fishermen who operate other types of vessels claim that the trawlers are lowering the price of fish and are slowly depleting the resource. Since trawlers secure their fish from lower depths not fished by traditional methods, there is little evidence to support this claim.

Part of the catch is dried, salted, and canned, but an increasing proportion is quick-frozen. Many vessels are equipped with complete refrigerating plants.

Lobster Fishing From Prince Edward Island to Massachusetts, tens of millions of lobsters are caught each year. Although the catch has been reduced by overfishing in the past, it has increased in recent years. Artificial propagation is now being used to increase the lobster population, and progress ·is being made. The eggs are artificially hatched, and the young lobsters are permitted to grow in ponds along the shore before being turned into the sea. Lobsters are taken in baited traps, called lobster pots, as they crawl about in shallow water looking for food. They provide the principal source of income for fishermen in New Brunswick and Prince Edward Island, and are important in Nova Scotia, Maine, and Massachusetts as well. Most of the catch is marketed alive or freshly boiled, or the frozen tail is sold.

Oysters, Clams, Quahaugs, and Scallops These occur in great numbers along the southern shore of New England and on Cape Cod. They are shell animals and live on the shallow sea floor or in beach muds. Taking them is more like harvesting than fishing. Individual ownership of the oyster beds is the rule. Some oysters are marketed locally in the shell, but because of costs most of them are shucked and marketed chilled or frozen. Recently there has been a marked increase in the take of sea scallops off Georges Bank by both Canadian and New England fishermen. They are scooped from the sea bottom with dredges.

Fishing Ports While almost every inhabited harbor area has its fishermen, the number of outstanding fishing ports is limited. The chief ones are Boston, New Bedford, Provincetown, and Gloucester in Massachusetts, Portland in Maine, and Halifax, Yarmouth, Clark's Harbor, and Lunenburg in Nova Scotia. However, fishing villages and fishermen's houses literally line the bay shores. In northern New Brunswick, for example, is Caraquet, said to be the longest town in the world. It consists of a continuous veneer of homes along the south shore of Chaleur Bay, 20 miles long and less than one block wide.

The Value of the Fisheries Despite continuous exploitation for more than four centuries, the western North Atlantic fisheries continue to provide a large and important supply of food—more than two billion pounds a year. Two-thirds of the total annual Canadian catch and about one-fifth of the total U.S. catch are from this area. Nova Scotia ranks second (to British Columbia) among the provinces and Massachusetts ranks third (to Louisiana and California) among the states in terms of total annual take.

Unfortunately the continued prosperity of the region's fishing industry is threatened by: (1) the growing scarcity of key species of fish in North Atlantic waters, causing increased operating costs; (2) conflict between the Fishermen's Union and the fish dealers, hindering the smooth operation of the industry; (3) increasing competition from foreign sources, particularly in the sardine industry; (4) lack of new vessels and modern equipment; and (5) decreasing market for salted cod in Europe.

Recreation

In the United States Recreation as a business started in this region about the middle of the nineteenth century, but it was completely revolutionized later by the automobile. Large numbers of tourists began to invade the New England segment, many going to private homes. Catering to tourists has proved to be a salvation to great numbers of people, both in rural areas and in small cities and villages. Northeastern Anglo-America is highly attractive to tourists, for it has: (1) fine scenery of mountains, bold cliffs, varied coastline, glacial lakes, and fast-running streams; (2) cool, bracing summers and cold, snowy winters; (3) excellent fishing in both inland waters and the ocean; (4) yachting and boating with continuous shelter; (5) skiing and tobogganing; (6) famous historic shrines and other attractions.

In New England most farmers produce special crops for tourists. Many are not farmers in the same sense that they would be if they lived in the Dakotas or Iowa, since agriculture constitutes only a secondary element of income.

The vacation industry has excellent prospects for expansion in this region, and in others, because of (1) the rising standard of living, (2) the increasing proportion of people in the upper age groups, (3) the increase in the paid-vacation movement, (4) the expanded amount of leisure time available to most Anglo-Americans, and (5) improved and speedier means of transportation.

The upland areas are endowed with practically all of the natural factors necessary for the development of a large resort industry. The cool, moist summers are ideal for summer vacationists, and the snowy winters are popular with winter-sports enthusiasts. In addition, the region profits from proximity to centers of dense population. "One fourth of the people of the United

States and Canada live within a day's drive ... and over half of the largest cities of the two countries lie within 900 miles of Mt. Washington." [20] The ease of access by people living in the crowded urban centers of the Northeast makes this one of the most popular recreational lands of the continent.

SUMMER SPORTS The Adirondacks and the Green and White Mountains began to attract summer tourists by the middle of the nineteenth century. As railroads were constructed into the mountains, more and more summer visitors came. Owing to the inconvenience of reaching the resort by train in those days, most tourists came for the entire summer, and there was a demand for large resort hotels. As the trade grew, many large summer hotels were built and equipped to provide every need of the visitor—swim-

[20] National Resources Committee, *Regional Planning, Part III—New England* (Washington: Government Printing Office, 1936), p. 37.

ming, boating, hiking, horseback riding, tennis, and golf (Figure 4-9), and were run on the American plan. Such hotels were expensive and appealed only to a wealthy clientele. Few facilities were provided for the low-income group because, before the days of the automobile, not many of that class of tourist reached the more remote places.

At first, the tourist business was confined to the summer months, and the hotels were closed during winter. In many instances the manager of a large hotel in the White Mountains or in the Adirondacks operated a resort hotel in Florida during the winter and moved seasonally with all of his domestic help, barbers, and bootblacks.

The automobile altered the summer resort industry considerably.

All-summer or month-long stays by a select few at a favorite hotel have tended to give place to short stops by nearly everybody in many hotels. Farmers and towns-

Figure 4-9. A large resort hotel in the White Mountains of New Hampshire. (Photo courtesy of the Balsams Hotel, Dixville Notch.)

folk who used to take in boarders now offer overnight accommodations to fleeting auto nomads. Villages still purvey groceries and meats, but they have added to the list ice cream and soda, gasoline and oil, and luncheon and tea.[21]

With the development of the automobile and good highways, the mountain country found itself at the crossroads between southern New England, French Canada, the Thousand Islands District, and the Maritimes.

State and national planning boards, park and forestry services have done much in recent years to develop the resort industry in this region. Several national forests have been established to preserve and restore the woods as well as to encourage summer resorts. Some of the recreational services for tourists now provided by the national forests include: (1) foot trails (more than 1,000 miles in White Mountain National Forest alone), (2) youth hostels, (3) bridle trails, (4) canoe routes, (5) hunting and fishing facilities, (6) golf courses, (7) camps, and (8) winter sports. Today this subregion is a playground for people from many economic groups—from those who spend their summers at large resort hotels to those who can stop only for the weekend, traveling by automobile and spending each night at a tourist home, cabin, or motel. The latter type of traveler has made it possible for many of the all-but-abandoned farms to revive.

In addition to mountains and lakes, the principal tourist attractions of New England include an unusual concentration of historical spots in and around Boston (and to a lesser extent in other areas), the dignity and charm of Cape Cod, luxury settlements like Newport and Bar Harbor, the spectacular rocky coast of Maine (especially

in Acadia National Park), and the general rural scene with its old farm houses, attached barns, and covered bridges.

WINTER SPORTS   Within the past few years, winter sports have developed rapidly, owing to (1) improved methods of clearing highways, (2) local promotion of winter sports, and (3) "snow trains" and "snow busses." The Northeastern Uplands are particularly favored for all types of winter sports. People living in cities are learning that the sun does shine in winter in the great outdoor recreational areas, and they are going to them by the thousands. The residents of the uplands keep roads open now that were never before plowed in winter. Also, some resort hotels stay open in winter and thereby increase their earnings.

Lake Placid, one of the best known areas in the Adirondacks, is important as a resort center in both summer and winter, but is particularly outstanding during the winter season. The village, located on the shores of Mirror Lake and Lake Placid, is surrounded by some of the highest peaks in the Adirondacks. In 1932 this was the site of the Winter Olympics.

Yet the resort business in New England is highly seasonal. Despite the great amount of publicity which has been given to skiing, autumn foliage, and hunting and fishing, much of the annual tourist trade still is confined to the months of July and August.[22]

In Canada   Maritime Canada is favored as a summer tourist center because it is near the densely settled parts of New England and New York; but it also suffers from this nearness, because the American section of Northeastern Anglo-America has similar attractions and better roads. Some of the points of particular interest, however, in the Maritimes include: (1) the Reversing

[21] American Geographical Society, *New England's Prospects: 1933*, Special Publication No. 16 (New York: 1933), p. 455.

[22] Council of Economic Advisers, Committee on the New England Economy, *The New England Economy* (Washington: Government Printing Office, 1951), p. 198.

Falls at Saint John; (2) the tidal bore of the Petitcodiac at Moncton; (3) sea cliffs and caves at Percé; (4) the Old World atmosphere of parts of the Gaspé Peninsula, where mountains approach the sea and French fishing villages add charm to the landscape; (5) the rural serenity of Prince Edward Island; (6) three scenic national parks, Cape Breton Highlands, Fundy, and Prince Edward Island; (7) the city and harbor of Halifax; and (8) many places of historical interest. The great majority of visitors come from the Maritimes or Quebec and make short stays; they are particularly attracted to the beach resorts of Prince Edward Island.

Mining

Coal While Nova Scotia has coal, the Dominion as a whole would benefit far more if these deposits were located in the more densely populated and industrialized parts of the provinces of Ontario and Quebec, where American coal is cheaper than Canadian. Some Nova Scotian coal, however, is transported economically by water to the cities of Quebec and Montreal during the navigation season. Nova Scotia contains only one per cent of the Dominion's coal deposits, but produces nearly one-half of that mined.

Nova Scotian coal has been mined for more than a century. There are four fields —two on Cape Breton and two on the mainland. All of the collieries are on or within a few miles of the coast, and more than one-half of the coal is actually mined beneath the Atlantic. The coal seams extend for many miles under the ocean. Because of the dip of the strata, the rock cover attains a thickness of 4,000 feet at about six miles from the coast. This makes support of the roof so expensive in effort, labor, and material that it is not profitable to work the seams at a distance of more than about four

miles from shore. As it is, some miners face a one-hour underground ride just to get from pithead to coal face. Under-ocean mining has many difficulties not encountered in mining under land. Since shafts cannot be sunk beyond the shore line, it is difficult to provide adequate ventilation, power and light for operation, and tramways to pull the mined coal to the base of the shaft.[23] The seams on Cape Breton Island vary in thickness from three to nine feet. The thickest seams, however, are in Pictou County on the mainland, where the principal seam in the Allan Shaft is 45 feet thick. The coal is of good quality and can be coked. Most of the coal that is not sent to Quebec and Ontario is used locally for industrial steam-raising or for production of metallurgical coke for steel-making at Sydney. In actuality much of Nova Scotia's coal mining industry survives only because it gets government subsidy for transportation to Montreal and eastern Ontario markets, where 40 per cent of the output goes.[24]

Gypsum and Salt Gypsum, which is used in the manufacture of plaster and plasterboard and as a retarder in cement has been mined in Nova Scotia since 1770, that province accounting for four-fifths of Canada's production. It is extracted at several localities in the central part of the province and is mostly exported to the United States.

The fisheries in the Maritimes are an important market for coarse salt, and the Malagash Peninsula has yielded rock salt for many years. Principal production now, however, is at Pugwash.

Asbestos Southeastern Quebec produces most of Canada's and about half the world's annual output of asbestos. These vast deposits were discovered in 1876, and for

[23] A. W. Currie, *Economic Geography of Canada* (Toronto: The Macmillan Company of Canada, 1946), pp. 72-73.
[24] Royal Commission on Canada's Economic Prospects, *Final Report* (Ottawa: Queen's Printer, 1958), p. 409.

many years were exploited only by open-pit mining methods. More recently, however, most large producers are using underground methods, even though the largest mine of all, at the new town of Asbestos, has been converted into a completely open-pit operation. Although a small amount of asbestos is mined in northern Vermont, immediately south of the Canadian border, most of the production is concentrated in a narrow strip of territory extending northeastward from the international boundary almost to the St. Lawrence River. In addition to Asbestos, the major producing centers are Thetford Mines, Black Lake, and East Broughton.

Asbestos is used primarily for roofing materials, as insulation for electrical equipment, and for automobile brake linings. Its chief properties are flexibility, incombustibility, and slow conduction of heat. The United States is the world's major consumer of asbestos.

Iron Ore Metalliferous deposits are dispersed throughout the upland area, but they are of relatively small commercial value. Most important are the magnetic iron-ore deposits found on the flanks of the Adirondacks. At present, five widely scattered areas are producing magnetite, mostly by open-pit methods. All of these mines have been in operation for a century or more, although production has been suspended frequently because of the high cost of transporting the ores to steel centers in Pittsburgh or on the Great Lakes. With increased demands for iron and steel at the outbreak of World War II, most of these properties were purchased by large companies such as Republic Steel Corporation, Jones & Laughlin Steel Corporation, and the M. A. Hanna Company. In most recent years New York has produced more iron ore than any state except Minnesota, Michigan, and Alabama, an indication that the Adirondacks may be able to compete to some extent with the Great Lakes ores. Great reserves of magnetite are still present.

Quarrying

The rocks that underlie most of Northeastern Anglo-America are dominantly igneous or metamorphic, consisting largely of granite, marble, slate, and others used universally as building stones. High-quality stone and nearness to large urban centers have made the region a leading producer in the building-stone industry. Although the Canadian part of the region is underlain with the same rock, its building-stone industry has not developed to any extent, no doubt because it is remote from markets.

Granite Granite, a hard, massive, and durable stone, is quarried extensively in central Vermont. The major producing area is in the vicinity of Barre, where the nationally famous "Rock of Ages" quarry is located (Figure 4-10). Because of its hardness and massiveness, granite is difficult to quarry. Drill holes are placed close together along a line in the bedrock, and into them wedges are driven. When the pressure from the wedges becomes sufficiently great, the granite block begins to crack along the line, and the stone is extracted in large blocks that are ideal for monumental and construction work. Small stones are used for paving or are crushed for road-building material. More than 100 plants for the manufacture of granite products are located in Barre, Montpelier, and adjacent Vermont towns. Numerous granite quarries have been opened in Maine, but their output is used chiefly for structural purposes. Since most of these quarries are located at or near tidewater, the stone can be shipped to Boston and New York City at a low cost.

Although Canada possesses one of the largest supplies of granite rock in the world, only an infinitesimal part is used, commercial development being confined to areas of southern Quebec near centers of popu-

Figure 4-10. Granite quarry near Barre, Vermont. The quarry covers more than 45 acres and is nearly 400 feet deep. The derricks of Douglas fir are 115 feet high with booms 100 feet in length. (Photo courtesy of Rock of Ages Corporation.)

lation. The major granite quarries are located immediately north of the international boundary near the village of Beebe.

Marble Vermont usually ranks first among the states in production of marble. Marble is a metamorphosed or altered limestone rock that has been hardened by heat and pressure. Although classified a hard stone, it is much softer than granite, and hence can be cut from the bed rock by powerful channeling machines. Blocks of quarried marble then go to the mills where they are sawed by smooth steel band saws into slabs and smaller pieces; these go to the finishing shops where they are carved and shaped for specific uses. The relative softness of marble makes it easy to work, but also keeps it from being a good building stone, particularly for exteriors. Nevertheless, it is quarried extensively, the chief producing centers being Rutland and Proctor. Vermont marble has the advantage of a wide variety of colors—pure white, red, gray, and green.

Slate Slate, also a metamorphosed stone, can be split into thin sheets. Hence it is highly prized as roofing material, for electrical panels, and for flagstones. Two of the more important slate-producing areas of the continent are in Maine, near the town of Monson, and on both sides of the Vermont-New York boundary. The slate from Monson is a black variety of high quality, used primarily in the manufacture of electrical panel boards and blackboards. The Vermont-New York product, occurring in several attractive colors, is used primarily for roofing. Some slate is quarried commercially in Richmond County in Quebec, but the industry there has declined in importance in recent years, because lower-priced fabricated building products or sheet metal are encroaching on the slate market.

Water-Power Production

This region possesses considerable water power—both potential and developed. The rocky north shore of the St. Lawrence below and including the Lower Saguenay has great power possibilities, but except for the St. Lawrence itself, most power sites are on the border of the Laurentian Shield. The south shore with numerous short streams having sharp descents also is favored. Nova Scotia and New Brunswick, because of their heavy precipitation, high altitude near the coast, and good storage facilities, have considerable power, although total power production in the Maritimes is more dependent on thermal generation than on hydro-generation. Most of New England's hydroelectric power is being generated in the upland of Maine, New Hampshire, and Vermont. Much of this power has been sent to industrial centers to the south in recent years.

Water power was an important factor in the early development of the upland, for the numerous small rapids and falls which characterize almost every stream were utilized by the early pioneers. Cheap hydropower was the basis for the paper and pulp industry, which is concentrated along the north flank of the upland, particularly in the Adirondacks.

Manufacturing

The highly industrialized areas of southern New England and of the Montreal district have been discussed in Chapter 3, *The American Manufacturing Region*. Therefore, only the industries which are not located within those manufacturing areas are considered here, and hence *Northeastern Anglo-America* is not of outstanding manufacturing significance. It does, however, have several highly specialized industries.

Pulp and Paper In the production of pulp and paper, few areas in the world surpass Northeastern Anglo-America. The distribution is largely a matter of geography: the pulp plants must be strategically situated with respect to the forest, cheap power, a dependable supply of soft, clean water, and good transportation facilities for the low-cost delivery of raw materials (sulphur, clay, soda). Fortunately, this region has large quantities of reasonably priced hydropower close to great supplies of superior pulpwoods—spruce, hemlock, pine, poplar, and fir. One hundred tons of pulpwood yield less than 30 tons of pulp, but this

production requires the power equivalent of about 120 tons of coal. Consequently most pulp mills are located at convenient power sites close to the forest. Also, 100,000 gallons of water are utilized in the production of one ton of pulp. Paper mills, on the other hand, are located in or near centers of population where the bulk of the output is used. The Canadian part of the region contributes pulp and paper about equally, but the New England segment produces more paper than pulp.

When the United States tariff on newsprint was removed in 1911, much of the newsprint paper industry migrated from the United States to Canada, where the pulpwood could be made into pulp and paper at a saving of about 10 per cent. Prince Edward Island does not participate in pulp and paper production, nevertheless this is the leading type of manufacturing in the Maritime Provinces. It is concentrated in a few large firms, and much of the production is for export.

The New England pulp and paper industry has expanded in recent years, largely as a result of technical developments that permit hardwoods to be utilized in pulpmaking.

Iron and Steel Ironmaking in the Maritime Provinces began in 1872, when the Sydney mills were built to supply steel rails for the rapidly growing Canadian railway system. Since 1918 the steel, coal, and related industries in the Maritimes have been administered by the Dominion Steel and Coal Corporation (Figure 4-11).

Sydney, the center of the industry, is a strategic locale for iron and steel manufacturing because: (1) it lies in the center of the coal area, (2) it has ample land on a commodious and well-protected harbor, (3) it is the eastern terminus of the Canadian National Railways System, and (4) it can get Wabana iron ore cheaply from Bell Island, Newfoundland.

Figure 4-11. The Dominion Steel and Coal Corporation plant at Sydney. (Photo courtesy Nova Scotia Information Service.)

Sydney has the lowest material-assembly cost of any steelmaking site in Canada.[25] The blast furnaces are within sight of the coal mine mouths. Not only is the quantity of coal enormous but the quality is good. Limestone and iron ore suitable for blast furnaces are obtained from Newfoundland. Despite the fact that the mines are 415 miles from Sydney by steamer, ore can be laid down economically at the steel mill because the water transport is inexpensive.

Markets are the major problem. Canada's steel has to pay a tariff to enter markets in the United States, and despite an excellent location on the Great Circle Route to Europe, it cannot invade that market. Consequently, Sydney steel is mostly restricted to the Canadian market, and must compete with production from Hamilton, which has a much more favorable market orientation.

Other Manufacturing Only a few other types of manufacturing are of any significance in northern New England and Maritime Canada. Sawmills are widespread, but, in contrast to pulp mills, are generally small. Fish processing is the second most important manufactural activity in each of the

[25] Donald Kerr, "The Geography of the Canadian Iron and Steel Industry," *Economic Geography*, Vol. 34 (April 1959), p. 152.

Maritime Provinces, and is also noteworthy along the coast of Maine. Small textile mills, mostly producing blankets and carpets, are found in various localities, and there is some shipbuilding of note in Halifax, Saint John, and on the northern New England coast.

Transportation

As the pioneers pushed farther into the wilderness, they naturally used the Indian trails, which for the most part followed the streams. When wheeled vehicles (ox cart) came into use, trails were widened where possible. Although the streams pointed the way through the forest, they seldom provided means of transportation. The same rapids and falls that aided the development of power hindered navigation. In the 1840's railroads penetrated the wilderness and caused some of the wagon roads to fall into disuse.

From the days of Cabot, Cartier, and Champlain, the St. Lawrence River has offered unique opportunities for water transport. Much of the trade of Canada moves in and out over this waterway.

River transportation was of considerable importance in the early settlement of New Brunswick, when the St. John and its tributaries were widely used. It is unimportant, however, now that other means of transport are better developed. The Maritimes have not benefited from St. Lawrence traffic.

The original settlements in Quebec were on the banks of rivers; those of the Maritimes and New England were along the coast. Everywhere they benefited from water transportation.

The New England railways are distinctive in that they serve directly only New England. More than in any other area in North America, tonnage consists of high-grade manufactures. Aside from forest and quarry products, the outbound movement of raw materials is almost negligible. Furthermore, food and industrial raw materials are carried eastbound into New England, but empty cars characterize much of the westbound traffic.

Prior to Canadian confederation in 1867, which resulted in the construction of the first transcontinental railway, the Maritime Region had little railway mileage. The Maritime Provinces were more interested in the Inter-Colonial Railway than in the confederation. They felt that this railway from the interior would greatly stimulate their ocean trade and their ports, especially in winter when the St. Lawrence could not be used. Prince Edward Island was the only part of the Maritimes to be indifferent, for it realized that such a route would not solve its local transportation problems. The extensions to the Maritimes are "weak thongs" in summer, but they become vital parts of the transcontinental systems in winter.

Railways have been constructed for some distance on both sides of the St. Lawrence east of Quebec City, but they are important only in winter.

The uplands profit from railroad development outside the subregion. The first railways were built from the Atlantic ports of Boston, New York, and Portland to participate in "western trade" and Great Lakes

trapping. The Champlain Lowland, however, which had always been a highway for traffic between New York and Montreal, soon secured through lines. Later, Canadian railways, seeking ice-free ports on the Atlantic, built several main lines across the uplands. The Adirondacks, northeastern Maine, and the highlands of eastern Canada were largely avoided, leaving many localities remote from rail connections.

In Acadia the earliest French adopted Indian methods, traveling by canoe on the rivers and by foot on the trails; in winter they used snowshoes and went by foot on both rivers and trails. Later, the French introduced the wheeled vehicle, which demanded roads.

The building of roads in the Lower St. Lawrence Valley entailed many difficulties. The forest was almost continuous, so that cutting trees and removing stumps was necessary. The rivers required bridges. The severe climate induced deep frost which, in spring, raised humps and broke holes in surfaced roads and caused deep mud on soft roads.

In New England, as population increased and farms wore out, the need for new lands became imperative. The migration which followed utilized streams or Indian trails. These paths were widened first into pack trails and subsequently into wagon roads. Thus arose a system of trails radiating from the seacoast.

Roads for wheeled vehicles came into existence during the turnpike era, which began in 1795 and reached its climax between 1830 and 1850. Turnpikes declined with the advent of the railroad.

Although many of them fell into disuse, those in the upland area survived longer than those in other areas. With the advent of the automobile, many old roads were improved and new ones constructed. The ever-increasing automobile traffic through the highlands has created a demand for

Figure 4-12. A toll station on a toll road in southern New England. (Photo courtesy of the Connecticut State Highway Department.)

good roads. Except in the most remote places, the region is well served by modern highways. The automobile highway has penetrated the mountain fastness to a greater extent than has the railroad.

Southern New England today has a network of highways that is denser than almost any other in the world. It includes the Merritt Parkway, first of the modern toll roads, and a variety of more recent tollways, such as the Connecticut Turnpike, the Massachusetts Turnpike, the New Hampshire Turnpike, the Spaulding Turnpike, the Maine Turnpike, and the Everett Highway (Figure 4-12).

The sea-level Cape Cod Canal, 17.4 miles long and 32 feet deep, was built to enable mariners to avoid the hazardous section southeast of Cape Cod and to shorten the distance between northern and southern New England. It is now operated by the United States Government, toll-free, as a link in the intracoastal waterway from Maine to Florida.

Ferry service is important in Maritime Canada, as the highly indented and irregular coastline provides few uninterrupted land routes. Regular ferries ply between New Brunswick and Nova Scotia across the Bay of Fundy, between Nova Scotia and Newfoundland across Cabot Strait, between Prince Edward Island and both Nova Scotia and New Brunswick across Northumberland Strait, and at several places between the north and south shores of the lower St. Lawrence River.

Commerce

So attractive were trade and shipping during colonial and Revolutionary times that maritime commerce became a leading activity. New England and Nova Scotian sea captains and sailors were recognized as among the ablest and most fearless to be found on the oceans.

Then came wars, followed by privateering and piracy. Speed in ships was imperative. Accordingly, the schooner became a clipper ship, and with it New England and Maritime Canada experienced the golden age of their salt-water activity. During this era—the first half of the nineteenth century —clipper ships dominated the seven seas, carrying the name of New England and of Nova Scotia to almost every port in the world. This continued until the advent of the iron ship. In 1860, United States vessels carried about two-thirds of the country's foreign trade; by 1890 the amount had fallen to one-tenth. Americans all but abandoned the sea, a situation attributable to (1) steamships made of iron, which displaced wooden sailing vessels; (2) national legislation whereby protection to American shipping was removed; (3) the Civil War; and (4) the development of the natural resources in the interior.

Although Boston, Providence, and some smaller cities still carry on a notable amount of oceanic shipping, they are thoroughly overshadowed by the port of New York. Commercial movements in New England are mostly on land, with motor trucks handling an increasing share of the traffic as the railroad's proportion decreases.

Halifax is easily the most important port in Maritime Canada, normally accommo-

dating more overseas shipping than any other Canadian city on the Atlantic coast except Montreal (Figure 4-13). Imported petroleum is the principal commodity handled, gypsum and wheat being the major exports. The only other important ports in the region are Quebec City, a general cargo port, and Sept Iles and North Sydney, both of which handle iron ore. Land movements of a commercial nature are not great in Maritime Canada, primarily because of the "backwater" nature of the region with respect to the rest of the nation. Less than one per cent of the total highway freight movements of Canada are accomplished in Nova Scotia, New Brunswick, and Prince Edward Island combined.[26] Rail freight

[26] Royal Commission on Canada's Economic Prospects, *Final Report* (Ottawa: Queen's Printer, 1948), p. 280.

Figure 4-13. The principal commercial port of the Maritimes is Halifax. Its extensive harbor is spanned by a single high-level bridge. (Photo by the Photographic Survey Corporation Limited of Toronto.)

service is also limited, in spite of federal subsidies. Moncton is the principal railway center, having a strategic location on the Chignecto isthmus.

The Outlook

In spite of an early history and a distinguished heritage, Northeastern Anglo-America has not been a favored region from the economic standpoint. Its natural resources are limited, and its position in the northeast and southeast corners of the two countries involved has cut it off from the mainstream of activity just enough to inhibit its commercial vitality. There is no reason to expect a change in this broad pattern.

The Maritime Provinces and Lower St. Lawrence have a disproportionately large number of people engaged in marginal activities in the fields of farming, fishing, and logging. There is a dearth of arable land that must circumscribe agricultural growth. Agricultural crop specialization (especially in orchards, tobacco, and poultry), and in some cases intensification, should have a salutary effect in some areas. Coal mining can anticipate increasingly competitive conflict with Canadian natural gas and United States coal for the central Canada market, and employment cutbacks are likely with increased mechanization of the mines. The forestry industries (lumber, pulp, paper) can probably anticipate gradual expansion. Fishing, a mainstay of the economy, remains precarious because of fluctuations in fish populations and the vagaries of foreign competition and markets. A decreasing market for salted cod in Mediterranean Europe may be compensated for by growth in Latin-American outlets. There is a rising trend in catches of lobsters, Atlantic salmon (after many years of decline), and scallops, which lends a hopeful note. Manufacturing and commerce will continue to be restricted.

The New England subregion has undergone repeated economic readjustments. Though forced to shift constantly to different types of economic enterprise, it has generally done so with more or less success, and will probably continue to do so. Water power might be further developed, and pulp and paper manufacturing should continue to be important. Agricultural specialization and industrial diversification are likely, though neither on a large scale. Farm abandonment, already a major feature of the agricultural scene, will continue. A tendency toward part-time farming and the combination of city and country life will increase. Poultry-raising, second only to dairying in agricultural importance, is expected to increase.

The activity with the brightest prospects on both sides of the international border is tourism. The Maritimes are being "discovered" by an ever-increasing number of both United States and Canadian tourists, and New England's long-established attractions will beckon more and more visitors. Summer tourism, lengthening slightly into the autumn, will undoubtedly continue to grow at a faster rate than the winter variety.

Cities

The cities of Anglo-America are listed for each region in this volume by means of tables which give the population for (a) the urbanized area and (b) the political city, as delineated in the 1960 census of the United States and the 1961 census of Canada. The cities in each table are arranged in alphabetical order; only the more important ones lying within the region under consideration are included. As the American Manufacturing Region is an overlapping region, its cities (marked with an asterisk) are listed with the regions it overlaps, and no table of cities follows Chapter Three.

The 1960 United States census definition states that "an urbanized area contains at least one city with 50,000 inhabitants or more in 1960 as well as the surrounding closely settled incorporated places and unincorporated areas that meet [certain] criteria." The 1961 Canadian census lists "metropolitan areas" which correspond roughly to the "urbanized areas" of the United States, and hence they are given in the same column of each table.

On the regional maps at the beginning of each chapter, the following urban places are shown: (1) Those with a population exceeding 250,000 (according to the 1960 United States and 1961 Canadian censuses)

TABLE 1

Selected Cities and Towns of Northeastern Anglo-America

City or Town	Urbanized Area	Political Center	City or Town	Urbanized Area	Political Center
Albany	455,447	129,726	*Montreal	2,109,509	1,191,062
*Arlington	......	49,953	*Nashua	......	39,096
*Attleboro	......	27,118	*New Bedford	126,657	102,477
Augusta	......	21,680	*New Britain	99,894	82,201
Bangor	......	38,912	*New Haven	278,794	152,048
Barre	......	10,387	*New London	......	34,182
Berlin	......	17,821	*Newport	......	47,049
*Boston	2,413,236	697,197	*Newton	......	92,384
*Bridgeport	366,654	156,748	*Norwalk	82,270	67,775
*Bristol	......	45,499	*Norwich	......	38,506
*Brockton	111,315	72,813	*Pawtucket	......	81,001
Burlington	......	35,531	*Pittsfield	62,306	57,879
*Cambridge	......	107,716	*Portland	111,701	72,566
*Cap-de-la-Madeleine	......	26,925	*Portsmouth	......	25,833
Charlottetown	......	18,318	Presque Isle	......	12,886
*Chicopee	......	61,553	*Providence	659,542	207,498
Concord, N.H.	......	28,991	Quebec	357,568	171,979
*Cranston	......	66,766	*Quincy	......	87,409
Dartmouth, N.S.	......	46,966	Rimouski	......	17,739
*East Hartford	......	43,977	Rome	......	51,646
*Fairfield	......	46,183	Rutland	......	18,325
*Fall River	123,951	99,942	Saint John	95,563	55,153
Fredericton	......	19,683	Schenectady	......	81,682
*Gloucester	......	25,789	Sherbrooke	......	66,554
*Greenwich	......	53,793	*Somerville	......	94,697
Halifax	183,946	92,511	*Springfield	449,777	174,463
*Hartford	381,619	162,178	*Stamford	166,990	92,713
*Haverhill	......	46,346	*Stratford	......	45,012
*Holyoke	......	52,689	Sydney	......	33,617
*Lachine	......	38,630	Thetford Mines	......	21,618
*Lawrence	......	70,933	*Trois-Rivieres	......	53,477
Levis	......	15,112	Troy	......	67,492
*Lowell	118,547	92,107	Utica	187,779	100,410
*Lynn	......	94,478	*Waltham	......	55,413
*Malden	......	57,676	*Warwick	......	68,504
*Manchester	91,698	88,282	*Waterbury	141,626	107,130
*Medford	......	64,971	*West Hartford	......	62,382
*Meriden	......	51,850	*West Haven	......	43,002
*Milford	......	41,662	*Woonsocket	......	47,080
Moncton	......	43,840	*Worcester	225,446	186,587

* Also in the American Manufacturing Region.

are indicated by a solid circle, and their names are shown in all capital letters (as BOSTON); (2) Those with a population between 50,000 and 250,000 are shown by a solid circle, and their names are in capitals and lower case letters (as Sherbrooke); (3) Those with a population of less than 50,000 that are mentioned prominently in the text are indicated by an open circle, and their names are in capital and lower case letters (as Bangor). To assure legibility, cities and towns that are distinctly suburbs of larger urban places are not shown.

Because of space limitation, the tabular method of treating the cities of each region was considered advisable. For the reader who wishes more detail on each city, however, two modern reference works, available in most libraries, are recommended: (1) *Webster's Geographical Dictionary*, and (2) *The Columbia Lippincott Gazetteer of the World*. A description of Bangor, Maine, (Northeastern Anglo-America) is given below as it appears in each volume.

Ban'gor (băng'gôr; -gẽr). **1** Commercial and industrial city, ⊗ of Penobscot co., E cen. Maine, at head of navigation on Penobscot river 60 m. NE of Augusta; pop. 38,912; lumbering, pulp and paper mills. Bangor Theological Seminary (1816; Congregational); Dow Air Force Base.[27]
Bangor City (pop. 31,588), Penobscot co., S. Maine, on W. bank of the Penobscot, at head of navigation, at mouth of Kenduskeag Stream, opposite Brewer; alt. 100 ft.; 44°48′ N 68°46′ W. Third largest city in Maine; mainly a commercial center with varied industries supplementing once-dominant lumber and paper milling; printing, lumber processing, mfg. (shoes, dental supplies, tools, machinery, furniture, clothing, food products). Port of entry. Ships lumber, woodpulp, paper. Gateway to Mt. Desert Isl. and to an extensive resort area of many

lakes. Seat of Bangor Theological Seminary and Northeastern Conservatory of Music. Settled 1769 on site probably visited (1604) by Champlain; town inc. 1791, city 1834. Developed in 19th cent. as flourishing shipping center handling lumber, furs, fish, ice.[28]

Selected Bibliography

Alcock, F. J., "The Isles of Fundy," *Canadian Geographical Journal*, Vol. 39, 1949, pp. 92-107.

Bennett, M. K., "The Food Economy of the New England Indians, 1605-75," *Journal of Political Economy*, Vol. 43, October 1955, pp. 369-397.

Bird, J. Brian, "Settlement Patterns in Maritime Canada," *Geographical Review*, Vol. 45, July 1955, pp. 385-404.

Brooke, Cornwall, "A Land-Use Reconnaissance of the Annapolis-Cornwallis Valley, Nova Scotia," *Geographical Bulletin*, No. 9, 1957, pp. 37-63.

Clark, Andrew H., *Three Centuries and An Island*. Toronto: University of Toronto Press, 1954.

Forbes, Charles B., "Historic Forest Fires in Maine," *Economic Geography*, Vol. 24, 1949, pp. 269-273.

Gentilcore, R. Louis, "The Agricultural Background of Settlement in Eastern Nova Scotia," *Annals of the Association of American Geographers*, Vol. 46, December 1956, pp. 378-404.

Gibson, J. Sullivan, "Prince Edward Island—Gem of the Maritimes," *Journal of Geography*, Vol. 59, October 1960, pp. 301-308.

Higbee, Edward C., "The Three Earths of New England," *Geographical Review*, Vol. 42, 1952, pp. 425-438.

Klimm, Lester E., "The Empty Areas of the Northeastern United States," *Geographical Review*, Vol. 4, July 1954, pp. 325-345.

Laing, Jean, "The Pattern of Population Trends in Massachusetts," *Economic Geography*, Vol. 31, July 1955, pp. 265-271.

Raymond, C. W., "Agricultural Land Use in the Upper Saint John River Valley, New Brunswick," *Geographical Bulletin*, No. 15, 1960, pp. 65-83.

[27] By permission. From *Webster's Geographical Dictionary*, copyright 1962 by G. & C. Merriam Co., Publishers of the Merriam-Webster Dictionaries.

[28] By permission. *The Columbia Lippincott Gazetteer of the World* (New York: Columbia University Press, 1962), p. 157.

Shaw, W. R., "Prince Edward Island—the Story of its Agriculture," *Canadian Geographical Journal,* Vol. 52, May 1956, pp. 182-203.

"The Maine Broiler," *New England Business Review,* Federal Reserve Bank of Boston, June 1961, pp. 1-4.

"The Roving Population," *New England Business Review,* Federal Reserve Bank of Boston, October 1960, pp. 6-7.

Thoman, Richard S., "Portland Maine: An Economic Urban Appraisal," *Economic Geography,* Vol. 27, 1951, pp. 348-367.

Wilder, D. G., "Canada's Lobster Fishery," *Canadian Geographical Journal,* Vol. 55, September 1957, pp. 88-107.

Zelinsky, Wilbur, "The New England Connecting Barn," *Geographical Review,* Vol. 48, October 1958, pp. 540-553.

chapter five

The Atlantic
Coastal Plain
and
the Piedmont

The Coastal Plain and the Piedmont are here considered as a single geographical region because the pattern of settlement and development is somewhat similar throughout. Differences in utilization of the unconsolidated sediments of the Coastal Plain, and the residual soils of the Piedmont, are of enough contrast, however, to establish two distinct subregions: (1) the Atlantic Coastal Plain, and (2) the Piedmont. Because of climatic differences it seems de-

sirable to subdivide the Piedmont into three areas (Figure 5-1). The entire region possesses a degree of unity, however, in that types of economic activities are similar even though local variations exist.

The Coastal Plain Subregion, which occupies a belt 50 to 100 miles wide along the Atlantic Seaboard from the eastern end of Long Island through northeastern New Jersey to central North Carolina, owes its economic life to the huge market for fruits and

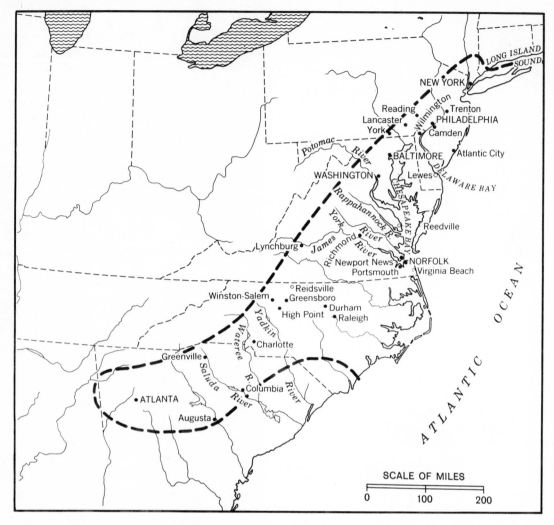

Figure 5-1. The Atlantic Coastal Plain and the Piedmont. A region of large cities, truck farming, tobacco growing, fishing, specialized manufacturing, and resorts.

vegetables created by the dense population between Norfolk and Boston. The southern boundary is drawn where cotton culture becomes dominant. The western boundary of this subregion, on the other hand, is marked by the Fall Line, which separates the crystalline rocks of the Piedmont from the softer sedimentaries of the Coastal Plain. This "line" is most pronounced along the streams where falls or rapids have developed, but in the interstream areas it becomes difficult to trace. The Fall Line is best shown by the string of cities that have grown up to utilize the power resources of the streams and to stand at the head of ocean navigation on those same streams.

Inland from the Atlantic Coastal Plain, between the Blue Ridge and the Fall Line Zone, lies the Piedmont, a long belt of foothills averaging about 100 miles in width. Extending from southeastern New York to Alabama, it reaches its greatest width in southern Virginia and North Carolina. Although not homogeneous throughout, it possesses considerable unity. The subregion may be divided into:

1. The Northern Piedmont (from southeastern New York across Maryland to north-central Virginia)—an area of general farming and dairying.

2. The Central Piedmont (central and south-central Virginia and north-central North Carolina)—especially noted for the production of tobacco and apples.

3. The Southern Piedmont (south-central North Carolina, western South Carolina, northern Georgia and northeastern Alabama)—an area of general farming with an emphasis on cotton.

The Physical Setting

Surface Features THE ATLANTIC COASTAL PLAIN was formerly a portion of the continental shelf that was raised above the sea without essential deformation. It is level to gently rolling. In relatively few places does the land rise more than 100 feet above sea level, though some of the long interstream areas rise to nearly 400 feet. Most of the cultural features, including roads and residences, are on these higher lands.

Poor drainage over much of the area is the principal surface condition limiting its use by man. Especially is this the case along the marshy coast of Virginia and North Carolina. In the embayed section of the Chesapeake Bay area, however, much of the land is rolling. The marshes and swamps, breeding places for mosquitoes, inhibit settlement.

The coast is broken by numerous peninsulas which are generally "splintered into smaller tongues," as an old document put it. The lands of Tidewater Virginia lie along four major rivers—the York, the James, the Rappahannock, and the Potomac. The head of tidewater on the last three lies at the Fall Line. The coastline is one of submergence, so that stream valleys are drowned and form broad tidal estuaries.

The seaward margin is fringed with an almost continuous succession of beaches and bars, the work of wave action. Incoming waves do not reach the shore, but break some distance out to form sand bars known as barrier beaches. Lagoons, varying in width from one-half mile to as many as eight miles, lie between these bars and the mainland. Most lagoons have been filled or are being filled with sand carried by streams from the mainland or blown from the beaches. Eventually the barrier beaches become so large that they prevent even the highest waves from washing over them. They are separated one from another by narrow inlets through which the tide enters.

THE PIEDMONT, a rolling, hilly area at an elevation of 100 to 1,500 feet, differs considerably from the lower level-to-undulating lands of the Coastal Plain. While called an upland, it is really an erosional plain with a few hills rising above its otherwise gently rolling surface. The divides, with few exceptions, rise to an even skyline. The Piedmont is smoothest along the interior border close to the Blue Ridge, where the full erosive power of the streams has not been felt. All the rivers are muddy and they fluctuate considerably in volume.

The Fall Line traverses the numerous rivers which flow from the Blue Ridge to the Atlantic. Where they pass from the older and harder rocks of the Piedmont onto the younger unconsolidated sediments of the Coastal Plain, there is a zone of rapids—the Fall Line. This Fall Line Zone has played a significant role in American history, since it determined the sites of a string of important cities from New York to Columbus, Georgia. Frequently rapids marked the head of navigation for sea-going craft; here bulk had to be broken. Moreover, water power was available for manufacturing.

Climate The mild, semi-marine climate is the *Coastal Plain's* most important environmental factor. Its warm spring makes the early maturing of vegetables and small fruits possible. The Gulf Stream, which moves northward along the coast, limits the range of temperature. The marine climate is emphasized by the numerous bays which seam the land.

Average annual precipitation varies from 40 inches in the north to 55 in the south, with the maximum in late summer and the minimum in autumn.

The long growing season, a result of proximity to the ocean, ranges from 190 days in the north to 240 in the south. Thus as many as four truck crops can be grown regularly on the same piece of land within a year.

Climatically, the *Piedmont* is a sort of transitional area between the North with its long, cold, snowy winters and the South with its short, mild ones. Obviously an area extending over so much latitude could not have an identical climate throughout. It is mostly on the basis of climate and the resultant land use that the Piedmont is divided into subregions. The growing season varies from an average of 160 days in the north to more than 230 in the south. The Southern Piedmont in winter averages 15° F. warmer than the Northern Piedmont.

Few agricultural areas in the United States receive so much precipitation; relatively few stations get less than 40 inches and some receive as many as 50. Maximum rainfall, in the form of thundershowers, comes in summer when crops need it most. These heavy downpours cause much soil erosion in a region where clean-tilled crops prevail. Hardly a week passes without a good rain, though this region, like most others, does have its occasional dry spells.

Soils The soils of the region show a disdain for broad generalization. The principal groups are of the podzolic-latosolic category, but to characterize them so broadly is to gloss over their individual variations. Three principal types may be noted: sands or sandy loams in the better-drained parts of the Coastal Plain, hydromorphic soils in

the numerous areas of marsh and swamp, and varied residual soils in the Piedmont. Despite the fact that agriculture occupies a high percentage of the land locally, the soils of the North Atlantic Coastal Plain *are not fertile*. This condition is not altogether the result of man's failure to rotate crops, fertilize the soil, and employ a scientific system of farming. Nature herself had "robbed" the soils long before the first colonist set foot upon the continent. In this subregion soil is considered primarily a medium through which to feed the crops. All soils require manure or commercial fertilizer to produce cash crops.

Viewed regionally, the soils of the Piedmont vary in quality from good to bad. Soil is, nevertheless, the most potent single natural environmental factor distinguishing this subregion. Lancaster County, Pennsylvania, is a notable exception, its fertile limestone soils being world-famous. From north to south, the Piedmont soils vary in texture from light to heavy. They are *residual;* that is, they are derived from the long disintegration, in place, of granites, gneisses, and schists—which underlie most of the region. Pedologists estimate that nature requires nearly 1,000 years to build one inch of topsoil. The only transported soils are confined to the valleys and are immature, having no relation to the underlying bedrock.

In colonial days, sandy loams seven to fifteen inches deep predominated, but these are now mostly gone, having been eroded from exposed slopes. Piedmont soils, never high in humus, have been depleted both by erosion and by leaching.[1] Leaching occurs throughout the year in the Central and the Southern Piedmont, especially in the latter; in the Northern Piedmont, however, the

[1] Land that is cultivated loses fertility through the draining away of those mineral elements which dissolve in water. Some leaching is inevitable, but it is increased by practices which leave the land bare throughout much of the year. It can be retarded by growing grass and cover crops.

ground is frozen during much of the winter and hence does not suffer so much.

Generous applications of commercial fertilizer must be used in this region to make the soil productive. The Southern Piedmont is one of the most heavily fertilized parts of the United States.

Natural Vegetation Originally, except for the coastal marshes and sand dunes, virgin forests of conifers or of deciduous species or of a mixture of the two characterized the Coastal Plain.

More than one-half of the area is still in forest and brush (not virgin), despite its early settlement by white men and its nearness to the great cities of New York, Philadelphia, Baltimore, Washington, and Norfolk. Some 1,200 square miles in southeastern and south-central New Jersey have almost no farm settlements.

The Piedmont, at the time of the first settlements, was an almost continuous expanse of forest—largely hardwoods. Into this pristine wilderness pushed the white man with his ax and fire, plow and seed. Soon, the original forest disappeared, being removed at a rate never before equaled in world history. It was an inexhaustible source of wood for fuel, fences and dwellings. But only a small part was taken for those uses. The rest went up in smoke, for the settlers regarded the forest as an enemy standing in the way of agricultural progress and burned it wantonly.

Today, much of the Piedmont is again in forests, but the trees are inferior second-growth stock. In spite of this, however, numerous small sawmills dot the landscape, showing an economic use of the forest that was not originally practiced. The forests of the present often occupy old fields which have been abandoned.

Settlement

The Atlantic Coastal Plain The Coastal Plain, especially Tidewater Virginia, was

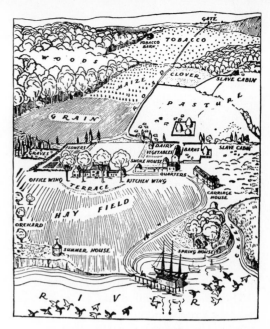

Figure 5-2. A typical eighteenth-century tidewater plantation. With miles of shoreline available and trackless forests inland, settlers located their plantations on the waterfront, relying almost wholly upon water transportation. (Courtesy Ginn & Company and the Maryland State Planning Commission.)

one of the cradles of Anglo-America. Colonial life centered in the plantation, rather than in the town, as in New England. The local isolation and economic self-sufficiency of the plantation were antagonistic to the development of towns. Prior to 1700, Jamestown was the only settlement in this region that really could be called a *town*, and it was actually nothing more than a village.

Nearly all settlements were located on navigable streams, and every planter owned a wharf which could be reached by the small ships of that day (Figure 5-2); in fact, one of the strongest reasons for which the planter selected his land was that it fronted on a water highway.

Plantations were governed geographically by the streams; counties were governed by the plantations; men thought in terms of plantations. . . . The growth of towns and cities was simply not a part of the scheme of society. When late in that first century men bethought themselves of the need of towns, it was too late. The rural system was so well established that it was impossible to overcome its influence.[2]

Within twelve years after the founding of Jamestown, plantations had spread 70 miles upstream, extending inland for several miles from either bank. Nowhere was there between rivers a land-reach greater than 20 miles, and frequently it was five miles or less. It would be wrong, however, to believe that colonial Tidewater Virginia and Maryland were entirely lands of plantations, slaves, and beautiful mansions.

There were several strata of society, but only the great landowners and the yeomen will be considered here. The wealthier and more intelligent planters occupied the more productive lands. Yeomen, for the most part poor, operated the medium-sized farms in the less productive areas. They found it both difficult and irritating to compete with Negro slaves. So powerful had the large plantation owners become that the yeomen experienced great difficulty in obtaining even small holdings. Hence the ablest migrated westward.

The Introduction of Slavery Slaves were first introduced because the tobacco growers of Tidewater Virginia and Maryland demanded them. In fields growing tobacco and corn, slaves working in gangs could be supervised easily. Women and children also worked. However, slaves could be used only where the work was set in simple and continuous tasks, where the winters were mild so that they could work out of doors twelve months in the year, and where the cost of living was low. Slavery never really became established in this region, however, as it did in the cotton and sugar areas to the south. It is thus apparent that the distribution of slavery throughout the United States

was based on geographical conditions and not on sentiment. By 1840 it was declining in both Maryland and Virginia.

The Piedmont The American Indians, who had occupied the Piedmont for a long time before the coming of the white man, were primarily hunters and hence had not changed the primeval character of the landscape. They had divided the hunting grounds into family-size portions and never trespassed unless forced to do so. Each family killed only the game it actually consumed. This system of occupance put no scars of exploitation on the land.

The Piedmont was settled from the older sections to the east—from the Chesapeake Bay and Albemarle Sound country and from Charleston, South Carolina—by people one, two, or three generations removed from the earliest settlers. It also received large numbers of Germans and Scotch-Irish who had followed the Great Valley southward and entered the Piedmont from the west. By 1750 most of the Piedmont had been occupied by white people.

Agricultural Activities of the Coastal Plain

Early Agriculture From the time of the earliest settlement, farming has been the predominant occupation. In colonial days it was assumed to be the necessary employment of all, and nearly everyone considered the ownership of tillable land the acme of "human earthly desire." Even those who were classed as merchants, fishermen, and manufacturers were really part-time farmers.

The colonies composing the North Atlantic Coastal Plain were not entirely self-sustaining; they had to produce something for exchange. They planted the European grape, but it failed; they introduced the mulberry and the silk worm, but unsuccessfully; they tried to rely on furs, but the supply was neither permanent nor plentiful.

[2] A. B. Hulbert, *Soil: Its Influence on the History of the United States* (New Haven: Yale University Press, 1930), pp. 111-12.

Something had to be found that was in demand and had high value per unit of weight or bulk. *Tobacco proved to be that product.*

TOBACCO The commercial production of tobacco began in 1612, and within a few years it was the leading crop. In fact, it was grown almost to the exclusion of foodstuffs. The continuous growing of a single crop on a given area, however, is soil robbery, and the history of early agriculture here is the history of land exploitation. Tobacco had not long been cultivated before planters found it necessary to acquire additional land. As soon as the soil showed signs of exhaustion, it was allowed to grow up in grasses and trees, and new fields were cleared. For this reason the large plantations came into being. The tobacco planter had to have considerable acreage on which to grow this crop, since it was necessary to reclaim new land from the forest as the soil lost its fertility. It was soon found that the soils were becoming depleted at so rapid a rate that few fields could produce more than three consecutive crops. To make matters worse, the neglect of the old fields encouraged washing and gullying. Thus tidewater counties were suffering from soil depletion as early as the First Census of 1790. About that time some planters began to move to the Piedmont. Though there was an agricultural revival during the 1850's when farm journals and soil chemists pointed out the value of commercial fertilizer,[3] deep plowing, and improved seed, Tidewater Virginia and Maryland were losing their Southern characteristics. The plantation was giving way to the small diversified farm, in which slavery had a steadily declining part. The truck farms were in sharp contrast to the large old-fashioned plantations from which they were carved.

Present-day Agriculture Since the earliest settlement, a selective process has been going on in the Coastal Plain—the best lands continuing productive, the bad ones reverting to wilderness. Tobacco no longer is important except in southern Maryland west of Chesapeake Bay, where it is a major cash crop. Wheat, corn, and hay occupy a considerable part of the land under cultivation. If proper rotations are maintained and moderate amounts of commercial fertilizer used, the yields are satisfactory—the average wheat yields compare favorably with the average for the United States.

The growing of vegetables, however, is profitable in many parts of the region. Vegetable consumption in Anglo-America has increased greatly since 1920, largely as a result of (1) dietary research—especially as regards the value of vitamins—and (2) the development of refrigeration, which permits perishable products to move great distances in season.

Only a fraction of the land available for truck crops is actually utilized in the North Atlantic Coastal Plain; nevertheless, this subregion is the world's foremost producer of commercial vegetables. The farms are small, because truck farming is so intensive that it is not profitable, normally, to work a large farm, since vegetables require 5 to 20 times as much labor as wheat. Ordinarily, as fast as one vegetable is harvested, the field is plowed, fertilized, and planted to another. Vegetable production nearly always is ahead of consumption.

The area is favored geographically for vegetable production by its long growing season, its level terrain, and its light, easily tilled soils that warm rapidly in the spring. A superb location with respect to the nation's outstanding markets for truck crops, along with almost unexcelled transportation

[3] The use of chemical plant food in the United States probably dates from 1830, when the first Chilean nitrate was imported. Production of mixed fertilizers was started in Baltimore in 1850, and the establishment of other factories along the Atlantic Seaboard followed. It is estimated that production was about 20,000 tons in 1856 and 50,000 tons in 1868.

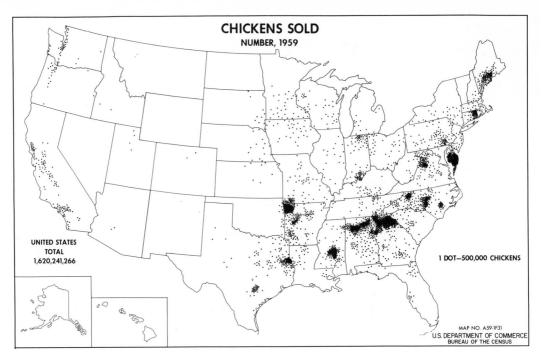

CHICKENS SOLD
NUMBER, 1959

UNITED STATES
TOTAL
1,620,241,266

1 DOT—500,000 CHICKENS

MAP NO. A59-1F31
U.S. DEPARTMENT OF COMMERCE
BUREAU OF THE CENSUS

Figure 5-3. Chickens sold in the United States. Broilers account for most of the sales. The Delmarva Peninsula is clearly a major commercial chicken-raising area.

facilities—rail, boat, and truck—add to its advantages.

FARM OPERATIONS   Output for the gigantic urban markets of the Northeast is the keynote for farming in the northern portion of the Coastal Plain. The intensive production of poultry, milk, and vegetables is the principal activity, although a great variety of crops is grown.

The chief farm enterprise north of Chesapeake Bay is raising poultry, mostly chickens (Figure 5-3). Almost every farm keeps chickens, but large-scale production is concentrated in eastern New Jersey (where there is considerable egg output), central Delaware, and the eastern shore of Maryland and Virginia (in which areas broilers are the principal product). The districts of more productive soil tend to be reserved for crop-growing, so that the very sandy soils generally contain the poultry farms. Feed for the chickens, and for the famous "Long Island ducklings" of New York's Suf-

folk County, mostly is shipped in from outside the region, constituting the major item of expense.

Dairying, second only to poultry on the farm scene of the northern Coastal Plain, is also confined to less productive areas, mostly the poorer-drained soils of southwestern New Jersey and northern Delmarva Peninsula. Output from these dairy farms is unusually large.

CROPS   Although many vegetables and potatoes are grown, the most common crops of the Coastal Plain are corn and small grains. However, it is market gardening and truck farming that provide much of the regional distinctiveness (Figure 5-4). Vegetables and horticultural specialties are raised in large quantities for the adjacent city markets, although much of the market garden area has become urbanized since 1940.

The sandy loams of southwestern New Jersey are particularly favored for vegetable production, and have given New Jersey its

Figure 5-4. Vegetables harvested for sale. The outstanding commercial vegetable growing areas in eastern United States are southwestern New Jersey and the Delmarva Peninsula.

reputation as "the Garden State" (Figure 5-5). A great many types of vegetables are raised in the area, but nearly one-third of the harvested value is in tomatoes. Asparagus is a strong secondary crop, followed by sweet corn, peppers, cabbage, and lettuce. Roughly 60 per cent of the output goes on the fresh vegetable market, and most of that is sold at local auctions. The remaining 40 per cent is contract production for the freezing and canning industry.

Potatoes and sweet potatoes are among the outstanding crops in other parts of the north Coastal Plain. They appear on the Northern market from late June to early August—after the peak of the season in the Carolinas but before the arrival of the Long Island crop. For the most part, potatoes are grown close to large population centers; in fact, maps of population and potatoes usually coincide remarkably well.

Figure 5-5. Harvesting snap beans on the New Jersey coastal plain. (Photo courtesy New Jersey Department of Agriculture, Trenton, New Jersey.)

Sweet potatoes, tropical or subtropical in origin, have been grown here since 1650. Favorable conditions are the sandy loam soils, long growing season, warm nights, and relatively high temperatures. Since 1909, commercial production has been concentrating in New Jersey, the Eastern Shore of Maryland and Virginia, and northeastern North Carolina.

Other commercial crops include sweet corn, cucumbers, cabbage, peas, peppers, onions, greenbeans, lettuce, celery, asparagus, tomatoes, and spinach. Some of these are sold as they ripen, while others are grown for canneries. When truck farmers grow fresh vegetables for sale, they make the most money by getting their crops to market early; hence they try to settle in the warmest part of the area.

Watermelons, cantaloupes, strawberries, blackberries, and raspberries are important locally. Delaware and Maryland are noted for strawberries as is southern New Jersey for cranberries.

South of Chesapeake Bay the pattern is somewhat different. Increasing distance from large urban markets diminishes the emphasis on market gardening, though truckloads of vegetables from southeastern Virginia make nightly runs as far as New York City. Corn, however, remains the dominant crop, and such specialties as tobacco, peanuts, and cotton are often of greater value than vegetables.

Tobacco is the distinctive and favored crop of the "New Bright Tobacco Belt" in the inner Coastal Plain of North Carolina and in parts of southern Maryland (Figure 5-6). It is a high-value crop, and the best drained, most fertile soils are devoted to it, as is a considerable amount of fertilizer.

Peanuts are important, especially in

Figure 5-6. Tobacco harvested. Note the heavy concentration on the Piedmont and the Inner Coastal Plain of the Carolinas, Virginia, and Maryland and in the Lancaster area of Pennsylvania.

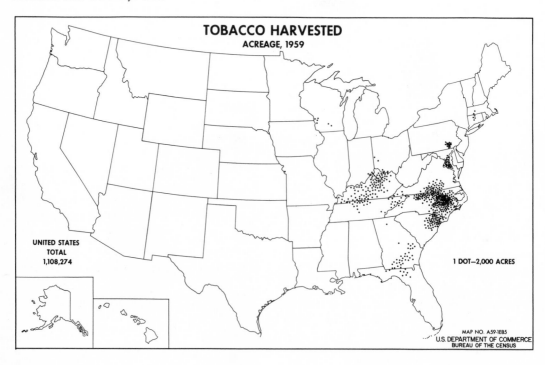

southeastern Virginia and adjacent North Carolina, where this crop has been cultivated longer and more intensively than in any other area in the country. Emphasis is on the large-podded variety for human consumption. This crop requires a long summer and a light-textured soil. Although a legume, peanuts do not add nitrogen to the soil if the nuts are harvested. Hay from the peanut plant is fully as valuable as alfalfa and clover. The peanut has helped to terminate the one-crop system of farming so long prevalent here.

Cotton is an important crop in the North Carolina portion, and hogs, the principal type of farm livestock, are notable throughout the southern Coastal Plain.

MARKETING Large-scale commercial production of truck crops became possible only in proportion to the availability of rapid and efficient transportation. The region everywhere is well served by rail, water, and highway. Moreover, within or adjacent to it is a long line of cities reaching from Boston to Norfolk whose inhabitants make up an amazingly large part of Anglo-America's total population. Probably no other region on earth possesses such an enormous and immediate city market for its products. The great resorts are an additional market; tourists in New Jersey alone number millions annually. The Hampton Roads district is more important than its population figure indicates, because of its military posts and naval bases, and because many commercial vessels replenish their supplies there. The importance of proximity cannot be overestimated—75 per cent of the vegetables sold in New York City come in season from farms within 100 miles.

Wherever you go, from farmhouse to farmhouse, the chief topics of conversation are not so much farm practices as markets, prices, supply and demand, cost of distribution, and similar problems. Farther west or south, these same items enter into conversa-

tions, it is true, but not on the day-to-day, almost hour-to-hour basis that they do in the Middle Atlantic States. . . . Many crops will start or not go to market on a twelve-hour basis. If the sweet corn market closes strong today, a farmer will hope that it will hold on the opening and start his truck rolling at midnight for the terminal. If the report states that broilers are in full supply and going into the cold-storage market, a poultryman will hold off for a few days in slaughtering that lot of five hundred which is about ready to go. Although milk prices are set at intervals, dairymen avidly follow their ups and downs by the day. A long trend downward may mean a meeting of farmers to protest to the milk administrator. It may mean a radical change in feeding and breeding. Likewise, the dairyman and poultryman want a daily report on the going price of feed.[4]

Agriculture of the Piedmont

Agriculture employs more people than does any other industry on the Piedmont, though in the area between Lynchburg and Atlanta manufacturing increased rapidly after 1930.

As already noted, the Piedmont was settled by farmers from the tidewater region and from the Great Valley. Upon clearing the forest, many of them planted tobacco, a row crop, successively for three, four, or even five years. When tobacco was no longer profitable, they grew corn until it would not pay for the labor expended. Then they abandoned the fields, cleared new land, and repeated the process.

The central and southern parts of the Piedmont are essentially areas of small farms. Many so-called "problem farms" have an average of only 18 acres in harvested crops. Much of the land is marginal or submarginal. Production is directed largely toward such cash crops as cotton and tobacco,

[4] By permission. Ladd Haystead and Gilbert C. Fite, *The Agricultural Regions of the United States* (Norman: University of Oklahoma Press, 1955), pp. 49-50.

whose prices fluctuate widely and occasionally bring misfortune to the farmer. The farm tenancy rate is the highest in Anglo-America; however, it is decreasing rapidly. Nowhere else do livestock, milk, and home-grown vegetables play so small a part in the farming enterprise. There are, however, local exceptions, especially around cities and towns, because of manufacturing and commerce.

The Northern Piedmont Lying north of the James River in the states of Pennsylvania, Maryland, and Virginia is an important dairy section. The farms, averaging 50 to 100 acres, are usually smaller than those in any other geographical region of their respective states. Dairying is so organized as to supply fluid milk to nearby cities; some goes as far as New York City. A secondary factor is that the soils are not sufficiently fertile nor the topography sufficiently flat for most successful general farming practices. Proximity to great markets has enabled the farmers to rise above the minor deficiencies of soil and topography. Much wheat is grown, partly for its cash value, but partly for the protection it offers against excessive soil erosion and leaching and for the straw it supplies for bedding dairy cattle. Barley is planted as a winter cover crop for the same reasons. Corn, grown for grain and silage, also is a major crop. The land, after it is laid by, is planted to winter wheat or barley. The hay crop is invariably a legume, either alfalfa or red clover.

Nearly all the farmers are white, because the plantation system never was important in Pennsylvania and did not extend beyond the Coastal Plain even in Maryland. Farmers of German descent, who follow scientific practices, are numerically important, especially in Pennsylvania, and the high standard of the dairy industry is in no small measure attributable to them.

LANCASTER COUNTY, PENNSYLVANIA Lancaster is one of the most scientifically farmed counties in the United States, and it merits separate treatment.

For the most part, this area is a broad undulating plain lying southeast of all the mountain ridges of Pennsylvania. The climate is highly favorable for farming. The growing season of 160 to 175 days is adequate for most middle-latitude crops. Winters are mild and summers hot. Precipitation averages about 40 inches, nearly two-thirds of which falls from April to September, inclusive, when the crops need it most. The fertile limestone soils—those that have developed from a residue resulting from the decay of limestone—are, undoubtedly, the best in the state.

Swiss Mennonites, followed later by Germans, were the original settlers. Today Lancaster County and Pennsylvania Dutch (German) are synonymous; three-quarters of the people in the county are of German ancestry. It is indeed significant that this area was settled by immigrants from western Germany whose ancestors for many centuries had cultivated one of the richest wheat-growing regions of Europe. They were used to soils with a high lime content, and Lancaster County appealed to them. Since settlement, these thrifty and diligent Pennsylvania Dutch have transformed the region into a highly fruitful one (Figure 5-7). Unlike farmers in other regions, generations pass through the same homesteads; sons follow their fathers on the same soil.

Lancaster County is above all an agricultural land. More than 90 per cent of it is in farms, and in some townships more than 80 per cent is in crops. There is little waste land. Farms are relatively small—averaging less than 60 acres—and are well cared for. Houses are well built but not ostentatious; barns are large and in excellent condition; all outbuildings and fences are painted. Roads everywhere are good and railroads numerous. The whole cultural landscape reflects prosperity.

Figure 5-7. A Lancaster County farm. Few areas in Anglo-America have been so richly endowed by nature and so well handled by man as Lancaster County. The Pennsylvania Dutch, predominant element in the population, have brought their lands to a high degree of productivity. (Photo courtesy Pennsylvania Dutch Tourist Bureau, Lancaster, Pa.)

Corn, winter wheat, hay, potatoes, and tobacco are the major crops. Tobacco, which fits into the system of diversified farming in Lancaster County, is one of the two money crops. Nevertheless, the least acreage is given to it, because it is a "robber" crop, draining fertility from the land, and it requires an abundance of labor from planting through harvesting and marketing.

Lancaster County tobacco, mild in aroma and flavor, is used primarily for cigar fillers, of which it contributes about two-thirds of the nation's supply. The county produces about 90 per cent of Pennsylvania's tobacco, and its per-acre yield is high. In order to procure this high yield, the crop is grown only on the better soils—especially the silt and clay loams—and these are well fertilized. Few other areas have solved their fertilizer problems so well. The fertilizer is the manure of steers and dairy cattle.

Wheat is the other cash crop, being widely distributed and grown on all soils. At least half is used within the county for livestock and human consumption. Corn, like wheat, is widely distributed. Corn cannot be shipped because of its low value, so most of it is fed to steers and poultry. Potatoes, low in value and perishable, are grown by nearly every farmer. The excellent location of this area with respect to large consuming centers favors commercial production of potatoes. Probably no other area in this country gets larger per-acre yields— about 600 bushels. Hay is an important rotation crop. Timothy, alfalfa, and clover all are grown. Legumes yield well everywhere. Nearly all the hay is fed on the farms where it is grown.

Dairying is not as important as one might expect, because its labor requirements are heavy and it would compete with tobacco for the farmer's time. It is for this reason that the county has gone in for fattening steers. Stockers come mostly from southwestern Virginia and West Virginia, areas growing insufficient corn to fatten them. In recent years, however, increasing numbers of cattle are being brought in from Texas and other western ranching areas. The extensive southeastern Pennsylvania holdings of the King Ranch of Texas is a notable example of this. Here the "Braford" (*Brahma* and *Hereford*) strain of beef cattle forms a conspicuous feature of the cultural landscape.

MUSHROOMS IN SOUTHEASTERN PENNSYLVANIA   In the southeastern corner of the Pennsylvania Piedmont lies the leading mushroom-producing area of the United States. The actual acreage devoted to the crop is negligible, since it is grown in beds within mushroom sheds. The chief observable forms of the industry are the rows of ventilated sheds with large piles of horse-manure compost alongside. The product is sent to Philadelphia, New York, and other large urban centers by truck or express.

THE APPLE AREA OF THE VIRGINIA PIEDMONT   Bordering the Blue Ridge from the James River to the Rappahannock River is one of the leading apple districts in eastern United States. The belt, with Charlottesville as the center, is approximately 45 miles wide and extends in a northeast-south-west direction. The industry began some 75 years ago when farmers planted apple orchards in the small, moist, fertile valleys (*coves*) at the foot of the mountain ridges. Location on slopes enabled them to benefit from air drainage. Many of them are on rough land and are called "mountain orchards."

The Central Piedmont—Land of Tobacco   The Central Piedmont is one of the continent's major tobacco-growing areas. Dark fire-cured leaf and air-cured leaf are grown in Virginia, and bright flue-cured in Virginia and the states south of it (Figure 5-8).

By Revolutionary times, tobacco had nearly exhausted the "second bottoms" of Tidewater Virginia and was moving up the valleys of the Virginia and North Carolina Piedmont. Tobacco was the staple, and every attempt to produce other export crops

Figure 5-8. A field of bright leaf tobacco in eastern North Carolina. (Photo courtesy North Carolina Department of Conservation and Development.)

such as silk, grapes, flax, hemp, and cotton failed. But not everyone on the Piedmont grew tobacco. Those who came from the Great Valley were opposed to slavery and hence did not grow tobacco, and the poor whites who migrated from the Coastal Plain were non-slaveholding.

DARK FIRE-CURED AND AIR-CURED TOBACCOS These types are grown on the heavier soils of the Virginia Piedmont—the former in the central part, the latter in the north-central portion. The fire-cured type is identical with that grown in early days of Jamestown, and the method of treatment is fundamentally the same as that employed by the Indians. The cured leaf of these types is dark in color, thick, tough, oily, and high in nicotine. Dark tobaccos are used for pipe-smoking mixtures, snuff, and chewing. The fire-cured types have been grown primarily for export and the air-cured types for domestic manufacture. The demand both in foreign and domestic markets is decreasing.

BRIGHT FLUE-CURED TOBACCO In 1852, near Durham, North Carolina, two farmers broke away from tradition and set their plants in light, sandy, siliceous, infertile soil. They heated some of the yield over hot flues and got a clear, rich, gold leaf that was mild and sweet to smoke. Thus was revived the social economy of the worn-out soil, and the lands that had been abandoned jumped in value many-fold.

Land used for tobacco is carefully selected, since soil is the dominant environmental factor contributing to aroma, flavor, and thinness of leaf. On any given farm, only a small acreage is planted in tobacco and but a fraction of this grows the highest quality. Light-colored and light-textured soils, with little clay and organic material in the subsoil, are best for cigarette and pipe tobacco. Most farmers devote from two to ten acres of highly prized land for tobacco and use it year in and year out. This type of farming has so ruined the land

that virgin soils are now at a premium. Legumes dare not be used to build up the soils, and manures must be used sparingly. The grower prefers to put his crop on almost sterile soil, to which he then may add plant foods in the right amount. It is little wonder then that this area is one of the largest consumers of commercial fertilizer.

Only a small acreage per farm is in tobacco because it is a back-breaking, highly technical crop to grow. It requires so much labor that little time is left for other crops. There is the seed bed, the preparation, the fields, transplanting, cultivating, topping (to prevent the growth of seeds), worming, suckering, spraying, harvesting, curing, stripping, and marketing. Tobacco is a crop that wears out men as well as the land.

Tobacco is hard on the soil because it is a clean-tilled crop that induces erosion. The rows are kept scrupulously free of weeds during the growing season. Finally, open winters and torrential summer rains on steeply sloping fields mean only one thing—soil loss.

Tobacco in the Central Piedmont is meeting some competition, especially from dairying, poultry raising, and beef fattening. Large numbers of beef cattle are now run on lush pastures. On the estates in the Virginia section the preference is for the Aberdeen-Angus breed, and today these sleek, black cattle form an integral part of Piedmont economy (Figure 5-9).

Corn is the outstanding crop in acreage and almost every farmer grows it. It yields best in river and creek bottoms but is grown also on steep hillsides. Like tobacco, it is a row crop that induces soil erosion. It is made into corn meal for human use and is used as feed for livestock.

The Southern Piedmont—Land of Cotton and Corn From central North Carolina to Alabama, cotton replaces tobacco as the principal cash crop. This area lying south of the July isotherm of 78° F. has a

Figure 5-9. Aberdeen-Angus cattle on a blue-grass pasture near Gordonsville, Virginia. (Photo courtesy C. T. Neale and the Virginia Aberdeen-Angus Association.)

growing season of 200 days or more. Its soils are heavier than those in the tobacco area to the north. Cotton, outstanding since 1820, was an excellent pioneer crop in the prerailroad era because high value enabled it to stand transport charges. Its production could also employ slaves.

The Southern Piedmont is one of the oldest cotton-growing areas in the United States but is no longer one of the best. The competition from the less humid cotton districts in Texas and Oklahoma is becoming more difficult to meet.

The natural environment in the Southern Piedmont is satisfactory for growing cotton. Rainfall is light in spring and early summer when cotton requires little moisture and great heat, and low in autumn when precipitation would discolor the lint in the opening bolls and retard picking. But cotton has been hard on the land. Thousands of ruined acres have returned to forest. Between 1954 and 1959 in the two Carolinas alone there was a decrease of more than 400,000 acres in cotton growing.

Corn, a subsistence and not a cash crop like cotton, is grown for both human and livestock consumption. Like cotton, however, corn is a clean-tilled crop which induces sheet and gully erosion and hinders systematic rotations. It also draws heavily on the soil nutrients. Corn and cotton have made much of the Southern Piedmont a problem area—a large portion of which should not be farmed at all.

Lespedeza, a deep-rooted perennial, is revolutionizing agricultural practices in the Southern Piedmont. It affords an excellent protective cover, makes the soil more absorbent, is a popular forage and, when plowed under, increases the yield of subsequent crops.

Some crop diversification is also of significance. More dairy cattle, but particularly more beef cattle, are being raised. Peaches are replacing cotton in many areas, especially around Spartanburg, South Carolina.

Soil Erosion Few areas have been so manhandled (Figure 5-10) as the Piedmont. Although the first cotton gin was not built until 1795 in the South Carolina Piedmont, significant soil wash was already noticeable by 1808,[5] indicating the brief period of time required for cotton cultivation to cause significant erosion. Soil erosion occurs on practically every acre of slope land, and the prevailing system of farming has not encouraged soil conservation. Hence nearly one-third of the Southern Piedmont has lost 75 per cent or more of its topsoil. Over large areas, crops are being grown on subsoil. Considerable land has been abandoned because it is submarginal—cannot produce crops at a profit.

Soil erosion is the great problem of much of the Piedmont. In the central and southern sections, thousands of farmers operating on slopes now stripped of topsoil cannot make a satisfactory living. Their families are "ill-fed, ill-clad, and ill-housed."

Conservation A national objective is to pass on to future generations a soil as nearly unimpaired as possible. The Soil Conservation Service is attempting to improve both the Piedmont and its people: little can be

[5] Edward Higbee, *American Agriculture: Geography, Resources, Conservation* (New York: John Wiley and Sons, 1958), p. 331.

accomplished without considering both. Some of the conservation practices being employed are:

1. *Contour farming*. The farmer plows around the hill rather than up and down the slope. Each small ridge and furrow helps to hold back rain water.

2. *Strip cropping*. Strips of close-growing crops alternating with rows of clean-tilled crops are grown on the contour. The strips of close-growing crops filter out the soil particles from the silt-laden water moving downhill. The water is obstructed, its velocity is checked, and the load is dropped. The water then has more time to soak into the ground and soil wash is diminished.

3. *Terracing*. Terraces act as impediments to the flow of water, thereby reducing its erosive power. They let surplus water run from the field in an orderly manner.

4. *Cover crops*. Close-growing crops are planted on steep slopes and bare ground to protect the land from erosion. One of the best crops for the Piedmont is lespedeza. On an experimental plot this crop lost only about one ton of soil per acre, as against

Figure 5-10. Soil erosion on the Piedmont. Prior to the Civil War this was productive land, but in the century since Appomattox the topsoil has been carried away and deep gulleys are tearing through the subsoil. (Photo courtesy Soil Conservation Service.)

28 for bare plots, 18 for cotton, and 7 for corn. Another cover crop which has been successful on the better-drained soils of the Piedmont is the perennial, kudzu, a deep-rooted, leguminous vine with a dense, broad-leafed foliage. Its rapid growth, as much as 50 feet in a single season, makes it especially desirable for protecting steep slopes from erosion,[6] although the riotous growth sometimes interferes with other forms of land use.

Topsoil contains the bulk of the life-giving humus and nitrogen. Since subsoil is only one-fourth to one-half as productive as topsoil, the need for conservation is obvious.

Rural Depopulation

Despite the importance of truck farming, fewer people in the Coastal Plain are engaged in agriculture today than a century ago. In fact, the more southerly part of the subregion passed the climax of its prosperity on the eve of the War for Independence. It suffered still more in the War of 1812. From 1820 to 1840 there was a heavy exodus. The principal cause of emigration was the opening of the cheap land and extremely fertile soils of the Middle West, with which Tidewater Virginia and Maryland could not compete. An additional factor was that the plantation system was so lacking in democracy that the family of small means could make little headway socially or economically, and the New West loomed as a beacon of hope.

The rural population in Tidewater Virginia and Maryland is only about half of what it was in 1810. The same is true in New Jersey, which has 400,000 acres of deserted farms; here, however, the urban pull

[6] R. Y. Bailey, *Kudzu for Erosion Control in the Southeast,* U.S. Department of Agriculture, Farmers' Bulletin No. 1840 (Washington: Government Printing Office, 1944).

is strong, and suburbs occupy much former farm land.

Tenancy

The Central and Southern subregions are capital examples of man's misuse of the land. Throughout the United States there is unmistakable correlation between tenancy and erosion. Tenancy had its inception after the Civil War. Planters with land and experience lacked funds for paying wages to their former slaves, and hundreds of thousands of newly freed Negroes were poor but knew the routine of caring for cotton under rigid direction. The tenant system brought these two interdependent groups together. The former slaves were given a share of the crop (usually half) for their part of the labor. At first only Negroes were croppers, but now there are about as many white tenants as there are colored. White croppers dwell mostly in the Southern Piedmont and are cotton growers. Some also occupy the tobacco lands of the Central Piedmont. Nearly all emanate from the adjacent mountain areas or from patches of poor land which were scattered between plantations before the Civil War.

Most croppers are little more than *peons*—many are poorly nourished. Dwellings, of two or three rooms, are poorly constructed, weatherbeaten and unsightly. Few tenants remain on the same piece of land for more than a year or two; in fact, one out of every three moves each year. Under such a system there is little incentive to conserve the land, which each year becomes more depleted and eroded.

One of the most encouraging trends in American agriculture, however, has been the precipitate decline of tenancy in recent years. Cotton is no longer a predominantly tenant crop; nor is tobacco. Broadened opportunity for urban employment has attracted large numbers of tenant and part-time farmers into the cities. Only in the "delta lands" of Mississippi-Arkansas-Tennessee and to a lesser extent on the Carolina Coastal Plain is tenancy still of much significance.

Present Inhabitants

South of Delaware Bay on the Coastal Plain, the farmers are of early American stock and 35 per cent are colored. North of Delaware Bay, especially in New Jersey, the farmers are largely of foreign origin: German, Irish, English, and Italian. European immigrants have long shunned the lands south of the Mason-Dixon Line because their higher standard of living would prevent them from competing with the Negro and because the social status of the agricultural laborer is unattractive.

The difference in the composition of the population north and south of Delaware Bay affects the tempo of life. To the north the manner of living is typically Northern, to the south typically Southern. In the latter area farming is not as scientific, and the standard of living is lower.

In Maryland and Virginia, Negroes generally occupy better lands than white farmers, for they work parts of former plantations which had to be sufficiently productive to support both the landlord and his slaves. Many of the white farmers attempt to farm sandy soils that were never very good.

Estates of the Piedmont

Settlement of the Piedmont followed that of the Coastal Plain. This was partly because the better lands of the Coastal Plain were occupied at an early date and partly because colonists realized that the soils of the Piedmont were more fertile. So long as settlement was confined to the Coastal Plain, plantation homes were erected with their front doors facing the water—their chief contact with Europe. In the Piedmont section, however, the spread of people did

not hinge so definitely on stream patterns. Homes occupied the higher and more attractive interstream areas.[7]

To this rolling and fertile Piedmont country came the Quakers and later the "Pennsylvania-Dutch" Mennonites to settle in Lancaster County; the English aristocracy to establish manor houses in Lord Baltimore's colony of Maryland; and the Cavaliers to the Virginia Piedmont. The type of settlement made by the Mennonites in Lancaster County has been discussed. The settlement of the Manor Counties of Maryland, and the appearance of that area today is vividly described in the following quotation:

> The Manor Counties of Maryland form one of the most distinctive and gracious communities in America. There the climate is hospitable, terrain comfortable, soils fertile and highly productive, resources varied and adequate, and the countryside peaceful and attractive. There, in the midst of plenty and prosperity, folks have learned long since the art of living abundantly and graciously, of entertaining delightfully, and enjoying to the fullest the loveliness and bounty of the land in which they live. There, American citizenship and patriotism have achieved a perfection that might well be envied and emulated throughout our country.
>
> From the deep, fertile soils of the farms on the rolling terrain of the lower Piedmont, farmers take heavy yields of wheat, and corn, and alfalfa; on the luxuriant pastures they raise prize-winning cattle, swine and sheep; in their productive orchards all kinds of luscious temperate fruits flourish and yield heavily and trustworthily; in their gardens they can grow any and all healthful vegetables; from the shallow, mild waters of the neighboring bay, they take varied fishes and oysters and crabs; from the streams they get shad and smelt and other finfish; wild fowl throng the marshes and bays, quail and pheasant find cover in the broom-sedge and cut-over woodlands, squirrel, and rabbit and raccoon haunt the brush and groves.

[7] Henry J. Warman, "Population of the Manor Counties of Maryland," *Economic Geography,* Vol. 25 (1949), pp. 34-35.

It is a land of rich and abundant living where tournaments, races, and riding after the hounds, enliven the days of toil. It is a land of fun and recreation as well as of industry and application to business. It is a land of superior transportation facilities, of capacious homes, of flourishing agriculture, and alluring landscape. It is a land of content and charm, as well as of vision and achievement. Men and women who dwell there, or who have been born and nurtured there, have made deep impress upon the institutions and history of America. The Manor Counties of Maryland grace America's rural life.[8]

The Virginia Piedmont closely resembles the Manor Counties of Maryland. Monticello, the plantation home of Thomas Jefferson, is a classic example of the "gracious living" practiced by the landed aristocracy. In recent years, many of these old plantations have been purchased by urban dwellers from Washington, Baltimore, Philadelphia, New York, and other large metropolitan centers. Low property taxes have in part attracted these large investments, and as a result many old plantations have been modernized and revived. Today, as one drives through the Piedmont, between long rows of white fences, one wonders how land that is not particularly fertile can support such magnificent and costly estates. The answer is, in most cases, that the estate is being supported by money supplied from the industry and commerce of the cities and not from farming. In Virginia a common statement is that "farms" have ordinary fences and "estates" have white painted fences. The result, however, is a very pleasing landscape such as could be found only in a land with great natural beauty and upon which outside wealth has been spent in a lavish manner.

The Piedmont of the Carolinas and Georgia was either developed under the cotton culture of the antebellum South or

[8] Editorial in *Economic Geography*, Vol. 25 (1949).

left largely as backwoods. With the collapse of Southern economy following the Civil War, little new money flowed into the area and the old estates were abandoned. Modern development has come largely in the form of manufacturing industries.

Mineral Resources

The Piedmont ranks rather low in minerals, though it does have several kinds of building stone of economic value. The first coal to be mined in the United States was dug near Richmond, Virginia, and, until the Gold Rush to California in 1849, Georgia was the country's leading source of gold. But no part of the Piedmont is important today for metallic minerals.

Most of the rocks are crystalline and are among the oldest in the world—granites, gneisses, schists, marbles, and slates. Granites of high quality are quarried widely throughout the region and are used in a number of Eastern cities as building and monumental stones, curbing and paving blocks. Broken granite is used as an ingredient of concrete, as railroad ballast, and as artificial sand. In the hilly Piedmont of northern Georgia is a narrow belt some 60 miles long and a few miles wide where one of North America's more important marble-working areas is to be found. Pure-white and pink marbles of high quality are quarried. Asbestos, chromite, copper, corundum, feldspar, gold, mica, serpentine, and talc are also produced.

Limestone, quarried in Pennsylvania, Maryland, and Virginia, is used for cement, burnt-lime, building stones, and as a flux in the iron industry.

Water Power

Water power is one of the leading resources of the Piedmont. The natural factors responsible for it are:

1. A heavy rainfall well distributed throughout the year.

2. Land mostly in slopes.
3. Forested watersheds.
4. Room for dam sites and storage reservoirs.

The Piedmont possesses more than 20 per cent of the developed hydroelectric power of the country, though it has within its boundaries only 7.6 per cent of the potential supply.

The principal part of the Piedmont's water-power development includes the Catawba-Wateree, the Yadkin-Pedee, the Broad, the Saluda, and the Tallulah-Tugaloo rivers. The Catawba, a remarkable stream, drops 1,058 feet in a distance of only 300 miles. One of the most interesting features of the hydro development in this stream is the use of dams and pools. So well planned is it that at many places the tailrace of one pond flows into the head of the next. Unfortunately, careless farming methods have resulted in silting up many of the reservoirs, thereby reducing the amount of water power available.

Manufacturing

The leading industrial centers of this region, New York City, Philadelphia, Baltimore, and Wilmington, already have been discussed in connection with the American Manufacturing Region. Other important cities, with the exception of Atlanta and Norfolk, mostly are associated with the Fall Line.

An impressive industrial "belt," encompassing nearly 10 per cent of the factories in the United States, is found in the Piedmont, extending from southern Virginia through the Carolinas and across Georgia. The heart of this belt is in North Carolina, where industrialization has taken place in several small cities (as Winston-Salem, Charlotte, and Greensboro), many smaller towns (as Reidsville and Shelby), and a surprising number of nonurban areas (especially in Gaston and Cabarrus counties). Manufac-

turing is not diversified here: its main components are cigarettes, textiles, chemicals, and furniture. The importance of manufacturing in the economy, however, should not be underestimated. Only in Connecticut and New Hampshire are greater proportions of the labor force employed in factories than in North and South Carolina. The principal types of manufacturing in the region are discussed below.

The Cotton-Textile Industry The South has become the center of the nation's cotton-textile industry and the Piedmont is the heart of it. The principal advantages of the South over the North have been the price differential and the longer working hours of labor. The price differential, however, is fast disappearing and the differential of working hours (of the individual worker) already has disappeared.

Piedmont mill workers are mountain whites and former croppers. Formerly, most of the mills occupied villages on the outskirts of towns, many lying only a short distance from the fields. However, the mill village is beginning to disappear from the textile scene. Older mills are finding it desirable to sell the houses to their employees on an easy-payment plan, and the newest mills (Figure 5-11) are making no attempt to construct villages for their employees.

Labor unions had little influence upon these workers before the New Deal, but since then unionization has made some progress, wages have been raised, and hours shortened. The labor supply is abundant, and workers can live at less expense than can those employed in Northern mills. The textile worker usually has a garden which supplements his income from the mill, and though he receives smaller wages than the New Englander, his dollars go further.

Nearness to raw cotton is not the chief location factor. Most of the bales used by the North Carolina textile mills are brought in from other states, largely from west of

Figure 5-11. A modern textile mill near Lancaster, South Carolina. The newer mills of the Piedmont make no attempt to build villages for employees as was formerly the custom. (Photo courtesy South Carolina Research, Planning and Development Board.)

the Mississippi. Thus Piedmont manufacturers, getting their raw cotton from the same sources as the New England mills, have but a slight advantage if the product moves all the way by rail.

As regards power, the Piedmont is as favored as New England. Moreover, its power is considerably lower in cost. Mills are free to locate anywhere because of the transmission of electrical energy over long-distance power lines. Atmospheric conditions of the Piedmont originally were less favorable than those of New England, but air-conditioning in the new ultra-modern factories has rendered this factor insignificant.

The Piedmont is not hampered by tradition or obsolescent power establishments, and its mills are located strategically. Most of them are close to the main line of the Southern Railroad, which has direct outlets to the North, the South, and the Middle West. The Piedmont differs from New England in that its mills are scattered and not concentrated. The *position* factor is of slight importance in the Southern Piedmont, one general area being about as good as another. It is the *site* factors that count, and they will

play an increasingly important role in the choice of industrial locations in the future.

In spite of declining trends in national textile output, the cotton-textile industry continues to be the outstanding type of manufacturing in the Piedmont. It is the leading industry in Georgia, both Carolinas (where it employs nearly half of the factory workers in the two states), and southern Virginia. The major production centers are Greenville, Greensboro, Charlotte, and Winston-Salem.

The Synthetic-Fiber Industry The South is the center of the rayon industry—Virginia alone accounting for a large part of the total production. Some of the plants are located in the Piedmont, which shares the following advantages with the Southern Appalachians: (1) a copious supply of soft water, (2) access to an ample supply of local labor capable of being trained quickly, (3) nearness to markets, (4) ready access to an abundant supply of raw materials, (5) sufficient level land for factory sites, and (6) efficient transport facilities and favorable freight rates.

Most of the factories are located in agricultural areas rather than in or near large cities where they would have to compete for labor with other activities.

The Cigarette Industry Cigarette manufacturing is the most notable industrial enterprise entirely created and owned in the South. It is rooted geographically in propinquity to the raw material—bright tobacco. Manufacturing on a large scale began in the period 1890-1900. North Carolina and Virginia together account for most of the cigarettes produced each year, and pay enormous taxes to the Bureau of Internal Revenue. The industry in this region is confined to the Piedmont between Richmond and Winston-Salem, including also Durham, Reidsville, and Petersburg.

The Central Piedmont is the logical place for cigarette-making, since, for the past century thousands of men have studied and solved the intricate problems connected with the production of bright leaf tobacco. There is little likelihood of any drastic relocation of this industry.

A unique feature of the cigarette industry is the great disparity between the cost of raw material and the price (including taxes) of the finished product. Even so, the industry pays attractive wages. The answer, of course, is large-scale production by machinery, requiring little labor. This industry is practically immune to depression.

The factories invariably occupy the hearts of their cities, since they were there early in the cities' development.

Manufacture of Fertilizer The Coastal Plain, strategically located with respect to large local markets for fertilizer and to ports that import fertilizer ingredients, ranks high in this branch of the chemical industry. In fact, this region has been important in the manufacture of commercial fertilizer since the middle of the nineteenth century. Fertilizer materials rank first in the import trade of several cities, such as Norfolk.

The Furniture Industry Although the furniture industry of the Piedmont began with the "Industrial Revolution of the South" in the 1880's, it was not until 1911 that the first meeting of the Southern Furniture Manufacturers' Association was held. Thus the industry is relatively young.

The major producing area lies in the Piedmont, with High Point as the hub, but other major centers are Martinsville, Winston-Salem, Lexington, Hickory, Morgantown, and Lenoir. This area accounts for more than 75 per cent of the region's output, and within it lie at least four of the country's largest furniture factories. Much manufacturing, however, is done in small factories scattered throughout the region in cities of less than 25,000 population.

Some advantages offered by the region to the furniture industry are: (1) an abundant supply of reasonably priced labor, (2) cheap hydroelectric power, (3) good transportation facilities, (4) a satisfactory supply of hardwood timber in the Piedmont and in the adjacent Appalachian Uplands, and (5) a tradition of skilled techniques.

Originally the industry supplied only the Southern market, which was at first small but which has grown at an amazingly rapid rate in recent years. As early as 1921, however, Southern furniture was shipped to the North. At first only cheap merchandise was made, but now high-quality furniture is manufactured along with medium-priced products. The region is the nation's chief producer of wooden household furniture, especially for dining room and bedroom. There is, however, an increasing tendency toward "full-line" manufacture, which includes both case goods and upholstered furniture.

Today the leading furniture companies own and manage their own forests, practicing efficient reforestation as they cut. They engage in every phase of the industry from logging to the shipping of the finished product.

The Pulp and Paper Industry   The manufacture of pulp and paper has become an important industry throughout the South, and a number of mills have been established in or near the Piedmont. There has been a general upsurge in the use of southern yellow pine for pulping (the sulphate process), and increasing amounts of southern hardwoods are pulped by means of a semichemical process. In addition to kraft paper (for heavy packaging), which is the leading product, a variety of other types is made, including cigarette paper made from flax brought into the region from the northern Great Plains or the Southwest Gulf Coast.

Canning   The Atlantic Coastal Plain is the greatest vegetable-canning area in the world, and Baltimore is the only large American city ranking high in that industry.

Canning does not depend on the surplus produce of the area—that which would otherwise spoil because of glutted markets. In Maryland 90 per cent of the tomatoes, sweet corn, and peas are sold to some 400 canneries. More than 90 per cent of the requirements of the canneries is grown and sold on a contract basis. In spring a contract is made whereby the farmer agrees to grow a specified number of acres of crops for a definite price. He guarantees that he will deliver only his own produce and that this will be all he raises, except for his own consumption. The best canneries watch their farmers closely, keeping inspectors constantly on the job, estimating yields and advising on scientific production. The farmer normally contracts with a cannery located nearby, to simplify the problem of transportation. Growers who produce without a contract must sell wherever they can and for whatever price they can get.

The tendency in the past was toward regional specialization in the growing of crops for canning. Only the market gardens, which lie close to great cities, grew a large variety of vegetables. Recently, however, the trend in truck farming has been toward greater variety.

From the growers' standpoint, the canning industry is a form of insurance. In years of glutted markets, they are saved by the canneries. Canning communities are invariably prosperous.

The canning industry has given rise to many subsidiary enterprises, for example, the making of crates, baskets, and boxes.

Quick-freezing   In quick-freezing, which has become important in the truck-growing areas of the Coastal Plain, vegetables are reduced to a temperature of about zero degrees Fahrenheit in an hour or less, and they must be kept at a sub-freezing temperature until ready for use. New York (Long Island), New Jersey, and Maryland are among the more important states in this method of food preservation.

Shipbuilding   Newport News has one of the largest and best-equipped shipbuilding yards in the world. It has constructed many of the nation's most powerful and formidable battleships as well as an imposing list of merchant vessels. In normal times it employs some 25,000 workers.

Fisheries

The variety in the catch from the fishing grounds of the Atlantic Coastal Plain subregion is more limited than that of New England. Shellfish (primarily oysters, clams, and crabs) and menhaden are the principal fish caught.

Menhaden, a fish little known to the general public, is caught in far greater volume by United States commercial fishermen than is any other product of the sea (Figure 5-12). In most years it amounts to more than 40 per cent by weight of the total United States catch, which is about 10 times as much as the second variety (tuna); however, it is a low-value fish, rarely providing more than 7 per cent of the total value of fish

Figure 5-12. A heavily laden menhaden boat being unloaded at a North Carolina fishing port. As is typical, both the hold and the deck of the fishing vessel are crammed with the catch. To unload, the fish are pumped through openings in the bottom of the hold, and are carried by pipes and hoses into the reduction plant. (Photo courtesy United States Fish and Wildlife Service Biological Laboratory, Beaufort, North Carolina.)

caught in the United States, thus ranking behind shrimp, tuna, salmon, and oysters.

Well over half of the total United States catch of menhaden comes from the waters off the Atlantic Coastal Plain, and a large proportion is actually taken in Chesapeake Bay. In part because of its extreme oiliness, menhaden is not generally considered as a food fish. It is used primarily as a source of oil and meal for the making of stock feed and commercial fertilizers. In spite of an annual catch in this region normally in excess of one billion pounds, the menhaden industry is in serious difficulty because of low world prices for fish meal and oil occasioned by a large increase in the manufacture of low-cost fish meal in Peru. To combat this, the menhaden fishermen are quick to adopt modern techniques that may increase their efficiency. They commonly use such refinements as airplane spotters, power blocks to haul in the nets, electric fields to guide the fish to desired areas, and pumps to take the fish from net to boat; and they are beginning to make greater use of the complex but effective pound net (though more than 90 per cent of the catch is still taken by purse seiners).

The Atlantic Coastal Plain has a long history as the leading oyster fishery of the continent, but this reputation is in serious jeopardy due to declining yields. The many bays, estuaries, and tidal flats of the region, with their relatively warm and shallow water, comprise an ideal location for oyster propagation.

Under favorable conditions the shell remains ajar. Water passes through the gills, bringing oxygen and food. It is said that an oyster pumps more than 15 gallons of water through its gills daily. A single female may produce millions of eggs at one spawning and several hundred million in a summer. The development of the oyster from the egg to the setting stage requires 13 to 16 days. The eggs, after being laid, float through the water and hatch in the drifting current. The ideal temperature for spawning and propagation is 68° F. or above. For a short time the spat or young oyster is a free swimmer. After about two weeks it cements itself to some hard, submerged object—a rock, an oyster shell, or debris—and begins to develop its own shell.

The Indians taught the white man to catch oysters with a forked stick. This method was too slow for the white man, however, and he soon used tongs, working from a boat. Later came the dredge and suction methods for extracting oysters. The oyster industry boomed from 1870 to 1890, when between 800 and 900 dredges sailed the Chesapeake region, scooping up oysters from the bottom of the bay and stripping the beds. In 1880 the catch in Maryland alone exceeded that of all the rest of the world. As a result of overfishing and pollution, the rich Chesapeake beds were nearly destroyed in two decades.[9] Oyster farming, or seeding, was begun in the hope of assuring a continuous supply. The oyster is readily cultivated, and thousands of acres of barren bottom were transformed into valuable food-producing areas.

Severe inroads by diseases and predators (oyster drill and starfish) have caused a drastic decline in oyster survival, particularly in Delaware Bay and Long Island Sound, but also in Chesapeake Bay. As a result the fishery is in its most critical period in history. Even so, more than half of the oysters produced in the United States come from this region. A long-term, unstable element has been the animosity between Virginia and Maryland oyster fishermen, especially concerning illegal dredging in the estuary of the Potomac River and in Chesapeake Bay.

[9] "The Oyster," *Fortune*, Vol. 2 (December 1930), p. 72.

Other fish of importance taken in the littoral waters of the region are scup, surf clams, blue crabs (mostly in Chesapeake Bay), shrimp (off the North Carolina coast), and flounder.

In total this region yields more than one-third of all the fish caught commercially in the United States, although the average value is low. Nearly 30,000 fishermen are involved, which is one-fourth of the national total. The major fishing ports are Reedville, Virginia, and Lewes, Delaware (normally the second and third greatest volume ports in the country, primarily due to menhaden). Also of significance are Beaufort, North Carolina; Norfolk and Chincoteague, Virginia; Crisfield, Maryland; Wildwood and Port Monmouth, New Jersey; and Montauk and Amagansett, Long Island.

Recreation

The coast, one of the leading summer playgrounds for the great industrial East, is dotted with scores of beach resorts including, among the better-known, Asbury Park, Atlantic City (Figure 5-13), Rehoboth Beach, Ocean City, Virginia Beach, and the

Figure 5-13. The beaches of this region attract visitors in almost every season. Strollers on the boardwalk of Atlantic City are well-bundled against the chill of spring in this Easter Sunday scene. (Photo courtesy New Jersey Department of Conservation and Economic Development.)

numerous beaches of North Carolina. The warm water and white sand make bathing far more pleasant here than in New England.

Atlantic City is the most famous beach resort. Its site was formerly low-lying, sandy, mosquito-ridden, and uninhabited. Now, with more than 1,000 hotels, many of which are elegant, it can accommodate more than 500,000 guests per day. It is reached by magnificent motor roads and fast railways.

This coast eventually may become almost solidly lined with cities and cottages as workers in manufacturing plants put in shorter hours and have more leisure.

What Atlantic City is to the northern part of the region, Virginia Beach is to the southern. In addition to the excellent bathing characterizing the entire coast, Virginia Beach is near many of the nation's top-ranking tourist attractions, such as colonial Williamsburg, Jamestown, and Yorktown, as well as Kitty Hawk, where aviation history began in 1903, and Roanoke Island, the site of the "Lost Colony" of 1585-87.

The Piedmont, with all the charm of its rural landscape, does not offer those inducements to tourists which require the establishment of large resort centers such as those along the coast. The long and colorful history of the area, however, has made it a tourist mecca for millions. Practically all Piedmont states have capitalized upon selling "history" to tourists, but Virginia, with hundreds of permanent historical markers along its highways, has done the most complete job. Revolutionary and Civil War battlefield sites are particularly notable.

Perhaps the greatest tourist attraction in this subregion, however, is Washington, D.C., and its National Capital Parks. These include The Mall, the Washington Monument, the White House, the Lincoln and Jefferson Memorials, the Chesapeake and Ohio Canal Parkway, the Mount Vernon Memorial Highway, and others. While figures are not available, the number of tourists visiting the National Capital is enormous, greater, perhaps, than the number visiting any city in the United States with the exception of New York.

Transportation

Because of the excellent water transportation and the difficulty and cost of north-south railroad construction in an area deeply cut by large rivers and estuaries, waterways provided the only means of transportation in the Coastal Plain for more than 150 years. Hence most north-south railroads and highways are in the Piedmont. There were other reasons for the slow start in the Coastal Plain. In Tidewater Virginia and Maryland, the estate-owners, the dominant population, did not wish their culture disturbed by an influx of outsiders attracted solely by economic motives. Furthermore, they owned the bulk of the wealth and they did not want to risk it in railroads, where financial success was uncertain. They were fairly well provided with transportation, considering that each plantation was largely self-sustaining so far as the necessities of life were concerned and that English merchantmen brought other items to their very wharves. Much later, railroads were discouraged because of the fear of competition from the hinterland.

In the Eastern Shore country, between Chesapeake and Delaware bays, conditions were substantially the same until the modern demand for rapid transportation caused the building of railroad lines between the truck farming areas and the large urban markets to the north. Fortunately, no large rivers or estuaries offered barriers to railroad and highway construction here as they did in Tidewater Virginia and Maryland. In recent years, the Delmarva Peninsula has developed an excellent system of railroads and highways to speed the movement of truck crops to market.

Compared with the Coastal Plain, the Piedmont in colonial days was retarded economically and socially because its rivers were not navigable. It did not come into its own until the advent of railroads, canals, and hard-surfaced roads.

The railroads which were built (1) to supplement canal and river transportation, (2) to haul agricultural products from the Piedmont to the Northeast in exchange for manufactured goods, (3) to deliver agricultural products to the Middle West in exchange for grain and manufactured goods, (4) to move coal to nearby ports, and (5) to transport cheap commercial fertilizers to the farmers, broke down the barriers of distance and isolation in the Piedmont.

The east-west railroads extend inland from New York, Philadelphia, Baltimore, or Hampton Roads, generally following the interstream divides. In addition, there are three major north-south railway routes in the region.

Until the 1880's there was considerable traffic on the canals of the Piedmont. The West was being opened up and prosperity beckoned to those able to tap its resources. New York led the way in 1825 with the Erie Canal; Pennsylvania, Maryland, and Virginia answered the challenge, but theirs was a poor reply.

The canals that were built during this period were:

1. The *Pennsylvania Canal,* opened in 1834. It was built in an attempt to secure some of the trade then using the Erie Canal. Its route consisted of a railroad from Philadelphia to Columbia, a canal from there to Hollidaysburg, another railroad over the abrupt rise of the Allegheny Front to Johnstown, and a canal from there to Pittsburgh.

2. The *Chesapeake and Ohio Canal,* begun in 1828, completed in 1850. It was 186 miles long and connected Washington (Georgetown) with Cumberland, Maryland. For decades this canal was an important link between the Ohio Valley and the Atlantic Seaboard. It had locks, aqueducts, and tunnels.

3. The *James River Canal,* one of the first

built in the United States. It extended westward from Richmond, on the Fall Line, to Lynchburg, the route being along the James River. It was further extended to Buchanan in 1851, but never got beyond that point because of the mountain barrier. The canal was abandoned after a damaging flood in 1877.

The northern portion of the Coastal Plain today has a dense network of roads, with four-lane, divided highways connecting the major cities. The greatest amount of intercity traffic flow in the world moves between Washington and Boston, particularly in the section between Philadelphia and New York. In New Jersey are two of the most successful of contemporary toll roads; the New Jersey Turnpike connects New York with Philadelphia and Wilmington, while the Garden State Parkway extends from New York down the east coast to Cape May. The Piedmont and the southern part of the Coastal Plain have a network that is less dense and less well developed, but still satisfactory.

Four of the major ocean ports of the United States are found in this region—New York, Philadelphia, Baltimore, and Hampton Roads (consisting of Norfolk, Portsmouth, and Newport News). Overseas and coastal shipping is a bigger business here than in any other region in Anglo-America.

The Outlook

Possibly no other region has an outlook so difficult to forecast. The part of the Coastal Plain being farmed will continue, perhaps for a century or more, to specialize in the commercial production of vegetables and fruits for the large urban markets. The increasing complexity of marketing arrangements and contract-farming agreements in this and other parts of the country will play a large role in determining the vitality of market gardening in the region. Most of the subregion, however, will probably remain in forest, with the area under cultivation actually declining, because the sandy soils are not well suited to staple crops and pasturage and because truck crops demand but small acreage.

The New Jersey portion will become more highly industrialized. The Coastal Plain might be suitable for the type of community that is strongly recommended by some regional planners—one combining farm work with factory work.

The tourist business should increase.

The Piedmont will continue to be important agriculturally. The growing of tobacco and cotton will decline, whereas dairying and crop diversification should increase. Farming will necessarily become more scientific and intensive. Stock raising, particularly the fattening of beef cattle, should become increasingly important. Soil erosion should be reduced as much marginal land is taken out of cultivation. Man has been practicing level-farming on rapidly eroding hills. For centuries he has been growing gully-stimulating crops—corn, tobacco, and cotton. Slope lands plus summer torrential rains plus clean-tilled crops constitute an ideal triad for erosion. Moreover, land destruction is worse in the Southern Piedmont since turf does not thrive in hot, humid areas. In the future, man must cultivate intensively only the level and gently rolling areas, terrace and strip-crop the more sloping fields, and place the remainder in pasture and trees.

Much of the Piedmont, however, is rapidly developing into a major manufacturing region. Especially is this true of that portion between Lynchburg and Atlanta, where factories literally dot the landscape. In this subregion there is a close balance between manufacturing and agriculture.

Unfortunately, one of the basic industries of the region, cotton-textile manufacturing, has been suffering from a national decline for several years, and shows no evidence of regaining its vitality. It is better entrenched in the Piedmont than in any other part of

TABLE 2

Selected Cities and Towns of the Atlantic Coastal Plain and the Piedmont

City or Town	Urbanized Area	Political Center
Alexandria	......	91,023
Anderson	......	41,316
Annapolis	......	23,385
Arlington County	......	163,401
Athens	......	31,355
Atlanta	768,125	487,455
*Atlantic City	124,902	59,544
Augusta	123,698	70,626
*Baltimore	1,418,948	939,024
*Bayonne	......	74,215
*Camden	......	117,159
*Chester	......	63,658
Charlotte	209,551	201,564
Charlottesville	......	29,427
*Clifton	......	82,084
Columbia	162,601	97,433
Danville	......	46,577
Durham	84,642	78,302
*East Orange	......	77,259
*Elizabeth	......	107,698
Gastonia	......	37,276
Greensboro	123,334	119,574
Greenville	126,887	66,188
Hampton	......	89,258
High Point	66,543	62,063
*Hoboken	......	48,441
*Irvington	......	59,379
*Jersey City	......	276,101
*Lancaster	93,855	61,055
Lynchburg	59,319	54,790
Marietta	......	25,565
*Mt. Vernon	......	76,010
*Newark	......	405,220
Newport News	208,874	113,662
*New Rochelle	......	76,812
*New York City	14,114,927	7,781,984
Norfolk	507,825	304,869
*Passaic	......	53,963
*Paterson	......	143,663
*Perth Amboy	......	38,007
*Philadelphia	3,635,228	2,002,512
Portsmouth	......	144,773
Raleigh	93,931	93,931
*Reading	160,297	98,177
Richmond	333,438	219,958
Silver Spring	......	66,348
Spartanburg	......	44,352
*Trenton	242,401	114,167
Washington	1,808,423	763,956
*Wilmington, Del.	283,667	95,827
Wilmington, N.C.	......	44,013
Winston-Salem	126,176	111,135
*York	100,872	54,504

* Also in the American Manufacturing Region.

the nation, but its stability is questionable.

Cigarette manufacturing may not expand greatly and it probably will not relocate. The furniture industry will become more important now that the forests are being conserved. Forestry systems are evolving whose purpose is to effect proper cutting and to treat trees as a crop. Manufacturing is becoming more varied, as many and diverse new industries appear: synthetic yarns, nylon yarns, plastics, paper and paper products, and chemicals.

Since few parts of the country have so many attractive small towns where labor, power, and efficient transportation are satisfactory, numerous new industries will be attracted. Community attitude toward industry is generally positive, and the relatively small amount of racial strife accompanying desegregation in such states as North Carolina provides an inducement for businessmen that few other parts of the South can match.

The northern part of the region inevitably will become more urbanized. The great and small cities of Megalopolis will devour the countryside with an insatiable appetite, and around their peripheries, as Gottmann has pointed out, the distinctions among rural, exurban, suburban, and urban will become increasingly less meaningful. The problems and the benefits of being an urbanite will multiply both in number and in kind.

Selected Bibliography

Emory, Samuel T., "North Carolina Flatwoods," *Economic Geography*, Vol. 2, 1946, pp. 203-219.

Gottmann, Jean, *Megalopolis: The Urbanized Northeastern Seaboard of the United States.* New York: Twentieth Century Fund, 1961.

Hawk, D. B., "Piedmont Landscapes," *Landscape*, Vol. 2, Autumn 1952, pp. 27-29.

"How Recessions Hit Philadelphia," *Business Review*, Federal Reserve Bank of Philadelphia, September 1962, pp. 3-15.

"Menhaden—Our Largest Commercial Catch," *Monthly Review*, Federal Reserve Bank of Richmond, August 1960, pp. 2-5.

"New Jersey's Fifty-Million-Dollar Vegetable Garden," *Business Review*, Federal Reserve Bank of Philadelphia, September 1962, pp. 16-23.

Northam, Ray M., "Recent Industrialization in the Appalachian Piedmont: The Case of Northeastern Georgia," *Northwestern Studies in Geography*, No. 6, May 1962, pp. 93-112.

"The Shipbuilders," *Monthly Review*, Federal Reserve Bank of Richmond, March 1958, pp. 2-5.

Van Burkalow, Anastasia, "The Geography of New York City's Water Supply: A Study of Interactions," *Geographical Review*, Vol. 49, July 1959, pp. 369-386.

Warman, Henry J., "Population of the Manor Counties of Maryland," *Economic Geography*, Vol. 25, 1949, pp. 23-40.

chapter six

The Appalachians
and
the Ozarks

The Appalachian Highlands and the Ozark-Ouachita Uplands are two disconnected segments of a single region, separated by the broad expanse of the Mississippi Valley (Figure 6-1). This region has three outstanding characteristics: (1) it is dominantly hilly or mountainous; (2) it is everywhere surrounded by broad, flat lowlands; and (3) it presents a great variety of adaptations by man, ranging from the modern, progressive agricultural and industrial communities of the densely settled lowlands to the isolated and backward communities of the sparsely settled mountains that only recently have begun to feel the impact of modern civilization.

The Appalachian Highlands extend from central New York State, south of the Mohawk Valley, to central Alabama, where they terminate on the Gulf Coastal Plain. The general trend of the mountains and their intervening valleys is northeast-southwest.

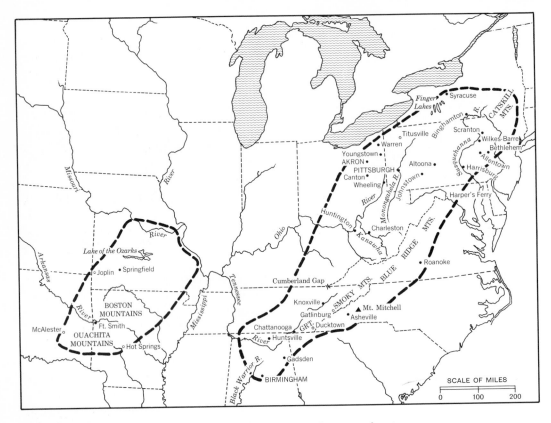

Figure 6-1. The Appalachians and the Ozarks. A region of mining, farming, electricity development, manufacturing, and resorts. The two parts of the region —the Appalachian Highlands and the Ozark-Ouachita Uplands—are separated by the Mississippi Valley. The subregions are shown in Figure 6-2.

Geographically, the eastern boundary of this subregion is the contact between the low, rolling Piedmont and the Blue Ridge-Great Smoky Mountains. The western boundary is the western edge of the Appalachian Plateau where the upland gives way to the Central Lowlands. The subregion (Figure 6-2) is divided into (1) an eastern mountain province, the Blue Ridge-Great Smoky Mountains; (2) the Ridge and Valley country; and (3) the Appalachian Plateau, which is further subdivided into a northern part called the Allegheny Plateau and a southern part known as the Cumberland Plateau. The Allegheny consists of a glaciated portion in New York, Pennsylvania, and northeastern Ohio, and an un-glaciated area in southwestern Pennsylvania, southern Ohio, West Virginia, and eastern Kentucky.

The Ozark-Ouachita Highlands represent in many respects a smaller replica of the Appalachian Area. They are completely surrounded by lowland plains and are subdivided into (1) the Ouachita Mountains and (2) the more extensive Ozark Plateau (Figure 6-2). The total area of this subregion is more than 50,000 square miles, and like the larger Appalachian Highlands, it has densely settled lowlands with modern agricultural and industrial culture and sparsely settled mountain areas where the older culture of the mountain folk is still dominant.

Although the two parts of this region are

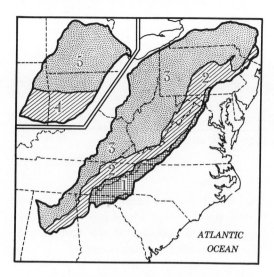

Figure 6-2. The subdivisions of the Appalachians-Ozarks Region. (1) The Blue Ridge-Great Smoky Mountains. (2) The Ridge and Valley Area. (3) The Appalachian Plateau. (4) The Ouachita Mountains. (5) The Ozark Plateau.

separated by extensive lands which do not belong within the regional boundaries, it seems desirable to consider them as forming one region because of their remarkable similarity both in physical appearance and in agricultural responses.

This is a diversified region—topographically, climatically, and economically. Nevertheless, a thread of internal unity holds the several parts together, making them one major geographical region. The most densely settled areas, those with more than 100 persons per square mile, are the valleys, while the sparsely settled areas, with less than ten inhabitants per square mile, are those of broken relief. The opportunities available to the inhabitants are closely associated with the distribution and utilization of natural resources. Considerable discrimination is shown in the selection of places for settlement, especially regarding the suitability of the land for crops. Since most of the population consists of farmers and miners, the

inhabitants of the Appalachian Uplands are everywhere conscious of their dependence upon nature.

The Natural Environment [1]

The Blue Ridge—Great Smoky Mountains The Blue Ridge consists largely of crystalline rocks of igneous and metamorphic origin—granites, gneisses, schists, diorites, and slates. Extending from Pennsylvania to Georgia, the Blue Ridge exceeds all other mountains in the East in altitude. North of Roanoke it consists of a narrow ridge cut by numerous gaps; south of Roanoke it spreads out to form the Great Smoky Mountains, a tangled mass of mountains and valleys more than 100 miles wide. The mountains are steep, rocky, and forest-covered. The highest peak is Mount Mitchell in North Carolina (6,684 feet).

Some of the gaps through the Blue Ridge enable railroads to penetrate the barrier; outstanding is the one at Harper's Ferry, through which the Baltimore & Ohio passes.

Because of heavy rainfall, the Blue Ridge was clothed with magnificent forests, the original covering consisting of hardwood trees, especially oak, chestnut, and hickory. The greater part of the original forest was logged years ago, part of it being converted into charcoal for iron furnaces in the nineteenth century. Much of the area has been cut repeatedly and a great deal has been badly burned. However, most of the subregion is still cloaked with extensive forest.

The Ridge and Valley This subregion consists of the Great Valley, which is made up of several broad longitudinal valleys such as the Shenandoah Valley and the Valley of East Tennessee, and the Ridge and Valley Section, which is a complex folded area of parallel ridges and valleys, well-

[1] Based largely on Nevin M. Fenneman, *Physiography of Eastern United States* (New York: McGraw-Hill Book Co., 1938), pp. 163-342, 631-89.

APPALACHIAN PLATEAU   VALLEY RIDGES   BLUE RIDGE

GREAT VALLEY

HORIZONTAL SEDIMENTARY ROCKS   FOLDED SEDIMENTARY ROCKS

Figure 6-3. Cross section of the

developed in Pennsylvania and southwestern Virginia (Figure 6-3).

The Great Valley, a nature-chiseled groove that trends northeast-southwest from the Hudson Valley of New York to central Alabama is one of the world's longest mountain valleys. In no sense a rugged area, it is broad and relatively flat-bottomed. The divides between its several streams are rolling.

The Great Valley has numerous segments. Near the Delaware, it is called the Lehigh Valley; north of the Susquehanna, the Lebanon Valley; south of the Susquehanna, the Cumberland Valley; in northern Virginia, the Shenandoah; in Virginia as a whole, the Valley of Virginia; and in Tennessee, the Valley of East Tennessee.

It has long been the great north-south highway in the Appalachian region as well as one of the most productive agricultural areas in the East. It has never been of outstanding industrial importance, though several of its cities, particularly in Pennsylvania and Tennessee, have important manufacturing establishments.

The eastern and western confines of the Great Valley are definite: the knobby wooded crest of the Blue Ridge towers above the valley floor on the east; the wild, rugged, though less imposing Appalachian ridges bound it on the west.

Gray-brown podzolic soils prevail over all but the southern part, where red and yellow soils rule. The most productive are the transported soils of the larger flood plains and those derived from limestone. Having developed largely under a forest cover, they contain little humus and are acid in reaction. Some leaching has occurred.

The Ridge and Valley Section of this subregion (Figure 6-2) consists of a belt of land between the Great Valley on the east and the Appalachian Plateaus on the west. It is characterized by a series of roughly parallel ridges and valleys, variable in width and in number of component ridges. From an airplane, the forested ridges show up as dark parallel bands and the cleared valleys as light ones.

The ridges are not everywhere the same; some are low and narrow, others high and fairly broad. Most of the valleys are narrow, flat to undulating, and cleared. Gaps appear in all of the ridges. South of Knoxville the Appalachian Ridge and Valley Section merges with the Great Valley.

Since more land is in sandstone, shale, and conglomerate ridges than in limestone and shale valleys, most of the soils are infertile.

This area gets less rainfall than other parts of the Appalachians—about 40 inches. This difference is due to the sheltering effect of the Blue Ridge on the one side and the Allegheny-Cumberland Escarpment on the other. The seasonal distribution is quite even, though autumn is somewhat drier than spring; about half the precipitation falls during the growing season, the average length of which varies from 176 days in the

PIEDMONT

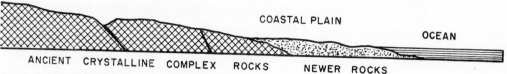

Appalachian Highlands (after Atwood).

north to more than 200 days in the south.

The natural vegetation of the valley lands consisted primarily of oak and hickory, with sycamore, elm, and willow near the streams. On the ridges it was similar to that found on the Blue Ridge Mountains to the east. Some of this magnificent forest was destroyed by the pioneers who settled in the area, but the ridges are still tree-covered, even though much of the cover is second and third growth. There were also areas of grassland in the broader river valleys—the result of annual burning by the Indians.

The Appalachian Plateaus The western division of the Appalachian Highlands is a broad belt of land known as the Appalachian Plateaus. Along its eastern edge it has a bold, high escarpment, the Allegheny Front, which is so steep that roads and railroads ascend it with extreme difficulty. Most of the layers of rocks comprising the plateaus lie flat, one upon the other. This subregion extends from the Catskill Mountains to north-central Alabama, and from the Allegheny Front to the Interior Lowland. The plateau is everywhere dissected, but not identically throughout. Geographically, this area is divided into (1) the Allegheny Plateau (glaciated and non-glaciated sections) and (2) the Cumberland Plateau.

THE GLACIATED ALLEGHENY PLATEAU Rugged topography puts its stamp on most of this area, which on the north is bounded by the Mohawk Valley and Ontario Plain. The nearly flat-lying sandstones and shales

are much dissected by streams that have cut down and back into the plateau. In the northern part, the Finger Lakes country, six slender lakes trending north-south occupy the valleys of preglacial streams that were modified by ice erosion and blocked by ice deposition. Here is an area of rolling terrain. In northeastern Ohio and adjacent northwestern Pennsylvania, the plateau was modified by the ice, and the relief is gentle, with broad divides. Northeastern Pennsylvania consists of a hilly upland with numerous streams, lakes, and swamps.

Gray-brown podzolic soils characterize the entire area. These are mostly derived from sandstone and shale, are acid in reaction, and are not outstanding in fertility. Locally, limestones and calcareous shales occur, and the soils derived from them are more fertile.

THE UNGLACIATED ALLEGHENY PLATEAU Topographically, this plateau is more rugged than its glaciated neighbor to the north. Most of this area might properly be regarded as hill country, for the plateau has been maturely dissected. In the Kanawha Valley, the streams lie 1,000 to 1,500 feet below the plateau surface. Some of the valleys are so narrow and canyonlike as to be uninhabited; some have inadequate room even for a railroad or highway.

Gray-brown podzolic soils prevail here, but in the eastern portion, near the Allegheny Mountains, the soils are infertile and stony. Most have developed from sandstone and shale, are light in color, are classed as sandy and silt loams, and are deficient in lime and humus. Along the larger streams lie patches of sandy alluvium.

THE CUMBERLAND PLATEAU   This plateau is mostly rugged hill country that is so maturely dissected that practically none of its former plateau characteristics remain except locally, as in parts of Tennessee. It is reached only with great difficulty—from the east by relatively few gaps through the steep Cumberland Front and from the west by tortuous and labyrinthine valleys from the Blue Grass Area and the Nashville Basin. No sharp boundary separates it from the Allegheny Plateau to the north. In fact, the boundary is arbitrary. Thus, the Cumberland Plateau is regarded here as beginning in southern Kentucky (the upper reaches of the Kentucky River) and extending to the Gulf Coastal Plain. It includes parts of southeastern Kentucky, eastern Tennessee, and northern Alabama.

The northeastern part of the Cumberland Plateau is less dissected than the Unglaciated Allegheny Plateau to the north. Streams have etched it into an elaborately branching system of steep-sided valleys separated by narrow, winding ridges. There is a dearth of level upland, especially in the northern part, and not a great deal of level lowland except narrow strips along the streams. To the northwest a belt 40 miles wide and 300 miles long, extending from Kentucky to Alabama, is in sharp contrast to the maturely dissected northeastern part. This area, a true tableland, is undulating to rolling, and is crossed and cut into by V-shaped valleys. The southern part of the Cumberland Plateau, which lies entirely in Alabama, is rolling to hilly, with here and there roughly dissected parts. Its physiographic character is like that to the northwest, except that the bluffs are lower and hence less effective barriers.

The Ozark-Ouachita Uplands   The Ozark-Ouachita Subregion is composed of two major subdivisions: (1) the Ozark section, consisting mainly of plateaus such as the Salem and Springfield plateaus and two hilly areas, the St. Francois Mountains in Missouri and the Boston Mountains in Arkansas (Figure 6-4); and (2) the Ouachita section, including the Ouachita Mountains,

Figure 6-4. A typical autumn scene in the Boston Mountains of northwestern Arkansas. (Photo by Johnnie M. Gray; courtesy Arkansas Highway Department.)

a lens-shaped folded and faulted upland—
and the Arkansas Valley, a broad structural
trough corresponding to the Ridge and
Valley Section of the Appalachians. The
Ouachita Mountains reach their highest
elevation—about 2,800 feet above sea level—
near the Arkansas-Oklahoma border.

Settlement of the
Appalachian Highlands

Most of the people who live in the Blue
Ridge and Great Smoky Mountains are of
old colonial stock. Their ancestors were
crowded out of the tidewater by slave labor
and plantation management. The pressure
of population in the Great Smoky Mountains is so great that every arable spot is
now pre-empted, and in many areas the
once productive soil has become depleted
by overcropping or hopelessly ruined by
sheet erosion and gullying. Much of that
being cultivated should be in forest.

In the maturely dissected area the people
are very poor. Their houses are crude, indoor plumbing is scarce, and, in most instances, water is carried from nearby springs.
The standard of living is low and inbreed-
ing common. Yet there is something to be
said in favor of their way of life.

> They do not make elaborate preparations
> to enjoy life but begin at once, and if their
> scheme of things is simple, it is no less satis-
> fying. Mountain man will hardly slave
> through a sunny spring day when he longs
> to enjoy the weather in order that he may
> take a vacation in the same sunshine some-
> where else later on. His affairs are not so
> pressing. As soon as he thinks of it, he will
> probably pick up a chair, tilt it back against
> the sunny side of the house, tip his hat down
> over his eyes, and start in on the business of
> enjoying the day.[2]

Since the small mountain farms of the
Blue Ridge cannot be subdivided indefi-

nitely, children from the large families find
it necessary to migrate to the lowlands.
Sometimes the entire family moves onto the
Piedmont to work in textile mills.

The Ridge and Valley Area was settled
largely by English, Scotch-Irish, and Germans. Because of their craving for independence, the Scotch-Irish particularly made
admirable frontiersmen. The Germans chose
the rich limestone soils, the Scotch-Irish the
slaty hills. Hostile to the Virginian and
North Carolinian way of life, the Germans
and Scotch-Irish made the Valley one of
relatively small holdings, diversified farming, and free labor. Slavery never was so
important here as in the valley areas to the
east and south.

The Allegheny Plateau was settled in the
latter part of the 18th century and the early
part of the 19th century by colonists from
eastern Pennsylvania or from overseas. At
first, settlement was confined to the fertile
valley, although some pioneers chose upland localities in order to utilize grazing
and forest lands. The uplands contained salt
licks, fish, and game and therefore provided
an almost ideal habitat for a self-contained
culture. Although coal was discovered in
the Allegheny Plateau as early as 1750, it
seemed to have had little effect on localiz-
ing the original settlements.[3] Unlike the
Cumberland Plateau, the Allegheny served
as a route for land traffic flowing through
the deeply entrenched river valleys to the
more fertile lands of Ohio. Settlements in the
uplands, therefore, did not become dominant and did not develop the type of culture found in the Cumberland. With the
industrialization of the valley areas, as
around Pittsburgh (Chapter 3), isolation
was broken down in this part of the Appalachian Plateau at an early date.

The Cumberland Plateau has been iso-

[2] Muriel Earley Sheppard, *Cabins in the Laurel*
(Chapel Hill: University of North Carolina Press,
1935), pp. 157-58.

[3] Ralph H. Brown, *Historical Geography of the
United States* (New York: Harcourt, Brace &
World, Inc., 1948), p. 184.

lated because of the influence of its topography upon the transportation pattern. Most of the main railroad lines avoid it by going north and south of the Appalachian barrier. Roads and truck transportation, however, are doing much to overcome its isolation.

Even before the Revolutionary War, the frontier was moving westward. Some of the pioneers migrated through the gaps in the Appalachians. Large numbers continued on their way, but many dropped like seeds into the coves of the Appalachians.

The first settlers occupied the valleys, where they built cabins and grew crops. Isolation forced upon them a subsistence type of agriculture. They combined farming with stock raising, hunting, and fishing. As their numbers increased, they found it necessary to work back into the hills. The forests are now largely gone, most of the game has been destroyed, and the topsoil has been swept from the steep cultivated slopes by torrential rains. As a result, poverty has settled down upon the people, hope has departed, and they have been cast into a mold of helpless inactivity.

The hill folk are not inferior. They are of Anglo-Saxon and Celtic stock and as intelligent and resourceful as the people elsewhere in Anglo-America, but nature denied them nearly all means of making a livelihood except farming.

Considering the type of terrain, the Appalachian and Ozark highlands include some of the most densely populated parts of Anglo-America. Many valleys in this area, devoted almost entirely to farming, contain more than 200 persons to the square mile. Frequently such valleys are hemmed in by slopes having no resident population whatsoever. Population pressure here is a grim reality.

Living Conditions Some of the farm homes are virtually unlivable by present standards, and many are in a pitiable state of disrepair. Many of them are small, one-storied, log cabins or simple board shacks of one or two rooms. Seldom is one painted. The chimney is made of rough stones and mortar. In general, however, conditions are changing. The cabins and shacks are being replaced by small frame houses. Some of the houses are covered with a false-brick sheathing, and the "brown-brick appearing" shack is now somewhat common. Some houses are painted white. The cheap electricity of the TVA is reflected also in the presence of the washing machine on the front porch of many rural homes, and television antennae sprout from the roofs of some of the humblest of dwellings.

Changes Through Improved Transportation For generations the Southern Appalachians were a sort of land-locked island, isolated from the rest of the country. Most rivers were too swift to be used for transportation, and the rugged terrain caused railroads and highways to avoid it. Even today most of the railways are branch lines built solely to exploit the coal and timber resources. Until lately, highways were dirt roads and some, mere trails hewn from the forest. Recently improved roads have contributed significantly to breaking down the isolation.

In Kentucky, which probably had the most "back-woodsy" areas in the plateau, were many counties where pioneer culture and primitive living persisted for a long time. The most striking changes came to the area when WPA money was used for building "farm to market" roads, and today change is coming rapidly. Thus, with improved highways, better agricultural methods are being introduced by farm agents. Home demonstrations in canning, sewing, and household management, along with 4H Clubs, are bringing better living conditions. The handicrafts of the hills are now being sold in Asheville, Gatlinburg, Berea, and Spruce Pine, as well as in many large stores in the metropolitan centers of the North.

Improved roads are leading to the consolidation of schools.

And the attractions of urban living have become known to many of the hill people. The availability of industrial employment and urban amenities has drawn tens of thousands of inhabitants from the Appalachians to live in Nashville, Louisville, Cincinnati, Pittsburgh, Cleveland, and especially Detroit and Chicago. There they tend to settle in relatively closely-knit neighborhood communities, maintaining a strong flavor of "hill-billy" living in the midst of the city until time eventually wears away the traditions.

Settlement of the Ozark-Ouachita Uplands

The earliest white settlements in the Ozark-Ouachita Uplands were those of the French along the northeastern border in Missouri. They were only feeble attempts and were based on the presence of minerals, especially lead and salt. Since silver, the one metal they wanted, was lacking, the French did not explore systematically or try to develop the subregion. The first recorded land grant was made in 1723. The French, who never penetrated far into the Upland, were reduced to a minority group by English-speaking colonists toward the close of the eighteenth century. After the purchase of this territory in 1803 by the United States, settlement proceeded rapidly.

The Upland was occupied before settlements were made in the lowland prairies to the northwest, west, and southwest. The area immediately to the west was set aside by the United States government between 1820 and 1837 as the Indian Territory and was not opened to white settlement for many years. The Kansas-Nebraska prairies to the northwest and the Texas prairies to the southwest, however, could have been occupied by these pioneers had they wished to settle there. Several factors attracted

them to the Upland: (1) the climate was more humid and the winters less severe than on the adjacent plains; (2) the plateau was timbered, thus providing the pioneer with wood for construction and fuel; (3) the soils were believed to be more fertile; (4) hillside springs were abundant and supplied good potable water; (5) wild game was plentiful; and (6) Indians were less numerous than on the plains. After the first settlements in the Missouri, Mississippi, and Arkansas River valleys, succeeding pioneers entered the rougher and more remote sections of the Upland and remained there. The hilly forested habitat that provided so amply for the needs of the pioneers later retarded their development by isolating them from the progress of the prairies.

Hunting, once dominant, is no longer. Subsistence farming and the raising of livestock, particularly sheep and low-grade cattle, are the principal occupations in the more rugged areas, supplemented by such household handicrafts as weaving, basketry, pottery, and furniture-making. Before the middle 1920's, when the Missouri and Arkansas state highway systems were constructed, the mountaineer of the Ozarks was truly a backwoodsman, largely living out of touch with the outside world. Even today his life is simple and his wants few. His farm consists of a few acres of bottomland in which he grows corn and other food crops and of timbered hillsides which furnish feed for cattle, sheep, and hogs. His house, usually in a valley bottom but occasionally on a ridge, is a one- or two-room cabin made of roughly hewn logs or roughly sawed boards.

Soon after the Anglo-Saxon pioneers entered the Upland, other settlers came from Germany. They occupied the northeastern borders of the Upland, particularly in the Missouri section; later they moved down into the valleys and into the cities. The Germans developed a better type of agriculture, partly because of their inherent skills and partly because of the fertility of the valleys in which they settled. Agriculture in these border sections has kept pace with the modern development on the prairies beyond the Upland. The farmsteads of the Springfield Plain resemble those of the Kansas Prairie or the Missouri River Lowlands.

World War I was an important factor in the breakdown of isolation in this subregion. The draft and the appeal for volunteers caused many ridge dwellers to leave the hills to join the armed forces. High wages in the cities during the War also enticed them away from their mountain fastnesses. After the war, those who returned brought back new ideas. However, the depression following 1929 had a regressive effect, for many who went to the cities lost their jobs and returned to the Upland, and a large part of the plateau population went on relief when various relief agencies were developed under the New Deal.

World War II repeated the effect of the first World War, Selective Service and high wages, particularly in munitions and aircraft factories in St. Louis, Kansas City, Tulsa, Dallas, and Fort Worth, attracting many of the younger persons away from the hills. Most of these individuals are still in the cities and will probably remain there.

Since much of the land still is in timber, soil erosion has been less serious than in the Southern Appalachians. The pioneer Anglo-Saxon who came into this Upland a century ago succeeded in establishing a home and making a living, and his descendants, too, will no doubt work out their destiny in this environment that they understand and love.

As in the Southern Cumberland Plateau, modern highways and the automobile, more than any other factor, are influencing the lives of the people; they not only bring in outsiders, especially to the resort areas, but also make it possible for the mountaineer to get into the village or town with comparatively little effort. Some of the products of home industry, particularly pottery and baskets, find their way with ease to crossroad stores, resorts, or to stands on through highways, where they are sold to tourists.

This is the principal general farming region of the United States. Specialty crops are limited. The agriculture is broad and diverse, but it exhibits certain similar characteristics throughout. The most decisive control of land use is exercised by relief, with soil variations of equal significance in some areas. Principal crop output is typically, although not invariably, from valley bottomland. Farms tend to be small, and cropped acreage per farm is limited. In many areas, average farm size is decreasing (contrary to the national trend) due to fragmentation of larger properties, but most farms are operated by their owners. Farm mechanization lags behind the rest of the country. Corn is the most common row crop, although rarely is it grown for commercial purposes. Hay production is widespread, mostly utilizing alfalfa, clovers, and lespedeza. Tobacco is the most typical cash crop, though acreages are quite small on the average. Livestock is very significant and often produces the majority of the farm income. Beef cattle, dairy cattle, sheep, poultry, and hogs are widely raised. Normally the steep slopes are kept in forest or pasture; the moderate slopes are kept in a rotation of corn, small grains, and pasture; and the flat lands are reserved for intensive growing of corn and tobacco. Residential and part-time farming are common in this region.

Agriculture

Blue Ridge—Great Smoky Mountains While agriculture is the most important economic activity in the Blue Ridge and the Great Smoky Mountains, the area does not favor commercial farming. Much of the land, both in the north and south, is rugged and stony and should be forever the stronghold of the forest. In the southern Blue Ridge, small patches of arable land called locally "coves" or "hollows" are given over to growing corn, apples, and sorgo (sweet sorghum for syrup). The coves vary in size from those able to support only a single family to those capable of sustaining 40 to 50 families. Commercial apple orchards were started in this area near Afton, Virginia, as early as 1890. Most of the orchards of Virginia, Maryland, and Pennsylvania are confined to the gravelly loams on either side of the Blue Ridge, primarily to guard the trees against spring frosts—the slopes assuring good air and water drainage. Access to both the Great Valley and the Piedmont enables the crop to be delivered without difficulty. In the more isolated sections, large quantities are converted into applejack. Corn, the leading crop, is grown by agile farmers on amazingly steep slopes or in the narrow valley bottoms. Though grown mainly for subsistence, when made into whiskey, the corn becomes a cash "crop." The value of corn in proportion to its bulk is so low that the mountain farmers cannot economically deliver the grain to market, but by converting it into whiskey, only one-thirtieth as bulky, they can sell it at a profit. Moonshining, "the hidden industry of the hills," has been important in this region since colonial times, and its significance continues today, although there is evidence of a trend from "subsistence" to "commercial" operations.[4]

The Ridge and Valley   Most of the Great Valley is in crops or pasture, and the majority of the people make their living from agriculture. General farming predominates,

[4] Loyal Durand, Jr., "Mountain Moonshining in East Tennessee," *Geographical Review,* Vol. 46 (April 1956), pp. 168-81.

though dairying is important near cities and towns, and most farm income is derived from livestock products.

The Shenandoah Valley is Virginia's leading agricultural area. In this valley, one of the best general farming areas in the entire Appalachian Highlands, the density of the population is considerably lower than in the less fertile and more rugged neighboring subregions. This means that general farming requires more capital and smaller units of labor than does subsistence farming.

Crops such as wheat, corn, hay, and apples predominate from Pennsylvania to Alabama. For a century after the Shenandoah was occupied it was a leading wheat-growing section. Wheat was well suited to the fertile limestone soils, and most farmers made it their chief crop, but as cheap, fertile, and relatively level land was put under the plow in the Middle West, the valley farmers were forced out of competition. Nevertheless, winter wheat still is an important rotation crop, and helps in equalizing the seasonal distribution of labor.

Corn fits into every rotation system. Though grown on both level and rolling terrain, it is more concentrated on alluvial bottom lands where the highest yields are procured.

Hay provides feed for livestock, supplies fertility by adding humus and nitrogen to the soil, needs little labor as compared with apples and other clean-tilled crops, and provides excellent fall pasturage.

The Shenandoah Valley is one of the country's outstanding apple-growing sections, and the business of producing and selling apples is uppermost in the people's minds. Though apples have long been grown, commercial orcharding has been important only during the past six or seven decades. While some failures have occurred where air drainage was poor or where soil was not suitable, the soil, climate, topography, and access to market make the area well-suited to this crop. Orchards are found along mountain slopes and foothills, and on level and rolling land. The most famous area is "Apple Pie Ridge," which extends through Frederick County, Virginia, to Berkeley County, West Virginia—an almost unbroken series of apple orchards—for a distance of 25 miles.

Burley tobacco is an important cash crop in the southern two-thirds of the valley, although the average allotment (tobacco is grown under a strict federal acreage allotment system) is less than one acre per farm.[5] A little cotton is raised in the extreme southern end of the valley, in the vicinity of Chattanooga.

With splendid pastures during six to eight months of the year and with large urban centers not far away, dairying has become an outstanding activity, and is growing rapidly in importance.

Beef cattle are raised in large numbers in the Virginia-Tennessee portion—often on lands too steep for crops. Formerly large numbers of beef cattle were exported alive to Europe; now, however, they are shipped to local markets and to Lancaster County and other areas of the Piedmont for winter fattening.

The general trend toward increased poultry production is felt in the Shenandoah Valley. Rockingham County in northern Virginia is perhaps the leading turkey-raising area in the nation, and broilers are important as well.

In the minor valleys and ridges of this subregion about one-half of the land is in farms, but of this only a small part is actually under the plow. The broken surface insures wooded slopes and abundant pasture land; hence the raising of livestock is important. Settlements are scattered along the valleys and lower slopes. The ridge farms, as well as those in many extremely

isolated canoe-shaped valleys, are definitely submarginal and should be replaced by forest.

Often the valleys are so narrow that farmers find it difficult to make room for even a small field. Where limestone valleys occur, they are wider and more fertile, a few of many examples being Burkes Garden in Virginia, Greenbrier Valley in West Virginia, and the Central Limestone Valley in Pennsylvania. In Pennsylvania, the large, fertile Nittany and Kishacoquillas Valleys, floored with limestone, are, in places, as highly productive as Lancaster County. Some of these valleys are miniatures of the Great Valley.

By and large, however, the Ridge and Valley is not an area of big barns and well-kept homes such as characterize the Shenandoah Valley, but rather it is one of small farms and poor homes and barns. Erosion has been robbing the farmers of their richest topsoil, and scarred fields characterize most holdings.

In an area with rugged terrain, with soils of only fair fertility, with cool, moist conditions favoring luxuriant grass, and with limited transportation, the production of livestock is an outstanding economic activity. Where the land is not too steep for pasture and yet too rugged for growing crops, beef cattle predominate. Over much of this area natural blue grass clothes the slopes as soon as the timber is removed. On slopes too steep for cultivation and the grazing of heavy cattle, sheep are being raised in increasing numbers. Sheep are effective destroyers of weed seeds and demand little labor.

The Appalachian Plateau General farming prevails over much of the glaciated section, but fruit, truck, dairy, livestock, part-time, and self-sufficing farming also are common.

The Finger Lakes District of New York is nationally famous for its fruits, vegetables,

---

[5] Department of Agriculture, *Soil*, Yearbook of Agriculture, 1957 (Washington: Government Printing Office, 1957), p. 563.

and dairy products. A large grape industry is supported here, especially on the slopes of Lake Keuka. The care of the vines is a year-round job, for there are about 680 individual vines on a single acre. A large part of the crop consists of the Concord variety. Along the shores of the lakes are also fine orchards of apples and peaches.

In the northern part of the Finger Lakes District is one of the few truck-farming areas in the East comparable with that of the North Atlantic Coastal Plain. It produces two-fifths of the cabbage and a large part of the beets, beans, peas, asparagus, and sweet corn of New York State. Many of these are grown for canning factories.

In southern New York and adjacent northwestern and northeastern Pennsylvania, as well as in northeastern Ohio, is an outstanding dairy section. Hay, oats, winter wheat, corn, and potatoes are grown. Potatoes and fresh milk are in demand in Cleveland, Buffalo, Rochester, Syracuse, Pittsburgh, New York City, and Philadelphia. This area also is the country's leading buckwheat producer. The crop does well here because it is quick-growing and hence can do well even with a short, frost-free, season. It matures if sown as late as July.

The farmland of the rest of the Allegheny Plateau is much like that in the glaciated area to the north except that it is more rugged and the soils are less fertile. More than one-half of the land is in forest, about one-fifth is in pasture, and only one-fifth is in crops. Much of the land is too hilly or too infertile for growing any crops. Where the land is arable general farming prevails; the chief crops are winter wheat, corn, oats, and hay. Much land is impoverished by long cultivation, the owners failing to realize that inch by inch the topsoil has been slipping away.

Throughout the region, some of the farm buildings are falling into disrepair and taxes are becoming delinquent. A great deal of marginal and submarginal farmland has been abandoned, or purchased by county and state agencies, often for reforestation. In New York State alone nearly 1,000,000 acres have thus reverted to the public. As a result, open space is actually increasing in the northeast, despite increased population; this is possible because the people have been migrating to cities and concentrating in urban agglomerations.

Sheep have their greatest stronghold in the East in western Pennsylvania, southeastern Ohio, and northern West Virginia, mostly, though by no means exclusively, in the unglaciated parts of this area. Steep slopes and soils derived largely from sandstone and shale discourage agriculture. Thus the eastern boundary of the Corn Belt halts abruptly upon reaching the Allegheny Plateau. Sheep thrive better on steep slopes than do cattle. Moreover, the climate favors sheep, winters are relatively mild, and only a small amount of feed is necessary.

In the northeastern part of the Cumberland Plateau, farming is the predominant occupation. However, in spite of the fact that nearly all the arable land is in use, it is incapable of supporting the large population. Much of the area is submarginal—sterile and very steep. Level land is lacking except along the larger stream courses. Fields, accordingly, extend around the steep hillsides. A cornfield on a 55 per cent slope is not unusual. Most of the hillsides are too steep for wheeled implements, and homemade sleds must be used. After several years of this type of farming, the land is eroded beyond repair and must be abandoned. Yet many a barren field continues to be doggedly tilled as the only means of family subsistence.

Poor land is farmed because it is cheap land, and this is the only kind poor people can acquire. Fertile land is so expensive as to be beyond their reach. In southeastern Kentucky the average hill farm has about ten acres in crops, three-quarters of which is in corn.

In the northwestern part of the Cumberland Plateau, where the surface is not deeply dissected by rivers and creeks, farming encounters few physical obstacles. Though machinery may be used, the area is poorly developed agriculturally and only about one-fourth is in farms. This situation is hard to explain. Some attribute it to shallow, rocky soils, but isolation appears to be the dominant factor. Roads, now penetrating the highland, eventually will make it more accessible.

In the southern section of the Cumberland Plateau, agriculture is more advanced. Warmer weather permits the growing of cotton. Since cotton farms are small, owing to the restricted acreage of cultivated land, the population is dense. Within the past three or four decades, this section, together with the adjacent Tennessee River Valley, has become the leading cotton-producing area of Alabama.

The Ozark-Ouachita Uplands The agriculture of this subregion consists of two distinct types: (1) subsistence farming as practiced by the mountaineers on the upland ridges or in the narrow valley bottoms, and (2) modern commercial farming in the Arkansas Valley and the Springfield Plateau. In the latter peripheral areas, crops are grown for outside markets and sold for cash. Most farms are prosperous and resemble farmsteads in better localities elsewhere. The same contrasts exist here as between those of the Blue Ridge and the Great Valley in the Appalachians.

Because of climatic conditions and nearness to the great cotton-producing lowlands of southeastern Arkansas, the Arkansas Valley could be considered an extension of the Cotton Belt. Although there is some diversity, cotton in normal times constitutes the principal cash crop. Good transportation by railroad and highway facilitates marketing this crop at Little Rock and other Cotton Belt cities lying along the eastern border of the region.

North of the Boston Mountains the open land resembles the rolling terrain of the Virginia Piedmont more than the hilly areas of the Ozarks. This Springfield Upland or Southwestern Ozark Plateau has developed

Figure 6-5. A dairy herd going out to pasture in southwestern Missouri. (Photo courtesy Massie—Missouri Commerce Commission.)

Figure 6-6. Dairying is a major activity in southwestern Missouri. This plant at Monett has a production capacity of 500,000 pounds of milk per day. (Photo courtesy Producers Creamery Company.)

into an important fruit-growing region, the leading crops being grapes, apples, strawberries, and tomatoes. The production of milk (Figure 6-5) and broilers is also notable.

Grape production for years was confined to fresh grapes for the city markets in the surrounding territory. Nevertheless, there are many small wineries in this part of the region.

This portion of the Ozarks is one of the few places in the South able to grow a good table apple. Like the grape industry, however, apple production suffers from a lack of large nearby markets.

Canning of tomatoes for local consumption began in northwestern Arkansas and adjacent counties of Missouri about 50 years ago, and until recently they were the only vegetables processed. In the 1930's, however, diversification became important and today there are more than 30 kinds of canned items coming from the area, although green beans, spinach, and tomatoes dominate the industry. Springdale, Arkansas, is the chief canning center.

The Ozark-Ouachita Uplands have long produced wild game and semiwild hogs (razorbacks), but, until recently, few domestic animals were produced for the outside market. In some areas sheep have been raised largely for wool to be sold in urban markets. More recently, cattle and poultry have been introduced. Cattle fed on native grasses are shipped as stockers and feeders into the Kansas City area of the Corn Belt, where they are fattened before being slaughtered. Those fattened on corn from the better farms in the valleys go directly to packing plants in Kansas City, East St. Louis, or Chicago. Poultry and dairy cows have taken the place of sheep and cattle in some of the more favored districts and, for the subregion as a whole, rank next to meat animals as a source of farm income. In areas near St. Louis and Springfield, however, dairying has become a major enterprise. Nearby markets for fresh milk are limited, though, and refrigerated tank trucks occasionally deliver as far away as southern Texas. A steadier outlet is provided by condensed-milk plants that have been established in the area (Figure 6-6).

The bulk of the region is less well suited to agriculture than is the Arkansas Valley or the Springfield Upland. Most of the soils have a considerable chert content, which, while imparting resistance to erosion, makes tillage difficult and inhibits the retention of soil moisture. Farms, generally small, are located in the valley bottoms. In some areas, however, as in the Boston Mountains, they occupy the crests of hills and ridges, and only rarely are found in the narrow valleys.

Corn and hay are the most commonly grown crops, with cotton significant only in the Ouachita Mountains, where the growing season is sufficiently long.

Logging and Lumbering

Practically all of the Appalachian Highland Area was forested and at some time or other supported logging and lumbering activities, but the last great area to fall before the woodsman was in the southern highlands, within the confines of the present Great Smoky Mountains National Park. A description of the logging activity in that area will illustrate that activity throughout the Appalachians.

Logging and lumbering came late in the Great Smoky Mountains area because the roughness of the terrain made it too expensive to build roads and logging railroads as long as timber could be secured on the more accessible lowlands. The increase in demand for hardwoods, however, and the depletion of the supply in the Great Lakes area, caused commercial logging to begin in the Great Smokies in the 1890's. At first only the precious cabinet woods (walnut and cherry) or the choicest construction timbers (basswood, yellow poplar, and white pine) were cut. Portable saw mills, some of them cutting up to 100,000 board feet a day, were erected near timbered tracts. By 1905 the finest of the cabinet woods and the soundest of the construction timbers had been culled, and throughout the area logging and lumbering began to decline. The establishment of the Great Smoky Mountains National Park and the several national forests in the area have caused logging to be restricted severely in recent years in the Southern Appalachians.[6]

In the Ozark-Ouachita Uplands, lumbering never has been important commercially,

[6] Edwin J. Foscue, "Gatlinburg: A Mountain Community," *Economic Geography*, Vol. 21 (April 1945), p. 197.

except in a few restricted areas, because of the difficult terrain over which logs have to be transported and because of nearness to the important lumber-producing Cotton Belt. Cutting, however, has taken place over most of the forests, the timber being used for railway ties, firewood, and barrel staves. Much of the area still is in forest—mostly second growth. The chief lumber mills are located in the small valleys of the Ouachita Mountains, up which logging roads have been built to secure hardwood trees for flooring mills and furniture factories.

Mineral Industries of the Appalachians

Mining and quarrying are important, though less so than farming.

Copper and Zinc Numerous small deposits of metallic ores yielding copper, zinc, and small quantities of other metals are worked along the western flanks of the Great Smoky Mountains. In the Copperhill-Ducktown District of southeastern Tennessee are located the mines and the smelter of the Tennessee Copper Company. This area produces blister copper and zinc concentrate.

Iron Ore Large deposits of both brown ores and red hematite ores underlie portions of the southern part of the Valley in Alabama. These form the basis of the iron and steel industry of Birmingham, and their extraction places Alabama in third place among the iron-producing states of the nation.

Cement Widespread limestone deposits encouraged industrial development in the Appalachians, especially the manufacture of cement. Pennsylvania's Lehigh Valley produced more than one-half of the nation's supply a half century ago. Today it produces only a fraction of that proportion, although its actual output has increased considerably. The reason for its relative decrease in production is that the cement industry is now decentralized, for the market is nationwide and the product is of relatively low value and great weight. Freight rates accordingly set a definite limit on the area a given source can serve.

Nevertheless, with many good sources of argillaceous limestone or of ordinary limestone and silica, the principal raw materials needed in cement making, the Appalachian Region is relatively significant as a producer of cement. Other notable production occurs in the Pittsburgh area, in the Kanawha Valley of West Virginia, and at various places along the Ohio River.

Slate and Marble Additional stone-working enterprises include the quarrying of slate in the Lehigh Valley, which produces a large share of the United States total, and of marble in the Knoxville district of east Tennessee.

Anthracite Coal In the extreme northern end of the Ridge and Valley country in northeastern Pennsylvania lies the great anthracite coal field of Anglo-America. It is unique in being engaged almost exclusively in mining; it is not a farming area merely interrupted by sporadic evidences of mining. The anthracite region, characterized by narrow valleys, is clogged by large mine buildings, enormous piles of waste, and many railroads. Though only 480 square miles in extent, this area produces almost 100 per cent of the anthracite of the United States.

As a result of folding and faulting as well as of the presence of much earthy material, anthracite is neither so easily nor so cheaply mined as the bituminous coal of western Pennsylvania (Figure 6-7). Accordingly, more labor is required in mining and separating the coal from slate. Both strip and underground mining are carried on, but the latter is more important.

The first record of the practical utilization of anthracite was for blacksmithing in 1768. Until the use of Connellsville coke and the establishment of Pittsburgh as the center of ironmaking, the American metal-

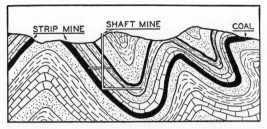

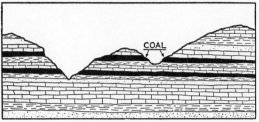

Figure 6-7. Cross section of anthracite and bituminous coal beds. Mining is difficult and costly in the highly folded seams (*above*) of the Pennsylvania Anthracite District, while it is much simpler and more economical in the horizontal bituminous beds (*below*) of the Appalachian Plateau.

lurgical industry was concentrated in the anthracite region. The area lost this, its chief market, after 1875. Anthracite, because it is smokeless, was long in great demand for domestic heating. It is at present suffering from intense competition, however, with natural gas and petroleum, particularly the former.

The anthracite industry reached its peak in 1917 and has been declining ever since, particularly since World War II. Current production is less than 20 per cent of the 1917 output, even though the reserves are far from exhausted. Despite Pennsylvania's monopoly of this resource, the anthracite district is economically in distress. It has suffered from four decades of chronic unemployment, and attempts to attract industry to utilize the available labor have not been particularly successful. Several large manufacturing facilities have been established, but they mostly produce apparel

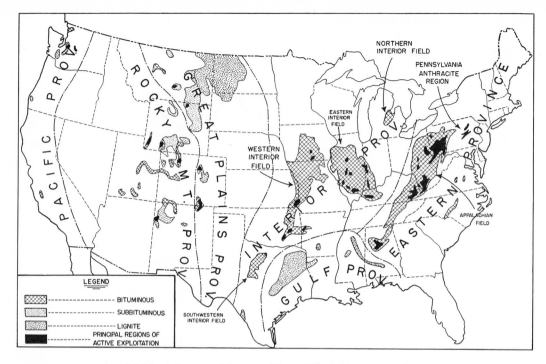

Figure 6-8. Major coal fields of the United States. (From Nels A. Bengtson and William Van Royen, *Fundamentals of Economic Geography*, 3rd ed., p. 389. Englewood Cliffs, N.J.: Prentice-Hall, Inc., 1956.)

and textiles, thus employing mostly women workers at low wages, which does not alleviate the problem significantly.

Bituminous Coal Most of the Appalachian Bituminous Coal Province, greatest in the world, lies in the dissected Allegheny Plateau (Figure 6-8). Nearly the entire area is underlain by bituminous coal, which is interbedded with layers of sedimentary rocks. The seams vary in thickness from a few inches to more than ten feet. The bulk of the mining is carried on in beds four feet thick or more.

When the plateau was being formed, there was so little deformation of the strata that neither the coal beds nor the rock between them was disturbed. Over much of the area, streams, in cutting toward base level, have exposed the seams on the sides of the valleys. This has made possible the low-cost drift type of mining, where the

miners tunnel into the outcrop at the side of a hill.

In traveling over the area, one is not always aware of the importance of coal mining, since scores of mines are tucked away in the hills and are thus invisible from the main highways.

The coal for the most part is of high quality. The Pittsburgh bed in western Pennsylvania, eastern Ohio, and West Virginia is the world's largest deposit of high-volatile gas and coking coal. So excellent is much of this fuel that it set the standard for coke-making. The bulk of the high-quality coking coal of the continent is here, as well as most of the so-called "smokeless coals."

Nearly all of the mining is done by machinery. In underground shafts, mobile drills prepare the way for explosives or compressed air blasts to shatter the coal seam, or continuous mining machines tear the coal out at eight tons per minute. The coal is brought out of the shafts by electric shuttle cars or extensible conveyor belts. In strip mining, gigantic scoop shovels exploit seams close to the surface, while extremely efficient horizontal power augers denude a coal seam without the expense of removing the overburden or sinking a shaft. These machines are expensive and result in decreased mine employment, but gains in productivity make their use worthwhile.

As the coal is cut, it is placed in cars, which are brought to tipples at the mine mouths. Here it is sized and dumped into railway cars or river barges. When the distance to market is not great, trucks may be used.

The Unglaciated Allegheny Plateau is the source of most of America's coal. Pennsylvania and West Virginia alone contribute nearly one-half of the total bituminous coal output.

Petroleum   Petroleum has long been important in Pennsylvania, Kentucky, New York, and Ohio. In fact, the first oil well sunk, the Drake Well, was put down near Titusville in northwestern Pennsylvania in 1859, and that state led all others in the production of crude oil until 1895. Before the Drake Well, petroleum, which had been called "Seneca Oil," was gathered from the surface of springs with blankets. Following the completion of the first well, land values soared; land formerly valued at $5 an acre became worth $50,000 or more. Pennsylvania reached its peak about 1891 when it produced 31,424,000 barrels of petroleum. Though still productive, the area is outstanding more for the high quality of the lubricants derived from the oil than for the quantity of production. Today less than two per cent of the country's petroleum is produced in the Appalachians and Ozarks, and only one of the sixty leading oil fields (the Bradford-Allegheny field in Pennsylvania and New York) is in the region.

Mineral Industries of the Ozark-Ouachita Uplands

For an upland area, the Ozark-Ouachita Subregion is poor in minerals with two exceptions. The northeastern section, one of the oldest mining areas of the United States, nevertheless, is a major producer of lead. In the northwestern plateau lies the famous Tri-State (Missouri-Kansas-Oklahoma) Zinc and Lead District, one of the leading zinc producers of the country. Aside from these two metals, however, there are few valuable minerals. In the western part of the Ouachita Mountains are some small deposits of anthracite coal that were worked profitably in the past. Some coal is still mined near McAlester, Oklahoma. The great production of petroleum and natural gas in the region surrounding the Upland leaves little demand for coal as a fuel. In the southeastern part of the Ouachitas, near Hot Springs, is a small but unique whetstone industry that quarries Arkansas novaculite. Since it must compete with artificial abrasives, this enterprise has declined in importance.

The Lead District of Southeastern Missouri   Lead was discovered here by French explorers in the early part of the eighteenth century. Except for spasmodic interruption during the early years, production has been continuous since 1725. It is the largest single lead-mining area in the United States, supplying 41 per cent of the total domestic output in 1958. Prior to 1869, nearly all the lead was obtained from shallow workings in solution pits and caves, but with the perfection of the diamond drill, ore was procured from greater depths. Since then the output has increased greatly.

The low metallic content of the ore necessitates large-scale operations. When conditions are normal, nearly 29,000 tons of ore are handled each day. In recent years the mines have been consolidated; two companies now produce almost the whole output.

In the vicinity of Flat River, about 60

miles south of St. Louis, are located the major lead-producing mines of the United States. Practically all workings of this mine are deep underground; only the few buildings around the mine shaft and the large piles of ore waste (tailings) give any indication of the magnitude of the subterranean activities. Below ground no mine props are used and no timber is visible; the roofs of the vast chambers, ranging up to 200 feet in height, are supported by huge limestone columns.

The Tri-State Zinc-Lead District   Lying along the northwestern edge of the Ozark Plateau is the Tri-State Zinc-Lead District of southwestern Missouri, southeastern Kansas, and northeastern Oklahoma. Although its presence has been known for a long time, large-scale production has been carried on only during the past half century. The district mainly produces zinc and has yielded from 50 to 80 per cent of the total for the United States and nearly 30 per cent of that for the world. Production is confined to small units of varying size, separated from each other by cultivated land. Hence the entire district is pitted with mine shafts. (Figure 6-9) Principal production is from Oklahoma. While zinc is the chief metal mined, lead, which was worked first, has

been produced in sizable quantities. Nearly all the zinc and lead ores are shipped to Joplin for further processing. Production in the Tri-State District has been decreasing steadily in recent years. The district generally is a high-cost producer of relatively low-grade ore, so that during periods of low zinc prices operations are curtailed considerably.

Other Minerals   Small quantities of copper and silver are recovered from working the lead and zinc ores.

The iron-mining district in southeastern Missouri, where production began in 1845, is of only minor importance today.

In southeastern Missouri and northeastern Arkansas is also located the nation's chief producing area for barium sulphate (barite). This white, inert mineral is used in sludge for oil wells, and it replaces white lead in paints.

In the east-central Missouri Ozarks is a major producing area for diaspore aluminum, which is used in the manufacture of the high-grade refractory clay products of the St. Louis industrial area.

The Tennessee Valley Authority

The TVA is perhaps the greatest experiment in socioeconomic planning and devel-

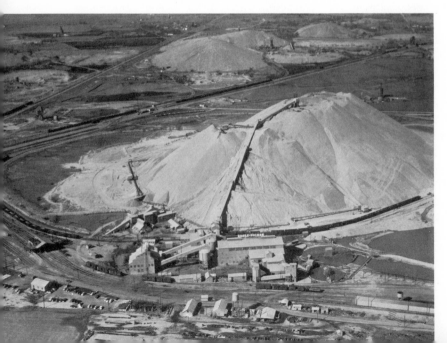

Figure 6-9. The largest zinc and lead mill in Anglo-America is at Cardin, Oklahoma, in the Tri-State District. Here the ore is crushed, the waste rock is eliminated, and the zinc and lead are separated from one another. The pile of waste rock (called "chat" or "tailings") is 300 feet high and contains more than 10,000,000 tons of material. (Photo courtesy the Eagle-Picher Company, Cincinnati 1, Ohio.)

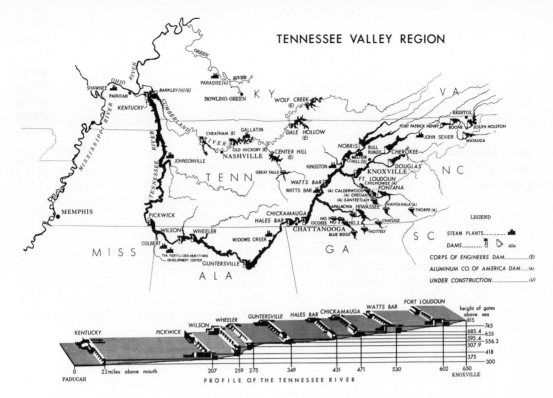

Figure 6-10. The T V A. (Courtesy of the Tennessee Valley Authority.)

opment thus far carried out by the federal government.[7] It was created in 1933 to aid in controlling, conserving, and utilizing the water resources of the area. It deals with such diverse problems as flood control, power development and distribution, navigation, fertilizer manufacturing, agriculture, afforestation, soil erosion, land planning, housing, and manufacturing. Dams were constructed along the Tennessee River and some of its headwater tributaries, backing up the river in a series of contiguous reservoirs throughout almost its entire length.

The area of the Tennessee Valley Authority (Figure 6-10) encompasses the watershed of the Tennessee River and its tributaries—more than 40,000 square miles. It lies in seven states and contains 3 million people in its watershed and an additional 5 million

in adjoining territory. This area was selected because of its relation to navigation, flood control, and power production. Except that it is a drainage basin, it is not a unified region, because land utilization, agriculture, manufacturing, transportation, and the economical distribution of hydro-power all cut across the drainage boundary.

Nevertheless the TVA area has many of the things necessary for a well-developed economy: hydro-power, coal, petroleum, metals, chemicals, pigments, abrasives, ceramic materials, fertilizer ingredients, lumber, and farm lands.

Power In potential water power this is one of the richest areas in eastern United States. For example, in the vicinity of Muscle Shoals, prior to the building of Wilson Dam in 1916, the river dropped 134 feet in 37 miles. Generating plants are now located at the foot of each of its dams. The water flows through raceways against the blades

[7] The TVA is not confined to the Valley, but the most important part lies within it, so it is discussed here.

151

of giant turbines, which generate electricity for the transmission lines. Behind the dams are artificial lakes, some more than 70 miles long, for storing water.

The TVA markets power by underselling private corporations, yet it is claimed by some who are disinterested that the government does not know the *exact cost* of this power, since part of the expense is charged to flood control and navigation.

In recent years the TVA has developed a number of steam plants to supplement hydroelectric power. By the 1960's hydroelectricity in the Valley was less important than coal-generated thermal electricity.

Navigation The Tennessee River connects southeastern United States with the Mississippi Valley. Existing navigation facilities on which commerce may move now include nine reservoirs and their connecting locks. With the completion of the nine-foot-deep channel to Knoxville, a moderate volume of barge traffic began moving along the waterway.

Soil Conservation Nearly one-third of the three million people in the TVA area live on farms. Man has cut down the forest and farmed steep slopes as though they were flat land. The productivity of hill-country farms is low in many areas since farmers are working steep and eroded acreages and are becoming poorer each year. There has been too much dependence upon the one-crop system; diversification must now be practiced. Another major aim of the TVA is to conserve soil: first, to give farmers a higher standard of living; second, to retard the filling-in of reservoirs behind dams. Much remains to be done to assure soil conservation and optimum sustained productivity. Changes in land-use are also needed which will reduce the acreage of row crops and increase the amount of land in legumes, small grains, and pastures.

Flood Control A major purpose of the TVA is to control floods that formerly destroyed millions of dollars worth of property, took many lives, and left desolation and poverty in their wake. It is alleviating flood damage not only in the Tennessee Valley but in the Mississippi Valley as well.

Manufacturing

Manufacturing is less important in the Blue Ridge-Great Smoky Mountains Area than in the neighboring Southern Piedmont. Some textile, rayon, and paper mills and furniture factories are situated in those localities where timber, labor, power, and transportation are available. Copper smelting, one of the few industries based upon Blue Ridge mining, is carried on at Ducktown, Tennessee. Handicraft industries, such as weaving, woodworking, and pottery, are typical of mountain areas. Until revived in the Southern Appalachians by settlement schools and other philanthropic organizations, they were an almost forgotten art. Schools of the type established in Gatlinburg, Tennessee, in 1911, not only revived these native arts and crafts but aided the mountaineers in marketing their products throughout the nation. While Gatlinburg is perhaps the best known of the southern Appalachian handicraft centers, there are numerous others.

In the Ridge and Valley province, the dominant industrial development is associated with the TVA and its hydroelectric power. The principal industrial centers are Knoxville, Chattanooga, Kingsport, and Bristol. Cotton textiles constitute the main product, but metalworking industries are also important.

In the extreme south, at Birmingham, Alabama, is an important iron and steel industry. This is the only district in the United States that lies astride all three raw materials for ironmaking; on the east is red hematite ore; on the west, good coking coal; in the valley bottom, dolomite and limestone. About one-fourth of the mined ore is self-fluxing—carrying 38 per cent iron oxide and 20 per cent lime. This district is reputed to have the lowest assembly costs in the country, though it uses larger quantities of both iron ore and coal than other districts. Gaps through the ridges give ready access to and from the rest of the country. Though Birmingham is not actually on navigable water, it lies only 18 miles from Birmingport on the Black Warrior River. The two are connected by a short railroad, owned by the Federal Government, which functions (so far as freight rates are concerned) as though the channel of the Black Warrior extended to the Birmingham mills. Despite these many advantages, Birmingham has not rivaled Pittsburgh, the Chicago area, or even Youngstown, because it is considerably removed from the major markets for iron and steel. Hence its advantage in assembly cost is partially offset by the expense of marketing when it sells pig iron and steel north of the Ohio River. Birmingham is strategically located, however, for supplying structural steel and oil-field equipment to the rapidly growing industrial South, for shipping to the Pacific Coast, and for engaging in the export business. Moreover, its largest mills are owned by the United States Steel Corporation, which gives it many market advantages. The nearby town of Gadsden is also a steel producer.

Manufacturing in the Appalachian Plateau Subregion is highly developed in the northern section around the great industrial centers of Pittsburgh, Youngstown, Akron, Canton, and Charleston; these industrial developments have been discussed in Chapter 3, *The American Manufacturing Region,* and will not be considered further here.

In the southern Cumberland Plateau of Kentucky and Tennessee, handicrafts constitute the dominant industry just as they do in the Blue Ridge—Great Smoky Mountains Area, although they are not so well-developed as around Gatlinburg or Asheville.

Manufacturing in the Ozark-Ouachita Uplands is confined largely to handicrafts, and to food processing, as, for instance, in the canneries and wineries of northwestern Arkansas. In the Tri-State Area the lead and zinc industries are dominant. As more electric power is developed in this subregion, manufacturing will increase in importance but the area will never become outstanding industrially.

Transportation in the Appalachians

The Blue Ridge offered a partial barrier to the westward movement of the pioneer from the Coastal Plain and the Piedmont, but the numerous water gaps through the mountains made it possible for him to cross into the Ridge and Valley Area and beyond at an early date.

A Great Highway Pioneers westward-bound had to find a way across, through, or around the Appalachian Uplands. The most famous early route was through the Great Valley. Prior to the Revolutionary War it was used by the English Quakers and German colonists from eastern Pennsylvania in their migrations southward. Some pioneers left the Great Valley near Shippensburg, Pennsylvania, and went over the mountains to Pittsburgh. Most of those from Maryland, Virginia, and North Carolina, en route to the Kentucky Blue Grass, followed the Great Valley to the headwaters of the Tennessee to a notch in the Cumberland Mountains, the Cumberland Gap. From here on was the famous Wilderness Road.

During the Civil War the Valley was the roadway by which the Southern Army moved north and the Northern Army marched south. The Confederate Army reached its most northerly point in the Great Valley at Carlisle, a few miles south of Harrisburg. It was following the line of least topographical resistance. The Valley's strategic location with reference to objective points of both armies is well known: Richmond, capital of the Confederacy, was the goal of the Army of the Potomac, while Washington was the goal of the Army of Virginia.

Few areas saw so much fighting or devastation as the Shenandoah Valley. Winchester was taken and retaken 72 times during the conflict.

The present "Valley Pike" (the old Indian Road) was the first macadamized highway in Virginia, having been built between 1830 and 1840. For decades it was the main line of travel for farmers of this and adjacent areas.

Rugged land presents many obstacles to transportation in the Ridge and Valley Area. In the pioneer period, travel was by horse and wagon and followed the valleys. The chief barriers to transportation were not broken down until the advent of railroads which came to exploit the coal, iron ore, and lumber. Main lines invariably follow the transverse stream valleys.

The Wilderness Road Roads, which were the first improved means of transportation, were scarcely better than trails hewn from the forests. Most famous of the early ones was the Wilderness Road blazed by Daniel Boone in 1775. This road led from the Ridge and Valley province through the Cumberland Mountains to the Cumberland Plateau. For about 30 years it served as the main link connecting the new settlements in Kentucky with the Atlantic Seaboard. The rise of the Wilderness Road was attributable to the fact that the easiest and best route, the Mohawk Valley, was blocked by the powerful and hostile Iroquois. The route through Pennsylvania to the Ohio led to a stream that was uncharted and hence dangerous. The country south of the Appalachian barrier was controlled by the warlike Cherokees. Because Kentucky was a neutral ground, the first important settlements west of the mountains took place

there, and the Wilderness Road, the only feasible route to the west, was followed. From 1775 to 1800, 300,000 people went through the Cumberland Gap and over the Wilderness Road through the long miles of mountainous desolation. The importance of the Road declined when the power of the Indians was broken and better routes could be utilized.

Modern Roads Today there exists a comprehensive network of all-weather roads. Those in Pennsylvania and Virginia are especially good. Many of the highways follow the prevailing northeast-southwest trend. One of the most notable highways in Anglo-America, the Pennsylvania Turnpike, crosses the Appalachians in its east-west traverse of Pennsylvania (Figure 6-11). It was not the first of the modern toll roads, but it was early (first opened in 1949), extensive (total length, including extensions, is 450 miles), and eminently successful (ordinary roads through central and western Pennsylvania are characteristically narrow and winding, so that the Turnpike is extremely attractive to both automobile travelers and truckers). The Pennsylvania Turnpike represents the most important link in the toll-road system that today enables a motorist to travel from Chicago to New York without meeting a traffic light or a cross-road.

The physical contrast between the northern and southern parts of the Appalachian Plateau had a profound effect upon the building of highways and railroads. The northern (Allegheny) portion, with its through-flowing streams, such as the Ohio, provided easy grades for highways and railroads, while the southern (Cumberland) portion, lacking large streams, presented a great barrier to transportation. In addition, over the Allegheny Plateau lay the logical route for railroads between the major port cities—New York, Philadelphia, Baltimore—and the rapidly growing Agricultural Interior south of the Great Lakes; whereas the

Figure 6-11. The Pennsylvania Turnpike is the longest, and one of the earliest and most successful of the modern toll roads. (Photo courtesy the Pennsylvania Department of Commerce.)

Cumberland Plateau, located between Charleston, South Carolina, and the Nashville Basin and Lower Mississippi Valley, was not an essential link between its neighbors, for traffic from the Mississippi settlements could move easily to the Gulf Coast or go around the southern end of the Appalachian Mountains.

Railroads The northern portion of the Appalachian Subregion is well served by railways, in spite of topographic hindrances. Trunk lines from New York, Philadelphia, Baltimore, and Norfolk cross the Appalachians to tap the Agricultural Interior, and receive important revenue from the products of the mine, quarry, and factory that they obtain within the region. Coal is the most significant and greatest revenue-producing commodity hauled on American railroads, so it is logical to expect that rail lines serving the coal regions of Pennsylvania, West Virginia, and Kentucky would have a healthy income.

Water Transportation Only a few rivers in the subregion are consistently navigable. Most important by far is the Ohio, which is traversed from source to mouth by barges that carry a variety of items, but especially coal and other mine products. Certain tributaries of the Ohio, particularly the Monongahela, also are notable for coal haulage. As mentioned previously, there is a modest amount of traffic on the Tennessee River, and a little on the Black Warrior.

Transportation in the Ozark-Ouachita Uplands

While parts of this subregion continue to present a picture of remoteness, isolation is gradually being broken down. Soon after the middle of the nineteenth century, railroads began to penetrate the subregion to tap important lead mines or to connect St. Louis with the rapidly growing prairie lands to the west and southwest. The mining roads were usually short and did not reach far into the hills. The through railroads were built around the upland area and for the most part avoided the hill country. The Arkansas Valley, however, provided a good westward route from Memphis between the Ozarks and the Ouachitas (Figure 6-1). In recent years highways have been built into some of the remote areas which were never reached by railroads. And one of the nation's main trans-

155

continental highways passes through the northern part of the subregion, between St. Louis and Tulsa, as a link between Chicago and Los Angeles.

Resorts and Recreation

The Blue Ridge-Great Smoky Area From north to south the Blue Ridge is becoming famous for its resorts. Hotels, camps, and summer homes are common in Pennsylvania's Blue Ridge, which is relatively near New York, Philadelphia, Baltimore, and Washington.

In the South the national parks attract large numbers of tourists. Shenandoah National Park, with its beautifully timbered slopes and valleys, is well known for picturesque Skyline Drive, a paved highway extending along the crest of the Blue Ridge between Front Royal and Waynesboro. Farther south it connects with the Blue Ridge Parkway. The southern segment of the Appalachian Trail, which extends from Maine to Georgia, follows the crest of the Blue Ridge. One of the country's leading regional planners, Benton MacKaye, who conceived the Appalachian Trail, has called it "the backbone of a primeval environment,

a sort of retreat or refuge from a civilization which was becoming too mechanized."

The establishment of the Great Smoky Mountains National Park in 1926, with its lofty mountains clothed with dense forests of spruce, fir, and hardwoods, transformed a relatively remote part of the country into one of the most accessible and most popular resort areas in eastern United States. The completion of a paved highway across the mountains between Gatlinburg and Asheville diverted many tourists through the area and across Newfound Gap for the first time. Gatlinburg, designated as park headquarters, is today the best-known tourist center in the Appalachians (Figure 6-12).

The Ridge and Valley Country The Valley is a great highway connecting the North and the South. It is rich in limestone wonders such as Natural Bridge and numerous famous caverns, is one of the country's most historic areas, and is productive agriculturally. In few other parts of Anglo-America are historical episodes presented so clearly and accurately to the traveler.

The Appalachian Plateaus Until the establishment of the TVA, there were relatively few resorts developed either in the

Figure 6-12. One of the larger resort hotels in Gatlinburg, gateway to Great Smoky Mountains National Park. (Photo courtesy the Greystone Hotel.)

Allegheny or the Cumberland Plateaus because of inaccessibility and the lack of tourist facilities. With the formation of large lakes by the completion of the Norris Dam and similar structures in the TVA area, and with the construction of picnic grounds, shelter houses, and overnight accommodations, the tourist is being attracted to the plateaus. It is doubtful, however, if this area will be able to compete in the tourist trade with the loftier and more scenic mountains to the east.

The Ozark-Ouachita Uplands The recreational possibilities of this subregion were recognized by Congress as early as 1832,[8] but the resort industry as it exists today is a recent development. Although Hot Springs and other centers became important locally in the 1890's, the present development had to wait until better railroads and highways were built into the mountains and until the urban centers in surrounding regions attained sufficient size to support a large nearby resort industry. Both of these goals have now been achieved, and the Ozark-Ouachita Uplands today occupy the unique position of being the only hilly or mountainous area within a day's drive of such populous urban centers as Kansas City, St. Louis, Memphis, Little Rock, Monroe, Shreveport, Dallas, Fort Worth, Oklahoma City, and Tulsa. The most remote of these lies less than 300 miles from the center of the subregion.

The climate is only reasonably favorable for resorts, and this tends to offset the advantages of location and mountain scenery. Winter temperatures are cold and there is considerable snow on the higher slopes, but not enough for winter sports. The spells of hot, humid weather in the summer are far from desirable in a resort area.

[8] An area around Hot Springs was set aside as a federal preserve some four decades before Yellowstone, normally considered to be the first of the national parks, was established.

The establishment of the Ouachita and Ozark national forests has greatly improved conditions for the resort industry, because the Forest Service has not only opened up much inaccessible territory through the construction of good secondary roads but has also built recreational facilities in various scenic parts.

As in other parts of the Southeast and Gulf Southwest, some of the most successful recreational areas have developed around the large, dendritic reservoirs that have been constructed artificially in various river valleys. Water sports, in the form of boating, fishing, swimming, and skiing, are now very much a part of holiday living for hundreds of thousands of families in an area where natural lakes are almost nonexistent. Most important as a recreational center is Lake of the Ozarks in Missouri, but also notable are Lake O' the Cherokees (Grand Lake) in Oklahoma, Lake Ouachita in Arkansas, and Table Rock Reservoir, Bull Shoals Lake, and Norfolk Lake on the Missouri-Arkansas border.

The Outlook for the Appalachians and the Ozarks

The future of the valley areas and the Glaciated Allegheny Plateau, which have satisfactory environmental conditions for farming or for certain types of manufacturing, promises to be a continuation of the present. The rest of the Uplands is largely a problem region. As thousands of acres were destroyed by soil erosion, much of the land became submarginal and the standard of living of the inhabitants fell. The majority of these people have never known prosperity in any form.

Most of the major mineral resources—coal, petroleum, natural gas, lead, and zinc—are used in the American Manufacturing Region. While they enrich outsiders, they have done little to ameliorate the living conditions of the hillsmen. Eventually, most of the coal-mining settlements will become "ghost towns," since they have nothing to sustain them once the coal is gone. Exhaustion locally is already resulting in abandoned communities hopelessly stranded. Coal mining has been a problem industry for many years, and in order to keep it commercially worthwhile it will undoubtedly be necessary to increase efficiency, utilize more machinery, and employ fewer people. The peak of production in both petroleum and natural gas has long since been passed.

While the struggles of the people in the Blue Ridge, the Unglaciated Allegheny Plateau, the Cumberland Plateau and the Ozark-Ouachita Uplands have made a brave human story, it is a story that violated all the rules of careful stewardship of land. For the most part the outlook is dark. The region is now definitely overpopulated. The problems facing these people today are beyond their individual wills or efforts and call for careful regional planning. To improve their lot, whether they be miners or farmers, is a big task, and the solution is not easy. The one outstanding example of geographic and social planning is the TVA, where the Federal Government has undertaken a comprehensive development of the entire watershed of the Tennessee River. It is not yet possible to forecast with assurance the result of this experiment, but it is an attempt to keep an area viable. The economy of the region has been helped in no small measure, but the basic question is, "Would this tremendous investment in public money, time, resources, and productivity have benefited more people in more ways if it had been invested in some other manner or in some other region?"

Certain advantageous trends can be predicted for the region. There will be increasing agricultural specialization, which will result in more efficient and profitable output. It will be most notable in livestock, particularly beef cattle, poultry, and dairy

TABLE 3

Selected Cities and Towns of the Appalachians and the Ozarks

City or Town	Urbanized Area	Political Center
*Akron	458,253	290,351
*Allentown	256,016	108,347
*Altoona	83,058	69,407
Anniston	......	33,657
Asheville	68,592	60,192
*Ashland	......	31,283
Bessemer	......	33,054
*Bethlehem	......	75,408
*Binghamton	158,141	75,941
Birmingham	521,330	340,887
Bristol, Tenn.	......	17,582
Bristol, Va.	......	17,144
*Canton	213,574	113,631
*Charleston	169,500	85,796
Chattanooga	205,143	130,009
*Cumberland	......	33,415
*Elmira	......	46,517
Fayetteville	......	20,274
Florence	......	31,649
Fort Smith	61,640	52,991
Gadsden	68,944	58,088
*Hagerstown	......	36,660
*Harrisburg	209,501	79,697
Hot Springs	......	28,337
*Huntington	165,732	83,627
Huntsville	74,970	72,365
*Ironton	......	15,745
Johnson City	......	31,187
*Johnstown	96,474	53,949
Joplin	......	38,958
Kingsport	......	26,314
Knoxville	172,734	111,827
*Massillon	......	31,236
McAlester	......	17,419
*McKeesport	......	45,489
*Munhall	......	17,312
Muskogee	......	38,059
Oak Ridge	......	27,169
*Parkersburg	......	44,797
*Pittsburgh	1,804,400	604,332
Roanoke	124,752	97,110
*Scranton	210,676	111,443
Springfield	97,224	95,865
*Steubenville	81,613	32,495
*Syracuse	333,286	216,038
*Warren	......	59,648
*Weirton	......	28,201
*Wheeling	98,951	53,400
*Wilkes-Barre	233,932	63,551
*Youngstown	372,748	166,689

* Also in the American Manufacturing Region.

cattle. Increasing cultivation of forage and hay crops will accompany this, and better care of the soil will result. Specialty cash crops will also increase, particularly tobacco, vegetables, apples, peaches, and berries. The number of noncommercial farms and part-time farmers, however, will continue to grow, particularly near towns where there are urban employment opportunities. Secondary industries will continue to be attracted to valley sites in the region, because reliable power resources are available and because the surrounding hill country is one of the last reservoirs of underemployed workers in the nation. Tourism will grow, and could grow significantly, if coordinated efforts were exerted.

By and large, however, the outlook for the region as a whole is not particularly promising. It is likely to remain a region of poor farms, eroded soil, underworked mines, unemployment, and attractive scenery for some time to come, with only slow changes for the better.

Selected Bibliography

Burchfiel, William W., Jr., "Land of the Smokies," *Journal of Geography*, Vol. 45, 1946, pp. 297-308.

"Coal: An Industry Survey," *Monthly Review*, Federal Reserve Bank of Richmond, May 1962, pp. 2-7.

Crisler, Robert M., "Cities of Central Missouri," *Economic Geography*, Vol. 23, 1949, pp. 72-75.

———, "Recreation Regions of Missouri," *Journal of Geography*, Vol. 51, 1952, pp. 30-39.

Deasy, George F., and Phyllis R. Griess, "Geographical Significance of Recent Changes in Mining in the Bituminous Coal Fields of Pennsylvania," *Economic Geography*, Vol. 33, October 1957, pp. 283-298.

Durand, Loyal, and E. T. Bird, "The Burley Tobacco Region of the Mountain South," *Economic Geography*, Vol. 26, 1950, pp. 274-300.

Ford, Thomas R., *The Southeastern Appalachian Region: A Survey*. Lexington: University of Kentucky Press, 1962.

Foscue, Edwin J., "Gatlinburg: A Mountain Community," *Economic Geography*, Vol. 21, 1945, pp. 192-205.

Guernsey, Lee, "Outlook for Coal in the United States," *Focus*, Vol. 10, November 1959, pp. 1-6.

Hewes, Leslie, "Cultural Fault Line in the Cherokee Country," *Economic Geography*, Vol. 19, 1943, pp. 136-142.

———, "The Oklahoma Ozarks as the Land of the Cherokees," *Geographical Review*, Vol. 32, 1942, pp. 269-281.

Kersten, Earl W., Jr., "Changing Economy and Landscape in a Missouri Ozarks Area," *Annals of the Association of American Geographers*, Vol. 48, December 1958, pp. 398-418.

Miller, E. Willard, "Penn Township—An Example of Local Governmental Control of Strip Mining in Pennsylvania," *Economic Geography*, Vol. 28, 1952, pp. 256-260.

———, "The Southern Anthracite Region: A Problem Area," *Economic Geography*, Vol. 31, October 1955, pp. 331-350.

———, "Strip Mining and Land Utilization in Western Pennsylvania," *Scientific Monthly*, Vol. 69, 1949, pp. 94-103.

Moke, Irene A., "Canning in Northwestern Arkansas; Springdale, Arkansas," *Economic Geography*, Vol. 28, 1952, pp. 151-159.

Rich, John L., "A Bird's Eye Cross Section of the Central Appalachian Mountains and Plateaus: Washington to Cincinnati," *Geographical Review*, Vol. 29, 1939, pp. 561-586.

"The Changing Ozarks," *Monthly Review*, Federal Reserve Bank of St. Louis, Vol. 39, February 1957, pp. 17-24.

chapter seven

The Cotton Belt

For many decades the Cotton Belt has been considered to be that part of southeastern United States where, largely because of a suitable climate, cotton has been the principal cash crop and a dominant factor in the lives of the agricultural population. To some extent this is still true, but instead of being a virtually continuous belt of cotton from the Carolinas and Georgia to western Texas, several disconnected areas of intensive cotton production stand out

(Figure 7-1). Cotton is grown in the intervening areas, but is of secondary importance to other crops. Acreage reduction has obliterated the old Cotton Belt in the sense of a vast continuous cotton-producing region (if it ever existed in that form), but increasing yields and increasing prices have offset acreage decreases to the extent that the gross regional income from cotton is approximately the same as it was a few decades ago.

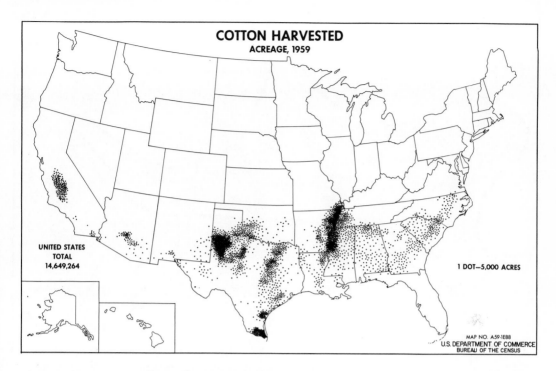

Figure 7-1. Cotton production in the United States. Although certain areas outside the boundaries of the Cotton Belt Region produce large quantities of cotton, the older cotton-growing areas are still of prime importance.

The regional boundaries of commercial cotton production are largely climatic, though areas of intensive production within these boundaries are primarily responses to superior soils. The northern limit coincides roughly with the line of a 200-day growing season—the time between the last killing frost in the spring and the first killing frost in autumn. Cotton production north of that line is speculative.

The western boundary is located where cotton must be irrigated. This boundary is a transitional zone between the cotton and the range areas, although, as more drought-resisting varieties have been developed, cotton production has been pushed farther west. The growing of cotton by well-irrigation on the High Plains of west Texas and New Mexico, and in the irrigated valleys of New Mexico, Arizona, and California is discussed in Chapters 11, 13, and 14.

The southern boundary is drawn approximately on the line of 10-inch autumn rainfall. Where the rainfall is greater in that season, cotton may be beaten down and discolored and picking seriously hindered. This rainfall boundary, paralleling the Gulf Coast 75 to 100 miles inland, separates the Cotton Belt from the Subtropical Gulf Coast.

The eastern boundary is indefinite. The boll weevil has rendered much of the South Carolina-Georgia coast unproductive to cotton, and much of this land has reverted to wilderness. More recently, however, small areas here have been returned to production through the growing of truck crops and rice.

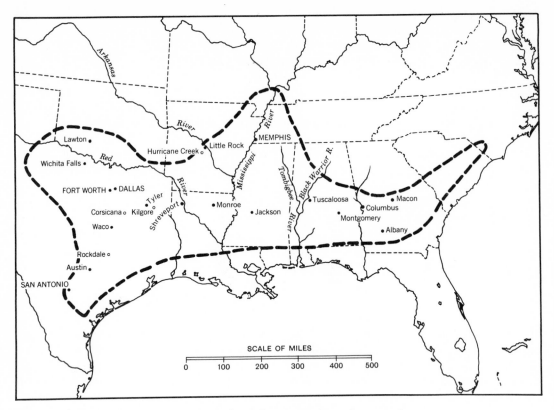

Figure 7-2. The Cotton Belt. A region of diversifying agriculture, forest products, minerals, and manufacturing.

The Physical Environment

Except for the Red Prairie of Texas and Oklahoma, the Cotton Belt lies wholly within the physiographic province known as the Atlantic–Gulf Coastal Plain (Figure 7-2).

Most of the Cotton Belt is a broad plain composed largely of sedimentary materials brought down by streams from the Appalachian Mountains or the Ozark-Ouachita Highlands. The rivers cross through low-lying and even swampy areas, particularly in the southern section. Flowing southward and dividing the region almost equally is the Mississippi River.

Climate The rainfall of the Cotton Belt, largely of the convectional thundershower type, varies from 20 inches on the west to more than 50 on the east. A mild, windy spring with light frequent showers precedes a moderately moist summer that is hot by day and warm by night. This is followed by a dry, cool, and prolonged autumn and a winter that is short and relatively mild, but with occasional spells of severe weather.

Soil Except in northwest Texas and southwest Oklahoma, most Cotton Belt soils are pedalfers. By far the largest part of the region is covered by red and yellow soils. Red soils occupy areas of good drainage where the water table lies many feet below the surface, whereas yellow soils lie in flat areas where ground water comes near the surface. These are all forest soils. They are predominantly sandy in the surface horizons.

The soils of the Black Belt of Alabama-Mississippi and of the Black Prairie of Texas are mostly rendzinas that are derived from marl or limestone. In the Black Belt of Alabama, however, the prairie soils are no longer black, the top dark layer having

162

been washed off through excessive sheet erosion; and the lighter-colored parent material is becoming exposed in many parts of the Black Prairie as well.

The dominant soils along the Mississippi River and its tributaries are of alluvial origin, rich in organic materials, and usually dark in color, having been derived from materials transported in part from the northern prairies or the Great Plains. Cotton is grown on almost every type of Cotton Belt soil but yields are greatest on the dark-colored types.

Natural Vegetation The Cotton Belt was originally a timbered region characterized by southern pines (longleaf, loblolly, shortleaf, and slash) on most of the interfluves and southern hardwoods (gum, oak, cypress) in the stream valleys, with a proportion roughly half pine and half hardwood. Exceptions were the treeless prairies of Alabama and Texas, which later became two of the most productive cotton districts of the South. Although much of the land has been cleared for agriculture, the Cotton Belt landscape is still predominantly a forested one, the woods rather than the cotton fields providing the landscape unity.

Historical Geography of Cotton Production

When this region was first settled, the colonists thought they were in a tropical country and assumed that white men could do little physical labor. Accordingly, Charleston and Savannah became great slave-importing cities. The first crops raised with the help of slave labor were rice, indigo, sugar cane, tobacco, and some cotton. In 1786, long-fibered Sea Island cotton was introduced and was successfully grown along the coastal lowlands.

In 1793, Eli Whitney invented the cotton gin, which soon revolutionized the cotton industry. Until then cotton had been one of the more expensive vegetable fibers, because its separation from the seed was so difficult that large-scale operation was impossible. The textile industry in northwest Europe began to demand increasing quantities of raw cotton. Southern planters (of the Carolinas and Georgia), having had little success with crops previously grown, then saw new opportunities in cotton. More acreage and more slaves were needed, and the plantation system began to expand rapidly in this region.

Westward Movement of Cotton Westward expansion of cotton growing was blocked temporarily by Indian tribes in western Georgia, Alabama, and eastern Mississippi. At the beginning of the nineteenth century, the white settlements that composed the "cotton" South were confined to a relatively narrow strip along the Atlantic Coast and to the Southern Piedmont. Acquisition of Louisiana and the opening of the bottom lands along the Mississippi and its tributaries, however, made large areas available for the establishment of the plantation system. The intervening areas were also thrown open to settlement. It was at this time that the Black Belt of Alabama and Mississippi became the heart of the Old South. With the separation of Texas from Mexico, the establishment of the Republic, and its annexation to the United States in 1845, cotton migration continued westward until it reached the treeless prairies of central Texas, where it halted, owing to (1) the pioneer's distrust of grasslands, (2) the heavy soil that was difficult to till with the iron plow then in use, and (3) the lack of protection from nomadic, warlike Indians. Thus during the first half of the nineteenth century cotton became "king" in the area between the Atlantic Ocean and the Texas prairies.

The Civil War and Its Effects By the time of the Civil War many southern planters realized that slavery was no longer economical. Had some practical method been suggested at that time for compensating the owners in part for their heavy investments in slaves, secession might have been averted. However, the strong agitation of the radical abolitionists of the North caused these planters to resolve to hold their slaves, even at a financial loss. At that time most planters had many more slaves than were needed as laborers or as domestic servants.

In 1860 the United States shipped more than four million bales of cotton to Europe, as against 779,000 supplied by the rest of the world. By 1864, federal blockade of all Southern ports and decreased production due to the war reduced exports to 241,000 bales (most of these smuggled out), while foreign regions supplied 2,300,000.[1] Thus began foreign competition in the production of cotton. It did not become serious, however, for nearly fifty years, and immediately upon the resumption of normal trade after the Civil War, the South again became the greatest cotton-producing area in the world.

Two other factors must be considered as consequences of the war: (1) the freeing of slaves, and (2) the abandonment of many plantations in the southeast which resulted in a second westward movement. The southern planter, as soon as he became reconciled to the fact that he no longer owned slaves, set about rebuilding his farm economy. If his land had not become worn out by continuous cotton cultivation, he subdivided the plantation into small plots to be tilled by former slaves who refused to leave even though free. This led to sharecropping, a Southern heritage that still exists. It was a natural outgrowth of the former plantation-slavery system. Throughout much of the Old South it was the only solution. The Negro farmer had no experience in planning for himself, nor did he

have land and the financial backing necessary for independent farming.

In many cases, however, the old plantation was so completely ruined and the planter's family so broken up that he could only move westward to make a new start. Some planters settled in unoccupied lands of east Texas, some moved to the Black Prairie and with the help of ex-slaves again planted cotton, while still others went farther west where they engaged in the cattle business on the High Plains.

The Boll Weevil and Its Effects Another westward shift in cotton production took place in the early twentieth century with the invasion of the boll weevil. Since the weevil thrives under the more humid conditions of the eastern Cotton Belt, many areas were abandoned in favor of the dry lands to the west and northwest. The boll weevil, a native of the plateau of Mexico and Central America, first appeared in the United States in 1892 near Brownsville, Texas. By 1894 it had spread through southern Texas. By extending its range annually from 40 to 160 miles, it had reached virtually every part of the Cotton Belt by 1921.

When the boll weevil first appeared, it damaged as much as 50 per cent of the crop, creating panic among cotton planters. Later, this loss was reduced considerably by the use of insecticides and by burning or plowing under, in autumn, cotton stalks which otherwise would be used by the weevils as hibernation shelters.

The pink boll worm, also a native of Mexico, first appeared in Texas in 1920. Its effect on the cotton industry, while not so severe as that of the boll weevil, has brought about the division of infested areas into districts with varying regulations for its control. Cotton seed is treated as it is ginned, and both the fiber and seed are shipped under regulation.

The Decline of the South's Supremacy in Cotton Production When Southern farm-

[1] E. J. Kyle, "Cotton Farmers at the Crossroads," *Cotton Trade Journal, International Edition,* 1938, p. 158.

ers first began growing cotton more than 100 years ago, they had the best natural conditions for the crop and hence became the world's most important producers. Nature favored a prosperous agriculture, but economic factors such as exorbitant interest rates, high ginning costs, and high transportation and marketing costs took a heavy toll.

During the Civil War, Southern cotton growers were cut off from foreign markets, a situation that greatly stimulated foreign production. Nevertheless, as pointed out, the South resumed its lead after the war. World War I then had adverse effects. At its close, as prices of farm products collapsed, cotton farmers, hoping to offset low prices, increased their plantings. But foreign demand had decreased, for the financial positions of the United States and Europe were reversed, and Europe, as the debtor, experienced difficulty in purchasing cotton. The years after World War I were marked not only by economic difficulties, but by the ravages of plant diseases and insect pests, particularly the boll weevil.[2] Moreover, the widespread effects of soil erosion were felt throughout the Cotton Belt. During the economic depression of the early 1930's, cotton prices were so low that the financial return hardly justified the investment.

In 1933 government controls limiting acreage planted and controlling prices were established which lasted until after the beginning of World War II. One important effect of this period was the Soil Conservation Service's program to institute better agricultural practices through incentive payments, subsidizing farmers when they adopted recommended practices. The great demand for cotton, along with competition from foreign areas, forced farmers to improve methods of production. Yet, these measures were not enough to maintain United States dominance, and today it is one among several leaders in cotton production. The trend of cotton production is still westward, with more than half of the crop now being grown west of the Mississippi River, and increasing proportions being raised in the dry lands of California and Arizona.

Areas of Intensive Cotton Production

Cotton has been grown on practically all the better-drained lands of the Cotton Belt, but it has become outstanding in those areas characterized by particularly fertile soils (Figure 7-3). Some of these areas now have importance which is merely historical.

Areas of Historic Importance Only The Sea Island District of Georgia, South Carolina, and northern Florida was the first important cotton-growing area in the United States. Both the coastal islands and the mainland grew the long-staple "Fancy Sea Island" variety which commanded a high price because of its superior quality. Because of the boll weevil, very little cotton is grown in the South Atlantic coastal area today; in fact little of anything is grown there.

The Black Belt of Alabama and Mississippi is no longer one of the South's important cotton districts. The dark, calcareous soils formerly produced heavy yields, but, as a result of soil erosion and depletion, boll weevil ravages,[3] unstable markets, and high cost of production, there are few counties in central Alabama where cotton occupies as much as five per cent of the cultivated land. With the decline of cotton, the mainspring of Black Belt agriculture, the area suffered a severe blow. The readjustment problem has not yet been completely solved,

[2] Merle Prunty, Jr., "Recent Quantitative Changes in the Cotton Regions of the Southeastern States," *Economic Geography*, Vol. 27 (April 1951), pp. 189-207.

[3] The boll weevil problem was unusually serious here because the heavy, poorly drained soils made it very difficult to plant cotton early enough to reduce weevil damage to a reasonable level.

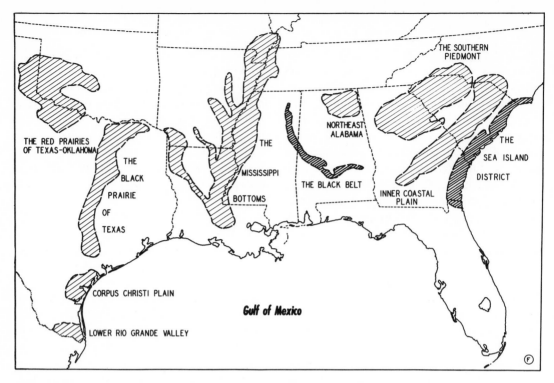

Figure 7-3. Areas of intensive cotton production of importance today (light shaded), and those of historic significance only (dark shaded).

but the raising of livestock has become an important activity, and in certain areas the growing of truck crops, watermelons, and peanuts has provided a partial solution.[4]

Areas of Present-Day Importance THE INNER COASTAL PLAIN OF THE CAROLINAS AND GEORGIA, an old cotton-producing area, has suffered greatly from soil erosion and the ravages of the boll weevil. Nevertheless, it is still an important producer of cotton, principally because nearness to the textile mills of the Southern Piedmont gives it an advantage in the marketing of the crop. The use of much fertilizer on the old depleted soils has enabled the area to rank high in per-acre yield.[5]

THE MISSISSIPPI BOTTOMS, which include the floodplains of the master stream and its

[4] J. Allen Tower, "Cotton Change in Alabama, 1879-1946," *Economic Geography*, Vol. 26 (January 1950), pp. 6-27.
[5] Prunty, "Recent Quantitative Changes in the Cotton Regions of the Southeastern States" pp. 198-200.

tributaries, form a belt of alluvium that occupies parts of seven states. The better-drained soils, rich in lime and organic matter, are devoted to cotton, the highest yields being obtained in the Yazoo Valley and in the Mississippi River bottom lands of Tennessee, Missouri, and Arkansas. Flat bottom lands, fertile soils, and heavy rainfall permit this area to lead in the production of upland long-staple cotton.

THE BLACK PRAIRIE OF TEXAS, an area of heavy cotton production, is about 300 miles long from north to south, and from 40 to 70 miles wide. It is nearly twice as large as the State of Maryland and throughout is composed of black calcareous soil, well-suited to cotton production. Practically the whole area is arable, and the heavy black soils are reputed to be the most fertile of the entire trans-Mississippi region. The climate favors cotton production because of (1) rainfall of between 30 and 40 inches, (2) a growing season ranging from 230 days in the north to 260 days in the south, and (3) long, hot summers. Cotton still is an important crop in the Black Prairie, but corn, wheat, and livestock are competing, and the acreage in cotton is tending to decline.

THE RED PRAIRIE OF TEXAS AND OKLAHOMA owes its importance largely to the damage caused by the boll weevil in the more humid sections of the South. Its semiaridity makes it an unfavorable habitat for this pest.

In the western part are some rough, badly-eroded areas, locally known as "breaks," which are unsuited to cultivation. The brown and red soils are of fair fertility. The annual rainfall of 23 to 30 inches is offset by high summer temperatures, high wind velocities, and low humidity. Production is limited by frequent summer droughts. The cotton plant can stand drought better than many crops, because it stops growing during dry periods, resuming growth and putting out new bolls only after a good rain.

OTHER COTTON-PRODUCING AREAS border the Cotton Belt. In these districts cotton is important, but it is of secondary significance in the total economy of the adjacent regions (Figure 7-1).

The Southern Piedmont and Northeastern Alabama, important cotton-growing areas because of their proximity to southern textile mills, are considered parts of the Atlantic Coastal Plain-Piedmont Region and the Appalachian-Ozark Region. The Corpus Christi area and the Lower Rio Grande Valley lie in the Humid Subtropical Coast Region. The irrigation of cotton in the High Plains of Texas has created a relatively new producing area which lies outside the Cotton Belt and within the Great Plains Region.

Quantity Production

Of the five leading cotton-producing states, only Mississippi, Arkansas, and part of Texas are located in the Cotton Belt. The trend is definitely westward. Texas, the leading cotton-growing state for many decades, has experienced significant internal production shifts, but remains the principal producer by far. Although its average yield per acre is the lowest of any major state, it accounts for nearly one-third of the national harvest in most years. California ranks second, with an output that is not quite half as great as that of Texas, but is continually rising. Mississippi and Arkansas each produce a steady 11 per cent of the total. Arizona's share is 5 per cent, and increasing. Alabama and Tennessee harvest approximately 5 per cent each; Georgia, 4 per cent; Louisiana, 3 per cent; Missouri fluctuates from 1 to 4 per cent; and no other state produces more than 2 per cent of the national total.

The Production of Cotton from Seed to Bale

Although mechanization has made significant inroads in recent years, much of the cotton is still produced by traditional methods that involve much back-breaking labor. Plowing is followed by bedding the land into ridges, usually three or four feet apart; several days later the cottonseed is dropped into the furrows. In some backward areas planting is still done by homemade planters which are operated by hand.

Cotton begins to come up from four to six days after it has been planted, depending upon the warmth and moisture of the soil. The plants then have to be thinned, generally with hoes. "Cotton chopping" is followed by almost two months of weeding and cultivating. At about the end of June or early July the cotton plant begins to bloom. Three days after the flowers appear, they fall off and a pea-sized boll is left which will develop within the next forty or fifty days into a mature boll with its cotton fiber and seed. There must be no delay in picking the cotton, for the plant is sensitive to

Figure 7-4. Although the mechanical picker becomes increasingly important each year, much cotton is still picked by hand. (Photo courtesy Waco Chamber of Commerce.)

sudden changes in the weather and one rain may seriously injure the quality of the fiber and materially lower its market value. Much picking is still done by hand (Figure 7-4); however, on the larger farms in the Mississippi Bottoms and in the western areas of the Cotton Belt an increasingly large percentage of the cotton is picked by machine.

After the cotton has been picked, it still is not ready for the market until the seeds have been removed at the gin. (Figure 7-5) The cotton comes out of the gin in a bale weighing about 500 pounds gross. For every 500 pounds of cotton baled, about 825 pounds of seed remain to be processed later

in the cottonseed and cottonseed-oil industries.

Plants known as "compresses" reduce the size of the bale and are usually located at interior markets or railroad concentration points. The standard 500-pound square bale (density, 12 to 15 pounds per cubic foot) is so bulky as it comes from the gin that only 30 to 35 bales can be loaded into a box car. In order to be shipped, they are compressed to a density of 22 to 24 pounds per cubic foot, enabling 65 to 75 bales to be loaded into a box car. Some exporting ports have "high density" compresses that make the bale still smaller, giving it a density of 35 pounds or more per cubic foot.

Figure 7-5. A cotton gin in operation. (Photo courtesy The Murray Company of Texas.)

Mechanization of Cotton Picking

Cotton is one of the few major crops which has not been completely mechanized. Most planting is done by machinery, as is a certain amount of cultivation. Thinning and weeding ("cotton chopping"), however, are difficult to mechanize (even though some weeding is accomplished by machine-applied herbicides), and it is likely that hoe-wielding workers will continue to be an integral part of cotton farming.

Picking offers several drawbacks to mechanical processes, and since much of the crop is grown on small farms cared for by the farmer and his family, the expense of buying and maintaining machinery is often prohibitive. In the last two decades, however, mechanization has proceeded at a rapid rate on the larger farms of the region.

Many types of mechanical pickers have been used with varying degrees of success. An early type involved a series of mechanical fingers or whirling nozzles attached to a section tube which was applied to the individual cotton bolls. Another machine sucked off the open fiber in the manner of a huge vacuum cleaner. Pneumatic pickers, however, failed because of the great amount of power required to operate them; because of the leaves, trash, and dirt sucked in by the vacuum; and because they had to be applied directly to the individual cotton boll by hand, making them about as slow as hand picking. Some years ago, the High Plains of northwest Texas had a large crop of cotton going to waste because pickers could not be secured. Late in the season a farmer experimented with a piece of picket fence which he dragged through his field to snap off the bolls. While his implement was crude and he gathered a mass of cotton burrs, stalks, and dirt along with the cotton, it was the forerunner of the cotton sled that has been used extensively on the High Plains. Many improvements have been made in the machine now called the "stripper-harvester," and two implement-manufacturing companies have developed types that are successful. Several agricultural implement houses have developed various spindle-type pickers mounted on tractors, and they have been used very successfully (Figure 7-6). These machines pick at the rate of one acre per 1¼ hours and are almost as precise and efficient as hand picking, taking the lint from 95 per cent of the open bolls

Figure 7-6. A two-row, self-propelled cotton picker at work on a plantation in Mississippi. (Photo courtesy International Harvester Company, Chicago, Illinois.)

but leaving the trash in the field. Furthermore they do not harm growing plants and unopened bolls.

Farm Labor

In spite of pronounced trends toward mechanization, the raising of cotton remains one of the principal labor-requiring activities in American agriculture. Cotton farms employ nearly one-fifth of all farm workers in the nation and more than one-third of the hired seasonal farm workers.[6]

Cultivation (primarily chopping) of cotton in early summer and harvesting (picking) in late summer and early autumn engage a large number of temporarily hired local workers in Cotton Belt states, as well as more than 100,000 migratory workers who enter the Cotton Belt for short-term farm work. Most of the local workers are Negroes, although the rural Negro population in the South is rapidly decreasing. Migrant workers normally move about in organized and contracted groups, going from one short job to another. The great majority are either Americans of Spanish descent from southern Texas or Mexican nationals (*braceros*) who cross the border under international agreement for a specified period.[7]

The Future of Cotton

Soil Erosion and Depletion For more than a century and a half cotton has dominated the agricultural picture as the most important cash crop of the American farmer. Since the First World War, however, certain factors have been forcing gradual changes upon the cotton economy.

With the alternate growing of crops such as cotton and corn year after year, soils have deteriorated here more rapidly than in any other part of the nation. The natural factors—rolling lands, open winters, and heavy rainfall—are conducive to soil erosion; but if fewer row crops were alternated, erosion could be reduced.

The South averages more than twice as many thunderstorms as the North. Moreover, in the North, nearly all thunderstorms occur in late spring and summer, while in the South they occur throughout the year. Most Southern stations have received at some time or other more than 8 inches of rain in 24 hours; 29 stations have received more than 15 inches; and 7 have received more than 20 inches.[8]

These intense rains cause serious damage to the soil. Upon even slightly sloping land, the waters run off in torrents that carry away large quantities of soil. Already much sloping land that was once farmed has been abandoned or rendered unproductive by soil loss. Level land, too, is injured by excessive rainfall, for in sandy areas it leaches out the mineral plant food. Thus the South uses more fertilizer than the North.

River bottom lands at times become flooded and covered with mud or other sediment. Sometimes this makes the land more fertile, but more often, perhaps, damage exceeds improvement, because the run-off carries not only fertile topsoil but also infertile subsoil and even sand and gravel.

The Cotton Belt has become accustomed to the gully and has accepted it as the symbol of erosion, but the process that precedes

---

[6] During the peak month of employment there are about 3,000,000 hired workers on United States farms. Some 700,000 of these are regular year-round employees, and the remainder are seasonal workers. Approximately one-third of the seasonal workers are migrants; the rest remain in their local areas to work. See U.S. Department of Labor, *Farm Labor Fact Book* (Washington: Government Printing Office, 1959).

[7] More than 90 per cent of the 450,000 foreign migratory farm workers in the United States each year come from Mexico. In addition, several thousand West Indian Negroes normally work in Florida, a few thousand Canadians participate in the Aroostook Valley potato harvest, and small numbers of Japanese and Filipinos work in California.

[8] S. S. Visher, "Torrential Rains as a Serious Handicap in the South," *Geographical Review*, Vol. 31 (October 1941), pp. 644-52.

gullying—sheet erosion—went unnoticed in most places for a long time. At a Soil Conservation station in east Texas, it was found during a four-year period of experimentation that a farm planted continuously in cotton lost 105 times more soil than one planted in grass and 237 times more than one planted in trees.

Thus it may be seen that the torrential rainfall and the traditional system of farm economy, with two dominant row crops occupying most of the cultivated land, conspired to accelerate soil erosion and soil depletion in the Cotton Belt. Millions of acres in this region, no longer fit for cultivation, are being changed to pasture and forest.

Conservation Since 1933 the Soil Conservation Service and various other government agencies have made great progress in introducing better agricultural practices to the South. Many measures are used, including terracing, contour plowing, strip cropping, and the planting of cover crops to be plowed under for fertilizer. Many crops introduced either to conserve soil or to provide the farmer with a commercial product have been found to fit into the cotton economy, and their production has continued.

The trend during recent years has been toward more effective land use. Livestock grazing is more important today than at any other time in the history of the Cotton Belt. Much needs to be done to effect a balance between prevailing agricultural practices and better farm management, but considerable progress has been made in soil-erosion control and the use of fertilizers.

The Market With present world conditions, cotton is in high demand, but the sharp decline of the export market for American cotton and the development of competition in the domestic market from paper and from synthetic fibers are bringing new problems which may become more acute when world economy is stabilized. In recent years cotton acreage has been curtailed in an attempt to limit production, but suitable crop replacements have not yet been found. Consumption of cotton has remained somewhat stationary while the yield per acre has increased.

To meet the loss of the export market and to meet domestic competition, production costs must be reduced and quality of the product improved. While mechanization is proceeding at a rapid rate in some areas, in large sections of the Cotton Belt the cost of equipment to the small farmer is prohibitive. In addition, much of the land is rolling terrain on which heavy machinery operates with difficulty. Mechanization and the inability of the small farmer to maintain himself when cotton prices fall have caused part of the farm population to leave the area. To date the exodus has affected proportionately more Negroes than whites.[9]

This would seem to indicate that the Cotton Belt is today in a state of flux. If the cost of cotton production can be lowered to meet foreign competition and increasing domestic competition from synthetics, and if current trends toward a more diversified economy can be stabilized, then the Cotton Belt should emerge in its most healthy economic position of the past century.

Cotton Belt Farming— Changing or Changed?

For at least three decades social scientists have made much of the "changing South," listing tendencies and prognosticating trends in economic and sociological matters that will make a "New South" out of the "Old South." Many of the predicted changes have long since materialized, and in no field have they been more striking than in agriculture.

The cotton-and-corn plantation duocul-

[9] John Fraser Hart, "The Changing Distribution of the American Negro," *Annals of the Association of American Geographers*, Vol. 50 (September 1960), p. 266.

Figure 7-7. Pastures and cattle are a dominant part of the farm scene in the Cotton Belt today. This scene is from Georgia. (USDA-SCS photo.)

ture (never merely a cotton monoculture) that characterized primary production in the South for several generations has given way to a diversification of considerable proportions. As Merle Prunty, Jr., one of the foremost students of the region, has said, "Southern agriculture has already diversified; now it is intensifying." Crop rotation, improved soil management and fertilization, supplemental irrigation, variation in field crops, and increased mechanization are all part of the scheme, but the most pronounced aspect is the shift toward mixed farming, with pastures for cattle as the dominant feature of the landscape (Figure 7-7). Cropped acreage, especially of cotton, has decreased, and many eroded fields have been restored to useful production by the planting of forage and pasture.

With the decline of cotton as undisputed king, many attendant evils have also diminished. Soil erosion and fertility loss have been decreased. The established and practical, but patently unsavory, triumvirate of absentee ownership, tenancy, and sharecropping has been broken, presumably forever (Figure 7-8). The general dietary level in the region has been raised; southern cookery, tasty but lacking in nutritive value, is

diversifying with the availability of more land for food growing. And the feast-or-famine economy that was utterly dependent on world cotton prices has been moderated.

The plantation is not gone, however; it is merely concealed with a disguised appearance and perhaps a pseudonym, as "ranch" or "neoplantation." Higbee describes the transformation of an Alabama plantation in the following terms:

In 1940 this property of 3600 acres had living on it 51 Negro tenant families totaling 235 persons. At that time 500 acres were in cotton, 615 in corn, and 100 in soybeans, oats, and peanuts. Except for 18 acres of kudzu, there were no improved meadows. Thirteen years later this same plantation had not a single acre of cotton, and only three Negro families remained. Cattle and fine pastures had entirely replaced croppers, cotton, and corn. Three hundred acres of oats had been planted for grain and grazing. Two thousand acres of improved meadow lands were partially sown to crimson clover, Bermuda grass, and sericea lespedeza, of which 175 acres were under irrigation, although the monthly rainfall seldom drops below 2 inches.[10]

[10] Reprinted by permission. Higbee, *American Agriculture: Geography, Resources, Conservation*, pp. 327-28.

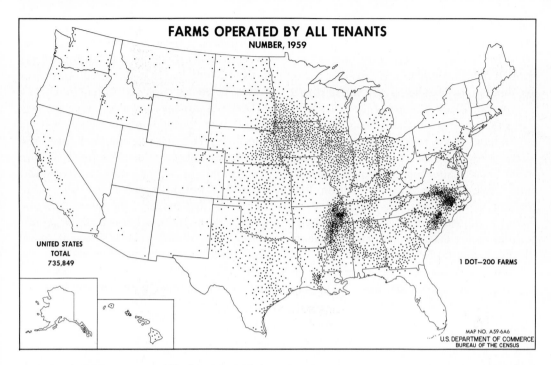

FARMS OPERATED BY ALL TENANTS
NUMBER, 1959

UNITED STATES
TOTAL
735,849

1 DOT—200 FARMS

MAP NO. A59-6A6
U.S. DEPARTMENT OF COMMERCE
BUREAU OF THE CENSUS

Figure 7-8. Tenant farming is much less pronounced in the Cotton Belt than it used to be. The principal concentration now is in the middle valley of the Mississippi River.

Indeed, Prunty points out that the southern plantation has experienced a significant renaissance as the number of farms has increased that have much land, large fields, mechanization, and centralization of administrative and cultivating power.[11]

Other Agricultural Products of the Cotton Belt

Corn The principal system of farming in the Cotton Belt has been based on two crops, cotton and corn, virtually every farmer growing both. Since 1938, however, total corn acreage has been decreasing; [12]

[11] Merle Prunty, Jr., "The Renaissance of the Southern Plantation," *Geographical Review,* Vol. 45 (October 1955), pp. 459-91.
[12] Merle Prunty, Jr., "Land Occupance in the Southeast: Landmarks and Forecast," *Geographical Review,* Vol. 42 (July 1952), pp. 448-49.

this decrease has been greatest in the western areas where corn has been largely replaced by grain sorghums and small grains. During the same period, the yield per acre has increased materially, and further increase on an even more reduced acreage seems to be the trend for the future. With corn, as with cotton and some other crops, definite rotation systems are not common. Fields that are well adapted may be planted more or less continuously to it, and high yields are obtained even over long periods if adequate fertilization and other good management practices are followed. It is interesting to note that two Cotton Belt states—Georgia and Arkansas—are among the leaders in corn yield per acre.

While a large percentage of the corn now produced in the Cotton Belt is grown for commercial use, the South still imports grain and feed and could easily absorb local increases in corn production.

Wheat In the western part of the Cotton Belt, wheat tends to replace corn as the second crop. In Oklahoma and the northern part of the Black Prairie of Texas, wheat occupies almost as much land as does cotton. In terms of the major crop, much of this border area might be considered as a part of the Great Plains Region growing cotton, rather than as a part of the Cotton Belt growing winter wheat. The grain elevator shares with the cotton gin a dominating position in the cultural landscape of many Oklahoma and north Texas towns.

Grain Sorghums In the drier parts of this region in Oklahoma and Texas, the grain sorghums—kaffir corn, milo maize, feterita, and hegari—also share acreage with cotton. These drought-resisting crops serve as stock feed in an area that is too dry for corn.

Soybeans The soybean became significant in the Mississippi Valley during the early 1930's when its introduction was encouraged by the Soil Conservation Service as a legume soil-building crop. Yields per acre were low and the soybean was not in any way considered a rival to cotton. Faced with a shortage of labor during World War II, cotton farmers, attracted by the adaptability of soybeans to mechanized farming and by their value as a cash crop, began to increase acreage. Continued research to improve the quality and productivity of the bean and to extend its utilization has resulted in such an increase in areal distribution that the Mississippi Valley today is the second largest soybean-producing area in the United States. In certain parts of the valley, the threat to cotton's supremacy has resulted in a soybean-cotton cultivation adjusted to the prevailing land tenure system. Soybeans do not rob the soil of its fertility, and can be grown continuously on the same fields for many years, often with increasing yields. The Mississippi Valley has been, and is, primarily a cotton-producing area; however, it seems probable that because of the many advantages that this dual cultivation offers, it can be expected to continue.

Other Legumes Several important legumes grown throughout the Cotton Belt are used for green manure, for stock feed, and for human consumption. The production of the *peanut,* a legume that is frequently classed a nut because of its flavor, was nearly trebled between the years 1929 and 1948. The increased demand for vegetable oils during World War II brought about the displacement of prevailing crops in the sandy lands of the Cotton Belt; this was particularly true of cotton districts in southwestern Georgia and southeastern Alabama which today produce more than half of the nation's crop of peanuts. Scattered former cotton-growing lands of central Texas and central Oklahoma form another important producing area. The major limiting factor in peanut production seems to be a lack of sufficient soil calcium and magnesium.[13] Research into the utilization of peanut hulls, nuts, and oil is continuing, and plants are being constructed near all the leading centers to process these products. *Cowpeas* are grown largely for stock feed and as a cover crop. The areas of major production lie in the inner coastal plain of South Carolina and Georgia, and in Arkansas, Louisiana, and Texas. *Velvet beans* are grown for green fertilizers and stock feed in southern Georgia and Alabama.

Tree Crops Peaches lead all other fruits in importance. Georgia, "The Peach State," is an important producer, as is South Carolina. Another typically southern tree crop is the pecan. Although native pecans are grown throughout the Cotton Belt, large commercial orchards are restricted to east Texas, Louisiana, and especially southern Alabama and southern Georgia. While these

[13] *Soil, the 1957 Yearbook of Agriculture,* p. 582.

two tree crops have brought a good revenue to many growers, the total amount of land planted to each is limited by market demand.

Truck Crops Although the Subtropical Gulf Coast produces the major part of the truck crops of the South, the Cotton Belt produces a wide variety, and they are significant cash crops. The most important are onions, tomatoes, cabbage, snap beans, watermelons, cantaloupes, and muskmelons. *Onions* are grown widely for local use, but in the northern part of the Black Prairie of Texas a large commercial industry has developed. *Tomatoes* are notable in central and northeastern Texas and in southern Georgia. The outstanding concentration of *cabbage* raised commercially within the limits of the Cotton Belt is in southwestern Mississippi. In the same portion of Mississippi and in the extreme eastern end of the Cotton Belt in South Carolina are concentrations of *snap-bean* (pole and bush) production, and there is a lesser concentration in southern Georgia. *Watermelons* are probably the most distinctive of the Southern truck crops. Production for local use is found in every state, and there is much commercial production in the Black Prairie and Western Cross Timbers of Texas, in southern Georgia, and in South Carolina. The latter two also carry on much commercial production of *cantaloupe* and *muskmelon*. The major forces involved in the creation and expansion of these specialized truck areas are the growth of frozen-food and canning industries and the increasing urbanization of the Cotton Belt. *Sweet potatoes* and *yams* are also grown as truck crops, but their principal production is for subsistence or industrial purposes.

Rice The leading crop of this region during colonial times was rice. Today most of the nation's rice is grown outside the Cotton Belt in the coastal areas of western Louisiana and southeast Texas, as well as in central California. Producing approximately as much as any one of these three states is an area in eastern Arkansas within the Cotton Belt. Much swampy river bottom land has been cleared of forest to make way for the rice, which is often rotated with pasture. Elaborate irrigation and drainage systems are generally necessary.

Roses Rose growing in East Texas has become a unique and a highly successful agricultural enterprise. With Tyler as its center, the area in a normal season ships more than 20 million plants all over the country. While the marketing of rose bushes is the principal source of revenue, the sale of cut flowers has potentialities for greater expansion. Freezes sometimes cause great damage, but recovery in the past has been rapid.

Livestock Although cotton farms in the Cotton Belt have always maintained a small number of work animals, milk cows, and chickens, it is only in recent years that the raising of livestock has become important commercially. The Black Belt of Alabama led the way when it was forced to abandon much of its cotton acreage because of boll-weevil infestation and soil erosion. During World War II high prices for beef accentuated the trend in other areas and more recently advances in mechanization have released acreage previously devoted to sustaining work animals. While in some ways the entire South has gone into the cattle business, and no particular section is outstanding, cattle raising seems best developed in the following portions of the Cotton Belt: the Black Belt, the alluvial Mississippi Valley from Baton Rouge northward, and the northern Black Waxy Prairies of Texas. In association with cattle raising, the acreage of grass and legume meadows for pasturage has been greatly increased. However, a considerable amount of grazing is carried on in the fairly open forest that characterizes more than half of the region. It is estimated that five-sixths of the forested area is grazed.[14] The most widespread beef breed is the Hereford, but Angus, Brahman, and Santa Gertrudis are also popular.

Poultry In the past, poultry raising—particularly chickens—has been of importance for home consumption and local market only; however, there are certain areas in the South today where the raising of poultry for commercial consumption dominates farm activities. There is some emphasis on producing chicken eggs, frying hens, and turkeys, but the principal product is broilers, and these constitute more than two-thirds of all poultry consumed in the United States. Much of this industry is handled under a contractual agreement whereby a feed merchant or meatpacker provides chicks, feed, vitamins, medicines, and market, while the farmer supplies only housing and labor. The contractee is benefited by needing little capital and having an assured market; the contractor, by having an assured supply of dependable quality; and the consuming public, by lower poultry prices. Skyrocketing poultry consumption has resulted, but an insecure national market, labor disputes at packing plants, and cutthroat competition have combined to inhibit stability in the industry. Commercial poultry raising is widespread in the Cotton Belt, but it is particularly concentrated in Georgia, eastern Texas, and Arkansas.

Dairying Dairying is a new but growing activity in the Cotton Belt. Small dairies for years have supplied the needs of southern cities, and in many cases large milk-products plants developed in the cities as urban markets grew. Urban population has increased greatly in the past two decades, and production of dairy products has also increased, but it does not meet the demand.

[14] F. J. Marschner, *Land Use and Its Patterns in the United States,* Agriculture Handbook No. 153, U.S. Department of Agriculture (Washington: Government Printing Office, 1959), p. 85.

No part of the Cotton Belt is comparable to the dairying areas of Wisconsin or Vermont; however, with the climatic advantage of mild winters and long frost-free seasons, this activity should increase until it adequately meets the demand.

The Processing of Agricultural Commodities

Agricultural by-products, which were once considered of little importance, are today providing industry with a large proportion of its raw materials. Agriculture is dealing more and more directly with the processing plant, and the field of chemurgy, now in its primary stages, offers with continued research almost limitless possibilities.

Cotton Fiber One of the purest forms of cellulose is found in cotton fiber, but the stalks and hulls also contain large amounts of cellulose. When partly refined, it is used in the manufacture of paper, building- and insulating-board, and absorbents. When freed of impurities and converted into cellulose compounds, it is used in the making of rayon, lacquers, plastics, cellophane, explosives, and many other products.

Cottonseed Products Before the Civil War period, cottonseed was considered a waste product and those seeds not needed for planting the next season's crop were destroyed. During the Reconstruction Period, large quantities of seed were used in the South for fertilizer and stock feed.

Although some extraction of oil from cottonseed was done before the Civil War, the industry did not become important until 1879, when it was learned that the oil could be made edible by a new purifying process using fuller's earth. Because cottonseed deteriorates rapidly in storage, the industry is of necessity highly seasonal, coinciding with that of ginning. Oil mills operate as near to capacity as possible to offset the large overhead cost of the mill, which remains idle for the greater part of the year.

With the expanding use of cottonseed oil as food, and with the increase in the number of mills, intense competition for seed has developed. Manufacturers and refiners, to protect themselves on the supply, price, and quality, bought out and combined the managements of many of the crushing plants and also acquired control of many gins. Soon the industry became concentrated in the hands of several large companies that operated chains of mills throughout the entire Cotton Belt. During the first World War there was a great inflation in cottonseed prices ($65.59 per ton in 1919) and an overexpansion of the industry. The deflation that followed ruined many oil plants and necessitated a complete reorganization of the industry. A second price collapse came in the depression years of the early 1930's when cottonseed reached an all-time low of $8.98 per ton.[15] Since then no other agricultural product has fluctuated in price more than cottonseed.

Cottonseed yields four primary products —oil, linters, hulls, and cake or meal. Oil, the most valuable, is a base for vegetable shortening, salad oil, sardine packing, and soap. Linters, the residual fibers left on the seed after ginning, are used in making absorbent cotton, felt, and rayon. The hulls and other solid material left after oil extraction, are pressed into a cake, ground into meal, and sold as stock feed and fertilizer. With further development of chemurgy, additional uses will be found for cottonseed products.

Plastics Within recent years the manufacture of plastics, one of the fastest-growing industries of the United States, has become important in the South. It utilizes a great number of waste products from both farm and forest.

The plastics industry is probably the best example of man's ability to improve on nature. Many of these products leave the mould finished, not requiring further treatment such as varnishing or painting. The bulk of organic plastics can be made from forest and farm products.

As yet this industry in the South is small, but expansion seems assured because of the great variety of raw materials available.

Soybean Products The processing of soybeans usually results in two products: soybean oil and the residue called oil meal or cake. The oil is used in the production of shortening, oleomargarine, and salad dressing. Flour, animal feed, and fertilizer are made from the residue. In industry, soybean oil is used as a semidrying agent in paints and varnishes, in the making of soap, and in many other ways.

Forest and Forest-Products Industries

The Cotton Belt lies largely in the southern part of what was once one of the greatest stretches of timber in the world—the eastern forest. With the exception of the prairie areas, every part of the Cotton Belt was originally forested. Demand for cotton land, coupled with reckless burning, reduced the standing timber long before lumbering began. It is becoming increasingly evident to land owners that forests produce a valuable crop, and the forest industries today are second only to agriculture in their contribution to the economy of the South. Southern forests produce about 35 per cent of the nation's lumber, 60 per cent of its pulpwood, and virtually all of its naval stores.[16] Georgia is the leading producer of the region in all three categories. More attention is being paid to better cutting practices, and restocking is proceeding more rapidly. Too much of the forest, however,

[15] Department of Agriculture, *Agricultural Statistics, 1951* (Washington: Government Printing Office, 1951), p. 122.

[16] Forest Service, *Timber Resources for America's Future,* Forest Resource Report No. 14 (Washington: Government Printing Office, 1958), pp. 526-27.

still is being exploited rather than farmed. Only a very small portion of the forest lands of the Cotton Belt, or of the South as a whole, is publicly owned. Roughly half of the forest acreage is in small farm woodlots (which, taken as a group, are characterized by poor timber management), and most of the remainder is owned by large corporations. Softwoods make up about 90 per cent of the commercial wood grown in the Cotton Belt, although, during World War II, the use of hardwoods expanded. The hardwood forests, particularly in the bottom lands of Arkansas, Louisiana, and Mississippi, have been more completely destroyed than the softwood, and since they grow more slowly, they cannot restock themselves as rapidly.

Lumbering The lumber industry removed the better timber first in the Upper Lakes District and then in the South. Its traditional policy has been to cut the best timber as fast as possible and then to abandon the location. This policy was followed throughout most of the Cotton Belt, which today is scarred as a result of destructive lumbering. The system of taxation based on standing timber was in part to blame, since it encouraged cutting the timber as soon as possible and moving it from the land.

The South is favored, however, over other lumber-producing sections of the country in that a long growing season and heavy rainfall assure rapid tree growth. A forest planted with pine seedlings can be thinned for pulpwood after only 15 years, and a mature crop of saw timber can be harvested after about 40 years. New growth from voluntary seedlings and reforestation has maintained a large lumber industry, although the annual balance between cut and growth is still precarious. Many wood-products industries are installing trained personnel to improve forest management practices (Figure 7-9).

The Hardwood Industries A considerable part of the southern forest consists of hardwoods such as oak, hickory, cypress, and gum. These hardwoods have been in great demand for furniture, veneers, and

Figure 7-9. A wood products plant in southeastern Arkansas. In addition to its sawmill (foreground) the Crossett Division also operates a chemical plant (left background) and a paper-mill (right background). (Photo courtesy of the Georgia-Pacific Corporation, Crossett Division.)

shingles. Since the best stands were in the Mississippi bottoms, Memphis, the largest nearby city, became the leading hardwood center in the nation. At first the industry cut only choice large trees that were suited for furniture. The railroad crosstie industry has used many smaller and less desirable hardwood trees, but after the discovery of the protective qualities of creosote, it began using pine, also. Although most southern pulp mills use pine, some pulp is being made from hardwoods: in papermaking the long fibers are preferred for strength, but the short fibers of the hardwoods give smoothness and opacity, and are often mixed into the papermaking formula. The increased use of hardwoods in pulp mills is important to better timber utilization, because it eases the pressure on the more desirable pines, and permits more orderly growth of the industry.

The Pulp and Paper Industry   The manufacture of pulp and paper in the South has grown with amazing rapidity in recent years. The Cotton Belt, particularly, gives promise of becoming the nation's great future source of pulp and paper. With the copious rainfall, abundant sunshine, and long growing season, conifers grow four or five times faster than the spruces of New England, the Lake States, or Quebec. In 1911 a small mill—the first in the South—was established at Orange, Texas, to produce sulphate pulp for wrapping paper. Today the majority of the pulp and more than one-third of the paper of the United States is produced in the South as a whole, and the industry is still expanding.

Today the southern pines and southern mills yield most of the kraft paper made in the United States; only since 1939 has the manufacture of paper for newsprint and other light paper gained a foothold. For a long time, sulphate pulp was thought impossible to bleach because of its resin content, and was made into bags and wrapping

paper. Ultimately it was discovered that only the older trees—those more than 25 years old—have large amounts of resin, it being a pathological substance produced following injuries, and that the younger trees have relatively little of it. It is significant that most trees in this region are less than 25 years old, the older ones having been removed by the lumber industry some time ago. This means that the best supply of trees for pulp in the whole nation is to be found in the South, and bleached pulp has become an important southern product.

Minerals of the Cotton Belt

Geographic regional boundaries, which seldom are determined by mineral distribution, frequently cut across mineralized areas. Thus, many minerals of the South, such as iron ore, phosphate, sulphur, salt, and coal, lie largely, if not entirely outside the boundary of the Cotton Belt and hence are not considered in this chapter. In fact the only ones of major importance in this region are those hydrocarbons—petroleum and natural gas—that are found largely in the trans-Mississippi portion. In addition, some bauxite, lignite, iron ore, and salt are mined.

Iron Ore   In recent years the mining of the iron ore of East Texas has given added impetus to the increasing industrialization of the Gulf Southwest. From the beginning of the settlement of East Texas, the obvious existence there of a large quantity of easily available iron ore has encouraged the belief that an iron and steel industry could be developed. Before the Civil War some pig iron was produced by small furnaces, but all of them were closed by 1910. The building of two large blast furnaces at Houston and Daingerfield, in the Cotton Belt, brought about a revival in production in 1943. While the plant at Houston uses some imported ores and scrap, the Lone Star Steel

Company at Daingerfield uses the brown iron ores mined from the open pits in its immediate vicinity. The East Texas ores exist in large quantities, although no definite estimate of tonnage can be made, and usually occur in strata forming the cap rock of low hills.

Bauxite Although more than three-quarters of the bauxite ores used in the United States still are imported, largely from Jamaica, Surinam, British Guiana, Haiti, and the Dominican Republic, domestic production is also important. All domestic supplies now being worked lie within the boundaries of the Cotton Belt region. Two counties in central Arkansas, near the boundary of the Ozark-Ouachita Subregion, account for more than 95 per cent of domestic production; three counties in Alabama and Georgia supply the remainder. In the Arkansas district, about three-quarters of the production comes from open pit mines.

Most bauxite is consumed in the aluminum industry, although an increasing amount is being used for abrasives, chemicals, and oil refining. It is replacing fuller's earth for decolorizing lubricating oils.

Lignite Lignite is widely distributed in two formations which extend from the Rio Grande across Texas into Arkansas and Louisiana. Prior to the discovery of the abundance of oil and natural gas, the lignite deposits of Texas were worked extensively, but by 1950 lignite mining had almost ceased. Output is on the rise again now, however, for production of electric power, most of which is used by the Alcoa aluminum-reduction works at Rockdale. The easy availability of lignite, usually by the strip-mining process, and its proximity to centers of population, are factors which indicate that the future development of these reserves could be extensive.

Petroleum Commercial petroleum production in Anglo-America began with the discovery of the Drake Well in northwest-

ern Pennsylvania in 1859 and soon spread westward into Ohio and Indiana, and later into most parts of the United States and to many foreign countries. Oil from numerous seeps was used locally throughout the country. One such locality, Texas' Nacogdoches County, in the southwestern part of the Cotton Belt, procured oil from an open pit as early as 1867. It was used on harness leather. The development of the large Mid-continent Oil Province, which lies partly in the western Cotton Belt and partly within the Great Plains Region, began in Kansas, later spreading to Oklahoma, Texas, Arkansas, and Louisiana.

The first commercial production in the Gulf Southwest began in the 1890's, with the discovery of oil in a well being drilled for water near Corsicana, Texas. Texas production climbed from 50 barrels in 1895 to nearly 66,000 in 1897. In the following year it reached 546,000 barrels, and the great oil industry of the Southwest was under way. Although numerous small fields were brought in during the next decade, no important development took place within the Cotton Belt until 1911, when the Electra Field, near Wichita Falls, Texas, was discovered. Many large fields were then discovered in rapid succession, including such famous producers as Ranger, Burkburnett (the field that caused the Red River boundary controversy with Oklahoma), Mexia, and Powell in Texas; numerous fields in southern Oklahoma; Smackover and El Dorado in Arkansas; and some important ones in Louisiana. Although each presented new problems of overproduction, the industry in the Southwest and the nation as a whole continued to postpone the "evil day" when oil wells would have to be prorated and production limited. Such conditions might have continued had not the East Texas field, the largest in the world, been developed in the early 1930's. Its enormous potential production threatened to wreck the entire petroleum industry. The size and importance of this field warrants a more detailed description.

THE EAST TEXAS OIL FIELD Some time before the discovery well was brought in, geologists had condemned the area as an oil producer because it did not show any of the common structures present in other developed fields. Accordingly no major companies had leased large tracts of land, and the whole area was in the hands of small land owners. A veteran "wildcatter," C. M. (Dad) Joiner, brought in the discovery well (3,592 feet deep) in the southern part of the field in Rusk County on September 8, 1930. It was the third well he had drilled, the other two having been dry holes. Since it produced only about 300 barrels per day, it all but discouraged further drilling in that section. But less than four months later the second well was brought in, yielding between 10,000 and 15,000 barrels a day. This started the boom in the East Texas field. Table 4 indicates the rapid rate of well drilling in the following decade.[17] Since most of the land in East Texas was privately owned, almost everyone owning property within the field drilled a well if he could secure financial backing. Ultimately the boundaries of the producing area were determined by the marginal dry holes. At its maximum extension, the field proved to be about 42 miles long and nearly 9 miles wide. Within an area of 300 square miles, more than 27,000 producing wells were drilled. Small cities, such as Gladewater or Kilgore, had more than 300 wells within their boundaries. Although production has been severely curtailed almost from the beginning, this field easily leads the nation.

So great was the production from these many wells in the East Texas field that soon the market was flooded with oil and prices declined. Oil that brought $1.10 a barrel when the discovery well came in dropped to ten cents by the following spring. The Texas Railroad Commission (the controlling agency) provided a total allowable of 70,000 barrels a day for April, 1931, but by the time the order became effective, the field was producing 140,000 barrels per day. On April 9, the Commission increased the daily allowable to 90,000 barrels, but the field was then producing 195,000 barrels daily. On May 7, the allowable was placed at 160,000 barrels daily, but the field was already producing 340,000 barrels daily. The average price of oil by that time was between ten and fifteen cents per barrel. The entire American petroleum industry faced ruin. Finally on August 17, 1931, the Governor of Texas called out the State National Guard and completely closed the field until September 5. During that period the Railroad Commission conducted hearings to determine the best method of proration, since it definitely had been proved necessary for the future welfare of the industry. These first proration orders considered among other things the proper spacing of wells and the limitation of production per well. Unfortunately, through the ignorance of some and the greed of others, this first attempt at control was unsuccessful. Many people were determined to get their oil to the re-

TABLE 4

Wells Drilled by Years in East Texas Field

Year	Oils Wells Completed	Gas Wells Completed	Dry Holes
1930	5	0	0
1931	3,299	0	41
1932	5,723	6	64
1933	2,424	6	27
1934	3,696	6	60
1935	3,999	4	121
1936	2,509	1	117
1937	2,380	2	84
1938	1,765	0	41
1939	417	0	8
Total	26,217	25	563

[17] *Kilgore Oil Carnival, The Kilgore News Herald* (Kilgore, Texas: October 1940).

fineries at all costs, and thus began a new development—"hot-oil running."

INFLUENCE OF OIL ON THE CULTURAL LAND-SCAPE The sandy lands within the East Texas oil field that previously had little value suddenly became almost priceless. The new industry was purely extractive and had no interest in community betterment. Its workers came with a single motive—to exploit the oil resources.

The conservation laws in Texas which were enacted to remedy conditions in the East Texas field have since proved of great value to the entire oil industry and to the nation by increasing recovery of oil and preventing waste. East Texas, still the largest oil field in the nation in total production (Table 5), has settled down to a normal existence, although an average of more than 400 new wells is still drilled each year.

Many towns in and near the East Texas

TABLE 5

Production of Leading United States Oil Fields [*]

Rank	Field	State	Production since Discovery (barrels)	Rank Based on Production in 1960
1	East Texas	Texas	3,453,903,000	1
2	Wilmington	California	883,953,000	2
3	Midway-Sunset	California	883,367,000	14
4	Coalinga	California	842,752,000	5
5	Long Beach	California	823,536,000	65
6	Oklahoma City	Oklahoma	716,651,000	79
7	Bradford-Allegheny	Pennsylvania-New York	695,244,000	51
8	Huntington Beach	California	666,737,000	9

[*] Data Source: Bureau of Mines, *Minerals Yearbook, 1960*, Vol. 2, pp. 378-379. Washington: Government Printing Office, 1961. American Petroleum Institute, *Petroleum Facts and Figures*, 1961 Ed., p. 36. New York: American Petroleum Institute, 1961.

field, however, still bear the marks of the early oil-boom days.

Kilgore, in the heart of the field, illustrates the remarkable development of an oil-boom town. Before oil was discovered, it was a small, rural business center in a cotton-farming district of low productivity. It was unincorporated and hence was not listed in the 1930 census; estimates placed its total population at a few hundred.[18] The community had been hard hit by the depression, and its economic outlook was far from bright. By the close of 1930, however, when the East Texas field was definitely established, the quiet conservative spirit of Kilgore had disappeared almost overnight, and in its place the tone was that of an ugly, dirty oil camp, overrun by a multitude of strangers whom the town was ill-equipped to serve. Since Kilgore was on productive property, oil wells were drilled on almost every lot (Figure 7-10). As the boom subsided and the oilworkers moved on to other parts of the field, the town began to spend its newly acquired wealth on new

[18] William T. Chambers, "Kilgore, Texas: An Oil Boom Town," *Economic Geography*, Vol. 9 (January 1933), pp. 72-85.

Figure 7-10. A forest of oil derricks in the heart of Kilgore, Texas. (Photo courtesy the Kilgore Chamber of Commerce.)

buildings, street paving, and beautification. Though Kilgore today is a modern small city, it still retains the forest of steel derricks that represent its lifeblood. Nowhere else, save in a town dependent upon minerals, logging activities, or fishing, can one find a single industry dominating the life of such a large proportion of the population.

PRESENT CONDITIONS In spite of severe foreign competition, major retrenchments in the domestic petroleum industry, and allowable flow of as few as eight days per month in the state, the East Texas field is still an area of superlatives. Not only has it yielded more than 5 per cent of all the oil ever produced in the United States, but in most years its production is well over twice that of the second most important field in the nation. Normally, only eight states have an annual production that exceeds that of the East Texas field.

Other Cotton Belt Petroleum Production The five "western" states of the Cotton Belt are all among the the national leaders in petroleum production (Texas, 1st; Louisiana, 2nd; Oklahoma, 4th; Mississippi, 9th; and Arkansas, 13th). Other than the East Texas Field, there are three principal areas of production: (1) north-central Texas and south-central Oklahoma, centering on Wichita Falls and Ardmore; (2) the northwestern corner of Louisiana and the southwestern corner of Arkansas, with adjacent portions of northeastern Texas, centering on Shreveport and El Dorado; and (3) northeastern Louisiana and adjacent portions of Mississippi.

Natural Gas Although most oil wells contain gas, its presence after lifting the oil to the surface has, until recently, been a liability.

In many old oil fields, large gas flares told the story of man's waste of this valuable natural resource. As a result of legislation, oil operators must send it to market by pipelines, utilize it in drip gasoline plants or put it back into the ground. Many long gas pipelines from southwestern fields serve communities at a great distance, but much gas still remains below ground.

Pipelines When the oil industry was first developed in the Southwest, most petroleum was shipped in tank cars. Some oil still moves by rail, and a large part of the refined gasoline is transported by motor truck; however, the bulk of the crude petroleum, natural gas, and gasoline today flows to refineries and markets by pipelines. These pipelines are of two kinds: gathering, which collect crude oil and funnel it to refineries; and distributing, which carry refined petroleum products from refineries to market centers (cities).

Manufacturing Industries of the Cotton Belt

In the past, the Cotton Belt has been primarily an agricultural region with certain localized manufacturing industries. During World War II the process of decentralization from the vulnerable eastern and western coastal areas accelerated industrial developments in the region. Since the war many industries have expanded and new ones have entered the region. The textile and garment industries have long had a foothold in the Cotton Belt, but heavy industries, such as iron and steel, aluminum, and aircraft, constitute more recent development.

Textiles Cotton textiles are manufactured throughout the South, and many large mills lie within the bounds of the Cotton Belt. They are mostly in smaller cities and towns, such as Columbus, Georgia. The combination of inexpensive labor, low taxes, availability of cotton, and cheap power has attracted the textile industry to the Cotton Belt just as it has to the southern Appalachian Piedmont.

Garments The garment industry is characteristically associated with larger cities, where labor, market, and transportation are most likely to be available. In the Cotton Belt the leading garment-making center is Dallas, but San Antonio, Fort Worth, and Memphis also have significant outputs. Traditionally located in multistoried buildings in the older parts of central business districts, the industry in recent years has begun to relocate in suburban communities peripheral to the major metropolitan areas, and, on a lesser scale, in more distant small towns.

Aluminum One of the most spectacular industrial developments in the Cotton Belt during recent years has been the expansion of the aluminum industry. Two alumina plants, at Hurricane Creek and Bauxite, in Arkansas, and three aluminum-reduction mills, at Rockdale in Texas and Jones Mills and Arkadelphia in Arkansas, are now in operation. The principal attractions are available bauxite and inexpensive natural gas for power generation (although the Rockdale plant.uses lignite-generated thermal electricity).

Aircraft-Missile-Electronics The most dynamic manufacturing industry in Anglo-America today is the complex comprising aircraft, rocket, spacecraft, and electronics production. This complex has merged almost completely the previously individual fields of airplane and electrical-equipment manufacture. The Cotton Belt can claim two important centers of this industry— Dallas and Fort Worth. Aircraft manufacturing was established in Texas during World War II, because of strategic decentralization demands and the availability of land and labor.[19] The industry essentially ceased production after the war, but then started again, and, in spite of fluctuations, is now in a strong position.

Food Processing As in most parts of

[19] Tom L. McKnight, "Aircraft Manufacturing in Texas," *Southwestern Social Science Quarterly,* Vol. 16 (March 1957), pp. 39-50.

Anglo-America outside the American Manufacturing Region, the leading manufacturing industry in the Cotton Belt is not novel; rather, it is the prosaic and necessary processing of foods. In most of the major cities and towns (as Memphis, San Antonio, Little Rock, Shreveport, Jackson, and Montgomery) food processing is the principal type of manufacturing, and even in Dallas and Fort Worth it is a major component of the industrial structure.

Transportation

Rivers and Canals Prior to 1811, there was considerable traffic downstream on the Mississippi by flatboat and by raft, but real trade developed with the appearance of the steamboat, for steam power made the journey upstream possible. A period of heavy steamboat traffic began in 1811 and lasted until the 1850's, when the railroads began to offer serious competition. From the close of the Civil War to the beginning of the twentieth century, traffic on rivers almost vanished.

The creation of the Inland Waterways Commission in 1907 marked the approach of a new era in river transportation. Yet even with the improvements that have been made on the Mississippi and its tributaries (including TVA work on the Tennessee), the traffic moving by water cannot compare with that moving by rail or motor truck. Shipments by water benefit from cheaper rates, but they are also much slower. No other water transportation of significance is found today in the Cotton Belt except on the Tombigbee and Black Warrior Rivers of Alabama.

Flood Problems on the Mississippi For many years the building of levees along the banks of the stream was the only means of preventing floods in the lowlands. For most high-water stages, these winding levees served well, but unusually heavy floods occasionally broke the levee at some weak point—usually on the outside of a bend—and flooded extensive bottom lands. The banks of the river lay in six states—Missouri, Arkansas, Louisiana, Kentucky, Tennessee, and Mississippi—and with no unified federal action, these states could not agree on a plan. The severe flood of 1927 showed the necessity of federal aid, and plans were soon made to treat the flood problems of the lower Mississippi as a unit. There were many facets to the solution, but probably the most significant was the establishment of major emergency floodways to carry off excess floodwaters and to reduce the level of the main stream. Another method of protection has been the straightening of the river by dredging cutoff channels. These cutoffs, navigable at all times, have not only reduced distances, but have also increased the velocity of the stream, thereby reducing flood hazards. The effectiveness of these methods in the years since their inception has demonstrated the soundness of the master plan.

Other Methods of Transportation   With the decline of river traffic at the close of the steamboat era, industries required better rail transportation. Southern railroads (in the Cotton Belt and in the Subtropical Gulf regions) have developed rapidly within the last 60 years and today no part of the area lies far from the railroad. The last three decades have seen also the establishment of a network of modern highways throughout the Cotton Belt. With the expansion of commercial aviation to provide excellent connections with all major points of the United States and Latin America, transportation facilities are keeping pace with the industrial and population growth of the region.

The Outlook

The Cotton Belt is no longer the one-crop region it has been in the past. Instead of giving an impression of a more or less con-tinuous cotton field as it might have in earlier times, the region today is marked by areas of intensive cotton production and areas where cotton is secondary to other crops.

For the entire region, per-acre cotton yields have increased steadily, while the total acreage in the crop has declined. The outlook is for continued consolidation of properties, which will result in more mechanization, fewer acres in cotton (without a decrease in cotton yield), and further crop diversification.

Cattle raising will continue to replace cotton farming as the chief agricultural activity in many areas. And since improved permanent pasture is the key to a livestock system in such a climate, there will be a continual expansion of grass and legume meadows, in some cases at the expense of good timberland. Cattle feeding will become more important too, utilizing cottonseed meal, sweet potatoes, corn, and enzyme-enriched grains.

Dairying will increase slowly, as will the acreage devoted to peanuts and soybeans. The raising of specialty products, as poultry, tree crops, and vegetables, will probably intensify. Supplemental irrigation will become commonplace to carry crops vigorously through short dry spells and to increase over-all yields. Contract-farming agreements will become more numerous. The permanent farm population will continue to decline, but migratory workers are likely to increase in numbers.

Production from timberlands will become increasingly important, both for lumber and for pulp. This trend will be enhanced as forestry becomes more scientific, and as education and increased social consciousness act to reduce the incidence of forest fires due to arson, the major cause.

The economic outlook in nonagricultural fields is generally promising, but less so in some areas than in others. One potentially

TABLE 6

Selected Cities and Towns of the Cotton Belt

City or Town	Urbanized Area	Political Center
Albany	58,353	55,890
Alexandria	......	40,279
Altus	......	21,225
Arlington	......	49,775
Austin	187,157	186,545
Blytheville	......	20,797
Bossier City	......	32,776
Columbus, Ga.	158,382	116,779
Columbus, Miss.	......	24,771
Dallas	932,349	679,684
Denton	......	26,844
Dothan	......	31,440
Florence, S.C.	......	24,722
Fort Worth	502,682	356,268
Garland	......	38,501
Grand Prairie	......	30,386
Greenville, Miss.	......	41,502
Hattiesburg	......	34,989
Irving	......	45,985
Jackson, Miss.	147,480	144,422
Jackson, Tenn.	......	34,376
Jonesboro	......	21,418
Laurel	......	27,889
Lawton	61,941	61,697
Little Rock	185,017	107,813
Longview	......	40,050
Macon	114,161	69,764
Memphis	544,505	497,524
Meridian	......	49,374
Monroe	80,546	52,219
Montgomery	142,893	134,393
North Little Rock	......	58,032
Phenix City	......	27,630
Pine Bluff	......	44,037
San Antonio	641,965	587,718
Selma	......	28,385
Shreveport	208,583	164,372
Texarkana, Ark.	......	19,788
Texarkana, Tex.	53,420	30,218
Tuscaloosa	76,815	63,370
Tyler	51,739	51,230
Vicksburg	......	29,143
Waco	116,163	97,808
Wichita Falls	102,104	101,724

have significant repercussions on economic growth. Race relations are likely to get worse before they get better.

The continued decrease of rural population, both white and Negro, is more likely to be a blessing than a curse to the region. The marginal agriculturalists thus displaced are likely to find more satisfactory urban employment (both within and without the Cotton Belt) and either machinery or migrant workers can take up the labor slack on the fewer but larger remaining farms.

The attraction of the Cotton Belt to manufacturing industries is solidly based on inexpensive labor, expanding markets, certain types of raw materials in abundance, low power and fuel costs, and miscellaneous financial considerations (as reduced taxes or direct subsidies by local governments). While manufacturing in the Cotton Belt is unlikely to rival the adjacent Humid Subtropical Coast Region in growth, it will undoubtedly play an increasingly important role, particularly in the western part.

Urban growth, and associated commercial expansion, seems assured. Some of the nation's fastest-growing medium-sized cities and large towns are in this region.

Selected Bibliography

"Broilers: Production Boom Benefits Consumers," *Monthly Review*, Federal Reserve Bank of Richmond, May 1960, pp. 2-5.

Foscue, Edwin J., "East Texas: A Timbered Empire," *Journal of the Graduate Research Center*, Southern Methodist University, Vol. 28, 1960, pp. 1-60.

Hill, Herbert, "Recent Effects of Racial Conflict on Southern Industrial Development," *Phylon Quarterly*, Vol. 20, Winter 1959, pp. 319-326.

McDonald, S. L., "On the South's Recent Economic Development," *Southern Economic Journal*, Vol. 28, July 1961, pp. 30-40.

McKnight, Tom L., "The Distribution of Manufacturing in Texas," *Annals of the Association of American Geographers*, Vol. 47, December 1957, pp. 370-378.

stifling factor is the unsettled nature of race relations in the region. Agitated by both white and Negro extremists, almost any part of the Cotton Belt, with the exception of central Texas and southern Oklahoma, could experience social violence that would

Nicholls, W. H., "Industrialization, Markets and Agricultural Development," *Journal of Political Economy,* Vol. 49, August 1961, pp. 319-340.

Prunty, Merle, Jr., "Land Occupance in the Southeast: Landmarks and Forecasts," *Geographical Review,* Vol. 42, 1952, pp. 439-461.

———, "Recent Expansions in the Southern Pulp-Paper Industries," *Economic Geography,* Vol. 32, January 1956, pp. 51-57.

———, "Recent Quantitative Changes in the Cotton Regions of the Southeastern States," *Economic Geography,* Vol. 27, 1951, pp. 189-208.

———, "The Renaissance of the Southern Plantation," *Geographical Review,* Vol. 45, October 1955, pp. 459-491.

———, "The Woodland Plantation as a Contemporary Occupance Type in the South," *Geographical Review,* Vol. 53, January 1963, pp. 1-21.

Soday, Frank J., "Southern Industrial Growth and the Textile Industry," *Commercial and Financial Chronicle,* Vol. 188, August 14, 1958, pp. 599-623.

Stokes, George A., "Lumbering and Western Louisiana Cultural Landscapes," *Annals of the Association of American Geographers,* Vol. 47, September 1957, pp. 250-266.

"The Distribution of Natural Gas," *Business Review,* Federal Reserve Bank of Dallas, Vol. 46, September 1961, pp. 1-6.

"The Situation of Cotton," *Monthly Review,* Federal Reserve Bank of St. Louis, Vol. 40, November 1958, pp. 135-139.

chapter eight

The Humid
Subtropical
Coast

The production of early vegetables, citrus fruits, and other subtropical crops, as well as a phenomenal industrial growth in recent years, characterizes the Humid Subtropical Coast, which extends from the Atlantic Coast of the Carolinas, Georgia, and Florida to the Mexican border in the Lower Rio Grande Valley (Figure 8-1). Although it includes the southern part of the Atlantic Coast, it is largely dominated by the Gulf of Mexico. The region is bounded on the north by the Cotton Belt, on the southwest by the southern Great Plains (where ranching becomes dominant), and on the east and south by the Atlantic Ocean and the Gulf of Mexico.

The Physical Setting

Relief of the Land Since this region represents the outer portion of the South Atlantic and Gulf Coastal plains, its physiography is similar to that of the Cotton

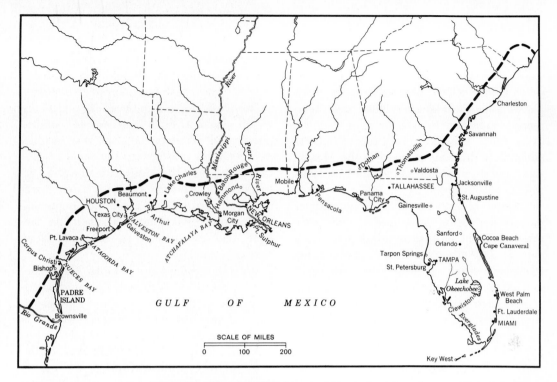

Figure 8-1. The Humid Subtropical Coast. A region of sugar cane, rice, citrus fruits, truck crops, stock-raising, minerals, manufacturing, commerce, fishing, and resorts.

Belt, except that its terrain is definitely flatter. No part of the region lies more than 500 feet above sea level; some large areas along the Gulf Littoral are only a few feet above high tide. Interior swamps, coastal marshes, and lagoons occupy a considerable part of the region, giving it a huge area of wet lands needing drainage. Much of the coast line is bordered by barrier beaches. North-central Florida, a gently rolling area with underground drainage, rises to about 100 feet above sea level. Elsewhere, except on the Mississippi Delta, the land gradually increases in elevation toward the interior.

Climate The humid subtropical climate of the region is characterized by a heavy rainfall and a long growing season (from 260 days in the north to the almost frostless areas of southern Florida and the Lower Rio Grande Valley). The total annual precipitation decreases from more than 60 inches in southern Florida and along the east Gulf Coast to less than 30 inches in the southwest. Over most of the region the rainfall is evenly distributed throughout the year, but the maximum comes during the summer and early autumn—thunderstorm and hurricane seasons. The torrential rains (most stations in this region have experienced more than 10 inches of rain in a 24-hour period) coupled with winds of high velocity have caused considerable damage to crops and wrought great destruction to many coastal communities at some time or other. Weather forecasting is now so efficient that people can learn of coming storms in ample time to protect themselves and, to some extent, their property. From the psychological standpoint, mild, sunny winters largely offset the hurricane menace and thus enable this region to capitalize on climate in its agriculture and resort business. However, severe, killing frosts affect part of the region almost every year.

189

Soils and Vegetation The Humid Subtropical Coast is characterized by infertile, sandy soils, which predominate in most places. The Florida Everglades and other marshy areas have hydromorphic bog or muck soils. Alluvium, often fertile but inadequately drained, is found in the Mississippi and Rio Grande deltas, and in some smaller river valleys.

Because of heavier rainfall, the eastern part of the region is covered largely with forests, mainly slash or longleaf pine, with cypress and other hardwoods dominating the poorly drained areas. The principal grasslands are in southernmost Florida and southeastern Louisiana. West of the Mississippi Delta, coastal marshes appear; the inland areas there, however, are dominated by pine forests. Still farther west, along the coast of Texas, is a prairie that has long been important in the raising of cattle.

Sequent Occupance of the Region

The Humid Subtropical Coast was one of the first regions explored and settled by Europeans. The oldest city of the United States, St. Augustine, was founded by the Spaniards in 1565. In colonial times parts of the region were controlled by Spain, France, and Britain. To the British, rather than to the Spanish or French, belongs much of the credit for the permanent occupance.

Because of their commercial significance, New Orleans and the Mississippi Delta became important at an early date. French colonists, supplemented later by Acadians, began the cultivation of sugar cane during the eighteenth century. Except on the southwest coastal plain where a few Spaniards had established large *ranchos,* the Texas Gulf Coast remained largely unoccupied.

The Anglo-Saxon trek to Texas came almost entirely by land, colonization being confined to the inner margin of this region. After the establishment of the Republic of Texas in 1836, many Mexican (formerly Spanish) settlers abandoned their holdings on the Texas coast and allowed their cattle to run wild. Then followed a period in which Spanish cattle (longhorns) multiplied rapidly. Before the Civil War, people in this remote coastal area hunted wild cattle, taking only the hides and allowing the carcasses to become carrion. Later there grew up along the Texas coast some 32 cattle ports that shipped animals "on the hoof" to New Orleans, Havana, and New York.

With the opening of the Great Plains following the Civil War and the building of railroads to the frontier, the Texas coast became the chief source of cattle. Soon the great cattle drives began; records show that between 1866 and 1880, 4,223,497 cattle were driven northward from Texas.[1]

When the western ranges proved to be superior for cattle, ranching decreased in importance along the Gulf Coast. The introduction of the hardy Brahman cattle, however, has revived interest in ranching. From Florida to Texas large numbers of cattle now graze on the grasslands scattered throughout the timbered areas and on the coastal prairies.

The major development of the Humid Subtropical Coast Region came, however, after the beginning of the twentieth century, as a result of a number of factors, including: (1) improvements in transportation facilities and ports; (2) increasing demands for early vegetables and subtropical fruits and other crops; (3) the discovery of oil, gas, salt, sulphur, phosphate, and other minerals; (4) the development of the petrochemical industries; and (5) the location of many new manufacturing plants on the coast to benefit from cheap freight rates and

---

[1] Clarence Gordon, "Report on Cattle, Sheep, and Swine," *Tenth Census of the United States, 1880,* Vol. 3 (Washington: Government Printing Office, 1880), p. 975.

inexpensive fuel. The impressive industrial growth of this region since 1940 is equaled by few other parts of Anglo-America.

Agriculture

Farming is by no means continuous throughout the region. High-value specialty crops characterize many areas. Although terrain hindrances are nil, agriculture is frequently handicapped by drainage problems. In addition, soils tend to be infertile, and considerable fertilizer, strongly laced with trace elements, must be applied, especially in Florida. The subtropical environment is quite permissive of insect pests, frost damage is sometimes heavy, marketing is often complex, and overproduction sometimes occurs. Regional agriculture, then, faces a host of problems; but a long growing season, adequate moisture, and relatively mild winters act as compensating factors, with the result that a considerable quantity of high-quality (and often high-cost) crops is grown.

Seasonal laborers are major necessities, and many migrants work in the region each year. There is a regular movement of Negroes from the Cotton Belt to Florida horticultural areas each winter. In addition, a good many Spanish-Americans, considerable numbers of Mexican nationals, and a few West Indians work in the region at harvest time. Florida alone utilizes some 65,000 migratory workers annually.

Cotton Some cotton is grown in this region (Figure 7-1), but it is of minor importance except in limited areas along the south coast of Texas. Heavy autumn rains make the crop highly speculative elsewhere, for an entire year's work may be destroyed in a single rainstorm. Since cotton cannot be important, staple crops—sugar cane, rice, grain sorghums, and flax—replace it except in the Lower Rio Grande Valley.

Sugar Cane Sugar-cane growing in the delta country of Louisiana began in 1751,

when Jesuits introduced the crop from Santo Domingo. The first successful sugar mill, built on a plantation near New Orleans in 1795, inaugurated the industry in that area.

The Acadians who came to Louisiana in 1757 took up the cultivation of sugar cane and spread its production westward. After the decline of indigo in the Carolinas and Louisiana, cane became the leading crop, though little was grown outside the delta for more than 100 years. Toward the close of the nineteenth century, production spread into the Texas coastal prairies and into the Lower Rio Grande Valley. Cane cultivation was discontinued in the latter area, however, during the first World War, because transportation was more difficult and because fruits and vegetables became more profitable. In the Sugarland area near Houston, it remained an important crop until about 1923, when production was discontinued because the large refinery there found it cheaper to import Cuban raw sugars.

In recent years, there has been a considerable development of sugar cane in the Florida Everglades. In 1931 the United States Sugar Corporation acquired and expanded the properties of a small producer on the south side of Lake Okeechobee, constructing its large mill at Clewiston. In the Everglades area it is unnecessary to replant each year as must be done in Louisiana, where killing frosts occur almost every winter. In Cuba and other tropical cane-producing regions, from 10 to 12 crops may be cut from a single planting; in the Everglades, from six to seven crops may be secured. Even so, the Florida cane area is much smaller than that of Louisiana, and the latter state produces about four-fifths of the 7,000,000 tons of cane harvested annually in the United States. (Figure 8-2).

In recent years there has been a tendency toward consolidation of many small mills into larger mill-plantation units, which have

Figure 8-2. The sugar cane has been harvested and stripped of its leaves. A mechanical loading device scoops up the cane stalks and deposits them in the tractor-drawn wagons, which will be pulled to the mill. This scene is near Clewiston, Florida. (Photo courtesy Florida State News Bureau.)

proved to be economical, since most of the small mills were obsolete. This type of consolidation has made it possible in the Louisiana delta country for many small, run-down plantations to operate today at a profit. The day of the small cane-sugar producer in the United States is definitely at an end; only large, well-organized companies can hope to compete with foreign producers of cane and domestic producers of beet sugar, and even the large companies depend upon domestic price supports.

The refining of sugar yields several useful by-products, including molasses and bagasse. Molasses is one of the basic sources of industrial alcohol. It is also mixed with feedstuffs as a fattener for livestock. Bagasse is the sugar-cane stalks as they are left after extraction of the juice, and it is the source of celotex, a construction material that has proved satisfactory for insulating purposes. In addition, small quantities of sugar cane are grown widely in the region for local sirup production.

Rice In colonial times the coastal areas of South Carolina and Georgia produced large quantities of rice. Although grown in Louisiana for more than a century, rice did not become an important commercial crop until after 1880, when the introduction of

harvesting machinery permitted large-scale farming on the prairies of southwestern Louisiana and southeastern Texas.

When the Acadians spread westward along the coast of Louisiana, they occupied first the higher, lighter, and more easily drained lands along the streams, leaving unoccupied the heavier prairie soils of the interfluves. These prairie areas, where the surface is underlaid by an impervious claypan, were covered by thousands of shallow ponds that held water after each rain. When these were drained by ditching, they made ideal areas for the cultivation of rice.

The flat relief permits subdivisions of the fields by small levees, a necessity since the field must be covered with about six inches of water during much of the growing period. Heavy rainfall, supplemented by artesian wells and surface streams, provides ample water. With proper drainage, the water can be taken from the fields when it is time for mechanical equipment to harvest the crop, or when heavy rains flood the area.

When railroads were built across the prairies in the 1880's, they began advertising the value of the land for growing rice. Many of those who came were Middle Western grain farmers, accustomed to using farm machinery. Harvesters similar to those used in the wheat regions were employed with great success. At first they were drawn by draft animals and later by tractors, and now self-propelled combines accomplish most of the work.

The usual rotation is one year of rice and two years of pasture. Principal soil problems involve drainage and a relatively low fertility level due to nitrogen and phosphorus deficiency.[2] An important adjunct to rice growing is the airplane. It is used to broadcast seed, spread fertilizer, dispense pesticide, spray weed-killer, distribute desiccants (to assure uniform ripening), and frighten birds during the ripening season. Harvesting, which takes place in late summer or early autumn, is almost the only activity for which the farmer needs to set foot on the field.

[2] *Soil, the 1957 Yearbook of Agriculture,* p. 532.

Mills, concentrated largely in Crowley, Lake Charles, and Beaumont, are equipped with complicated machinery for drying, cleaning, and polishing the rice and for utilizing its by-products. Favorable geographical conditions and complete mechanization enable this region to grow rice at a low per-acre cost.

Between 1940 and 1945 the acreage in rice increased markedly, particularly along the Texas coast as far southwest as Matagorda Bay (Figure 8-3). Approximately one-half of the United States rice crop is grown in this area, divided about equally between Texas and Louisiana.

Grain Sorghums Before World War II, grain sorghums were used largely for feed, but in recent years they have become a source of industrial raw materials such as protein and cornstarch. The major grain-

Figure 8-3. Rice-producing areas of the United States. Note the concentrated production along the Texas-Louisiana coast, with secondary centers in eastern Arkansas and the Sacramento Valley of California.

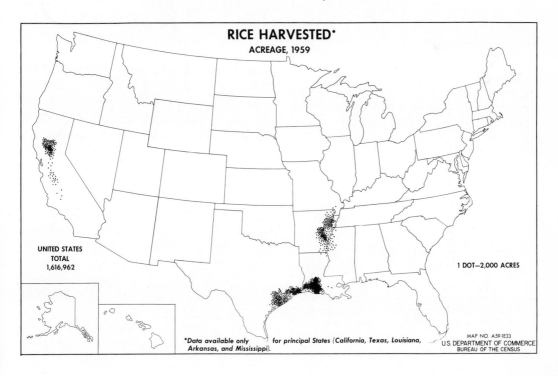

Figure 8-4. Aerial view of the Corn Products Company plant at Corpus Christi. The buildings, constructed without walls, make this a well-ventilated, blast-resistant factory. It is well adapted to the subtropical climate of the Gulf Coast. (Photo courtesy the Corn Products Company.)

sorghum area of the United States is in the Great Plains Region and will be considered in Chapter 11. However, the heavily producing area along the Gulf Coast in southwest Texas is favored by transportation advantages in reaching important domestic and foreign seaboard markets, and this led to the building of the Corn Products Company's plant in Corpus Christi to process millions of bushels every year (Figure 8-4).[3]

Flax A new crop in the Humid Subtropical Coast Region is flax. It has developed rapidly in southwest Texas. Grown as a winter crop, it can take advantage of rainfall and soil moisture, and can be produced on the same land which is planted to cotton or grain sorghum in the summer. Flax provides three commercial products: (1) linseed oil for paints, varnishes, oil cloth, and patent leather; (2) linseed meal for stock feeds; and (3) fiber from flax straw for cigarette papers and fine writing

papers. Total production is minor in comparison with that of the Great Plains.

Truck Farming With increasing demands for fresh vegetables, the Humid Subtropical Coast has become one of the major regions producing early truck products of the continent. Aside from parts of southern California and the gardens under glass in the North, nearly all of the nation's winter vegetables grown for sale come from this region, particularly from Florida and the Lower Rio Grande Valley. Other commercial vegetable-producing areas are in the vicinity of Corpus Christi in Texas, Dothan in Alabama, Thomasville in Georgia, and Charleston in South Carolina. Climate is the dominant factor affecting the growth of early vegetables, and soils help to determine the specific locations. In Florida, the best truck crops are produced on muck or other lands having a higher organic content than the sandy soils which characterize much of the state. Vegetable growing in the Lower Rio Grande Valley is confined largely to the alluvial lands of the delta.

Climatically, most of the region is suited to the production of early vegetables. In the southern parts of Florida and Texas,

[3] John H. Martin and M. M. MacMasters, "Industrial Uses for Grain Sorghum," *Crops in Peace and War, The Yearbook of Agriculture, 1950-1951* (Washington: Government Printing Office, 1951), pp. 349-52.

some winters have no killing frosts. However, even here an occasional cold spell or "norther" may sweep down from the interior and kill the more sensitive vegetable crops. Production is circumscribed by economic rather than geographical conditions. Winter markets can consume only a limited amount of truck crops. Therefore, the growing of winter vegetables, even in the most favored places, is highly speculative, although sometimes highly remunerative.

GREEN BEANS Beans are grown extensively in the Florida Peninsula, as well as in South Carolina, southern Louisiana, and Texas. In Florida, which produces the bulk of the nation's early crop, the rolling lands in the north and the southeast coast are particularly suitable.

CABBAGES Early cabbage comes largely from southern Texas and eastern Florida, although southern Louisiana, southern Georgia, and coastal South Carolina are also producers.

ONIONS Commercial production of early onions, particularly the Bermuda variety, is confined to the Lower Rio Grande Valley and the Corpus Christi area.

TOMATOES Most of the commercial crop of early tomatoes is grown in Florida and the Lower Rio Grande Valley, which, together with southern California, produce almost the entire early crop.

WATERMELONS Especially important in Florida, watermelons are shipped from early in April until the middle of July. Although not a winter crop, they add significantly to Florida's total truck production.

STRAWBERRIES The centers of early strawberry production are the Plant City district of Florida and the Hammond area of Louisiana. Louisiana, the leading producer, also has an important berry-freezing industry.

OTHER EARLY TRUCK CROPS AND THEIR MAJOR PRODUCING AREAS are: (1) celery—the Plant City and Sanford districts of Florida, (2) early white potatoes—the Hastings area of Florida, and to a lesser extent the Lower Rio Grande Valley, (3) beets and carrots—the Lower Rio Grande Valley, (4) peppers—the New Iberia district of southern Louisiana, and (5) cucumbers—north Florida. Lettuce, potatoes, escarole, eggplant, romaine, squash, okra, Brussels sprouts, mustard, spinach, parsley, cauliflower, broccoli, and green corn are produced locally throughout the region.

The Humid Subtropical Coast is also an important producer of figs, particularly that section of Texas between Houston and Beaumont, which, with California, produces nearly all of the nation's crop. Pecan production is scattered throughout the region except in southern Texas and southern Florida. Various tropical and subtropical plants can tolerate brief frosts, so in southern Florida there is some commercial production of avocados and pineapples and even a few papayas, mangos, and guavas are grown.

Citrus Fruits Citrus fruit trees cannot endure below-freezing temperatures for even a few hours at a time without serious damage, and hence are grown only in those parts of the United States where killing freezes seldom occur. The major citrus-producing areas of the nation are in southern California, Arizona, the Rio Grande Valley of Texas, and central Florida.

Oranges, most resistant to cold of the citrus family, are found in all the areas listed above, as well as in a small area in the Mississippi Delta of southeastern Louisiana (Figure 8-5). Grapefruit, next in resistance to cold, are grown commercially in this region only in Florida and the Lower Rio Grande Valley (Figure 8-6). Lemons, having still less resistance to freezing temperatures, are not produced commercially in this region. Limes, the most sensitive, cannot withstand frost and hence are grown commercially in the only absolutely frost-free part of the region, the Florida Keys.

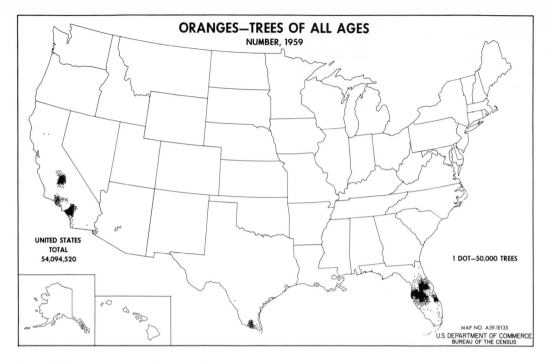

Figure 8-5. Orange trees in the United States.

Figure 8-6. Grapefruit trees in the United States.

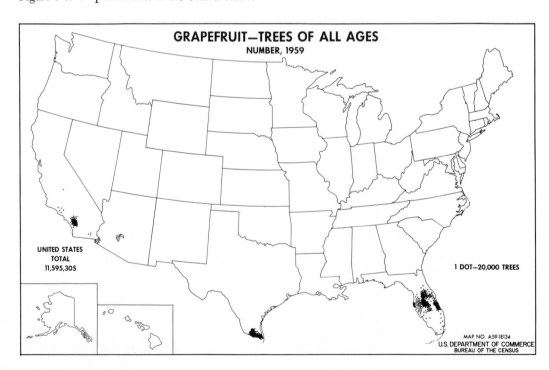

Tangelos, crosses of tangerine oranges and grapefruit, are grown on a small scale for the commercial market in Florida.

Florida is the outstanding citrus producer, supplying more than 70 per cent of the national orange crop, over 80 per cent of the grapefruit crop, and all of the limes and tangelos. Early Spanish settlers introduced citrus to the state, and Indians propagated it for their own use. "Some of the first commercial groves in nineteenth century Florida were the result of budding strains on the pruned stock of earlier Indian plantings." [4] The "Big Freeze" of 1894-95 caused a relocation of the industry, for most groves in northern Florida were destroyed, and the northern third of the state was essentially abandoned for citrus. Commercial groves are now mostly in the gently-rolling, sandy-soiled lakes district of central Florida (Figure 8-7). Surface drainage, air drainage, [5] and the warming effect of the lakes are all beneficial in combating frost danger.

[4] Higbee, *American Agriculture: Geography, Resources, Conservation,* p. 346.

[5] A 30-foot hill at Avon Park has recorded temperatures as much as 18 degrees higher than those in a "frost pocket" 150 yards away. See Higbee, *American Agriculture: Geography, Resources, Conservation,* p. 348.

In addition, oil-burning heaters are employed when the air temperature drops below about 27° F. The land is expensive, the yields are good, and production is steadily increasing. A major problem in Florida citrus groves is the Mediterranean fruit fly, which causes nausea in people who eat infected fruit. The menace is met by strict quarantine of infected areas and aerial spraying of a potent poison.

Transportation and marketing are often complicated. Roughly half of all citrus harvested in Florida is now sold as processed products.[6] Canned juices and canned salad are among these, but easily the most important is frozen concentrated juice. There has also been some success in transporting fresh orange juice directly to New York in a glass-lined refrigerated tanker ship. Citrus waste (pulp and peelings) is generally fed to cattle, although the flavoring oil is sometimes removed to be used in the manufacture of table wines and salad oils.

The Texas citrus area is located on the terraces of the Lower Rio Grande Delta. Practically all production is based on irrigation water diverted from the river. Severe

[6] Marschner, *Land Use and Its Patterns in the United States,* p. 87.

Figure 8-7. Harvesting oranges in the lake country of central Florida. (Photo courtesy the Florida Citrus Commission.)

frost occasionally damages the groves, sometimes so badly that new trees must be planted. On such occasions the horticulturists usually raise cotton or vegetables for a few years until the groves become re-established. Seedless pink grapefruit is the specialty of the Valley, which, in most years, produces more than 10 per cent of the national grapefruit crop; it also produces about 3 per cent of the orange crop. Considerable canning and freezing are done here, as in Florida.

A small quantity of oranges is grown commercially in southeastern Louisiana. The quality is high, but limited area prohibits large-scale production.

Tung Production The tung tree produces one of the best quick-drying oils for use in the manufacture of paints and varnishes. The oil is extracted from the kernels of the fruit of the tree, which is prolific. Tung trees were introduced into the United States from the Far East in 1905, but the first commercial orchard was not started until 1924. The first oil-extracting mill was placed in operation near Gainesville, Florida, in 1928. From this slow start the production of tung fruit increased rapidly, from a little more than 1,000 tons in 1939 to 88,000 tons in 1949, yielding about 26 million pounds of oil. By the early 1960's, production exceeded 150,000 tons.

The tree requires at least 45 inches of rainfall, evenly distributed through the year. Dormant, well-nourished trees have withstood temperatures as low as 8° F., but protracted periods of subfreezing temperatures prove disastrous. The fruit, which is about the size of a small apple, matures and drops to the ground late in September or October.

Because of the tree's exacting climatic requirements, the tung-producing area is limited to a belt about 100 miles wide that extends from eastern Texas along the Gulf of Mexico to the Atlantic Coast. Over half of the total production is from the Pearl River district of Mississippi.

Transportation and Marketing Marketing the winter truck crops in this region is a serious problem. Recent improvements in highways and railroads have made possible the shipment of much of the early crop to the northern markets in time to command a high price. Cooperative marketing associations have helped, but as yet the region is not so well organized in this respect as is California. Vegetable canning has aided in utilizing much of the crop that cannot be marketed fresh. The vegetable-freezing industry, which began about 1929, has grown rapidly in recent years because freezing alters the fresh character of foodstuffs least of all preserving methods.

The Livestock Industry

The Humid Subtropical Coast Region has been an important producer of beef cattle since French and Spanish colonial times. However, after the Great Plains were opened to grazing in the 1870's, the poorer pastures of the Gulf Coast found difficulty in competing. For several decades cattle raising was all but abandoned except in the Acadian French country of southwestern Louisiana and the coastal grasslands of southwestern Texas. In recent years, through the introduction of new breeds, particularly the Brahman, the cattle industry has expanded to other parts of the coastal region.

Brahman or Zebu cattle (*Bos indicus*) were brought from India to the Carolina coastal country more than a century ago, because cattlemen thought they would be better adapted to the hot, humid, insect-ridden area than were the English breeds common in the rest of the country. The oversized, hump-shouldered, lop-eared, slant-eyed, flappy-brisketed newcomer has been a thorough success, and is often crossbred to produce special-purpose hybrids. One of these hybrids, the Santa Gertrudis, meticu-

Figure 8-8. A mixed herd of Florida cattle, predominately "Brahma Cross." These artificial pastures are partially irrigated during dry seasons. (USDA-SCS photo by Hermann Postlethwaite.)

lously developed on Texas' gigantic King Ranch, is considered to be the only "true" cattle breed ever developed in Anglo-America. It is five-eighths Shorthorn and three-eighths Brahman. While there are many purebred Brahmans, as well as Herefords, Santa Gertrudis, and other breeds in the region, most of the beef cattle are of mixed ancestry, and their physiognomy usually reveals the presence of some Brahman inheritance (Figure 8-8).

The Humid Subtropical Coast Region, with large areas of grassland, plentiful rainfall, and mild, open winters, should be able to expand its cattle industry in the future, especially since crossbreeding has produced animals more nearly immune to tick fever.

One of the most interesting developments in the region has been the rapid rise of the beef-cattle industry of peninsular Florida. Today the ranching area extends from the lakes district in the northern part of the peninsula to lands south of Lake Okeechobee. In this area more than 1,600,000 head of beef cattle are roaming the range. Because of this rapid expansion, Florida now ranks among the leading cattle-raising states of the nation, ahead of every state west of the Great Plains except California and Montana. Livestock markets and packing houses are developing in the state, and sections of Florida, as the area around Kissim-

mee, where extensive ranches have been cut out of the undergrowth and swamp, are definitely taking on a "western" appearance.

Florida's spectacular growth as a beef producer can be attributed to (1) improvements in pastures, through the introduction of Bermuda, Bahia, Pangola, and other nutritious grasses, as well as trace-element fertilizers; (2) improvements in breeds of cattle; and (3) the discovery that citrus pulp and citrus molasses, formerly waste products, make excellent cattle feeds.

The Fishing Industry

The Gulf Coast is less important for commercial fishing than either the Atlantic or the Pacific Coasts. Its accessibility to the interior of the continent, however, plus the fact that several delectable varieties of fish found in Gulf waters are scarce elsewhere, make this region one of growing importance.

The most important catch are shrimp and red snapper, although sheepshead, pompano, and grouper are also highly prized. Few species are caught in large quantities in Gulf Coast landings. Shrimp are the most valuable variety of fish in the United States, and nearly nine-tenths of the total national landings are in Gulf waters, especially off Texas. Most of the small white and brown shrimp are caught in lagoons, and in recent years the industry has invaded offshore banks for the larger Brazilian, or red, shrimp. The shrimp to be sold fresh are iced, and those to be canned are boiled. Sun-dried shrimp are marketed abroad. The by-products of this industry are used to make meal for feedstuffs or for fertilizers. The only recurrent major problem in the shrimp industry is fluctuating prices caused by irregular foreign competition.

Two-thirds of the fish taken in the Gulf are menhaden, but their value is comparatively small. Oyster fishing is carried on in almost every bay and lagoon along the coast. Red snapper is a favorite food fish for restaurants, and mullet and crabs are caught in considerable quantity.

Sport Fishing Sport fishing has assumed great significance all along the Gulf Coast, and is particularly important in Florida waters where it has taken on the proportions of a multimillion dollar industry. The chief game fishes include the tarpon, shark, and sailfish, most of which have no food value.

Trapping

Several Gulf Coast areas produce furs, including mink, otter, skunk, muskrat, and nutria. The swamps of southern Louisiana provide the best home for muskrats, and nearly three-fourths of Anglo-America's supply is trapped here even though the area has relatively mild winters.

The trapper at the end of the day returns to his cabin in the marshes with his load of muskrats. He skins them and hangs their pelts on a rack by the side of the house to dry. Fur buyers visit these trappers, select and grade the furs they wish to buy, and pay cash for the pelts.

The muskrat is extremely prolific, and there seems to be little danger of extermination, despite the average catch of more than six million a year. Mink and otter are trapped to some extent in Louisiana, but the total value of their peltries does not equal that of the muskrat.

Nutria, originally imported from South America, are larger than muskrats and hence their pelts bring a higher price. They are multiplying rapidly and may some day replace the muskrat in the Gulf Coast fur industry.

Lumbering and Forest-Products Industries

Except for the prairie sections of east Texas and Louisiana, and the Florida Everglades, most of this region was originally forest-covered. Accordingly, such forest products as lumber and pulpwood have been important. These have been discussed in the previous chapter. The picture in this region is similar to that in the Cotton Belt, with the additional fact that some of the larger pulp mills have tidewater sites, as at Mobile and Houston.

Another forest product that is of only minor significance in the Cotton Belt but of major importance in the Humid Subtropical Coast is naval stores. These are the tar and pitch that were used before the advent of metal ships to calk seams and preserve ropes of wooden vessels. They come from the South Atlantic coastal area. When it was discovered that turpentine and resin could be distilled from the gum of southern yellow pine, many new uses were found for these products—as in paints, soaps, shoe dressing, and medicine.

The normal method of obtaining resin is to slash a tree and let the gum ooze into a detachable cup that can be emptied from time to time (Figure 8-9). A more recently developed method that is in great favor is to shred and grind stumps and dead branches (formerly considered as waste) and put them through a steam-distillation process. A considerable amount of naval stores also is obtained as by-products from the sulphate process of papermaking.

Extensive forests and high-yielding spe-

Figure 8-9. Extracting naval stores from southern yellow pines in Lowndes County, Georgia. The resin drips out of a slash in the tree, and is caught in a metal container. It is then scraped into barrels and taken to a processing station. (Photo courtesy U. S. Forest Service.)

cies of trees permit this region to produce more than half of the world's resin and turpentine. The principal area of production is around Valdosta in southern Georgia and adjacent portions of northern Florida.

Mineral Industries

Phosphate Rock Florida is Anglo-America's most important producer of phosphate rock, accounting for nearly 90 per cent of the total. A little hard rock phosphate is dug, but most of the production comes from unconsolidated land-pebble phosphate deposits east of Tampa Bay. There are 14 mines, all open-pit, in Polk and Hillsborough counties. The deposits average about 30 feet thick and have 5 to 20 feet of overburden. Large holes (often ponded because of the high water table), spoils banks, and considerable smoke from the processing plants (a council on air-pollution control has been established) are characteristic landscape features in the mining area. Phosphate mining began in 1888 in Florida, and there are still abundant reserves. Most of the output is used in fertilizer manufacture.

Sulfur Coastal Louisiana and Texas produce more than 90 per cent of the continent's native sulfur. The deposits are found in the cap rock overlying certain salt domes;

most of the domes however, do not contain sulfur in paying quantities. Although sulfur (brimstone) is found at moderate depths 500 to 1,500 feet below ground, commercial exploitation by shaft mining proved unsuccessful, because of danger from cave-in of the overlying sands and gravels. When the Frasch process was perfected in 1903, commercial success was assured, and the Gulf Coast soon took first rank among the world's sulfur-producing regions.

The Frasch process is based on the fact that crystalline sulfur melts at 240° F., only slightly above the boiling point of water. Wells are drilled into the deposits on top of the salt plugs. Superheated water is pumped into the deposit, and the sulfur is converted into a liquid. Compressed air is used to force the molten material to the surface (Figure 8-10). The pipes are heated to prevent the sulfur from solidifying until it reaches the vats on the surface. The vats, constructed of wood or of steel sheeting, are 1,200 feet long, 50 feet high, and 160 to 200 feet wide. The molten sulfur solidifies immediately upon being poured into the vat. When the gigantic bin is filled, the sides are stripped off, exposing a huge block which can be blasted. The fragments of almost chemically pure sulfur are loaded into open freight cars by power shovels and

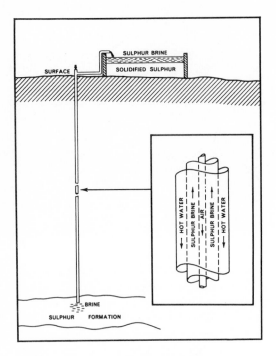

Figure 8-10. Generalized diagram of the Frasch Process. A well is drilled down to the sulfur formation and three concentric pipes are inserted into the hole. Hot water is forced down one pipe and compressed air down another. The water melts the sulfur and the resulting brine is forced back up the third pipe to the surface, where it is stored and allowed to solidify before shipping.

hauled to the shipping port, to be loaded on coastwise or ocean vessels for the large industrial consuming markets. A considerable amount of sulfur is shipped by barge up the Mississippi River system to the cities of the interior. A recent innovation, which is becoming more common, is the transport of sulfur to the processing plant in molten form by specially constructed pipelines or boats. Less than 10 per cent of the 230 known salt domes have been productive by the Frasch process,[7] and it is not anticipated

[7] Bureau of Mines, *Mineral Facts and Problems* (Washington: Government Printing Office, 1960), p. 825.

that other productive domes will be discovered on the Gulf Coastal Plain. In offshore waters, however, there are undoubtedly great reserves. The first offshore dome went into production seven miles from the Louisiana coast in 1960. Molten sulfur is taken by heated pipeline to the port of Grand Isle, then transshipped by tanker to Port Sulphur.

Some sulfur is used in elemental form in the manufacture of rubber and insecticides, and a large tonnage is converted into sulfur compounds for use in making such products as paper pulp. Most of the total supply, however, is converted into sulfuric acid which is then used to manufacture fertilizers, industrial chemicals, paints and pigments, and for petroleum refining.

The sulfur industry of the Louisiana-Texas Gulf Coast is one of Anglo-America's major mineral industries. Nearly two-thirds of the total world output of native sulfur is produced here, although foreign competition is increasing.

Salt The entire region from Alabama westward is underlaid by deposits of rock salt. The deposits occur mostly in salt domes of almost pure sodium chloride. Mining is limited to Louisiana and Texas, which are among the four leading salt-mining states in the nation. The reserves are enormous. Though only a few domes are being mined in the region at present, they are producing great quantities of salt, and none is approaching exhaustion.

The mine usually lies at the top of the salt dome, 600 feet or more below the surface. A shaft is driven down and large chambers are excavated. Mine props do not have to be used, because large supporting columns of salt are left in place. The chambers are sometimes more than 100 feet high. Some salt is extracted in brine solution by a modified Frasch process. While the Gulf Coast has no monopoly in salt production, it has sufficient reserves to make it an important producer for a very long time. There are many known salt domes (some of them now producing petroleum or sulfur) where salt can be obtained when needed.

Shells Although oyster and clam shells have been used for many years as a road-building material, the big development in this industry did not begin until the heavy chemical industry started its phenomenal growth in the 1940's. Today, one sees large mounds of gray, gravelly material piled up at many industrial establishments, which are oyster shells which have been dredged from the shallow bays along the Gulf Coast. With the nearest source of limestone in Texas more than 200 miles from the coast, oyster shells from dead reefs provide industry with a cheap and abundant supply of lime. Lone Star Cement opened its Houston plant in 1916 using oyster shells in place of limestone for fluxing, and in 1934 Southern Alkali Corporation of Corpus Christi began using shells as a source of lime for their process. Today shells provide road ballast as well as raw materials for making lime and cement at many coastal factories. The chief dead oyster reefs being dredged today are in Atchafalaya Bay in Louisiana, and in Galveston, Matagorda, and Nueces bays in Texas.

Petroleum and Natural Gas

The Humid Subtropical Coast includes the entire area known as the Gulf Coast Petroleum Province, one of the continent's major oil producers. It normally yields about 20 per cent of the United States total flow. The oil fields, almost exclusively in salt domes, are scattered along the west Gulf Coastal Plain from the mouth of the Mississippi to the mouth of the Rio Grande (Figure 8-11). Numerous new discoveries are being made, and some fields have been developed in the shallow coastal margin of the Gulf of Mexico. This province not only

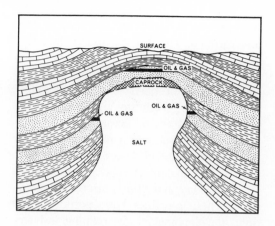

Figure 8-11. Generalized diagram of a salt dome, showing typical reservoirs of oil and gas.

holds the record for the first large gusher, but it also has the largest number of productive deep wells in the United States, some of which reach depths below 20,000 feet.

Following the discovery of oil at Spindletop, near Beaumont in 1901, many other fields in the Gulf Coast were opened. Geologists, however, found it difficult to locate possible oil structures, since no rock outcropped on the flat expanses of prairie, marsh, and forest lands. Some salt domes gave slight surface indications of their presence by forming small hills on the flat terrain, and they were drilled first. Further scientific prospecting was impossible until some means could be devised for discovering deeply buried plugs. Between 1901 and 1922, this region became a "wildcatter's paradise" for despite the crude methods of exploration employed, 39 of the 46 domes discovered during that period were producers.[8] During the 1920's, sophisticated geophysical prospecting devices and techniques were developed for detecting poten-

[8] Virginia Bradley, "The Petroleum Industry of the Gulf Coast Salt Dome Area," *Economic Geography*, Vol. 15 (July 1939), pp. 399-400.

tially productive structures that may be deep underground. This has expanded the scope of salt-dome discovery and exploitation considerably. Boats, "marsh buggies," and helicopters have all been useful in enabling technicians to penetrate and traverse the poorly drained coastal areas.

Since much crude oil is transported today by pipelines, the Gulf Coast port cities have become the termini of most pipelines from the Gulf Coast and Mid-continent Oil provinces. These pipelines have permitted the rapid development of the refining industry along the West Gulf Coast between Baton Rouge and Corpus Christi. Enormous quantities of both crude and refined petroleum are shipped also by tankers to the North Atlantic Seaboard and to foreign countries.

Continental Shelf   The Continental Shelf off the Gulf Coast is broad and shallow, and underlaid by geologic structures of the same types as those of the Coastal Plain. Accordingly, salt domes, with their associated petroleum, natural gas, and sulfur, are thought to be widespread in the "tidelands," as the shelf has come to be called. Many favorable structures have been discovered geophysically, and some wells have been sunk. Off-

shore drilling is quite expensive, averaging more than half a million dollars per well, largely because of the elaborate, self-contained drilling towers (Figure 8-12) that have to be anchored in place, sometimes miles from land.[9] Drilling, therefore, is never undertaken unless there is considerable assurance of success. As a result, relatively few offshore wells have been attempted—though a rapid increase saw more than 500 of them drilled in 1961—and the drilling success ratio has been about three times higher than that on land. Tidelands oil work has been slowed down by the protracted litigation between federal and state governments over ownership of the mineral rights. Ruling has been made in favor of state ownership out to the three-mile-limit,[10] but it is unlikely that the controversy has been finally settled. More than 95 per cent of the tidelands drilling so far has been off the Louisiana coast, and most of the few dozen wells attempted off the Texas coast have been unsuccessful.

[9] One well is 70 miles off the Louisiana coast, but the water is only 180 feet deep.
[10] Ten and one-half miles in the case of Texas and the Gulf Coast of Florida.

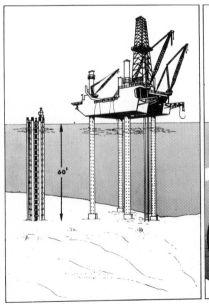 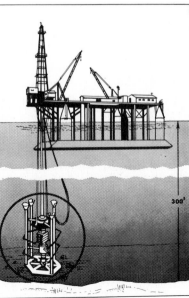

Figure 8-12. Two types of offshore oil-drilling rigs. The left diagram shows a conventional rig that rests on the sea bottom and can only be used in shallow water. The right diagram portrays a floating drilling vessel with a system for completing wells on the ocean floor by remote controls from the surface. (Courtesy Shell Oil Company.)

Natural Gas in the Humid Subtropical Region The Humid Subtropical Region contains one of the greatest producing areas and also one of the largest reserves of natural gas in the United States.

Conservation problems, however, are important. Although gas flares are still common, their numbers have been reduced considerably through the activities of the Texas Railroad Commission and the Louisiana Conservation Commission. Further reduction will be made when new laws are enacted which require a report on the disposal of gas from each well. Great quantities of gas are being piped to industrial and metropolitan areas in the North and East. As yet this represents surplus gas which is not needed locally. However, as industry continues to expand along the Gulf Coast and continues to use gas as a fuel and as a raw material for petrochemicals, greater demands will be made to keep the gas in the coastal area.

Manufacturing

Since the beginning of World War II, the Humid Subtropical Coast Region has advanced rapidly in industrial development. A few large industries moved in the 1930's to Mobile, New Orleans, Houston, and Corpus Christi, but the large-scale development came in the 1940's. Some advantages this region offered were (1) large supplies of basic minerals such as sulfur, salt, lime (oyster shells), magnesium (from sea water), and natural gas; (2) an abundant supply of natural gas for fuel; and (3) tidewater location to provide cheap ocean rates for bulky manufactured products. Other factors such as labor supply and availability of capital were also important, but they were of less significance in attracting industry.

The manufacturing industries of this region are of various types, but the major ones may be classified as:

1. *Food-products industries,* such as rice cleaners and processors, sugar refineries, and specialized processors of grain sorghums and flax.

2. *Wood-products industries,* including sawmills and pulp and paper mills.

3. *Refineries,* producing gasoline, lubricating oils, and similar products from petroleum and natural gas.

4. *Organic chemical industries,* which utilize petroleum and natural gas to produce such items as acetate salts, formaldehyde, nylon salts, and synthetic rubber.

5. *Inorganic chemical industries,* producing soda ash, caustic soda, chlorine, and sulfuric acid from salt and sulfur.

6. *Metallurgical industries,* extracting magnesium salt from sea water and refining it into metallic magnesium, or producing zinc, tin, and iron and steel from ores or concentrates imported largely from overseas.[11]

All these types of industries represent an outlay of more than a billion dollars—some of it private capital invested before World War II, much of it government money spent on war plants now operating under private control, and an increasing amount of it postwar investment by private capital from other parts of the United States.

The first three classes of industries have been considered with agricultural production, forest products, or minerals, and hence only two of these types will be discussed here. Space limitations prohibit any detailed analysis of the many large industries under each class, so for brevity only one type illustration will be given.

The Petrochemical Industries The demand for aviation gasoline has revolutionized petroleum refining and indirectly created many new-products industries. Along the west Gulf Coast in the early 1940's,

[11] Edwin J. Foscue, "Industrialization of the Texas Gulf Coast Region," *Southwestern Social Science Quarterly,* Vol. 31 (January 1950), pp. 7-8.

Figure 8-13. Aerial view of a part of the Humble Oil & Refining Company's plant at Baytown, Texas, The principal product from this portion of the installation is synthetic rubber. (Photo courtesy Roy M. Huffington and the Humble Oil & Refining Company.)

leading oil companies built subsidiary plants to process the by-products of aviation gasoline. Included were butadiene plants for the manufacture of synthetic rubber (Figure 8-13), toluene plants for the manufacture of a basic ingredient for trinitrotoluene (TNT), and many others. Recycling plants that "strip" natural gas of gasoline, butane, and other hydrocarbons, also were established. Another important industrial product made from natural gas is carbon black, about 80 per cent of which is produced by Texas, although not all of this comes from the coastal region.

As a result of these by-product industries, an entirely new group of industries, known as petrochemicals, has developed which produce an amazing number of synthetic products from oil and natural gas—chiefly the latter.

Although the industry is concentrated in five areas along the coast, (1) Baton Rouge, (2) Lake Charles, (3) Port Arthur—Port Neches—Beaumont, (4) Texas City—Freeport, and (5) Houston (Figure 8-1), many petrochemical plants are scattered through the region from Baton Rouge on the east to Brownsville on the southwest. One of the largest and most interesting of the petrochemical plants is the industrial establish-

ment of the Celanese Corporation of America at Bishop, some 45 miles southwest of Corpus Christi.

As early as 1932 the Celanese Corporation, one of the three largest producers of rayon yarns in the United States, began a research program to develop a process of securing acetic acid from natural gas. The company felt this was essential in order to have an unlimited supply of this basic raw material for its process. By 1941 the process was developed well enough so that a small plant was established at Cumberland, Maryland. Then came World War II and with it a demand by the War Production Board for rapid expansion of the process to supply additional products—particularly butadiene for the synthetic rubber and chemical programs. Accordingly, Celanese built its plant at Bishop, near large supplies of natural gas. Construction was started in 1944 and completed the next year, and initial operation began in April, 1945. The war ended before the Bishop plant got into the production of butadiene, but with slight alterations the entire establishment was converted to manufacture acetic acid and acetone, the two chief chemicals required in the production of cellulose acetate.

Some 200,000 gallons of propane and

butane (from natural gas) are required daily to supply the plant with its basic raw materials. These are piped largely from the La Gloria Field about 25 miles to the southwest. In addition this field furnishes 40 million cubic feet of dry gas (methane) per day for fuel to drive the compressors. Water needed in the process is piped from the Nueces River about 26 miles away. The 550-acre industrial site provides ample open space for long-range expansion.

Acetic acid and acetone, the two major chemicals produced at Bishop, are consumed entirely by company plants in the manufacture of textiles and plastics, which are marketed as Celanese products. In addition, a number of other chemical products, including formaldehyde, methyl alcohol, and propyl alcohol, are sold to outside organizations for the production of textiles, plastics, solvents, and antifreeze mixtures. All products are shipped from the Bishop plant in specially designed railroad tank cars and move either directly by rail to the ultimate consumer or by rail and water. In spite of a high degree of mechanization, nearly a thousand men are employed at the plant.

Metallic Industries For a long time the lack of a suitable coking coal prohibited the development of an iron and steel industry along the Gulf Coast, although low-grade brown iron ores from East Texas were available and there were ample supplies of scrap in the Gulf Southwest. Lime from limestone or from oyster shells was also available. The first plant was not constructed, however, until 1942, when Sheffield Steel, a subsidiary of Armco Steel Corporation, opened a large mill on the Houston Ship Channel. This plant has been enlarged several times and today uses scrap, east Texas ores, and some high-grade ores from Brazil.

The Gulf Coast area has had a locational advantage with regard to alumina plants, since most of our supply of bauxite comes from northern South America or from the West Indies. The first plant of this type was constructed by Alcoa at Mobile. Just prior to World War II, a similar plant was built at Baton Rouge by the government but was sold to the Kaiser interests after the war. Increasing demands for metallic aluminum caused a revolution in the industry. During the war period a number of aluminum plants were located on the West Coast. With the cessation of hostilities, however, Reynolds Metal Company and Kaiser Aluminum Company began expansion programs, locating some of their new plants on the Gulf Coast to utilize natural gas as a fuel for generating electricity needed in the reduction of the ore. Alcoa also expanded its production in the Gulf Coast area by constructing a plant at Point Comfort near Port Lavaca, Texas. In a short time, Reynolds built two large units on Corpus Christi Bay, utilizing natural gas as a fuel. The alumina plant is securing its supply of bauxite from newly discovered deposits in Jamaica, and the adjacent refinery is converting the alumina to metallic aluminum. After purchasing the reduction plant at Baton Rouge, the Kaiser interests built a large aluminum metal refinery in New Orleans, thereby establishing another completely integrated industry on the Gulf Coast in two cities less than 100 miles apart. More than three-quarters of the alumina production and about 20 per cent of the metallic aluminum reduction in the United States is now located in this region (Figure 8-14).

Numerous other metal industries are located along the coast primarily because of cheap fuel and cheap water transportation. In practically every case the ore is imported from overseas or from inland domestic sources. The only exception is the magnesium plant of Dow Chemical Company at Freeport, Texas, where metallic magnesium is extracted from salts dissolved in the waters of the Gulf of Mexico.

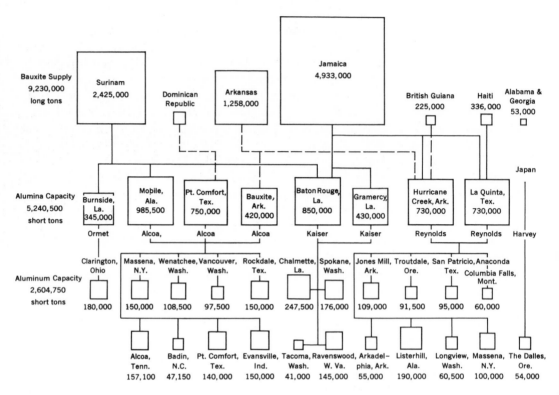

Figure 8-14. Generalized flow diagram showing aluminum production in the United States. The top level represents raw material supply, the second level represents alumina plants, and the two bottom levels represent metallic aluminum plants. (Adapted from Bureau of Mines, *Mineral Facts and Problems,* 1960 ed., p. 17. Washington: Government Printing Office, 1960.)

Industrial Centers On the Texas coast between Texas City and Bishop there are many large factories in scattered locations, often some distance from the nearest town of any size. Only in *Corpus Christi* is there any concentration of plants. In other parts of the Humid Subtropical Coast Region, however, manufacturing facilities tend to be clustered in isolated nodes, normally in association with the larger urban areas. *Houston* is the largest city in the entire South, as well as its major commercial and industrial center. The extreme importance of petroleum in Houston's economy is shown by the fact that three of the four leading industries in the metropolitan area are asso-

ciated with it—petroleum refining, petrochemical production, and manufacture of oil-field machinery and equipment.[12] Most of the larger factories are located on the banks of the winding, dredged Houston Ship Channel. Nearby smaller centers of industrial significance are *Baytown* and *Texas City.* The extreme southeastern corner of Texas is an area of major industrial activity. It is the leading oil refining center in Anglo-America, and other industries of importance include wood products and rice

[12] Tom L. McKnight, "Distribution of Manufacturing in Texas," *Annals of the Association of American Geographers,* Vol. 47 (December 1957), p. 376.

Figure 8-15. The industrial complex of Baton Rouge, a leading petroleum refining and petrochemical center. The state capitol is in the foreground, with the Mississippi River in the left background. (Photo courtesy Baton Rouge Chamber of Commerce.)

milling at *Beaumont,* petrochemicals at *Port Arthur* and *Port Neches,* and shipbuilding at *Orange. Baton Rouge* is a beehive of petrochemical activity and petroleum refining, and has the second largest alumina reduction works in the nation (Figure 8-15). *New Orleans,* second most populous city in the region, is not heavily industrialized. Food processing and textiles are its leading manufacturing industries. *Mobile* has a few large plants of major significance. Papermaking, shipbuilding, and alumina reduction are notable. There has been a recent upsurge of industrial activity in the eastern Gulf Coast, particularly in such places as *Orlando, Pensacola,* and *Tampa.* Specialized industries of note include cigarmaking at *Tampa* and shipbuilding at *Charleston.*

Resorts

The Humid Subtropical Coast is one of the major resort regions of Anglo-America. In addition to Florida, the coast of Mississippi, the Sea Island section of Georgia, and to a lesser extent the Texas coast, have a resort business which is increasing in importance. The entire coast of Mississippi from Pascagoula to Bay St. Louis is almost a continuous resort town. Principal resort areas in Texas focus on Galveston, Corpus Christi, and parts of Padre Island.

Florida Resorts The resort industry is of great importance throughout Florida. In the southern half of the state it flourishes primarily in the winter, with a secondary, smaller peak in the summer; while in the northern half business is greatest in the summer. Winter tourists begin coming in large numbers about the middle of January, increase steadily until the last of February, and begin to leave soon after the first of March.

Visitors come from practically every state and from many foreign countries, but the majority are urban dwellers from east of the Mississippi and north of the Ohio and Potomac rivers. They come in all kinds of conveyances—steam yachts, airplanes, streamlined trains, busses, and automobiles.

Toward the close of the nineteenth century Henry M. Flagler built a large modern hotel (The Ponce de Leon) at St. Augustine and made plans for others along the east coast. He also built the Florida East Coast Railroad to Palm Beach, Miami, and ultimately to Key West—more than 100 miles beyond the end of the peninsula. The tourist industry in Florida has experienced more

Figure 8-16. Miami Beach, an all-year vacation resort, stretches for ten miles along the Atlantic Ocean. (Photo courtesy Miami Beach News Bureau.)

than one major setback, and is still over-extended at times, but is now solidly based and is the most important revenue-producing activity in the state. The principal concentration of resorts is along the southeastern coast, focusing upon the extravagant hostelries of Miami Beach (Figure 8-16), but extending as far north as Palm Beach. Peripheral attractions include Everglades National Park, the various islands of the Keys, and tourist-oriented Seminole Indian settlements.

Other east coast resort centers are at Cocoa Beach (good swimming and nearness to Cape Canaveral spacecraft launching sites) and St. Augustine-Jacksonville (swimming, fishing, and historical interest).

The west coast has developed considerable tourist business, but on a smaller scale. The principal center is the Tampa-St. Petersburg-Bradenton-Clearwater-Sarasota complex, which attracts many retired people as well as resorters. The Panama City area in the panhandle has probably the finest beaches in the state, though it is lacking in surf.

Interior tourist centers, of which there are many, are mostly founded on special water features, such as clear springs, abundant fish life, or special water shows.

Transportation and Commerce

The Humid Subtropical Coast has a number of important ports, including Charleston, Savannah, Jacksonville, Miami, Tampa, Mobile, New Orleans, Lake Charles, Beaumont, Orange, Port Arthur, Galveston, Houston, Corpus Christi, and Brownsville. These, in varying degrees, carry on an important coastal and overseas trade for this region and also for the Cotton Belt. Houston is one of the outstanding ports of the continent, normally ranking second only to New York in tonnage handled. It is primarily an export port, shipping oil, cotton, grains, and other bulky items, mostly in coastwise traffic. Houston's access to the Gulf is via a 50-mile-long dredged channel. Galveston is somewhat hampered by an island location but nevertheless is a major shipper of cotton, sulfur, and wheat. New Orleans, although more than 100 miles from the Gulf, is favorably situated for serving the great interior hinterland of the nation. It is particularly significant as a receiving port for such Latin-American exports as sugar, bananas, coffee, and sisal.

Rivers, particularly the Mississippi and Tombigbee, have played an important role in transporting freight from the interior to Gulf Coast ports, and coastal waterways have grown in importance in recent years.

The Intracoastal Waterway was originally planned to extend from New York to Brownsville as a continuous channel, utilizing lagoons behind barrier beaches where possible, and cutting through the coastal plain where necessary. The link across northern Florida was never completed. One part of the canal, relatively little used, now runs down the east coast as far as Key West and another begins in western Florida and extends to Brownsville. Between Mobile Bay and New Orleans, and between New Orleans and Galveston Bay, considerable heavy barge traffic traverses the canal, which is linked with the Mississippi River system. Southwest of Galveston some traffic moves to Corpus Christi, but little goes beyond that point. Canal links connect with New Orleans and Baton Rouge, but Morgan City is the principal crossroads of east-west and north-south traffic.

Railway transportation in the region is mostly of the port-serving type, the routes generally extending northward into the interior. New Orleans is the major terminus, with direct-line connections to Chicago via the Illinois Central and to California via the Southern Pacific.

Roadways form a more complete network, except in some of the swampy areas and in the sandhill country of south Texas. Outstanding highways of the region include the four-lane, divided "Gulf Freeway" between Houston and Galveston; the Tamiami Trail connecting Fort Myers with Miami across the Everglades; the Overseas Highway to Key West, which has replaced the original Flagler railway; U.S. Highway #1, the principal tourist route, extending the length of east coastal Florida; and the Sunshine State Parkway, the modern and costly toll road extending northward from Miami.

Air transportation is also well developed. The three major air terminals, Houston, New Orleans, and Miami, are outstanding international air hubs.

Most large petroleum refineries are located on tidewater. Mid-Continent and Gulf Coastal oil fields are connected with Gulf ports by a maze of pipelines, through which flows a major part of the petroleum from southwestern fields, as well as considerable quantities of refined gasoline. Practically all crude oil that is not refined at Gulf ports is shipped by tanker either to eastern seaboard cities or overseas.

The Outlook

The Humid Subtropical Coast Region remained one of the most backward parts of Anglo-America until almost the beginning of the present century. Prior to 1900 its chief activities were forest exploitation, agriculture, and ranching. The few badly run-down ports were in need of modernization.

With the discovery of oil at Spindletop, and the development of phosphate, sulfur, salt, and lime (oyster shells), the coastal region began to attract industry, although no major development took place until the 1940's. In this region industry has found a favorable habitat.

In addition to deep water, the Gulf Coast offers many advantages to certain classes of industry. During times of peace, it is superior as an industrial region in some respects to either the Atlantic Coast or the Pacific Coast, but in times of war it has the additional advantage of being the most remote and hence the least vulnerable of our three coastal areas from an aerial attack by a possible transpolar enemy.

Few parts of Anglo-America present a brighter outlook for manufacturing than this Humid Subtropical Coast, where one finds the world's most extensive industrialization of a subtropical region. Specialized farming will continue to occupy an important place in the economy; forestry, mineral extraction, and cattle raising are likely to become more important; and commerce will expand as the population increases; but continued industrial growth will be the major stimulus to the economy in most parts of the region.

The attractions of mild winters and out-door living have brought this region the second fastest rate of population growth on the continent, as newcomers flock in to visit, to work, or to retire, especially in Florida. Rapid population growth and a continu-ally-expanding tourist trade will be major elements in the economic and social geog-raphy of the region for some time to come.

TABLE 7

Selected Cities and Towns of the Humid Subtropical Coast

City or Town	Urbanized Area	Political Center
Baton Rouge	193,485	152,419
Beaumont	119,178	119,175
Biloxi		44,053
Brownsville		48,040
Charleston	160,113	65,925
Clearwater		34,653
Coral Gables		34,793
Corpus Christi	177,380	167,690
Daytona Beach		37,395
Fort Lauderdale	319,951	83,648
Galveston	118,482	67,175
Gulfport		30,204
Harlingen	61,658	41,207
Hialeah		66,972
Houston	1,139,678	938,219
Jacksonville	372,569	201,030
Key West		33,956
Lafayette		40,400
Lake Charles	89,115	63,392
Lakeland		41,350
Miami	852,705	291,688
Miami Beach		63,145
New Orleans	845,237	627,525
Orlando	200,995	88,135
Panama City		33,275
Pasadena		58,737
Pensacola	128,049	56,752
Port Arthur	116,365	66,676
Prichard		47,371
St. Petersburg	324,842	181,298
Sarasota		34,083
Savannah	169,887	149,245
Tallahassee		48,174
Tampa	301,790	274,970
Texas City		32,065
Valdosta		30,652
West Palm Beach	172,835	56,208
Wilmington		44,013

Selected Bibliography

Alliston, James R., "Industry's Golden Strip," *New Orleans Port Record,* March 1959, pp. 26-30.

"Baton Rouge to the Gulf," *Fortune,* January 1961, pp. 104-114.

Camp, A. T., R. C. Evans, and L. G. Mc-Dowell, *Citrus Industry of Florida.* Tallahas-see: Florida Department of Agriculture, 1954.

Carson, Robe B., "The Florida Tropics," *Eco-nomic Geography,* Vol. 27, 1951, pp. 321-339.

Finch, L. Boyd, "The Florida Swamp That Swallows Your Money," *Harper's,* February 1959, pp. 77-82.

Foscue, Edwin J., "Industrialization of the Texas Gulf Coast Region," *Southwestern So-cial Science Quarterly,* Vol. 31, 1950, pp. 1-18.

———, "The Ports of Texas and Their Hinter-lands," *Tijdschrift Voor Economische en Sociale Geografie,* Vol. 48, January 1957, pp. 1-14.

Jensen, James E., "The Continental Shelf—a Petroleum Frontier," *Business Review,* Fed-eral Reserve Bank of Dallas, Vol. 43, May 1958, pp. 1-6.

Lounsbury, John F., "Recent Developments in the Aluminum Industry of the United States," *Journal of Geography,* Vol. 61, March 1962, pp. 97-104.

Madigan, La Verne, "The Most Independent People . . . ," *Indian Affairs,* No. 31, April 1959.

Parsons, James J., "Recent Industrial Develop-ment in the Gulf South," *Geographical Re-view,* Vol. 40, 1950, pp. 67-83.

Post, Lauren C., "The Old Cattle Industry of Southwest Louisiana," *The McNeese Re-view,* Vol. 9, Winter 1957, pp. 43-55.

Schlesselman, G. W., "The Gulf Coast Oyster Industry of the United States," *Geographical Review,* Vol. 45, October 1955, pp. 531-541.

Stephen, L. LeMar, "Geographical Role of the Everglades in the Early History of Florida," *Scientific Monthly,* Vol. 55, 1942, pp. 515-526.

"The Houston Complex," *Fortune,* February 1958, pp. 125-133.

Ziegler, John M., "Origin of the Sea Islands of Southeastern United States," *Geographical Review,* Vol. 49, April 1959, pp. 222-237.

chapter nine

The Agricultural
Interior

The world's greatest storehouse of farming wealth, a region ideally fashioned by nature to become the home of a thriving population is the Agricultural Interior (Figure 9-1). It produces more corn and oats and meat than any other area of equal size. It also produces much hay, winter wheat, barley, soybeans, tobacco, fruits, vegetables and dairy products. During World War II, it served as the bread basket of the United Nations. The Agricultural Interior falls al-most wholly within the United States. Canada has no agricultural Middle West; instead it has the inhospitable Canadian Shield, which does not give way to arable lands until it meets the Manitoba Basin. Even so, a large proportion of Canada's general farming and a considerable share of its population are to be found in the relatively small portion of Canada included in this region.

The influence of the Agricultural Interior

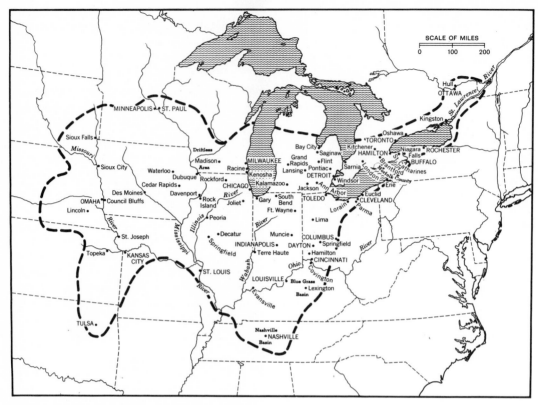

Figure 9-1. The Agricultural Interior. A region of prosperous agriculture and important industrial enterprises. The "core" of the region is the Corn Belt.

on the United States politically, economically, and socially cannot be overestimated. Of all the regions in Anglo-America, this one is indisputably the most self-contained and independent. It is basically agricultural, although its eastern half overlaps the western portion of the American Manufacturing Region, and thus encompasses a major share of the industrial activity of both the United States and Canada.

Boundaries

The Agricultural Interior occupies only part of the vast interior plain of North America; it is set off from adjoining regions to the west and north by rather indefinite boundaries that have been shifting because of improved strains of corn (hybrid), earlier maturing and drought-tolerant varieties of

grains, new methods of tillage, and moisture conservation.

On the west the region merges with the Great Plains; scanty rainfall separates the prairie margin from the short-grass country of the Great Plains at about the 98th meridian. Here precipitation is inadequate for the profitable production of corn, except in eastern Colorado, and the crop tends to be replaced by those that are more drought-resistant. On the east lies the rugged Allegheny Plateau with its prevalence of relatively infertile sandstone and shale soils which produce little corn for sale (Figure 9-2); here livestock, particularly sheep, dominate the agriculture. On the north lie the Northern Continental Forest, characterized by the relatively infertile soils of the Canadian Shield and a less important agri-

214

culture, and the Spring Wheat Subregion, which is now in a stage of transition from wheat growing to dairying. On the southwest, it is bordered by the Cotton Belt, the Ozark-Ouachita Uplands, and the Hard Winter Wheat Subregion. This last boundary is drawn where the rainfall and hot summer winds favor the growth of wheat and grain sorghums instead of corn.

The Subregions

The Agricultural Interior, despite its homogeneity, falls into several subregions— the Corn Belt, the Corn and Winter Wheat Belt, the Hay and Dairy Subregion, and the Tobacco and General Farming Subregion.

The presence of these subregions within a universally recognized region, such as the Agricultural Interior, indicates that even the most closely knit region is but relatively homogeneous.

Appearance of the Region

There is a certain similarity in the landscape from boundary to boundary; but similarity here is not synonymous with absolute uniformity. The best way to get the "feel" of this region is to fly over it—particularly in late spring. The landscape then unrolls like a map and it is a beautiful sight. The flat to undulating terrain is laid out in squares and looks like a checkerboard (Figure 9-3). The roads are laid out at right angles and mostly cross at one-mile intervals. Here are deep green fields of winter wheat, pale green pastures, and still paler green blocks of oats just coming through the earth; and there lie squares—

Figure 9-2. Corn acreage. Corn is the great American cereal, and the Agricultural Interior grows the bulk of it. The Corn Belt Subregion alone produces nearly one-half the national total.

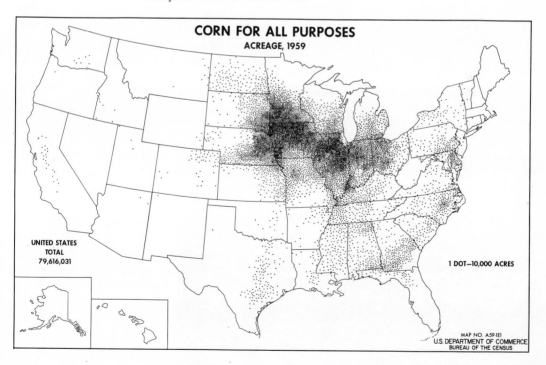

CORN FOR ALL PURPOSES
ACREAGE, 1959

UNITED STATES
TOTAL
79,616,031

1 DOT—10,000 ACRES

MAP NO. A59-1E1
U.S. DEPARTMENT OF COMMERCE
BUREAU OF THE CENSUS

black, brown, and tan (depending on the type of soil)—plowed and ready to be planted to the ubiquitous corn. Most of the land is under cultivation with very little in forest or wood lot.

The farms, as a result of the system of homesteading, contain about 160 acres or one-quarter of a square mile; a few are smaller, and the number of larger ones is increasing. For the most part, the larger ones are to be found on former prairies, the smaller ones on former wooded areas. Everywhere, however, the tendency is for greater size. Many small part-time farms are near the cities. In the cattle-producing portions, the buildings consist of large barns, often painted red, and small houses. The farmhouses suffer in comparison with the architectural gems of New England, New York, eastern Pennsylvania, and Maryland, but the total farmstead is large and impressive. The farmhouse, normally ringed with trees, is dwarfed by the large, imposing, and generally well-kept barns, corn cribs, silos, machine sheds, chicken houses, and other outbuildings.

The Physical Setting

Few, if any, large agricultural regions in the world have a more favorable combination of climate, terrain, and soils, or had a superior cover of natural vegetation.

Climate As a result of interior location, the area has a humid continental climate (mostly long summer phase), which is characterized by a wide range of temperature. Winter temperatures have fallen as low as −40° F., whereas those of summer have soared as high as 110° F. Summers are nearly always hot; even the nights are warm. Winters, especially in the western and northern parts, are severe though changeable. Because winter temperatures are mostly below freezing in the northern part of the region, there is a minimum of soil leaching; in the southern part, where freezing and thawing occur daily, the reverse is true. In pioneer days, winter storms (blizzards) were things of terror, but with coal, petroleum, and natural gas for fuel, closed automobiles, cleared roads, and better houses, this is no longer true.

The growing season is long—about 140 days along the northern border and 200 along the southern.

Precipitation varies between the east and west boundaries, being about 18 inches near the western boundary and 40 at the eastern border. Rain falls during every month in the year, with the maximum in

Figure 9-3. Characteristic checkerboard arrangement of fields over the interminable acres of the Corn Belt. The farms here are more closely spaced than those in the wheat regions to the west and northwest. Note the village in the foreground and the straight roads. (Photo courtesy of the *Daily Pantagraph,* Bloomington, Illinois.)

spring and early summer; about three-fourths of the rain falls in the frostless season—a significant factor in a great agricultural region. Summer precipitation is predominantly of the thundershower type.

Thunderstorms, which travel in an easterly direction, are both harmful and beneficial, but the good they do far outweighs the bad. The value of such a storm depends on when it arrives: coming when crops are suffering from a prolonged dry, hot spell, a single thundershower may increase the average yield of corn several bushels per acre and hence be worth millions of dollars to the farmers of a given area.

Occasionally, severe summer droughts reduce crop yields and turn pastures brown.

In the northern part of this region, snow characterizes the winter precipitation. Although single snowfalls tend to disappear quickly enough, others follow so soon and regularly that the ground is covered practically all winter. Southward the precipitation falls either as rain or snow; the snow generally melts quickly.

Floods are so common in this region as to have become an accepted part of the natural spring and early summer environment for farmers living on the flood plains of the Mississippi, Missouri, Illinois, Ohio, Wabash, and other rivers. Sometimes they result from heavy spring rains falling on frozen ground, but often they happen because of prolonged rain with rapid runoff.

Terrain Most of the Agricultural Interior is a plain characterized by level to gently rolling land. Exceptions are the lands south of the limit of Wisconsin glaciation which are often quite hilly, the comparatively rugged Driftless Area, and the rims around the Blue Grass area and the Nashville Basin. The part known as the Corn Belt is topographically one of the best-suited agricultural areas in the world.

The physiographic uniformity is due in part to the nearly flat-lying rocks and to the fact that most of the region was invaded several times by ice during the glacial period (Figure 9-4). The glacier left lasting traces; it sometimes planed off the hilltops 100 feet or more and filled up old gorges and deep valleys, covering both with glacial drift often to a depth of 100 feet. The greater part of the Agricultural Interior is thus indebted in no small part to the ice age for its flat lands and productive soils.

In southwestern Wisconsin and adjacent Minnesota, Iowa, and Illinois lies the Driftless Area—an unglaciated island in a sea of glacial drift. Missed by the continental ice sheets, it differs from the surrounding territory both topographically and economically. In fact, its landscape is like that which existed before the glacier came, consisting mostly of low but steepsided hills.

The Kentucky Blue Grass area and the Nashville Basin have long been outstanding in the geography of the nation. They are areas of relatively smooth to undulating surface separated from each other by the hill country of eastern Kentucky.

Soils Nowhere else on the continent can be found a large area such as this that combines highly fertile soils with a humid climate. This combination is at its best in the region's kernel—the Corn Belt. The Blue Grass area and the Nashville Basin also are highly productive. Some of the soils, however, as in central Michigan and central Wisconsin, in the Driftless Area and in the Highland Rim of Kentucky and Tennessee, are far from rich.

Most of the region is characterized by gray-brown podzolic soils and prairie soils. While the former, which develop under deciduous forest in the milder of the humid continental climates, are among the best of the pedalfers, the fact that they are forest soils means that they are in general less productive than the dark-brown to black prairie soils. Nevertheless some of the forest soils, such as those in western Ohio and

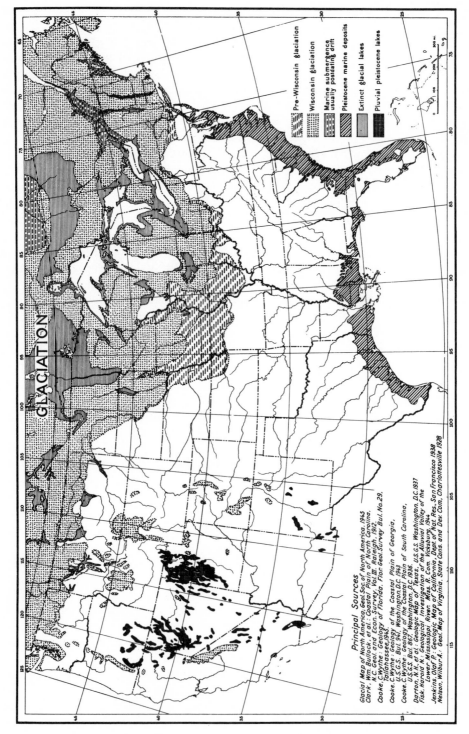

GLACIATION

Principal Sources

Glacial Map of North America. Geol. Soc. of North America. 1945
Clark, Wm. Bullock, et al.: Coastal Plain of North Carolina.
    N.C. Geol. and Econ. Survey, Vol. III. Raleigh, 1912.
Cooke, C. Wythe: Geology of Florida. Flor. Geol. Survey Bul. No. 29.
    Tallahassee, 1945.
Cooke, C. Wythe: Geology of the Coastal Plain of Georgia,
    U.S.G.S. Bul. 941. Washington, D.C. 1943.
Cooke, C. Wythe: Geology of the Coastal Plain of South Carolina,
    U.S.G.S. Bul. 867. Washington, D.C. 1936.
Darton, N.H., et al.: Geologic Map of Texas. U.S.G.S. Washington, D.C. 1937.
Fisk, Harold N.: Geological Investigation of the Alluvial Valley of the
    Lower Mississippi River. Miss. R. Com. Vicksburg, 1944.
Jenkins, Olaf P.: Geologic Map of California. Dept. of Nat. Res. San Francisco 1938
Nelson, Wilbur A.: Geol. Map of Virginia. State Cons. and Dev. Com. Charlottesville 1928

Pre-Wisconsin glaciation

Wisconsin glaciation

Marine submergence
usually postdating drift

Pleistocene marine deposits

Extinct glacial lakes

Pluvial pleistocene lakes

Figure 9-4. Conditions in the United States and southern Canada during the Pleistocene ("the Ice Age"). The continental ice sheets penetrated further south in the Agricultural Interior than anywhere else. Soils derived from glacial deposits in the Corn Belt generally are fertile. (Map prepared by Agricultural Research Service, U.S. Department of Agriculture.)

218

north-central Indiana, yield about as well per acre as the prairie soils. It may be said that forest soils which develop on calcareous till or on limestone, granite, gneiss, and schist are superior to those which evolve from shale and sandstone. All forest soils, however, are permanently leached, acid in reaction, and poor in humus.

The true prairie soils are generally fertile. They develop in cool, moderately humid climates under the influence of grass vegetation, are characterized by a dark-brown to black topsoil underlaid by well-oxidized subsoils. Being relatively well supplied with moisture, they are moderately leached and acid in reaction, and they lack a zone of lime accumulation. They are mostly silt loams and clay loams in texture and are derived largely from glacial till.

Much of the western part of the region is covered with *loess*, a fine wind-deposited material with a somewhat obscure origin that usually develops into fertile soils.

In summarizing, it may be said that: (1) most of the soils of east-central Minnesota, central Wisconsin, and the northwestern part of lower Michigan are too sandy for the profitable production of crops; these areas also have numerous deposits of peat and muck,[1] which without drainage are unsuited to growing crops; (2) the soils of the Corn Belt, of the Kentucky Blue Grass, of the Nashville Basin, and of western, southern, and eastern Wisconsin, southern Michigan, and southern Ontario, all in considerable part derived from limestone, are very fertile; (3) the soils of the Driftless Area and of the Highland Rim are of medium fertility.

[1] *Peat* is unconsolidated soil material consisting largely of undecomposed or slightly decomposed organic matter accumulated under conditions of excessive moisture. *Muck*, on the other hand, is fairly well decomposed organic soil material, relatively high in mineral content, dark in color, and accumulated under conditions of imperfect drainage.

It should be emphasized that there is a high degree of correlation between soils and types of farming in the Agricultural Interior. The kind of soil broadly determines the kind and quality of the crops that can be grown. Thus the Corn Belt coincides closely with the prairie soils, especially the dark-brown silt loams, and the principal dairy areas are found on the stony loam podzolic soils of the Hay and Dairy Subregion.

Natural Vegetation The Agricultural Interior's original vegetation consisted of forest and grass. The eastern part was forested; western Ohio, southern Michigan and Wisconsin, and southern and west-central Illinois all were a part of the oak-hickory southern hardwood forest, while the Kentucky Blue Grass and the Nashville Basin were a part of the chestnut, chestnut-oak, yellow-poplar southern hardwood forest.

The forest near the northern boundary of the region was characterized by conifers on the sandy soils and by magnificent stands of hardwoods on the clay lands; elsewhere the forest consisted wholly of hardwoods.

Southern Minnesota, all of Iowa, central Illinois, northern Missouri, eastern Nebraska and Kansas, and northeastern Oklahoma composed the prairie [2]—a vast billowy sea of virgin grass without timber except along the streams. It was *tall* grass with long blades and stiff stems, growing to a height of one to three feet and frequently six to eight feet. Men and horses could be lost in it. The trees growing along the streams were chiefly cottonwoods, oaks, and elms in the western portion, with occasional sycamores and walnuts farther east.

The true prairie extended from Illinois (small patches existed in western Ohio and northern Indiana) to about the 98th merid-

[2] The French, who had never seen such large areas of grassland, called them *prairies*, which in French means "large meadows."

ian, where it was gradually replaced by the short grass of the steppe. The boundaries of the prairie were never sharply defined. They were not the meeting place of two contrasted vegetation belts; rather were they broad mobile zones that moved with pronounced changes in precipitation. Many interesting theories for the origin of the prairie have been advanced, but none as yet has been wholly acceptable to botanists, plant ecologists, and plant geographers.[3]

Settlement

Settlement in the Agricultural Interior flowed from three fountainheads: (1) New England, whose Puritans came by way of the Mohawk Valley; (2) the South [4] whose frontiersmen broke through the mountains of Kentucky and Tennessee via Cumberland Gap,[5] and (3) Pennsylvania, whose Scotch-Irish and Germans came via Pittsburgh and the Ohio River country as well as by way of Cumberland Gap. Thus, whereas only a million Americans were living west of the Appalachians in 1800 (less than 50,000 of this total in Ontario), their numbers had increased by 1820 to 2,500,000 and by 1830 to 3,500,000. Settlement was by single families, scattered groups, or small companies.

European immigration is commonly divided into two groups: (1) that from northwestern Europe, consisting of English, Germans, Scandinavians, Bohemians, and Dutch—land-hungry people whose goal was to acquire a piece of unoccupied land that through tillage would insure a living; and (2) later immigrants—Poles and southern Europeans who settled largely in urban

centers in the eastern half of the region to become industrial workers.

The American pioneers, whose forbears had come from humid, forested Europe, had experience with forest rather than grassland. Hence when they met the prairie in their migration westward, they were surprised and puzzled by the fact that the land was clothed with grass rather than forest. They were even suspicious, reasoning that soils bearing no timber must be inferior. Hence for the most part they avoided the prairie. In 1836 Alby Smith, an Illinois pioneer, lost an election because the voters decided that anyone so stupid as to settle in the prairie should not be entrusted with the responsibilities of public confidence.[6]

The early settlers who took prairie land, took that which was contiguous to forest land, which they made the real base of the farm establishment. Several reasons have been advanced for the retarded settlement of the prairie, some of which apparently apply to different kinds of grassland: "wetness, difficulty in plowing grass sod, low degree of fertility, prevalence of disease, lack of water, of wood, of navigation, and of protection against the hazards of climate." [7] There was also the menace of prairie fires.

The taming of the prairie was not easy, for the iron plows then in use would not "scour" in the heavy soils and many of them broke. The soil stuck till the plow couldn't move in the furrow. The prairie was really not conquered until 1837, when John Deere, a blacksmith living in the tiny village of Grand Detour, Illinois, invented the steel plow.

In one respect the settlers were particularly fortunate; a British breed of beef

[3] James C. Malin, *The Grassland of North America* (Lawrence: University of Kansas Press, 1948), pp. 295-298.
[4] Virginia, Maryland, North Carolina and South Carolina.
[5] The absence of a strong Indian tribe at or near the western end of this gap accelerated the westward movement.
[6] Harlan H. Barrows, "Geography of the Middle Illinois Valley," *Illinois Geological Survey, Bulletin 15* (Urbana: 1910), p. 78.
[7] James C. Malin, "Ecology and History," *Scientific Monthly*, Vol. 70 (May 1950), pp. 47-54.

cattle, the Hereford, found the grassland environment so well suited to it that it ultimately dominated the entire area from Canada to Mexico.

The Present Occupance Of all the varied regions of the United States, the great ethnic mixing bowl, the most completely assimilated part of the continent is the Agricultural Interior. Here, through migration and westward movement, the first immigrants became in reality Americans rather than transplanted Europeans. The melting pot has melted most here—more in the western than in the eastern part and more in rural than in industrial areas. It was here that the challenge of opening up and settling a continent was first met. This blending of different peoples is also true in the Canadian portion of the region, though to a lesser degree. In any case, southern Ontario is Canada's largest area of fairly intensive land use, its density of settlement is high, and in general the occupance is on the grid pattern.

The population north of the Ohio River contains foreign as well as American stock, the principal nationality other than British in the rural communities probably being German. There are, however, large numbers of Bohemians, French, Poles, Scandinavians, and others. South of the Ohio the white stock is almost all native. The large Negro population, with its low standard of living, has discouraged European immigrants from settling there, because they were loath to accept the subordinate social status implied in manual employment. Lower wage rates have been a contributory factor also.

The average population density is higher in the eastern portion than farther west as a consequence of the many large cities and the smaller farms. The larger of these cities, however, owe their importance to the Great Lakes and to manufacturing rather than to agriculture.

Farming has become so highly mecha-

nized that all the children can no longer remain on farms. Hence large numbers of youths annually migrate to the cities and bolster up the low urban birth rate. It is estimated that one out of every three American urban workers comes from villages and farms. Despite the drop in farm population, however, production of crops and livestock steadily increases.

THE CULTURAL LANDSCAPE The Agricultural Interior is not static. In fact a veritable revolution is noted from census to census. Changes occur continuously in both the natural and cultural landscapes: soil erosion increases; farm woodlots are cut and the land used for crops; the original prairie has almost disappeared before the plow; and annual floods take their toll.

Farms, too, are becoming fewer in number but increasing in size. Technological advances in farm machinery, plant and animal breeding, and transport facilities all are altering the cultural landscape.

Education, religion, and social life have shared in the inevitable change. The rural school and the village church, in fact the village itself, all are changing.

Yet the Agricultural Interior is a farming region, and its fine farms still are the broad enduring base upon which much of the economy of the entire nation rests.

The Region's Political Power In National Affairs Probably no single region wields so much power in Washington as this one. During years of prosperity, when prices for agricultural commodities are high, life moves smoothly, and for this condition "the President residing in the White House . . . claims credit, even though the good times be due to rainfall in the Middle West." [8] During years of depression, however, or when lack of rain and burning sun bring small crops, or when a lavish nature gives too plentiful harvests with resultant

[8] William F. Ogburn, *Machines and Tomorrow's World* (New York: Public Affairs Committee, Inc., 1938), p. 3.

low prices, this region rumbles ominously. In times of low prices, political instability develops and people vote for him who promises the most. In recent years farms generally have yielded well; corn cribs have been filled to overflowing, elevators strained under burdens of wheat, and large herds of beef cattle and swine have dotted the landscape. Few economic or political panaceas contrived by man have not been tried out at some time.

Agriculture

The leading business is farming, for which the natural environment is highly favorable. The land is not too hilly or stony, the precipitation is generally adequate for all crops, the growing season is sufficiently long to mature all products save those needing more than six months free from killing frost, and the soil is generally fertile. But even though agriculture dominates, no simple system of farming such as once characterized the Cotton Belt exists.

Throughout the greater part of this region the country appears to be under complete cultivation, with four or five farmsteads to each square mile in the eastern portion, and two or three in the western portion. The farms are based on the subdivision of sections—half-sections, quarter-sections, and 40-acre plots. Corn, winter wheat, spring oats and hay are almost universal crops, with soybeans gaining annually in acreage. Tobacco and fruits are important locally, and much land is in pasture. The region not only grows tilled crops but supports the densest population of cattle and swine in Anglo-America.

Systems of Farming Mixed farming characterizes much of the region, with a major emphasis on corn in nearly all parts. Since the climatic range of corn on a commercial basis is more restricted than that of other crops grown, it nearly always gets first choice of the land. Corn is a very pro-

ductive crop, yielding two, three, or more times as much value per acre as wheat and oats. Corn yields the largest money return of any of the cereals. Other crops are grown (1) to equalize the seasonal distribution of labor, (2) to provide balanced feed for livestock, and (3) to improve the soil—the rotation preferably including a legume.

The most widely used rotation consists of (1) a tilled crop, (2) a small grain, and (3) a legume or grass crop, grown in this order. On the choicest soils a five-year rotation is followed—(1) corn, (2) corn, (3) oats or soybeans, (4) winter wheat, and (5) clover.

The flat to undulating land which favors the use of labor-saving machines has contributed much to the formation of larger farms. By utilizing a great number of different kinds of machines, the larger acreage can be handled without additional labor.

The average farmworker today produces 2½ times as much as his counterpart of only a generation ago. That American agriculture, centered primarily in this region, has been revolutionized is indicated by the fact that more farm implements and techniques have been invented, discovered, or perfected in the past hundred years than during all the preceding centuries of human history.

Winter wheat dominates the subhumid western margin; spring wheat, the northwest border; hay and oats for dairy cattle, the cool moist northern border; tobacco, parts of Kentucky, Indiana, Wisconsin, Tennessee, Ohio, and Ontario. Fruits and vegetables are important on the light soil and lake-locked peninsulas of Michigan and Ontario.

In the southern part of the region, as a result of significant physiographical differences, no one or two crops predominate, though corn, wheat, and hay are most important. In several counties in the Nashville

Basin and the Blue Grass area, tobacco is the crop of greatest value.

Seven types of farming characterize the region:

DAIRY SUBREGION	1. *Dairy farms.* These contribute fresh milk for urban centers but also specialize in the production of butter, cheese, and canned milk.
CORN BELT	2. *Livestock farms.* More than one-third of all the farms in the Corn Belt Subregion are livestock farms which specialize in swine and beef cattle for meat.
	3. *Cash-grain farms.* Almost one-fifth of all the farms are cash-grain farms that specialize in the growing of corn, soybeans, and feed grains for cash sale.
	4. *General farms.* About one-fourth of all farms are regarded as general farms, which derive less than half their gross cash income from any one type of farming.
CORN AND WINTER WHEAT BELT	5. *Subsistence farms.* Two-fifths of the farms are of this type, where more than half of what the farm produces is consumed by the family.
	6. *Cash-crop farms.* In certain areas the farms specialize in a particular cash crop, as tobacco in the Nashville Basin.
OTHER	7. *Specialty farms.* These do intensive growing of specialty crops, particularly fruits and vegetables; they are especially notable near metropolitan areas and on lakeshore sites.

A Corn Belt Farm Within the smaller subdivisions of regions, farmsteads are similar, but within a large and diversified region, they are dissimilar. Thus farmsteads in the Dairy Belt, the Corn Belt, and the Corn and Winter Wheat Belt differ considerably.

Within the Corn Belt are innumerable exceptional farms—marvels to behold. In this area farms are scattered along the rural roads at an average of about two per mile. The average square mile of farm land includes three farms of about 210 acres each. This does not mean, of course, that there are not variations, and it is clear that average farm size is increasing.

Size depends upon many things: whether the farm lies in the part originally in forest or originally in prairie; the type of farming practiced; the total investment; the amount of mechanization; and the government programs of paying farmers to grow less corn, oats, and wheat. Competition is today so keen that it forces farmers to adopt a farm size that is reasonably efficient.

The average farm is square or rectangular in shape; it is thus highly compact. It contains the operator's house, his barn, and sheds for livestock, storage of feeds, and protection of tools and machinery, truck and automobile. Adjacent to the barn, invariably the largest building, are the feed pens and yards. Nearly always there is a farm garden and occasionally a farm orchard. If the farm consists of approximately 160 acres, it might have, during a given year, 50 to 80 acres in corn, and the same acreage divided among winter wheat, oats, and hay. More and more farms include soybeans in the rotation. There is invariably a block of land in pasture—usually the least desirable piece from the standpoint of crop production. It may be too rough for crops, too poorly drained, too infertile, or too stony.

In many instances a farm has been in the same family for many years. Often there is no debt on the property. In other instances, the farms are heavily burdened by mortgage. While most of the farms are operated by their owners, considerable numbers are rented to tenants; this is particularly true in the richer areas. Such farms represent a large investment of capital, mostly for land and machinery; the income is substantial and the standard of living is high. This family type of farm is deeply rooted in American life.

The Influence of Machinery on the Region's Agriculture

As recently as three generations ago, with hand tools and a team of oxen or horses, the farmer was fortunate indeed if he was able to grow enough food for himself and three other persons. Hence, it is small wonder that so many sons of the soil were lured to the cities, for they afforded about the only escape from the backache and drudgery of this so-called man-and-horse type of farming. In the 1920's, a 25-foot combine, pulled by 28 horses and manned by a crew of 3, could harvest only about 35 acres of wheat in a 10-hour day; today that same field could be harvested in the same time by one man operating a 12-foot self-propelled combine, and modern trucks would haul the grain directly to the elevator.

The farmer of the Agricultural Interior today is essentially a machine tender and a power user. Many of the machines now so indispensable to the farmers have been contributed in large part by the very young men who left the farms for the cities. They understood the problems involved and were interested in reducing the drudgery of farm work. Today the farmer grows enough for himself and two dozen other people, and he does it with less effort and in less time than ever before.

In the Agricultural Interior, *every* farm, on the average, has a tractor, a truck, and an automobile. Not only these relatively ordinary machines, however, have revolutionized farming in the region. There are all kinds of others—combines, corn pickers, seeders, high-wheeled platforms for detasseling corn, sprayers, mechanical hay balers, hydraulic loaders, manure spreaders, flame weed killers, push-button-operated auger feeders, liquid manure handlers, automatic conveyor-belt feed dispensers and egg gatherers for poultry houses, potato dig-and-bag machines, and many others. In Illinois and Iowa, for example, there is an average of two tractors per farm, and two-thirds of the farms in these states have mechanical corn pickers. All these things lower the cost of production and reduce the demand by millions for man-hours of labor.

Mechanization, by making it profitable to farm on a larger scale, is a major cause of the increasing size of farms. It takes larger acreages to cover the first high cost of machinery and at the same time keep production costs low. In turn machinery encourages new farming methods.

Science and Farming in the Agricultural Interior

Production per acre and per man is greater now than it has ever been. Science is the answer to the question *"How do they do it?"* The significance of machinery, usually considered the biggest single contributing factor, has already been discussed. Additional factors are better farming practices, modern methods of soil management, improved seed, and greater use of commercial fertilizers and insecticides, pesticides, and similar substances.

The Use of Fertilizer The Agricultural Interior was originally extremely fertile, but many decades of cropping have been depleting the soil of its plant-food reserves. Hence the farmers are using fertilizers in ever-growing quantities. This is necessary because of the widespread adoption of new high-yield strains of hybrid corn, oats, and soybeans and the present high prices for farm crops. More fertilizer is used in growing corn than in growing any other crop in the nation; since the Agricultural Interior is the leading corn-growing region, its importance as a market for fertilizer is readily apparent.

Very great yield increases, estimated at from 25 to 50 per cent depending upon the situation, result directly from the application of fertilizers. The use of fertilizers enables farmers to plant more high-yielding, high-nutrient-demanding seed per acre and hence to reap a greatly multiplied yield per acre.

Use of Insecticides and Fungicides Farmers are engaged in a constant battle against insects that can multiply with incredible speed and adapt to almost any condition and an endless variety of foods.

Pest control in the United States used to be relatively simple, involving only the use of lead, arsenic, sulphur, nicotine, and later of rotenone. The picture is different now. This results largely from the fact that pests develop a tolerance to a given insecticide and that modern, highly specialized farming methods with their large-scale production aggravate the problem; apples in orchards covering a square mile obviously present a more serious pest problem than does a single apple tree in the farm yard.

However, the specter of partial destruction of the most productive farming region in the world by such pests as the corn borer is no longer very likely. Not only is a continuing stream of new and sophisticated pesticides being developed, but techniques and equipment for dispensing the sprays and mists and powders are also continually being refined. This is not to say that there will not be occasional severe crop losses, but in general no other large agricultural region in the world is so thoroughly under control from an entomological standpoint.

Plant Breeding Because many farmers have seen the prospect of an abundant and profitable crop ruined before the onslaught of an insect pest before which they were powerless, scientists have worked on the

problem of developing crops or varieties that could be planted with reasonable assurance of freedom from destruction by one or another insect. Several examples are the breeding of winter wheats resistant to the hessian fly and rust and of lines of corn that are resistant to the earworm, European corn borer, chinch bug, and stored-grain insects. The victory is not yet complete, but such strains suffer only one-tenth to one-fourth as much injury as the most susceptible lines.

Scientists also discovered a fundamental law of nature when they learned in their experiments with tobacco that many plants can flower and produce seed only when the duration of light, that is, the length of day, is right for a particular plant.

Hybrid corn is possibly the most discussed contribution of the plant breeders. It has now replaced open-pollinated varieties on a major portion (almost 100 per cent) of the corn acreage in the Corn Belt Subregion and on about 25 per cent of the national acreage. This popularity is deserved, for hybrid corn has greater vigor, greater resistance to lodging, plant diseases, and insects, and increases the yield per acre. The increase is 10 to 20 per cent in the Corn Belt and, on thousands of farms, as much as 50 per cent. Because of their resistance to lodging, the hybrids are particularly well adapted to the use of the mechanical picker (Figure 9-5).

The farmer who grows hybrid corn for the market does not usually grow the seed for the corn himself. He purchases it from other farmers who breed corn for hybrid seed. In fact, in this region, the production of hybrid seed is a special business carried on by large concerns. In Urbana and De Kalb, Illinois, are two of the largest. The market for their seed is good, for farmers must purchase their seed corn every year; the old farm scene of seed corn hanging on the windmill to dry or hanging on racks on

Figure 9-5. A two-row, tractor-mounted corn picker working in central Illinois. (Photo courtesy International Harvester Company, Chicago, Illinois.)

the porch is no longer a part of the Agricultural Interior.

The producer obtains hybrid seed by crossbreeding two different strains each of which he has inbred for several generations to assure that they possess selected desired characteristics that they can transmit. He covers the tassels and the silks as soon as they appear; then he places the pollen from the tassels of each strain on the silks of the other. He covers the ears again and allows them to ripen. At maturity, the kernels on the plants of both strains are hybrid seed. These he harvests and sells to the farmer. They carry the best of the inheritance from both inbred strains and thus give rise to a product superior to either parent.

Supplemental Irrigation The artificial watering of crops has long been an accepted necessity in much of western Anglo-America, but only in recent years has irrigation become important in the East. Average annual precipitation is adequate for most midlatitude crops east of the Mississippi River, but variations from the average, as well as seasonal fluctuations, have resulted in decreased vigor of growth and even in crop failures on occasion. Supplemental irrigation can eliminate these hazards.

Supplemental irrigation has been developed unusually rapidly in the Agricultural Interior; and this, when combined with fertilization and seed selection, has boosted crop yields enormously. Studies in Indiana, Illinois, Wisconsin, and Iowa, for example, have shown that irrigation of corn may double or triple the output per acre.[9]

Sprinkler irrigation is by far the most common, utilizing lightweight aluminum pipes and whatever water source is available. It is an expensive operation, costing an average of about $100 per acre to install, and $25 per acre annually to operate, plus the cost of obtaining the water. However, the positive results are notable.

Soil Conservation

Only a small proportion of the Agricultural Interior is flat—the bulk of it being undulating or rolling and much possessing a considerable gradient. With heavy summer rains, and with the wide adoption of clean-tilled crops, soil erosion is bound to be serious, except in the northern portion during winters.

[9] "Irrigation in the Midwest," *Business Conditions,* Federal Reserve Bank of Chicago, December 1956, p. 14.

A moderate amount, however, such as occurs with a rotation including corn, wheat, oats, and clover is actually beneficial, for it keeps the soil *young*, utilizing the enormous reserves of plant nutrients in the subsoil. It is only when topsoil is removed faster than it can be formed under good farm management that erosion is dangerous.

The region as a whole has not suffered nearly as much from accelerated erosion as the Piedmont or the Cotton Belt, but in many specific areas soil loss has reached tragic proportions. A much less obvious but perhaps more insidious problem is the loss of plant nutrients that accompanies each leaching rain, as well as physical loss of topsoil in fields planted to row crops. Thus fertilizer application is often used to boost yields, but sometimes much fertilizer must be used just to maintain yields at normal levels.

Floods In the Agricultural Interior floods annually cause much damage to land, crops, livestock, buildings, equipment, and roads (Figure 9-6). Even human lives are lost. Such floods result from many factors, among which are type and occurrence of precipitation, the soil-vegetation complex which in-fluences the amount of run-off, and the topography of the drainage basins.

THE MISSOURI The Missouri or "Big Muddy" rises in the Rockies, is fed by many tributaries, and debauches into the Mississippi above St. Louis.

The river has two regular flood periods annually, usually in March-April and again in May-June, during which time parts of the flood plain suffer.

With its headwaters and upstream tributaries originating in the "violent weather regions" of the Rocky Mountains and Great Plains, the Missouri probably has a record of more frequent rampages than any other major river in Anglo-America. As a result of its capriciousness a great many plans have been broached for "controlling" the Big Muddy. The two principal dam-building agencies of the federal government, the Corps of Engineers and the Bureau of Reclamation, have worked up a rivalry in attempting to prepare ever more grandiose schemes for the Missouri basin. Such schemes mostly involve the building of dams, the erection of artificial levees, and the straightening of channels by cutting across meanders.

Figure 9-6. The Missouri River in flood at Kansas City. (Photo courtesy Union Pacific Railroad.)

Implementation and financing a comprehensive scheme are the two stumbling blocks. It has been proposed that an MVA (Missouri Valley Authority) be established along the lines of TVA. The two federal agencies have produced the Pick-Sloan Plan, a "shotgun marriage" of their individual ideas, for over-all basin development, but it has not been implemented. Meanwhile, various individual projects have been undertaken.

It is clear that a plan for the entire watershed would be most useful, but it is not clear that the benefit-cost ratio could ever justify such an operation. Flood control, electricity generation, and provision of recreational areas would all be worthwhile; but neither increased irrigation nor improved navigation would seem to be in the national interest, in comparison with the tremendous cost required.

In terms of flood control, one of the major reasons for harnessing the river, two basic hydrologic facts need to be appreciated: (1) The way to start controlling floods is to protect the vegetation (whatever it may be) of the watershed. Ever-bigger dams and higher levees are only adjuncts to this. (2) Large rivers in humid, mid-latitude regions must be expected to flood at occasional intervals, no matter what upstream or downstream provisions are made to minimize the crests. If man expects to escape danger from floods, then man must be intelligent enough not to live on floodplains.

OTHER RIVERS The Missouri is only one of many major rivers in the Agricultural Interior. Flooding problems are also associated with the Ohio, the Wabash, the Mississippi, the Illinois, and others.

Drainage In most parts of the Agricultural Interior, particularly the northeast and the northwest, there are drainage problems. These areas, generally on old glacial lakebeds or till plains, normally did not require complete reclamation, as in many coastal zones. But the establishment of artificial drainage as an adjunct to a deficient natural system of surface and internal soil drainage has been one of the surest methods of increasing cultivated acreage and/or yields.

Crops

One reason that this is such an outstanding agricultural region is that most of the land can be and is cultivated (Figure 9-7).

Corn Corn (maize) thrives under the favorable conditions of hot, humid summer weather, fertile, well-drained, loamy soils, and level to rolling terrain. No other country has this favorable combination of growing conditions over so wide a territory. Thus the United States produces one-half to two-thirds of the world's corn, most of which is grown in this region (Figure 9-2). Corn to be grown commercially has rigid temperature requirements; it should have an average night temperature above 55° F., an average summer temperature of 70° to 80° F. up to the time of ripening, and a growing season of at least 130 days. Corn benefiting from frequent showers and warm nights in June, July, and August has been known to grow as much as two to five inches in one night. In fact there is an old saying in the Corn Belt that "it's so hot you can almost hear the corn growing." It is a fact that corn makes 80 per cent of its growth at night.

Soils for corn should be deep, well-drained, fertile, and rich in humus. The terrain should be level or undulating to permit the utilization of labor-saving farm implements and to retard soil erosion—always destructive on slopes where clean-tilled crops are grown. With this favorable combination of environmental conditions, yields are of 100 to 150 bushels per acre on the richer soils. The high yields obtained in the Corn Belt Subregion are mostly attributable to the almost universal adoption of hybrid

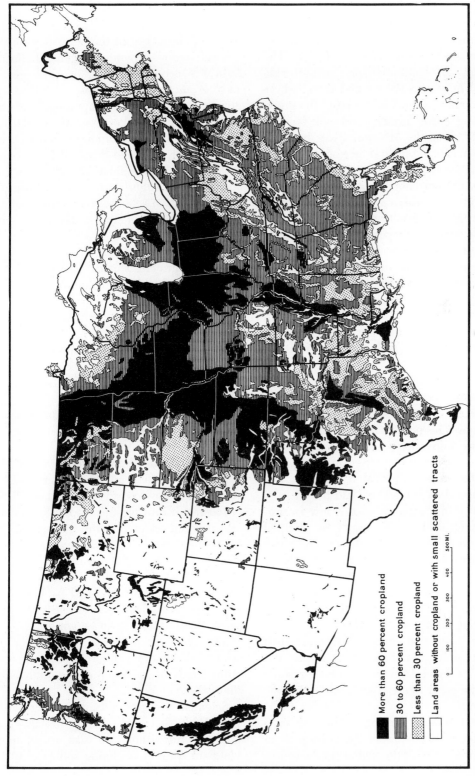

Figure 9-7. Principal cropland areas in continental United States, as shown by the proportion of the land used for crops. In most of the Agricultural Interior more than 60 per cent of the farm land is cropped. (Map prepared by Agricultural Research Service, U.S. Department of Agriculture.)

■ More than 60 percent cropland

▥ 30 to 60 percent cropland

▦ Less than 30 percent cropland

□ Land areas without cropland or with small scattered tracts

0   100   200   300   400   500 MI.

corn, to the rotation which always includes a legume, and to rather generous use of manure and commercial fertilizers. The heaviest concentrations of corn-growing are (1) in central Illinois and Iowa, where considerable corn is sold for cash, the growers being grain farmers and not feeders, and (2) along the Missouri River between southern Minnesota and northern Kansas. Most of the Corn Belt grows corn for feed. Corn is the only important feed grain produced in the southern and southeastern part of the region, oats not being grown because of high summer temperatures. In order to maintain soil fertility, a rotation of corn for one or two years, followed by a year in oats or wheat, and finally by one or two years in hay—usually clover but sometimes timothy or alfalfa—is followed. Corn production per man and per farm increases from east to west well into the state of Iowa.

The seed is planted mechanically by a corn planter and is "checkrowed," that is, dropped so as to be equally spaced in two directions. This permits both lengthwise and crosswise cultivation by cultivator. The two-row lister is also widely used in corn planting. The crop is cultivated three to five times and then the field is "laid by" in July.

Because the value of corn is low in proportion to its bulk, it cannot be shipped long distances as many other crops. Since more than three-fourths of it is fed to hogs, cattle, horses, and poultry, it is patent that a very close correlation exists between the distribution of hogs and cattle on the one hand and of corn on the other.

In the Corn Belt proper about one-fourth of the total farm land and about 40 per cent of the cropped land is in corn. In some areas the latter figure rises to more than 60 per cent.

Winter Wheat An important cash crop is winter wheat. Most of the acreage is in the southern half of the region—in the southern Corn Belt and the Corn and Winter Wheat Subregions. In the latter it is one of several crops grown on general farms. Wheat is secondary to corn over the greater part of the region, because it is less restricted in its range of adaptation. It is produced to equalize the seasonal distribution of labor, being seeded in autumn after corn cultivation is over and threshed before corn is harvested. Thus since wheat harvesting interferes but slightly with corn cultivation, the competition is not serious. Winter wheat also helps to control erosion during the winter months. Moreover, it is planted to provide a "nurse crop"; when sown with hay, its quick growth shields the young hay plants from the blistering summer sun. The grain is cut sufficiently early to allow the root systems of grass to withstand the succeeding winter.

On the better soils corn is more profitable than wheat, but even where corn finds optimum conditions, wheat remains a strong potential competitor. Important also in this competition is the fact that usually wheat yields are higher here than elsewhere in Anglo-America.

Wheat *can* be grown over much of the region. Exceptions are those parts where the winters are too severe or where there is too much rain in June and July. Winter wheat is not adapted to the frequent showers that so greatly favor the successful production of corn. In the Agricultural Interior winter wheat must compete with both corn and oats, both of which yield far better. In the heart of the Corn Belt wheat is less preferred than oats—a spring-sown grain.

Though most Canadian production of winter wheat is in southern Ontario, it constitutes only five per cent of the total Canadian wheat crop.

Scientists are gradually improving wheat varieties in their resistance to disease—particularly rust; they are also maintaining yields in spite of declining soil fertility by widespread use of nitrogen fertilizers and permitting extension into areas of high risks and low average yields.

Oats The Agricultural Interior, especially the northwestern part of the Corn Belt, is the most important oats-growing area in Anglo-America. Unlike other small grains, oats during seeding, harvesting, and threshing do not compete with corn but fit into the characteristic crop rotation. Oats are seeded in the spring before work on the corn crop begins and are cut in summer when corn cultivation is about over. Thus the farmer is kept busy throughout most of the summer. Oats, often used as a "nurse crop" for clover, alfalfa, and timothy, are grown primarily as feed for livestock; they are fed directly to horses, ground with corn for young animals, and fed to beef cattle in a ration. Oats are fed mostly on the farms where produced. This results from the crop's low value per unit of bulk and its limited industrial uses, which discriminate against its entering trade channels. Only about 3 per cent of the crop is utilized for human consumption.

Oats are ordinarily a crop of cool, moist areas. Yet the northern Corn Belt, which is not cool in summer, ranks as possibly the world's leading oats-grower. It must be admitted that the Corn Belt is not ideal climatically: early summer is too warm, frequent and severe thunder showers cause "lodging," the rich soils facilitate rank growth of straw, and occasional droughts result in low yields. Hot, dry weather even for a few days, at the critical period of development, may greatly reduce the yield.

The huge acreage in oats in this region results from the crop's high feed value and the fact that no other small grain fits so well into the labor-use pattern. As with corn, Iowa is the principal oats-producing state, followed by Minnesota, Wisconsin, and Illinois.

Except in the southern part of the region, oats generally follow corn in the rotation, since corn is customarily harvested too late in the season for the sowing of winter wheat. When oats follow corn, plowing is not necessary in preparing the seedbed in the spring, discing sufficing. The crop is threshed in July and early August.

Alfalfa The legume, alfalfa, is well adapted to the region—especially to the prairie portion, where winter rainfall is less abundant and the soils less leached and hence higher in calcium. It thrives only on soils rich in lime. The crop has greatly increased in importance in the Corn Belt and the Dairy Belt since 1920—even in the eastern part of the Agricultural Interior. When grown in such areas, however, due consideration must be given to soil conditions—especially to the availability of phosphates and to drainage.

Since alfalfa is harvested several times each season and recovers quickly after cutting, the per-acre yield exceeds that of any other hay crop.

In the short-summer, dairy portion of the region, alfalfa becomes a very significant crop. Wisconsin, for example, grows almost as much alfalfa as corn. In most years Wisconsin and Iowa vie with California as the leading grower of alfalfa.

Clover Another crop of major importance is clover, which is well suited to the hot humid summers, limy soils, and level to rolling terrain. Especially is it important in the northern and eastern sections where precipitation is heavy and where droughts and hot sun do little damage. Clover produces hay of excellent quality—rich in protein and mineral content.

Timothy This is the most widely cultivated hay grass in Anglo-America. Since it has the same general soil and climatic adaptation as red clover (much moisture and good soil drainage), the two are often seeded together. Especially is this crop important in the Dairy Belt and the northern

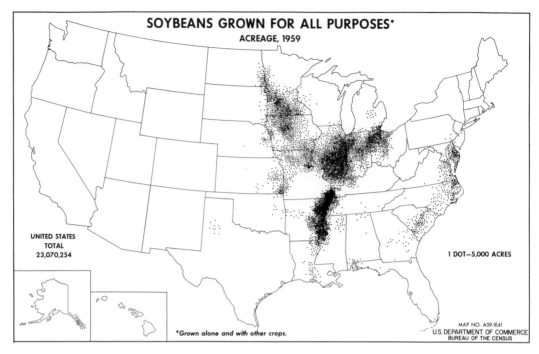

SOYBEANS GROWN FOR ALL PURPOSES*
ACREAGE, 1959

UNITED STATES
TOTAL
23,070,254

1 DOT—5,000 ACRES

*Grown alone and with other crops.

MAP NO. A59-1E41
U.S. DEPARTMENT OF COMMERCE
BUREAU OF THE CENSUS

Figure 9-8. The United States is the world's leading producer of soybeans and the Agricultural Interior is its outstanding growing region. The great expansion in soybean acreage was a significant wartime change in American crop production.

Corn Belt. Since timothy cannot tolerate the combination of high summer temperature and high atmospheric humidity, the crop is relatively unimportant in the Corn and Winter Wheat Belt and its production declines considerably even in the southern Corn Belt. Nearly all the crop in the Agricultural Interior is produced north of the Ohio River.

Soybeans Soybeans were introduced into the United States as early as 1804 but became a major crop only during the 1920's and reached really high acreage levels during and since the 1930's. Probably the greatest stimulus came when it was recognized that soybeans could be processed for oil.

The soybean, a shallow-rooted legume, is a heavy feeder on the elements of plant food in the surface soils. It is popular because it yields a heavy crop of beans, is valuable for meal and oil, makes good hay, silage, and pasturage, has few diseases, and is not attacked by pests. Every part of the plant is useful.

The soybean belt is approximately coextensive with the Corn Belt (Figure 9-8). The crop's climatic and soil requirements are about the same as for corn. Of the region's crops, only corn brings in more money. Illinois, the leading producing state by far, has 60 per cent as much soybean as corn acreage. The two crops together occupy more than 70 per cent of the state's cultivated land. To the casual traveler, crossing Illinois is like crossing a big field of succotash.

There are three principal reasons for the stimulated interest in soybeans in recent years. (1) Demand for soybean oil and meal has increased significantly. Domestic usage has doubled in the past decade, and exports have grown by 500 per cent. (2) Soybeans are an attractive alternative crop. There are no government-imposed acreage restrictions or marketing quotas, so land that has been diverted from production of restricted crops can be planted to soybeans. (3) The same farm equipment normally used in handling small grains can be used for soybeans, whereas net returns from the latter are generally substantially above returns from the former.

Tobacco In northern and central Kentucky and in northern Tennessee, lies one of the most important tobacco-growing areas in Anglo-America. Southern Wisconsin and southwestern Ontario also are impressive producers. In this part of Anglo-America tobacco competes neither with corn nor winter wheat for the best land, except in the Bluegrass and the Nashville Basins.

The Blue Grass Basin of Kentucky is the most important tobacco-growing area in the Agricultural Interior. The limy soils, high in phosphorus, are among the best in Anglo-America. In the Inner Blue Grass, though more than 90 per cent of the land is improved and has been producing for generations, little soil depletion has occurred. Of the three minerals essential to most crops, potassium, nitrogen, and phosphorus, tobacco requires greatest quantities of the first, less of the second, and only modest amounts of the third. Maximum yields of white burley tobacco are obtained on the silt loams and level to undulating terrain. The same type of tobacco—burley—is grown under almost identical conditions in the Nashville Basin. This light, aromatic, "air cured" leaf was grown originally for use in plug chewing tobacco but now is blended with other tobaccos in the manufacture of cigarettes and pipe-smoking mixtures.

Since labor requirements for tobacco are large and the work back-breaking, and since it can be raised profitably on almost any size farm, a given family cultivates only a limited acreage. Less than five per cent of the farmland in the subregion produces tobacco. Whereas most tobacco farms are operated by owners, much of the production is in the hands of share-croppers who rent 5 to 20 acres of land—the size of the tract depending mostly upon the number in the cropper's family. Under this system the landlords furnish land and advance money for the crop. However, many owners of small farms grow their own tobacco; often it serves as their only cash crop.

Dark-fired tobacco, the leaves of which are cured by the use of open fires and smoke, is grown on the rather fertile rolling lands north of the Highland Rim, whose climate is relatively free from extremes and whose location is favorable with respect to markets. In this area tobacco is the pivot crop, and around it revolves the whole system of farming. A four-year rotation is employed by the more progressive farmers, in which tobacco is followed by wheat, hay (frequently the legume, lespedeza), and corn. In the area as a whole, corn leads in acreage.

Lying between the burley and dark-fired growing areas is that specializing in dark air-cured leaf, which is used for making chewing tobacco and snuff. Total production is small, however, less than two per cent of the national tobacco output, and is declining because of the lessened demand for these two products.

While tobacco is not generally considered an important Canadian crop, it is the leading one in several counties bordering on Lake Erie, particularly in Norfolk County. The nation's first commercial tobacco production (heavy varieties) was on the clay and loam soils in the western counties of Ontario. Now production is centered considerably eastward. Three-fourths of the soils of Norfolk County are sandy—poorly adapted to most crops, but well suited to growing flue-cured tobacco. The climate, too, is favorable; killing frosts are conspicuously rare between the first week in May and the last week in September. Harvesting and curing are done by temporary workers in August and September. Some 65,000 laborers participate each year, about one-third coming from the Maritime Provinces.[10] Tobacco is the most valuable cash crop in Ontario.

Vegetables The farm vegetable garden is so universal that one may assume that vegetable production is to be found wherever there are farms. But the products from these farms are consumed mostly on the home farm. The areas of densest vegetable production in the region are those engaged in commercial production. Almost invariably these areas are close to large cities—Cleveland, Toledo, Cincinnati, Indianapolis, Detroit, Chicago, Milwaukee, Louisville, St. Louis, Hamilton, Toronto.

The Dairy Belt and the Corn Belt do not grow the same vegetables. The former's cool summers and light soils make it outstanding for growing peas, beans, cabbage, asparagus, and sweet corn. The short frostless season is excellent for growing sweet corn for canning, inasmuch as the cool days and nights keep the kernels in the milk stage. Sweet corn is grown in the Corn Belt, but the hot weather makes the ears dry and tough. The Corn Belt's hot, humid summers and heavy soils, however, enable it to be a major tomato-growing area. The north shore of Lake Ontario is also an important vegetable area, especially for tomatoes.

Fruit The commercial growing of fruit is not a widely distributed enterprise but is concentrated in definite localities—mostly those originally forested, for the fruits do not need extremely fertile soil. Tree fruits, more exacting in climate than in soil requirements, frequently suffer from extremes of temperature. Hence the areas best suited

are those with a minimum of danger from late spring and early fall frosts—notably peninsulas, hillsides, and the leeward sides of lakes. This tempering effect of a large body of water has given rise to a fruit belt on the eastern shore of Lake Michigan, where peaches and cherries are of great importance, and on the southern shore of Lake Erie, where grapes, peaches, and apples are dominant crops. The Niagara Peninsula in Canada, benefiting from the same climatic principle, is famous for fruits —particularly grapes and peaches. The narrow lake plain between Hamilton and the Niagara River is one of only two major areas in Canada where tender fruit crops can be produced. Its location in the most rapidly growing area of Canada makes available a ready market, but urban and industrial expansion in the so-called "Golden Horseshoe" have caused fruitlands to be subdivided at a rapid rate.[11]

Pasture In a region where most of the crops are grown for feeding livestock and where dairying is important, pastures of necessity play a prominent role in the systems of farming.

Pastures fall into two main classifications: (1) *permanent pastures*—areas covered with perennial or self-seeding annual plants that are pastured by livestock, and (2) *improved pastures*—areas planted with domesticated plants. Permanent pastures, which are seldom plowed or cultivated, comprise a large percentage of the pasture area in the Dairy Belt and the Corn and Winter Wheat Belt and even a considerable percentage in the Corn Belt. Since nearly every farm has some livestock, it must reserve some land for pasture. Moreover, a portion of nearly every farm is unsuitable for cultivation and can be utilized most advantageously for permanent pasture. The

[10] Marcus Van Steen, "Tobacco: Another Canadian Achievement," *Canadian Geographical Journal,* Vol. 61 (July 1961), p. 13.

[11] Ralph R. Krueger, "The Disappearing Niagara Fruit Belt," *Canadian Geographical Journal,* Vol. 58 (April 1959), pp. 102-17.

combined acreages of cultivated hay and pasturage approximate those in corn and small grains in Illinois, Iowa, and Minnesota and exceed them in Indiana, Michigan, Missouri, Ohio, and Wisconsin.

The Livestock Industry

The Agricultural Interior concentrates on growing feed for livestock rather than on food for man. In few areas elsewhere in the world is the system of farming based to so large an extent upon livestock. From two-thirds to three-fourths of the income from Corn Belt farms comes from livestock—a situation in sharp contrast with that in most other outstanding agricultural areas.

The farmers here have several possible choices for the utilization of their corn. Accordingly certain well-defined areas of corn-use have arisen. The "cash-grain" areas (central Illinois and parts of northern Iowa, and, to a lesser extent, parts of northern Ohio and Indiana) sell corn as grain to industry; this is possible in part because of low freight rates to nearby cities. Here, obviously, swine and beef cattle are relatively less important than elsewhere in the Corn Belt. In the eastern Corn Belt swine and dairy cattle predominate, though some beef cattle, too, are raised. Fresh milk finds a ready market in the large cities. In the western Corn Belt (western Iowa and eastern Nebraska), both beef cattle and swine are important. It is significant that the less weathered soils in the Agricultural Interior grow crops high in protein and hence lead in beef cattle, whereas the more weathered soils in the humid half of the region grow carbohydrate crops and lead in swine. A leading agricultural geographer has analyzed the situation as follows:

Except for the complications introduced by chickens, most of the Midwest (except for the northeast and west) has a hog-beef cattle-dairy cattle combination. Going toward the northeast, first beef cattle and then hogs drop out as the dairy area is entered. Going toward the west, first hogs and then dairy cattle drop out as the beef area is entered.[12]

Beef Cattle Beef cattle are most numerous in the central and western parts of the region, the old prairie portion, for, unlike swine, they are essentially grass eaters. Only 15 per cent of our total beef production tonnage is made from grain, though grain finishing contributes much to improving the grades of beef.

Since cattle lose more weight in transportation than do hogs, the tendency is to fatten them on farms within a single night's journey of the great markets. Few live cattle are now sent from the western part of this region as far east as Buffalo, Cleveland, and Pittsburgh. The development of good highways and the universal adoption of the truck have altered the method of getting livestock to market (Figure 9-9).

Contrary to the common notion that the range states provide only the grazing and breeding lands and the Corn Belt the fattening areas, the fact is that about two-thirds of the animals slaughtered within the Corn Belt are bred in it.

Feeding is a major agricultural enterprise in the western part of the region, the animals being carried through the winter on hay and other home-grown feeds and fattened on corn. There are twice as many cattle on feed in Iowa as in any other state. Illinois and Nebraska rank next. Most cattle feeders keep swine, which run with the cattle and act as scavengers. These animals root out of the ground and manure the corn which has spilled from the feeding bunks and which the cattle will not touch.

Swine Of all domesticated animals, swine convert corn into meat most effi-

[12] John C. Weaver, *et al.*, "Livestock Units and Combination Regions in the Middle West," *Economic Geography*, Vol. 32 (July 1956), p. 259.

Figure 9-9. Hauling livestock by truck. Most cattle and hogs are trucked to the packing plants. (Photo courtesy Automobile Manufacturers Association.)

ciently and rapidly. Spring shotes, for example, are ready for market in approximately eight months. During the feeding period, they gain in weight from one to one and one-fourth pounds per day. Three-fourths of the swine in the United States are raised in this region, where the density is about four times the average for the rest of the country (Figure 9-10). Where swine are most numerous is where corn is cheapest and can, therefore, move to market advantageously in the concentrated form of live or slaughtered animals. It is much more economical to ship one pound of hog than five pounds of grain (roughly the quantity required to produce one pound of live weight).

Formerly the Corn Belt specialized in the lard type of hog. Now, because of the competition of vegetable oils and shortenings, emphasis is placed on dual-purpose swine—

animals that produce plenty of lard but at the same time are noted for their high-quality meat.

Swine are kept in several kinds of movable houses placed near the barn and corn crib. Adjacent to each group of houses are self-feeders into which the feed drops from above. This method is much safer for the small pigs than the old swill trough with its excessive crowding and pushing of animals.

Dairy Cattle   In the heart of the Agricultural Interior, mixed farming based on corn and meat animals is the most profitable enterprise, though nearly every farmer keeps milk cows for home use, for the sale of fresh milk to nearby urban markets, and for utilizing pasturage advantageously. Moreover, dairy cows provide the farmer with profitable winter work which would be impossible if crops only were grown. Except for the fertile level plain on either side of the Illinois-Wisconsin line, which specializes in fresh milk rather than in corn and meat, the portion of this area west of Lake Michigan generally goes in for manufactured dairy products—butter, cheese, evaporated milk, and casein. The farther a farm lies from a city, the higher the transport cost on fluid milk, which, being 87 per cent water, is the most expensive of all dairy products to ship.

It is in the Dairy Belt, however, that dairy cattle are most numerous (Figure 9-11) and where the dominant system of farming is built around them. Here the short growing season and cool summers limit the growth of many crops; much land is in marsh, swamp, and lake; large areas are too wet for tillage but are satisfactory for pasture or marsh hay; and much soil (where there are podzols) is of low fertility or strewn with glacial boulders and stones. This combination of geographical conditions tempted the immigrant Germans, Swiss, and Scandinavians toward dairying rather than toward crop production. Most

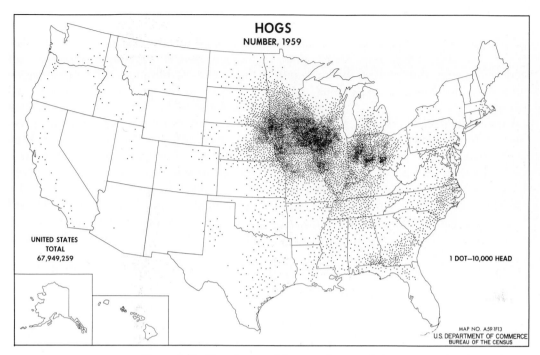

Figure 9-10. Distribution of hogs in the United States. Note the close relationship of the distribution of hogs and corn (Figure 9-2).

Figure 9-11. Distribution of cattle in the United States. The greatest concentration occurs where there is an overlap of beef cattle from the Corn Belt with dairy cattle from the Hay and Dairy Belt.

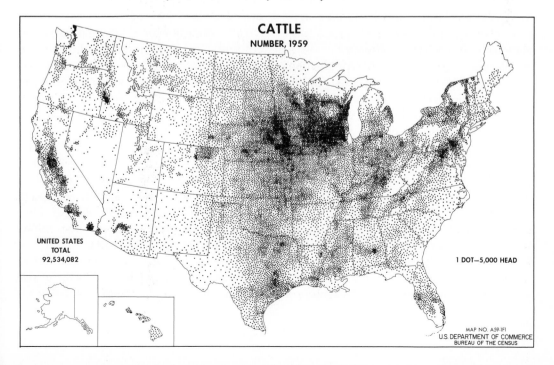

of the land here had been logged, then worn out by several successive crops of wheat, and before the arrival of the immigrants, virtually abandoned. Using grass and small grains, they revived the land, and ultimately developed a prosperous dairy industry.

Other Livestock Although far less important than cattle and hogs, other forms of livestock are widely raised in the Agricultural Interior. Ordinarily the region contains approximately one-fourth of the sheep (mostly in Iowa, Ohio and Michigan), one-fifth of the horses (the total is decreasing each year but this proportion remains the same), more than one-third of the farm chickens (but less than 10 per cent of the broilers), and one-fourth of the turkeys in the United States.

The National Government and the Farmer

In both Canada and the United States, agriculture, that "last stronghold of free enterprise," is becoming ever more dependent on the government. Within the last two decades a bureaucracy of astounding magnitude has evolved, doing many noble things for the farmer, but enmeshing agriculture in an endless series of quotas, regulations, and artificial conditions.

The major problem is overproduction, and resultant unstable markets. While people go hungry in many parts of the world, the agriculturalists of Anglo-America, despite sharply declining numbers of farms, farmers, and cultivated acres, continue to produce crop surpluses that are almost too enormous to visualize.

Direct government influence on farming comes about in many ways, and is somewhat different in the two countries involved. However, the geography of agriculture is most likely to be affected by the following practices:

(1) COST SHARING OF CONSERVATION PRACTICES An interested farmer can obtain from the government advice, plans, technical assistance for soil conservation. Also, the government pays approximately half the cost of establishing certain conservation practices on his land. In addition, he can take some of his acres out of cultivation and receive direct payments for not growing crops. All these measures have been beneficial for overused and eroded land. But, at the same time, the high productivity of intensified farming on the better-cultivated land has offset the tendency toward decline in total production that would be an anticipated effect of conservation practices.

(2) FARM CREDIT The United States and Canadian governments make loans to their qualifying farmers who cannot obtain credit from conventional sources.

(3) CROP INSURANCE The governments have set up crop insurance agencies to indemnify farmers for crop losses due to "acts of God."

(4) ACREAGE ALLOTMENTS AND MARKETING QUOTAS Most major crops are now grown under some sort of allotment and quota system, whereby maximal acreages are designated for each year's harvest.

(5) PRICE SUPPORTS Several basic agricultural commodities in both countries achieve what amounts to a guaranteed sale on the basis of federal price supports, regardless of national or international market conditions. This, more than any other part of the farm program, has contributed to the astronomically mounting stored surplus. In the United States by the early 1960's there was more than ten billion dollars' worth of surplus crops stored, transportation, storage, and interest charges alone amounting to approximately one million dollars per day (Figure 9-12).

What to do about the complex federal farm programs (which have been grossly oversimplified in this brief discussion) is

Figure 9-12. Corn being transferred into Commodity Credit Corporation storage bins at Rochester, Illinois. (Photo courtesy Illinois Information Service.)

enigmatic. Friend and foe alike agree that they are too big, too all-pervading, and too expensive. And yet neither Republicans nor Democrats nor Progressive Conservatives nor Liberals nor Social Crediters nor Independents have been able to devise a scheme for getting government out of agriculture without wrecking the farm economy.

Minerals

In this outstanding agricultural region, mining is in many localities also a cardinal enterprise. Coal, petroleum, natural gas, salt, clay, sand, gypsum, and building stones provide a livelihood for large numbers and simultaneously supply the sinews for rail and motor transport and for manufacturing.

Coal Coal deposits are widely distributed, and one of the nation's leading provinces—the Eastern Interior—is in this region (see Figure 6-8). While this coal, generally speaking, is not of such good quality as that mined in the Appalachian Province, its location near numerous manufacturing cities insures cheap fuel and hence supplies a large part of the industrial requirements of the Midwest. Most of it is stripmined. The Eastern Interior Province is second (though distantly) only to the Appalachian Province as a coal producer.

Illinois produces about 10 per cent of the United States total, and ranks third among the states in total volume produced since the inception of coal mining in the United States. The fields of western Kentucky and southwestern Indiana together yield slightly more coal than those of Illinois, and the trend in mining is steadily eastward and southward, reflecting the increasing importance of those two states and the decline of production in central Illinois. Total output from the five states of the Western Interior Province, while locally important, amounts to less than 2 per cent of the national output.

Petroleum and Natural Gas Important oil and gas reserves have been tapped in Michigan, Ohio, Indiana, Kentucky, and Illinois. Production is scattered, however, and the region as a whole yields but 7 per cent of the total United States output, about half of this coming from Illinois. Oil flow in Illinois continues to increase, particularly in response to the technique of waterflooding and deeper drilling.

The only oil and gas of any consequence in eastern Canada are found in this region, somewhat scattered in extreme southern Ontario. Oil output amounts to less than 1 per cent of the national total, but further modest discoveries are anticipated. The proportion of the national output of natural gas is somewhat higher.

Limestone In south-central Indiana, in the Bedford-Bloomington area, are the famous limestone quarries that supply a superior limestone used in buildings throughout the East and Middle West. About three-fourths of the dimension (block) limestone of the country comes from these quarries. The building-stone business is declining, however, for it suffers in competition with cheaper materials—concrete, brick, and lumber.

Salt Salt occurs widely in Anglo-America, but major deposits are in the vicinity of the southern end of Lake Huron. Michigan is the leading state and Ontario the leading province in salt output of their respective countries. The salt is obtained in the solid state by underground digging and in the dissolved state by the modified Frasch process. There are several mines in Michigan, but the principal output is actually within metropolitan Detroit (beneath the city). The Ontario mines are at Goderich, Watford, Sarnia, and Windsor.

Manufacturing

Approximately one-half of the American Manufacturing Region overlaps this region. The industrial development of that area has been discussed in Chapter 3. Analysis here is confined to those parts of the Agricultural Interior outside (essentially to the west of) the Manufacturing Region.

As might be anticipated, the bulk of the manufacturing of the region is oriented toward agriculture, either by using farm products as raw materials or by producing items for sale to farmers.

Meat packing is probably the principal type of food processing, following the well-established trend of decentralization toward the source of raw materials, in this case toward the areas of cattle and hog raising. Omaha has displaced Chicago as

the premier slaughtering center of the continent, and other meat-packing localities of prominence include South St. Paul, Sioux City, Waterloo, St. Joseph, Kansas City, and Tulsa.

Flour milling is the other outstanding food-processing activity in the region, part of the wheat coming from the Agricultural Interior but most of it coming from the Great Plains to the west. Minneapolis and Kansas City have maintained major milling enterprises for decades; they normally rank just behind Buffalo in national statistics.

The farm populace serves as a market as well. Although Chicago has no rival as a farm-machinery producer, major manufacturing centers of farm implements are located in Minneapolis, the Tri-Cities (Davenport – Rock Island – Moline), Des Moines, Waterloo, and Kansas City. Nashville is an important producer of farm fertilizer.

Diversified manufacturing, oriented primarily for the wholesale markets, is also characteristic of Minneapolis—St. Paul, Kansas City, and Nashville.

Transportation and Trade

No region, subregion or district can advance far in *commercial* agriculture without an abundance of efficient and relatively economical transportation. Lacking it, the area, unless it be fortunate enough to produce an exotic product, must be doomed to *subsistence* agriculture.

In the Agricultural Interior, which constitutes the crossroads of the nation, transportation is now of the best. Until a railroad web was developed over the region, interior location was a distinct handicap and hardship.

Before 1850 the principal avenues for the disposal of farm products were (1) the Mississippi and its navigable tributaries and (2) the Great Lakes with their eastern connections.

The first railroads in the Middle West were not built as competitors to navigable waterways but as links connecting them. The rapid extension and improvement of railway facilities after 1850, however, profoundly changed agriculture and revolutionized the whole course of internal trade. Railroads, by spanning the great interior with a network of steel rails, also stimulated the growth of cities and the development of manufacturing.

Roads The truck and the automobile have revolutionized transportation in the twentieth century almost as much as the railway did in the nineteenth. Approximately one-third of the nation's total mileage of highest-type surface roads is in the Middle Western states. This region is laced by a network of all-weather highways. One of the main problems connected with agriculture in this region is the provision of adequately coordinated distribution. Good roads are a prime factor in bringing the farm nearer the major centers of consumption. Nearly every farmer has a car or a truck or both; some even have several of each.

Over much of the region, highways tend to run in east-west or north-south lines 100 miles at a stretch. Most roads follow section lines and are a mile apart.

The lone disadvantage of such a road system is that distance is increased to towns and villages for farms that are not in one of the cardinal directions from them.

Hamlets and Villages

Within the Agricultural Interior there are an amazing number of hamlets and villages scattered throughout the region at about five-mile intervals. A *hamlet* is a small agglomeration of people (20 to 150) at a crossroads, with its houses and work units sufficiently prominent to indicate a node in the rural landscape. The typical *village* (both incorporated and unincorporated), of which there are thousands, consists of a combination of brick and frame buildings irregularly spaced along a street or streets bordered by trees and concrete or brick sidewalks. It usually contains a railroad station, a post office, one or more churches, a bank, a garage or two, a cream station, a feed store, grocery, hardware store, drugstore, and bakery. The most imposing building, invariably built of brick, is the school. Along the railroad tracks are a grain elevator and livestock loading pens (Figure 9-13). There are usually no factories or mills. The average village supports what it considers to be the essential minimum in

Figure 9-13. A small village (Graymont, Illinois) in the Corn Belt. Hundreds of such villages with their buildings and trees rise prominently out of the checkerboard fields of crops and pastures. (Photo courtesy of the *Daily Pantagraph*, Bloomington, Illinois.)

amenities of life. If the village prospers, it adds a library, an historical society, and more adequate health facilities. The majority of the inhabitants are apt to be retired farmers, who have rented or sold their holdings. Most everyone has a vegetable garden.

The frequent roads in the area focus on the scattered villages. During the great depression, many of these villages declined as the result of the attraction of large cities for the younger people and the widespread ownership of the automobile, which enables a person to go 20 miles as easily as he formerly went 5 with a horse. Some students of planning in this region believe there is an excess of such villages, and many of them do seem to be "withering on the vine." Their role in the region must not be underrated, however. They are the base of supplies for the surrounding farming area, the market place for a large portion of the output, and the hub of a considerable territory whose inhabitants depend upon them for a number of services. Farm villages have no urban ambitions. Most of them are destined to remain small communities.

The Outlook

The future of the Agricultural Interior as a whole must depend upon agriculture more than upon any other activity. The big problem is not one of production but rather one of marketing the output at a profit. Current trends of fewer farms, larger farms, decreasing acreage, increasing yield, and increasing surpluses will probably continue, at least in the short run. Market fluctuations, occasioned in part by the revived European economy, are likely to keep "natural" prices soft, to be firmed up only by government supports.

There will be occasional years when the farmer will suffer, for even the most efficient operator, making the best possible use of agricultural methods, is subject to the

TABLE 8

Selected Cities and Towns of the Agricultural Interior

City or Town	Urbanized Area	Political Center
*Alton	......	43,047
*Anderson	......	49,061
*Ann Arbor	115,282	67,340
*Aurora	85,522	63,715
*Bay City	72,763	53,604
*Berwyn	......	52,224
Bloomington, Minn.	......	50,498
*Brantford	......	55,201
*Buffalo	1,054,370	532,759
Cedar Rapids	105,118	92,035
*Champaign	78,014	49,583
*Chicago	5,959,213	3,550,404
*Cicero	......	69,130
*Cincinnati	993,568	502,550
*Cleveland	1,784,991	876,050
*Cleveland Heights	......	61,813
*Columbus	616,743	471,316
Council Bluffs	......	55,641
*Covington	......	60,376
Davenport	227,176	88,981
*Dayton	501,664	262,332
*Dearborn	......	112,007
*Decatur	89,516	78,004
Des Moines	241,115	208,982
*Detroit	3,537,709	1,670,144
Dubuque	59,447	56,606
*East Chicago	......	57,669
*East St. Louis	......	81,712
*Erie	177,433	138,440
*Evanston	......	79,283
*Evansville	143,660	141,543
*Flint	277,786	196,940
*Fort Wayne	179,571	161,776
*Gary	......	178,320
*Grand Rapids	294,230	177,313
*Granite City	......	40,073
*Green Bay	97,162	62,888
*Hamilton, Ohio	89,778	72,354
*Hamilton, Ont.	395,189	273,991
*Hammond	......	111,698
*Hull	......	56,929
Independence	......	62,328
*Indianapolis	639,340	476,258
*Jackson	71,412	50,720
*Joliet	116,585	66,780
*Kalamazoo	115,659	82,089
Kansas City, Kan.	......	121,901
Kansas City, Mo.	921,121	475,539
*Kenosha	72,852	67,899
*Kingston	......	53,526

* Also in the American Manufacturing Region.

TABLE 8 (cont'd)

Selected Cities and Towns of the Agricultural Interior

City or Town	Urbanized Area	Political Center
*Kitchener	154,864	74,485
*Lakewood, Ohio	......	66,154
*Lansing	169,325	107,807
Lexington	111,940	62,810
Lincoln	136,220	128,521
*London	181,283	169,569
*Lorain	142,860	68,932
*Louisville	606,654	390,639
*Madison	157,814	126,706
*Milwaukee	1,149,997	741,324
Minneapolis	1,377,143	482,872
Moline	......	42,705
*Muncie	77,504	68,603
Nashville	346,729	170,874
*Niagara Falls	......	102,734
*Oak Park	......	61,093
Omaha	389,881	301,598
*Oshawa	......	62,415
*Ottawa	429,750	268,206
*Parma	......	82,845
*Peoria	181,432	103,162
*Pontiac	......	82,233
*Racine	95,862	89,144
*Rochester	493,402	318,611
*Rockford	171,681	126,706
Rock Island	......	51,863
*Royal Oak	......	80,612
*Saginaw	129,215	98,265
*St. Catharines	......	84,472
*St. Clair Shores	......	76,657
St. Joseph	81,187	79,673
*St. Louis	1,667,693	750,026
St. Paul	......	313,411
Sioux City	97,926	89,159
Sioux Falls	66,582	65,466
*Skokie	......	59,364
*South Bend	218,933	132,445
*Springfield, Ill.	111,403	83,271
*Springfield, Ohio	90,157	82,723
*Terre Haute	81,415	72,500
*Toledo	438,283	318,003
Topeka	119,500	119,484
*Toronto	1,824,481	672,407
Tulsa	298,922	261,685
*Warren	......	89,246
Waterloo	102,827	71,755
*Waukegan	......	55,719
*Wauwatosa	......	56,923
*West Allis	......	68,157
*Windsor	193,365	114,367

whims of nature—drought, flood, tornado, hail, freezes, and insect pests—mostly beyond his control.

The exodus of young people from the farms to the cities will no doubt continue, despite the fact that farming is now profitable. However, agriculture never will be able to pay wages comparable with those paid in manufacturing and commerce. Furthermore, young people in large numbers are no longer needed on farms.

The importance of this region to Anglo-America cannot be overestimated. It includes the heartland of the United States, and it encompasses that relatively small part of Ontario that makes Canada solid (and British). Thanks to benignancy of nature and enterprise of man, the region generally has had a prosperous past. Its future should be similarly bright.

Selected Bibliography

Anderson, Edgar, "The Cornbelt Farmer and the Cornbelt Landscape," *Landscape,* Vol. 6, Spring 1957, pp. 3-4.

Baker, Joseph E., "The Midwestern Origins of America," *American Scholar,* Vol. 17, 1948, pp. 58-68.

Brownell, Joseph W., "The Cultural Midwest," *Journal of Geography,* Vol. 59, February 1960, pp. 81-85.

Dahlberg, Richard E., "The Concord Grape Industry of the Chautauqua-Erie Area," *Economic Geography,* November 1957, pp. 150-169.

Edwards, Everett E., "American Agriculture—The First 300 Years," *Yearbook of Agriculture, 1940,* pp. 171-276. Washington: U.S. Government Printing Office, 1940.

Fox, Rodney, "A Landscape in Transition," *Landscape,* Vol. 8, Spring 1959, pp. 1-5.

Garland, John H., ed., *The North American Midwest: a Regional Geography.* New York: John Wiley & Sons, 1955.

"Irrigation in the Midwest," *Business Conditions,* Federal Reserve Bank of Chicago, December 1956, pp. 13-16.

Krueger, Ralph R., "Changing Land Uses in the Niagara Fruit Belt," *Geographical Bulletin,* No. 14, 1960, pp. 5-24.

Malin, James C., "The Adaptation of the Agricultural System to Sub-Humid Environment," *Agricultural History*, Vol. 10, 1936, pp. 118-141.

———, *The Grasslands of North America, Prolegomena to Its History*. Lawrence, Kansas: Privately printed, 1948.

———, "Mobility and History: Reflections on Agricultural Policies of the United States in Relation to a Mechanized World," *Agricultural History*, Vol. 17, 1943, pp. 177-191.

"Soybeans—An Alternative Crop," *Monthly Review*, Federal Reserve Bank of Kansas City, February 1962, pp. 11-15.

Van Steen, Marcus, "Tobacco: Another Canadian Achievement," *Canadian Geographical Journal*, Vol. 61, July 1960, pp. 10-17.

Wallace, H. A., "Corn and the Midwestern Farmer," *Landscape*, Vol. 6, Spring 1957, pp. 9-12.

Weaver, John C., "Changing Patterns of Cropland Use in the Middle West," *Economic Geography*, Vol. 30, January 1954, pp. 1-47.

———, "Crop-Combination Regions in the Middle West," *Geographical Review*, Vol. 44, April 1954, pp. 175-200.

———, Leverett P. Hoag, and Barbara L. Fenton, "Livestock Units and Combination Regions in the Middle West," *Economic Geography*, Vol. 32, July 1956, pp. 237-259.

Wood, Harold A., "The St. Lawrence Seaway and Urban Geography, Cornwall-Cardinal, Ontario," *Geographical Review*, Vol. 45, October 1955, pp. 509-530.

chapter ten

The Northern Continental Forest

Anglo-America's largest region (Figure 10-1) is mostly an interminable coniferous forest, with a sprinkling of broad-leaved trees, covering an area of flat to rolling terrain. A map showing distribution of population superimposed on a map indicating regional boundaries will show the area's relative emptiness. Maps of terrain, soils, and climate show *why* there is a paucity of human beings. Much of this region consists of the Canadian Shield, a land of Pre-Cambrian crystalline rock, rounded hills almost devoid of soil, fast-flowing rivers, and innumerable lakes, swamps, and muskegs. Long, cold winters characterize most of the region; its amazingly short growing season makes agriculture relatively unimportant. On the mainland proper, true agricultural settlements persist only in the pioneer fringes. From boundary to boundary, most of the inhabitants are engaged overwhelmingly in *extractive* pursuits. The

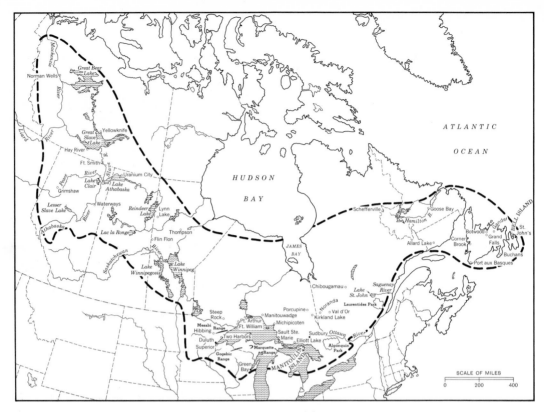

Figure 10-1. The Northern Continental Forest. A region of logging, trapping, mining, resorts, and wilderness.

natural environment discourages most other types of enterprises. Much of this region remains as it was originally—a land of the Indian. The central part, however, in the Clay Belt and in the mining region, is a part of settled Canada.

The Northern Continental Forest Region of Anglo-America falls logically into three geographical subregions: 1) Newfoundland and Coastal Labrador, 2) the Mainland Taiga,[1] and 3) the Upper Lakes.

Newfoundland and Coastal Labrador

This subregion occupies a strategic position across the mouth of the Gulf of

St. Lawrence and along the trade route connecting America and northwest Europe. It is advantageously situated with respect to important fishing grounds. Newfoundland, the most important part of this subregion, has long been the western terminus for transatlantic cables, wireless stations, steamer lanes, and airplane crossings. More recently the island has become one of the most important places for naval and air bases in eastern Anglo-America. But strategic location is no substitute for a viable economy, and in general this subregion is impoverished.

The Natural Environment

Terrain Newfoundland has rolling plateaus 500 to 1,000 feet above sea level, with elevations above 3,000 feet in the Long Ranges. The Labrador coast is the rugged,

[1] The vast forested area extending from interior Labrador to the lower Mackenzie Valley is referred to in this book as the Mainland Taiga. It includes most of the area known as the Canadian or Laurentian Shield, as well as the forested northern portion of the Great Plains.

246

elevated, fjorded edge of the Shield. Glaciation left much of the area studded with lakes, almost soil-bare, and swampy. Southeast of Newfoundland, the ocean bottom consists of a submarine plateau or tableland—the Grand Banks, already discussed as one of the major fishing banks of the entire world. Geologists affirm that Newfoundland had a small independent ice cap of its own.

Climate The climate is largely the result of a clash between continental and oceanic influences, with the former dominating. The winters are much colder than those in British Columbia or Britain in the same latitude. Altitude plays its role, as evidenced by the replacement of forest by tundra at elevations exceeding 1,000 or 1,200 feet.

The ocean is ever near (no point in the subregion is more than 70 miles from salt water), but its relative coldness and the prevailing westerly winds (which bring continental influences) do not permit much amelioration of the temperatures. In the Gulf of St. Lawrence all harbors freeze over in the winter, the Strait of Belle Isle being completely blocked by ice. The bays on the Labrador coast and large areas of the adjacent sea freeze solid by October or November. Summers everywhere are cool, because the Labrador Current, laden with floe ice and icebergs, moves southward along the east and south coasts.

Considerable snow falls: except for the south coast of Newfoundland, the entire subregion gets more than 100 inches of snow in winter. Ice storms, more common here than elsewhere in Anglo-America, occur when a south wind sets in. Rain freezes as it comes in contact with the colder ground. Fog is prevalent on the coasts and on the Grand Banks, but no more so than on the southern coasts of Nova Scotia.

Surface winds may change direction suddenly, and are sometimes so strong that houses must have double walls, double doors, and double windows to keep the wind and fine snow out. Even shoreline trees are affected by these winds and are stunted as a consequence.

Natural Vegetation The natural vegetation consists largely of coniferous forest—white spruce and balsam fir in the main body of the island. In the southwest is a small area of mixed forest—red maple and yellow birch. On the Long Peninsula is forest tundra—black spruce and reindeer moss. The coast of Labrador is almost completely lacking in forest, though the sheltered stream basins support some tree growth, particularly in the Hamilton River Valley.

Settlement

The Newfoundland-Labrador Subregion was the first part of Anglo-America to be discovered and used by white men. Though Newfoundland was England's oldest colony, for many generations it was considered unfit for human habitation. Moreover, settlement was discouraged, because the mother country wished to use it exclusively for the fisheries, which in turn served as "a school of seamanship" for the British Navy. Speaking of a group of naval recruits who arrived in England in the summer of 1941, Wallace Reyburn said:

> There could be few men better fitted to take on the duties of the Navy than these hardy Newfoundland lads. Having spent all their lives in this island colony off the east coast of Canada, they have the sea in their very bones. At an age when the average English youngster is attending preparatory school, these boys are out in their tiny fishing boats off the coasts of Newfoundland and Labrador, living up to the Newfoundlanders' claim of being the best fishermen in the world.[2]

[2] The British Library of Information, *Bulletin from Britain,* No. 40 (June 4, 1941), p. 4.

When settlement finally did get under way in the eighteenth century, practically all the population became concentrated along the coast near the fishing grounds. Today more than 90 per cent of the inhabitants live there.

Most Newfoundlanders are small in stature but wiry, and are of English, Scottish, and Irish extraction. Their standard of living is low; families are large and incomes small. The interior is unsuitable for farming and is plagued by myriads of mosquitoes during the two or three warm months. Among Britain's North American possessions, Newfoundland alone failed to become primarily a colony of settlement.

Economic Geography

This subregion has three principal sources of income all of which are based upon the exploitation of natural resources —the fisheries, the forest, and the mines. The soil contributes little, since agriculture is little-developed.

Fishing Some authorities declare that French and Portuguese fishermen came to the banks before Columbus reached the New World. Whether this be true or not, it is known that fishermen from Europe were on the banks in the sixteenth century. Permanent settlement by fishermen, however, did not begin until the close of the eighteenth century. Certainly commercial fishing goes back to the days when small sailing vessels carried to Europe commodities having immediate sale and bringing large returns. For 400 years fishing was Newfoundland's only industry: it was solely a summer enterprise, and codfish were always to be caught off the Grand Banks and at the mouth of the St. Lawrence.

Fishing employs more people than any other occupation, although the numbers have been declining during the past century. There are three principal types of fisheries: (1) inshore, (2) Labrador, and (3) bank. *Inshore* fishing, most important of the three, is carried on particularly along the east and south coasts of Newfoundland and accounts for about three-fourths of the catch. The fisherman operates as an individual unit using a dory or motorboat and returning home each night with his catch. Most of the fish are caught in June and July. *Labrador* fishing is carried on along the shore of Labrador by Newfoundlanders who travel north each summer, and by a very small number of resident fishermen or *Liveyeres*. There is also some fishing by schooners on the offshore banks. *Banks* fishing is conducted by schooners of up to 150 tons which make about three trips to the Grand Banks each season. A schooner carries about 20 to 25 men who, once on the fishing grounds, leave the vessel to fish from dories.

Some of the cod are salted when the ships are at sea and dried when the men are fishing close to shore. However, trawlers and draggers are becoming common since they can make more rapid trips from the banks. The fresh-fish trade is important, but so is fish processing. There are about twice as many fishermen as there are workers in the processing plants.

Although Newfoundland, with its relatively small population, is the third leading fishing province in Canada, the industry is facing hard times. Personal income is low, equipment frequently is outmoded, new capital investment is scarce, and Mediterranean markets for salted cod are declining.

Lumbering Newfoundland's forests are one of her most valuable resources and provide her people with much employment and revenue. In fact, since 1930 forest products have been more important than fish. About 47 per cent of the land area, some 17,150 square miles, is forested, of which about 83 per cent is exploitable.

The best timber, consisting of mixed stands of conifers and broad-leaved decidu-

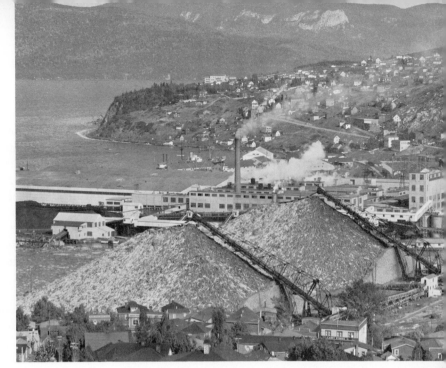

Figure 10-2. The Bowater Pulp and Paper mill at Corner Brook, Newfoundland. Note the two large piles of pulpwood waiting to be used. (Photo courtesy the National Film Board, Ottawa.)

ous trees—predominantly balsam fir, white spruce, and birch—lies in the interior, particularly on the better-drained valley slopes. The trees are inferior to those grown along the Pacific Coast, in Eastern Canada, the Lake States, or New England. Trees cannot attain large proportions when temperatures are low and winds strong. Though some lumbering is carried on, the bulk of the forest is better suited for pulp and paper.

In Labrador, exploitable or commercial forest occurs only in sheltered valleys on well-drained slopes in the interior.

Pulp and Paper The forest, dominated by spruce and fir, supplies the raw material for pulp and paper. The industry benefits not only from accessible timber, but from cheap hydro-power, transport of logs by stream, and from a plentiful supply of labor.

Newfoundland's first paper mill was built at Grand Falls in 1909, where there were both forest and power. The mill is still in operation, as is one situated at Bishop's Falls, just downstream from Grand Falls. Both are connected by rail with Botwood, the summer shipping point at the head of the Bay of Exploits.

One of the largest mills in the world

(Figure 10-2), built in 1924 at Corner Brook, almost at tidewater on the estuary of the Humber River, is well located with respect to its raw material and export markets. Logs are obtained from some 7,000 square miles of holdings and stream-driven to the mill. Hydroelectric power is generated nearby. Ice locks the bay from January to the end of April, at which time the mill's products move by rail southward to ice-free Port aux Basques.

Mining Mining is one of Newfoundland's three principal economic enterprises. However, despite a rich endowment, mining is retarded by the high cost of development. Hence there are only two major producing areas.

BELL ISLAND in Conception Bay is the location of one of the most valuable iron ore deposits and mines in the world. The ore was discovered by accident. Some sailors had picked up heavy stones for ballast and left them in their dories while at anchor in St. John's. A canny Englishman, who suspected these stones were iron ore, had them assayed, and found that they contained about 55 per cent metallic iron.

Since 1899, the mines have been operated

by the same interests as the iron and steel industry in Sydney, Nova Scotia. Their plant has reduced more than half of the 60 million tons so far mined. Annual production is about 10 per cent of the Canadian total. Nova Scotia and the United Kingdom are the principal markets. No ore is smelted in Newfoundland itself.

The workable beds are mined on the northwest side of the island, and mining extends out for a distance of 2½ miles under Conception Bay. The underwater mines, with reserves of about 2½ billion tons, contain ore in three beds separated from one another by thick layers of rock. The room-and-pillar method of mining is employed.

THE BUCHANS MINES, located five miles north of Red Indian Lake in the center of the island, yield zinc-lead-copper sulphide ores. New reserves are now being exploited.

In addition, *fluorspar* is mined at coastal sites on the Burin Peninsula and in southwestern Newfoundland, which produce more than three-quarters of the total Canadian output.

Agriculture   There is practically no agriculture in Coastal Labrador,[3] and even in Newfoundland it plays but a minor role. The people here have always looked *to the sea* and *away from the land*. The natural environment—short growing season, acid podzol soils, rugged terrain—is hostile to farming. Moreover, the planting and fishing seasons conflict. Farming is largely of the subsistence type, being carried on mainly by the families of fishermen and of loggers on small holdings. Seldom does a farm exceed 50 acres, and most farms comprise but a few acres. However, some commercial farming is carried on in the Avalon Peninsula and in the valleys of the west coast, near the larger urban centers. Limited transport facilities also restrict commercial

---

[3] Subarctic specialist F. K. Hare has said, "The Hamilton River Valley is Labrador's principal agricultural area; it has one farm."

farming. Owing to the small humus content of the soils, considerable fish and compost must be used to make the soils productive.

What agriculture there is falls into the hay, dairy, root-crop system. More than half the arable land is in hay and pasture. Actually less than one-half of one per cent of Newfoundland's surface is devoted to crops. Hay and potatoes along with hardy vegetables (cabbages, beets, carrots, and parsnips) and fruits (currants, gooseberries, raspberries, and strawberries) are the leading crops.

Trade   Newfoundland is dependent upon trade for its existence. The fish, pulp and paper, iron ore, copper, lead and zinc concentrates, and fluorspar are exported, but unfortunately the prices of all, especially of fish, upon which so large a proportion of the people depend, fluctuate widely, and poor prices enforce a standard of living dangerously low. About two-thirds of the food and consumers goods are imported, mostly from other parts of Canada.

Transportation

So long as Newfoundlanders engaged solely in fishing and lived in settlements along the coast, the sea was the highway. As exploitation of the island's other resources took place, however, man had to go into the interior. The railway (now a part of the Canadian National) was begun in 1881 and completed in 1896. The main line and its branches consist of 935 miles of narrow-gauge track.

There are less than 7,000 miles of all types of road on the island. Most of this mileage consists of gravel highway; the only hard-surface roads are on the Avalon Peninsula. There is not a mile of hard-surface road in coastal Labrador.

Sea transportation is of major significance in connecting the subregion to the outside world. St. John's is the chief port, but Port aux Basques is also important, chiefly because of its nearness to Nova Scotia.

The subregion's significance in air transportation is based upon two international airports, at Gander and at Goose Bay, where many transatlantic flights make first and last stops in North America.

The Outlook

Grim climate, poor soils, and immature drainage, all conspire to discourage any bright future for this subregion. The coasts of Labrador and of northern Newfoundland are frozen solid from December till late in June, though the Atlantic coast of the island has ice floes and is frozen part of the time. Agriculture and manufacturing, the two economic enterprises over the earth that sustain the largest populations, have in this subregion little future. And the enterprises that do have a future—fishing, logging, pulp- and papermaking, and mining—do not give opportunities and jobs to many persons. Despite the importance of the mines, they give employment to and affect but a relatively small number of persons. For the total capital invested and the value of the output, mining the world over gives employment to but a small part of a nation's or a region's total population.

Some expansion can be anticipated in all the extractive activities, although the structure of the fishing industry will probably undergo a considerable reorganization, causing further economic hardship, before rejuvenation can take place. Even with limited expansion, however, the economy of the subregion and the life of its people will not be changed materially.

The Mainland Taiga

This subregion consists essentially of the mainland portion of the Canadian taiga. It includes the Canadian, or Laurentian, Shield, a vast expanse of forest, water, and bare bedrock that is underlaid by an ancient crystalline basement complex, as well as a southwestern extension of the great forest that is undergirded with sedimentary deposits.

This is the land of great coniferous forests that for a long time was considered to be worthless wilderness except for the furs it supplied. It was practically unknown except to trappers and fur traders, to lumbermen, prospectors, and sportsmen—people whose numbers always are small. So inhospitable was much of the subregion that, despite determined efforts to put roads across the rocky, shallow soil and the filigree of lakes and rivers, Canadian expansion was deflected around the southern rim. Thus the Canadian Shield stood as a wall between eastern and western Canada, denying the nation the strength, vigor, and development which come from geographical and political unity. This situation has changed in the past half century, however, with the tapping of the area's wealth of forest, minerals, and water power. What had been a liability to the country has now become an asset. Even its soils are being utilized locally, especially in the Clay Belt, though for agriculture the area is precariously marginal.

The subregion, although enormous in size, is isolated. Its location has been and ever will be a handicap to development. The thin soils devoid of humus, the poor drainage, hostile climate, and pestiferous insects magnify the unattractiveness to the average immigrant. The Shield is a magnet only to people of the pioneer type or to those interested in quick wealth.

The Natural Environment

Terrain The Canadian Shield, a vast U-shaped peneplain of ancient crystalline rocks (granites, gneisses, and metamorphosed sedimentaries), covers one-half of

Canada, its rim towering above the St. Lawrence and Ottawa Valleys and the coast of
Labrador and reaching southeast of Georgian Bay and west of Lake Superior. It was
so thoroughly glaciated that its rivers were
dammed, forming numerous lakes and rock
basins. Drainage is poor; swamps or muskegs are extensive. Lakes are so numerous
that the country might almost be described
as water with land between it. The rocks
have been reduced to a peneplain of relatively uniform height over a considerable
area, although the whole subregion is far
from flat. Though there are local hills and
valleys, there is little difference in elevation, the average being approximately 1,000
feet.

In addition, the ice cap, which carried
enormous quantities of debris, deposited
this material as the ice melted after the last
invasion—an event estimated to have occurred about 10 thousand years ago. A
veneer of glacial till is a prominent feature
over the Shield and is the basis of the soils.
In some parts the land was scraped bare
even over extensive areas (Figure 10-3).
Within the Shield, however, are areas of
reasonably level terrain and fair soils that

owe their origin to old glacial lakes. Lake
Ojibway (Clay Belt) and the Lake St. John
Lowland are examples and are favorable
for settlement.

To the southwest and west of the hard-
rock Shield is a broad lowland of vast extent that is underlaid by softer sedimentary
materials. It has been built up by deposition of sands and silts washed off the
Rockies and the Shield. Consisting for the
most part of a plain with scattered hilly districts, it is almost as poorly drained as the
Shield, with the result that water features
(rivers, lakes, muskegs) are commonplace.
Some of the largest rivers (Mackenzie,
Slave, Athabaska, Saskatchewan) and lakes
(Great Bear, Great Slave, Winnipeg) in
Anglo-America are found here (Figure 10-
4). Most of the sedimentary plain, sometimes referred to as the "forested northern
Great Plains," drains northward to the Arctic Ocean via a complicated hydrologic
system that is dominated by the Mackenzie
River.

Climate In so enormous an area, important differences of climate from north to
south or east to west might be expected,
but actually the differences are relatively

Figure 10-3. Ice-scoured
rock on the Clearwater River,
Richmond Gulf, Quebec.
The stand of trees here is
thin, for the area is near the
northern limit of tree growth
and close to the Tundra.
(Photo courtesy the Royal
Canadian Air Force.)

slight. Everywhere the climate is continental —the result largely of interior location, great distance from oceans, and the barrier influence of the Cordilleras, which keep out the moderating effects of the Pacific Ocean. This continentality is the dominating feature of the Shield's natural environment. Winters are dark and cold and long; summers short and mild, with occasional hot spells. The total precipitation is light in most places, and well distributed through the year.

Soils Since no complete survey has been made of the soils of the Shield, the area pedologically speaking is *terra incognita*. Owing to the fact that the soils have been subjected to rain and cold for thousands of years, a large part of them are podzols, whose reputation for agriculture is not enviable. Grey, wooded soils are found in the west, and clay, alluvial, or high-lime soils occupy local areas. Most soils are poorly drained.

Permafrost Roughly the northern half of this subregion is subject to permafrost problems, although the distribution is erratic. Permafrost consists of permanently frozen subsoil, a condition that precludes soil-water percolation during the summer. Soil freezing and thawing are intimately associated with the vegetational cover, and its removal results in structural movements that may inhibit cultivation and almost invariably make construction of buildings and roads exceedingly difficult.

Natural Vegetation The distinctive natural vegetation of the Shield is coniferous forest with a deciduous admixture. From south to north the trees become smaller, those in the extreme north being small and scraggly. The forest has been known in detail only since the advent of aerial photography. The northern limit is determined mostly by climate and partly by drainage. The poor drainage which characterizes the flat land south of James Bay and the west coast of Hudson Bay makes this area so

Figure 10-4. The Slave River in the Northwest Territories. Deciduous trees in the foreground appear as light-colored spots against the dark matrix of conifers. Small ponds and marshes beyond the river give evidence of the poor drainage that is characteristic. (Photo courtesy Canadian Government Travel Bureau.)

water-logged that tree growth occurs only along the rivers.

This *taiga*, or great northern forest, is characterized by relatively few species, those of the greatest commercial value being spruce, with much pine, fir, and aspen on the southern side; in the subarctic belt, before it merges with the *tundra*, is to be found considerable scattered and slow-growing spruce of little commercial value. Much of the "Granite Shield" (in the east and center), where lakes and marshes are widespread, is covered by muskegs, consisting of boggy basins filled with peat or sphagnum moss; these are normally surrounded by dense stands of black spruce or tamarack.

There is a stand of hardwoods in the southeastern part of the Shield, but this forest, until recently, was little utilized. The increased demand for hardwood lumber and mechanical improvements in logging equipment have at last, however, enabled these forests to be tapped economically. The leading hardwood tree is the yellow birch.

Native Animal Life Native animal life was originally abundant. Fur-bearing animals have had the greatest geographical and economic influence because of the trapping carried on by natives and "outsiders" alike. The beaver, distributed throughout the subregion, has been the most important species, but also notable are the muskrat, various mustellids (ermine, mink, marten, otter, fisher, wolverine), canids (wolf and fox), the black bear, and the lynx. Another significant group is the ungulates. Woodland caribou occupy most of the subregion, and vast herds of barren-ground caribou often spend the winter in the taiga. Moose and deer are also found.

Bird life is abundant and varied in summer. Many species of fish inhabit the lakes and rivers. Insects, especially flies and mosquitoes, are so numerous as to make life for man and beast almost unbearable. Insects constitute an outstanding handicap to settlement and exploitation.

Water Power Few areas in the world have better water-power sites than the Canadian Shield. Large rivers and small rivers seldom run more than a few miles without tumbling over a fall or rapid. Moreover, most of them have their sources in lakes which serve as excellent storage reservoirs. Many, too, have storage lakes along their courses. About 80 to 85 per cent of the developed and roughly 60 per cent of the Dominion's potential water power are in the so-called acute fuel area—the provinces of Ontario and Quebec—where native coal is economically unavailable. Much of the undeveloped water power lies far from centers of population, but the developed power lies largely within the *ecumene*.[4]

The abundance of hydro-power is re-

flected in low rates and in the types of industry utilizing the power. The extremely low rate in Quebec results from huge sales to the pulp and paper industry, to aluminum plants, to other electrochemical and electrometallurgical industries. Wholesale rates are made to Ontario and the United States.

It is this power that has become the mainspring of Canadian industry and has contributed so much to Canada's recent metamorphosis from an almost pure agricultural and extractive economy to one of industrial prominence.

The Occupance

The Indian Before white men came, the Taiga was occupied by nomadic Indians who subsisted by hunting and fishing. It is not known whether they ever tried agriculture, but if they did it was unsuccessful, since the climate is too severe for maize.

Their numbers were small—possibly 500,-000 for all Anglo-America north of the Great Lakes.[5] The density of population has been estimated at approximately two to five persons for each 100 square miles at the time the white man came. It is significant that these inland Indians were, by area, even less numerous than the Eskimos along the shore of the Arctic.[6] This relative scarcity of inhabitants was due to a war-like social tradition and to the fact that hunting and trapping always preclude a dense population, since they entail the great disadvantage of uncertainty: today game may be plentiful, tomorrow it may be lacking. Hence life was precarious, poverty extreme, and starvation not uncommon.

These Indians, backward Algonquins in the east and south, Athabascans in the north-

---

[4] The land within ten miles of a railway.

[5] A. L. Kroeber, *Cultural and Natural Areas of Native North America* (Berkeley: University of California Press, 1939), p. 164.

[6] Kroeber, *Cultural and Natural Areas of Native North America*, p. 145.

west, and Crees in the Clay Belt,[7] were highly mobile both within and among their tribal areas. Culture here was lower than in the American Southwest. The paucity of formidable barriers east of the Rockies meant in general terms a similarity of environment and of culture.

With the coming of white men, trapping for furs became important. So keen was the competition for peltries between the French and English traders that Indian tribes warred upon one another.

Many Indian women, particularly Ojibwas and Crees, whose hunting territory was where most of the fur trade was carried on, intermarried with whites, especially in the earlier years of contact. The offspring of such unions are called *Metis*. They normally acquired a cultural background similar to that of the Indians, and lived like Indians. The prevalence of Metis is such that there are today relatively few full-blooded Indians among the hunting tribes of the Taiga.

The submarginal portions of the Canadian Taiga still are the land of the Indian, whose way of life demands a thorough knowledge of the habits of wild animals and ability to move over wide areas in pursuit of food and peltries. Some tracts are now specifically reserved where only Indians may hunt and trap.

White Settlement   The wide scope of this book does not permit a detailed treatment of white settlement in the Taiga. One of two motives actuated those who dared enter the wilderness: (1) to utilize the natural resources or (2) to make homes there and build new societies. The fur trader, miner, and forester exemplified the first, the farmer the second.

Though the land never can accommodate many settlers, nevertheless, much money and time have been spent in a fruitless effort to push the frontier beyond its natural lim-

its. By 1855 the better lands of eastern Canada had been acquired and settlement was approaching the Shield. At this time and for decades afterwards the Shield was known only superficially.

As in the Intermontane Basins and Plateaus (Chapter 13), two interests were working against each other: one, trying to administer the natural resources in the wisest way, was desperately attempting to keep settlers from those areas where they would do more harm than good, whereas the other used all its power to encourage settlement.

That the Taiga is a restrictive environment seems proved by the fact that after a century following pioneer penetration, the Crown still has title to all but a minuscule percentage of the land. Many who did settle have moved away from the pines and rocks. It is now generally believed that pioneers should be discouraged from engaging in marginal colonizing. Public acceptance of such an idea is difficult to obtain, for one of the deepest-seated human instincts is that the land is for the people. Despite difficulties, however, portions of the Taiga are being settled.

Present Population   The first whites were French explorers and fur trappers who did not settle permanently on the land. Later French immigrants, whose descendants are the present French Canadians, occupied the St. Lawrence Valley between Montreal and Quebec as well as several tributary valleys. As a result of the limited arable land and the high birth rate, some of these spilled over into adjacent areas and now make up a considerable part of the Shield's population. Later came English fur trappers and traders, rivals of the French. The transfer of Canada by France to England increased the number of Anglo-Saxons in Canada, though most of these went into southern Ontario or later into the Prairie Provinces. Some, however, were drawn onto the Shield by its timber, minerals, and, to a lesser de-

[7] Kroeber, *Cultural and Natural Areas of Native North America*, p. 194.

gree, its agriculture. More recent immigrants are the Germans, Finns, Hungarians, Italians, Russians, Poles, Slovaks, and Swedes. In the Taiga these nationalities tend to segregate into blocks, as they do in the large metropolitan centers of eastern United States.

The introduction of mining started an influx of peoples from all types of climates, some well fitted and some poorly fitted to cope with the harsh environment. Those who remained had to develop initiative and resourcefulness.

The population of the Taiga is less than 10 per cent of the Canadian total, and even these 1,300,000 people live for the most part on the southern margin of the Shield. It can hardly be expected that the area ever can support any appreciable proportion of the total Canadian population, even though the Indians and Metis are the fastest growing ethnic group in the nation, increasing at a rate of about three per cent per year.

Economic Development

Much of the Taiga remains undeveloped, but that portion lying immediately north of the St. Lawrence River and the Great Lakes is now partially conquered, and small but increasing numbers of people are finding their way into the Mackenzie Valley. Regardless of whether man has engaged in fur trading, lumbering, mining, farming, or pulp-and papermaking, his activities have been dominated by the forest. The explorer and fur trader, unable to go cross-country on foot or horseback because of the forest, had to take to the canoe and river. To lumbermen and pulp manufacturers the forest was a great natural resource from which they desired to keep out all but themselves. The prospector and the farmer, however, did not look kindly upon the forest; to them it was an enemy that had to be destroyed. The prospector saw in the forest simply a covering that prevented his knowing what kind

of rock underlay his feet. Extractive industries have held and probably always will hold sway on the taiga. Agriculture will expand briefly but will be relegated to a secondary place unless science makes contributions now unknown.

Subsistence Hunting and Fishing In the past both Indians and Metis led nomadic or seminomadic lives, depending on wildlife and fish for subsistence, sometimes with trapping as a sideline for trading. Within the Taiga today there is still a moderate amount of these activities, but nomadism is generally a thing of the past. The introduction of modern arms and ammunition has had the predictable effect of making it easier to kill game at first but much more difficult in the long run, due to overutilization of the faunal resources. The deer, moose, and caribou that once supplied most of the meat have been greatly depleted, and the problem of feeding a large family (the average Metis or Indian family is nearly half again larger than the average for all Canadians), plus supplying meat for the ubiquitous sled dogs, is increasingly difficult. Most native and half-breed breadwinners have to depend upon part-time jobs, supplemental income from trapping, and the ever-welcome government relief check.

Trapping Fur trading began along the coast of Canada, but it never attained great proportions there, because the short rivers were poorly suited to transportation and because the population was concentrated along the coast. The enterprise really became important and migrated onto the Shield in the latter part of the sixteenth century, when beaver hats became fashionable in Europe. Beavers were most numerous in the more northerly forested parts of the Shield, where agriculture and manufacturing had little chance of success and where the environment provided a favorable habitat for fur-bearing animals. The beaver was not a migrant, and its destruction in any locality

Figure 10-5. Hurricanaw River Indians with a trapped beaver. The spruce boughs are used for removing the snow and ice that cling to the animal's fur. (Photo courtesy National Film Board, Ottawa.)

forced the hunters to enter new areas. Prime furs were taken only in winter and in the more northerly parts of the forest (Figure 10-5).

Fur hunting still is important here; Canada ranks as one of the world's two chief suppliers of furs, though this subregion does not furnish the entire output. Total catches have shown an erratic decline in recent years, reflecting scarcity of animals, competition from fur farms, and the vagaries of fashion.

When possible, the animals are caught in snares or traps to avoid damaging the pelts. Because fur is longer and thicker in winter, Indians and Metis (very few whites are permitted to trap because the furs are so important to native livelihood and the resource is limited) at that time scatter out along the streams, sometimes going hundreds of miles to get their pelts. The more desirable animals—the beaver, otter, mink, and muskrat—live along the streams. Moreover, waterways are highways, even in winter, when they form ready-made hard sled roads.

The valuable beaver is still the most important fur-bearer caught. About one-third of a million beaver pelts are taken in an average year, which amounts to more than one-third of the value of all wild pelts in the nation. Mink ranks second, approximately half as significant as beaver. Muskrat is third and the lowly squirrel fourth in total value of catch. Ontario is the leading trapping province by far, followed by Alberta and Saskatchewan.

When ice melts in the spring, hunters take their catch to trading posts. Birchbark canoes and larger boats are used. Many of the fur-trading posts belong to the historic Hudson's Bay Company, oldest company in Anglo-America (established in 1670), which accounts for nearly half of Canada's furs. It has more than 200 trading posts strategically located with respect to navigable water. Some of its posts are found more than 600 miles north of the Arctic Circle.

Fur Farming The raising of fur-bearing animals for pelting got its start on Prince Edward Island about 1887 and in Quebec in 1894. Found to be an excellent adjunct to agriculture, because it was winter work, it was usually practiced by farmers. It was a major commercial activity on Prince Edward Island for several decades, but is practically gone from there today. The fur-farming trend in Canada, however, is decidedly upward. The proportion of the pelt value from fur farms, of the total pelt value (wild and farmed), has increased steadily

258

258 THE NORTHERN CONTINENTAL FOREST

from about 35 per cent in the late 1940's to more than 60 per cent in the early 1960's.

Foxes, mainstay of the early fur farmers, are rarely raised today. Mink farms make up more than 90 per cent of the total farms, and chinchillas most of the remainder. Fur farms are found in every region and every province of Canada, but they are characteristic of the Northern Continental Forest, with Ontario as the leading producer.

Forestry Logging and lumbering superseded trapping in the more accessible territory when the beaver were destroyed. The industry has been based largely upon the pines which grow as far north as the Hudson Bay drainage. Trees grow slowly in cold, windy climates and on thin, rocky soils and poorly-drained land. Thus about 100 years are required for a tree in such a habitat to reach sufficient size to be used for saw timber.

Lumbering in the Taiga has declined in importance in recent years because of (1) the competition of British Columbia and of northern Europe, whose forests are more accessible (Figure 10-6); (2) the exhaustion of the best pine near the St. Lawrence; and (3) the high tariffs in the United States. If the forests of British Columbia should be removed as have those of the St. Lawrence

Figure 10-6. Most of Canada's commercial forest land is accessible, particularly in the eastern provinces. (Courtesy of U.S. Forest Service.)

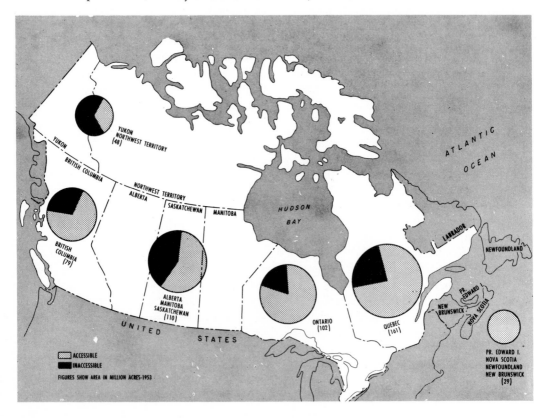

Figure 10-7. Tractor pulling a sled load of logs from the woods to a waterway. Scene is near Atikokan, Ontario. (Photo courtesy Caterpillar Tractor Company.)

Lowland, the Taiga would become a more important source of lumber, though in the northern part species dwindle in number and size.

Logging depends upon snow in this region of long cold winters. The cutters begin their work in autumn. Where small trees, destined for pulp mills, are cut, the work must be done before the snow buries the forests. The logs must be moved out while the ground is frozen. Ice-roads are built up by continual sprinkling with water over terrain absolutely impassable in summer. Tractors pull the sleds laden with logs to rivers, where the cut is piled awaiting the spring thaw and the freshets, which transport the logs by the hundreds of thousands to strategically located mills (Figure 10-7). River-driving is an economical method of transporting logs, though this applies almost entirely to softwoods (Figure 10-8). Logging employs the workers (mostly Slavs, Swedes, Finns, and French Canadians) for only about 100 days per year. Some of the lumberjacks are farmers who must supplement the living they eke from the land by other means.

PULP AND PAPER is Canada's leading industry, and Canada is now the world's largest manufacturer and exporter of newsprint.

Figure 10-8. Loggers breaking up a "jam" with pike poles and peaveys on the Desert River, a tributary of the Gatineau. (Photo courtesy National Film Board, Ottawa.)

Beginning in 1866, the industry grew steadily until the termination of the first World War, then boomed between 1920 and 1930, when new towns sprang up over-night, huge water-power projects were installed, and thousands of persons became employed. Much of the industry is controlled by American capital. The United States, the world's largest consumer of newsprint, is interested in Canada (the Shield in particular) because it is nearby and because newsprint since 1911 has been admitted free of duty. A great deal of pulp and some pulpwood also are exported.

At first, the paper companies, which engaged only in manufacturing, purchased their pulpwood. So great, however, became the demands that they were unable to meet the requirements by purchase and hence were obliged to get either freehold or Crown grants. Fortunately for Canada, 90 per cent of the forested area is retained by the Crown, whereas in the United States 80 per cent is in private ownership. Canadian pulp and paper manufacturing, however, is not restricted to the Shield, though it leads all other parts of the country by a wide margin.

The pulp and paper industry is located advantageously with respect to the spruce-balsam forests and to the distribution of water power. Spruce, though existing as far north as trees can grow, really reaches its optimum along the Hudson Bay Divide. So extensive is this forest that it would appear to be able to supply present needs in perpetuity, provided reasonable conservation is carried on. The method of transporting pulp logs is similar to that used by the lumber industry.

Cheap power is an important factor in the location of pulp plants, as is shown by their distribution. A string of mills (all water-driven) lines the southern edge of the forest from the mouth of the St. Lawrence to Lake Winnipeg. If, in addition to power and to proximity to resources of wood of superior quality for the manufacture of newsprint, the mill has abundant and dependable supplies of clean, fresh water, can receive river-driven logs, and lies on navigable water so that imported raw materials can be secured cheaply and finished products be shipped economically, its location may be considered strategic. A paper mill is a huge and costly plant which cannot afford to migrate even if its tributary area is denuded of forest cover. The practice now is to follow reforestation as a means of insuring a continuous and permanent supply of pulp wood. A company having a large area with trees at all stages of growth has little to worry about, if fires can be avoided. Moreover, the large-scale processes and the enormous cost of the plants have a good psychological effect upon the people who live in the region, for they look upon this industry as a permanent one—one not out to exploit or mine the forest, as has been the case with too many sawmills.

Commercial Fishing   In the last decade, commercial fisheries have developed in several of the large lakes of the western Taiga. The industry is on a small scale compared with oceanic fishing, but adds measurably to the local economy. It is a year-round activity, but emphasis is on winter ice-fishing and gill-netting. Transportation is significantly simplified during the cold months when tractor trains can reach the remoter lakes over frozen ground that would be soddenly impassable in summer.

Great Bear Lake is too deep and cold and barren to provide a commercial fishery, but Great Slave Lake has an expanding industry centered at Hay River. Whitefish and lake trout are caught, primarily for export to eastern United States. Lake Winnipeg is a major fishing ground, and commercial operations are found also on Lakes Athabaska, Clair, Lesser Slave, Winnipegosis, Reindeer, and Lac la Ronge. While export markets take most of the catch, the fur

Figure 10-9. Urban contrasts in the Mainland Taiga Subregion. The top photo shows the main street of Sudbury, Ontario, a town that is well-established and has much more permanence than is usually associated with mining settlements. The lower photo shows a residential section of Thompson, Manitoba, a new community that has mushroomed on the site of recent mineral discoveries. (Photos courtesy Ontario Department of Travel and Publicity, and Manitoba Department of Industry and Commerce.)

farms in the Taiga are taking a growing proportion of rougher species.

Mining The Canadian Shield is world-famous for its mineral wealth—metals, not coal or petroleum. Prospecting over much of the area is facilitated by (1) bareness of the rock, (2) accessibility by canoe routes or lakes for airplane landings, and (3) the existence of an accurate geological map for areas along stream courses. Had the region not been glaciated, prospecting would have been far more difficult. Several of the outstanding mineral deposits were discovered by chance—mining having begun as a by-product of railroad building, the fundamental purpose of which was the development of agriculture in the Clay Belt of northern Ontario.[8] Much prospecting today

is done by airplane and helicopter, the greatest single aids to the extension of mining. This is a far cry from those early days when the prospector roamed over the Shield. Now discovery and actual mining depend upon geological science, precision instruments, and the diamond drill.

When a mineral is discovered in a wilderness such as the Shield, the men at first live in camps. Life is grim and hard. Bread and water are expensive. But if conditions essential for successful and profitable mining be present in sufficient force, the camp grows in size to a village, town, or perhaps even a city. In this way began such thriving centers as Sudbury, Rouyn-Noranda, Kirkland Lake, Timmins, Cobalt, Val d'Or, and many others (Figure 10-9).

Power, essential for operating the mines and mills, was at first supplied by wood, but as nearby forested areas were cut off, the cost of using wood became too great. Water

[8] Harold A. Innis, "Settlement and the Mining Frontier," *Canadian Frontiers of Settlement*, Vol. 9 (Toronto: The Macmillan Company of Canada, Ltd., 1936), p. 372.

power accordingly replaced it, being first used for this purpose in Ontario in 1906. Today the mines are among the chief users of hydroelectric power. Among the Shield's more important minerals are nickel, copper, platinum, gold, silver, iron, uranium, lead, and zinc. They are produced from a variety of localities in some three dozen mining areas. On the basis of relative location, the areas can be grouped into three principal mineral districts, plus several isolated centers.[9]

SUDBURY-CLAY BELT DISTRICT Considering the magnitude of the Shield, this is a district of rather closely spaced mining activity. Many metals are recovered, but mostly nickel, copper, and gold.

Modern mining began in Canada after the discovery of the Sudbury nickel-copper ores in 1883. It is decidedly the outstanding metal mining area in Canada, producing more than half the world's supply of nickel, and considerable amounts of copper, silver, and cobalt. Both open-pit and shaft mining are employed, and most of the smelting is carried on within the area. Although no metal mining center can be considered as being permanent, Sudbury certainly approaches the goal of permanency. It has both tremendous reserves and a steady market.

In the Clay Belt country, straddling the Ontario-Quebec boundary is a major gold-copper zone that extends from Porcupine on the west 200 miles to Val d'Or on the east. There are dozens of gold mines in the area, with principal output at Porcupine, Kirkland Lake, and Larder Lake (which has Canada's largest gold mine). The Noranda area is a major mining and smelting center for copper.

What is regarded as the world's largest known reserve of uranium is that at Elliott

Lake, on the north shore of Lake Huron's North Channel. It contains more than 90 per cent of Canada's known reserves. The value of uranium production (largely from Elliott Lake) in the late 1950's exceeded that of any other metal in Canada. However, production began to be curtailed in 1960, as a considerable oversupply led the United States (the principal buyer by far) to decide not to purchase any more uranium after 1962. Arrangements were made to allow the producing companies to "stretch out" their deliveries until 1966, so production will continue at least until that time. Elliott Lake, "the city of tomorrow" in 1955, is well on the way to becoming a modern and elaborate ghost town by 1966, one of the first peace-time casualties of the nuclear age.

WESTERN ONTARIO DISTRICT This is a district of widely dispersed mines. Gold, the principal mineral produced, has a history of fluctuating output. Siderite iron ore has been dug at Michipicoten since 1899; production has increased in recent years as low-grade ores became more valuable. New copper mines were recently opened in the vicinity of Manitouwadge.

WESTERN MANITOBA DISTRICT Although copper-zinc ore was discovered in 1915 at Flin Flon, exploitation was not begun until a rail line was built from The Pas in 1928. Flin Flon, a well-established center, is a major copper producer, and yields considerable zinc, gold, and silver as well. Other producing centers are located northeast of Flin Flon and north of the railway line to Churchill. Lynn Lake yields nickel and copper. Snow Lake produces gold and various base metals. But the outstanding development is at the planned town of Thompson, a "Second Sudbury" 200 miles northeast of Flin Flon, which began producing nickel in 1961. It is expected to become the world's second largest nickel producer, with reserves to last at least a century.

[9] E. Willard Miller, "Mineral Regionalism of the Canadian Shield," *The Canadian Geographer*, No. 13 (1959), pp. 17-30.

ISOLATED MINING DISTRICTS At other localities on the Shield are mining centers that consist of either: (1) a rare mineral of particularly high value, or (2) a massive deposit of an ore that has an assured world market.

In the former category are the gold mines of the Yellowknife district on the north shore of Great Slave Lake and the Uranium City development on the north shore of Lake Athabaska, which grew from nothing in 1952 to a town of nearly 6,000 in 1958, but must now readjust to the loss of market for uranium.

Two sources of iron ore in the eastern Taiga represent the massive deposit type. An ilmenite-hematite ore has been mined at Allard Lake, Quebec, 25 miles inland from the Gulf of St. Lawrence and north of Anticosti Island. Both titanium and iron are obtained from the ore.

But the most exciting mineral development in Canada since Alberta's Leduc oil field was the discovery and development of extensive and rich iron ore deposits on the Quebec-Labrador border. This deposit is regarded as one of the great iron ore discoveries of all time.

The discovery was especially timely because the Mesabi's high-grade ore will soon be depleted as a result of two exhaustive world wars in a period of about a quarter century. While American companies have access to rich ore deposits in Chile, Brazil, Venezuela, Peru, and Liberia, the American iron and steel industry, which accounts for more than one-third of the world's steel production, dares not be wholly or even largely dependent upon such distant sources.

Transportation was the big problem until the completion of the railway. So difficult is the terrain that, during construction, bulldozers and other heavy equipment, food, supplies of all kinds, as well as men, had to be flown into the area. The railway, 360 miles long, follows the winding Moisie River for part of the way from the mines at Schefferville to Sept Isles on the shore of the Gulf of St. Lawrence. The cost of the railway averaged in excess of $100,000 per mile.

OIL AND GAS The sedimentary deposits of the western Taiga have no metallic wealth, but their possible store of hydrocarbons is considerable. Significant production to date has been only from the Peace River district and has consisted mostly of natural gas. Both natural-gas and crude-oil pipelines from the Peace River area serve the southern British Columbia market and link up with lines into the United States.

Petroleum has been obtained from the Norman Wells field, at 66° North Latitude on the Mackenzie River, for more than two decades. Oil prospecting continues apace throughout the Mackenzie District and parts of the Yukon Territory; in the early 1960's, there were 400 to 500 men and 60 aircraft searching for oil in the northern sediments.[10]

Agriculture It has been reliably estimated that 94 per cent of Canada is unsuited to farming and that only 6 per cent is arable. Nevertheless, following the common belief that all forest lands could be used for farming, Canadians during the nineteenth century pushed into the northern wilderness of the Upland, which someone has called "an agricultural no man's land." Most settlers believed that the plow would immediately follow the woodman's axe. Later impetus to farming was given by the construction of railways, by the rise of mining, and by paternalistic provincial governments. Accordingly, large tracts of forest were cleared that have since proved to be ill-suited even for subsistence farming. The agricultural pioneer has actually

[10] William C. Wonders, "Economic Change in the Mackenzie Valley Area," *Canadian Geographical Journal*, Vol. 63 (October 1961), p. 143.

penetrated the Taiga in only a few favored places, such as the Lake St. John Lowland, the Clay Belt, and the Peace River district. The Taiga climate is not conducive to farming. Winters are long and extremely severe, and the growing season varies in length from year to year, although it is always short. The rainfall (20 to 35 inches) is ample, but crops often are ruined by the drizzle and dampness as they stand in the field. If livestock are kept, the long, cold winters necessitate costly feeding and shelter. One advantage is the long duration of sunlight during the growing season. It is estimated, for example, that wheat planted in extreme northern Alberta will mature a month faster than the same crop in central Alberta.[11]

Most of the farming (except where local markets exist) is of the subsistence type. The mining and the pulp and paper industries have brought in their wake an increased population which has stimulated agricultural development in nearby areas. The principal crops, hay, barley, oats, potatoes, and vegetables, are of the hardy type. Since it is extremely difficult to live solely from the land, some farmers work during the winter (their off-season) in a lumber camp, a mine, or a pulp mill.

LAKE ST. JOHN LOWLAND   This small isolated agricultural area lies in the midst of 41,000 square miles of rugged, forested plateau country. Dairying is the chief farm activity, in spite of the long winter shelter period that is required. Since the lowland opens to the St. Lawrence by the fjord-like Saguenay, which has an important aluminum industry, the farms are satisfactorily located with respect to markets. More than half the people in the area are urban dwellers.

THE CLAY BELT   The Clay Belt remained almost empty for two centuries following

its discovery. This area, like an island in the ocean, is separated by the wedge of the Shield from Toronto (450 miles), Montreal (600 miles), and Winnipeg (1,000 miles). Its isolation may always be a distinct handicap.

The Clay Belt is more than a mere pocket in the Shield, but it does have notable limitations. The better land is quite restricted in extent and occurs for the most part in narrow strips along stream courses, on ridges, swells, or flats underlaid by sand and gravel. Drainage is a problem.

Settlers first came into the Clay Belt about 1910, when the better lands near the Great Lakes became fully occupied. Expanding northwards, they noted the overwhelming poverty of the soils of the Shield. They also observed that, about 150 miles north of the southern edge of the Shield, the character of the soils changed considerably—the sterile granites giving way to white clay interspersed with much peaty material. Settlement is difficult, farming is fraught with physical dangers, and market problems are well-nigh insurmountable.

Transport costs usually tend to swallow up all the profits. One of the best informed men on the area believes the future lies in combining forestry with farming, "for much of the area can produce better 'harvests' of spruce than of any other crop." [12]

Many middle-latitude crops cannot be produced because of the short growing season. The principal agricultural products are oats, barley, hay, and hardy vegetables. Some dairy and beef cattle are raised to meet local requirements and for some of the mining districts which border on the area to the south. But the market provided by mining towns has been insufficient to support a sound agricultural economy, even though

[11] Clifford Wilson, ed., *North of 55°* (Toronto: Ryerson Press, 1954), p. 138.

[12] G. A. Hills, "Pedology—The Dirt Science and Agricultural Settlement in Ontario," *Canadian Geographical Journal*, Vol. 29 (1944), pp. 106-27.

it has caused a shift in emphasis from general farming to dairying and market gardening for local sales. Settlement generally has advanced much more on the Quebec side (Abitibi) than on the Ontario side (Cochrane), presumably because of the paternalistic attitude of the Quebec government in contrast to the *laissez faire* approach of the Ontario government.[13]

It is believed that the Clay Belt will not become a "rural slum" as have some other sections of the Shield. At the same time, it is as certain that the area will not become of primary agricultural importance to the Dominion.

PEACE RIVER DISTRICT In the northwestern part of Alberta and adjacent British Columbia is a 25,000-square-mile enclave of black soil and grassy parkland that is Canada's northernmost area of satisfactory commercial agriculture. The Peace River District, as it is called, was first entered by settlers as long ago as 1879, but it was only sparsely occupied until well into the twentieth century, particularly after a rail line was laid from Edmonton to Grande Prairie in 1916.

[13] George L. McDermott, "Frontiers of Settlement in the Great Clay Belt, Ontario and Quebec," *Annals of the Association of American Geographers*, Vol. 51 (September 1961), p. 273.

Mixed farming is characteristic, with an emphasis on cash grains (especially barley, oats, and wheat) in the older areas, and livestock (particularly beef cattle and hogs) in the newer ones. The climate differs little from that of the northern portion of the Spring Wheat Belt, 150 miles to the south, so that grain crops can be harvested in most years and hay thrives (Figure 10-10).

Completion of the Pacific Great Eastern Railway connection in 1958 gave the Peace River farmers access to the markets of southern British Columbia for the first time. This improved transportation has accounted for a considerable increase in production of feed grain for sale to ranchers west of the Rocky Mountains.

The pioneer fringe of agriculture is being pushed slowly northward toward Great Slave Lake as mechanical bush-clearing equipment is used ever more frequently. The wisdom of further marginal encroachment on the forest, however, is questionable.

Manufacturing The few factories of this vast subregion are usually large and located on the southern fringe, in Ontario and Quebec, generally at hydroelectric-power sites or in mining towns. The principal industries are wood-using plants (sawmills, pulp mills, paper mills), which are scattered all along the fringe; aluminum plants,

Figure 10-10. Combining grain in the Peace River country, with a storm building up in the background. This scene is near Pouce Coupe, B.C. (British Columbia Government Photograph.)

in the Saguenay Valley; and nickel-copper smelters, particularly at Sudbury and in the Clay Belt.

Canada's outstanding aluminum-reduction complex (at least until Kitimat production is brought up to planned capacity) is in the Saguenay Valley of eastern Quebec. The plants are located at Arvida and Ille Maligne. All raw materials must be imported by ship to Port Alfred, and transshipped by rail for the remaining 20 or 40 miles to the two production centers.

Transportation The first transportation in this area was by canoe in summer and by dog team and sledge in winter. The maze of waterways with only short portages enabled the canoe to go unbelievable distances, and the accumulation of snow due to the absence of thaws in winter made sledging relatively easy. These relatively primitive modes of travel are still important in the Taiga, although not so vital as they once were.

Railway construction was begun as a means of encouraging agricultural settlement and, in the case of the Hudson Bay Railway, to enable the wheat growers of the Prairie Provinces to compete more favorably in world markets with Argentina and Australia. Other lines were built into areas known to have minerals, as a means of stimulating mining. The lines to Flin Flon, Noranda, and elsewhere are notable examples of this type. The mining industry, in turn, creates a demand for high-grade produce, supports an important traffic, and tends to encourage mixed farming in its tributary area insofar as nature permits. The Hudson Bay Railway (part of the Canadian National Railway) was built by the Dominion Government, is owned by it, and did not have as its primary purpose the opening up of mineral lands. Yet the line serves as the key to the mining possibilities over a vast stretch of the Shield. This is because the government builds branches to

mining developments, as at Lynn Lake, as the need arises.

The Grand Trunk Railway (included in the Canadian National Railway System), which the government constructed, went through empty land all the way to Winnipeg. Later, however, the line was found to have tributary to it valuable mineral country and the fairly good soils of the Clay Belt.

For a long time after mining was developed in the Shield, the traffic was heavy only one way, inbound, and it was not until 1918, with the boom of the pulp and paper industry, that outbound or southbound traffic became more important than inbound or northbound traffic.[14]

Not a single mile of railway existed in Labrador and southeastern Quebec until the line was constructed from Sept Isles to the Schefferville iron mines in the 1950's. Railway building here encountered all the construction problems of the Canadian North—low temperatures, terrific windchill, permafrost, and, in summer, poor drainage and insect pests.

The long-held dream of a railway connection from the prairies to the Mackenzie country will probably become a reality in the 1960's. Previous contact involved either travel by rail from Edmonton to Peace River and then by road to Hay River, or by rail from Edmonton to Waterways and then down the Athabaska and Slave Rivers by boat to Great Slave Lake (summer only). Conflict between advocates of an eastern or a western route for the railway apparently will be resolved in favor of the western route.[15]

Locally, very important water transport is accomplished on the Athabaska and Mackenzie Rivers during the limited navi-

[14] Innis, "Settlement and the Mining Frontier," p. 372.
[15] Jane Lancaster, "A Railroad to Great Slave Lake," *Professional Geographer,* Vol. 13 (September 1961), pp. 31-35.

gation season. Two large companies provide reliable service on the latter waterways.[16]

There are still relatively few roads and highways in the Taiga, except in a few parts of southern Ontario and in Quebec's Saguenay Valley. In the west there is one major all-weather road, the Mackenzie Highway, which runs 385 miles north from Grimshaw, Alberta, to Hay River on the south shore of Great Slave Lake, and then another 280 miles around the western end of the lake to Yellowknife on the north shore. "Winter only" roads have been bulldozed in some places for use by trucks and tractor trains.

Without doubt, the most important development in the history of the Canadian North was the introduction of the airplane, about 1920. It has revolutionized communications and accelerated the whole pattern of economic and social progress. There are still only a few scheduled flights into the Taiga, mostly in the Clay Belt and the Mackenzie Valley, but the nonscheduled, bush-pilot type of flying is significant. Light aircraft can be equipped with pontoons, skis, nose warmers, and other devices to permit operation into almost any area, both summer and winter. And the use of the slower but more flexible helicopter has further benefited the subregion.

Recreation

The recreational activities of the subregion are of two principal types: (1) brief winter and summer visits from nearby population centers, and (2) more extensive expeditions involving considerable travel.

Most of the Taiga is far removed from large population clusters, but part of the fringe of the Shield lies close to the St. Lawrence Valley and southern Ontario plain, where most Canadians live. Principal areas of attraction include the Laurentides Park area (particularly for the people of Quebec

City); the Central Laurentians, favored for skiing as well as summer activities (especially for Montrealers); Algonquin Park, notable for fishing and canoeing (near Toronto); the lake country of southern Manitoba and Riding Mountain National Park (for Winnipeg); Prince Albert National Park (near Saskatoon); and Elk Island National Park, a wildlife preserve within picnicking distance of Edmonton.

The abundant fish and wildlife resources of the Taiga are major attractions for sportsmen both north and south of the international boundary. They make long trips, frequently by air, to fish in remote lakes for trout, whitefish, pike, perch, etc., and to hunt moose, caribou, bear, and deer. There is even a Northwest Territories Tourist Association in operation at Yellowknife!

The Outlook

The Taiga is primarily an empty subregion, so far as human occupancy is concerned and, logically, will remain so. However, it represents the Canadian frontier, and as long as there are frontiers, there will be men trying to push them back.

The agricultural frontier is still edging northward in the Peace River District, and it will probably creep into the Hay River and perhaps even into the Liard River drainages. Farming will probably expand somewhat in the Prince Albert area north of Edmonton and erratically (partly balanced by farm abandonment) in the Clay Belt. But raising crops and livestock can never be a major enterprise in this subregion; there are too many physical and transportation handicaps.

The timber resources will continue to be significant. Canada's pulp and paper industry doubtless will grow, although part of the United States market probably will be lost to Cotton Belt producers; the small, but formerly steady, Cuban market is now be-

---

[16] Wonders, "Economic Change in the Mackenzie Valley Area," p. 144.

ing supplied by the Soviets and by Cuba's own bagasse.

Mining has been and will continue to be the key to the North. Where economically recoverable ores are found, development will take place and transportation will somehow be provided. Uranium is no longer an attraction, but lead and zinc (as at Pine Point, near Hay River), nickel and copper, and oil and gas (important discoveries are quite likely in the Mackenzie Valley) will create more "miracles in the bush," like Sudbury, Flin Flon, Thompson, Yellowknife, and Schefferville.

And as transportation improves (railways to Chibougamau, Hay River, perhaps Lake Athabaska; roads to Fort Smith, perhaps to Churchill and Norman Wells), the recreational advantages will be further developed. Genuine tourists will begin to appear where only fishermen and hunters now go. There is only a short time-lag in Anglo-America between the completion of any fairly negotiable road and the appearance of motels, trailer camps, picnic tables, roadside litter, and new money.

The Upper Lakes Subregion

The Upper Lakes Subregion includes northeast Minnesota, northern Wisconsin and Michigan, and a part of Ontario lying north of Lakes Huron and Superior (Figure 10-1).

Typical of the Northern Continental Forest Region as a whole, the primary industries are extractive—fishing, trapping, logging, and mining.

The Natural Environment

Terrain The American part of this subregion, often called the "cutover area," was treated roughly by the continental glaciers. The ice gouged out the softer rocks, the depressions later forming thousands of small lakes; it also deranged the drainage and

threaded the area with a filigree of rivers. It mellowed the terrain over which it moved. Thus low hills characterize much of the land, though high steep hills, locally called "mountains," lie along the shores of Lake Superior.

The rocks are much like those noted in the Canadian Shield, of which this area is geologically a part; they are ancient, tightly compressed, and severely metamorphosed.

Climate The climate, being continental, is subject to the severe variations that characterize the interiors of large land areas in middle latitudes. Winters are long and cold, summers short and cool. The growing season varies from 90 to 100 days, though at Marquette and other places on the south shore of Lake Superior it is 158 days. There are large sections where the first autumn frost arrives early in September. Precipitation varies from 25 to 35 inches, falling mostly as rain. Though only 10 to 20 per cent is snow, the whole area is snow-covered for 90 to 120 days—a longer period than in any other area of comparable size in the United States.[17]

Soils The soils, like those elsewhere in the region, are poorly suited for growing standard crops. They are also distributed in intricate patterns, with pockets of fertility scattered here and there in the huge wilderness of non-productive land. The mature soils, gray podzols, are light in texture and acid in reaction, since they are derived from crystalline rocks and lie in a humid climate. Some areas are strewn with glacial granitic boulders, while others are charcterized by deep, sterile sand or peat and muck.

When the frontier was moving over the Upper Lakes Subregion, no soil surveys had been made and nothing was known regarding the suitability of the soil for crops. Accordingly, settlers took anything that was

---

[17] National Resources Committee, *Regional Planning—Part VIII, Northern Lakes States* (Washington: Government Printing Office, 1939), p. 9.

cheap, believing that crops would grow wherever trees did. The result was an irregular, inefficient, and illogical pattern of land use.

Natural Vegetation When the explorers and fur traders broke into this subregion, they found a virgin forest consisting of conifers in the northern and northwestern part and mixed forest in the southern part. White pine was the principal commercial tree, but jack and Norway pine and even spruce and fir were associated with it. In the southern portion were beech, birch, and maple, interspersed with the conifers. The hardwoods grew on the better soils; the conifers, in the more sandy sections. The best of the forests was in northern Michigan, northeastern Wisconsin, and central and northern Minnesota.

The Occupance

During the first half of the nineteenth century, settlement spread rapidly over the trans-Appalachian region as far as rainfall would permit crop production. The Upper Lakes Area was less disturbed, remaining an unbroken forest for two centuries after its discovery—the only development of any sort being the trapping and trading of furs.

The virgin wilderness abounded in furbearers, with winters long and cold enough to put the furs in prime condition. The early *voyageurs* who came by way of the Great Lakes found ideal conditions for their vocation. The interior location and the great distance from Europe meant that only products that were valuable, easily conveyed, and in great demand could bear the costly transportation. This enterprise was the principal business for two centuries after the discovery of the subregion.

Lumbermen rather than farmers finally opened up the subregion. They bought the land, built transport facilities, cut off the timber, and got out. Their business was timber, not land.

Lumbering

This subregion had Anglo-America's largest and densest stand of white pine. When forests of this highly prized tree had been "mined out" of New England and the Middle Atlantic States, lumbermen led the onslaught into the Northern Lakes Area. Contributing factors were the rapid urbanization of the Middle West and improvements in transportation—the Erie Canal and the building of railroads. Yet the real mass attack on the forest did not begin until the termination of the Civil War. By 1870, Michigan ranked first in the production of lumber, and reached its peak in the decade 1880–1890. In 1896 a traveler covering 40 counties and going 2,000 miles wrote that:

> The heart of the white pine country, from Manistee on the west to Saginaw on the east (is) an almost continuous succession of abandoned lumber fields, miles upon miles of stumps as far as the eye can see....[18]

The horde then moved into Wisconsin and finally into Minnesota, which took leadership, attaining its peak in 1900. This army of lumbermen had one-track minds: they sought but one resource—*pine*. They cut any tree so long as it was big, and they were not concerned when young growths were ruined by the fall of the tree they were cutting. Stripping the forest, leaving only slashings and stumps in their wake, they moved on.

Whereas in 1890 these three Lake States produced 35 per cent of the nation's total, by 1910 they could not supply their own needs, and today they produce only three per cent, the bulk consisting of hardwoods. By 1920 even the best hardwoods had been cut off.

Reforestation was hardly considered.

[18] W. N. Sparhawk and W. D. Brush, "The Economic Aspects of Forest Destruction in Northern Michigan," *Technical Bulletin No. 92*, United States Department of Agriculture (Washington: Government Printing Office, 1929).

Figure 10-11. A burned-over area in Minnesota. These charred stumps and trunks are the remains of once-wonderful forests. (Photo courtesy U.S. Forest Service.)

Everyone thought that, with so vast an area of dense growing timber and with much yet to be cut, the forest was inexhaustible. Accordingly the land was repeatedly burned over (Figure 10-11). These fires destroyed the seedlings and the forest litter and so ruined the topsoil that in many localities white pine can no longer grow. Carl Sauer, one of the pioneers in land-utilization surveying in Michigan, estimates that these sand-pine lands will require 500 years undisturbed by man to produce a pine forest like the original one. The growing and selling of Christmas trees has become an important, and for some people a highly profitable, business in this area.

Fishing

Fishing was a flourishing enterprise in Lakes Huron, Michigan, and Superior, antedating lumbering and mining. Whitefish and lake trout in 1880 made up 70 per cent of the catch. Since then, however, they have declined steadily as a result of overfishing, depredation by the destructive sea lampreys, destruction of immature fish, the fouling of waters by city sewage and industrial waste, and changing physical conditions in the lakes; today they make up less than 5 per cent of the total catch.

The major feature in Upper Lakes fishery development recently has been the beginning of effective lamprey control. The sea lamprey is an adaptable, anadramous, parasitic, eel-like species that has moved up the St. Lawrence and into the Great Lakes from the Atlantic Ocean. It destroys fish by attaching itself to them with its sucker mouthparts, and feeding on them. After essentially wrecking the lake trout and whitefish fishery of the Lower Lakes, it is now doing the same in the Upper Lakes. However, fishery technicians have developed a two-pronged attack that appears to be capable of controlling the menace. A selective poison is spread in upstream lamprey spawning grounds, and electric gates are installed at the stream mouths with the current turned on during times of lamprey migration into and out of the lakes. It is an expensive and difficult program, but one that promises to yield positive results.

The three lakes today account for only 33 per cent of the commercial fresh-water catch in the United States and less than 2 per cent of the combined fresh- and salt-water catch. Comparable proportions for the Canadian Upper Lakes fishery are 5 per cent and 1 per cent, respectively. The principal species caught are chub, carp, smelt, and other low-value varieties, plus lake herring. Most commercial fishing is done in summer, although ice-fishing is carried on in a number of localities during the winter.

Mining

The Upper Lakes Subregion is one of Anglo-America's richest in minerals—not in variety, but in quantity, and of the type most in demand by industry. Southwest and northwest of Lake Superior lie the continent's best, largest, and most favorably located iron ores. On the Keweenaw Peninsula are the richest and longest used, though not the most profitably mined, copper accumulations. On the west shore of Lake Huron are valuable deposits of metallurgical limestone.

Mining is the outstanding economic enterprise in this subregion today. Billions of tons of red hematite ore have been found in the Lake Superior district. These deposits lie in elongated east-west extending beds. They were formed during an ancient mountain-building period, but erosion has long since worn down the mountains and the terrain is now almost flat.

In the Mesabi Range, the ore deposits, shallow and extensive, are covered by glacial till to a depth of 10 to 150 feet. Mesabi ore is an example of deposition and concentration of ores in small valleys between hills.

In the Gogebic Range, the iron deposits lie hundreds of feet below the surface. Its ores exemplify the deposition and concentration of ore by circulating waters in underground channels. The famous "Lake Superior iron-ore region," which accounts for 80 per cent of American production, comprises eleven counties (three in Minnesota, five in Michigan, and three in Wisconsin). Minnesota alone contributes two-thirds of the total. Upon the Mesabi Range, the greatest body of iron ore in the world, has been built the extensive American iron-ore and lake-shipping businesses, and indirectly most of the steel manufacturing of the Lower Great Lakes area. Billions of tons already have been removed, and the high-grade ore is now nearly gone. Data on reserves are not dependable, however, for the steel companies give out no more information than necessary, since they report no more taxable property than the public authorities require.

Production on a large scale began about the time the lumber industry was declining. Shipments from the Marquette Range (the only producer until 1877) started in 1854, and those from the Mesabi in 1892, when the first railroad reached it.

At first, mining in the Lake Superior area was done underground. Later, large deposits of high-grade Mesabi ore in loose form were discovered near the surface. These ores could be mined with power shovels after the glacial overburden had been removed. Thus open-pit mining, the

Figure 10-12. A typical open pit mine on the Mesabi Range. "Natural" ore from such mines as this can no longer compete successfully with higher grade ores and concentrates from other sources. (Photo courtesy Pickands Mather & Company, Duluth.)

fastest and most economical method known, came into use (Figure 10-12). This mode of mining can be used only in summer. Underground mining elsewhere in the area is carried on the year round, the ore being stockpiled during winter.

As mining went forward, the richer and better ore was removed. Today, in order to send high-grade hematite down the lakes, the lower quality ores must first be sent to beneficiation plants which upgrade the ores by screening, crushing, washing, and concentrating them. There are more than 80 such plants in the iron ranges.

The Mesabi Range contributes nearly four-fifths of the total production of the Lake Superior area. Since 1892, it has sent down the lakes more than two billion tons of ore. The greatness of the Mesabi Range is due to (1) large size, (2) nearness of ore to the surface, (3) quality of the ore, (4) proximity to Lake Superior, and (5) ease of mining. The ore was first recovered with hand shovels; later came steam and finally electric shovels, which remove 16 tons at a single bite.

In getting the ore out of the huge man-made caverns, railways were used at first—the tracks being built into the pits. Later came crawler trucks on giant rubber tires. Now much of the ore moves out in a continuous stream on conveyor belts directly to concentration plants. The world's greatest single mine, the Hull Rust at Hibbing, Minnesota, is 350 feet deep, from one-half mile to one mile across, and two and one-half miles long, with an area of 1,100 acres.

Taconite The quantity of ore removed from the Lake Superior region, particularly from the Mesabi, in the past two world war periods, and more recently during the rearmament program, took a terrific toll of American high-grade iron-ore reserves. No one knows exactly how long the remaining top-grade ore will last, but the estimates indicate only a short time. Adjustments are

being made by shifting to lower quality ores.

Taconite is a dense, hard rock containing only 25 to 35 per cent iron and a considerable amount of such impurities as silica, quartz, and oxides. The iron oxide is finely dispersed (like specks of pepper) in the silica and firmly held by it. Since there are billions of tons of taconite in the Lake Superior area, the perfection of an economic method of extracting this iron oxide from it has been a high priority job.

Taconite and similar but nonmagnetic ore called jasper (mostly found in the Michigan iron ranges) are now being mined, concentrated, and pelletized in large volume. Beneficiation, while expensive, produces a concentrate that is about two-thirds iron and that will yield more pig iron with less blast-furnace cost than will other ores (Figure 10-13).

Estimates are that by 1966 the iron ore used in the United States will be one-third imported (mostly from Venezuela, Canada, Peru, and Liberia), one-sixth Lake Superior taconite and jasper concentrates, one-third other Lake Superior ores, and one-sixth other domestic ores.[19] By 1975 it is thought that more than half of the Lake Superior iron-ore output will be taconite and jasper.[20]

Taxation of Iron Ore Most of the inhabitants in this subregion live in mining communities, and the mines are largely owned by steel interests in the East. Minnesota counties, especially, have been taxing these absentee owners heavily. As a result, tourists are amazed at the fine roads and well-equipped schools in an otherwise exceedingly poor region. The State of Min-

[19] Clyde F. Kohn and Raymond E. Specht, "The Mining of Taconite, Lake Superior Iron Mining District," *Geographical Review*, Vol. 48 (October 1958), p. 538.

[20] "Iron Ore Beneficiation," *Monthly Review*, Federal Reserve Bank of Minneapolis, October 1957, p. 11.

Figure 10-13. A taconite beneficiation plant at Hoyt Lakes, Minnesota. (Photo courtesy Pickands Mather & Company, Duluth.)

nesota has a commission of experts in mining accounting, mineralogy, geology, and mining engineering who permit no discovered ores to escape assessment. The iron and steel manufacturers complain bitterly, pointing out that Minnesota's mining tax is ten times as great proportionately as that for the nation as a whole.

On the other hand, public sentiment in Minnesota, whence comes 60 per cent of the ore, is averse to sending millions of tons of the red metal down the lakes each year, leaving in place of the rich heritage vast holes in the ground. Ore shipped down the lakes means only a few dollars or so to the state—a mere fraction of its value when converted into iron and steel at Gary, Cleveland, or Pittsburgh. Minnesota used this as a major argument in getting the United States Steel Corporation to construct the plant at Duluth.[21]

Whereas Minnesota taxes all known high-grade ores, Michigan levies only against the exploited ones, those adjacent to them, and those most evident. It would appear that the different mode of taxing in the two states is (1) a political expression of Minnesota's

[21] C. Langdon White and George Primmer, "The Iron and Steel Industry of Duluth: A Study in Locational Maladjustment," *Geographical Review,* Vol. 27 (January 1937), pp. 82-91.

predominant agrarianism—indicated by the fact that the taxation on a dollar invested in a mine is twice that on a dollar invested in a farm, and (2) a desire on the part of Michigan ore owners to compete with Minnesota ore, which has certain natural advantages.

Steep Rock About 140 miles northwest of the head of Lake Superior and relatively near the international boundary, lies Canada's Steep Rock Mine. Before mining could begin here, Steep Rock Lake had to be drained, for the ore lay beneath its waters. The lake was 130 feet deep. Drainage required a year to complete, and 120 billion gallons of water were removed. Big power shovels then began scooping out enormous bites of rich hematite ore averaging 60 per cent metallic iron. Open-pit mining, however, is done no deeper than 400 feet from the surface. Below 400 feet, mining must be done underground for reasons of safety.

This is the second largest iron-mining operation in Canada, accounting for between 10 and 15 per cent of national output.

Moving Iron Ore Down the Lakes Ore from the Minnesota mines is loaded into cars, which are made into trains and taken to weighing and classification yards before continuing on their way to Duluth, Supe-

Figure 10-14. Ore boat and loading docks at Marquette, Michigan. (Photo courtesy Michigan Tourist Council.)

rior, or Two Harbors. The distance from the mines to Duluth is only 60 to 80 miles, and the trains coast much of the way. The railroad charge for delivering ore this distance is more than the freighter charge for carrying it ten times as far. Hence all three states ship nearly all their ore to Lower Lake ports by water.

The docks jut out into the lake like huge peninsulas. The trains, after being moved onto the docks, dump their ore into "pockets," from which it drops by gravity through hatches into the holds of the lake vessels (Figure 10-14). Ordinarily three to four hours are required to load a vessel, but the job has been done in much less time. When a boat reaches a Lower Lake port, the ore is discharged in four or five hours by means of huge clam-shaped unloaders.

The Great Lakes can be utilized for only seven or eight months, because in the winter the connecting links such as the "Soo" Canals are locked by ice (Figure 10-15). No time is lost by a vessel during the season of navigation. Every effort is made to complete as many round trips as possible—the number usually being 23 to 30. It is a race against time to accumulate enough ore

Figure 10-15. Ore boats locked in ice. Subzero temperatures trapped these down-bound vessels in six-inch channel ice. The boats are waiting for a Coast Guard icebreaker to free them. The shipping season on the lakes normally begins in April and ends in early December, when insurance rates become prohibitive due to the hazards of winter navigation. (Photo courtesy Don Walker and the *Detroit News*.)

at the Lower Lake ports to keep the mills operating throughout the year. Numerous collisions occurred prior to 1911 in hot summer months when fog was bad. Vessels on the down trip are now required to follow a slightly different course from those on the upbound voyage. Thus steamers passing on the open lake are at least five miles from each other, and are also separated as far as possible in rivers and channels.

The traffic tonnage moving through the "Soo" Canals is almost unbelievable. In a normal year it exceeds that of the Panama, Suez, Welland, and New York State Barge Canals combined. Nowhere else in the world is so much bulk traffic handled.

In an effort to procure a return cargo, principally coal, a much lower rate is offered by northbound carriers. Most coal moving northbound from Toledo and other Lake Erie ports, however, is destined for such industrial areas as Detroit, Chicago, and Milwaukee, or for Canada, rather than for the Upper Lake ports. Only a small percentage of the lake carriers haul coal up the lakes.

The "Soo" Canals, from the standpoint of tonnage, are the most important artificial waterways in the world. The St. Mary's River, connecting Lakes Superior and Huron, is about 63 miles long, and at Sault Ste. Marie has a stretch of rapids three-fourths of a mile long and a fall of 17 to 21 feet, depending on the stage of water in the two lakes. In order to afford passage for deep-draft vessels, canals and locks 25 feet deep had to be built through this barrier. So important are these canals that when they freeze in winter, Great Lakes ore traffic comes to a halt.

The first "Soo" Canal was built on the Canadian side by the Northwest Fur Company in 1797-1798 for the passage of small boats. The first canal on the American side was built by the State of Michigan in 1853-1855, following the discovery of iron ore in the Lake Superior area. This canal was transferred to the United States Government in 1881 when the Weitzel Lock was built. So great has Lake traffic become that four locks have been built on the American side. The Canadian government constructed a lock and canal in 1895, but nearly all the lake carriers use those on the American side. During the season of navigation a vessel is locked through the "Soo" Canals about every 15 minutes day and night.

Will the New Situation in Iron Ore Cause the American Iron and Steel Industry to Move? It has been pointed out that the end is in sight for ores that can be shipped directly to the mills. Since the Lake Superior area has supplied about 80 to 85 per cent of the iron ore utilized in the United States, new sources of ore must be found and got ready before the existing top-quality open-pit deposits give out.

About 90 per cent of the nation's steel-ingot capacity is located in the states tributary to the Great Lakes, and these plants now rely almost wholly upon Lake Superior iron ore. Moreover, a tremendous proportion of our secondary steel fabrication capacity and of our steel consumption is centered in the Lower Lakes area, close to the open hearths, Bessemers, and electric furnaces. Because of these facts, along with the abolition of the basing-point system, the extreme possibility that the American iron and steel industry might move to tidewater would have a momentous effect on American industry. Most men in the steel industry, however, expect that most of the industry will remain where it is, though they recognize that some new capacity must be added to the Atlantic, Gulf, and Pacific seaboards. One of the best informed men in the industry expresses it as follows:

> . . . the customer eventually will come to the maker of steel rather than the other way round. You can't shove a huge business like steel around like a pawn in a chess game.

Limestone   In four counties of Michigan lies Anglo-America's leading source of metallurgical limestone. The quarries lie so close to the lake shore that, despite the fact that they are geographically 300 miles from the blast furnaces, they are economically only 30 miles away, since water rates are only one tenth as much as rail rates. Accordingly, this area has become the largest and the cheapest source of stone for the great iron and steel plants of the Great Lakes area, as well as for cement and chemical factories. Limestone is used in blast furnaces to remove from the ore such impurities as silica and alumina, which have a stronger affinity for lime than for iron.

The quarry of the Michigan Limestone & Chemical Company at Calcite has nine and one-half miles of vertical quarry side from which electric power shovels of 23 tons capacity remove the stone. This company has its own harbor and loading slip. As the stone is brought from the quarry, it is crushed into pieces less than nine inches in their maximum dimensions. Conveyor belts then carry it to storage, where it is sorted into piles according to its ultimate disposition: open-hearth furnaces, blast furnaces, cement plants and chemical companies. Within the same pile the stone is further graded as to both size and chemical composition. The boats used to transport this particular limestone are "self-unloaders"; they all carry "pickaback" a great steel boom, an unloader.

Copper   Michigan is also a producer of copper. Mines in three counties in the Upper Peninsula yield about six per cent of the national output. There is a long history of copper mining in this area, some of it carried on by Indians before the advent of the white man. Steadily declining ore quality has caused a decrease in production since the peak year of 1916, although there has been an upturn since the 1940's, and new, large low-grade ore bodies are under development.

Agriculture

Not more than 10 per cent of the Northern Lakes Subregion is in crop land now, and possibly not more than 20 per cent ever can be utilized for agriculture. The crop acreage per family is too low and the tax burden too high to permit successful farming. Paucity of markets is a severe handicap in this essentially forest environment.

Unfortunately, poor lands as well as good lands were sold through high-pressure salesmanship to all kinds of people—miners, factory workers, former city white-collar employees, and Corn Belt farmers. Some accidentally obtained good land but most did not, since they "found themselves in possession of (1) outcrops of crystalline rock, of undrainable peat bogs and marshes, or of stump land covered with granite boulders [or] of (2) soil so light and sandy that, when cleared, it was blown about by the wind." [22]

Many of the farmers who first entered the area worked part-time in mines, mills, or logging camps. The amount of improved land on most farms (25 to 30 acres) has been so small that a living could not be made solely by growing crops.

It is unfortunate that no soil maps or agricultural experiment farms *preceded* immigration. Knowledge came only through trial and error and the crushing of human beings by a relentless environment. A large proportion of the farmers remaining are foreign-born or of foreign parentage, being mostly Scandinavian, Slavic, or Finnish. The Finns assert that they came into this area because they were shipped up to supply labor. They took to agriculture during periods of industrial inactivity. As "part-time" farmers they have made a fair living from the soil despite the short growing season, and they usually do better than most other nationalities, as

[22] National Resources Board, *Maladjustments in Land Use in the United States,* Part VI (Washington: Government Printing Office, 1935), p. 27.

indicated by their rejuvenation of farm lands abandoned by settlers of other ethnic stocks.

The Finns grow primarily hay, potatoes, and root crops and leave much land in pasture. Wheat, formerly of considerable importance, is no longer grown because the area cannot compete with better lands to the west and south. Most of the feed grains used on the farms are raised locally but practically none is produced for market. A typical clearing carved out of the forest consists of 20 to 30 acres planted largely in hay and smaller plots in barley, oats, potatoes, and other vegetables. Cows and pigs are kept, the latter being fattened on skim milk or whey. Dairying is not prosperous, because the cows require expensive winter housing and feeding. Moreover, all farm production suffers from the dearth of nearby markets. Much of the farming is submarginal. Away from the lakes, the short growing season is a greater handicap than are the soils, for even on the better lands frost precludes the growing of most crops.

In many instances it is as necessary to supplement the farm income now as it was in the beginning of settlement; hence much farming is "part-time." Many farmers cut pulpwood, ties, and poles from their land. The income on the average farm is too low to maintain the American standard of living. There is a scarcity of doctors, nurses, and hospitals: hence there is much neglect of medical and dental care, and what service there is must be largely at public expense. Few homes have electric lights or running water.

Farming is somewhat more prosperous on the Canadian side, where pockets of good soil are being utilized and the poor areas have not been settled. For example, in the Rainy River district, north of Minnesota, farms average 50 to 100 acres cleared and produce good crops of oats, hay, and flax. The chief source of agricultural income is from the sale of livestock and livestock products.

Manitoulin Island in Lake Huron, said to be the largest fresh-water island in the world,[23] is predominantly agricultural, even though much of the farming is marginal. Cattle and turkey raising and fur farming are specialties.

Manufacturing

Manufacturing is not well developed in the Upper Lakes Subregion because of the small population and the great distance from the continent's principal markets for fabricated products. The chief industries are those making chemicals, lumber, pulp and paper, iron and steel. Throughout the entire subregion, the general trend of industrial employment is downward, except in the Port Arthur-Fort William area of Ontario, where industry has been expanding.

Iron and Steel Duluth, Minnesota, and Sault Ste. Marie, Ontario, are iron and steel centers. Although neither district is a major development in the continental picture, Sault Ste. Marie is outstanding to Canada. Whereas most Anglo-American iron and steel districts are located close to coal and have iron ore brought to them, these districts do just the reverse. Their low assembly cost is a result of the desire on the part of ship-owners to have a return cargo; accordingly, the cost for shipping coal up the Lakes is appreciably less per ton than for bringing ore down. It is a truism that the location of iron manufacturing is primarily a matter of freight charges, not on raw materials alone but also on the finished products to points of consumption.

THE DULUTH DISTRICT In 1915, when the plant was completed in Duluth, many journalists enthusiastically wrote, "Pittsburgh is moving west." But today Duluth still carries on only as a minor producer. The United States Steel Corporation, which built the plant, did not wish to do so, realizing that

23 Donald F. Putnam and Donald P. Kerr, *A Regional Geography of Canada* (Toronto: J. M. Dent & Sons, 1956), p. 289.

Duluth was not a scientific location. Before construction, it stated that the total demand for steel in Duluth's tributary area would not keep the plant busy three months in the year. Public sentiment in Minnesota, however, threatening higher taxes, forced the issue. The district's past unimpressive record resulted from remoteness from great markets. The industry here may well gain in importance as a result of need for steel in the oil fields of the Williston Basin and Alberta and the need for pipe to transport crudes and gas. Certainly the industry in Duluth looks more promising than it did in the late twenties and early thirties.

THE SAULT ST. MARIE DISTRICT   A steel industry was established here about 1898. The main plant, occupying an area of 185 acres on the bank of the St. Mary's River, is strategically located for assembling raw materials and shipping finished products by water. Iron ore was originally obtained from Michipicoten, to the northward on Lake Superior, but now comes chiefly from Mesabi and Steep Rock.

Pulp and Paper   The principles involved in the location of pulp and paper manufacture for Canada have already been presented. The Upper Great Lakes states—Michigan, Wisconsin, and Minnesota—and northern Ontario are outstanding in this industry. Mills became established in both peninsulas of Michigan, in northern Minnesota, in the valleys of the Fox, Black, Wisconsin, and Chippewa Rivers in Wisconsin, and along the northwestern shore of Lake Superior in Ontario. Because spruce is scarce, almost no newsprint is made, emphasis being placed upon the manufacture of fine grades of paper. So thoroughly cut and burned-over was this area that it produces only a fraction of the nation's wood output.

The pulp mills on the south shore of Lake Superior, as at Munising, get much of their pulpwood from Canada in huge rafts pulled by tugs, which move at the rate of about two miles per hour provided there is no storm. An effort is made to deliver these rafts during that part of the summer when winds are weakest.

Transportation

The Great Lakes provide the finest system of inland waterways in the world. Their traffic consists almost entirely of bulky products—iron ore, coal, wheat, and limestone. The vessels that move them are built solely for service on the Great Lakes and their connecting waterways. They would be useless for ocean service, as severe storms would break them in two. A ship of the largest class can carry 18,000 to 20,000 tons. Some are self-unloaders. These carriers average 11 to 13 or more miles per hour, making a round trip in approximately a week. Since large carriers are more economical than small ones, those being constructed now are of the more efficient 600-foot type. These are also speedier and can be loaded and unloaded in faster time. Such a vessel involves an investment of several million dollars.

Rail and highway transportation are available, though the former is relatively unimportant, since there are few main lines. An exception is the main lines of Canadian roads into Port Arthur and Fort William.

The net of branch lines built during the lumbering era is now largely abandoned, and in many instances the rails have been removed and sold for scrap. The significance of iron-ore shipments is well indicated by the fact that 99.75 per cent of the cars return empty to the mine area. This traffic situation probably will not change, since much of the mining country appears incapable of important agricultural or other development.

Hard-surface roads have had a remarkable development in the past half century, though much remains to be done if the sub-

Figure 10-16. The Mackinac Bridge, which connects the Upper and Lower peninsulas of Michigan. This $99,000,-000 structure is 8,300 feet long and required four years to build. (Photo courtesy Mackinac Bridge Authority.)

region is to capitalize on its recreation possibilities. Especially must attention be given the scenic roads along the shores of Lakes Superior, Michigan, and Huron.

For many years there was no through road across the Shield north of Lake Superior. A gravel road was finally completed in 1942, making the first transcontinental link across Canada by road. It is now paved, as part of the Trans-Canada Highway.

There are two narrow necks of water that have impeded land transportation in the subregion—the Straits of Mackinac (outlet of Lake Michigan) and the St. Mary's River (outlet of Lake Superior). The former has been bridged from the Lower to the Upper Peninsula of Michigan (Figure 10-16), and the border-crossing journey between Sault St. Marie (Michigan) and Sault Ste. Marie (Ontario) can now be made by bridge.

Recreation

Recreation is important now and undoubtedly will be the leading business in the future. In the 1920's it was first realized that too much time, effort, and money had been wasted in farming worthless lands and that agriculture had no future. About the same time the once-rich timber and copper began to play out. On the other hand, the area has all the necessary features for a great playground—woods, lakes and streams, fish, wildlife, cool summer climate, many good roads, and resort facilities. Eighty per cent is forest land, nearly half being publicly owned. The "cut-over area" is within easy driving distance from the densely populated centers of the Middle West, whose summer climate is so trying as to drive people to the "North Woods." But the tourist season is short, lasting only from early July to Labor Day. Hay-fever sufferers often remain somewhat longer.

The recreation industry gives employment to a considerable number of people: to farmers who furnish milk, eggs, and vegetables, and to others who sell petroleum products, rent cottages, boats, and fishing tackle, or act as guides. It is, however, a highly seasonal industry and cannot alone sustain the population. Winter sports are of some importance but less so than in New England, the Adirondacks of New York, and parts of the West. Summer tourism, fishing, and fall hunting (more than 300,000 deer are shot in this subregion each year) are the dominant activities.

The Outlook

The Upper Lake Subregion is a problem area to the United States. Both from a state

TABLE 9

Selected Cities and Towns of the Northern
Continental Forest

City or Town	Urbanized Area	Political Center
Arvida	......	14,460
Ashland	......	10,132
Chicoutimi	......	31,657
Corner Brook	......	25,185
Dawson Creek	......	10,946
Duluth	144,763	106,884
Eau Claire	......	37,987
Flin Flon	......	11,104
Fort William	......	45,214
Grande Prairie	......	8,352
Hibbing	......	17,731
Kenora	......	10,904
Marquette	......	19,824
North Bay	......	23,781
Pembroke	......	16,791
Port Arthur	......	45,276
Prince Albert	......	24,168
St. Cloud	......	33,815
St. John's	90,838	63,633
Sault St. Marie, Mich.	......	18,722
Sault Ste. Marie, Ont.	......	43,088
Sudbury	110,694	80,120
Superior	......	33,563
Timmins	......	29,270
Val d'Or	......	10,983
Wausau	......	31,943

and national viewpoint, these lands possibly will always be poor. Many people migrated after removing the timber and finding the land ill-suited for farming. Others, mostly unemployed miners, stayed on in the cut-over areas and now comprise stranded populations. The cost of local government in this land of few people and large open spaces is too high to justify isolated rural living. Recently, science has made considerable progress in developing crops that mature early and thus need only a short growing season. Perhaps onions, potatoes, cauliflower, carrots, celery, and other truck crops could be grown and marketed successfully.

The major problem, that of unemployment, has been caused by regression of the principal enterprises—particularly lumbering and farming. Some persons believe that forest-development work offers the only large-scale employment possibility for thousands of families in the cut-over area; this is possible with reforestation and protection from fires.

The large-scale development of taconite should contribute to stability of employment, to increasing payrolls, to stimulating all business activity in Minnesota, and to extending the life of iron mining for several generations. The revival of copper mining is also encouraging.

The proximity of the area, with its numerous lakes, streams, and forests, to the Middle West, with its hot summers, guarantees a growing importance for the subregion as a vacation land. Tourism and outdoor recreation, although strictly seasonal, will contribute mightily to the economy.

Selected Bibliography

Ballart, Albert G., "Commerce of the Sault Canals," *Economic Geography*, Vol. 33, April 1957, pp. 135-148.

Bennett, M. K., "The Isoline of Ninety Frost-Free Days in Canada," *Economic Geography*, Vol. 35, January 1959, pp. 41-50.

Black, W. A., "Population Distribution of the Labrador Coast, Newfoundland," *Geographical Bulletin*, No. 9, 1956, pp. 53-74.

Brown, R. J. E., "The Distribution of Permafrost and Its Relation to Air Temperatures in Canada and the U.S.S.R.," *Arctic*, Vol. 13, September 1960, pp. 163-178.

Bucksar, Richard G., "Elliott Lake, Ontario: Problems of a Modern 'Boom-Town,'" *Journal of Geography*, Vol. 61, March 1962, pp. 119-125.

Charles, J. L., "Railways March Northward," *Canadian Geographical Journal*, Vol. 62, January 1961, pp. 3-21.

Gill, C. B., "Manitoba's Northland Rediscovered," *Canadian Geographical Journal*, Vol. 63, November 1961, pp. 149-157.

Greening, W. E., "Some Recent Changes in the Economy of Newfoundland," *Canadian*

Geographical Journal, Vol. 55, October 1957, pp. 128-149.

Hare, F. Kenneth, "The Climate of the Island of Newfoundland: a Geographical Analysis," *Geographical Bulletin,* Vol. 2, 1952, pp. 36-88.

————, and Svenn Orvig, *The Arctic Circulation,* Arctic Meteorology Research Group Publication in Meteorology, No. 12. Montreal: McGill University, 1958.

Herbert, C. H., "The Development of Transportation in the Canadian North," *Canadian Geographical Journal,* Vol. 53, November 1956, pp. 188-197.

Humphreys, Graham, "Schefferville, Quebec: a New Pioneering Town," *Geographical Review,* Vol. 48, April 1958, pp. 151-166.

Hustich, Ilmari, "On the Phytogeography of the Subarctic Hudson Bay Lowland," *Acta Geographica,* Vol. 16, 1957, pp. 3-48.

"Iron Ore Beneficiation," *Monthly Review,* Federal Reserve Bank of Minneapolis, October 1957, pp. 8-11.

Litterer, Oscar F., "District Dairy Industry in Transition," *Monthly Review,* Federal Reserve Bank of Minneapolis, December 1961, pp. 2-7.

Miller, E. Willard, "Mineral Regionalism of the Canadian Shield," *The Canadian Geographer,* No. 13, 1959, pp. 17-30.

"Mining Capital Sees Future in District Taconite," *Monthly Review,* Federal Reserve Bank of Minneapolis, May 1962, pp. 12-14.

Rowe, J. S., *Forest Regions of Canada,* Forestry Branch Bulletin 123. Ottawa: Department of Northern Affairs and Natural Resources, 1959.

Seeley, Sylvia, "The Thompson Project," *Canadian Geographical Journal,* Vol. 63, November 1961, pp. 149-157.

Sim, Victor W., "The Pas, Manitoba," *Geographical Bulletin,* No. 8, 1956, pp. 1-21.

Twidale, C. R., "Recent and Future Developments in the Labrador Peninsula," *Australian Geographer,* Vol. 7, May 1958, pp. 103-112.

Valentine, V. F., and R. G. Young, "The Situation of the Metis of Northern Saskatchewan in Relation to His Physical and Social Environment," *The Canadian Geographer,* No. 8, 1954, pp. 41-55.

Vanderhill, Burke G., "The Decline of Land Settlement in Manitoba and Saskatchewan," *Economic Geography,* Vol. 38, July 1962, pp. 270-277.

————, "The Farming Frontier of Western Canada: 1950-1960," *Journal of Geography,* Vol. 61, January 1962, pp. 13-20.

————, "Observations in the Pioneer Fringe of Western Canada," *Journal of Geography,* Vol. 57, December 1958, pp. 431-441.

de Vos, A., and A. T. Cringan, "Fur Management in Ontario," *Canadian Geographical Journal,* Vol. 55, August 1957, pp. 62-69.

"White Pine Project Spurs Economy," *Monthly Review,* Federal Reserve Bank of Minneapolis, April 1962, pp. 2-4.

Wonders, William C., "Economic Change in the Mackenzie Valley Area," *Canadian Geographical Journal,* Vol. 63, October 1961, pp. 138-145.

Wooding, F. H., "Draculas of the Great Lakes," *Canadian Geographical Journal,* Vol. 55, July 1957, pp. 2-13.

chapter eleven

The Great Plains

The Great Plains Region as discussed in this volume corresponds roughly with the Great Plains physiographic province,[1] although in places it extends eastward into the Central Lowland and southward into the Coastal Plain to include areas of extensive production of crops such as winter and spring wheat and areas of ranching activi-

[1] Nevin M. Fenneman, *Physiography of Western United States* (New York: McGraw-Hill Book Co., 1931), pp. 1-91.

ties beyond the borders of the Great Plains, as near the southwest Gulf Coast of Texas (Figure 11-1).

The eastern boundary corresponds roughly with the zone of crop land where corn, cotton, or other intensively grown crops become dominant over wheat. The western boundary is the foot of the *Front Range* of the Rocky Mountains, from southern Canada to central New Mexico, and the western margin of the Pecos River Valley from that

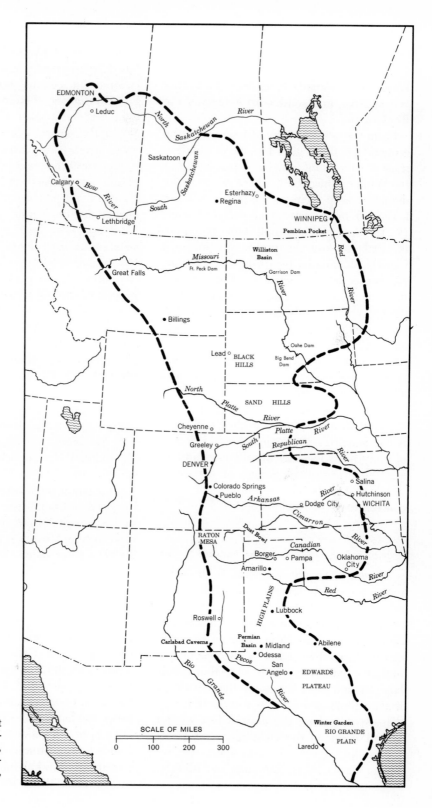

Figure 11-1. The Great Plains. A region of winter and spring wheat, grain sorghums, irrigated crops, ranching, and mining.

point southward to the Mexican border. To the north the region extends into the Prairie Provinces of Canada to include the Spring Wheat Area, and southward it reaches the Rio Grande.

From the point of view of land use or the economy of the region five major subdivisions or subregions may be recognized: (1) the Winter Wheat Belt, where wheat is the dominant crop, being sown in the fall and harvested in the spring or early summer; (2) the Spring Wheat Belt, lying largely in the Dakotas and the prairie provinces of Canada, dominated by spring-sown wheat; (3) the cotton and grain sorghum area of the Southern High Plains, dominated by those two extensively grown crops; (4) the many small irrigated areas, found largely along the stream courses throughout the region, which specialize in such intensively grown crops as vegetables, sugar beets, and alfalfa; and (5) the vast expanses of grassland grazed by cattle, sheep, or goats.

Although somewhat diversified in its economic activities, the region shows a degree of unity in its level terrain, its low rainfall, and the ever-present danger of dry years which makes the area a problem of great concern to all of Anglo-America.

The Physical Setting

Terrain   The wheat-growing parts of this region are mostly level to rolling, the slight relief being attributable in large part to the almost horizontal strata and to peneplanation. The fact that 90 per cent of the area can be farmed by labor-saving machinery indicates that there is little rugged or rough land, though there is some in the "Breaks"— in the valleys of the North and South Canadian Rivers, along the eastern face of the Staked Plains in the Oklahoma and Texas panhandles, and in the Bad Lands of Nebraska, the Dakotas, Montana, and Alberta.

A small part of this region was once the bottom of glacial Lake Agassiz, which came into existence when the continental ice sheet covered the country north of the present Lake Winnipeg, thereby forming a natural dam across the Red River of the North. When the ice retreated, the lake drained away, leaving an extensive plain.

The western, semiarid part of the Great Plains was formed by the retreat of the great inland Cretaceous Sea. Subsequent erosion and deposition modified the original landscape. The heavier rainfall and more severe erosion in the mountains to the west has caused thick layers of sediment to be deposited on the plains in broad overlapping alluvial fans. Near the mountain front, some of these deposits have been removed by later erosion so that a trough appears between the mountains and the High Plains to the east. This trough is locally known as the Colorado Piedmont. The southern part of the Great Plains (the High Plains), with an average elevation of 4,000 feet, is dissected by several through-flowing rivers: (1) the North and South Platte, (2) the Republican, (3) the Arkansas, (4) the Cimarron, and (5) the Canadian. Almost all these streams have cut their valleys several hundred feet below the plain surface. South of the Canadian River, in western Texas and eastern New Mexico, is an area of more than 20,000 square miles (the Llano Estacado) which is practically untouched by stream erosion.

From south to north the physiographic subdivisions of the western Great Plains are (1) the Rio Grande Plain, (2) the Edwards Plateau, (3) the High Plains, (4) the Raton Mesa, (5) the Sand Hills, (6) the Black Hills, (7) the Bad Lands, and (8) the Northern Great Plains. Of these, the Raton Mesa, the Sand Hills of Nebraska, the Black Hills of South Dakota, and the various Bad Lands have distinctly hilly to mountainous terrain. In addition, in central Montana and in Wyoming there are several distinct but isolated mountain ranges that are some distance east of the Rocky Mountain front. All of these features of considerable relief are included in the Great Plains geographical region because of their location in it.

Climate The climate of the Great Plains is continental; the precipitation ranges from 15 inches in the northwest to 35 in the southeast, and varies greatly from year to year. There are periods of dry years when the westerly margins become almost desertic. The growing season varies from about 120 days in the north to about 300 days in the south. Summers are very hot; the maximum temperature for a typical station is more than 100° F., and it is the maximum rather than the average which harms crops. Thus, whereas temperature and growing season are adequate for most staple crops, the low rainfall, combined with hot dry winds, discourages the growth of most crops. In the western part of the region wheat gives way to pasture, and, along the southwestern boundary, to the grain sorghums and cotton.

Within the Spring Wheat Belt the climate varies from subhumid to semiarid. The precipitation ranges from about 13 inches in the west to 22 inches along the eastern border. Forty to 50 per cent of the precipitation falls in the three summer months and greatly favors the growth of wheat.

Winters are bitterly cold and dry, and therefore very hard on such perennials as cultivated hay and fruit trees. The differences in temperature between winter and summer are so great as to give this region the distinction of having the greatest range of any region in Anglo-America.

Precipitation is the most important climatic factor of the Great Plains. The rainfall is less than 20 inches annually throughout most of the area (hilly and mountain regions excepted), and it has wide annual variations. In a humid area an annual variation of approximately 15 inches would not be significant, but here, where the average

is less than 20, a decrease of only a few inches may create an extremely critical situation. Wet and dry years tend to run in periods of varying lengths and intensities, but data are not yet sufficient for climatologists to determine the exact nature of them nor to forecast future conditions with any degree of reliability. Evidence indicates that the period between 1825 and 1865 was relatively dry, with few wet years. After settlers began keeping meteorological records in the late 1860's and early 1870's, an increase in rainfall was observed. Pioneers concluded that their settlements were responsible and offered many fantastic theories to prove their contention.[2] Then came the dry cycle during the 1880's and early 1890's, causing great distress among settlers and wholesale land abandonment. Since that date wet and dry periods have alternated, and the variations have always been serious. The dry period of 1933-1938, which probably caused the most widespread damage, created the Dust Bowl.

The high evaporation, ranging from 68 inches in southwest Texas to 37 inches in northern Montana, is due to high wind velocities and to a maximum of sunshine. These factors also reduce the precipitation effectiveness.

High winds, besides increasing evaporation and reducing rainfall efficiency, frequently assume destructive velocities, especially in the former Dust Bowl area.

Summer winds are so hot and dry and those of winter so biting and cold that nearly every farm needs a windbreak to reduce surface wind velocities. However, in the western part of the region, from Colorado northward, the winter weather is sporadically ameliorated by *chinook* winds. These warming, drying, downslope winds from the mountains bring periods of relative

[2] Walter Kollmorgen, "Rainmakers on the Plains," *The Scientific Monthly,* Vol. 40 (February 1935), pp. 146-52.

Figure 11-2. Hail and rain damage in a corn field in eastern Colorado. Violent weather conditions are agricultural hazards in the Great Plains. (USDA Photo.)

mildness that are a welcome relief to both man and livestock.

The Great Plains has the highest incidence of hail of any region in Anglo-America. The crop-destroying nature of the ice pellets is so intense that hail insurance is important to most farmers, particularly in the northern portion (Figure 11-2).

But probably the most notable aspect of Great Plains climate is its striking variety within short distances and abrupt changes over brief time spans. Indeed, in spite of gross regional unity, the Great Plains presents a variety of contrasts—not only in climate, but in other physical and cultural aspects as well. The words applied by two Oklahoma geographers to the Oklahoma panhandle are applicable to the entire region:

> Within this area means are insignificant, averages misleading, and generalizations are often invalid. Flat plains alternate with dissected semi-badlands; bitter cold and snow vie with blistering heat and dust; fertile calcareous soils contrast with sterile blow sand; bounteous grain yields alternate with crop failures; huge ranches compete with small subsistence farms; emigration meets immigration.[3]

[3] Arthur H. Doerr and John W. Morris, "The Oklahoma Panhandle—a Cross-Section of the Southern High Plains," *Economic Geography*, Vol. 36 (January 1960), p. 70.

Soils   The soils of the wheat belts, among the most fertile in Anglo-America, are mostly chernozems, though black prairie soils characterize the eastern margin and chestnut soils the western portion. They have a *lime zone*, a layer of calcium carbonate, at two to five feet beneath the surface, within reach of plant roots. Because of the scanty rainfall, these soils have not had the lime leached from them. Their fertility, combined with greater rainfall, makes them the most productive zonal soils in the world, although there is less humus than in the types of grassland soils to the east.

Not all soils throughout the wheat belts are equally good, since considerable areas possess types ill-suited to wheat or any other cereal. In southern Saskatchewan, within a radius of 20 miles, occur the province's most productive lands as well as some that may have to be abandoned for crops.

A distinct correlation exists between the distribution and density of population and soil types. Thus the population is densest on the excellent black soils which lie north and northeast of the brown soils. It is relatively sparse on the brown soils (many of which are submarginal) of the open semi-arid treeless plains which extend from as far north as Edmonton to southwestern Saskatchewan and southern Alberta and on across the border into adjacent parts of the United States.

Though the quality of wheat is little influenced by soil, the crop, for successful production, requires better soils than does any other small grain.

The semiarid grazing section of the Great Plains lies entirely within the pedocalic soil group, but local soils vary widely in physical characteristics, particularly in their moisture-holding capacity. In general these soils have good texture and high fertility and need no lime or other commercial fertilizers. However, moisture deficiency prohibits their being used successfully for crops except under irrigation.

Natural Vegetation Between the forests on the east and the mountains on the west lie the prairies and the steppe. The prairie, whose grasses attain a height usually of one to three feet, characterizes areas with 20 to 25 inches of precipitation in the north and 35 to 40 inches in the south.

They are practically identical with the area of the wheat belts except that there is a "park area" in the northeastern portion in Canada where bluffs of poplar and willow are interspersed with the heavy growth of grass. Merging with the prairie on the semiarid fringe to the west is the steppe, whose grasses are of low stature and whose rainfall is less than 20 inches.

The native vegetation of the semiarid grazing portion of the Great Plains is dominantly short grass, with grama and buffalo grasses most conspicuous. Along stream courses and on higher elevations such as the Black Hills, trees are dominant. Before the introduction of beef cattle in the 1870's, luxuriant native grasses (mainly western wheat grass) covered extensive areas. Overgrazing, however, has reduced thousands of square miles to a semi-desert. Extensive wheat farming during the periods of the two World Wars has ruined large areas of grazing land which may not be able to

graze livestock for some time. The white man seems to have done everything possible to make this subregion a desert.

Wildlife The Great Plains Region was the principal habitat of the American bison, with an estimated 50 million of these magnificent beasts occupying the region at the coming of the white man. Once white penetration of the region got underway in earnest, practically all of the vast herds were exterminated in less than a decade.

Other hoofed animals—pronghorn antelope, mule deer, whitetail deer, elk, and mountain sheep—were also common. They suffered a lesser fate than the bison, being pushed into the mountains to the west as settlement advanced.

Although this is a subhumid region, fur-bearers were numerous along the streams. Beaver, muskrat, mink, and otter were great attractions to the trappers and fur-traders, who were, with the exception of a few explorers, the first whites to penetrate the region.

A tremendous number of small, shallow marshes and ponds dot the glaciated terrain of the Dakotas and Prairie Provinces. These poorly drained areas provide an excellent muskrat habitat and are used as summer breeding grounds for myriads of waterfowl.

Sequent Occupance of the Great Plains

When the region was first traversed by European explorers, they found millions of buffalo, antelope, and other animals grazing on the vast steppe. The Indian had not disturbed the balance of nature by destroying either the native animal life or the grassland vegetation. Had this simple type of land occupance continued, wind-erosion problems such as we know today would not have affected the region.

The land was originally "Indian country." Though the Indians were not at first mobile, they became so after acquiring horses introduced by the Spaniards. With the arrival of the white man, the Indians were dispossessed, their game was killed off, and cattle were introduced. After the brief but spectacular era of the cattleman on the open range, that part of the Great Plains included within the Hard Winter Wheat Belt was homesteaded.

Settlement of the Eastern Part of the Region The first farmers believed that country unable to grow trees could not be good for agriculture. They shunned the prairie as they migrated westward, and they clung to the woodlands and river bottoms. The eastern part of the region was originally tall-grass country. Once crops were grown successfully on the prairie, newcomers arrived in large numbers; but settlement on a large scale had to await the arrival of the railroad.

No part of the world before had been conquered so rapidly for agriculture; clearing was unnecessary. True prairie soils, however, were not successfully turned over until the advent of the steel plow. Iron plows clogged so thoroughly in the tough, thick sod of the prairies that they frequently broke. Steel, on the other hand, sliced cleanly through the soil because it had a smoother and less porous finish.

Adjustment was difficult. The settler encountered extremes of temperature and variable rainfall. In some areas water was unobtainable at ordinary depths. Except at the edge of the forest, firewood and logs for homes were scarce or procurable only on a distant river bank. Where timber was scarce or lacking, a house made of sod had to meet the immediate need. But even this called for some wood. From the aesthetic point of view, the sod house was ugly; but, though cold in winter, it was cool in summer, and it cost practically nothing.

Scarcity of timber, except along stream courses, made fuel-gathering a problem.

Settlement, as well as travel, normally stayed close to the valleys for this reason. Whites soon adopted the Indian custom of burning buffalo chips, but the source of the chips was wiped out as settlement advanced.

The westward movement was in full swing and soon pioneer farmers had pushed beyond the tall-grass into the short-grass country. Their failure to understand the significance of short vs. tall grass proved to be an important factor, for they soon learned that rainfall on the steppe was inadequate for most crops and that tragedy would be widespread. The steppe was to prove itself less desirable for agriculture than the prairie.

The lands included in the Spring Wheat Subregion were originally inhabited by Indians who carried on some farming in the more favored spots but depended mostly upon the hunting of buffalo for a living. The Hudson's Bay Company later controlled the area.

The Dominion of Canada in 1870 took over the territories which the Hudson's Bay Company held by Royal Charter. The settlers had to learn by trial and error the agricultural possibilities of their country. It was known that the climate was dry, that the soil was fertile, that there were few obstacles to cultivation, since neither stumping nor stoning was required, and that crops might suffer from late spring and early summer frosts; but it was not known how variable the rainfall would be from year to year.

Settlement in the real sense did not begin until steel rails made their way across the continent. The Canadian prairie was settled long after its American counterpart—the lag being due to the dearth of wagon trails across the sterile Canadian Shield.

As a result of natural barriers, the older settled provinces of Canada appeared to have reached their limits of agricultural expansion even before Confederation. The so-called "Northwest" offered the only possible outlet to the area hemmed in by the Great Lakes on the west and the Canadian Shield on the north. As late as 1870 the Northwest area contained a scanty population. Settlement was limited largely to the shadows of the trading posts. The Canadian Pacific Railway, which became the great colonizer, did not span Canada from the Atlantic to the Pacific until 1885. To speed up settlement, agents were sent out. They enticed settlers by promising them free land. The railway here did not follow population; instead population followed it. For half a century the Canadian Pacific worked feverishly to spread settlers over the prairie. It alone of all Anglo-America's land-grant railroads actually colonized; the others merely sold land.

Struggling against scanty and irregular precipitation and a short growing season, the settlers ultimately triumphed—winning with quick-maturing varieties of wheat such as Marquis, Garnet, and Reward, and with the moisture-conserving practice of dry farming. At times rust played havoc with their crops, but again they triumphed by developing rust-resisting wheats.

The governments of Canada and the United States, along with their railroads, so encouraged immigration, although little was known of the area, that thousands of people poured into the Spring Wheat Belt and began to grow wheat. A mistake made by many was to locate too far from railroads. The market price of wheat determines how far the crop can be hauled. Moreover, during unusually favorable years when good crops could be grown, many immigrants settled on what later proved to be submarginal land. With the return of normal weather, crops failed and much land had to be abandoned.

Considering the numerous difficulties that have had to be overcome, the Spring Wheat Belt—American and Canadian—was trans-formed rapidly and on the whole successfully from the domain of the fur trader to that of the farmer.

Settlement of the Western Part of the Region Few people attempted to emulate the accomplishments of the Spanish explorers of the sixteenth century, in crossing this vast steppe, then considered a part of the Great American Desert. They found the plains to be a barrier to the westward movement that was seeking lands in Utah and Oregon. The first large party, the Astorians (1811-1813), followed the Missouri River to a point east of the Black Hills and then crossed westward into Wyoming. The following year a second group crossed the plains along the route of the North Platte River and established the Oregon Trail. A substantial migration to the Oregon Territory began about 1843. The next major trek was that of the Mormons (1846-1847), who followed the valley of the Platte from Omaha westward, but turned southwestward into the Salt Lake area after crossing the mountains. Soon after the Mormon trek came the California Gold Rush of 1849 and succeeding years. In addition to the well-established Oregon Trail, several others were used, but intermittent rivers with their water holes always marked the route. The rapidly growing population in California demanded closer contacts between the east and west coasts, resulting in several means of communication being developed—the stage coach, the pony express, and, most interesting of all, the camel caravans across the southern part of the Great Plains in Texas.

The completion of the Union Pacific Railroad in 1869, followed by several others in the 1870's and 1880's, ushered in the cattle era. A brief stage of buffalo hunting intervened, when for a few years white men with high-powered rifles all but exterminated the vast herds. By 1889 not more than a thousand head remained. The thousands of square miles of pasture lands left vacant immediately encouraged cattle drives from the Texas Gulf Coast. Although many cattle were driven northward to railheads at Abilene and Dodge City, during the 1880's large numbers also were driven into the northern Great Plains to establish the industry there.

The cattle era on the Great Plains was the most romantic stage in its utilization. Before the advent of barbed wire and its general use on the plains, the land was entirely open range. Individual cattle were branded and then allowed to run with the herds until the next season, when surplus animals were cut out and sent to market and calves were branded.

From the close of the Civil War period until about 1886, large herds grazed on the open range—a single open pasture thousands of square miles in extent. The increasing demand for meat both at home and abroad and improvements in transportation and refrigeration made the raising of livestock on the open range a highly profitable activity. Money poured into the region to establish large ranches and to increase and improve the herds. Much of this came from Europe, particularly from England and Scotland. Renewed interest in the range industry brought a demand for better strains of beef cattle, and several new varieties were introduced. Increasing numbers of cattle were being pastured and the open range was approaching its capacity. In some sections herders pastured large numbers of sheep on the open range. The closer grazing of sheep led to clashes between sheepmen and cattlemen over water holes and pasture rights.

The series of dry years which began in 1886 inaugurated a period of large fenced ranches. Before the development of barbed wire, fencing of the range would have been impossible even had it been desirable. A barbed-wire fence does not involve so much material as to make its cost prohibitive even on extremely large pastures.

The "cattle barons" attempted to secure from the Government all the land around a water hole; they had their cowhands do likewise. They would then fence in the entire area, sometimes more than they owned. Frequently they completely enclosed small ranchers or farmers within their fences, who retaliated by "fence cutting." The large ranchers then ordered their cowhands to ride their fences and shoot anyone found cutting them. Conditions became so bad that laws were passed to prevent "fence cutting" and "fence riding," and the large rancher was required to provide gates at intervals.

There was only a slight increase in cattle on the plains after 1890. The encroachment of the wheat farmer curtailed the amount of land available for cattle ranches, and overgrazing on the drier western parts still further reduced the area.

After 1910, several new influences made themselves felt in the region. The development of the tractor, combine, and other power machinery made feasible the planting and harvesting of a much larger acreage of land than formerly had been possible. Numerous drought-resisting crops, especially wheat, and the grain sorghums, were planted on the plains. The high prices during both World Wars resulted in further expansion of the wheat area, and many overstocked and overgrazed native pastures were plowed up and planted.

Errors Made in Settlement It is always easy to see errors after they are made. Settlers coming into the region homesteaded quarter-sections, the amount permitted the head of a family in accordance with the Homestead Act of 1862. They ploughed up the grass on land that was unsuitable for cultivation. They soon learned that they could not make a satisfactory living growing wheat on 160 acres, especially in the western margin. A family needed more land here than in humid regions where intensive methods were practicable. Accordingly thousands of families met disaster—losing their money, their labor, and finally even hope. They had gambled and had lost.

In 1904 the Kincaid Act increased to 640 acres the amount that could be homesteaded in western Nebraska, and in 1909 the Enlarged Homestead Act established the 320-acre homestead over a large area. But even these enlarged homesteads, including those made possible by the Stockraising Homestead Act of 1916, proved to be little more than gestures in the right direction. The great weakness of all these acts was that they did not fit conditions west of the 100th meridian, and 20-inch rainfall line. The desire for small farms within semiarid Anglo-America was tenacious but untenable. In 1934 and 1935 all remaining unreserved and unappropriated public lands were withdrawn from homesteading by the federal government.

Unlike areas farther west, however, most of the Great Plains Region was already in private ownership. Some dry and rough lands in Montana and state-owned lands in west Texas, as well as several Indian reservations, are exceptions to the general rule of private ownership. Abandoned farmsteads are common both east of and west of the 100th meridian. In most cases the land has been incorporated into other farms. This reduction in the number of farms was accelerated by drought and depression.

The Mennonite settlers of Kansas, Manitoba, and Montana were a notable exception to these failures, for they brought with them from Russia drought-resisting varieties of wheat. Up to this time only the varieties adapted to the humid East had been grown.

Possibly the biggest mistake of all was made during the first World War when the price of wheat skyrocketed and it was every farmer's patriotic duty to feed the Allies and win the war. This meant growing wheat and more wheat. Millions of acres that had never been anything but grazing land were attacked with tractor-drawn plows and seeded with wheat. Improved machinery enabled large amounts of power per man to be employed in crop production. The increase in wheat acreage took place mostly as a western extension outside the so-called Winter Wheat Belt. The yield was favorable at first, for the soil was fertile, rains were plentiful, and there was much moisture in the subsoil. Farmers grew wheat year after year. Before long, however, the soil-binding quality of the humus became depleted by continuous cropping. Livestock were turned in to graze the poorly developed crop, and their hoofs pulverized the ground. Then in the spring of 1934, winds began to blow the soil. Great clouds of dust swept eastward from this land largely devoid of anchoring vegetation. Thus must the nation pay a high price for having grown wheat on grazing land. Yet that is what might be expected from a people who had inherited the deeply rooted idea that in America land was practically unlimited and soil inexhaustible.

THE DUST BOWL at its greatest extent covered 16 million acres. Here during the months December to May (the blow season), fine fertile soil particles were whisked hundreds of miles away, forming "black blizzards." The heavier particles remained as drifts and hummocks. Sand dunes attained heights of 20 feet. The atmosphere was choked with dust; in some areas people had to put cloth over their faces when going out of doors. The vegetation in the fields was coated and rendered inedible for cattle, and whole groups of counties became almost unlivable.

But the Dust Bowl has been shrinking due to greater and better-distributed rainfall, to the regrassing of extensive areas, and to the erosion-preventive measures or

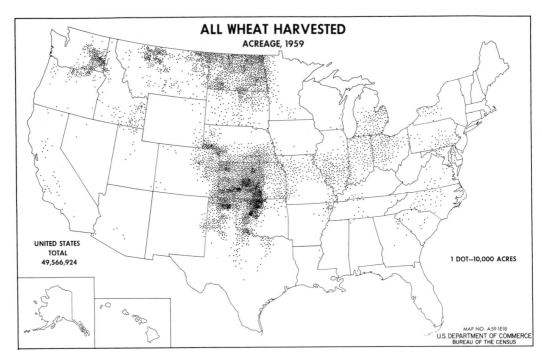

Figure 11-3. Distribution of harvested wheat in the United States. The Winter
Wheat Belt and the Spring Wheat Belt of the Great Plains are conspicuous.

new farming techniques of the Soil Conservation Service and other federal and state organizations. New techniques, including contour plowing and strip cropping, have been devised to utilize all the rain that falls.

From the national point of view, the Dust Bowl has been one of the most uneconomic farming areas in all Anglo-America. The drier and sandier portions should be returned to grass, as a means of controlling soil drifting, for grass more than anything else ties down the soil during the years of recurring droughts. A combination of factors caused dust storms to appear again in the northern Great Plains in 1945 and in the southern High Plains in the early 1950's. Dust storms are by now a common springtime occurence.

Present Distribution of Population A current map of population distribution would show a fairly open and even pattern, generally decreasing from east to west. In detail, the irrigated river valleys stand out as distinct population clusters. The topographically unfavorable areas, such as the Sand Hills, various Bad Lands, and mountain outliers, are quite barren of population.

Wheat Farming

Wheat is grown widely throughout the United States and Canada, but the two most important areas are (1) the Hard Winter Wheat Belt in Kansas, Nebraska, Colorado, Oklahoma, and Texas, and (2) the Spring Wheat Belt in the Dakotas, Montana, western Minnesota, and the Prairie Provinces of Canada.

The two wheat-growing areas are not contiguous (Figure 11-3). Between them is a belt (in southern South Dakota and northern Nebraska) where little wheat is grown.

This is the Sand Hill country, a disordered arrangement of grass-covered slopeland, unsuited to cultivation.

The Winter Wheat Area The typical farm in the Winter Wheat Belt is large—it has to be. The size is greater in the western than in the eastern part. In central Kansas, the heart of the area, farms approach 1,000 acres. Many farmsteads have windbreaks on their windward sides, and these are conspicuous features of the landscape. Windbreaks offer, among other advantages, protection from the cold, dry northwest winds of winter and the hot southwest winds of summer.

Most of the land in crops is in wheat, though grain sorghums are probably more important on those farms in the southwestern part of the area. One may look in any direction and see little else growing in the fields than wheat. Actually only about a quarter of the land is in such crops as grain sorghums, alfalfa, and barley. Alfalfa and sorghums remove so much water from the subsoil that they cannot be grown continually on the same land.

Hard wheat is a variety having more and better gluten, a protein, than *soft wheat*. Flour made from it imparts adhesiveness to dough, which is desirable for making bread. Hard wheat flour is more desirable also because, measure for measure, it produces a larger loaf than does soft wheat flour. Dough containing hard wheat flour can better withstand severe treatment in mechanical mixers. On the other hand, soft wheat is more desirable for hot biscuits, crackers, and pastries. Other advantages of hard wheat are its higher market price and its greater per-acre yield.

There is a steady movement northward of winter-wheat growing. In eastern Wyoming spring wheat is hardly grown at all. In South Dakota spring wheat is still the leader, but winter varieties are rapidly gaining in favor. In the plains areas of Montana there is actually more winter than spring wheat grown. This trend is a response to the development of varieties of winter wheat that can better tolerate colder weather. Only in North Dakota, eastern Minnesota, and the Prairie Provinces does spring wheat still hold undisputed sway.

The Spring Wheat Area The entire Spring Wheat Area grows hard wheat. Great progress has been made in both plant exploring and plant breeding, scientists having been challenged to develop high-protein [4] types which mature early, yield well, and resist drought and rust.

Canadian spring wheat is mainly of the hard red type, though considerable durum is grown in the east where the hazard of rust is greatest. Canadian spring wheat is considered the world's best, because it provides a higher flour yield, a bushel outweighing by several pounds one bushel of American spring wheat, and because it has a higher protein content, desirable in bread.

Farms of the Spring Wheat Area are large, but they are larger south of the international border than north of it. They also increase in size from east to west. The tendency is toward still larger holdings. The average North Dakota farm contains about 800 acres. In the drier part three, four, or sometimes as many as seven sections are required to support the family unit. This means, of course, a thinner population in the western than in the eastern portion.

The spring-wheat farmer, particularly the Canadian, reaps the advantages and disadvantages of specialization. His production costs (land and labor) are low; at the same time he is a great gambler, since he "carries all his eggs in one basket." Moreover, the Prairie Provinces suffer because of their de-

---

[4] The percentage of protein is commonly employed for determining the milling and baking qualities of wheat. The protein content is said to be dependent upon climatic conditions—being high if dry weather prevails during the six weeks preceding harvest.

Figure 11-4. Wheat farms near Portage La Prairie, Manitoba. (Photo courtesy National Film Board, Ottawa.)

pendence on foreign markets (Figure 11-4).

In the eastern part of the region, particularly the United States segment, the wheat acreage is being reduced in favor of diversified farming, with emphasis on dairying. This is true also in the Winnipeg area, where longer settlement, more moisture, and larger population are encouraging mixed farming and dairying. A diversified and fruitful agriculture has developed in Manitoba's "Pembina Pocket," southwest of Winnipeg, which is to that province more or less what the Annapolis Valley is to Nova Scotia, the Niagara Peninsula to Ontario, and the Okanagan Valley to British Columbia.[5]

Diversification is also developing in the western part of the subregion as far north as Edmonton and especially in the foothills. Here crops are grown under irrigation; alfalfa forms the basis of important winter feeding of range cattle and sheep. Sugar beets, too, are grown, there being two sugar factories at Lethbridge. The growing and

[5] W. R. Leslie, "The Pembina Pocket," *Canadian Geographical Journal*, Vol. 63 (September 1961), pp. 76-83.

canning of vegetables, especially peas, is also being developed.

Systems of Farming Commercially, the Winter Wheat Belt is a one-crop area dominated by wheat. The heaviest concentration is in central and southwestern Kansas and in northwestern Oklahoma, where the cereal is grown on a large scale.

Farmers build up their systems of farming around wheat. The best ones diversify, producing feed crops for livestock on part of the acreage. Diversification gives employment throughout the year, brings in constant returns, and maintains the fertility of the soil. Rotation in the eastern and central parts of the Hard Winter Wheat Belt includes alfalfa, sorghum, corn (on the better lands), oats or barley, and wheat, in this order, resulting in higher yields. Rotations are more difficult and less satisfactory in the western part of the subregion, for here wheat may be grown for a longer period on the same land without suffering losses in yield, and fewer other crops can be raised. The best rotation consists of one year each of a grain sorghum, preferably kafir or milo, and fallow, followed by two or three years of wheat. Where wheat is the only crop, probably the best system consists of one year of fallow and two or three years of wheat. About one-third or one-fourth of the acreage intended for wheat should be fallowed. When land is in fallow, it is cultivated but not sown. Weeds are thus controlled and moisture is conserved. Care must be taken not to pulverize the soil, for a surface of clods absorbs water more effectively than a surface of mulch and is less given to blowing. Fallowing is advantageous because it increases yields and because it better equalizes the seasonal distribution of labor, since the land is prepared in the slack period before harvest.

In the Spring Wheat Area, wheat gets first choice of the land, though oats, barley, hay, flax, and corn (for silage) are grown as rotation crops. In the very dry areas, the rotation followed (if it may be called a rotation) is summer-fallow and wheat. Alternating strips from 6 to 20 rods wide are oriented at right angles to the prevailing wind. In preparing summer-fallow, the mould-board plough has been replaced by several types of cultural implements that destroy vegetational growth, but leave the stubble on the surface of the land to aid in the control of soil drift. Only during about the last two decades has this "stubble mulching" method of cultivation in the drier areas been generally adopted. It is proving very effective in checking soil drift. In the more humid parts, oats and barley may follow wheat. Because of the difficulty of growing row crops and controlling weeds, north of the international boundary, fallow is more popular than south of the boundary. In North Dakota, where corn does not thrive, one-third of the crop area is devoted to wheat.

Harvesting Problems To equalize the seasonal distribution of labor is difficult anywhere but particularly in a monocultural region. In the early days of wheat growing, labor was scarce, especially during harvest. Accordingly migratory workers—lumberjacks, hoboes, and college students—tempted by substantial wages and a relatively short working period, poured into the area. They started in Texas and Oklahoma, where the harvest begins in early June, and moved northward at the rate of about 100 miles a week. They arrived in Nebraska in early July and in the Dakotas in August. Some of them went on to the Prairie Provinces of Canada, where the harvest begins in September. Such labor was expensive, but when the kernels are ripe, wheat must be harvested, threshed, and put under cover before rain falls. The upward trend of wheat prices from 1896 to 1920 was terminated by the close of the first World War. Falling prices necessitated a saving in cost of production, and machinery, especially the combine, was the solution. Having reduced by more than one-half the per-acre cost with only one-fourth the manpower, combines have been a potent factor in increasing the size of farms and in opening up to wheat growing those lands near the southwestern border of the area.

Migrant workers have been important in wheat harvesting for many decades. They operate as custom-combining crews, working northward throughout the long summer, and returning to their homes and families, usually in Texas, for the winter. After World War II there was a decided decline in custom combining, as wheat farmers accumulated sufficient wealth and land to make it feasible for most of them to own their own combines (Figure 11-5). Since the mid-fifties, however, federal wheat acreage controls have caused a swing back to custom combining. Some 50,000 men work as combine crews following the northward harvest trail.

Sidewalks and Suitcases Extensive wheat growing lends itself easily to absentee ownership. If no livestock are kept on

Figure 11-5. Combining wheat in southern Alberta. (Alberta Government Photograph.)

the farm, a resident operator is not needed. Work needs to be done only at seeding and harvest times, and even this can be custom-contracted. Thus special terminology has come into being to identify certain types of wheat farmers. A "sidewalk farmer" lives and works in a nearby town, but can drive to the farm when there is work to be done there. A "suitcase farmer" is likely to live farther away, perhaps in another state, and pay only occasional visits to his wheat property. Sometimes he will own land in both Winter and Spring Wheat belts, migrating back and forth with his machinery at planting and harvesting times.

Surplus One of the most striking characteristics of Anglo-American wheat growing is the astounding surplus that has accumulated. Since the end of World War II wheat production in both countries has generally exceeded the amount needed for domestic use or export. Supplies increase in four out of five years, on the average, and the more than two billion bushels carry-over on hand in the early 1960's was equivalent to a three-year supply.[6]

Prospects for holding the line on sur-

6 "The Wheat Surplus Problem," *Monthly Review,* Federal Reserve Bank of Kansas City, November 1960, p. 10.

plus production are dim. Per capita domestic consumption has been declining at about the same rate as population has been increasing. And although exports have increased notably in the last two decades—more in the United States than in Canada[7] —the surplus continues to mount. Acreage allotments have been in effect for most years since 1950. This has decreased the planted acreage, but has not appreciably slowed down the continued upward trend of yields, which is due to improved wheat varieties and cultural practices.

Both national governments have maintained price-support programs to improve farm income, which abets the surplus problem. Although acreage allotments and marketing quotas have been in effect intermittently, they have not held down overproduction, because the incentive of price supports persuades farmers to apply more

7 The United States disposes of wheat by loans, gifts, and acceptance of local currencies in payment, as well as by normal commercial exports. Canada, on the other hand, sells for dollars only. [See John T. Seywell, ed., *Canadian Annual Review for 1960* (Toronto: University of Toronto Press, 1961), p. 229.] The avowed United States policy is to interfere as little as possible with normal commercial relations of other wheat-exporting nations, but some displacements, and considerable ill feelings, inevitably occur.

capital and effort per acre, thus increasing yields. So the wheat surplus, a major bi-national scandal, continues to mount and the end is not in sight.

Transportation of Wheat Since the population in this region is so small and wheat production is so great, the bulk of the crop is shipped elsewhere (except for the surplus that ordinarily goes to nearby, newly constructed storage bins). Accordingly wheat regions must have good transport facilities. The crop is first carried by truck from the farm to one of the many small country elevators distributed throughout the wheat belt alongside the railroads. From there it goes by rail to some large primary market. Getting the grain to elevators before rains set in has long been a major problem, necessitating the bringing in of freight cars by the tens of thousands.

In the United States the wheat is taken from the elevators to larger primary markets by rail. That destined for domestic consumption continues via train to the milling centers. Export wheat normally is shipped from Great Lakes ports during the summer season of navigation. Some also is exported year round from Atlantic coastal cities, and barge traffic down the Mississippi (for transshipment on ocean-going vessels from Gulf ports) accounts for further exports.

The Prairie Provinces ship most of their wheat from field to country elevator, nearly 6,000 of which dot the Canadian Prairie. Elevators occupy railway sidings, and many small towns consist of little else (Figure 11-6). A large part of the grain moves to Winnipeg for grading, whence it is hauled to Port Arthur and Fort William for shipment by lake carrier to Montreal or Buffalo.

From Montreal, St. John, and Halifax, the grain is exported to Europe, from Buffalo it goes to New York City for transshipment. An appreciable quantity of wheat from the Prairie Provinces is exported from Vancouver as well as from Victoria and Prince Rupert via the Panama Canal to Europe. Some also travels over the Hudson Bay Railway to Churchill. Much of America's spring wheat goes to Minneapolis, which is the leading terminal storage center. Some also moves via lake carrier to Buffalo.

Because of the Spring Wheat Area's interior location and because water transportation is cheaper than rail, enormous grain

Figure 11-6. Other buildings in wheat belt villages and small towns are dwarfed by the grain elevators that characteristically stand along the railroad tracks. This is Indian Head, Saskatchewan. (Photo courtesy National Film Board, Ottawa.)

elevators have been built at strategic points on navigable water; for example, Fort William and Port Arthur have some of the largest and finest elevator equipment in the world. Duluth and Superior also are well equipped, as are Montreal, Vancouver, and Churchill.

Rail rates for comparable distances are lower in Canada than in the United States. This is a matter of charter provisions: in return for a subsidy and a land grant, the Canadian Pacific Railway agreed to reduce rates from western Canada to Lake Superior wheat ports by three cents per 100 pounds and to maintain these rates in perpetuity.

Milling Between 1855 and 1870, flour mills of three types evolved:

1. *Custom mills*, which ground the farmer's grain, making a definite charge per barrel.

2. *Exchange mills*, which exchanged flour, already ground, for wheat. The farmer usually got about 25 to 30 pounds of flour for a bushel of wheat. Most of the mills were of this type prior to 1870 and were largely a response to the extremely bad and often impassable roads of winter.

3. *Merchant mills*, which bought the grain and sold the flour and by-products outright. The roller process of milling sounded the death knell of the small custom and exchange mills. Today nearly all, if not all, are of the merchant type—either (a) *interior*, which mill flour for the local market, or (b) *terminal*, which mill flour for distant markets, including those in foreign countries.

Prior to 1892 the bulk of the Hard Winter Wheat Belt's grain was shipped to the ultimate market for milling, since freight rates were so regulated that wheat could be shipped more cheaply than flour. Some milling took place within the area, but it was mostly confined to the eastern part, to the larger cities, and, to the transportation terminals. To a certain extent this is still true. The dominant centers today in the Hard Winter Wheat Belt are Wichita, Salina, Hutchinson, and Oklahoma City.

When Minneapolis became the world's leading milling center, the grist mill "struck a snag." Whereas soft winter wheat made a beautiful white flour, hard spring wheat and hard winter wheat made a dark, distasteful flour. This was attributable to flinty particles and to friction caused by the buhrstones, which completely crush wheat kernels.

The hard-wheat flour, therefore, was sold at a great disadvantage in the East, and even the wheat from which it was made sold for about 20 cents a bushel below soft winter wheat. Something had to be done, and the roller mill resulted. The steel-roller process, which revolutionized flour milling, was invented in Budapest (1820), then the world's leading milling center. It was a trade secret, but Hungarians were induced to come to Minneapolis. The essential feature of the roller process was the iron or porcelain rollers that were used instead of buhrstones. Smooth rolls were unsuccessful, however, and porcelain tended to chip. Accordingly, a corrugated roll was perfected which produced more flour from the wheat and performed 30 per cent more work on 47 per cent less power. Other contributions to milling were the dust collector, for preventing explosions; the purifier, for eliminating middlings (flinty particles); the "middlings purifier," for separating the dust and fluffy particles or bran from the middlings; and the bolting machine, for sifting the flour through a very fine silk cloth.

Though this region is the world's leading producer of wheat, it is not outstanding in milling, because (1) the domestic demand (Canada) for flour is small, (2) ocean freight rates are lower on wheat than on flour, and (3) foreign countries want the by-product for animal feed.

Other Crops of the Great Plains Region

Grain Sorghums With the exception of a small but concentrated area along the coastal plain of south Texas, most of the grain sorghums of the United States are grown along the western margin of the Winter Wheat Area on the High Plains of Texas, Kansas, Nebraska, and Oklahoma. These drought-resisting crops, introduced into the United States from the semiarid parts of Africa, have grown in importance in the southwestern part of the area, where they are being used for fodder and as a binder crop in strip and terrace cultivation (Figure 11-7). In dry years grain sorghums produce a partial crop for feed and cover even when wheat withers and dies. They have been known to grow on as little as ten inches of annual rainfall. Moreover, the stubble stands erect against the wind, thereby reducing erosion. Since the sorghums require much heat, they are less important north of the Arkansas Valley.

Figure 11-7. A field of grain sorghums on the Texas High Plains. (Photo courtesy Texas Agricultural Extension Service.)

Sorghum acreage has continued to increase. In Oklahoma it is about one-quarter, and in Kansas and Nebraska, about one-half that of wheat acreage; in Texas, it is two and one-half times greater than the wheat acreage (Figure 11-8). Rather severe acre-

Figure 11-8. Distribution of grain sorghum in the United States. Most production is in the southern half of the Great Plains.

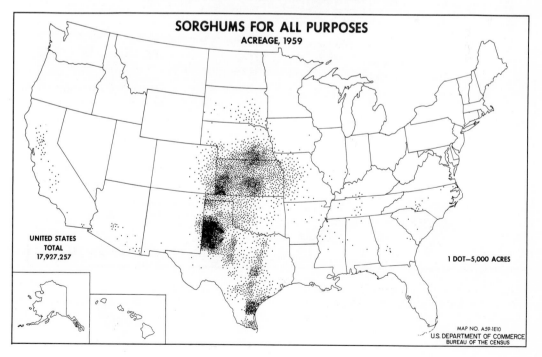

SORGHUMS FOR ALL PURPOSES
ACREAGE, 1959

UNITED STATES
TOTAL
17,927,257

1 DOT—5,000 ACRES

MAP NO. A59-1E10
U.S. DEPARTMENT OF COMMERCE
BUREAU OF THE CENSUS

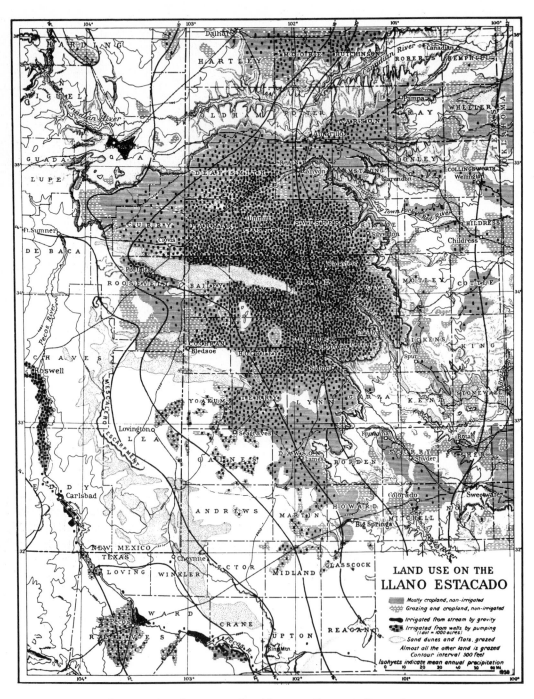

Figure 11-9. Land use on the Llano Estacado. (Courtesy Economic Research Service, U.S. Department of Agriculture.)

age limitations were instituted in 1961, which decreased the amount of land planted to sorghums for the first time in a decade. Sorghums are now second only to wheat (proportionally) as a surplus crop, and further government restrictions are to be expected.

Some of the more important varieties of grain sorghums grown on the Southern High Plains include the kafirs, milos, feterita, darso, and hegari.

Cotton   The southern part of the Great Plains, which is an important cotton-producing area, is included frequently with the lands of the Cotton Belt (Chapter 7), but in this text the cotton grown here is treated as one of the crops of the Great Plains.

When the potentialities of the High Plains [8] area for cotton production became known, the acreage increased rapidly, and by the close of World War I, it had developed into a great cotton-growing area. At first practically all of the crop was grown by dry-farming methods, but in time much of the cotton area was irrigated by means of shallow wells. This has changed the appearance of this area from a land of ranches and extensively cultivated cotton and grain sorghums, to one of intensive cultivation of cotton through irrigation methods (Figure 11-9). Growing cotton under irrigation, however, has reached its maximum development in the Great Valley of California and hence will be considered in detail there (Chapter 14). Since most of the water for irrigation in the South Plains Area comes from wells drilled into water-bearing sands which have no large surface outcrop, and since this area lies within a region of low rainfall, it is clear that the underground water source is being depleted at too rapid a rate and that the number of wells drilled in the area should be regulated so that the

supply of irrigation water will not be exhausted. Texas now has more than 15,000 pumped irrigation wells, mostly on the High Plains. These once-shallow wells currently have an average depth of more than 125 feet, and the average is growing each year as the aquifers are further depleted. Even so, only about 10 per cent of the harvested cropland of Texas is irrigated, the lowest proportion of any of the twelve "western" states. In many years Lubbock County is the greatest cotton producer in the nation. The city of Lubbock is one of the fastest-growing in the world.

Small Grains   The northern plains constitute Anglo-America's major producing area of barley and rye, as well as an important secondary producer of oats. The leading barley growers are North Dakota, Alberta, and Saskatchewan; rye is most important in South Dakota, North Dakota, and Saskatchewan; oats are most notable in Alberta, Saskatchewan, Minnesota, and North Dakota.

Flax   In the northern plains flax is also an important crop. Ninety-five per cent of the United States crop and 99 per cent of the Canadian crop is grown here. The valley of the Red River of the North is the principal area of cultivation, especially in North Dakota (Figure 11-10) but also in South Dakota, Minnesota, and Manitoba. Major production also occurs in southern Saskatchewan and Alberta. The crop is grown almost exclusively for seed (linseed), but its short, hard fibers are occasionally used in the manufacture of cigarette paper.

Irrigation on the Great Plains

Irrigation was practiced in the Southwest long before the coming of white men, but, except for that developed by the Spaniards in the middle Rio Grande Valley, the reclaimed area was increased only slightly. The first irrigation project to be established on the Great Plains dates from 1870, when

[8] This area goes by a number of names, including the *South Plains*, the *High Plains*, the *Staked Plains*, and the *Llano Estacado*.

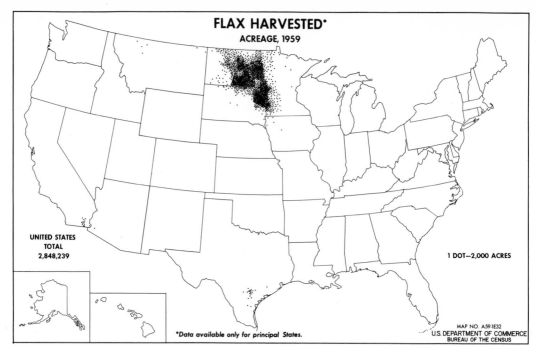

Figure 11-10. Distribution of harvested flax in the United States.

the Greeley Union Colony developed a large tract of land in northern Colorado by using water from the South Platte and Cache la Poudre rivers.

Irrigation projects are developed under four principal types of ownership and management: (1) mutual irrigation companies, such as the Greeley Union Colony, where every farmer is automatically a part of the organization; (2) commercial irrigation, where privately owned companies construct all facilities and sell services to water users at a profit; (3) irrigation-district movements, involving public support but depending upon private capital for construction financing; and (4) federal irrigation districts, organized under the National Reclamation Act of 1902, where the government bears all construction costs and the settlers pay for their land and water rights on comparatively easy terms. Of these, the first and fourth have been the most successful, although the third type has been responsible for the irrigation of much land in the West. In 1936 the President's Great Plains Com-

mittee found that counties with adequate irrigation systems had only five per cent tax delinquency while adjacent counties had as high as 95 per cent tax delinquency, despite the fact that irrigated lands had tax valuations ten times as great as those of dry farming or grazing lands.

Great Plains Irrigation Districts The irrigation districts of this region are too numerous to list, since almost every stream flowing from the Rocky Mountains provides water for some project. The Federal Bureau of Reclamation has under construction or active operation on the Great Plains a number of large projects, but there are many more under other types of ownership. In Texas, where the federal government owns little public land, the Bureau of Reclamation has made no improvement. However, some land in Texas is supplied with water from the federal Rio Grande project. The irrigated area of Texas is scattered throughout the arid parts of the State and in the rice-growing areas of the coastal plain, but more than half of the developed area lies

302

within the Great Plains grazing area. On the High Plains more than one million acres depend upon wells. In south Texas, the Winter Garden area utilizes artesian water, and the Laredo district draws upon the Rio Grande.

Other outstanding irrigated areas are along the Pecos River in New Mexico; the Arkansas River in eastern Colorado and Kansas; much of the northeastern corner of Colorado, primarily in the South Platte drainage; along the Platte River in Nebraska; along various parts of the Missouri River in eastern Montana and the Dakotas; in the valley of the Red River of the North; and along portions of the Bow and Saskatchewan rivers in the Prairie Provinces.

All irrigated areas have much in common, but there are many varied problems involved in their construction and maintenance. A brief description of the Colorado–Big Thompson project in northeastern Colorado follows.

THE COLORADO–BIG THOMPSON PROJECT The more than 600,000 acres in this project lie in northeastern Colorado and include the lands of the Greeley Union Colony that have been "under the ditch" since 1870. Water shortage in the area led the Bureau of Reclamation to undertake construction of this project at a cost originally estimated at 44 million dollars, one-half to be assumed by the federal government for power development, and the other half to be repaid by farmers in the Northern Colorado Conservation District. Besides being the largest single irrigated area on the Great Plains, this project has several unique features. The natural watershed of the Big Thompson River could not meet the needs of the irrigated lands, and since the waters of other streams on the east slope were already appropriated, sources on the west slope of the mountains had to be tapped. It was therefore necessary to drill one of the longest tunnels in Anglo-America. The tunnel is

13.1 miles long, has a diameter of 9.5 feet, and is capable of carrying 550 second-feet of water. Under the summit of the Continental Divide it is nearly 4,000 feet below ground. To prevent water users on the western slope from losing their water supply, reservoirs were constructed to supplement the volume of Grand Lake so that it can be maintained at a constant level. All reservoirs and tunnels lie outside the Great Plains, but the irrigated lands are within the region. In the area to benefit from this project live more than 250,000 people who derive their livelihood directly or indirectly from farming. Because of the severe water shortage during the 1930's, farmers in this area suffered an annual loss of nearly seven million dollars. This project is designed to meet all irrigation needs.

Because of changes in original plans, miscalculations, and the increased costs of labor and materials due to inflation, the original estimate of 44 million dollars may reach 200 million before the project is finally completed. Because of these costs, many people have expressed grave doubts over the economic practicability of the project, and considerable opposition has arisen within the State of Colorado concerning the entire project. Some have gone so far as to suggest its abandonment. Under the original estimates the farmers within the district could have paid their share, but with construction costs amounting to several times the original estimate, queries have arisen as to the soundness of the undertaking. If the farmers have to increase their share of the cost it will place them under a financial burden far above their ability to pay. Since the Bureau of Reclamation cannot abandon the project without subjecting itself to severe criticism, the only solution seems to be for the federal government to assume all costs over and above the original estimate, and hope that the sale of electricity will ultimately pay for the project. Some electrical engineers, how-ever, have expressed misgivings concern-ing the possibility that the sale of electricity may pay the balance.[9]

Pick-Sloan The Pick-Sloan plan for "taming" the Missouri River was introduced in Chapter 9. Many of the major construc-tion projects have been or will be built on the Great Plains. Four huge dams—Ft. Peck in Montana, Garrison in North Dakota, and Oahe and Big Bend in South Dakota—as well as many small ones are included.[10]

In spite of obvious local benefits, many people question the wisdom of expending so much effort and money for dubious gains. Flood control will be beneficial, re-creation benefits may be noted, power gene-ration is secondary, and more irrigated acres in these days of crop surpluses are definitely nonessential. As for stimulating the local and regional economy, one agri-cultural specialist has said,

> The establishment of specialized irrigated farm units which are not individually inte-grated, each with a much larger area of dry land, will not mitigate the uncertainties of climate which plague the owners of dry land. Irrigated units which are not inte-grated with dry land are like isolated oases. They cannot stabilize the fluctuations caused by drought on the dry lands around them. Without integration they are more of an appendage than a functional aid to farmers and ranchers on the dry lands.[11]

The Major Irrigated Crops The length of the growing season within this region varies from more than 280 frost-free days in the Winter Garden and Laredo districts of south Texas to less than 120 in northern Montana and southern Canada. The most extensively grown crop is *alfalfa*, which is

[9] Harold A. Hoffmeister, "Middle Park and the Colorado-Big Thompson Diversion Project," *Eco-nomic Geography*, Vol. 23 (1947), pp. 228-30.
[10] Fort Peck, Oahe, and Garrison, in that order, are the three largest earthfill dams in the world.
[11] Higbee, *American Agriculture: Geography, Re-sources, Conservation*, p. 212.

used for supplemental winter feeding of livestock. Alfalfa occupies the largest acre-age of any irrigated crop from southern Colorado northward. The Winter Garden and Laredo areas in the extreme south pro-duce early *Bermuda onions, spinach* and other winter truck crops.

On the several irrigated areas of the Pecos Valley in southern New Mexico, *cot-ton* has become dominant, although con-siderable acreage is devoted to alfalfa. On the High Plains of the Texas Panhandle, large acreages of cotton are irrigated by water from deepening wells.

From Colorado northward, in addition to alfalfa, sugar beets occupy a large acreage. This crop is grown throughout the irrigated West, but northeastern Colorado and west-ern Nebraska, the second and fifth leading producing states, respectively, are outstand-ing in the Great Plains.

SUGAR BEETS belong fundamentally to a cool-summer region, where summer tem-peratures do not average above 70° F. Beets produce best on dark-colored silt and clay loams. The major requirement, however, is moisture, and since a uniform supply is needed at all times, the crop in this region must be irrigated. The average field of sugar beets requires from three to seven irrigations each season (Figure 11-11). Un-like sugar cane, the raising of sugar beets requires considerable farm equipment. The principal implements needed are beet-seed drills, beet cultivators, mechanical thinners, chemical sprayers, beet lifters, and special trucks for hauling the roots to the loading station or factory. Beet seeds are planted with drills in rows about twenty inches apart and covered to a uniform depth. As soon as the rows can be followed, they are cultivated and the beets thinned out so as to stand 7 to 12 inches apart. During the early growing period beets are cultivated to keep down weeds. When the plant becomes large enough for the leaves to cover the

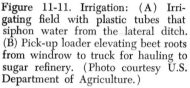

Figure 11-11. Irrigation: (A) Irrigating field with plastic tubes that siphon water from the lateral ditch. (B) Pick-up loader elevating beet roots from windrow to truck for hauling to sugar refinery. (Photo courtesy U.S. Department of Agriculture.)

ground, the crop is "laid by," and no further work is done until the beets are fully mature. Warm days and cool nights are essential for satisfactory maturing of the beets.

The crop is harvested by lifting the roots from the soil and placing them in piles. They are then topped, loaded into trucks, and transported to the sugar factory or loading station. Beets should not be hauled more than four or five miles. If farms are more remote from the factory, loading stations are provided by the railroads.

Sugar beets, an intensively grown crop, require a large amount of labor, especially during thinning and harvesting. Formerly, most beet areas depended on migratory Mexican labor for their activities, but the industry is rapidly becoming mechanized and "field hands" are of less importance.

In the sugar factories, which are large establishments, the beets are cleaned, sliced, and placed in cylinders for the extraction of the sugar. Ultimately the sugar is separated from other liquors or molasses. At most factories the beet pulp (wet or dry) is sold to stockmen for feed. The tops and crowns left in the field are also used as stock feed. The beet-sugar industry is an exacting one, but it has proved to be very remunerative in irrigated areas throughout the West.

The Range Livestock Industry

Cattle, sheep, and Angora goats dominate the range of the Great Plains Region. Although cattle are the most widely distributed, overgrazing has resulted in their elimination from some areas. Sheep, introduced later than cattle, were pastured on the poorer lands, but have become dominant in parts of Montana, Wyoming, and southwest Texas, where formerly only cattle were considered of value. Many cattlemen, especially in southwest Texas, found it more profitable to run sheep than cattle on their ranches, although it hurt their pride to do so. Angora goats are raised almost exclusively on the Edwards "Plateau" of central Texas.

The Range Cattle Industry Despite the fact that the Great Plains Region has fewer range cattle today than formerly, ranching is still important. The demand for better-quality meat and the practice of fattening stock on farms before slaughtering them has resulted in the Agricultural Interior having more cattle than the western ranges.

Throughout the Great Plains the carrying capacity of the range varies widely. Practically all the region has been overstocked—a temptation that becomes greater during years of high prices, particularly if the rainfall has been good and pastures are greener than normal. Conservative cattlemen, however, have learned the approximate carrying capacity of their land and do not run more cattle than can be fed in dry years.

The size of the cattle ranches varies from less than 2,000 acres to more than 800,000 acres. One of the largest cattle ranches in the Great Plains Region is the Matador Ranch, located along the breaks of the plains in the Texas Panhandle. The three properties controlled by the Matador interests, containing more than 800,000 acres, constitute one of the largest areas of the continent producing top-quality beef. Each year more than 9,000 beef cattle and 10,000 calves are shipped to market from this large-scale, well-managed "beef assembly line." The Matador was the last of the large High Plains ranches owned by foreign capital (Scottish) although at one time millions of acres of the Great Plains from Canada to Mexico were held by absentee owners in Great Britain.

The small ranches are usually located near the eastern margin of the region or adjacent to irrigated areas, and they grow much of their own feed. Often stock and wheat farming are carried on together. A subsidiary cattle enterprise can be the wheat farmer's best insurance policy. Some ranchers fatten their cattle and market them directly at the packing houses. Most of the range cattle, however, are raised on large ranches (Figure 11-12).

The High Plains subregion has year-long grazing. North of the Texas Panhandle, snows temporarily interrupt winter grazing (Figure 11-13), necessitating supplemental feeding to prevent or reduce losses. In dry years, however, feed must be given in both summer and winter to prevent wholesale starvation. During those periods the cattle industry is unprofitable.

Throughout the region, stockmen utilize

Figure 11-12. Herefords being driven across the Old Man River near MacLeod, Alberta. (Alberta Government Photograph.)

Figure 11-13. Spreading hay for winter feed on a Wyoming cattle ranch. (Photo courtesy Union Pacific Railroad.)

native pastures as much as possible in order to reduce the expense of supplying hay or cottonseed cake. If beef cattle can be shipped out to the Agricultural Interior with little or no expense for supplemental feed, the ranchman can, as a rule, make a fair profit.

Over much of central and southern Texas a deep-rooted scrubby tree called Mesquite (*Prosopis juliflora*) has extended its range by usurping overgrazed grasslands, to the marked detriment of the forage resources. Stringent control campaigns, involving poisons, burning, and especially uprooting with heavy equipment, have restored much of the area to its original grassland cover.

Some of the best grazing land is found isolated in the wheat areas. The Flint Hills of central Kansas, for example, are a little too rough for cultivation but support a fine cover of bluestem grasses that are coveted for grazing. Much of the area is rented out to western and Texas cattlemen for temporary use. Nebraska's Sand Hill country, situated between the Winter and Spring Wheat Belts, is another excellent ranching area. The rolling, grassy hills are unsuited for cropping, and there are many wet depressions where wild hay can be harvested.

A TYPICAL LARGE CATTLE RANCH A prime requisite for successful ranching is a good supply of water. An insufficient water supply prevents the utilization of thousands of acres of grazing land. At first ranchmen supplied their reservoirs (tanks) from natural sources—springs, seeps, and surface streams. The development of cheaper drilling methods and the perfection of the windmill added many square miles to the ranching area of the Great Plains. Water is piped to a dirt tank or watering trough some distance from the well or natural spring to prevent the cattle from contaminating the supply.

Winter care of stock is an important item. In the southern Great Plains, timber and broken terrain (breaks) afford sufficient protection. In the northern Great Plains, however, protection is provided by sheds, usually constructed with an open side. These open sheds face away from the direction of the prevailing winds, and they suffice for even the most severe blizzards. Other desirable equipment includes (1) pens for branding, (2) chutes for cutting out (separating) cattle from the herd for shipment, and (3) dipping vats for treating animals affected by ticks, lice, or other pests.

In early days each cowhand furnished his own "outfit"—horse, saddle, bridle, blanket, and bedding. Today, however, most large ranches furnish horses and equipment. While well-trained horses and good equipment may add to the initial investment, they decrease expenses in the long run. At the time of the roundup, cowhands must use a number of horses, sometimes two to four a day.

WORKING ON THE RANGE In small pastures or on ranges bounded by natural barriers, cattle cannot become widely scattered; hence comparatively little labor is involved. On large ranches, however, the annual or semi-annual roundup is a big job. Often neighboring ranches combine their cowhands. In this way cattle on the unfenced range which belong to different ranches can be separated, and driven back to their owners' ranges or to some shipping point.

Roundup time varies with different sections of the Great Plains Region. If the ranch ships grass-fat cattle instead of feeders, the roundup is scheduled to hold cattle a minimum of time prior to shipment as a means of preventing loss of weight.

A considerable part of the cowhand's time on a big ranch is spent in cutting out steers that are to be sent to market or to northern feed lots, and in branding calves. On the better-equipped ranches, branding is usually done in corrals. The brand must be recorded according to the laws of the state in which the ranch is located. To be successful, the brand must not burn the hide but must mark the animal permanently.

SHIPPING TO MARKET When beef cattle destined for market have been cut from the herd, they are driven to loading chutes built along the railroad tracks. Formerly long drives over cattle trails were necessary. As the railroad net grew throughout the cattle country the drives were reduced and today they are seldom more than a few miles long. Upon reaching the loading chute, the animals are driven up an incline into waiting cattle cars. Formerly cowhands rode the cattle trains to their destination in order to supply the animals with feed and water, prevent their being trampled, and

assure their arrival in good condition. The railroads now take care of the animals.

The Sheep Industry Sheep ranches on the Great Plains are similar to cattle ranches; in fact, many cattle ranches today also run large numbers of sheep. The sheep industry, most concentrated in southwest Texas and northern Colorado, is also important in Montana. Since sheep graze closer than cattle and require less water, they can be pastured on lands where the latter cannot survive. In some respects sheep are easier to handle, although they usually require continual surveillance, whereas cattle can be depended upon to shift for themselves most of the time. In the northern Great Plains, sheep must be driven in summer long distances to mountain pastures and returned in winter to the plains. The ranchman works hard throughout the winter to protect and feed his flocks. Constant vigilance is necessary during extreme cold and heavy snow to prevent sheep from drifting with the wind and perishing in the deep snows.

SHEARING The sheep of the Great Plains are raised chiefly for their wool. The period of greatest activity on a ranch, therefore, is shearing time, which usually takes place in late spring or early summer, after all danger of further freezes has passed. In the Southwest a second shearing is sometimes made in early autumn, but the wool is never so good as that cut at the close of the winter season. The wool is sorted, cleaned, and baled before it is shipped to market.

Angora Goats The hill country of central Texas yields more than 95 per cent of the nation's mohair. Goat ranching is similar to sheep ranching, except that goats, being browsing animals, can subsist on pastures not good enough for sheep. Most of the pasture land used by Angora goats is in the brush country where scrub oak and other small trees and shrubs supply browse (Figure 11-14). Goats are clipped during

Figure 11-14. Angora goats on a ranch in the central Texas "hill country." (Photo courtesy *Sheep and Goat Raiser*, San Angelo, Texas.)

March and April and again in September and October. The mohair is shipped mainly to New England, though some is exported. Since 1927, Texas alone has produced more mohair than the Republic of South Africa, the former leader.

The Mineral Industries

Mineralogically, the Great Plains Region consists of two structural associations: (1) hilly to mountainous areas composed of intruded masses of igneous rock, as in the Black Hills, and (2) flat to gently rolling land, underlaid by sedimentary rocks. The first type contains metallic minerals such as gold, silver, copper, lead, and zinc, while the sedimentary areas yield nonmetallic and fuel minerals, such as petroleum, natural gas, helium, coal, and potash.

Metallic Minerals The first gold discoveries in the Black Hills (1874) were placers. The news of the strike, widely publicized in Eastern newspapers, created a gold rush. Conflicts with the Indians in the Black Hills, at the time a part of the Sioux Reservation, caused the federal government to attempt to exclude white men. Prospectors entered the Reservation, however, and before they could be ejected they had succeeded in extracting considerable placer gold. A persistent demand to open the "hills" to prospecting led to a withdrawal of military regulations. In 1877, the entire area was thrown open to white occupation. The first settlements were made around the placer deposits near Custer, but when richer strikes were uncovered at Deadwood Gulch, Custer's population of 11,000 fell to about 100. Deadwood at the same time grew from nothing to a population of 25,000. This rich placer ultimately led to the discovery of lode gold.[12]

THE HOMESTAKE MINE The original Homestake claim, made in 1876, was purchased the following year for $70,000 by George Hearst, who organized the Homestake Mining Company. This mine, the largest gold producer in the United States, had operated continuously until it was closed down by the federal government during World War II. Its production up to that time exceeded 440 million dollars. Owing to isolation, mining was greatly handicapped during the first decade, but in time railroads were built into the area. In the early part of the twentieth century, when the cyanide process was introduced, the Homestake Mine improved in efficiency. Deep-shaft mining prevails, operations being carried on from the 3,200- to 6,200-foot level. In haul-

[12] Paul T. Allsman, "Reconnaissance of Gold Mining Districts in the Black Hills," *Bureau of Mines Bulletin 427* (Washington: Government Printing Office, 1940), pp. 6-7, 12-13.

ing ore from the stopes to the mine shafts, 73 miles of narrow-gauge railroad track and 36 compressed-air locomotives are used. In addition to its mining property at Lead, the company holds extensive water rights, owns a coal mine in Wyoming, and has large timber holdings. It is easily the major industrial establishment of the Black Hills. After the end of the war Homestake Mine was reopened. By 1949 it had forged ahead to make South Dakota again the leading gold-producing state. In most years the Deadwood-Lead area produces one-third of the gold mined in the United States.

Numerous other mining properties have been developed in the Black Hills, but in most cases they have failed after a short period of prosperity or hope. The names of some of these describe the wild and adventurous life of the early mining community: Deadbroke, Two Bit, Gilt Edge, Holy Terror, and Legal Tender. Some of these still are worked from time to time, but the majority are only memories of the wild and glorious days of the gold rush.

Petroleum The Great Plains Region, because of its extensive size and because most of it is underlaid with sedimentary rocks that probably bear oil, has many producing oil fields. Among the 14 states and provinces of which portions are included in this region, only South Dakota, Minnesota, and Manitoba lack significant production.

Nearly half of all Texas petroleum production, amounting to one-sixth of the national output, is from West Texas fields, particularly the Permian Basin. Major yields are obtained also in parts of Oklahoma and Kansas, in the increasingly prolific fields of Wyoming (particularly the Elk Basin), in scattered Montana localities, in the Williston Basin of North Dakota, and in the skyrocketing production areas of Alberta and Saskatchewan.

The Canadian Prairie Provinces' oil fields are among the newest in Anglo-America and represent a potentially gigantic reserve of petroleum. The discovery well blew in on a cold day in February, 1947. This well was located at Leduc, a few miles southwest of the city of Edmonton. The section in which this well was drilled is in the heart of the Spring Wheat Belt, which was dependent almost entirely upon one-crop farming. The impact of this new wealth on the economy of the wheat-farming area is interesting to watch.

The two dozen or so principal fields in central Alberta and southwestern Saskatchewan have provided Canada with significant petroleum output for the first time. Most of the exploratory work and an overwhelmingly large part of the present development has been carried on by American companies and their affiliates. Edmonton and Calgary have grown rapidly since oil was discovered. Refinery needs in the area caused one Canadian oil company to dismantle a wartime refinery at Whitehorse, 1350 miles to the north, ship it by truck and rail to Edmonton, and reassemble it. The cost was as great as that of a new refinery, but its construction required much less time. Pipelines have been built eastward to the head of Lake Superior at Duluth and on to Sarnia and Toronto, southward to Montana, and westward across the Rocky Mountains to Vancouver. An interesting feature of this new oil area is that the Canadian provincial governments control most of the mineral rights on the land. As a result, provincial financial problems have essentially been solved. In Alberta, for instance, personal taxes are nil, and the provincial government occasionally gives a cash bonus to each citizen.

Natural Gas The Prairie Provinces also have a surplus of natural gas, particularly in the fields of Alberta and the Peace River District. The 2,300-mile Trans-Canada pipeline from Alberta to Montreal (with a Midwestern spur from Winnipeg to the United

States) was completed in 1958. A west coast line goes from the Peace River country 700 miles to Washington State, and a 1,400-mile pipeline has been completed from Alberta to California.

Natural gas is also a major product from Wyoming, Kansas, Oklahoma, and west Texas, the Panhandle gas field of the last three states being the largest producer of natural gas in the world. At first the demand for natural gas within the area was very limited, and hence it was allowed to escape and was burned. However, the great quantities of cheap natural gas attracted industries, and by 1930, 24 carbon-black plants, 53 natural-gasoline plants, and one helium plant were using the gas from this area. With an increasing number of gas wells being completed, pipelines were built to the major urban centers of the East and Midwest, thus providing ready markets for the increasing gas production.[13]

Helium The major helium-producing area in the world is located within the Panhandle gas fields. Originally helium was used mostly as a lifting gas for dirigibles, but it now has a multitude of atomic, spacecraft, medical, and industrial (particularly for helium-shielded arc welding) uses. Of the five plants in the United States producing helium, four are in the Great Plains Region. The long-range helium outlook is for increasing demand and decreasing supply. No new reserves of significance have been discovered since 1943.

Potash The Great Plains Region in west Texas and southeastern New Mexico contains a major supply of potash salts.

For nearly a century the Stassfurt Mines of Germany and the deposits in Alsace dominated the world market. At the outbreak of the first World War, the United States,

lacking potash, began searching desperately for a domestic source. The price jumped from $40 to $500 a ton. Large investments were made in plants to extract the mineral from certain salt lakes in Utah and California and in the western Sand Hills of Nebraska. When the war ended, however, Germany, and France (which then controlled Alsace) again dominated the world market, and most American production was discontinued. Congress, however, appropriated a small sum (2 million dollars) to continue the search for potash within the United States. The western Texas deposits of polyhalite (the best-known potash-producing salt) had been known since 1912, but because of the German monopoly and because of the remoteness of this deposit from the large consuming area, little development took place. Even during the emergency of the first World War, the government felt that extraction of potash from salt lakes and even from kelp (seaweed) was more satisfactory than working the Texas deposits. Later, oil prospectors discovered sylvite deposits more than 250 feet thick in Eddy County, New Mexico, at depths of from 1,200 to 1,400 feet. Sylvite is a potash-bearing mineral containing more than 60 per cent potassium oxide. Germany's famous Stassfurt deposits consist mainly of polyhalite carrying less than 20 per cent potash. Moreover, the German area extends over only about 24,000 square miles, whereas that in Texas-New Mexico covers more than 70,000. The United States now produces about one-fourth of the world's output, more than any other country. Most of this yield comes from the deposits just described, where extraction is accomplished by both shaft mining and brine-solution drilling.

An even larger and richer supply of potash is currently under development in southeastern Saskatchewan, at Esterhazy. A shaft mine has been sunk 3,000 feet, partly through heavily water-logged rock formations, to

---

[13] John R. Stockton and Stanley A. Arbingast, *Water Requirements Survey: Texas High Plains* (Austin: Bureau of Business Research, University of Texas, 1952).

reach the deposit. The potash mostly is taken by rail to Vancouver, whence it is exported to Japan and elsewhere in the Far East.

Coal The great Plains Region contains several large fields of subbituminous or semibituminous coal and an enormous deposit of lignite. The lignite is found in the Dakotas, eastern Montana, and Saskatchewan. Despite domestic demands for fuel in that area of severe winters, little lignite is mined.

The bituminous deposits, although of low grade, are worked in several places for local use. The most important bituminous-producing areas are the Assiniboine district of Saskatchewan, the Judith Basin of Montana, the Powder River district of Wyoming, the Denver area of Colorado, and the Raton Mesa area of southern Colorado and northern New Mexico. The coal in most of these areas lies in thick seams near the surface and is strip mined, particularly in Montana and Wyoming. In the Denver field, coal seams lie some distance below the surface and are therefore shaft mined. In the Raton district, the coal has been exposed on the eroded sides of the mesa, and a type of drift mining, similar to that of West Virginia, is practiced.

Manufacturing

While agricultural processing industries such as flour mills and meat-packing plants have been important for many years on the Great Plains, a relatively recent industrial development has taken place in those areas where large supplies of petroleum and natural gas have been available. This is particularly true in the Panhandle of Texas, and more recently in the Prairie Provinces of Canada. These industries include (1) petrochemical plants, using oil and natural gas as the base for the manufacture of organic acids, alcohol, glycerine, butadiene, carbon black, and many other products; (2) specialized plants that depend upon cheap natural gas for fuel, as exemplified by zinc refineries in the Amarillo area; and (3) oil refineries and catalytic cracking plants. These petroleum-oriented industries are located at a variety of places, but there are two districts of concentration—the Amarillo-Pampa-Borger area of the Texas Panhandle, and the eastern outskirts of the city of Edmonton.

There are four other nodes of some industrial importance in the Great Plains: (1) Wichita is one of the leading aircraft-manufacturing centers of the continent. Its position is based largely upon a wartime decentralization of Seattle's Boeing Aircraft Corporation. In addition, however, Wichita today is the leading producer of light private and business aircraft. (2) Pueblo is the site of the oldest steel mill west of the Mississippi. It uses coal from the Raton Mesa and iron ore from southern Wyoming. Limited market is its major problem. (3) The booming Denver area is the center of industrial expansion along the inland side of the Southern Rockies. Much of the growth is in defense-oriented industries, stimulated in part by the presence of the North American Air Defense Command headquarters and the Air Force Academy at Colorado Springs, as well as major air bases in the vicinity. Although Denver's largest factory produces missiles, its industrial structure reflects a strategic position as the most populous city of the Plains, processing local materials and fabricating for the regional market. (4) Winnipeg is the largest city in central Canada and has a diversified industrial structure similar to that of Denver. Both Edmonton and Calgary have similar developments on a smaller scale.

Transportation

The Great Plains Region has served primarily as a transit land. Most of the freight and passenger traffic passes through the region enroute to and from the Pacific Coast. Thus, the transportation lines of the region show a predominance of east-west railways, highways, and airways. The only important north-south traffic flows along the western edge, at the foot of the Rocky Mountains where the major population is concentrated, or in the wheat belts where a well-developed network of railroads and highways appears. On the whole, the region is sparsely settled, but the major concentrations of population are found either in the eastern parts of the wheat belts, or along the extreme western edge near the foot of the Rocky Mountains. The cities of the western margin of the Great Plains, such as Roswell, Pueblo, Colorado Springs, Denver, Cheyenne, Billings, Great Falls, Calgary, and Edmonton, serve both the Great Plains and the Rocky Mountains— their industries reflecting the major economic activities of each. Although they are frequently associated with the mountains, they are cities of the plains.

Resorts

The Great Plains Region, with its extensive area of level to gently rolling lands and with its continental climate of hot summers and very cold winters, offers few attractions for the tourist and hence is not important as a resort region, despite the fact that it is crossed by thousands of tourists each summer, seeking a vacation in the mountains to the west. Three areas within the region, however, are of significance: (1) the Black Hills, (2) the Carlsbad Caverns, and (3) the Edwards Plateau of southwestern Texas —the last becoming an important dude ranch area, particularly for the winter season.

Of these areas, the most scenic and most important is the Black Hills. With its forest-clad mountains, attractive Sylvan Lake area, Wind Cave National Park, Custer State Park with its friendly wildlife, and man-made Rushmore Memorial, the Black Hills area annually attracts thousands of tourists.

In southeastern New Mexico, in an area where the surface of the land is unattractive, lies the world-famous Carlsbad Caverns National Park, with its extensive subterranean caves. As one of the most popular tourist attractions of Anglo-America, it is visited by great numbers of people each year. The area, however, does not encourage the tourist to tarry long, and in most cases it is visited for a short time by persons on their way to more attractive resort centers.

Several cities on the western margin of the Great Plains have become important summer tourist centers because they are gateways to the mountains beyond. Colorado Springs, Denver, Cheyenne, and Calgary are particularly notable in this respect.

Hunting and fishing activities are limited in this region, with two important exceptions. The central Texas hill country contains one of the largest and most accessible deer herds in Anglo-America. The central and northern plains have a heavy population of ring-necked pheasants, an introduced exotic that has prospered fantastically. It is a leading hunter's quarry from Colorado northward, but is especially concentrated in South Dakota.

The Outlook

Agricultural maladjustment has been the ruination of many people in the Great Plains. All too often the sod has been broken on marginal land that should have stayed in grass. In spite of bleak chapters in its history, however, the region can boast of fertile farms, impressive ranches, and mushrooming cities.

Agricultural prosperity in the future will be in part (but not always necessarily) determined by activities and controls of the two national governments. In general, however, one can look forward to decreasing wheat acreage and increasing wheat yield, with a consequential increase in the surplus.

TABLE 10

Selected Cities and Towns of the Great Plains

City or Town	Urbanized Area	Political Center
Aberdeen	......	23,073
Abilene, Tex.	91,566	90,368
Amarillo	......	137,969
Aurora	......	48,548
Big Spring	......	31,230
Billings	60,712	52,851
Bismarck	......	27,670
Borger	......	20,911
Boulder	......	37,718
Brandon	......	28,166
Calgary	279,062	249,641
Carlsbad	......	25,541
Casper	......	38,930
Cheyenne	......	43,505
Clovis	......	23,713
Colorado Springs	100,220	70,194
Denver	803,624	493,887
Edmonton	337,568	281,027
Englewood	......	33,398
Enid	......	38,859
Fargo	......	46,662
Fort Collins	......	25,027
Grand Forks	72,730	34,451
Great Falls	57,629	55,357
Greeley	......	26,314
Hobbs	......	26,275
Hutchinson	......	37,574
Jasper Place	......	30,530
Laredo	......	60,678
Lethbridge	......	35,454
Lubbock	129,289	128,691
Medicine Hat	......	24,484
Midland	63,274	62,625
Minot	......	30,604
Moorhead	......	22,934
Moose Jaw	......	33,206
North Platte	......	17,184
Odessa	84,285	80,338
Oklahoma City	429,188	324,253
Pampa	......	24,664
Ponca City	......	24,411
Pueblo	103,336	91,181
Rapid City	......	42,399
Red Deer	......	19,612
Regina	......	112,141
Roswell	......	39,593
St. Boniface	......	37,600
Salina	......	43,202
San Angelo	......	58,815
Saskatoon	......	95,526
Wichita	292,138	254,698
Winnipeg	475,989	265,429

In the more humid areas, there should be further displacement of wheat by corn and by dairy and beef cattle. On the semiarid margins, more acreage will be occupied by cattle raising and by sorghums.

Irrigation promises to expand throughout the region, partly as the result of large government reclamation projects and partly through more intensive use of local waters by individuals and groups. One sure result will be the lowering of the High Plains water table until it becomes increasingly less economical to pump from the aquifers. With more irrigation will come more specialized crops.

The petroleum resources are extensive; they continue to be developed and to play an increasingly important role in the regional economy. Although the Great Plains is not destined to become an industrial region, manufacturing continues to grow, and its growth will be accompanied by rapid urban expansion, especially in west Texas, the Colorado Piedmont, and Alberta. The large and medium-sized communities will grow ever larger; the smaller settlements often will "wither on the vine." Rural landholdings should continue to grow larger, and mechanization increase.

Prosperity can be expected to wax and wane, but the region will maintain its essential character. The landscape will be dominated by a mixture of extensive and intensive agriculture; the population will never be very dense except in a few urban areas; and it will always be an important transit land, lying as it does across all transcontinental routeways.

Selected Bibliography

Baker, W. B., "Changing Community Patterns in Saskatchewan," *Canadian Geographical Journal*, Vol. 56, February 1958, pp. 44-46.
Borchert, John R., "Climate of the Central North American Grassland," *Annals of the Association of American Geographers*, Vol. 40, 1950, pp. 1-39.

Calef, Wesley, "Problems of Grazing Administration in the Basins of Southern Wyoming," *Economic Geography*, Vol. 28, 1952, pp. 122-127.

"Cattle Feeding—A Dynamic Industry," *Monthly Review*, Federal Reserve Bank of Kansas City, March 1958, pp. 3-9.

Eggleston, Wilfred, "The Short Grass Prairies of Western Canada," *Canadian Geographical Journal*, Vol. 50, April 1955, pp. 134-145.

Francis, E. K., *In Search of Utopia*. Glencoe, Illinois: Free Press, 1955.

"Grazing Is Big Business in the Tenth District," *Monthly Review*, Federal Reserve Bank of Kansas City, February 1958, pp. 9-15.

Hanson, Eric J., *Dynamic Decade*. Toronto: McClelland & Stewart, 1958.

Hargreaves, Mary W. M., *Dry Farming in the Northern Great Plains, 1900-25*. Cambridge: Harvard University Press, 1957.

Hewes, Leslie, "Wheat Failure in Western Nebraska, 1931-1954," *Annals of the Association of American Geographers*, Vol. 48, December 1958, pp. 375-397.

——, and Arthur C. Schmieding, "Risk in the Central Great Plains: Geographical Patterns of Wheat Failure in Nebraska, 1931-1952," *Geographical Review*, Vol. 46, July 1956, pp. 375-387.

Jackson, J. B., "High Plains Country," *Landscape*, Vol. 3, Spring 1954, pp. 11-22.

Knudtson, Arvid C., "The Range Area," *Monthly Review*, Federal Reserve Bank of Minneapolis, Vol. 15, September 1960, pp. 2-14.

——, and Rex W. Cox, *Upper Midwest Agriculture: Structure and Problems*, Upper Midwest Economic Study Paper No. 3, 1962.

Kollmorgen, Walter M., and George F. Jenks, "Sidewalk Farming in Toole County, Montana, and Traill County, North Dakota," *Annals of the Association of American Geographers*, Vol. 48, December 1958, pp. 375-397.

——, and George F. Jenks, "Suitcase Farming in Sully County, South Dakota," *Annals of the Association of American Geographers*, Vol. 48, March 1958, pp. 27-40.

Kraenzel, C. F., *The Great Plains in Transition*. Norman: University of Oklahoma Press, 1955.

Leslie, W. R., "The Pembina Pocket," *Canadian Geographical Journal*, Vol. 63, September 1961, pp. 76-83.

Morris, John W., and Arthur H. Doerr, "Irrigation in Oklahoma," *Journal of Geography*, Vol. 58, December 1959, pp. 421-429.

Ryan, Robert H., and Leonard G. Schifrin, *Midland: The Economic Future of a Texas Oil Center*. Austin: Bureau of Business Research, University of Texas, 1959.

Shaw, Earl B., "Esterhazy and Its Potash," *Journal of Geography*, Vol. 61, January 1962, pp. 31-35.

Smith, P. J., "Calgary: A Study in Urban Pattern," *Economic Geography*, Vol. 38, October 1962, pp. 315-329.

"The Wheat Surplus Problem," *Monthly Review*, Federal Reserve Bank of Kansas City, November 1960, pp. 10-16.

Villmow, Jack R., "The Nature and Origin of the Canadian Dry Belt," *Annals of the Association of American Geographers*, Vol. 46, June 1956, pp. 211-232.

Watts, F. B., "The Natural Vegetation of the Southern Great Plains of Canada," *Geographical Bulletin*, No. 14, 1960, pp. 25-43.

Weaver, J. E., and F. W. Albertson, *Grasslands of the Great Plains: Their Nature and Use*. Lincoln: L. Johnson Publishing Co., 1956.

Webb, Walter P., *The Great Plains*. Boston: Ginn & Co., 1931.

Weir, Thomas R., "Land Use and Population Characteristics of Central Winnipeg," *Geographical Bulletin*, No. 9, 1956, pp. 5-22.

Wonders, William C., "River Valley City—Edmonton on the North Saskatchewan," *Canadian Geographer*, No. 14, 1959, pp. 8-16.

chapter twelve

The Rocky Mountains

The Rocky Mountain Region is an extensive upland lying between the Great Plains to the east and the Intermontane Region to the west (Figure 12-1). The general trend of the mountains, which consist of a series of linear ranges with intervening basins, or trenches, is from south-southeast to north-northwest.

Origin of the Rocky Mountains

During the Cretaceous Period most of the area of the Rocky Mountain Region as well as that of the Great Plains was covered by a shallow sea that extended from the Gulf of Mexico to the Arctic Ocean.[1] At the close of that period the Rocky Mountain Area was uplifted, and the waters drained off. Sediments with a thickness of perhaps 20 thousand feet were involved in this first great uplift.

A long period of erosion followed this early uplift, during which time much mate-

[1] Atwood, *The Physiographic Provinces of North America,* pp. 294-328.

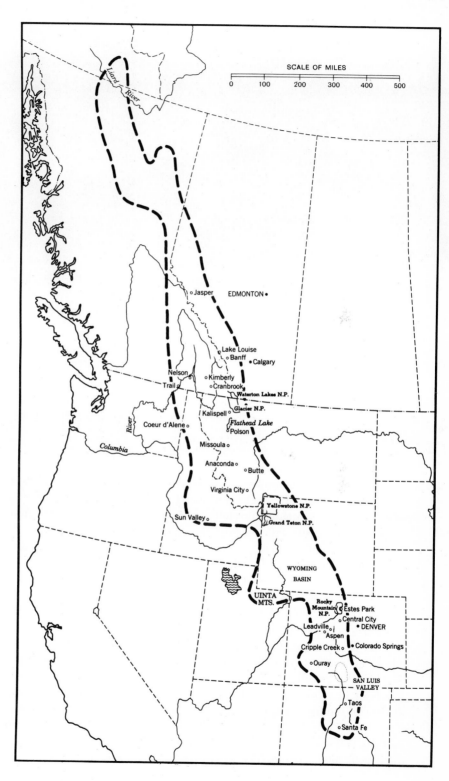

Figure 12-1. The Rocky Mountains. A region of mining, grazing, farming, logging, and outdoor recreation.

Figure 12-2. The glaciated Canadian Rockies—Maligne Lake in Jasper National Park. (Photo courtesy Canadian Government Travel Bureau.)

rial was removed from the summits and deposited in the basins. Later (Tertiary Period), the Rocky Mountains were subjected to another period of uplift, accompanied by considerable volcanic activity, and followed by still another period of leveling. The region's master streams, flowing over sediments that had buried the mountain ranges, established courses which they continued to hold after they had cut into older rocks, forming the major gorges and canyons through the front ranges. Mountain glaciation followed, which further deepened the valleys and greatly eroded the peaks. Glaciation was more extensive in the Northern Rockies and still is active there. In the Southern Rockies it was not so extensive and only a few small remnants of glaciers exist today.

The Rocky Mountains may be subdivided into three sections: (1) the Southern Rockies, (2) the Middle Rockies, and (3) the Northern Rockies. The Southern and Middle Rocky Mountains appear quite different from the Northern Rockies, which begin north of Yellowstone National Park and continue well into Canada. The ranges of the Southern and Middle Rockies are for the most part linear features, with their granitic cores generally flanked by steeply dipping strata forming hogback foothills such as the Flatirons of the Boulder area in northern Colorado. In contrast, the Northern Rocky Mountains, composed mainly of sedimentary rocks, are not so linear, but appear more like lofty plateaus that have been severely carved into majestic alpine peaks and deep U-shaped valleys by valley glaciers (Figure 12-2).[2]

Scattered about in the Southern and Middle Rockies are a large number of relatively flat-floored basins, generally called "parks," which are mostly not timbered and present a distinct change in landscape from the surrounding mountainous terrain. The largest of these is the Wyoming Basin, which separates the Middle from the Southern Rockies. Other notable basins include the San Luis Valley, South Park, Middle Park, and North Park; and there are a host of smaller parks. In the Northern Rockies the circular

[2] Fenneman, *Physiography of Western United States,* pp. 92-93.

318

basin is less common; more distinctive landscape features in this subregion are long linear valleys of structural origin. The most conspicuous of these is the Rocky Mountain Trench, which extends for 1,000 miles from the vicinity of Montana's Flathead Lake to the Liard Plain in northeastern British Columbia.

Climate, Vegetation, and Soils

Altitude modifies temperature and rainfall to a great extent in this region. The Southern and Middle Rocky Mountains have sufficient precipitation to support dense forests of pine and other conifers, whereas the adjacent plains have a short grass or desert vegetation. The basins of this region are usually covered with grass, making them suitable for ranching. The tree line decreases in altitude from 12,000 feet in southern New Mexico to 10,000 feet in northern Wyoming. In the Northern Rocky Mountains the contrast in vegetation between the lowland and the upland is also sharp, although in these more northerly latitudes timber sometimes appears on the plains and floors of intermontane basins. The tree line in the Northern Rocky Mountains decreases from 10,000 feet in Montana to the level of the adjacent plains in northern Canada.

Because of the great contrast in altitudes and its wide latitudinal extent, this region presents a range of plant associations varying from the Sonoran Zone to the Tundra. The various plant zones that may be seen in any part of the mountains are well shown in the Rocky Mountain National Park in northern Colorado. The valleys or basins (Estes Park) are covered with short grass. As one ascends the lower slopes into the mountains, large western yellow (ponderosa) pines appear. At higher altitude are found the smaller but denser-growing Engelmann spruce, lodgepole pine, and limber pine. Still higher is a transitional area between the forest and alpine meadows—the tree line (Figure 12-3), which has been described as follows:

In the struggle for existence in the vegetable world, the tree line pushes as far up the mountain as conditions of climate and soil will permit. Then comes a season of fiercer storms, intenser cold and invading ice upon the peaks. Havoc is wrought, and the forest drops back across a zone of border warfare—for war belongs to borders—leaving behind it here and there a dwarfed pine or gnarled and twisted juniper which has sur-

Figure 12-3. Gnarled and twisted trees near timberline on the slopes of Mt. Evans in Colorado. (Photographed by D. C. Hopwood, courtesy the State of Colorado.)

vived the onslaught of the enemy. Now these are the stragglers in the retreat, but are destined later in milder years to serve as outposts in the advance of the forest to recover its lost ground. Here we have a border scene which is typical in nature—the belt of unbroken forests, growing thinner and more stunted toward its upper edge, succeeded by a zone of scattered trees, which may form a cluster perhaps in some sheltered gulch where soil has collected and north winds are excluded, and higher still the whitened skeleton of a tree to show how far the forest once invaded the domain of the waste.[3]

Above timber line lies the alpine meadow and tundra, surmounted by bare rocky peaks and permanent snow fields.

Because of steep slopes and excessive erosion, only the basins and valley bottoms within the Rocky Mountain Region have mature soils. Even so, the alluvium in most basins is comparatively fertile and becomes quite productive when water is available either through rainfall or irrigation. The lower mountain slopes, although rocky and almost devoid of soil, usually support a fair stand of timber.

Boundaries

The eastern boundary is marked by the break between the Great Plains and the Rocky Mountains (Figure 12-1). From central New Mexico to northern Alberta the mountains rise abruptly from the plains, except in central Wyoming where the Wyoming Basin merges almost imperceptibly into the Great Plains. The western boundary, which marks the transition from the Rocky Mountain Region to the Intermontane Basins and Plateaus Region, is fairly definite in the southern and middle sections, but becomes somewhat vague in northern British Columbia, where the Omineca Mountains and the Skeena Mountains provide a

[3] Ellen C. Semple, *The Influences of Geographic Environment* (New York: Henry Holt & Co., 1911), p. 206.

"bridge" across the interior plateau to connect the Rockies with the Coast Mountains.

Early Exploration and Settlement

Except in the extreme southern part of the region which was penetrated by the Spaniards in the sixteenth century, the first white men to see the Rocky Mountains were the French fur-traders. They were followed in a short time by several military exploration parties sent out by the United States Government, such as the expeditions of Lewis and Clark in the Northern Rockies in 1803-1804, and Lieutenant Zebulon M. Pike in 1806-1807 and Major Stephen H. Long in 1820 in the Southern Rockies. Meanwhile, fur trapping became important throughout the Southern and Middle Rockies, particularly in the area of the Tetons in western Wyoming. This colorful period, however, did not last long, as the value of beaver fur declined in the 1840's, following changes in the style of men's hats. From that time until the discovery of gold in the late 1850's, the Rocky Mountains served only as a barrier to the westward movement—pioneers pushing through the lowest mountain passes as rapidly as possible on their way to the Oregon Territory or to California.

The discovery of gold at Sutters Fort in the newly acquired California Territory created a mad rush of gold seekers coming from all parts of the world. Although many prospectors went by ship from New York to San Francisco by way of Cape Horn, or by ship and caravan by way of Panama or Nicaragua, the majority braved the natural hardships and Indian dangers in the overland crossing of the continent. In crossing the Rocky Mountains, some of them prospected for gold in the stream gravels and found traces of the precious metal. Although most gold seekers went on to California, many returned within a few years to prospect further in the numerous mountain gulches.

It was not until 1859, however, that gold in paying quantities was found in the Rocky Mountains. John Gregory's discovery near Central City, Colorado, led to extensive explorations and many important gold discoveries throughout the region. Within the next two or three decades more people settled in the mountain country than in all its previous history. Practically every part of the Southern Rockies was prospected, and many valuable mineral deposits were found. Boom towns sprang up in remote valleys and gulches of the high country, and this in turn led to the development of a series of narrow-gauge railroads built at great expense per mile for the purpose of hauling out gold ore. As the higher-grade ores were exhausted, production declined in these camps and in time most of them became ghost towns.[4]

Lumbering and logging, grazing activities, irrigation agriculture, and the tourist trade have brought additional population to the mountains, but none has been so significant in peopling the region and in bringing its advantages to the attention of the rest of the country, as gold mining.

The Mining Industry

The history of Central City, Colorado, illustrates the early mining activity characteristic of the mountain region. Central City sprang up in a rich mineralized zone that a "forty-niner" discovered on his return to this region in 1859. Within a few months thousands of gold prospectors had come to the area. Almost overnight they also built the mining towns of Black Hawk and Nevadaville, but these did not reach the importance of Central City, which in the early 1870's was the largest urban center in the Rocky Mountain Region. Its growth and prosper-

ity continued for a decade or two, but toward the close of the century the decline began. Little by little, holdings were abandoned and the miners moved on to more productive areas. Nevadaville became a "ghost town," but Black Hawk and Central City retained a few inhabitants. Central City's famous Opera House, said to have been the West's finest show-house in the 1870's, has been reopened as a summer theater, and for three months of the year the steep and narrow streets are as crowded with automobiles as they once were with horses and burros.

Wherever rich mineralized zones were found, mining camps developed. Colorado was especially important, with its Central City, Ouray, Cripple Creek, Victor, Leadville, Aspen, Georgetown, and Silver Plume. Wyoming and New Mexico were relatively unimportant, but the southern part of the Northern Rocky Mountains produced important minerals around Virginia City in southwestern Montana, in the vicinity of Butte and Anaconda, in the Coeur d'Alene area of northern Idaho, and in the Kootenay district of British Columbia. While gold was the mineral chiefly sought, valuable deposits of silver, lead, copper, tungsten, and molybdenum have been found.

Mining Today In a region so complex as the Rocky Mountains, with its many mineralized areas, a discussion of all districts is impossible in this volume. Therefore only five leading districts are selected: (1) Leadville, Colorado—a gold, silver, lead, zinc, and molybdenum district; (2) Cripple Creek, Colorado—a gold mining area; (3) Butte, Montana—copper, silver, lead, and zinc; (4) Coeur d'Alene, Idaho—gold, silver, lead, and zinc; and (5) Kootenay, British Columbia —lead and zinc.

THE LEADVILLE DISTRICT One of the oldest and most important mining areas of the entire Rocky Mountain Region is located at Leadville in a high mountain valley near

[4] Muriel Sibell Wolle, *Stampede to Timberline: The Ghost Towns and Mining Camps of Colorado* (Boulder, Colo.: University of Colorado Press, 1949).

the headwaters of the Arkansas River at an elevation above 10,000 feet. Following the discovery of gold in the Central City area, prospectors searched the numerous mountain valleys of practically all highland Colorado. In the spring of 1860 placer gold was found in California Gulch near Leadville. News of the discovery immediately spread and by July of that year more than 10,000 people were in the camp. The first gold vein was discovered in 1868, and soon after that the first stamp mill was put into operation.[5]

In 1874 silver-lead mining began and gold soon ceased to be the dominant metal. With waning gold production, most of the 10,000 miners departed and Oro City (Leadville), the original settlement, was virtually deserted. At that time, the site of the present city of Leadville was an unbroken wilderness, the existence of the rich silver-lead and zinc ores there being unsuspected. The rich discovery at Fryer Hill led to the rapid development of the district. The first shipment of lead carbonate went out from the region in 1875, by wagon to Colorado Springs, and thence by rail to St. Louis. Within the next five years 10 million ounces of silver and 66 million pounds of lead were produced with a total value of nearly 15 million dollars. Following this, the real mining boom began. Railroads were completed into the city in 1880 and 1887. The decline in the price of silver in the early 1890's from $1.17 an ounce to 61 cents curtailed production, but silver-lead mining was revived somewhat after the Panic of 1893.

Copper production began in the 1880's but never became very important. Zinc, although discovered in 1885, was unimportant until after the close of the nineteenth cen-

tury. In 1902 the zinc output exceeded that of lead and in 1903 that of silver.

In 1877 Leadville had a population of 200 persons, the business houses of the town consisting of a grocery store and two saloons. Within two years it had an estimated population of 15,000 and an assessed property valuation of 30 million dollars. In 1880 the city had 14 smelters and 30 producing mines. Since then its population has fluctuated, as shown by the following census figures:

1890	10,384
1900	12,455
1910	7,508
1920	4,959
1930	3,771
1940	4,774
1950	4,078
1960	4,008

Leadville continues to be an important mining district, producing all of its former metals and adding molybdenum from the rich ores of the Fremont Pass area. Lake County (Leadville) is not the leading producer of a single mineral except molybdenum, although it ranks second among Colorado counties in total mineral output. There is production at seven major mines and a large smelter yielding molybdenum, lead, silver, gold, copper, and some by-products. The great development of the Climax Molybdenum Company at Fremont Pass, 13 miles north of Leadville, deserves special consideration.

Molybdenum became important in recent years only after it was discovered that the metal imparts the properties of toughness and fatigue strength when used as a steel alloy for machine tools and for automobiles and airplane motors. The Climax Mine lies at an altitude of more than 11,000 feet. Because of the difficulties of working at that level, the mining company built a model town in the hope that more comfortable living conditions might induce the miners to stay longer on the job. Unlike most min-

[5] Charles W. Henderson, "Production, History, and Mine Development," *Geology and Ore Deposits of Leadville Mining District, Colorado,* United States Geological Survey Professional Paper 148 (Washington: Government Printing Office, 1927), pp. 109-37.

ing boom-towns, Climax was established by a single producing company that owned all the land and constructed all the buildings. Instead of typical miners' shacks, well-built residences housed the miners. The company also constructed a large hotel, school, gymnasium, and recreation hall for its workers and their families. However, after several years, the company in 1960 dismantled the town, and now the miners reside in Leadville and other nearby communities.

The company is the world's largest producer of molybdenum, accounting for nearly 90 per cent of the Free World's output.

THE CRIPPLE CREEK DISTRICT   Gold in paying quantities was discovered in the Cripple Creek District of the Front Range of the Southern Rockies in 1892, and for several decades that area produced fabulous amounts of the precious metal. The mining area developed rapidly, and numerous towns including Victor and Cripple Creek were established. In 1894 the mining district was connected by the Colorado Midland Railroad to Colorado Springs via Divide. In

1901 the scenic Cripple Creek Short Line was completed which provided a second railroad for shipping gold ore from the mining district to Colorado Springs. In 1905 the Golden Cycle Mill was built in Colorado Springs to treat Cripple Creek ore. The smelter was located on the plains some fifty miles from the ore-producing areas, because large quantities of coal and other heavy materials were needed in the smelting process and it was more economical to move gold ore downgrade to the smelter than to haul these heavy materials up to the mining areas. For a long time both railroads carried large quantities of ore, reaching peak production in 1914. Following the decline in gold mining during World War I, the Cripple Creek Short Line Railroad was abandoned and dismantled, leaving the Cripple Creek–Victor Area with only the longer railroad outlet via the town of Divide (Figure 12-4). This, along with highways that had been built into the mining camps, continued to serve the area. All gold mining was suspended during World War II (gold

Figure 12-4. The Cripple Creek gold-mining district of Colorado. The railroads shown are: (a) the Colorado Midland; (b) the branch of the Colorado Midland built in 1894 to connect Cripple Creek with Divide; (c) the Cripple Creek Short Line, built in 1901 to haul ore directly to the Golden Cycle Mill (GCM on map); (d) the Denver and Rio Grande; and (e) the Santa Fe. When the new Carlton Mill (CM on map) was completed, the Golden Cycle Mill was destroyed, and all railroad connections between Cripple Creek and Colorado Springs were abandoned.

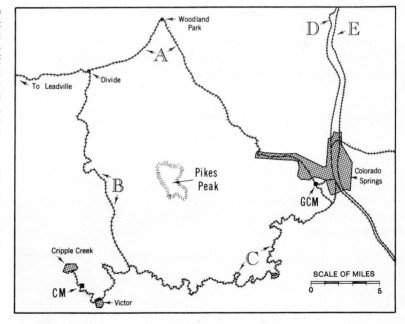

being a nonessential metal for the prosecution of the War), but production was started in 1946 and heavy ore-trains again rumbled down the long grade to the smelter in Colorado Springs.

By that time, however, revolutionary changes in the process of treating gold ore eliminated the need for large quantities of coal and other heavy materials. The increased production of ore in tailings around the old mines of Victor and Cripple Creek, together with discoveries of new ore veins, led to the closing and dismantling of the Golden Cycle Mill at Colorado Springs and the building of the new Carlton Mill at a site halfway between Victor and Cripple Creek. Meanwhile, the Colorado Midland Railroad was abandoned and dismantled, leaving the Cripple Creek District without rail connections.

Today the district is an active mining area with 19 mines in operation, but without the colorful prospectors who frequented the mountain gulches of the early mining days. Gold mining is now a scientific and systematic industry. The new mill handles some 100,000 tons of ore each year in an economical manner, with only the gold bullion being shipped out of the area. The Cripple Creek District should remain a profitable gold-mining area for many years.

THE BUTTE–ANACONDA DISTRICT, MONTANA
In western Montana is located a copper-mining district that is normally the third most prolific producer in the nation. The Anaconda Copper Company, which owns the mining properties at Butte and the large smelter at Anaconda, dominates the Montana copper production and also produces most of its silver, gold, lead, and zinc.

The large hill upon which Butte is built is honeycombed with mine tunnels that have produced more than two billion dollars' worth of metal within the more than 90 years of operation, giving it the name "The Richest Hill on Earth." For a long time the smelter was located at Butte, but injurious fumes from its stacks destroyed so much vegetation in the city that it was removed to Anaconda, 23 miles to the west. The Anaconda smelter, famous for having the world's tallest smokestack (585 feet), throws the fumes high into the air. Since the smelter's removal from Butte, the city has had some success in growing trees and grass.

Mining in Butte's Summit Valley District goes on 24 hours a day. Electricity is used in all operations, including the hauling from stopes to mine shafts. The district has always been famous for its deep-shaft mines, but increasing proportions of the output, amounting to about 50 per cent in the early

Figure 12-5. An open pit mine at Butte. (Photo courtesy Montana Highway Commission.)

1960's, are from open-pit operations (Figure 12-5). Lead, zinc, gold, and silver are produced, as well as copper. The copper ore is transported to the Anaconda smelter, where it is converted into blister copper.

THE COEUR D'ALENE DISTRICT   This mining area, one of the richest of the Northern Rocky Mountains, lies in northern Idaho. There are more than two dozen active mines in the district, yielding major outputs of silver, lead, and zinc, as well as some copper, gold, and miscellaneous by-products. Since Coeur d'Alene became active in 1884, minerals to the value of more than one billion dollars have been extracted.

The lead, silver, and zinc ores of the Coeur d'Alene District are so complex that effective recovery has been difficult. The gravity process used before 1922 was extremely wasteful because of the almost identical weights of lead and zinc. In 1922 the selective-flotation process was introduced, which made possible the extraction of the metals through their varying affinities to oils and chemicals after the ores had been ground to a fine powder. The concentrates are smelted either in the district or in the Pacific Northwest.

The Pine Creek area, lying to the east of the city of Coeur d'Alene, is one of the oldest mining areas of northern Idaho. Diffi-

culties of access, however, and the complexity of the ores, made development very difficult. In recent years new techniques have been perfected to separate economically the components of the complex ores; and a network of modern roads has been built to the various mines, making them accessible to the large zinc reduction plant and smelter at Kellogg, only a few miles away.

THE KOOTENAY DISTRICT   In the southeastern corner of British Columbia lies an important lead- and zinc-mining district. Most of the ore comes from the great Sullivan mine at Kimberly, but significant yields also come from mines at Riondel, Salmo, and Invermere.

Concentrates from the Kootenay district, as well as from other parts of western Canada and some foreign sources, are treated in the Consolidated Mining and Smelting Company refinery at Trail, which is one of the world's greatest nonferrous metallurgical works (Figure 12-6). Its principal products are lead, zinc, silver, gold, fertilizer elements, and heavy water. Unfortunately, nuisance emanations from the smelter smokestacks have caused problems with international ramifications. For years Trail has been pervaded by an unpleasant odor, and the vegetation on the surrounding hillsides

Figure 12-6. The metal refining complex at Trail. The Columbia River is at left. (Photo by George Hunter; courtesy Consolidated Mining & Smelting Company.)

Figure 12-7. A typical ghost town in the Colorado Rockies. Ashcroft, near Aspen, was a thriving settlement during the boom mining days. (Photograph by D. L. Hopwood; courtesy the State of Colorado.)

has been killed by the toxic effect of atmospheric pollution. Further, the smelter fumes characteristically are wafted southward down the Columbia Valley into Washington State, where natural vegetation and fruit orchards were damaged and soils became hyperacidic. Several lawsuits were successfully enjoined against the company as a result. During the last decade expensive treatment units have been installed to cleanse the fumes, with favorable results.

Although the mining industry has been declining throughout the Rocky Mountain Region for several decades, some people think that many valuable deposits are yet to be discovered. However, if new discoveries are made, it seems unlikely that new boom towns will evolve. Discoveries in the future can be made only on properties already privately owned, or on government lands without mineral rights to the individual. The cost of working minerals with modern mining methods also precludes the possibility that the individual prospector may acquire great wealth through methods used in the last decades of the 19th century. The ghost town (Figure 12-7), the abandoned mine shaft, and the dilapidated miner's hut located far in the mountain fastness provide mute romantic reminders of a picturesque phase in the occupance of the Rocky Mountain Region.

Forestry

The lumber industry never has been as important in this region as in the Upper Lakes Area, the South, or the Pacific Northwest, but logging has occupied the time of man in a number of places. The best-developed lumber camps are in the Northern Rockies where large trees occupy the lower slopes and are easily accessible. Owing to the steady demand for mine timbers and railroad ties from the great mining developments in the Butte and Coeur d'Alene Districts, northern Montana and Idaho have carried on profitable sawmilling for some years. Most of the large mills are located in the towns of Missoula, Polson, and Kalispell. Only about one-fourth of the merchantable stand is privately owned, the bulk being in the national forests. Some five per cent of the total timber cut in the United States is from the Northern Rockies, only a fraction of one per cent being from the Middle and Southern Rockies.

The traditional logging area of western Canada has been coastal British Columbia, but in recent years increasing timber supplies have come from the interior of the province, partly from the Rocky Mountain Region. Pulping is very limited, but sawmilling is a major activity at such places as Fernie, Cranbrook, Nelson, Golden and McBride.

Throughout the Rocky Mountain Region most of the timber cut was used for mine props and for dwellings—frame houses in the mining camps and log cabins in the more remote areas. As a result of the limited market, large areas are still covered with virgin timber. Since most of the land never was occupied or claimed by individuals, it remained in the hands of the governments, which made it comparatively easy to establish national forests (Figure 12-8), national parks, and provincial parks. Today there are more square miles of national forests in the Rocky Mountain Region than in any other area of equal size on the North American continent.

The establishment of forest reservations has done much to preserve the natural beauty of the region as well as to protect the trees from reckless logging and destructive fires. Despite government vigilance, fires frequently burn over considerable areas before they can be checked. In many places throughout the region one can see the charred remains of former magnificent forests. While many fires are started by lightning and hence are unpreventable, far too many are due to sparks from sawmills, incendiarists, careless campers, and cigarette smokers.

Agriculture and Stock Raising

In any consideration of Rocky Mountain agriculture and ranching, it must be remembered that the region consists mostly of forested or bare rocky slopes. The occasional level areas are utilized for irrigation farm-

Figure 12-8. National Forests of the United States. Most are located in the West. (Courtesy U.S. Forest Service.)

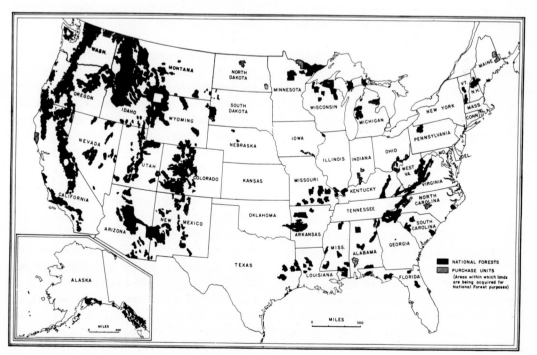

ing, dry farming, or ranching, and thus attain an importance out of all proportion to their size.

When the Spaniards settled in the Santa Fe area of the Southern Rockies at the beginning of the seventeenth century, they were primarily prospecting for gold and silver. Finding little mineral wealth, they soon turned to ranching in broad basins of the upper Rio Grande Valley. They received large land grants in the San Luis Valley from Spain, and for the next two centuries the area was dominated by "cattle barons." After the close of the Mexican War and the annexation of this territory by the United States, the large land holdings were broken up. Because of semiaridity, ranching has remained the principal occupation of the San Luis Valley, although considerable acreages are irrigated. Native grasses and alfalfa are dominant, and crops generally are supplemental to ranching. Because of the high altitude (above 5,000 feet) and the resulting short growing season, corn cannot be grown successfully. This was a great disappointment to settlers from the Corn Belt. In the absence of corn, wheat and potatoes became the chief crops. Though profitable at first, wheat yields have declined, and potatoes now constitute the main cash crop. In addition, there is a considerable amount of truck farming based upon the hot sunny summers and abundant irrigation water from artesian wells. Migratory farm workers are important in the San Luis Valley.

Ranching began much later in the valleys and basins to the north, as most of this land remained unexplored and unoccupied by white men until trappers and prospectors entered the mountains. In time each grassy plot in the Middle and Northern Rockies was homesteaded and turned into a ranch. Many areas, however, have been given over to dry farming or to irrigation agriculture. As is the case elsewhere, the best lands were the first to be cultivated and the poorest and most inaccessible ones remained in pasture. In the Northern Rockies and in the higher mountain valleys where frosts are common even during summer, ranching has remained the major activity. On most ranches both cattle and sheep are raised. In many places sheep have become more important, as they are better adapted to the short grasses and can graze the higher slopes in summer (Figure 12-9). The government, through its permit system, cooperates with ranchmen, allowing them to pasture sheep and cattle within the national forests, but it attempts to see that the land is neither overstocked nor overgrazed. This *transhumance*—the driving of grazing animals to high mountain pastures in summer and back to lower valleys in winter—is almost universal throughout the Rocky Mountain Region (Figure 12-10).

The ranching industry received a great stimulus through the development of the "dude ranch." Dude ranches, neither summer hotels nor farms, are usually located in scenic areas containing mountains, lakes, and streams. They appeal to a summer clientele from the East who enjoy riding, hiking, fishing, hunting, and "roughing it" in the great open spaces of the West. The visitors are respectfully called "dudes," the ranch owner a "dude wrangler," and his cowhands and business associates the "outfit." The Jackson Hole country of western Wyoming is especially noted for its many excellent dude ranches.

Some ranches which do not cater to tourists profit by renting saddle horses to summer visitors at nearby lodges or hotels.

Irrigation Agriculture The establishment of mining towns throughout the Rocky Mountain Region which were isolated from the agricultural areas to the east, made it profitable to withdraw some of the more favored valleys and basins from pastures and plant them in wheat and other staple crops. High prices and a great demand also

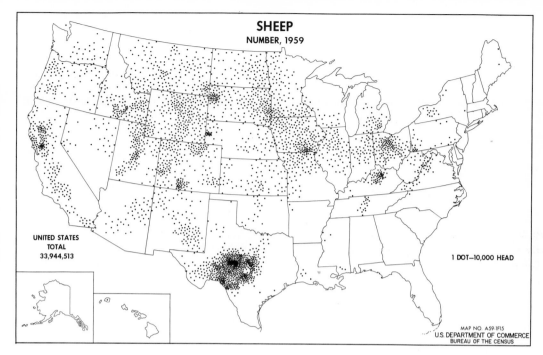

Figure 12-9. Distribution of sheep in the United States.

stimulated the production of vegetables by irrigation. Wherever water could be diverted for irrigation, additional land was placed under cultivation. At first all irrigation projects were either privately developed or under state supervision, but ultimately the United States Bureau of Reclamation established several projects within the region. One of the most interesting of these is the Uncompahgre Project in southwestern Colorado. Surplus waters from the Gunnison River, along which there is little land suited to irrigation, were diverted through a mountain range via a six-mile tunnel to the broad flat semiarid valley of the Uncompahgre River, thus making it irrigable.

Figure 12-10. Cattle grazing in a "park" or mountain valley in Colorado. They are often taken into the high country for summer grazing. (Photo courtesy Colorado Department of Public Relations.)

A more recent development of this type is the Colorado–Big Thompson Project which diverts, by means of a 13-mile tunnel, the surplus waters of the Grand River on the west slopes of the continental divide to the Big Thompson River on the east slope. Most of this water is used to irrigate land in the Great Plains east of the Front Range (Chapter 11).

The basic crop throughout the region is hay. Irrigated valleys yield valuable supplies of alfalfa and other hay crops for winter feeding of livestock. Some specialty crops are grown as well—pinto beans and chili peppers in New Mexico, miscellaneous vegetables in Colorado and Utah, sugar beets and grains in Idaho and Montana, fruits around Flathead Lake and in some of the Kootenay valleys, wheat in the Kootenay River Valley and around Cranbrook— but hay occupies the principal cultivated acreage almost everywhere.

Great sums of money have been invested by the national and state governments and by private concerns in the development of irrigation projects throughout the Rocky Mountain Region, but with the handicaps of a short growing season, restricted local markets, and costly transport charges to Middle Western and Eastern marts, it is doubtful whether some of the money has been spent wisely. In many cases these irrigated mountain farms are producing at greater cost the same crops as the Middle West with which their surplus must compete.

The Resort Industry

A tourist has been defined as "a vagabond with money to spend," and the type of industry which vacation travel supports is referred to as *tourism*.[6] Throughout the Rocky Mountain Region many communities derive their chief income from the tourist's money. Where tourism is confined to the summer season, as in most mountain areas, the resort business is concentrated into a relatively brief period. During the long winter season most resort centers are practically deserted except for the relatively few permanent residents. An illustration of this may be found in the resort town of Estes Park at the eastern gateway to Rocky Mountain National Park in Colorado. The permanent population of the settlement in 1960

[6] Clifford M. Zierer, "Tourism and Recreation in the West," *Geographical Review*, Vol. 42 (1952), pp. 462-81.

Figure 12-11. Sun Valley, Idaho, in winter. This is the principal winter sports resort in the Northern Rockies. (Photo courtesy Union Pacific Railroad.)

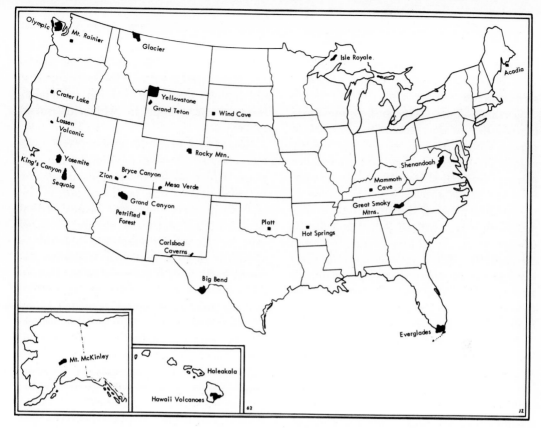

Figure 12-12. The National Parks of the United States.

was only 1,175, but each summer this small town with its many hotels, cabins, trailer camps, and other types of accommodation in the immediate tributary area supports a population of more than fifty thousand. The annual number of tourists passing through the entrance of the National Park has exceeded 1½ million for the past several years, which represents a heavy summer concentration since Trail Ridge Road across the mountains is closed to traffic because of snows for eight months each year.[7]

Summer Tourism The Rocky Mountain Region, with its high rugged mountains, spectacular scenery, extensive forests, varied wildlife, and cool summer temperatures, is a very popular vacationland. The location of the region between the Great Plains on the east and the Intermontane and Pacific Coastal areas on the west places it directly across lines of travel. With the building of transcontinental railroads and hard-surfaced highways, most of the Rockies has been made reasonably accessible.

The development of specific resort centers depended upon accessibility; thus the first resorts were those sponsored by the railroads. Others were developed after highways were built through the region. Only where some unusual natural or scenic feature presented itself were resort hotels and lodges built in remote places.

Throughout the Rockies there are places of interest for tourists, with interesting and spectacular scenery as the principal attraction. Many of the outstanding scenic areas have been reserved as national parks (Figure 12-12), which generally function as the key attractions of the region.

[7] Edwin J. Foscue and Louis O. Quam, *Estes Park: Resort in the Rockies* (Dallas: Southern Methodist University Press, 1949).

331

Seven of the most popular tourist areas, in terms of numbers of visitors, are described below.

SANTA FE–TAOS The southernmost portion of the Rocky Mountains, located in northern New Mexico, is not particularly rugged or spectacular, consisting mostly of pleasant forested slopes. However, its summers are considerably cooler than those of the parched plains of the Southwest. It is an area with a rich historical heritage that is manifested in the cultural landscape, and picturesque Indians still abound. As a result, the narrow, twisting streets of Santa Fe are jammed with tourist vehicles during the summer, and the Taos area is a center for dude-ranch and youth-camp activities.

PIKES PEAK AREA Colorado Springs is a city of the Great Plains, but its site is at the eastern base of one of the most famous mountains in Anglo-America. Pikes Peak, with a summit elevation of 14,110 feet, is far from being the highest mountain in Colorado, but its spectacular rise from the plains makes it a feature of outstanding prominence. The area roundabout contains some of the most striking scenery (Garden of the Gods, Seven Falls, Cheyenne Mountain, Cave of the Winds, Rampart Range), and some of the most blatantly commercial (Manitou Springs) tourist attractions in the region. Few tourists visit the Southern Rockies without at least a brief stop in the Pikes Peak area, as the overcrowding of even the unusually wide streets of Colorado Springs gives eloquent evidence.

DENVER'S FRONT RANGE HINTERLAND The Front Range of the Southern Rockies rises but a dozen miles west of Denver, and the immediate vicinity provides a recreational area for both residents of the city and visitors from more distant places. Denver maintains an elaborate and extensive group of "mountain parks," which are actually part of the municipal park system. There are thousands of summer cabins to be rented;

many streams to be fished; deer, elk, mountain sheep, and bear to be hunted; dozens of old mining towns to be explored; and countless souvenir shops in which to spend money.

ROCKY MOUNTAIN NATIONAL PARK Following many years of agitation by the people of Colorado for the establishment of a national park in the northern part of the state to preserve the scenic beauty of that section of the continental divide, a rugged area of 400 square miles was reserved by Congress in 1915 as Rocky Mountain National Park. It includes some of the highest and most picturesque peaks, glacial valleys, and canyons of the region, as well as extensive forested tracts which provide protection for numerous native wild animals. This park, one of the most accessible in the country, may be reached by excellent highways from Denver, Boulder, or Loveland on the east, or from Grand Lake on the west. Spectacular Trail Ridge Road traverses the park in connecting the tourist towns of Grand Lake and Estes Park, and reaches an elevation of 12,185 feet. Automobile touring is the principal activity in the Park, but hiking, climbing, and trail riding are also popular.

YELLOWSTONE – GRAND TETON – JACKSON HOLE In the northwestern corner of Wyoming is an extensive forested plateau, one area of which, 3,500 square miles in extent, has been designated as Yellowstone National Park; this was established in 1872 as our first national nature preserve. It is lacking in spectacular mountains, but contains a huge high-altitude (elevation 7,700 feet) lake, magnificent canyons and waterfalls, and the most impressive hydrothermal displays (geysers, hot springs, fumaroles, hot-water terraces) in the world. A few miles to the south is Grand Teton National Park, a smaller and more recently reserved area that encompasses the rugged grandeur of the Grand Teton Mountains, a heavily glaciated fault block that rises abruptly from the flat floor of Jackson Hole. Jackson Hole was an early fur-trappers' rendezvous that is now the winter home of the largest elk herd on the continent. The Tetons are particularly attractive to hikers and climbers, while Yellowstone is a motorists' park. The ubiquitous black bear and a great variety of other species of wildlife add to the interest of the area. In spite of its relatively remote location and short open sea the Yellowstone-Grand Teton country   cts more than a million visitors annually.

WATERTON — GLACIER   INTERNATIONAL PEACE PARK   Glacier National Park in Montana and Waterton Lakes National Park in Alberta are contiguous and have similar scenery. The mountains are typical of the Northern Rockies, with essentially horizon-

tal sediments uplifted and massively carved by glacial action. The area is a paradise for hikers, climbers, horseback riders, and wildlife enthusiasts, and contains one of the most spectacular automobile roads on the continent, the Going-to-the-Sun Highway which traverses Glacier Park from east to west.

THE CANADIAN ROCKIES The most magnificent mountains in the region are found west of Calgary and Edmonton on the Alberta—British Columbia boundary. The National Park system of Canada was started in 1885 when a small area in the vicinity of the mineral hot springs at Banff was reserved as public property. The famous resorts of Banff, Lake Louise, and Jasper were developed by the two transcontinental railways, and the Canadian Pacific and Cana-

Figure 12-13. The National Parks of Canada. Most are located in the Rocky Mountains. The key to the numbers on the map is as follows: (1) Mount Revelstoke, (2) Glacier, (3) Yoho, (4) Kootenay, (5) Jasper, (6) Banff, (7) Waterton Lakes, (8) Elk Island, (9) Wood Buffalo, (10) Prince Albert, (11) Riding Mountain, (12) Point Pelee, (13) Georgian Bay Islands, (14) St. Lawrence Islands, (15) Fundy, (16) Prince Edward Island, (17) Cape Breton Highlands, and (18) Terra Nova. (Map courtesy Canadian Department of Northern Affairs and National Resources.)

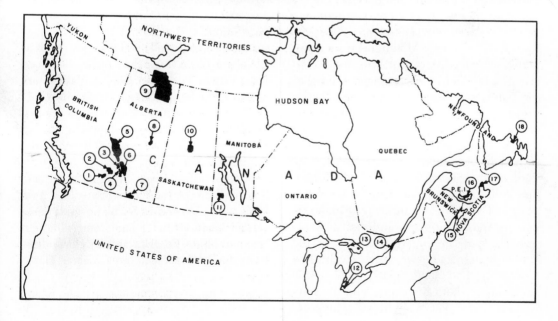

Figure 12-14. Banff Springs Hotel. This Canadian Pacific resort hotel faces across the Bow River and Banff Golf Course toward the Palliser Range of the Canadian Rockies. (Photo courtesy Canadian Pacific Railway.)

dian National are still major operators in the area. Today there are six national parks and three provincial parks with almost contiguous areas totaling 12,000 square miles—probably the largest nature recreational area in the world (Figure 12-13). Heavily glaciated mountains, abundant and varied wildlife, spectacular waterfalls, colorful lakes, deep canyons, the largest ice field in the Rockies, and luxurious resort hotels characterize the area (Figure 12-14).

Winter Sports Ever-increasing numbers of winter-sports enthusiasts are being attracted to the Rocky Mountains during the period of heavy snows, but, with the exception of a few famous resort centers, most of the winter-sports areas serve only nearby urban communities. The relative remoteness of the Rocky Mountain Region prohibits it from becoming outstanding for winter sports as has the Adirondack Mountains of New York or the Sierra Nevada of California. Sun Valley (Figure 12-11) in the Sawtooth Range of the Rockies in central Idaho, is perhaps the most famous and most glamorous "ski spot" in the western part of the United States. Its heavy snows, established reputation, and long, partly timber-free slopes attract both the expert and the novice. The Union Pacific Railroad, which de-

veloped the resort, provides excellent train services and hotel accommodations for the winter guests, and keeps the name "Sun Valley" before the public through its advertising literature. As a result, Sun Valley has become the "style center of the ski-fashion world, where celebrities are to be found along with spectacular scenery." [8]

The Colorado high country has the largest number of winter sports centers, primarily because the cities of the Colorado Piedmont (especially Denver) have a ski-conscious population sufficiently large to support them. Most of the major ski resorts (such as Loveland Basin, Arapahoe Basin, Berthoud Pass, Winter Park, and Hidden Valley) are within a two-hour drive of Denver; the only Colorado ski center that has developed along the lines of Sun Valley in attracting many out-of-state patrons is the revitalized mining town of Aspen.

In most other Rocky Mountain ski centers the bulk of the customers comes from local areas. Thus Taos Ski Valley and Santa Fe Ski Basin attract skiers from Albuquerque and Santa Fe, Alta and Brighton draw from the Salt Lake City area, various slopes

[8] Zierer, "Tourism and Recreation in the West," p. 469.

334

in western Montana are skied by Montanans, and the developments at Banff depend largely upon enthusiasts from Calgary.

Fishing and Hunting No other region in Anglo-America provides such a variety of faunal resources to tempt the sportsman. The fishing season normally lasts from May until September, with various species of trout as the principal quarry. Only diligent artificial stocking can maintain the resource in the more accessible lakes and streams where overfishing is rampant. The hunting season lasts from August to December in various parts of the region. The list of legal game is extensive, running the gamut from cottontail rabbit to grizzly bear and from pronghorn antelope to mountain goat. In an average year more than a quarter of a million big game animals and two dozen hunters are killed in this region.

Transportation

Like the Great Plains, the Rocky Mountains have been a major barrier to east-west travel. The early trails across the Rockies either passed around the southern end in New Mexico or crossed through the Wyoming Basin between the Southern and Middle Rockies. The first "transcontinental" railroad (the Union Pacific) used the Wyoming Basin route. Railroad surveying parties explored all possible routes, but in the end only nine lines succeeded completely in crossing the mountain barrier. Two of these, the Southern Pacific and the Santa Fe, were built through New Mexico, south of the mountains. Only the Denver and Rio Grande Western crossed through the highest part of the Rocky Mountains by way of Tennessee Pass (elevation 10,202 feet). Later, with the completion of the six-mile Moffat Tunnel, it succeeded in reaching the western slope by a shorter and lower route. Three "transcontinental lines," the Northern Pacific, the Great Northern, and the Chicago, Milwaukee and St. Paul, crossed the mountains in Montana. In Canada, only two lines were built: the Canadian Pacific to the south and the Canadian National farther north. Only these two are true transcontinental railways in that they link ports on opposite coasts, the Pacific ports of Vancouver and Prince Rupert with the Atlantic ports of Montreal, Halifax, St. John, and Sydney. Primary Canadian Pacific service crosses the Rockies at the relatively low Kicking Horse Pass from Banff to Yoho and then descends through the famous spiral tunnels in its westward route. Secondary service is over the more southerly Crows Nest Pass route. The route of the Canadian National Railway traverses the northerly but low-level Yellowhead Pass.

Highway development later followed similar routes, but the two southern routes and the one through the Wyoming Basin carry most of the traffic. Highways in the Canadian Rockies suffer from two difficulties that are uncommon south of the border: (1) Their routes are interrupted in several places by long, narrow lakes that occupy the structural trenches of the Northern Rockies. Automobile ferries span these lakes. (2) Every winter finds avalanches damaging or destroying sections of the highway. Thus summer maintenance and repair work are inevitably necessary.

Canada's most ambitious road-building program is the Trans-Canada Highway. Completed in 1963 and extending from St. John's in Newfoundland to Victoria in British Columbia, it is reputed to be the longest unbroken stretch of roadway ever built by one country (although the Cabot Strait and the Strait of Georgia are too wide to be bridged, and so must be crossed by automobile ferry). The most expensive and difficult section of the highway to construct was that crossing the Rockies, where many tunnels were cut and costs reached $1,000,000 per mile in some segments.

TABLE 11

Selected Cities and Towns of the Rocky Mountains

City or Town	Political Center
Anaconda	12,054
Bozeman	13,361
Butte	27,877
Coeur d'Alene	14,291
Cranbrook	5,549
Durango	10,530
Helena	20,227
Kalispell	10,151
Kellogg	5,061
Kimberly	6,013
Leadville	4,008
Livingston	8,229
Los Alamos	12,584
Missoula	27,090
Nelson	7,074
Rawlins	8,968
Rock Springs	10,371
Santa Fe	33,394
Trail	11,580

The Outlook

Permanent settlements in the region are based mostly on mining, logging, limited agriculture, and tourism. Mining will undoubtedly experience fluctuating fortune in different areas. Farming and ranching are developed almost to capacity and cannot be expected to change greatly. Logging activities are likely to expand particularly in British Columbia, Idaho, and Montana, though to some extent throughout the region. The dynamic future of the Rocky Mountains, however, appears to be intimately associated with that seasonal vagabond, the tourist. Natural attractions are almost limitless; recreational developments on federal lands have been accelerated by the National Park

Service's Mission 66 Program and the Forest Service's "Operation Outdoors"; [9] improvements in transportation facilities and accommodations are being made haphazardly but continually. The unprecedented growth currently characterizing tourism is expected to continue.

Selected Bibliography

British Columbia Lands Service, *The Kootenay Bulletin Area.* Victoria: Queen's Printer, 1958.

Foscue, Edwin J., and Louis O. Quam, *Estes Park: Resort in the Rockies.* Dallas: Southern Methodist University Press, 1949.

Harrington, Robert F., "The Kootenay Area of British Columbia," *Canadian Geographical Journal,* Vol. 63, December 1961, pp. 192-201.

Helburn, Nicholas, "Human Ecology of Western Montana Valleys," *Journal of Geography,* Vol. 55, January 1956, pp. 5-14.

Hoffmeister, Harold A., "Alkali Problem of Western United States," *Economic Geography,* Vol. 23, 1947, pp. 1-9.

———, "Middle Park and the Colorado—Big Thompson Diversion Project," *Economic Geography,* Vol. 23, 1947, pp. 220-231.

Knudtson, Arvid, "Ranching in the Rockies," *Monthly Review,* Federal Reserve Bank of Minneapolis, October 1961, pp. 2-11.

Lackey, Earl E., "Mountain Passes in the Colorado Rockies," *Economic Geography,* Vol. 25, 1949, pp. 211-215.

Zierer, Clifford M., "Tourism and Recreation in the West," *Geographical Review,* Vol. 42, 1952, pp. 462-481.

[9] These two programs are designed to expand significantly the provisions for visitors to national parks and national forests by constructing more and better roads, campgrounds, picnic areas, tourist accommodations, parking areas, and trails.

chapter thirteen

Intermontane Basins and Plateaus

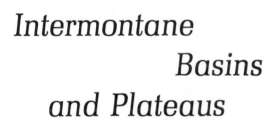

The relatively few occupants in this huge region (Figure 13-1) dwell mostly in valley oases and occasional mountain mining camps, which appear like islands in the desert wilderness. It is one of the most colorful regions in all Anglo-America.

By many regionalists it is considered several regions rather than one. Here, however, it is treated as one, since the whole is intermontane and in nearly every part evaporation exceeds precipitation. Water is problem

number one to every form of life, whether plant, animal, or man. Moreover, the following types of human adjustment recur from north to south and from east to west:

1. Where water is available for irrigation and where the land is sufficiently level, intensive farming prevails.

2. On bench lands and plateaus where the rain is sufficient for a crop once in two years, wheat and a few other crops are dry-farmed.

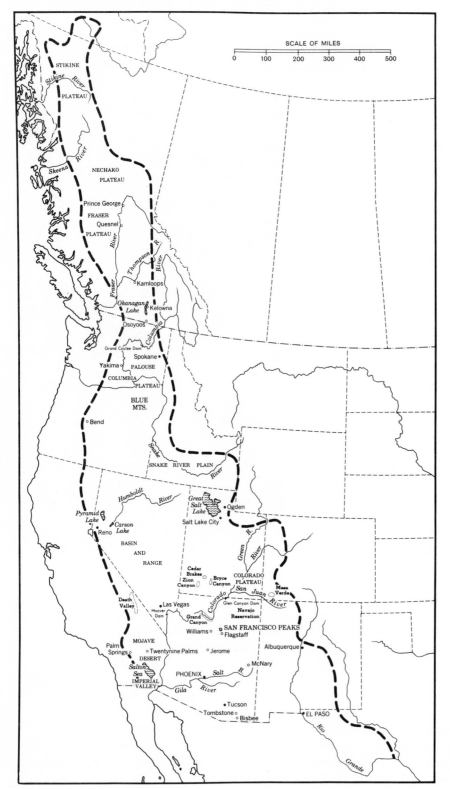

Figure 13-1. The Intermontane Basins and Plateaus. A region of mining, grazing, irrigated farming, and scenic attractions.

3. Where sources of irrigation water are wanting, and where the rain is insufficient for dry farming but the precipitation is adequate for grass and shrubs, grazing prevails —cattle and sheep using the semiarid areas and goats the strictly arid ones.

4. In mountains and on higher plateaus (Utah, Arizona, New Mexico, and especially British Columbia) too rugged for farming but receiving enough rain for trees to grow, a limited amount of lumbering is carried on.

5. Where minerals occur in paying quantities and where they are accessible to railways or highways, mining is locally important.

6. In a few favored locations, market towns have blossomed into rapidly growing cities, complete with a modest amount of manufacturing.

7. Here and there throughout the whole region are scenic attractions, such as the Grand Canyon, which have no counterparts anywhere else in the world. Most of these are now reserved as national parks, national monuments, or national forests which attract hundreds of thousands of tourists each year.

Climate

The greater part of this region is desert or semidesert. This, however, does not mean that it is everywhere a region of sand dunes and barren desolation. A desert is an area whose water supply is so small that agriculture is impracticable. "It is poor but not dead."

Climatically, the region falls into four realms: (1) the *subhumid,* (2) the *semiarid,* (3) the *normally* or *moderately arid,* and (4) the *extremely arid.*

The *subhumid* portion of the region occurs in the central and northern portions of the interior plateaus of British Columbia. A combination of heavier rainfall because of lower coastal mountains (in the Skeena district) and less evaporation because of lower summer temperatures results in a climate that shows little evidence of precipitation deficiency. Winters are long and cold; summers are short and cool. Precipitation maximum is in summer.

The *semiarid* climate is typified by the Fraser and Columbia plateaus (except along their western and eastern borders which are arid and subhumid respectively); precipitation ranges from 7 to 20 inches per year and falls largely in the late autumn, winter, and spring. The growing season varies from less than 100 days in central British Columbia to more than 200 in parts of Oregon.

The *normally arid* climate, characterized by most of the Great Basin, has periodic rainfalls—seasons of fairly regular, though limited precipitation, during which vegetation bursts into life and the water table is replenished. The precipitation at Elko, Nevada, a typical station, is 9.46 inches. The frostless season varies from 100 to 180 days.

In the *extremely arid* climate, the rainfall is episodic, coming largely in summer at irregular intervals and invariably as cloudbursts. The Mojave-Gila Desert exemplifies this type. Its annual precipitation is less than five inches—too little even for grazing. Almost the entire annual rainfall may come in a single downpour lasting but a few moments. So much water falls so quickly that little can penetrate the soil.

The diurnal range of temperature throughout the region is high. The days are generally very hot; and the nights are cool, even in summer. This is because the amount of cloud and water vapor in the air is so small that the sun's rays can reach the earth promptly in the morning and the heat can dissipate rapidly after sunset. Elevation is a factor, too—the Colorado Plateau experiencing slightly cooler days and cooler nights than the Great Basin. Exceptions as far as cool nights are concerned are the Imperial and Mojave Deserts. The highest official shade temperature ever recorded in the United States was 134° F. at Greenland Ranch in Death Valley.

Surface Features

Physiographically, this region consists of the Colorado Plateau, the Basin-and-Range Province, the Columbia Plateau, and the Interior Uplands of British Columbia.

The Colorado Plateau This enormous area consists of several strongly differentiated parts but has sufficient unity to justify separation from adjacent subregions. It stretches outward from the Colorado River and its branches in Arizona, New Mexico, and Utah. The greater part consists of a rather flat summit area, slightly warped or undulating as a result of earlier crustal movements, interrupted by erosion scarps in the eastern portions and fault scarps in the western parts. Physiographically, the area is distinguished by:

1. Great elevation; all the plateau except the bottoms of canyons and the highest peaks has an elevation of 4,000 to 8,000 feet. The higher areas comprise the plateaus of Utah, the San Francisco Peaks, White Mountains, Chuska Mountains, and Zuñi Uplift.

2. Remarkable canyons, hundreds of which thread the Canyon Lands of southeastern Utah and Mesa Verde. These make the Colorado Plateau the most dissected, most difficult to traverse, and least known of all the regions of the United States (Figure 13-2).

3. An amazing amount of erosion extending through thousands of feet; nowhere in the world is there so impressive an example as the Grand Canyon.

4. Numerous arroyos, which cut the region into a maze of steep-sided chasms, dry during most of the year but filled from wall to wall during the rare rains. (Not to be confused with badlands.)

5. Mesas, flat-topped islands of resistant rock found only on the borderline of arid and humid climates.

The Basin-and-Range Province To the northwest, west, southwest, south, and southeast of the Colorado Plateau, from southern Oregon to western Texas, is a vast expanse of desert and semidesert country that has notable physiographical similarity. Throughout this extensive area the terrain is dominated by isolated mountain ranges that descend abruptly into gentle alluvial piedmont slopes and flat-floored basins of interior drainage.

The mountain ranges characteristically

Figure 13-2. The Green River in extreme northwestern Colorado. The Colorado Plateau Subregion is characterized by flat-topped mesas, sheer cliffs, and deeply-incised canyons. (Photo courtesy Colorado Department of Public Relations.)

are rough, broken, rocky, steep-sided, and deep-canyoned (Figure 13-3). They tend to be narrow in comparison with their length, distinctly separated from one another, often arranged in parallel patterns (trending north-south in Nevada, New Mexico, and Utah; trending east-west in Arizona and Texas), and of only moderate altitude. Although their origins are somewhat diverse, most consist of tilted and block-faulted masses of previously folded and peneplained sedimentary rocks. The canyons and gullies that drain them are waterless most of the time, harboring intermittent streams only after a rain.

Near the base of the mountains there is normally an abrupt flattening out of the slopes, caused by stream deposition. As the streams reach the foot of the mountains, their gradient is sharply decreased, so that they can no longer carry the heavy load of silt, sand, pebbles, and boulders that they have brought down from the highlands (although the streams flow only intermittently, the amount of erosion they can accomplish is tremendous), and considerable deposition takes place. This piedmont deposition generally occurs in fan- or cone-shaped patterns (called alluvial fans) that become increasingly complex and overlapping (piedmont

alluvial plains) as the cycle of erosion progresses.

The fans become increasingly flatter at lower elevations, and eventually merge with the silt-choked basin floors. The basins themselves, often referred to as playas, frequently are without exterior drainage. Shallow lakes, mostly intermittent, may fill the lowest portion of the basins. They are saline, because they have no outlet and because the streams which feed them, like all streams, carry minute amounts of various salts. As the lake waters evaporate, the salts become more concentrated, and the complete disappearance of the water leaves an alkali flat or salt pan.

There are several large and relatively permanent salt lakes in the subregion, particularly lakes Carson and Pyramid in Nevada and Great Salt Lake in Utah. The latter expands and contracts according to the variation in precipitation in the mountains, its water source, and according to the rate at which irrigation water is drawn off. It is a shrunken remnant of prehistoric Lake Bonneville—a great body of fresh water that was as large as present Lake Huron. Probably several lakes filled the basin area and then retreated, perhaps desiccating completely. Though Lake Bonneville and the other lakes disappeared thousands of years ago, the old beach lines still remain strikingly clear on the sides of the mountains. The highest shoreline, the Bonneville, lies about 1,000 feet above Great Salt Lake.

There are only a few permanent streams in the region, and they generally can be classified as "exotic," because the bulk of their water supply comes from adjacent regions. Most conspicuous are the Rio Grande and the Colorado River. The latter, along with its left-bank tributary, the Gila, provides a significant amount of water for irrigation and for domestic use. The Salton Basin in southeastern California was partially flooded in 1906 when attempted irrigation permitted the Colorado River to get out of control. The river was re-established in its original channel the following year, but the Salton Sea still exists as a permanent reminder of the incident.

The Columbia Plateau The Columbia Plateau lies between the Cascade Mountains on the west and the Rocky Mountains on the east and north, and grades almost imperceptibly into the Great Basin to the south. While called a plateau, which popularly suggests a rather uniform surface, the area has quite varied relief features of mountains, plateaus, tilted fault blocks, hills, plains, and ridges. In general, this intermontane area is covered with lava flows which originally were poured out over a nearly horizontal landscape and interbedded with a considerable quantity of silts that were deposited in extensive interior lakes. After the outpouring of the sheets of lava and the deposit of the lake beds, the surface of much of the region was strongly warped and faulted so that the present surface of the lava varies from a few hundred feet above sea level to nearly 6,000 feet in elevation. Numerous tilted fault blocks and upfolded ridges, called somewhat ineptly the Blue Mountains, extend from southeast Washington across Oregon to within 40

miles of the Cascade Mountains and divide the lava-covered area into nearly equal halves. The balance of the subregion consists predominantly of basins surrounded by plateaus, hills, and ridges. Thus in southeastern Washington is the Columbia Basin surrounded by a rim of higher uplifted lava-covered country. The eastern part of the Columbia Basin, called the Palouse, consisting of rolling hills covered with loess, receives sufficient rainfall to make it a very productive farming area. The Deschutes-Columbia Plateau is a triangular-shaped area in north-central Oregon that slopes in general from the Blue Mountains to the Columbia River. The Snake River Plain or Basin extends across southern Idaho in a broad arc. In central Oregon, the Harney Basin and the Great Sandy Desert are shallow interior basins and flats between the Blue Mountains and the Great Basin. They may be considered a transition area between the so-called Columbia Plateau and the Great Basin.

The Interior Uplands of British Columbia The Canadian portion of the Intermontane Region consists of an extensive area of diversified but generally subdued relief (Figure 13-4). The Fraser Plateau in the south and the Nechako Plateau in the center are characterized by moderately dissected hills, occasional mountain protuberances, and a few large entrenched river valleys. Most notable of these entrenchments are in portions of the Fraser and Thompson Valleys and in the Okanagan Trench.[1]

North of the Nechako Plateau is a relatively complicated section of mountains and valleys that flattens out somewhat into a series of dissected tablelands, referred to as the Stikine Plateau, in the far north. The Stikine country is underlaid by lava, and is surmounted by several volcanic peaks.

[1] The spelling of this name differs in Canada and the United States. In the former it is "Okanagan"; in the latter, "Okanogan."

Figure 13-4. A view in the Nechako Plateau of central British Columbia. (British Columbia Government Photograph.)

Soils

Most of this region has not been carefully mapped, and little can be said of its soils except that the mature ones are all pedocals.

Columbia Plateau soils vary from heavy silt loams to fine sand and sandy loams, the former predominating. They are well supplied with potash and phosphorus but are deficient in nitrogen and humus. In the driest parts there is considerable damage from blowing. Palouse soils, true *chernozems,* and the most important in the Columbia Plateau, are exceptionally fertile, and, before their structure and organic content were destroyed by farming, absorbed moisture readily. They are presumably of loessial origin.

Palouse terrain is unique—wavelike in appearance. It is believed that it results largely from wind action and snowdrift erosion, or nivation, which scoops out cirque-like forms on northeast-facing slopes. The hills are asymmetric, the northeast slopes being more concave and steeper than the southwest ones. Although this unconsolidated material is extremely deep, erosion has been comparatively slow due to the cohesive qualities of loessial material, the fine particles being

bound together with grass roots. When this humus is destroyed by continuous cropping and fallowing, the soils erode readily.

Most true soils in the Basin-and-Range lie on alluvial fans, piedmont alluvial plains, and playas.[2] With water, the first two may become highly productive. The Basin Ranges have either a thin layer of soil or none whatsoever. The soils at the foot of the Wasatch (the Salt Lake Oasis) are dark-colored because the benches received enough precipitation to cause a vigorous growth of shallow-rooted vegetation. These soil constituents were carried originally by streams into ancient Lake Bonneville. Similar lacustrine materials occur around the eastern border of the Snake River Plains.

Much of the Colorado Plateau is devoid entirely of soils. When present, they are limy, light grayish-brown or gray in color, and contain little organic material. Where water is available for irrigation, those that

[2] Playas—both "wet" and "dry"—form in the lowest parts of desert basins. The former contain shallow bodies of water during rainy spells and are apt to be moist even during the nonrainy season. The latter occupy nonwatertight basins and their surfaces consist of hard, sun-baked clay.

are deep, well-drained, and free from an excess of salts become highly productive. The soils in the southern part of the Colorado Plateau are reddish in color and, like most desert soils, are rich in lime. When irrigated, they are highly productive and capable of growing a wide variety of crops, such as alfalfa, barley, corn, cotton, grain sorghums, and wheat.

The soils of interior British Columbia are varied, and strongly influenced by relief. Most have developed from glacial deposits. Gray wooded soils predominate, but the southern valleys have chernozemic and alluvial soils of considerable fertility.

Natural Vegetation

In so large an area and in one varying so greatly in land forms and hence in climate, marked differences in the natural vegetation occur. Some variations, however, as in the Great Salt Lake area of Utah, are due to physical and chemical properties of the soil.

Forests Western yellow pine and Douglas fir forests are confined mostly to the higher elevations where the rainfall is relatively heavy. As precipitation declines, forest changes to woodland, then to types associated with inadequate moisture—piñon and juniper—and finally to chaparral. There is considerable juniper in the area north and south of Bend, Oregon.

More than half the Colorado Plateau is clothed with trees of some kind, though the forest area containing merchantable timber is limited.

Western yellow pine contributes most of the saw timber on lands lying at altitudes of 6,000 to 7,500 feet in Arizona and New Mexico. Piñon and juniper along with chaparral occupy the belt below yellow pine but are most common in southern Arizona and southern California. For the most part they are not found north of the forty-fourth parallel. The forests in the higher western and southern margins of the Plateau are included in national forests.

Most of the British Columbia Intermontane section is forested. In the Fraser Plateau to the south, the forest is open and park-like, with ponderosa pine, lodgepole pine, and Douglas fir alternating with grassland. The Nechako forest is denser and is predominantly composed of Engelmann spruce, alpine fir, and aspen. In northern British Columbia the forest is similar to the Taiga, with white spruce as the dominant species and considerable areas of muskeg in evidence.

Grasslands Grasslands, more numerous than might be supposed, characterize the highlands of southeastern Arizona, New Mexico, and the Columbia Basin. Mesquite grass grows where temperatures are high, evaporation excessive, and annual precipitation low. Short grass characterizes large areas in the high plateaus of New Mexico and Arizona, as does bunch grass in the Columbia Plateau; and the noxious cheat grass is almost ubiquitous. In southern British Columbia, the valleys are mostly covered with natural grassland, and many of the slopes are grassed as well.

Desert Shrub Xerophytic plants characterize deserts—those areas where irrigation is essential for permanent settlement. Vegetation grows in even the driest parts. Most desert plants, usually dwarfed in size, have small leaves and therefore minimum transpiration. *Sagebrush,* which dominates as far south as southern Nevada, and has invaded much of southern British Columbia, grows in pure stands where soils are relatively free from alkaline salts. Especially is it abundant on the bench lands which skirt mountains and on the alluvial fans at the mouths of canyons. *Shadscale,* a low, gray, spiny plant with a shallow root system, grows on the most alkaline soils but never in dense stands. Much bare ground lies between the plants. It is especially prominent in Utah and Nevada and is believed to have a wider range even than sagebrush. *Greasewood*, bright green in color and occupying the same general region as sagebrush and shadscale, grows from one to five feet in height and is tolerant of alkali. *Creosote bush*, dominating the southern Great Basin as sagebrush does the northern, merges in the *chaparral* zone where it draws moisture from deep down under the surface. Creosote bush is a large plant, attaining a height of 10 to 15 feet. *Mesquite grass* also occupies a large acreage in southern New Mexico and Arizona and is especially abundant on the fertile soils along drainage channels. *Cactus* and *yucca* grow over much of the Arizona Highlands at slightly higher elevations than creosote bush. They characterize the loose soils covering the rough rocky hills and low mountains that have been badly eroded. Their grazing value is slight. Most desert plants live precariously and in lonely isolation.

Fauna

In spite of considerable barrenness and scarcity of water, the Intermontane Region has a surprisingly varied fauna. It was never an important habitat for bison, but the plains-dwelling American antelope, or pronghorn, is still found in considerable numbers in every state but California. In most of the Canadian section and in the mountains and rough hills of the United States portion, other ungulates are notable, including deer, elk, desert mountain sheep, moose (in British Columbia), caribou (in British Columbia), feral burros (particularly in California and Arizona), feral horses (especially in Nevada, Utah, Oregon, and British Columbia), and javelinas (in Arizona).

Fur-bearers are common only in forested portions of the northern half of the region. Most predators (as wolf, coyote, fox, cougar, and bobcat) are systematically poisoned and becoming increasingly scarce.

The relatively few rivers and lakes provide important nesting and resting areas for migratory waterfowl.

Land of the Indian

The Indians are discussed in greatest detail in this chapter because their numbers are greatest in this region and they have retained their heritage and way of life here better than elsewhere, except in the Northern Continental Forest and the Yukon-Kuskokwim Basins. But there they were forest Indians who were hunters; here, in the dry West where game was less abundant some were hunters and some farmers. Now some are also graziers.

The Indians are thus a part of the pioneer picture—the human element in the background against which the achievements of the pioneer whites are projected. Under these circumstances they must be studied.

In the arid Southwest the Indians reached the apex of their culture and civilization. Here they made considerable progress prior to the white man's arrival and it is here they are making their strongest stand today. So far as the United States is concerned, this is the only part of the country that remains true Indian country.

Land of the Navajos The scope of this book precludes treatment of all the tribes in the Southwest; hence only the Navajos, who typify the nomadic Indians, and the Hopis and Zuñis, who typify the sedentary ones, are discussed.

The Navajo country is a reservation comprising some 16 million acres. For the most part it is a sun-scorched, water-sculptured land—one of high plateau, flat-topped mesa, sharp, deep canyon, and sandy and gravelly wash. It is larger than the state of West Virginia.

The rainfall, of about 3 to 15 inches, comes in the winter and summer seasons. Summer rains, mostly torrential, have stripped the topsoil from scores of squares miles, which are now almost naked. Aside from the main arteries used by transcontinental tourists, motor roads are few and poor. Motorists from outside this region who have been caught on a dirt road in a summer afternoon downpour do not soon forget their nightmare. This then is more the land of the horse than of the motor car.

Water is scarce. Only five per cent of the Navajo country has permanent streams; man and beast depend upon pools, water pockets, or tanks.

Most of the land is classed as marginal by the land economist; little, however, is so desertic as to be positively worthless to sheep and goats.

When the Navajos first turned to the raising of livestock, the range was in good condition. But with increasing population, more animals were needed, and with more livestock came overgrazing. This has diminished the carrying capacity of the range and erosion has attacked it, gnashing it with gullies and seaming it with arroyos. Springs have dried up and the Navajos have been threatened with starvation or with becoming public charges.

DISTRIBUTION OF THE NAVAJOS   The Navajo Reservation, which looks almost deserted to the traveler, has a population density of about three persons to the square mile. Yet, because it has hardly ten inches of rainfall and severely lacks other natural resources, *it is overcrowded*. Much has been said about the Indians as the "vanishing Americans." This phrase certainly is not applicable to the Navajos, the largest Indian tribe in the United States, which has increased from less than 10,000 in 1870 to more than 70,000 in 1960.

This growth is amazing considering that the life expectancy of the Navajos is 20 years less than the national average. Welfare officials reveal that the health conditions among this Indian group are the worst in the nation —with deaths from dysentery, pneumonia, and tuberculosis being triple the national average.

GRAZING   North America was poor in domesticable animals: the bison, antelope, deer, and elk were not tractable and have never been domesticated. The Spaniards who settled in New Mexico attempted to domesticate the bison but failed.

Since grazing was a leading enterprise in their homeland, it was natural that the Spaniards should have brought their animals to the New World. Especially valuable to the Indian was the horse, which for the first time assured mobility.

Today the Navajos are essentially pastoralists (Figure 13-5), their flocks of sheep and goats being driven into the higher timber areas in summer and back into the valleys in winter. In arid areas with small relief, they drive the flocks into the highlands in winter because at that season water is available only in the higher places.

There are too many head of livestock on the reservation. The Navajo sheep are hardy, subsisting throughout the year on the open range; their wool is easy to card, spin, and weave by hand, and it makes a high-grade rug; however, the fleece is light, weighing but four pounds per head as compared with the average of eight pounds for the entire country. Furthermore, these sheep are poor meat animals. As a means of enabling the Navajos to reduce the size of their flocks and thus improve the grazing lands, the government has sought to improve the breed.

NAVAJO DWELLINGS   The Navajos have never been a pueblo people, have never lived in towns, and have never farmed very much. This is understandable, since formerly they were hunters and even now are mainly pastoralists. Their homes are well-adapted to the surroundings; so widely scattered are their hogans and so well do they blend with the landscape, they are seldom seen by unobservant passers-by. The *winter hogan* is constructed of logs, the cracks on

Figure 13-5. A mixed flock of sheep and goats in Monument Valley, Utah. These two species often forage together in Navajo herds. (Photo courtesy Utah Tourist and Publicity Council.)

the outside being chinked with earth; a hole is left in the roof for the escape of smoke. The door, formerly a blanket, is now made of wood. There are no windows. Hogans differ in size, the largest being about 15 feet across. They are dry, warm, and well-ventilated. Sheep skins cover the floor, serving as beds by night and seats by day. The *summer hogan,* made of brush closely piled against upright stakes, is shady and open to breezes but is unsatisfactory during rains.

TRIBAL CRAFTS   The Indians of the Southwest are skilled craftsmen. They get a considerable part of their income from the sale of art wares to tourists. For example, when a Navajo mother needs provisions and clothing for her babies, she makes a rug of the size that can be exchanged for the bill of goods (Figure 13-6). Though machine-made articles have to some extent displaced native arts, the federal government, through the Office of Indian Affairs, is trying to prevent the extinction of Indian crafts by acquainting the public with the richness of the wares, by developing markets, and by encouraging the Indians.

THE MODERN NAVAJOS   Modern living has had relatively little effect on the Navajos, but in a few ways civilization is impinging on their lives. An increasing number of oil and gas discoveries is being made in the Four Corners Country, part of which is in-

cluded in the Navajo Reservation. The mineral rights are owned by the tribe, so that the financial benefits are being widely dispersed. Under the auspices of the Navajo Tribal Council and the Employment Se-

Figure 13-6. The Navajo rug story at a glance. In the background is a flock of sheep and goats. In the foreground squaws card and spin the wool. The weaver is working on a rug on her hand loom. (Photo courtesy the Santa Fe Railway.)

curity Commission of Arizona, opportunities for jobs in industry are now more available to Navajos, who possess considerable innate manual dexterity. Such factory jobs are off the Reservation, especially in Flagstaff. Pickup trucks are now common among the Navajos, and their mobility is thus significantly increased.

The Hopis   Not all the Indians are nomadic graziers. One important sedentary group is the Hopis, who for many hundreds of years have occupied *pueblos*.[3]

The Hopis have been compared to the wild sheep which were compelled to move to mountain peaks because of fierce animals. Surrounded by the more numerous Navajos, the Hopis perched their picturesque pueblos atop lofty steep-walled mesas accessible only by one or two tortuous trails which they could defend against enemies. Here too, they kept food and water.

The Hopi house, made of stone and adobe bricks, is easily constructed, easily repaired, and inexpensive. Thick walls make it warm in winter and cool in summer. Roofs are always flat.

HOPI AGRICULTURE   Among the best farmers of the Colorado Plateau are the Hopis, who occupy lands in the southwestern part of the Navajo Reservation. Long ago they realized that their rainfall was inadequate for normal agriculture. In order to grow crops they learn the location of all moist soils for miles around their pueblos, and practice flood-water farming—placing their crops in valley bottoms near washes, or wherever moisture is available. The fields often lie far from their pueblos.

They plant their corn in hills, 15 to 20 kernels to the hill, about six feet apart to conserve water and six to eight inches deep to keep it from sprouting until rain falls. Occasionally, they erect small windbreaks

about 30 feet apart in parallel rows and at right angles to the prevailing winds. Because of the short growing season (the result of altitude) they have developed quick-maturing strains.

The Hopis, reputed to be the most skillful of all dry-land farmers, cultivate intensively, each farmer handling only 2 to 10 acres. Seldom is their land in one continuous piece.

RELIGION   The Indian religion is a practical one designed to be of help on earth rather than in an uncertain future. Since life in the dry plateau is at the mercy of sun and rain, the Indians are extremely religious. Their religion was from the beginning woven about their intimate observations of nature.

In the Southwest among those Indians who were farmers, as for example, the Hopis and the Zuñis, a deep reverence developed for those natural forces that control weather, especially rainfall. Following a custom inaugurated by their forbears at least 2,000 years ago, they pray for rain by dancing; the dances, little modified since first seen by whites 400 years ago, are held when crops are suffering from drought or when rain is needed to germinate newly planted corn. When, as often happens, rain begins to fall in the midst of the dance, the Indians whoop it up and prance with triumph.

Historical Settlement

The Arrival of the Spaniards   It is not definitely known when the first Spaniards came into the arid Southwest. About the middle of the sixteenth century, however, those in Mexico heard tales:

> Far to the north are cities that make the palaces of Montezuma look like beggars' hovels. The golden cities of Cibola they are called. And gold they are—houses three and four stories high shining in the desert sun. Their inhabitants eat from golden vessels and their doorways are studded with the blue of turquoise stones.

---

[3] The Spanish word *pueblo* means *people;* apparently, then, a pueblo had to be large enough to accommodate a sufficient number of people to justify the use of the term.

Led by the black slave, Estevanico, those swashbuckling Spanish eventually found Zuñi and opened up an empire. Etched against the blue New Mexican sky, rose tier on tier of what looked to be a city of gold. But it was not gold. It was only puddled adobe guilded by the bright desert sun. Nor did the inhabitants eat from golden vessels, but from skillfully made yellow clay pots.

Disgusted, the Spaniards pushed on up the valley of the Rio Grande.[4]

Later on, the Spaniards explored the entire Southwest and were responsible for the conquest of nearly one-third of what is now the United States. Unable to find precious metals, some remained to convert the Indians.

The Spaniards left an indelible influence on the history of the Southwest as well as upon American civilization. Their livestock formed the basis of the later American cattle and sheep industry, and their horses gave mobility to the Indians, the importance of which can hardly be overestimated. Small Spanish settlements and trading posts such as Santa Fe made up the population of the Southwest until the middle of the nineteenth century.

Anglo-American Explorers and Trappers British and American explorers began to filter into the region in the early nineteenth century. Actually, young Alexander Mackenzie had completed the pioneer traverse of British North America in 1793, and a string of fur-trading posts had been established across central British Columbia by 1807. Lewis and Clark entered the Pacific Northwest in 1804-05. Simon Fraser and David Thompson explored much of southwestern Canada in 1805-1808 and 1808-1811, respectively. The Astorians were active in 1811-1813; Smith penetrated the Great Basin in 1828; and Wyeth, the Pacific Northwest in 1832-1833. Bonneville in 1832 and 1836 traded in furs and casually explored the area drained by the Bear River, while Fremont

in 1845-1846 entered the Salt Lake Basin by way of the Bear River, becoming the first to examine it systematically. These are but a few of the many who explored the region.

Trapping, a powerful incentive to exploration, was, as a matter of fact, the main object of many of the men who explored the West in the early nineteenth century. The trappers were a special breed—self-reliant, solitary individuals—largely freebooters constantly striving to outwit their rivals, to supplant them in the good will of the Indians, and to mislead them in regard to routes. They lasted until fashion suddenly switched from beaver to silk for men's hats. The mountain-men trappers were then through. Nonetheless, they left an indelible stamp upon our history.

It was the Canadians rather than the Americans who were in control of the Northwest from 1813 until 1846. The intense rivalry between the Hudson's Bay Company and the North West Company ended with amalgamation in 1821. Although many American names are associated with it, no American fur company was dominant in the northern part of the Intermontane Region for any length of time. The "Snake Country" to the south was the great zone of conflict between the Americans and the Hudson's Bay Company.

The Farmer Invasion The outstanding example of farmer invasion was the Mormon migration to Salt Lake Basin in 1847.[5]

[4] Dorothy L. Pillsbury, "Golden City of Peace," *The Christian Science Monitor*, March 15, 1947.

[5] On June 23, 1847, the Mormon advance party under Brigham Young met the famous Rocky Mountain trader and trapper, Jim Bridger, on the Big Sandy River. They were strongly advised by Bridger not to settle in the Valley of the Great Salt Lake because they would find it difficult to grow crops there. He said it would be unwise to bring a large colony into the Great Basin until it was proved that grain could be raised there, and he offered to give a thousand dollars for the first ear of corn that matured in Salt Lake Valley. The Mormons received similar advice from others whom they met on the trail west of Fort Laramie. Bridger knew nothing of irrigation and hence based his thinking on the dryness of the Salt Lake Valley.

The Mormons had trekked from Ohio, Missouri, and Illinois to escape persecution and to find a sanctuary where they might maintain their religious integrity. To accomplish this, they felt impelled to establish themselves on the border of the real American Desert. The agricultural fame of the Utah colony was soon known far and wide. Utah is the only state in the Union that was systematically colonized. The leader, Brigham Young, sent scouts into every part of the "state" to seek lands suitable for farming. He personally selected the colonists, who were of sufficient number to build forts against Indian attacks and construct dams and canals for irrigation. He located all farm-villages near streams, for upon water the colonists depended for their very existence. Even before Utah was settled, he made several settlements outside to control territory and serve as a line of forts. Among his early outposts were Las Vegas, Nevada, Moab on Utah's Colorado Plateau, San Bernardino in California, Alamosa in Colorado, and Fort Lemhi in Idaho.

Before long all the arable land had been acquired; scouts were then sent outside Utah to seek new irrigable lands. Thus Mormons made the first permanent settlement in Idaho, and were the first Anglo-Saxons to arrive in the Grand Canyon country.

The California Gold Rush Following the explorers, trappers, and farmers came the gold-seekers of 1849. So large was the movement that it led to the establishment of trading posts and stations, where the migrants rested and refreshed themselves. The Salt Lake Oasis especially became a "Mecca" for the weary and exhausted. Farther west the wagon trains rested in Carson, Walker, and Mono basins. Important in the route through Nevada was the Humboldt River:

This is the paradox of the Humboldt, that it was almost the most necessary river of

America, and the most hated. Americans came this way to stand on the mountain passes and look far upon the Pacific; Americans came back. Emigrant and immigrant came this way, Mormon and miner and soldier, Pony Express and Overland stage, Overland telegraph and Pacific Railroad, cattleman and sheepman, highway and airline. Indians fought for life in the river bottoms while the West went mad as the Comstock poured out its bonanzas on the heights . . . The Humboldt was a way, a means; few settled here until they had to, until greener lands were occupied.[6]

Other precious metal discoveries had a significant influence on early settlement. Outstanding examples include the silver lodes of western Nevada (dating from 1859) and the Fraser River gold rush (beginning in 1858).

The Graziers Most of this region was favorable for the grazier. For some years after the Spaniards came, cattle raising was almost the only range industry, though Navajo Indians and Mexican colonists herded some sheep. Northward in Utah and Idaho as well as in the Oregon Country cattle raising held sway in nonfarming areas. In fact, the Columbia grasslands were major cattle-surplus areas for many years and shared the stocking of the Northern Great Plains ranges with Texas.

In the 1870's and early 1880's bands of Spanish and French Merino sheep were driven into the Southwest from California, furnishing a fine, short-staple wool in sharp contrast to the coarse, long wool of the Navajo sheep. Transhumance was practiced: in Arizona the cool northern mountains were used from May until August; then the flocks were moved to the lower desert ranges. Late spring found them once more among the mountain pastures. [7]

[6] Dale L. Morgan, *The Humboldt* (New York: Farrar & Rinehart, Inc., 1948).

[7] Transhumance today is carried on more extensively in the Great Basin than elsewhere in the Intermontane Region.

In Utah the self-sufficing Mormons raised sheep for homespun, and as early as the 1850's nearly every farmer possessed a few head.

Most parts of the range in this enormous region were overgrazed. The situation in Utah was typical: after only 35 years of use, the best pasture grounds showed scarcely a trace of the originally abundant grass and browse. By 1880 every locality west of the Wasatch Mountains showed the effects of overgrazing.

Errors Made in Settling Arid America

The Spaniards who settled in this region —one not fundamentally different from their Meseta—knew how to cope with its problems, and, as a result, Spanish colonization was successful. The Anglo-Saxons, on the other hand, encountered a distinctly new type of habitat, for they came from lands of ample rainfall. Even the federal government blundered, its laws having been framed for humid and not for arid and semiarid land; accordingly the Homestead Act's gift of 160 acres, adequate for the humid East, was inadequate for the arid region. Says Paul Sears:

> . . . a family might starve to death in the grazing country on a farm of one square mile, while a quarter or even an eighth of that would mean comparative comfort in the beautiful valley of Virginia.[8]

Only after the pioneer, through trial and error, had learned certain lessons, did the government act wisely and change the size of the Homestead unit from 160 to 320 acres. But this amount was inadequate for stock farming in the arid West. Investigators estimated that a family could support itself on 640 acres. Accordingly, after considerable agitation on the part of congressmen from the western states, the Stock-Raising Homestead Act was passed in 1916 allowing a family 640 acres.

Since nearly one-quarter of the area of continental United States is arid or semi-arid, it is obvious that greater knowledge of the region under consideration is needed. As a means of helping prospective settlers choose land more wisely, the Geological Survey and the Department of Agriculture are today classifying lands on the basis of their suitability for grazing, mineral production, crop production (with or without irrigation), or uselessness. That close settlement was pushed well beyond safe limits is proved by the hundreds of abandoned homesteaders' shacks. The history behind nearly every one is the same; land was offered for sale at low cost to people who never had lived in a dry region and hence knew nothing of its problems. Time and again people settled where they could not possibly make a living. In many instances they tried to grow crops totally unsuited to the climate. These people were not to blame so much as their government, which should have determined the true character of the land preceding settlement. It is significant that in 1878 Major John W. Powell, in reporting to Congress, pointed out that, for parts of the West, there was need for a special land policy that would allot 2,500 acres to each family.

Nowhere in the world was land in such enormous tracts acquired so rapidly.

> Almost over night, as history is reckoned, the white man moved into the territory that had been 'forever' reserved for the Indian, crossed the country that had been labeled 'impassable,' grazed, plowed, and settled the land that was 'uninhabitable' and on it built himself a thriving civilization. Within a few generations it was all over. The frontier was pronounced closed; the Wild West was domesticated.[9]

[8] Paul B. Sears, *Deserts on the March* (Norman: University of Oklahoma Press, 1935), p. 208.

[9] Harold McCracken, *Portrait of the Old West* (New York: McGraw-Hill, 1952).

352

Thus, within a century after the formation of the United States government, the Director of the Census announced that there was no longer a frontier. Accordingly, in 1935 the Homestead Policy, which really had long been obsolete, was brought to an end.

Population

What population there is in the Intermontane West congregates mostly in "islands" where (1) precipitation is adequate, (2) water is available for irrigation farming, (3) ore deposits permit commercial mining, or (4) transportation routes converge. In the entire region only six urban centers have 100,000 or more inhabitants: Salt Lake City, Spokane, El Paso, Phoenix, Tucson, and Albuquerque. The principal nonurban population concentrations are in the lower Salt River Valley in Arizona, the Imperial Valley of southernmost California, along the western Wasatch piedmont in Utah, at various places along the Snake River in Idaho, along the middle Columbia Valley in central Washington, and around the shores of Lake Okanagan in British Columbia.

This is a region of considerable population movement—migration into, out of, within, and across. And in recent years the rate of population growth has been very rapid. More than 1,000,000 inhabitants were added to the regional total between 1950 and 1960. Nevada's population gained 78 per cent and Arizona's 75 per cent during that decade.

The population includes several significant ethnic and religious elements.

(1) A large proportion of the population is of Mexican-American ancestry and Roman Catholic religion in the Basin-and-Range Subregion of Texas, New Mexico, Arizona, and southern California.

(2) Indians form a significant element of the population in Arizona, New Mexico, southwestern Colorado, central Oregon,

western Washington, and the Fraser and Skeena valleys in British Columbia.

(3) Negroes comprise a small but significant minority element in the population of southern Arizona and southeastern California.

(4) Utah is still predominantly Mormon, as are parts of southern Idaho, northern Arizona, and eastern Nevada.

Agriculture

Though agriculture is the dominant economic enterprise throughout the greater part of this region, only a fraction (three per cent in Utah, for example) of the total land area is in farms and of this, little is actually in crops. Moreover, this picture will not change greatly in the future on account of (1) aridity, (2) alkaline, rocky or poorly drained soils, (3) rugged terrain, and (4) remoteness from efficient and cheap transportation and from large markets. Submarginal areas where the rainfall is most unreliable, the soil poorest, the surface roughest, and land most remote from railroads are better suited for grazing than for growing grain and other crops, since animals can be walked to market or to a railway.

Dry Farming Dry farming is the growing of crops with water-conserving methods; it should be called "water-conservation farming." Usually only a single crop is grown in two years, the crop being alternated with summer fallow. In the Palouse, many farmers fallow only one year in three. Fallowing is one of man's devices for conserving moisture by eliminating weeds and retarding evaporation.

This method of farming was carried on by aborigines before 1000 A. D. in the Mesa Verde, San Juan country, and west of the Little Colorado River.

The first Anglo-Saxons in Anglo-America to practice dry farming were the Mormons. In 1863 a company of Danish Mormons left

Salt Lake City and founded Bear River City, some miles to the north, where they utilized the water of the Malade River to irrigate their fields. After repeated experiments, they became convinced that something was wrong with the water they were using (it contained too much salt), since their seed did not germinate. As the season was well advanced, they were desperate, and accordingly plowed up some sagebrush land on the bench above the ditch, planted grain, and awaited results. They obtained fair yields, which indicated that dry farming with an alternate fallow year could succeed.

The proportion of the region actually being dry-farmed is small indeed. That the area is so small is significant. Dry farming is highly uncertain, except in the Palouse, because the Intermontane Basins and Plateaus frequently have years of drought followed by periods when the precipitation is well above average. With more rainfall, dry-land crop production flourishes and is accordingly pushed farther into the more arid sections; then in the following period of less rainfall, the farmers blame the drop in production of these expanded areas on the lack of rainfall instead of on their poor judgment.

The Columbia Intermontane Area, [10] the White Wheat Belt, is one of the most noted dry-farming areas on the continent and is a major world wheat region. Most of the crop is dry-farmed, though along the eastern margin some is grown by customary farm methods. At any one time, about half the cultivated land is in fallow and wheat constitutes essentially the only crop in areas of less than 18 inches annual precipitation. In the moister parts, peas, barley, oats, clovers, alfalfa, and grass may be grown in

rotation with wheat. Thus the area is almost a one-crop region, and the yield per acre and the price per bushel for a given year are vital regional indexes of prosperity.

Large "ranches" (as the farms are called locally) and small population encourage the employment of machinery—tractors, gang plows, disks, weeders, and combines. By utilizing large power units, one man does the work of three.

Both spring and winter wheat are grown in this area—each in the part whose natural endowment is best suited to it. Some spring wheat, however, is grown in the winter wheat area when a dry autumn has prevented the germination of winter wheat or when snowfall is so light and winter temperatures so low as to have killed the planting of the winter variety. As in other parts of the United States, spring wheat is rapidly being displaced by winter wheat in the area as a whole.

The most popular wheats are the white varieties (both common and club). These have strong stiff straw, are resistant to lodging, have firm tough heads, and do not shell even in dry windy weather. These qualities enable harvesting to extend over a long period, and are extremely important where labor is scarce.

Most wheat produced in the Columbia Intermontane Area is soft and starchy and under modern baking practices is not well suited for bread making, so is mostly used for pastry flour.

A crop that has become extremely important since 1929, when seed was first planted in the foothills of the Blue Mountain area of eastern Oregon and Washington, is peas. In this former checkerboard area of wheat fields and summer fallow, peas now occupy considerable land on slopes of the Blue Mountains between 1,400 and 3,400 feet in elevation. The 2,000-foot variation in altitude permits a long planting season and a long harvesting season. The

[10] This discussion of wheat deals with but a small part of the Columbia Intermontane Area—the Palouse and Big Bend of Washington and north-central Oregon.

rainfall varies from 17 to 20 inches. Frost is a threat but only locally, the effect being spotty; some valleys may escape, whereas others may have fields that suffer heavy damage.

This crop uses less moisture than does wheat and, being a legume, puts nitrogen into the soil. The farmer replows and sows wheat for the alternate season as soon as the pea crop is harvested.

The pea grower must race against time: overexposure to heat and dust, for example, results in reduced moisture in the peas and affects adversely color, flavor, and texture. Hence, during the pea pack, both field crews and packing plants operate around the clock. Since the area is but sparsely populated, labor is somewhat of a problem. Accordingly, mechanization has been adopted wherever possible. Peas are grown primarily for processing.

Unlike the Blue Mountain district, which concentrates on green peas, the Palouse district raises dry peas. Peas fit in as an alternate crop with wheat instead of leaving the land in fallow. The area has highly favorable physical conditions for the crop— cool temperatures and adequate rainfall. And the same equipment is used as for wheat. Production of the crop is mostly concentrated in the eastern edge of the Palouse counties. This area is now the most important dry-pea area in the United States.

There are no other major areas of dryland farming in the region. Scattered patches of dryland wheat are found in Idaho, Oregon, Washington, and southern British Columbia. Dry beans are raised without irrigation in central New Mexico, southwestern Colorado, and southeastern Utah where there is sufficient summer rain.

Irrigation Farming The importance of irrigation farming to the Indians and Spaniards has been pointed out. The Mormons in Utah were the first Anglo-Saxons to practice it on a large scale on this continent

and by this means transformed an inhospitable desert into a productive oasis. Since 1847, when the first pioneers entered Salt Lake Valley, irrigation has been practiced wherever water was available. In the dry lands it is the water of the stream rather than the land itself that has value; hence he who controls the water controls the land.

Since irrigation is restricted to the smoother, less sloping terraces and to alluvial belts along rivers, and since the total amount of water is definitely limited, it is obvious that most of the Intermontane Basins and Plateaus—probably more than 95 per cent—can never be irrigated. Even so, there are now more than 9,000,000 acres under irrigation in the region. Nearly 2,500,000 acres are irrigated in Idaho, and more than 1,000,000 acres each in Arizona, Utah, Washington, and the Intermontane portion of California.

THE SILTING OF RESERVOIRS Farming and grazing on slopes have resulted in soil erosion, which has skimmed off much topsoil from an extensive area. Much of this silt has been transported into reservoirs which were built to store water for irrigation. Without these reservoirs only a pastoral civilization could be supported. Yet today the majority of the irrigation reservoirs below an altitude of 7,000 feet are in jeopardy of becoming silted up. [11] Since mechanical removal of silt costs 5 to 50 times as much as the original reservoir, the cost is too great to justify taking the mud out and letting the reservoir fill up again. This is a significant argument for fighting soil erosion throughout the West.

[11] An exception to this generalization is at Franklin D. Roosevelt Lake, behind Grand Coulee Dam, where silt is not a serious problem because most of the inflow is from glacial and snow water. In a check made above the dam in a sheltered spot after a 10-year period, the dried deposit was only $\frac{3}{16}$ inch deep. At this rate, more than 7,000 years would be required to fill the reservoir with silt.

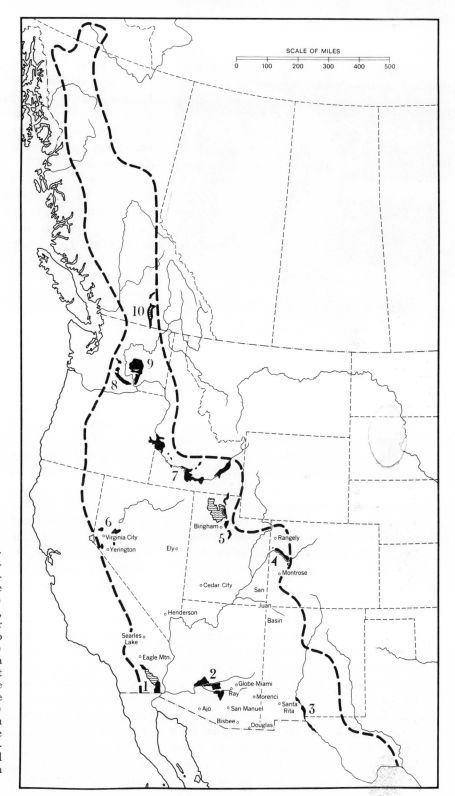

Figure 13-7. Major irrigated areas and mining towns in the Intermontane Region. The irrigated areas are: (1) the Imperial Valley, (2) the Salt River Valley, (3) the Rio Grande Project, (4) Colorado's "Western Slope," (5) the Salt Lake Oasis, (6) the Reno Oasis, (7) the Snake River Plain, (8) the Columbia Plateau Apple Valleys, (9) the Columbia Basin Reclamation Project, and (10) the Okanagan Valley.

SCALE OF MILES

0   100   200   300   400   500

Virginia City
Yerington
Ely
Bingham
Rangely
Montrose
Cedar City
San
Juan
Basin
Henderson
Searles
Lake
Eagle Mtn.
Globe-Miami
Ray
Morenci
Ajo
San Manuel
Santa
Rita
Bisbee
Douglas

Figure 13-8. Hoover Dam and the lower end of Lake Mead. (Photo courtesy Nevada State Highway Department.)

OASES   The principal irrigated areas are: (1) the Imperial Valley, (2) the Salt River Valley, (3) the Rio Grande Project, (4) Colorado's "Western Slope," (5) the Salt Lake Oasis, (6) the Reno Oasis, (7) the Snake River Plain, (8) the Columbia Plateau Apple Valleys (Yakima and Wenatchee), (9) the Columbia Basin Reclamation Project (Grand Coulee), and (10) the Okanagan Valley (Figure 13-7).

THE IMPERIAL VALLEY   From an economic standpoint the Imperial Valley, whose frost-free season is one of the longest in the United States, varying from 303 to 323 days, has a bright future. It occupies the cultivable part of the Salton Basin, and first attracted settlement more than a half century ago.

The Inter-California Canal was built down the slope of the delta through a part of northern Mexico toward the Salton Sea; but the river during a flood at the turn of the century cut around a head gate of the canal, enlarged the channel, and doubled the area of the Salton Sea. Imperial Valley farmers lived in fear from then until 1935, when the Hoover Dam was completed. This dam, one of the highest in the world, has formed behind it an artificial reservoir, Lake Mead (Figure 13-8). Water from the lake passes into the Colorado River. Some is drawn off at Imperial Dam, where it passes through desilting works; then it is carried to the valley through the All-American Canal. The All-American Canal was built to increase the irrigable area of the Imperial Valley. Some 80 miles long, it was constructed across the most forbidding part of the Great American Desert so that it would lie entirely within United States territory. It carries Colorado River water from 20 miles north of Yuma through sand dunes and across a desertic high tableland to the Valley. Drainage and salinity are ever present and are serious problems in the irrigated areas.

Most of the crops, with the exception of alfalfa, have a high value per acre and compensate for the high cost of water. Particularly important are the many early truck crops—carrots, lettuce, cabbage, cantaloupes, tomatoes, and peas. Vegetable growing is reputed to be more highly mechanized here than in any other area in the world. In recent years flax has ranked among the first two or three crops. Another leading money crop is the crisp head lettuce, which dominates the American market during the winter. Sugar beets and cotton also are important. Despite its type of climate, Imperial County leads all other California counties in the production of sugar beets. With a natural environment much like that of the Nile Delta, the Imperial Valley produces high-grade long-staple cotton. Alfalfa, which yields ten tons per acre and five to seven cuttings in a single year, is fed to livestock, and is shipped out in the concentrated form of dairy products and fat cattle and sheep.

Herefords and Brahman cattle are now being crossbred in an effort to get animals better able to withstand the midsummer heat. The sheep are range animals brought here specifically to be fattened. The Imperial Valley has one of the West's most important livestock-feeding industries.

Where water is to be had in sufficient amounts, two or more crops are grown on the same fields during the year—which is not common in the United States. Migrant workers, both *braceros* and Mexican-Americans, are vital to successful harvests.

THE SALT RIVER VALLEY First of the major irrigation projects undertaken by the Bureau of Reclamation and one of the most economically successful in Anglo-America is that in the Salt River Valley. Twentieth-century engineers have built near the inner margin of the desert of south-central Arizona the large Roosevelt Dam, which has converted the upper valley into Roosevelt Lake and has turned the lower valley into a great producer of citrus fruits, truck crops, alfalfa, and cotton. The site chosen was the narrow canyon of the Salt River just below the junction with Tonto Creek about 75 miles east of Phoenix. Behind the dam is impounded enough water to irrigate the fields for two years even if not a drop of rain should fall. Five additional dams have been constructed for providing storage and for the development of power.

The valley, physiographically considered, is not a valley but a detrital plain—very flat and with sediments many hundreds of feet deep.

Centuries before white men arrived, Indians had farmed this area. According to archeologists they settled in the valley very early in the A. D. era, reached their peak in 1200, and disappeared about 1400. It is believed they abandoned this area because the soil became water-logged and, lacking

pumps, they could no longer grow crops. So admirably planned and executed were some of their works that they would do credit to modern engineering. Since then the problem of wet land has been solved, the ground-water level being controlled by pumps.

Probably the main reason for the success of the Salt River Project is the long frostless season; 60 per cent of the land grows winter crops. Though agriculture is both intensive and diversified, a permanent system of farming has not yet evolved. At first alfalfa and dairying predominated; then Egyptian cotton became the leading crop as a result of high prices for long-staple cotton during the first World War. At present alfalfa occupies about half the cultivated area, though cotton, now short-staple or middling, remains important. Oranges and grapefruit are grown in large quantities, and safflower is becoming a very popular crop. In addition, the Phoenix area has become one of the outstanding cattle feedlot centers west of the Corn Belt.

Short-staple cotton is the chief cash crop. It is grown under irrigation on relatively large properties. Costs are high (Arizona has the highest cost irrigation of any state), but so are yields. The average farmer can expect to spend between $125 and $150 per acre to grow his crop, and picking costs must be added to that. The average yield is about 3 bales to the acre (sometimes as high as 5), and the bales can be sold for about $150 each. More than half of the crop is normally picked by machines; the remainder by migrant workers who visit the area each year.

An infestation of pink bollworm has caused some distress in the area in recent years, but the outstanding problem is water. Only a portion of the irrigation water comes from stream storage and diversion; more than half of Arizona's irrigation water is obtained from wells. And increased pumping has caused the water table to drop alarmingly. No other state utilizes such deep wells, on the average, as Arizona, and each year new wells must be drilled deeper. In some localities the water table is several hundred feet below the surface, and pumping is no longer feasible.

THE RIO GRANDE PROJECT The Middle Rio Grande Valley, above and below El Paso, constitutes one of the oldest irrigated areas on the continent, having been developed by pre-Columbian Indians. Three centuries of Spanish dominance did not materially change the systems nor extend the area "under the ditch." When the land became a part of the United States, some improvements were made by private capital. Since the federal government did not own any land in the area, it was not interested in development, even after the passage of the Reclamation Act in 1902. More and more water was diverted from the Rio Grande, and it became a dry stream immediately below El Paso. As a result, a considerable part of the total irrigated area—the Juarez Valley—was rapidly reverting to desert, and the Mexican government threatened suit unless their lands were provided with water and again made irrigable. After considerable negotiation, Elephant Butte Dam in southern New Mexico was constructed and a treaty signed guaranteeing the Juarez Valley 60,000 acre-feet of water a year delivered to the head of the International Diversion Canal. The Rio Grande Project then developed rapidly under federal auspices. Today it contains some 175,000 acres. At first it produced fruits and alfalfa almost exclusively, but its major crop now is long-staple cotton.

COLORADO'S WESTERN SLOPE In west central Colorado there are several major irrigated areas that utilize water flowing westward from the Rocky Mountains in such rivers as the Colorado and the Gunnison. Most notable is the Grand Valley

project near Grand Junction. Many different field crops, such as corn, small grains, alfalfa, sugar beets, potatoes, and vegetables, are grown; but the area's reputation is based on its fruit crop—primarily peaches, but also other orchard fruits and grapes. Intensive feeding of cattle and sheep is also common.

SALT LAKE OASIS Utah is of special interest to the geographer, for nowhere on the continent is there a closer adaptation of agriculture and its institutions to nature.

The Valley of the Great Salt Lake, one of the most favored spots in the entire West, was settled by the Mormon Church, which claimed a vast territory extending from the Sierra Nevada to the Rockies and from Oregon to Southern California. Settlement of much of it began immediately after hundreds of land-hungry immigrants from the East and even from Europe arrived. Brigham Young carefully picked leaders and families and sent them to definite locations; by means of these outpost colonies, based on irrigation farming, he systematically colonized Utah.

The area occupied by the Oasis in 1963 virtually coincides with that occupied in 1857 (10 years after the arrival of the Mormon pioneers), which indicates that land suitable for habitation was rapidly acquired. Some irrigated areas have been added as a result of surface water brought from outside the watershed and to a lesser extent from ground water. For the most part these have not changed the map of irrigated land very much.

The lofty Wasatch Mountains tower above the Oasis on the east; from their snow-clad slopes comes the life-giving water for the valleys below. The greater part of Utah is rugged. Hence the levelness of the area at the foot of the Wasatch and the depth of its fertile soils are additional reasons for the virtual restriction of settlement in Utah to the Salt Lake Oasis. As

Egypt is primarily the Nile Valley and Delta rather than the large political block portrayed on the map, so Utah is really but an insular strip of human habitation at the foot of the Wasatch. This, the heart of Utah, contains about three-fourths of the state's inhabitants.

At the mouth of almost every stream canyon, as it emerges from the Wasatch, is located a city or village girdled by green fields and adorned by orchards and shade trees. Each town is separated from its neighbors by five to ten miles of field, orchard, or pasture. Both north and south of the Oasis, where there is less water, the towns and irrigated farms lie at greater intervals.

Small holdings, cultivated thoroughly, prevail—a result of scarcity of arable land, a limited supply of water for irrigation, the early Mormon land system, and dense population. Here the birth rate is high—a consequence of high fertility and approval by the Mormon Church of early marriage and large families. In the decade 1950-60, Utah's average birth rate of 32 per 1,000 was 30 per cent higher than that of the nation as a whole.

Possibly 90 per cent of the farmers dwell in towns—the Church, the desert, and the canyon stream conspiring to produce this village concentration. Each town has its church and school buildings, its public hall and stores; each is compact and self-sufficient. Farms lie one to five miles from towns.

Crops are so diversified that farms resemble gardens, yet three-fourths of the cropped land is devoted to sugar beets, wheat, and hay (primarily alfalfa), the remaining one-fourth being devoted to fruits and vegetables. Most farmers concentrate on those products which give a high return per acre and can be sold locally. If distant markets are sought, products that can travel in concentrated form are grown, to reduce transport costs. Much farm land is in pasture, and dairying is outstanding. Milk is trucked from Salt Lake City to Colorado and even to California.

The water-logged land near Utah Lake is pastured by dairy cattle, and the alkaline soils near Great Salt Lake are grazed occasionally in winter by sheep if drinking water or snow is present for them. On the higher portions of the old lake plain and on the coarse soils of the benches are grown the irrigated crops (Figure 13-9). Most orchards occupy bench lands, since trees do well on coarse soils and benefit from air drainage. On lands above the ditch, con-

Figure 13-9. Intensive farming in a portion of the Salt Lake Oasis. Water from streams emerging from the Wasatch Mountains sustains hundreds of small farms. The light-colored material in the left foreground is a mud flow brought down from a canyon during a heavy rain. (Photo courtesy U.S. Forest Service.)

siderable winter wheat is dry-farmed. Such areas, however, are merely adjuncts of irrigated farms, and are largely devoid of dwellings and trees. There is an increasing drainage problem resulting from seepage of water into the low-lying farm lands.

THE RENO OASIS   On the west side of the Great Basin at the foot of the Sierra Nevada lies a beautiful and productive oasis fed by streams from melting snow. It is separated from the Salt Lake Oasis at the eastern end of the basin by hundreds of miles of desert. The most fruitful part of the Reno Oasis, the Truckee Meadows, is sustained by waters of the Truckee River. Here is a checkerboard composed of hundreds of small farms on which are grown alfalfa, wheat, and vegetables. Dairying too is important. The largest project, the Newlands, was created by the United States Bureau of Reclamation.

The greater part of the irrigable land, and, therefore, of the agriculture of Nevada, is confined to the valleys of the Humboldt, Truckee, Carson, and Walker rivers. Yet all this in the aggregate comprises less than one per cent of the area of the state. Elsewhere agricultural enterprises consist almost exclusively of grazing.

THE SNAKE RIVER PLAIN   Another important oasis in this region is the Snake River Plain. In many ways it is more productive agriculturally than the entire state of Utah. Nevertheless it is tributary to Salt Lake City. As compared with the Salt Lake Oasis, it lacks the productive nearby mines and possesses little focal quality with respect to transportation. It supports more than one-half the population of Idaho. Into this area from the Grand Tetons come two forks of the Snake River, pouring their waters through head gates into canals. The irri-

Figure 13-10. Distribution of Irish potato growing in the United States. The five principal producing areas are the Snake River Plain, the Red River Valley, the "eastern shore" of Virginia, Long Island, and the Aroostook Valley.

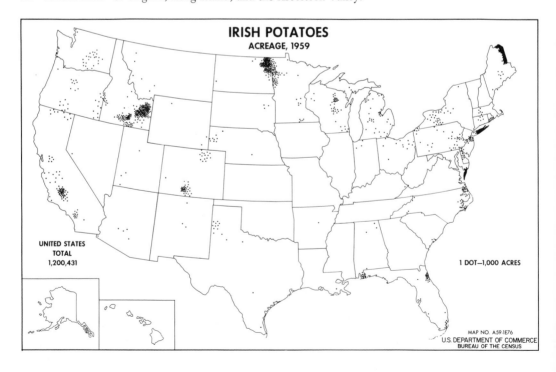

gable land totals more than 2,200,000 acres. The chief crops are alfalfa and other feed crops, potatoes, sugar beets, dry beans, and wheat. Idaho normally vies with Maine as the leading grower of potatoes (Figure 13-10) and ranks behind California and Colorado in sugar-beet production. Vegetables and fruit are important also—particularly near Ontario and Payette.

Some sheep and dairy cattle are raised, the sheep being grazed in the national forests in summer and on the plain in spring and autumn. They are fed in oases in winter. Large numbers of lambs are fattened for market.

Most of the products when converted into a concentrated form have high value, a necessity in an area located far from large consuming markets. A notable exception is the potato, a product that is both perishable and relatively inexpensive. Because of its superiority to all other Anglo-American potatoes for baking, the Idaho potato (grown from St. Anthony to Boise and Nampa) is in demand almost everywhere in the United States.

COLUMBIA PLATEAU APPLE VALLEYS In the rain shadow of the Cascade Mountains lies a series of disconnected oases—Anglo-America's most famous apple-growing area —the Yakima, Hood River, Wenatchee, and Okanogan valleys. Most of the irrigated land is in fruit, chiefly apples. Other important crops are alfalfa, asparagus, dry beans, grapes, hops, peppermint, potatoes, sugar beets, and vegetables, as well as soft fruits.

The Yakima Valley ranks high in agriculture in the state of Washington, in the Intermontane Region and nationally. A quality product, national advertising, and national and international markets are responsible. Yet this prestige has been attained solely by irrigation from the Yakima River and its tributaries, which are in a region receiving only 7.5 inches of precipitation per year, less than one-third of which falls during the growing season.

In the public mind, Yakima and fruit are synonymous, despite the great importance of open field crops. Most orchards are planted on slopes to benefit from air drainage. Apples occupy more land than any other fruit crop, though pears are very important. These two crops are grown mostly in the Upper Valley (upstream from Union Gap), a few miles southeast of the city of Yakima, and apricots, cherries, grapes, and peaches in the Lower Valley (downstream from Union Gap). There is less land favored by air drainage in the Lower Valley so that field crops are important—row crops (asparagus, corn, hops, peppermint, potatoes, and sugar beets), alfalfa, and small grains. The animal industries, involving cattle and sheep, also have attained prominence in recent years. Many bands of sheep are grazed in the Cascade Mountains in summer and fed during winter in the valley. Much hay and grain and pasture are available.

The Wenatchee Valley, which is typical of all apple-growing districts in this region, extends from the Columbia River to Leavenworth, a distance of about 22 miles. The part used for fruit varies from one to two miles in width but increases to six miles along the Columbia River at the city of Wenatchee.

The climate is highly favorable for apples: below zero temperatures are rare; the growing season approximates 200 days (apples need close to 150 frost-free days); and the high percentage of sunshine gives the fruit an attractive color. Most of the trees are grown on slopes to benefit from air drainage. Surveys made by the United States Weather Bureau show that on a frosty morning the temperature is sometimes 30 degrees higher 50 feet up a slope than at the base. The precipitation is both inadequate and badly distributed for tree growth without irrigation. The soils, while extremely varied, generally contain adequate nutriment, except nitrogen, for which deficiency alfalfa is grown. Most of the farms are small, 10 to 15 acres, and are operated by owners.

THE COLUMBIA BASIN RECLAMATION PROJECT (GRAND COULEE DAM) During the Ice Age the course of the Columbia River was obstructed by ice, forcing the river to cut a new channel in the State of Washington some 150 miles from the Canadian border. When the ice receded northward, the dam disappeared and the river resumed its former channel, leaving the old channel abandoned. It is now known as the Grand Coulee. The Columbia River Basin, a flat land of some two and one-half million acres, with rich volcanic soil in an arid and semiarid area, became important for wheat and livestock around the turn of the century. But a slight increase in rainfall made a

proportionately greater increase in yield, and after a year or two of good crops on marginal land farmers started to plow and plant even poorer land. Then followed a period of below normal precipitation and many farmers went broke.

In the winter of 1933–1934, the federal government began construction on the Grand Coulee Dam, one of the largest concrete dams in the world, aiming to create a new agricultural frontier and make irrigable some 1,200,000 acres of semiarid land in the Big Bend area of south-central Washington for the several hundred thousand "Okies," "Arkies," and others forced into migration by soil erosion. The Grand Coulee Dam was built on the Columbia River 92 miles west and north of Spokane and just below the head of the Grand Coulee (Figure 13-11). Here granite is exposed on both banks. Behind the dam lies Lake Roosevelt, a 151-mile-long storage reservoir, impounding

Figure 13-11. Grand Coulee Dam. A portion of the "Grand Coulee" itself is visible in the background. (Photo courtesy U.S. Bureau of Reclamation.)

Figure 13-12. Heavily-laden apple trees in the Okanagan Valley. The scene is near Osoyoos. (British Columbia Government Photograph.)

10,000,000 acre-feet of water—enough to supply New York City for ten years. More than 4,000 miles of main and secondary canals have been constructed. The irrigated area is actually about 50 miles from the Grand Coulee Dam. Although a wide variety of crops is grown—alfalfa, dry beans, onions, other vegetables, sugar beets, potatoes, and grapes—irrigation from the canals did not begin until 1952 and the agricultural pattern is still developing. The dam supplies water for irrigation agriculture and power for manufacturing, transportation, and domestic use.

THE OKANAGAN VALLEY One of Canada's most distinctive specialty crop areas occupies the long narrow trench of the Okanagan Valley. Extending for 125 miles north from the international border, the valley is only two or three miles wide except where it broadens a bit into tributary valleys in the north. Lakes occupy most of the valley floor, and farming is mostly limited to the adjacent terraces. Irrigation is necessary in the south, but general farming can be carried on under natural rainfall conditions in the north.

A variety of field crops, feed crops, and vegetables is grown, but fruit raising is the distinctive activity in the valley. The Osoyoos section in the south (Figure 13-12) is said to produce the earliest fruit in Canada. The Okanagan Valley, along with Ontario's Niagara Peninsula, is the only important grower of tender tree fruits in the country. Peaches, plums, pears, and apples are to be seen on heavily laden trees, whose limbs must be propped up with poles as harvest time approaches. Cantaloupes, berries, and grapes are grown also.

Grazing

In this region of rough terrain, light rainfall, sparse vegetation, and poor transportation, most of the land (if it is to be used at all) must serve as range for livestock (Figure 13-13). Probably not more than 3.5 per cent of the land between the Rockies and the Sierra Nevada-Cascades is in crops. Some of it cannot even serve as range; the ten-inch isohyet is said to separate grazing country from true desert. Disaster awaits him who settles in the latter. Grazing, however, is possible where the precipitation is less than ten inches providing the animals browse in winter when snow or rain occurs.

Ranches of 2,000 to 4,000 acres and more are usually necessary, for much of the land is so poor that 25, 50, and even 75 acres are needed to support one steer.

Obviously the pronounced differences in elevation cause differences in precipitation

363

Figure 13-13. A calf round-up on a cattle ranch in Nevada. The sagebrush country of the Intermontane Region is used primarily for grazing. (Photo courtesy Union Pacific Railroad.)

and in vegetation which, in turn, are reflected in the seasonal utilization of the range. Mountain pastures are strictly summer pastures; deserts are utilized mostly in winter when snowfall provides water for sheep and occasionally for cattle. Oasis pastures and feedlots are caring for more and more animals in winter (Figure 13-14).

The establishment of federal grazing districts by the enactment of the Taylor Grazing Act of 1933 had a significant effect on the pastoral pattern of the United States portion of the region. This legislation put an end to unrestricted grazing on the public domain, and has helped to stabilize the balance between forage resources and numbers of stock. Ranchers may lease portions of a grazing district for seasonal use. It is up to the Bureau of Land Management, the administering agency, to harmonize the carrying capacity of the range with the economic realities of the stockmen.

The interior plateaus of British Columbia comprise one of only two large areas of ranching in Canada. Stock raising has been carried on for more than a century here, and the ranching pattern is well established. Lowland ranches are the most favored and most common. They generally have sufficient bunch-grass range for spring and fall grazing. Summer grazing is usually on

leased Crown lands in the hills and mountains. Winter feeding is sometimes a problem, for putting up hay is the largest single item of expense in the ranching operation.

Sheep This region has been one of Anglo-America's leading sheep centers since 1893. Since sheep do well on rugged land and over a wide range of climatic conditions, their production has been especially successful in the sparsely populated arid West. Furthermore, they relish the shrubby and wheaty types of forage, which horses and cattle do not like.

After 1870 the sheep industry expanded rapidly in the West. In early days the only expense was for labor and supplies, the only investment in the animals themselves and in a camp outfit. Expansion continued until the range became overcrowded and overgrazed. Acquisition of land for dry farming also reduced numbers, for whenever dry farming enters an area, sheep give way to cattle.

Ranches handling sheep are nearly always located near streams or perennial waterholes. A man with a couple of dogs can manage and keep in good condition about 3,000 sheep. The herder is with his flocks constantly, directing grazing, preventing his sheep from straying, and protecting them against the depredations of wild animals.

364

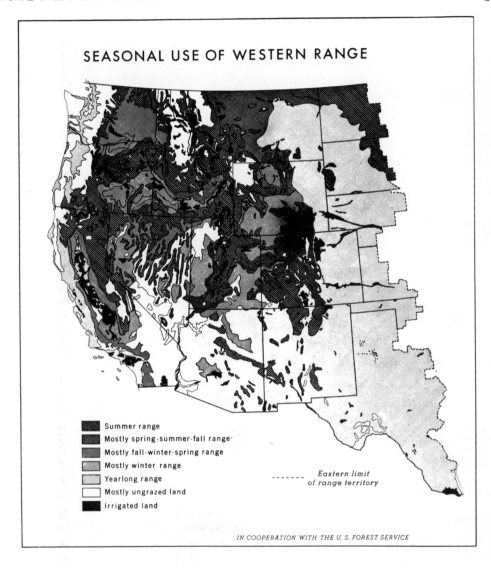

Figure 13-14. Seasonal use of western range land. The seasonal pattern is a complex one, but is based mostly on altitude and the availability of water. (Courtesy Agricultural Research Service, U.S. Department of Agriculture.)

He is aided by a camp tender who brings supplies and moves camp. Herding is a lonesome occupation, and before trucks became common, western states passed laws compelling herders to work in pairs. The sheep are raised for both wool and mutton, al-though emphasis is turning toward the latter.

Cattle Although beef cattle can graze on rough land and sparse vegetation, as a rule they are raised in areas of better forage. In summer they are driven into large areas of abundant grassland and abundant browse in the mountains. In winter they either are driven to valley ranches and fed on alfalfa, beet pulp, and grain or are shipped to California or the Corn Belt to be fattened. Historically, in the West more livestock have been raised than could be fattened on the feed produced, whereas in the East the reverse was true; hence the importance of stocker and feeder shipments from the West to the East. However, since 1925 a larger share of western marketings has been sent to western slaughterers. Phoenix, Ogden, and Salt Lake City have become important stockyard and slaughtering centers. This is true particularly of Ogden because of its location at the junction of major railroads. Thus the line of east-west movement (the boundary to which western packer-buyers must come from coastal points to purchase their slaughter livestock) has gradually moved eastward. The same trend holds for sheep and hogs.

Horses Outside the irrigated districts, this entire region is a land of the horse. In the Navajo Country, a family's wealth, prestige, and standing have depended on the number of horses owned. Horses are also significant on other Indian reservations, and continue to be useful on most ranches in the region.

Goats Angora and milk goats thrive in the high, dry lands of Arizona and New Mexico, where Indians run them with their sheep. Goats do well where cattle would starve.

Mining

From the Wasatch to the Sierra Nevada and from the Yukon to the Mexican border, the region is dotted with communities located solely to tap the mineral resources—communities that enjoy a mushroom growth so long as the mines produce, but decline precipitously and become ghost towns once the ores are worked out (Figure 13-15).

In several of the states, particularly Nevada, prospecting for minerals was the major factor in settlement and early development. Moreover, the total value of minerals mined during the history of the Intermontane Region still is said to be greater than that of any other single product of the region.

The first prospectors, mostly gold miners from California, sought only placers. Later, however, they worked vein outcrops. The Intermontane West is no longer the land of the lone prospector with his lowly burro,

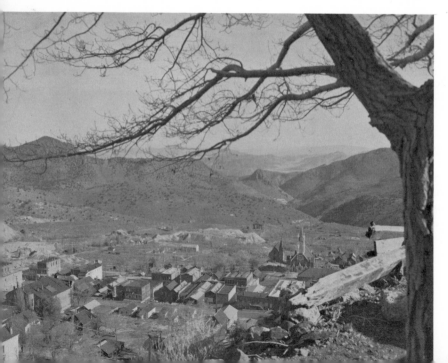

Figure 13-15. Virginia City, America's first big silver mining camp. Millions of dollars poured from the mines and the town boomed as few others have. At its height in 1880 Virginia City had a population of 10,917. Now it has less than 1,000. (Photo courtesy of *Dodge News*.)

Figure 13-16. The famous Utah Copper Company mine at Bingham. The operating area of this mine covers about 1,000 acres. There are nearly 200 miles of railroad track on the various levels. (Photo courtesy Salt Lake City Chamber of Commerce.)

pick and blankets, beans and bacon, searching for gold and silver. Rather is it the land of the large corporation taking great risks, investing fabulous sums of money, and employing eminent engineers and a large labor force. It is now concerned more with low-grade than with high-grade ores.

Copper mining is most important in this region, but its status of relatively recent date depended upon the revolutionary developments in the science of metallurgy. There was no question regarding the reserves. The big question was whether the ore could be moved profitably from mines to reduction plants. The operator had to make one of two choices—both necessarily bad—either (1) smelt almost the entire ore output, which means exorbitant fuel cost; or (2) discard so much of the low-grade material as to make the whole mining process unprofitable. The problem facing porphyry copper was almost identical with that facing taconite today. Porphyry copper was so named because it is finely dispersed in *porphyry*, a hard igneous rock. Today such ore can be successfully concentrated even when there is less than one ton of copper in each 100 tons of copper-bearing rock. This accomplishment has been one of the marvels of our time.

Major Districts in Utah There is a concentration of nonferrous mining near the Salt Lake Oasis. Location here is highly significant, for every mine, regardless of size, is near good transport facilities. A deposit of equal richness located in some parts of Nevada, however, might be held back permanently by high transport costs.

BINGHAM, lying in a canyon of the same name in a low Basin Range about 30 miles southwest of Salt Lake City, is one of the world's best-known and most profitable mining ventures. Historically, it is important because the first mining claim in the state of Utah was staked out there in 1863. Though several mines working copper, lead, silver, and zinc are located in Bingham, the most famous and most profitable is that of the Utah Copper Company. There the great electric shovels are tearing down an enormous mountain (1,400 feet high) of low-grade ore, about one per cent metallic copper. The mountain is girdled with levels of terraces, tracked, and completely electrified (Figure 13-16). Laden ore-cars are delivered to the mountain base, made into trains, transported to concentration mills, and later to the Garfield smelter. Copper is also mined in Bingham by the leaching and precipitation process.

Although the Mormons discovered and worked iron ore near Cedar City more than a century ago, accurate information regarding the reserves and distribution was unavailable until quite recently. World War II stimulated intensive research on this mineral. Iron ore is widely distributed throughout the West—much more so than coking coal. Each state in this region has sizable reserves with relatively high iron content, but the major deposits of the entire Intermontane Basins and Plateaus Region are west of *Cedar City* in Iron County. Eight mines yield essentially all of Utah's crude iron ore. It is shipped to steel plants in Utah, California, and Colorado.

Uranium is produced widely in Utah (the leading producing state), but the vast majority of all output is from several hundred small and medium-sized mines in *San Juan County*. The frantic boom of the 1950's has subsided, and the prosperity of this industry will depend upon needs of the federal government, which are currently oversupplied.

Some Mining Communities in Nevada In 1859 silver was discovered in Nevada, a state differing from others in the West in that its economic life and very existence have been derived from mining. From 1875 to 1877, Nevada produced more gold and silver than all the rest of the United States combined. Near the western border of the desert lies *Virginia City*, formerly the greatest silver-mining camp of all time and a rip-roaring prodigy of the wildest days of the West. The industry has now declined, and Virginia City owes its continued existence to the tourist business.

The Ely district, lying in eastern Nevada in the heart of the parched Great Basin, is the principal copper-mining area of Nevada. Its porphyry ores are very much like those at Bingham, the copper being disseminated in veins so small that crushing fails to separate the metal from the gangue. The

mineralized zone is about nine miles long and one-half mile to one and one-half miles wide, the ore being found in the igneous rocks which break through the sedimentaries. Mining began with the discovery of gold and silver-lead ores in 1868-1869.

The mines lie 140 miles south of Cobre on the Southern Pacific Railroad to which they are connected by the Nevada Northern Railway. The unproductive desert in the intervening land exerts a tremendous charge against the mines. This is in marked contrast to the situation at Bingham, which is close to the productive agricultural lands of the Salt Lake Oasis and hence benefits from transportation built and supported largely by farming.

Other important mining operations presently active in Nevada are at Yerington and near Henderson. There is a large open-pit copper mine at *Yerington*. Northeast of *Henderson* is an open-pit mine that is the principal domestic source of manganese for the United States.

Some Arizona Mining Districts The mines of Arizona furnish the bulk of the state's railway tonnage and support a large proportion of the state's population, which is thus the chief market for most of the state's farm products. Moreover, Arizona is the first state in copper production, yielding about half of the national total.

Since 1858 these mines have produced in excess of three billion dollars in metals, approximately 87 per cent of which was copper. Some of this copper is rich ore, though there is also much of the lower-grade type. As elsewhere in the region, copper mining requires heavy capital investments. Arizona prospers and suffers according to the price of copper. The exploitation of gigantic supplies in Chile, Peru, the Congo, Rhodesia, and Canada results in the periodic closing down of high-cost producing mines in Arizona. The critically short domestic copper output during the early years of the defense mobilization program witnessed the birth of many mines and the reopening of others which could not possibly operate during so-called "normal times."

Morenci, in the eastern part of the state, is the home of Arizona's largest copper mine. A low-grade ore body, it had been known for a long time but could not be worked profitably until the advent of modern technology. Now it is the second largest copper producer in the United States, annually yielding about half as much ore as the famous mine at Bingham, Utah. Open-pit mining is followed, gigantic electric shovels removing the ore and dumping it into trucks and trains.

The *Globe-Miami* district consists of a complex agglomeration of three large mines, a major waste dump water-leaching operation, and several types of concentrating and smelting works. Both shaft and open-pit mines are in operation. This is the fourth most prolific copper mining district in the nation (following Bingham, Morenci, and Butte).

Just across the Santa Catalina Mountains from Tucson is the recently developed *San Manuel* copper district. It consists of a large mine, a concentrator, a smelter, and a company town.

Bisbee, located in the steepest part of Mule Pass Gulch, is the center of one of the continent's richer copper-producing districts. It is located on the Southern Pacific Lines, which dominate rail transportation in the southern part of the region. Its ore is richer than that at Morenci. Mining is the sole support of Bisbee, whose history is the history of its mines. About 1900 the city boomed, and though output rose and fell with the demand for copper, the district has been one of the nation's leading metal producers for more than 80 years. There is a large underground mine and a smaller open-pit operation. The concentrated ore is processed nearby at the huge smelter in Douglas.

The town of Bisbee is unique, houses clinging to the slopes tier above tier.

Other major copper producers in Arizona include open-pit mines at *Ajo* and *Ray*.

Almost all of the copper operations also yield significant quantities of other metals, especially gold, silver, and molybdenum.

Much of the processing of Arizona ore is done within the state. Each major mine has a concentrator nearby. The concentrate is smelted at Hayden, Douglas, Morenci, Ajo, Miami, and Superior, and it is refined electrolytically at Inspiration, El Paso, and five coastal locations between New York and Baltimore.

Other Major Nonfuel Mining Districts
A variety of minerals is mined at many different localities in the Intermontane Region, but only a few others are of major significance.

At *Santa Rita* is produced most of New Mexico's copper from an open pit that also yields molybdenum, gold, and silver.

The second most important iron district in the West is at *Eagle Mountain* in California's Mohave Desert. Most of the ore dug from the open-pit mine goes to the Kaiser steel mill in nearby Fontana.

Several places in the Intermontane deserts yield salts of one kind or another, but the principal production locality is at *Searles Lake* in California's San Bernardino County. The lake is a remnant of an inland sea, and has a salt deposit 12 square miles in size containing a crystal mass whose surface is firm and compact. Brine is pumped from wells sunk in the lake, and surface deposits are also scraped off. Two chemical plants at opposite ends of the lake accomplish the primary processing. Many products result, but most important are boron, bromine, and potash.

Colorado vies with Utah as the leading domestic producer of uranium. Mining takes place in many localities in the western part of the state, but *Montrose County* yields about half of the total output, from more than 250 mines.

Mineral Fuels

COAL. Fortunately this region is well endowed with coal. Among the states included, Utah ranks first in reserves, in production, and in the importance of coal in a state's total economy. The coal is bituminous and subbituminous, though only the former is mined. The 46 underground mines yield 5 or 6 million tons annually, enough to give Utah first ranking among western states, although only tenth in the nation as a whole. Most of the output is from two counties, Carbon and Emery. This product has the highest heating value of any coal in the West, and is used to make coke for all the blast furnaces west of the Rockies.

PETROLEUM. Although the map of oil lands in this region is expanding, and although the amount of drilling is increasing, the Intermontane Region is but a minor producer, contributing less than five per cent of the national output. Principal production comes from the *Rangely* field in northwestern Colorado and the *San Juan Basin* in southeastern Utah and northwestern New Mexico. The latter area has experienced remarkable development in the last half decade, with pipelines to Los Angeles and Gulf Coast refineries providing excellent market outlets.

OIL SHALE. Some day oil shale will serve as a great source of petroleum. It is widely scattered over that part of the region in Utah south of the Uinta Mountains, in adjacent west-central Colorado, and southern Wyoming (partly outside the Intermontane Region). Actually these shales contain not petroleum but kerogen, which can be converted to crude oil by heating. At present, it costs more to distill a gallon of gasoline from shale than to refine or polymerize it from crude oil. However, continuing research will doubtless make it possible to utilize the oil shales in the future.

Development of Surface Water Resources

There are four major river systems in the Intermontane Region—the Rio Grande, the Fraser, the Columbia, and the Colorado. The latter two are involved in major development schemes, while the others have experienced relatively little dam-building in their courses through this region. The "harnessing" of rivers, primarily by the construction of dams and reservoirs, is normally a multipurpose operation, combining flood control, hydroelectricity generation, irrigation potential, and recreational facilities.

The Columbia. The Columbia-Snake-Kootenay river system has been dammed in many places, and is now the leading power-generating river in Anglo-America. Six large dams—Grand Coulee, Chief Joseph, Rocky Reach, Rock Island, Priest Rapids, and Mc-Nary—have been built on the Columbia in this region (two others are further downstream in the North Pacific Coast Region); another—John Day, ultimately planned to produce more electricity than Grand Coulee—is under construction; and the Ice Harbor Dam, on the Snake River 10 miles above its confluence with the Columbia, is now in operation. Grand Coulee is a dam of superlatives. It houses the largest hydroelectric power plant in the world, impounds the sixth largest reservoir (F. D. Roosevelt Lake) in the United States, is the fifth highest dam in the nation, and is designed to irrigate more than 1,000,000 acres. Other major proposals include Wells Dam on the Columbia and Mountain Sheep, Nez Percé, and Hell's Canyon Dams on the Snake.

The Colorado. Consideration of the Colorado River generally is divided into an "Upper Basin" and a "Lower Basin," with the Grand Canyon separating the two. There are four major dams blocking the river in the Lower Basin, three on the California—

Arizona border and Hoover Dam on the Nevada–Arizona border. At an altitude of 726 feet, Hoover Dam is the world's fourth highest dam, and its impounded reservoir, Lake Mead, contains more water than any other in Anglo-America. It generates more hydroelectricity than any other American dam except Grand Coulee.

In the last half decade, three other major dams have been started, all in the Upper Basin. Glen Canyon Dam, on the main river at the Arizona–Utah border, will rank just behind Hoover Dam in terms of superlative statistics. Flaming Gorge Dam is being built on the Green River in northeastern Utah, and Navajo Dam is under construction on the San Juan River near Farmington, New Mexico.

In an arid region, water is often the key to life, and the use of the Colorado River is disputed mightily. There is considerable conflict between the Upper Basin states (Colorado, Wyoming, Utah, New Mexico) and the Lower Basin states (Arizona, Nevada, California), but the most acrimonious debate is between California and Arizona. Complex litigation between these two states for water rights to the Colorado flow has dragged on for years.

Forestry

Forests are generally absent from this region, except on some of the higher mountains and in the north, so logging is not a major activity. Only three areas are notable: (1) central Arizona; (2) Intermontane fringe areas in Oregon, Washington, and Idaho; and (3) the interior plateaus of British Columbia.

The high plateaus and mountains of the Mogollon Rim country and the San Francisco Peaks of Arizona are clothed with vast forests of ponderosa pine, Douglas fir, and other coniferous species (Figure 13-17). Much of the area is within the boundaries of national forests or Indian reservations,

Figure 13-17. A pine forest in the White Mountains of east-central Arizona. Most of Arizona is arid, but the higher elevations receive sufficient precipitation to support abundant tree growth. (Photo courtesy Arizona Development Board.)

and logging practices are generally quite good. Exploitation mostly is limited to a few large timber-cutting operations and their associated sawmills, although a pulp mill has recently been brought into operation. Arizona logging and milling centers are at Flagstaff, Williams, and McNary.

A considerable amount of relatively open forest is found around the margins of the Intermontane region in the three northern states. The principal species involved is ponderosa pine. Logging here is usually on a small scale, except in a few instances, as at Bend, Oregon, which is a major pine sawmilling center.

Approximately half of the timber cut in British Columbia today comes from forest land east of the Coast Mountains, mostly in the Intermontane Region. Throughout most of this area forestry is the most important contributor to the economy. Douglas fir is by far the leading species cut, although several varieties of spruce and pine are also used. Logging is a year-round activity wherever possible, but heavy winter snows and rainy springs sometimes preclude activity for several weeks. Pulp, paper, and plywood mills are scarce, but sawmills and planing mills are common, with important concentrations at Kelowna, Kamloops, Quesnel, and Prince George. Less than 20 per cent of the sawn lumber is used in British Columbia, the remainder being shipped out to eastern Canada or the United States.

Manufacturing

The manufacturing industries that have been located here are in large part an adjustment to the region's isolation, and have developed almost entirely (1) to meet the requirements of the local community, such as bakeries and ice plants; (2) to convert bulky products of field, range, and mine for economical transportation to distant markets, as metal smelting, sawmilling, and sugar refining; or (3) to utilize hydroelectric resources, as aluminum refining along the Columbia River and chemical processing near Hoover Dam.

Principal Industrial Centers   No city in the region is a major manufacturing center. Phoenix, which has more factories than any other city in the Intermontane Basins and Plateaus, is exceeded in its industrial output by some 80 other cities in Anglo-America. Even so, the larger Intermontane metropolitan centers have certain industries of distinction.

The *Phoenix* and *Tucson* areas share certain handicaps and advantages in terms of industrial location. Although the areas lack raw materials (except from local irrigated farming and ranching) and have limited

markets, labor is available and inexpensive, the community attitude toward new industry is favorable, and the idea of "Southwestern living" is a major attraction for industrialist and worker alike. The most important components of the industrial structure are associated with aircraft and electronics production, which are based on less tangible location factors than materials and markets; nearness to but separateness from Los Angeles (leading aircraft-manufacturing center in the world) is significant. Metalworking factories, including an aluminum refinery, and apparel manufacturing are other industries that are externally oriented; while food processing and production of air-conditioning equipment got their start on the basis of local markets.

The *Salt Lake City* area is an outstanding nonferrous milling and smelting center. It produces blister copper, lead bullion, zinc oxide concentrates, uranium, sulfuric acid, and cobalt from Utah and Idaho ores. The only significant steel mill in the region is located at Geneva, 40 miles to the south. Flour milling, sugar refining, meat packing, canning and freezing, and oil refining are other industries of note.

El Paso is another metallurgical center. Copper, lead, and silver are produced in smelters and refineries here, from both domestic and foreign ores. Apparel manufacture, based on inexpensive female labor, is also characteristic.

Spokane has three notable manufacturing industries: aluminum refining, which utilizes local hydroelectric power; flour milling of Palouse wheat; and sawmilling of nearby timber.

Other manufacturing in the Intermontane Region is mostly small-scale and based upon local primary resources. Irrigated farming areas such as the Imperial Valley, the Snake River Plain, and the Okanagan Valley maintain many packing, preserving, milling, canning, and freezing plants for fruits, vegetables, and sugar beets. Various mining areas, especially in Arizona, have adjacent ore-processing facilities. The principal logging districts—central Arizona and southern British Columbia—are also wood-milling centers.

Transportation

The frontier could not advance unbroken over the barrier of the Rockies, but carved channels through it on the lines of least resistance, notably the Oregon Trail (early 1840's) and the Santa Fe Trail (1821). These trails were destined to become major rail lines of industrial flow to the Pacific Coast.

Pioneer Trails. The *Oregon Trail,* paralleled by the later Mormon Trail, was the best-known and the most used route to the Pacific. Each year, at the approach of spring on the Great Plains, hundreds of covered wagons prepared for the long trek to Oregon. This trail divided the American bison into northern and southern herds, leaving the route bare save during seasonal north-south migrations.

The *Santa Fe Trail* [12] began at Independence, Missouri, a short distance east of Kansas City, and extended some 850 miles to Santa Fe. Though primarily a traders' trail, it was nonetheless an important trailway for migrants from the East to the West. This trail contributed notably to the shrinkage of the Great American Desert and broke the policy permitting Indian occupation in the Southwest. In the early 1800's, Santa Fe was one of old Mexico's leading commercial distributing centers as well as a point from which trails and highways moved down the Rio Grande Valley.

At first, traders made only one trip a year, setting out in early summer as soon as the pasturage was promising. Later on, trade became so important that caravans set out every few days. A day's journey was usually about 15 miles. In 1866 approximately 3,000 wagons were working the Santa Fe Trail.

Prerailroad Transportation. The *Pony Express* carried the first mail to California. It began in 1860, lasted only 16 months, and ruined its promoters.

The *Stage Coach* delivered mail and passengers. Some coaches drove day and night, but others halted at night to enable their passengers to rest.

The *Camel Caravan* was used to open up the Southwest along a route extending from Texas through southern New Mexico and Arizona to California. Camels were tried out during 1857-1858 by Edward F. Beale, who reported them to be eminently satisfactory.

> I look forward to the day when every mail route across the continent will be conducted and worked altogether with this economical and noble brute.

However, the experiment failed. Though the animal could carry heavy loads and was adapted to desert conditions, he required patient, careful handling which American mule skinners would not give. The completion of the first transcontinental railway in 1869 sounded the death knell of the camel experiment.

Railroads. This region, more than any other, is dependent upon railroads, though only seven transcontinental routes cross it.[13] This paucity is striking, but if they get too close together, tapping the same trade territory, as do the Northern Pacific, the Great Northern, and the Chicago, Milwaukee, St. Paul, and Pacific at times, they cannot prosper.

Several of these transcontinental lines,

---

[12] The Santa Fe Trail lies entirely east of this region, but it is discussed here with other trails because of its historic significance and because the Spanish Trail was a continuation of it.

[13] Actually only the Southern Pacific may be considered transcontinental, because it reaches from the Pacific Ocean to the Gulf of Mexico.

however, prosper because they connect rich productive areas; service to the "revenue vacuums" in between is incidental. All western railroads face two major problems: (1) much of the country is mountainous, which causes high capital and operating costs; and (2) most of the flat country is so dry and sparsely settled as to yield a low traffic density.

Thus, while the people who dwell in the region dispose of many of their products and bring in much of what they use by rail, the bulk of the traffic is supplied by the terminal areas, and the arid region functions primarily as a transit land. Most of the west-bound freight trains are made up of empty cars.

It was in this region on May 10, 1869, that the first so-called *transcontinental* railroad in the United States was completed — Union Pacific–Central Pacific. At Promontory, Utah, just north of Great Salt Lake, a golden spike was driven into a crosstie to commemorate joining the rails of the Central Pacific (now the Southern Pacific), built eastward from Sacramento, and the Union Pacific, built westward from Council Bluffs. Princely land grants, used as bait to stimulate rivalry between the two roads, hastened construction.

Roads. Good roads reflect rich lands and dense population, for they are expensive to build and maintain and unproductive areas characterized by sparse population cannot support them. This region, therefore, has relatively few superior roads, except those connecting the Atlantic and Pacific Coasts built by the federal government in cooperation with the several states. They are, therefore, the result of a remarkable national program, existing primarily to serve the "automobile nomad" and bus and trucking interests.

While railroads carry the greater part of the interregional freight and much of the bulky products in intraregional trade, trucks are hauling an ever-increasing proportion of both.

Air Routes. Transcontinental air travel, especially that catering to passengers, grows daily and forms an important link connecting all of Anglo-America's regions. So far as this Intermontane Region is concerned, Salt Lake City is the focal point. Lines from Butte, Portland, San Francisco and Los Angeles converge here for the assembly and interchange of passengers with the trunk route east to Chicago and New York.

Tourism

The region under discussion is one of the most scenic in America, for within it are Bryce Canyon, Zion National Park, the Grand Canyon, Cedar Brakes, the Kaibab Forest, the Petrified Forest, the Painted Desert, Death Valley, Hell's Canyon on the Snake River, and the Columbia River Gorge. Fortunately the United States government has preserved most of these scenic beauties and has made them a part of its national parks, monuments, and forests.

Several generations ago only the rich and the indigent could see their country, the one in a Pullman, the other in a box car. The automobile, however, has brought a large tourist income to these states, which suffer from the fluctuations of mining. While most visitors spend only a few days in a given place, some settle down permanently.

The Grand Canyon of the Colorado. The Grand Canyon, a colossal chasm 250 miles long, 10 to 12 miles wide, and more than one mile deep, is too gigantic for the human mind to encompass (Figure 13-18). It is the world's choicest exhibit of erosion—the result of cutting and grinding of fast-flowing mud- and rock-laden water, abetted by frost, wind, and rain. It presents the world's most exposed geological timetable. The mile of rock from bottom to rim represents a period estimated at 700 million years. The

Figure 13-18. The Grand Canyon of the Colorado, as seen from the North Rim. (Photo courtesy Arizona Development Board.)

whole panorama is a riot of colors from the mineral stains and mineral salts originally in the sediments. To be appreciated, the canyon should be seen in the sunlight, moonlight, during a rain, and when the weather is cloudy. No color film, no brush, no pencil —no matter how inspired—can reproduce what one sees, and word pictures are completely inadequate.

Bryce Canyon National Park. The Bryce Canyon in south-central Utah is a significant amphitheatre. No other national park appears so fantastic, its bizarre forms being slender, dainty, bulky, or grotesque. Moreover, these forms are of many colors, but essentially pink, red, white, orange, and purple. Bryce Canyon also tells a story of erosion. One stands on the rim of a precipice and looks down on a forest of tall and erratically carved stone spires. The trails are comparatively easy to follow.

Zion National Park. Lying a short distance from Bryce is Zion National Park, consisting of a narrow, meandering canyon with vertical walls 1,000, 2,000, and 2,500 feet

high and with a maze of side canyons. It is banded with white and many shades of red. Some consider it the most inspiring sight in the world. Entering it through a long tunnel, one suddenly comes out into the narrow, towering canyon with its unbelievable colors. The Virgin River occupies the bottom of the valley.

Man-made Tourist Attractions. This region of colorful and spectacular scenery has an almost unlimited number of natural attractions. However, many of them are difficult of access, and most tourists will invest only a limited amount of time in sight-seeing off the beaten track. Consequently, various man-made attractions, which almost invariably are reached by excellent roads, draw considerable attention from visitors to the region.

There are many *historic towns* in the region, remnants of that romanticized and immortalized period in American history, "the Old West." Some of these, such as Bisbee, Tombstone, and Jerome in Arizona or Virginia City in Nevada, have capitalized on

Figure 13-19. Las Vegas at night. The flamboyance of gambling casinos and the inexpensive power of Hoover Dam combine to give Fremont Street the brightest lights in the Intermontane Region. (Photo courtesy Union Pacific Railroad.)

their heritage and built up a steady trade in historically-minded tourists.

The remarkable history of *Mormonism* in Utah, and the continued importance of Salt Lake City as headquarters of that Church, is another impelling tourist attraction. Various edifices and monuments in and around Salt Lake City are visited by hundreds of thousands of visitors annually.

Although Nevada has a colorful past, its present is in many ways even more flamboyant. As the only state that systematically utilizes *gambling* as a major source of revenue, the development of games of chance in Nevada has reached amazing proportions. Every town in the state has its cluster of "one-armed bandits," but Las Vegas (Figure 13-19) and Reno are the chief centers by far. As added attractions, these cities also specialize in glamorous entertainment, "quickie" marriages, and simple (though not speedy) divorces.

Man's engineering feats always seem to hold great interest for tourists, and the two great *dams* of the region are prime attractions. Grand Coulee Dam is particularly noted for its power plant, and Hoover Dam for its boating facilities on Lake Mead. Glen Canyon Dam, now under construction, gives promise of becoming a third engineering asset of major tourist interest.

Specialized Southwestern Living

The rapid population growth of the southern part of the Intermontane Region in recent years, matched only by Florida and southern California, is an obvious tribute to sunshine and health. Many modern Americans feel that sunny, mild winters and informal outdoor living provide sufficient satisfaction to counteract the problems of moving to a distant locality, even if that locality is characterized by scorching summers. Health benefits (some real, some imagined) are also derived for sufferers from respiratory afflictions in the dry air of the Southwest.

Thus, in southern Arizona, southern New Mexico, and southeastern California particularly, the ordinary summer tourist is a minor element in comparison with the frequent winter visitor, the new resident eagerly anticipating opportunity in a growing community, and the retired couple content to spend their last years in sunny relaxation.

It is on these three groups that the social, and to a considerable extent the economic, structure of the Southwest is turning. The significance of these groups is demonstrated nowhere quite as pointedly as in the growth of suburban Phoenix. Scottsdale, on the northeast, is a semiexclusive residential and resort suburb whose luxury hotels and elaborately picturesque shops and restaurants are geared specifically to the winter visitor. Deer Valley, on the north, is a sprawling desert scattered with large factories and ambitious subdivisions for the migrant from the eastern states. Sun City, on the northwest, is a specifically planned retirement community without facilities for children but with abundant amenities for "senior citizens."

Another facet of Southwestern living is the rise of the trailer camp. Throughout Anglo-America the mobile home is a sign of the times, but in the southern Intermontane region it is a way of life. Trailer camps are widespread, both as semipermanent installations in urban areas and as temporary expedients in "boom" districts which tend to be rurally located.[14] Trailer homes are not self-sufficient; they must cluster where they can get water, electricity, and sewers—hence the growing ubiquity of trailer camps. Such camps are now a transient but basic element of the cultural landscape—several dozen trailers parked side by side on small lots that focus on the cement block building that houses the toilets, laundromat (the central social institution), and manager's office; the amount of landscaping depends upon the permanency of the residents, but tricycles and portable gas tanks abound.

Southwestern living is relaxed, casual,

[14] Recent Southwestern booms have been triggered by uranium exploration, oil discovery, and major construction jobs. Farmington, New Mexico, and Cortez, Colorado, have experienced mineral-oriented booms, and Page, Arizona, is an excellent example of a town that has grown because of a construction project (Glen Canyon Dam).

and popular. It attracts people from all economic levels. It is not a temporary fad.

The Outlook

Man has accomplished much in this restrictive environment. No one can stand on the steps of the State Capitol Building at Salt Lake City and gaze at the green island that is the oasis without being impressed. Nevertheless there is a limit to what human beings can accomplish against a stubborn and relentless nature. Since water, which means life, is scarce, and much of the terrain is rugged, the greater part of the region is destined to remain one of the emptiest and least used on the continent.

Agriculture should become more important, though too great dependence on outside markets is a retarding factor. For this reason, the region must convert into concentrated form those products it cannot itself consume. Sugar beets in irrigated areas over much of the northern part of the region, though also in the Imperial Valley in the south, will continue to be an important crop, for they guarantee the farmers their "tax money." This will be true even if beet acreage declines in certain areas from time to time. The Bureau of Reclamation and the Corps of Engineers will probably continue to add to the irrigable area with enormous projects similar to the Grand Coulee, John Day, and Glen Canyon Dams. Such projects will increase the regional farm output and aid the local economy, but only at considerable cost to the general public.

Grazing cannot be expected to expand much, except perhaps in part of central British Columbia. But a trend toward intensification is probable. More feeding will be carried on, both at local ranches and at centralized feedlots. Hay and sorghum feeding will continue to dominate, but grains, often brought into the region, will increase in importance. More attention will be paid to breeding, too, with improved Hereford and Angus strains in the north, and more emphasis on Santa Gertrudis and Charolaise in the south.

Mining is an industry of fluctuating prosperity in the region, and will continue to be so. The most important commercial Intermontane mineral (copper) has an unstable market and suffers from antagonistic labor relations; the most dynamic Intermontane mineral (uranium) is in oversupply, at least in the short run; the best growth prospect is in gas and oil, but their prosperity will affect only limited areas (primarily the Four Corners country and the Uintah–Rangely district).

Forest exploitation will become increas-

ingly important in British Columbia and to a lesser extent in central Arizona, but it cannot have much effect on the rest of the region.

Manufacturing will continue to grow rapidly in a few urban places. Although such localities are limited, they are the population centers, and continued industrial growth will be impressive in the over-all economy.[15] It is a measure of the stability of the current population growth that industrial expansion is keeping pace.

Tourism in this region, as in most, is

[15] Already in Arizona manufacturing contributes more to the state income than does any of the four traditional C's—copper, cattle, cotton, or climate (tourism).

TABLE 12

Selected Cities and Towns of the Intermontane Basins and Plateaus

City or Town	Urbanized Area	Political Center	City or Town	Urbanized Area	Political Center
Alameda	......	10,660	Moses Lake	......	11,299
Alamogordo	......	21,723	Murray	......	16,806
Albuquerque	241,216	201,189	Nampa	......	18,897
Barstow	......	11,644	North Las Vegas	......	18,422
Bend	......	11,936	Ogden	121,927	70,197
Bisbee	......	9,914	Orem	......	18,394
Boise City	......	34,481	Palm Springs	......	13,468
Bountiful	......	17,039	Pecos	......	12,728
Brawley	......	12,703	Pendleton	......	14,434
Brigham City	......	11,728	Penticton	......	13,859
Caldwell	......	12,230	Phoenix	552,043	439,170
Chandler	......	9,531	Pocatello	......	28,534
Douglas	......	11,925	Prescott	......	12,861
El Centro	......	16,811	Prince George	......	13,877
El Paso	277,128	276,687	Provo	60,795	36,047
Farmington	......	23,786	Reno	70,189	51,470
Gallup	......	14,089	Richland	......	23,548
Glendale	......	15,696	Salt Lake City	348,661	189,454
Grand Junction	......	18,694	Scottsdale	......	10,026
Henderson	......	12,525	Sparks	......	16,618
Idaho Falls	......	33,161	Spokane	226,938	181,608
Kamloops	......	10,076	Tempe	......	24,897
Kearns	......	17,172	Tucson	227,433	212,892
Kelowna	......	13,188	Twin Falls	......	20,126
Las Cruces	......	29,367	Vernon	......	10,250
Las Vegas	89,427	64,405	Walla Walla	......	24,536
Lewiston	......	12,691	Wenatchee	......	16,726
Logan	......	18,731	Yakima	......	43,284
Mesa	......	33,772	Yuma	......	23,974
Moscow	......	11,183			

bound to expand. Summer is tourist time in the northern four-fifths of the Intermontane Basins and Plateaus, while winter visitors are more important in the southern portion. An abundance of natural allurements, a variety of man-made attractions, and improving transportation routes combine to assure a steady flow of tourists.

Population growth in the northern half of the region is slow, and it will probably continue to be so. In the southern half, population aggrandizement is faster than the national average, and is truly phenomenal in some areas. Mild winters, few clouds, dry air, informal living patterns, and the mysterious attraction of the desert will continue to exert their magnetic effects on dissatisfied, snow-shovel-weary citizens of northern states. "Suburbia in the Sun" is the drawing card for Albuquerque, Tucson, Phoenix, El Paso, and smaller settlements in the same latitude. And the "spillover" from Los Angeles will account for an accelerating growth rate in Palm Springs, Twenty-nine Palms, Thousand Palms, Palm City, and other mushrooming desert settlements in southern California.

This migration-fostered population growth probably will become overextended at times, outstripping a sound economic base; but generally it is likely to grow with soundness, for capital will accompany people in the migration. Water may be a long-run limiting factor, but in the short run it is no barrier, for urban growth is often at the expense of irrigated agriculture, and the former uses less water than the latter.

The southern Intermontane region, then, is in transition from desert to metropolis. Today one can find smog in Phoenix that would make a Los Angeleno proud, traffic jams in Albuquerque that would do credit to Chicago, and tension-induced psychiatric treatments in Salt Lake City that would be suitable for New York. Progress will manifest itself in the region in a nodal

fashion; the rural areas will never fill up, but the urban centers will continue to grow.

Selected Bibliography

Bernstein, Harry, "Spanish Influence in the United States: Economic Aspects," *Hispanic American Historical Review*, Vol. 18, 1938, pp. 43-65.

British Columbia Lands Service, *The Atlin Bulletin Area*. Victoria: Queen's Printer, 1961.

———, *The Kamloops Bulletin Area*. Victoria: Queen's Printer, 1958.

———, *The Okanagan Bulletin Area*. Victoria: Queen's Printer, 1957.

———, *The Quesnel-Lillooet Bulletin Area*. Victoria: Queen's Printer, 1957.

Carter, G. F., *Plant Geography and Culture History in the American Southwest*, Viking Fund Publications in Anthropology, No. 5. New York: Viking Fund Inc., 1945.

Claire, Justinian, "The Sheep Industry," Supplement to the *Monthly Review*, Federal Reserve Bank of San Francisco, September 1950.

Clawson, Marion, "Water Laws," *Farm Policy Forum*, Vol. 2, October 1945.

———, and B. Held, *The Federal Lands: Their Use and Management*. Baltimore: Johns Hopkins Press, 1957.

Garwood, John D., "An Analysis of Postwar Industrial Migration to Utah and Colorado," *Economic Geography*, Vol. 29, January 1953, pp. 79-88.

Hafen, LeRoy, *Old Spanish Trail: Santa Fe to Los Angeles*. Glendale: A. H. Clark Co., 1954.

Holmes, Charles H., "Factors Affecting Development of the Steel Industry in Intermountain America," *Journal of Geography*, Vol. 58, January 1959, pp. 20-31.

Horgan, Paul, *Great River: The Rio Grande in North American History*. New York: Rinehart Publishing Company, 1954, 2 vols.

Jackson, J. B., "The Four Corners Country," *Landscape*, Vol. 10, Fall 1960, pp. 20-26.

Jaeger, Edmund, *North American Deserts*. Palo Alto: Stanford University Press, 1957.

Jennings, Jesse D., "The American Southwest: a Problem of Cultural Isolation," *American Antiquity*, Vol. 22, October 1956, pp. 59-127.

Kelley, Tim, "The Taylor Grazing Act and the West," *Annals of the Association of American Geographers,* Vol. 39, March 1949, pp. 56-57.

Leech, C. J., "The Navajos Today," *Geographical Magazine,* Vol. 31, February 1959, pp. 479-492.

Leitch, Adelaide, "The Okanagan: Sagebrush Valley of Blossoms," *Canadian Geographical Journal,* Vol. 53, July 1956, pp. 12-21.

McCleneghan, Thomas J., "Bisbee, Historic City With a Future," *Arizona Review of Business and Public Administration,* Vol. 9, October 1960, pp. 1-14.

Meigs, Peveril, "Outlook for the Arid Realm of the United States," *Focus,* Vol. 4, December 1953, pp. 1-6.

Miller, Elbert E., "Outlook for Uranium," *Focus,* Vol. 10, March 1960, 6 pp.

Padfield, Harland, "The Arizona Seasonal Farm Worker: Some Theoretical and Practical Problems," *Arizona Review of Business and Public Administration,* Vol. 10, April 1961, pp. 2-14.

Tuan, Yi-Fu, "Structure, Climate, and Basin Land Forms in Arizona and New Mexico," *Annals of the Association of American Geographers,* Vol. 52, March 1962, pp. 51-68.

chapter fourteen

The Subtropical
Pacific Coast

The most diversified region in Anglo-America, one that is characterized by many different types of economic activity, is the Subtropical Pacific Coast. Agriculture is important in almost every segment, with cotton, fruits, and vegetables being leading crops, and with livestock and dairying important in areas ill-adapted to cultivation. Actually California means different things to different individuals; and this is as it should be, for actually there are many Cali-fornias—each having marked individuality—the result of its distinctive geographical conditions. In this book the entire state, with the exception of the Salton Trough, the Imperial Valley, the Northeastern Lava Plateaus, and the Northern California Littoral, is considered under the heading of the Subtropical Pacific Coast (Figure 14-1). This division lends itself well to the regional approach:

1. Southern California (from Santa Bar-

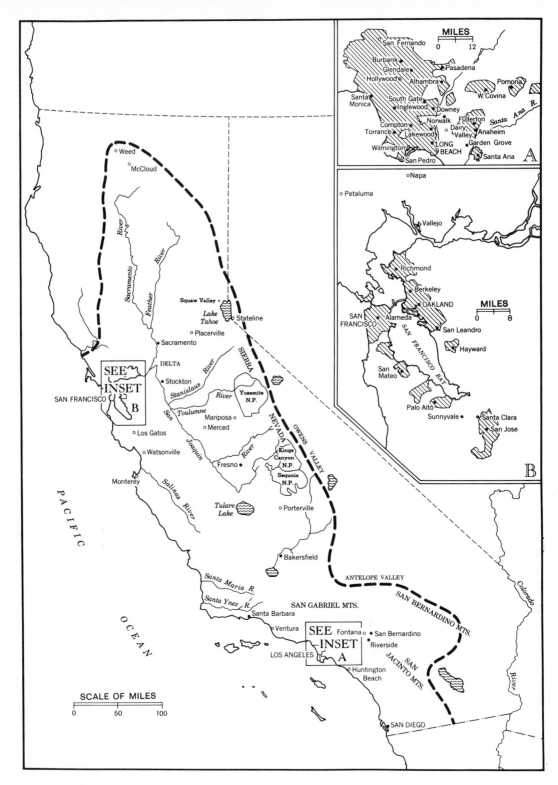

Figure 14-1. The Subtropical Pacific Coast. A region of diversified farming, ranching, fishing, logging, mining, manufacturing, commerce, tourism, and rapid population growth.

bara to San Diego and east to San Bernardino and Riverside).

2. The Central Valley.

3. The Sierra Nevada.

4. The Central Coast Ranges and Valleys, including the San Francisco Bay Area.

While these subregions show marked contrast in relief, climate, soils, natural vegetation, and economic development, they are nonetheless so interrelated and so mutually interdependent as to constitute one major geographic region.

In each of these subregions the people are adjusting themselves in their own particular way. The state now exceeds any other in total population. More of this growth in population results from heavy inmigration than from a high birth rate.

Water: Great Problem of the Region

Water is considered by nearly all authorities on California to be a major potential problem. California opposed several of the western states in order to effect federal construction of Hoover Dam on the Colorado River, and is still in litigation with Arizona over the apportionment of "Lower Basin" water. Owens Valley ranchers fought in real "wild West" fashion to prevent Los Angeles from using their water. They lost, however, for a Superior Court ruled that water must be used for the greatest good of the greatest number.

California receives sufficient rainfall as a state but the moisture does not fall in the right places at the right time in the right amounts (Figure 14-2). Thus, if one compares a map showing distribution of water availability with one showing population distribution, it becomes immediately apparent that man has not adapted himself to the pattern set by nature, for two-thirds of the available water is in the northern part of the state, whereas two-thirds of the population is in the southern half.

The problem is to get water from where there is too much to where there is not enough. Down through the years an effort has been made to do this. No state in the Union made such tremendous expenditures in reaching out for water. Yet, from some points of view, California is water-poor. It has taxed man's ingenuity seriously, having impounded surface waters, tapped underground sources, attempted to make rain by cloud-seeding, and even experimented with methods of freshening sea water at low cost. However, man in California is removing water faster than nature is replenishing it.

Such a problem would be serious if only the natural increase in population had to be considered, but California's population increase is far from normal. Population and

Figure 14-2. Rainfall in California. Precipitation varies markedly from place to place. In general the southern half of the state suffers from moisture deficiency, and the northern half sometimes is troubled by too large a surplus.

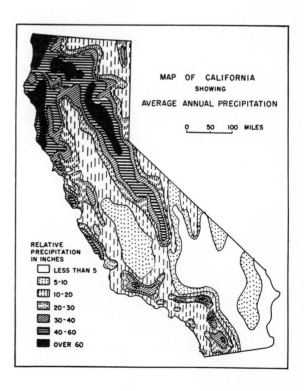

MAP OF CALIFORNIA
SHOWING
AVERAGE ANNUAL PRECIPITATION

0   50   100   MILES

RELATIVE
PRECIPITATION
IN INCHES

LESS THAN 5
5-10
10-20
20-30
30-40
40-60
OVER 60

manufacturing both are growing at rapid rates. Both, however, may be halted eventually by the insufficiency of water unless man can overcome the problem.

Under present conditions, it is believed that most of southern California will feel the pinch of water shortage by the early 1970's (the city of Los Angeles has a rosier outlook; its supply is thought to be ample until the 1980's). There are two possibilities to solve this problem when it arises: (1) Divert surface water from elsewhere, or (2) Make sea water potable.

Many schemes have been suggested to transport water from areas of surplus to southern California, but in 1960 the voters of California approved the so-called "Feather River Project," a 10-year 1.75-billion-dollar plan to channel excess water from the Sacramento–San Joaquin Delta and the Feather River to the areas of deficiency—the San Francisco Bay area, the San Joaquin Valley, the central coast region, and southern California as far south as San Diego. This might provide the necessary solution.

Many people believe, however, that desalinization of sea water will be more feasible and less expensive. In the early 1960's it was still too costly a process, but continued research will undoubtedly find techniques to cheapen it.

Whatever the proper solution, southern California must have more water if it is to prosper in the future.

Population: Sensational Regional Growth

For more than three centuries the people of the United States have had a reputation for moving from region to region. As pointed out earlier, Americans began carving out their homes in the wilderness (the empty country between their settlements and the Pacific Ocean), and the process continued for three centuries. "Like locusts they swarmed, always to the west, and only the Pacific Ocean stopped them." The exist-

ence of an area of free land, its continuous recession, and the advance of settlement westward, explain American development.

That westward trek is now stronger than ever, and California is the great Mecca. In the past two decades the population has been increasing at about five per cent per year. For Los Angeles County alone, the increase has amounted to 185,000 people annually. To cope with such a growth the county should open a new, fully-equipped elementary school every Monday morning. There is no obvious reason why this accelerated tempo should slow down.

The history of settlement in California has been characterized by a continuous movement in number and space marked by new forces finding expression in new forms of population distribution.

Southern California

This is the smallest of the subregions of the state, but it is one of the most important and one of the most intensively developed areas in all Anglo-America. It has a true mediterranean subtropical climate. With the rapid growth of metropolitan Los Angeles and San Diego, the area has become highly urbanized and highly industrialized.

The boundaries of this subregion are natural—both physiographical and climatic. The east-west range of the San Gabriel and San Bernardino Mountains excludes winds coming from the continental interior and confines the mediterranean climate to a small strip of coast. The San Jacinto–Santa Rosa–Laguna Mountains to the southeast separate this subregion from the Salton Trough and the Imperial Valley, parts of the Intermontane Basins and Plateaus Region.

The Natural Environment

The most distinct feature of the terrain is the east-west mountain range along the northern margin—the San Gabriel and San Bernardino Mountains. South of this rim of mountains lies the Los Angeles Lowland, which is subdivided into several smaller valleys such as the San Fernando and San Bernardino by a number of intervening ranges of hills.

Much of this lowland is covered with extensive coalescing alluvial fans formed of material washed down from the mountains. These fans slope from altitudes of 1,000 to 2,000 feet at the base of the mountains to 300 to 500 feet a few miles away. The streams forming these fans are broad, stony washes, becoming surface streams only during times of flood. They provide, however, an important supply of ground water for the area's large-scale irrigation development.

Much of this basin is now occupied by the extensive urban area of Los Angeles and by intensively cultivated citrus groves. South of this area lies a narrow coastal plain that extends to the Mexican border. This narrow plain forms a continuation of the Southern California agricultural area.

The coastline of Southern California is marked by low shelving beaches at points where the deltaic plains reach the ocean alternating with elevated beaches and bold promontories where the mountain spurs approach the coast. From 25 to 90 miles offshore lie a number of small rocky islands that are a definite part of the region.

The climate is a true mediterranean type, having a marked seasonal rhythm of rainfall. The precipitation (15 to 20 inches) comes almost entirely during the winter season. Desert conditions with a maximum of sunshine prevail during the dry and hot summers. Winters are mild and summers are hot, although near the Pacific Ocean the summer temperatures are modified by cool sea breezes. The high percentage of sunshine, even during the winter rainy season, has attracted tourists as well as many im-

portant industries. Southern California vies with Arizona and Florida in selling climate to the people of the rest of the continent.

The natural vegetation in this foothill and valley area consists largely of chaparral at elevations of 3,000 to 5,000 feet, with annual and perennial grasses forming much of the understory. Directly below, on the lower slopes, extend considerable dense thickets of chamisal. On the higher slopes, where the rainfall is greater, there was formerly an open stand of coniferous forest. Lumbering was a fairly important enterprise in the San Bernardino and San Jacinto Mountains in early days.

Settlement

Little is known about the Indians who inhabited Southern California. Records indicate that the area was occupied by scattered small tribes in a low cultural stage. When the Spaniards arrived, they subjugated the natives without difficulty.

The Spanish-Mexican Period (1542-1848)

In September, 1542, Rodriguez Cabrillo, the first European to visit the region, sailed up the west coast from Mexico and discovered San Diego Bay. After exploring the coast and offshore islands, he claimed every harbor for Spain. Some years later (1602), a second expedition under Sebastian Vizcaino explored the coast northward as far as Monterey. Following this, however, no further explorations were made and no settlements attempted in California for more than 160 years. Southern California seemed to offer little attraction to the adventurous gold-seeking *conquistadores*. Renewed interest was stimulated not by the possibilities of the region itself but by the rapid advance of Russian domination of the Pacific Coast south from Alaska. Although Spain considered the whole California area economically worthless, she felt that a buffer state should be established to prevent possible Russian encroachment upon her more valuable colony of Mexico. As a result, Spain renewed her interest in this region in 1769 through the establishment of a string of presidios and missions, followed later by the founding of pueblos or towns. The first mission was established at San Diego in 1769 and soon was followed by others. Later, towns were located near most of the missions.

Although some mineral wealth was found within the subregion, including quicksilver at Santa Barbara, little mining was practiced. The Spanish cattle brought in by the early settlers multiplied so rapidly that ranching became the chief occupation. Since there was no way to market cattle, they were slaughtered and the hides and tallow sold to New England traders, whose vessels put in at the ports of San Diego, San Pedro, and Santa Barbara. Though Spain prohibited this trade, she offered no substitute; hence the isolated colonists of Southern California continued to ship out animal products in exchange for manufactured goods brought in by Yankee clipper ships. Whaling vessels also visited the California ports to outfit for their long trips into the Arctic. During the last two decades of this Spanish-Mexican period (1828-1848), it is estimated that more than a million hides and more than 60 million pounds of tallow were exported from California.

The Early American Period (1848-1876) Toward the end of the Spanish-Mexican period, the Santa Fe Trail was extended to Los Angeles. The westward drift of settlement was moving toward California, but no great progress was made until gold was discovered near Sacramento in 1848. News of the strike spread rapidly, and soon the most spectacular mass migration in the history of the New World began.

Without gold, with poor harbors, and remote from routes of travel, Southern California had little chance to profit from this new migration. Eventually, however, some people, failing to find gold, drifted south-

ward. Through devious means many large *ranchos* were broken up and title to considerable land was obtained by these new American settlers. Cattle ranching continued dominant throughout the rest of this period.

In 1876 the Southern Pacific Railroad built a line from Oakland southward to Los Angeles, and five years later extended it eastward to New Orleans. In 1885 the Santa Fe Railroad completed its "transcontinental" line, making Los Angeles its Pacific terminus. These new connections with the outside world broke down the extreme isolation of Southern California—an isolation that had retarded its growth since the beginning of Spanish settlement.

The Commercial and Industrial Period (1876 to the present) Following the completion of the railroads, people moved into Southern California in great numbers, and for two decades most of them went into agriculture. Other important enterprises, however, began about the same time. Oil was discovered in 1880, and the petroleum industry began its phenomenal growth. This was followed in turn by the motion-picture industry, tourism, the commercial growth of the port of Los Angeles, and quite recently by manufacturing. This modern period, which will be described in more detail, evolved so rapidly that Southern California outgrew all other areas of comparable size on the continent during the past century. Los Angeles County, for example, jumped in population from 2,785,643 in 1940 to 6,038,771 in 1960, an increase of 117 per cent.

Agriculture

Prior to the 1849 gold rush, California agriculture, except for small irrigated areas near missions, was almost entirely pastoral. The great army of gold seekers, centered in northern California, created a demand for food at high prices and initiated a period of bonanza wheat growing. While most of this was confined to the Central Valley, some wheat was grown elsewhere, including Southern California lands.

Ranching, however, remained dominant until the severe drought of 1862-1863 brought death by starvation to thousands of cattle and other range animals. Until that time, most of the land in Southern California was in large land holdings, *ranchos*, which had been granted to early settlers by the Spanish crown or the Mexican government. This disastrous drought practically wrecked the livestock industry and forced many large landholders to sell at least a part of their acreage.

In the late 1860's, boatloads of prospective land-buyers went from San Francisco to Los Angeles. Land sales soon became so important that companies were organized to subdivide and sell ranches that had been acquired by foreclosure of mortgages. With the completion of railroads to Southern California, the land boom increased, and during the 1880's reached large proportions. Since the area was deficient in rainfall and most of the rain came during winter, many agricultural experiments were made. Among crops attempted were cotton, tobacco, and castor beans; even sericulture (growing of silkworms) was tried. Unfavorable physical factors, coupled with high transportation costs to distant markets, caused these early experiments to fail.

Ranching, however, was still important, especially on the rougher hill lands, and today is surpassed only by irrigation farming.

On the drier bench lands along the coast, barley and beans are grown without irrigation. Though occupying considerable acreage, their value is of minor significance in comparison with that of the irrigated crops.

Irrigation was practiced on a small scale by the early Spanish settlers, each mission having its irrigated plots. The limited amount of surface water, however, pre-

cluded any extensive development until additional supplies could be developed from wells or could be brought in from the outside. Until the coming of the railroads in the early 1880's, few surplus crops could be sold outside the region, and production was limited largely to the local market. Between 1850 and 1880, however, small shipments of fruits and vegetables were sent regularly by vessel from Los Angeles to San Francisco. The boom in irrigation agriculture started in 1880, and its importance has increased each decade since then. Irrigated lands have so encroached upon dry farming and ranching areas that today only the least desirable lands remain in lower-grade uses. It should be noted, however, that much land formerly irrigated has since been abandoned to non-agricultural uses because of the rapid growth of the Los Angeles and San Diego metropolitan areas.

The Irrigated Crops In surveying agriculture in each of the subregions, it will be seen that most crops are irrigated. Yields under irrigation nearly always are high. It is not surprising to learn, therefore, that California's cash farm income has ranked first in every year since 1929 despite the fact that many other states harvest larger acreages (Figure 14-3).

Truck Crops This subregion, along with the Subtropical Gulf Coast and the Imperial Valley, supplies most of the early truck crops for the United States. Although grown here under irrigation, the crops are cultivated similarly to those described in the other areas. The Southern California Subregion ranks high in production of lettuce, tomatoes, cauliflower, celery, and carrots. Because of the great expansion of the citrus-fruit industry in this subregion, however, the Imperial Valley of southeastern California (Chapter 13) has been able to surpass it in the production of truck crops.

Citrus Fruits While citrus fruits are grown over wide areas in California, by far

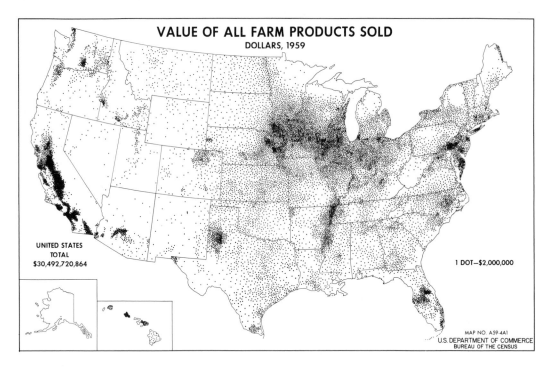

VALUE OF ALL FARM PRODUCTS SOLD
DOLLARS, 1959

UNITED STATES
TOTAL
$30,492,720,864

1 DOT—$2,000,000

MAP NO. A59-4A1
U.S. DEPARTMENT OF COMMERCE
BUREAU OF THE CENSUS

Figure 14-3. Value of all farm products sold in the United States. Gross income is higher on farms in the Subtropical Pacific Coast Region than in any other.

the major production is confined to the Southern California Subregion, making it one of the leading producers of the continent. Oranges and lemons predominate, although some grapefruit also is grown.

Extensive acreages of citrus groves dominate much of the landscape of Southern California (Figure 14-4), and no fruit district of the nation is more intensively cultivated or more productive. Since citrus fruits are produced by irrigation, this has created a tremendous demand for water. Aside from the fact that the fruits are irrigated, in contrast to those of Florida, production methods in the two states differ little.

Because of the great distance of this subregion from the large consuming centers of the East, marketing procedures must be very efficient.

During the early years of the commercial industry, oranges were bought outright by dealers who then shipped them to wholesalers in the East. These dealers developed their operations into large shipping and marketing concerns, and by the 1890's five or six such organizations practically controlled the business. These firms packed and marketed the oranges on a commission basis, consigning the fruit directly to commission merchants in the East.

Early attempts at cooperative marketing were unsuccessful. In 1893, however, some 60 orange growers organized a type of exchange which operated successfully for a while but was ultimately rendered impotent through loss of membership. Then came the Southern California Fruit Exchange, which, as an incorporated institution, established cooperative marketing of citrus fruit on a reasonably secure basis. Today this large organization, now called Sunkist Growers, Incorporated, functions for practically all citrus producers. Picking, packing, and shipping are now done by it, or under its supervision.

The Care of Orchards Groves belonging to members of Sunkist Growers, Inc., average from 10 to 15 acres in size. Protec-

388

tion from frost is largely the responsibility of the individual owner, although the United States Weather Bureau cooperates by broadcasting daily the expected temperatures. Owners must be on guard at all times during the frost season. Many of them have installed automatic signal systems that sound an alarm at the approach of a critical temperature. Growers have learned to plant trees on slightly sloping hillsides to benefit from air drainage, but at times temperatures fall so low as to necessitate the use of orchard heaters and wind machines.

Occasional hot dry winds, known as "Santa Anas," which blow into this subregion from the desert country to the northeast, inflict great damage on orchards. Although windbreaks have been used with some success, areas opposite canyon mouths, particularly Cajon Pass, are avoided by citrus growers because of the destructive force of these desert winds.

No citrus fruits are grown without irrigation. The amount of intensively cultivated land in Southern California is directly proportional to the amount of water available. Water costs are high and most water is controlled by mutual organizations of users. Nearly three-fourths of that used by citrus growers comes from wells. Orchards receive five to eight applications of water each year in addition to the scanty rainfall. Excessive irrigation in areas of poor drainage results in the accumulation of salts in the soil, which is detrimental to the citrus trees.

Picking and Packing the Fruit When the fruit reaches maturity, the job of picking usually is turned over to a local packing unit, which harvests the fruit economically by using crews of expert pickers. The packing plant lays down strict rules: all pickers must wear gloves to keep their fingernails from injuring the fruit, and all must use special clippers for removing the fruit from the tree. Special picking bags and carefully designed field boxes are used, to assure a

minimum of damage to the fruit. When the field boxes are filled they are taken by motor truck to local packing houses and the fruit is prepared for shipment. The organization provides the local packing houses with all the necessary supplies, such as wraps, labels, and boxes.

Decline of Southern California Citrus Citrus production in California has been declining for many years. Whereas 75 per cent of U.S. oranges were grown in the state in 1920, only 39 per cent were grown in 1950, and the proportion had dropped to 29 per cent by 1960, with Florida taking up most of the slack. Much of the decline has been in the Southern California Subregion, where urban subdivisions have been replacing orchards at a rapid rate. The southern end of the San Joaquin Valley is now dis-

Figure 14-4. Conflicting land use. An oil well being drilled in a lemon orchard near Ventura. Such conflicts among agricultural, residential, commercial, industrial, and transportational land use are commonplace in this region. (Photo courtesy Standard Oil Company of California.)

placing Southern California as the principal orange- and lemon-growing area.

Other Irrigated Fruit and Nut Crops *Peaches* are grown in a number of the valleys bordering the mountain zone. *Olives* are grown in portions of Los Angeles, Riverside, and San Diego Counties, but production is of minor significance compared with that in the valleys to the north. *Avocados* have recently become quite important, and large farms or "ranches" have been established to produce them for the ever-increasing national market.

Almonds are produced to some extent in the northern part of this subregion, though the bulk of the output comes from the coastal valleys of central California and from the Sacramento Valley. Southern California, however, is a leading producer of *English* (Persian) *walnuts*, although much walnut growing is being shifted to the Central Valley.

Food-Preparation Industries

California leads all states in the food-preparation industries.[1] While canning is statewide in its distribution because the ecological adaptations of many crops have quite definite climatic and soil requirements, there is nonetheless much concentration within a relatively few areas. This subregion is one of the areas of greatest concentration.

Food processing is conducted for the most part on a small scale compared with other outstanding branches of manufacturing. It could not, however, operate efficiently otherwise, for the sources of its raw materials are widespread and these materials are highly perishable. Moreover, the industry is seasonal, lasting for periods of six weeks to six or eight months. In the southern coastal area, the canning season is

[1] For the geographic principles involved in the location of such plants, see Chapter 24, "Food Preparation Industries," in Clifford Zierer, ed., *California and the Southwest* (New York: John Wiley and Sons, 1956).

long, whereas in the San Francisco Bay area, where the various products mature in a brief period, it is short. The long growing season and the great diversity of crops enable the canneries to utilize to better advantage costly plant equipment and to operate over a long season. A large part of California's pack of canned foods is fruits: apricots, peaches, and pears account for about 97 per cent of the total fruit canned. The seasonal aspect of canning also demands a pool of potential workers, mostly women, interested in seasonal employment.

The quick freezing of food has skyrocketed in growth in the past two decades. Frozen foods compete seriously with canned, dried, and even fresh fruits and vegetables.

Possibly the most interesting phase of the frozen-foods industry has been the freezing of citrus concentrate. Within only a few years it has had a terrific impact on the entire citrus industry. Traditionally, of course, California's orange growers marketed fresh fruit. The fine quality of the product assured financial success. But the meteoric rise of the frozen-juice industry in Florida forced California growers into the business. The cost of production is greater in California than in Florida. While labor is the big factor, tax costs are higher and irrigation is expensive.

Dairying

With a relatively compact, mostly urban population that exceeds 8,000,000 the Southern California Subregion provides a major market for dairy products, particularly fluid milk. The more than 800 dairy herds totaling 100,000 cows, of which more than half are in Los Angeles County, produce more milk than those of any other county in the nation.

It is mostly "dry lot" dairying, which means it is done on small land units that are not large enough to produce feed or to use as pasture land for the herds. Well over half a million tons of alfalfa are brought into Los Angeles County annually from the San Joaquin, Antelope, and Imperial Valleys to feed the cows. There are actually four cities in Los Angeles and Orange counties that have incorporated to protect the dairy areas from subdivision. The city of Dairy Valley, for example, had 3,500 people and 85,000 dairy cows within its 9 square miles in 1960.

Increasingly, however, the value of the land becomes so great that the dairymen cannot afford not to sell. Consequently, each year finds fewer dry-lot dairy farms in the urbanized areas, and more dairies moving out to less developed districts to the east of the coastal zone.

The Fishing Industry

Southern California is adjacent to one of the important commercial fishing regions of the continent. The major fishing grounds extend from Southern California waters southward along the coast of Mexico, Central America, Ecuador and Peru. Most fish are brought to the ports of Los Angeles and San Diego.

The establishment of a sardine cannery at San Pedro in 1893 marked the beginning of commercial fishing. The year 1905 found a temporary scarcity of sardines, and the fishermen experimented with the canning of albacore (tuna). By 1909 the canning of tuna had become so profitable that the packing of sardines was temporarily abandoned. When other types of tuna were caught and canned after 1918, the commercial fishing grounds were extended into the waters off Lower California. San Diego, the nearest port, profited greatly from this new expansion of the fishing grounds. By 1923 Latin American waters were supplying nearly half of the tuna landed at Southern California ports. High license fees for fishing in Mexican territorial waters caused the construction of larger sea-going tuna vessels that could fish in offshore waters, thereby avoiding the payment of the Mexican fees. The development of these larger ships has so expanded the tuna-fishing grounds that they now extend southward beyond the equator and westward as far as Hawaii. Most of this catch is handled by San Diego and Los Angeles canneries. Of the 111 million pounds taken in the peak year of 1930, San Diego handled about 60 per cent and Los Angeles the remainder.

The temporary stoppage of the European supply of sardines during the first World War led to the re-establishment of the sardine industry. Los Angeles soon became a major center, and has mantained its importance even in competition with European supplies. More recently, mackerel, a fish abundant along the Southern California coast throughout most of the year, is being canned, especially during months when tuna and sardines are not available.

About 1930, a tuna-canning industry patterned after that of Southern California was developed in Japan, and in 1933 more than 600,000 cases of Japanese tuna appeared on the United States market, despite a 30 per cent *ad valorem* tax. The duty was soon increased to 45 per cent, but even that, as a result of the differential between American and Japanese labor, was not sufficient to bar Japanese competition. Furthermore, Japan, through a subsidy, was making it possible for her canned tuna to be delivered to markets on the Atlantic Coast at a cost of only five cents per case more than that of California fish. Despite apparent advantages Southern California seemed to enjoy in the tuna industry, Japanese competition was a serious threat to future expansion. Peru is now marketing canned tuna in the United States also.

"Fish Harbor" is an artificial basin developed on Terminal Island at the time Los Angeles Harbor was being constructed.

Here are located all of the fishing docks and canneries. Eight large fish canneries and associated oil and meal plants line the docks at Fish Harbor, along with marine-oil and gasoline stations and with ice plants and other supply plants for outfitting the fleet.

Because the fishing industry in Southern California is so new, vessels and equipment are very modern. With the construction of sea-going fishing ships to work the offshore and distant tuna grounds, modern Diesel-powered tuna clippers have been developed. These craft, built exclusively for catching tuna at sea by means of hand lines (Figure 14-5), are equipped to refrigerate the fish for several weeks while the vessel is away from port. More recently, there has been a marked trend to convert tuna clippers into purse seiners. The use of power blocks and strong synthetic fiber seines allows a purse seiner to take a capacity load of tuna in about a month, in comparison with an average of 80 days for the same vessel equipped with hand lines.

Tuna are caught mostly from June to September, and sardines from November to March; mackerel are primarily a winter catch, though some are taken in other seasons. This seasonal distribution provides all-year employment for the canneries and

has made Los Angeles one of the best-organized fishing ports in Anglo-America.

At the present time San Pedro (the harbor for Los Angeles) lands 60 per cent of the tuna, 60 per cent of the mackerel, and 50 per cent of the sardines caught by United States commercial fishermen. Comparable statistics for Santa Barbara are 2, 7, and 10 per cent, respectively. San Diego is primarily a tuna port, landing 20 per cent of the national catch.

Petroleum and Natural Gas

The Southern California Subregion contains some of the most productive oil fields on the North American continent, and, despite its small areal extent, the region accounts for approximately seven per cent of the United States production. Two of the three major California oil districts are located in this area, the Coastal district with more than 18 producing fields and the Los Angeles Basin with more than 15 fields.

Oil was discovered in the Los Angeles Basin as early as 1880 with the completion of the Puente Hills field, but despite miscellaneous drilling, no further important development occurred until 1902, when the Brea-Olinda field was brought in about seven miles west of the center of Los An-

Figure 14-5. Hauling in tuna off the coast of Southern California. Once the school is sighted, live bait is thrown into the water and the tuna strike at brightly colored feather jigs attached to the fishing lines. (Photo courtesy San Diego Convention and Tourist Bureau.)

geles. Extensive drilling began throughout the basin, but, after reaching a peak in 1909, drilling declined until the close of the first World War. By that time rotary drilling was replacing drilling by cable tools, and deeper levels could be explored. The big oil boom for Southern California came in 1921 and 1922 with the completion of three large fields at Huntington Beach, Long Beach (Signal Hill), and Santa Fe Springs. In 1936 these fields, the three largest in the Los Angeles Basin, contained one-half of the producing wells of the area. In 1939, seventeen years after they were brought in, they were producing more than 37 million barrels, or nearly one-third the total for the basin. Only the Wilmington field of the Los Angeles Basin and the Ventura field in the coastal district surpassed these in production.

Three of the ten leading oil fields in the United States are in Southern California. The Wilmington Field (Long Beach—Los Angeles Harbor) is second only to the fabulous East Texas Field in output. The Ventura Field ranks fifth and Huntington Beach is ninth. However, California oil production has been declining steadily since 1953. Oil prospects in the state are reasonably well known, and it is believed that the two best prospects for increasing production are (1) more intensive exploitation of the Wilmington Field, particularly by waterflooding; and (2) offshore exploration, which will exploit the only favorable area virtually undrilled.

Probably the most interesting geographical aspects of the Southern California fields are those concerned with land utilization. In general, oil fields have been brought in on lands having little surface value. In the Los Angeles Basin, however, much of the land was being used intensively before oil was brought in. With rapid increases in land values due to the phenomenal growth of the City of Los Angeles, some of the less

productive fields are being abandoned. Although some of the fields are in brush-covered hill lands, many are either in irrigated agricultural lowlands or in crowded urban territory. Those along the Pacific Coast compete with bathing beaches and in some cases have been forced out into the water. Nowhere else have oil wells had such keen competition for surface rights. Clifford M. Zierer [2] classes the fields of the Los Angeles Basin into three types according to location: (1) hill districts, where fields have been developed on brush-covered hill lands devoted largely to grazing activities; (2) urban districts, where oil wells, drilled on building lots (50 by 120 feet or less in size), have resulted in the greatest crowding of derricks to be found anywhere; and (3) rural districts, largely irrigated and planted in citrus orchards or intensively cultivated truck crops. In the last-named type, the oil fields have had to compete with high-value surface rights, and serious conflicts in surface development frequently take place.

In the Wilmington and Huntington Beach fields, oil and gas wells are spaced closer together than they are anywhere else in the world. Derrick legs almost overlap in some instances. In part, this is due to wasteful exploitation, a result of small surface-land ownership plots, but in most cases it is an expression of whipstocking, or directional drilling. Modern drilling techniques allow wells to be drilled at any angle from a single location, so that much offshore drilling can be whipstocked from dry land.

A unique problem has developed in the Long Beach area, primarily as a result of oil and gas extraction in the Wilmington Field. Remarkable land subsidence has taken place, causing the surface to sink as much as 30 feet in some places. This has

[2] Clifford M. Zierer, "An Ephemeral Type of Industrial Land Occupance," *Annals of the Association of American Geographers,* Vol. 26 (1936), pp. 125-56.

394

caused untold damage to constructional and engineering features in the Long Beach harbor area and in downtown Long Beach itself.[3] Extensive litigation has been initiated, and attempts to stop the subsidence by re-pressurization and waterflooding are under way.

Nearly all fields in the region are accompanied by considerable gas pressure, but the large urban market of metropolitan Los Angeles consumes practically the total production. Natural gas is now being piped into California from Texas, New Mexico, and Utah.

Refining and Shipping Petroleum Refining petroleum and the shipping of it are important industries in Southern California. Because of the chance distribution of the oil fields within a 25-mile radius of Los Angeles Harbor, most refining is done on the coast. Oil and refined gasoline, above the requirements of Southern California, have moved out of the port by tank steamer to Alaska, to the East Coast (via the Panama Canal), and to the Pacific Coast of South America. About 60 per cent of California's refining capacity is in Los Angeles County.

The Motion-Picture Industry

The Motion-Picture Industry

What Pittsburgh is to steel and Akron to rubber, Hollywood is to the motion-picture industry: it is the movie capital of the world. One-half of the studios are either in Hollywood or Los Angeles proper, though in recent years there has been some decentralization out of these centers and into Culver City, the San Fernando Valley (Burbank), Studio City, and Westwood. The principal

[3] Buildings planned for a civic center two miles from the center of subsidence have been designed with a built-in lean, on the theory that continual subsidence will make them plumb. See Howard J. Nelson, "The Spread of an Artificial Landscape Over Southern California," *Annals of the Association of American Geographers,* Vol. 49 (September 1959), p. 98.

attraction of the San Fernando Valley is availability of land in large tracts and at lower cost than in the older areas.

The original studios were attracted to Southern California by the sunny mediterranean climate and the great variety of scenery to be found within the immediate area—mountains, deserts, tropical vegetation, and seacoast. This early start enabled the area to retain the industry even after natural advantages were no longer so significant. Early photography required good sunlight, and before the advent of sound-films, most pictures were taken in the open, which required periods of protracted sunlight with a minimum of rain that might damage the equipment. Today most movies are staged in studios, and since a large part of the lighting effect is produced artificially, Southern California sunshine is no longer a controlling factor. Nevertheless, the industry is firmly entrenched here because of the early concentration of talent, skills, and reputation.

At the present time an increasing number of motion pictures are being filmed outside Southern California, often on location in foreign countries. However, the booming television industry has also found a home in Los Angeles, particularly for "canned" (filmed) shows.

The concentration of these entertainment industries in the subregion has been a powerful attraction for tourists and job-seekers alike.

Manufacturing

This subregion, long famous for its agriculture and climate, is also justly famed in manufacturing. Especially is this the case in the great conurbation that occupies the Los Angeles lowland. Los Angeles today is the third largest industrial center in Anglo-America. San Diego, though considerably smaller, has been growing at a faster rate than any other industrial center in the United States since World War II.

Aircraft Part of the rapid development of this industry is due to World War II and the gigantic demand for military aircraft, but the industry was entrenched in Southern California before the outbreak of the war. The 1937 *Census of Manufactures* reported 24 establishments for California and only 17 for New York, which until then had been the leading state. Possibly nowhere else in the world is there so large an aggregation of airframe plants. Within a ten-mile radius in the Los Angeles industrial area are located the principal plants of four of the seven largest American aircraft producers.

The finished airplane is the result of the combined efforts of the three main groups of manufacturers: (1) engine manufacturers who construct the vital power plants which are to propel the machine; (2) manufacturers who provide literally thousands of parts and sub-assemblies for each airplane; and (3) manufacturers who build the frames of the airplanes and assemble into them the necessary engines, propellers, parts, and accessories. Many of the engine and propeller plants remain at or near their original sites in the East, where materials and skilled labor are at hand. California's favorable flying weather is no inducement to them.

Before the United States began to prepare itself for national defense, the aircraft industry was heavily concentrated in Los Angeles, Seattle, Baltimore, and Buffalo. After 1939, however, the business grew so fast and changed so much that statistics applicable to that year are of interest only to the historian. For military reasons, the total capacity of the industry on the coast fell from 77.3 per cent of the nation's total to 42.3 per cent. Los Angeles' share was reduced from 28.4 per cent to 11.8 per cent—a situation attributable to economic causes and to the desire to lessen the vulnerability of the industry to possible air attack.

Climate appears to be the most important single location factor affecting this industry. Snow and freezing temperatures are of very rare occurrence in Southern California, and there is an abundance of sunshine. The mild climate is advantageous in four ways: (1) the good flying weather permits year-round flight testing of airplanes; (2) the warm and relatively dry climate permits the storage of parts and equipment out-of-doors; (3) mild temperatures reduce heating needs and consequently construction costs—an important factor where hangars covering millions of square feet are used; and (4) outdoor work may be carried on all year round, a factor of special importance because the final assembly process of airframe production requires a great amount of space owing to the huge wing span of modern planes. These several advantages make it possible for most work to be done out-of-doors, thus saving the cost of constructing huge sheds (Figure 14-6).

The second most important location fac-

Figure 14-6. A Southern California aircraft plant. Prime aircraft contractors need plenty of room both inside and outside their buildings. (Photo courtesy Douglas Aircraft Company, Inc.)

tor is availability of a large pool of skilled labor. Los Angeles and San Diego developed such a pool, and as a result, other airframe plants and allied industries established themselves nearby in order to draw on the supply. Most of the important centers are now able to utilize such supplies. Skills take a long time to develop. The time required for and the expense of training inexperienced workmen and the high wage rates necessary to move skilled workers from already producing areas make difficult the task of locating in new areas to meet changed conditions. Many women are employed in this industry.

Taxation may be an important locational factor. The high taxes are proving an incentive for the decentralization of the airframe industry to communities surrounding the large cities, such as Santa Monica, El Segundo, Long Beach (Douglas), Culver City (Hughes), Burbank (Lockheed), Inglewood (North American), and Hawthorne (Northrop).

Los Angeles is the world's leading aircraft manufacturing center, with nearly 200,000 workers in the industry. The huge windowless plants of the prime contractors are invariably located adjacent to an airport (Los Angeles International, Santa Monica, Long Beach, or Burbank). San Diego has about one-fourth as much production as Los Angeles, but vies with Flint (automobiles) and Wichita (aircraft) as the most specialized industrial city in the nation, for more than 70 per cent of its factory workers are employed in aircraft plants.

All of the large aircraft makers are also involved in missile and spacecraft work. This complex supports many ancillary subcontractors, especially in electronics and instrument production.

Electronics The complicated field of electronics is well represented in Southern California. A product largely of the last decade, this industry has tended to concentrate in the San Fernando Valley, but is also found in other areas.

Iron and Steel At Fontana, 50 miles inland from Los Angeles, is the only completely integrated iron and steel plant on the Pacific Coast. It emerged during World War II, when American railroads were laboring under the strain of supplying the terrific demands of the two-ocean war. There was urgent need for building ships on the Pacific Coast. The water route via the Panama Canal, however, was menaced by German submarines, and the railroads could carry no more overland traffic. Henry J. Kaiser, who built the plant, wanted to locate it on tidewater, but naval security seemed to require that it be built inland. Nearness to market and easy access to tidewater were the dominant location factors. The plant, which cost originally about 100 million dollars, has been expanded and now includes several of the nation's largest blast furnaces, by-product coke ovens, open-hearth furnaces, and other facilities.

The enterprise gets its fuel from Kaiser-owned coal mines in Utah some 800 miles away, its iron ore partly from mines 175 miles away in San Bernardino County and partly from mines in Utah, its limestone from a local quarry, and its scrap from the region at large. Los Angeles is the largest scrap source on the Pacific Coast. Water is purchased but is reused by cooling. Since the plant is only 50 miles from the Los Angeles industrial area, it has a good market (Los Angeles normally uses 43 per cent of the Western steel output). In its proximity to market, Fontana differs from the Colorado and Utah industries. Indeed, it is well located for supplying the entire Pacific Coast.

In addition to the Fontana plant, there are in the Los Angeles area subsidiaries of some of the big eastern corporations. They are of a size and type, however, typical of those usually found when dependence is preponderantly on local supplies of scrap.

Compared with Pittsburgh, Gary, Youngstown, and Birmingham, the California iron and steel industry is unimpressive, but to the state itself, it means much. Moreover, the industry is growing rapidly.

Sports Wear In certain lines of clothing, Southern California poses a real threat to both New York and Paris. Hollywood greatly influences style trends because of the popularity of the motion-picture stars. But it is in sportswear that the state, particularly Southern California, is surging ahead spectacularly. Californians are said to have invented outdoor living. Assuredly, the climate does encourage living out-of-doors. Hence, designers make it a point to understand outdoor fabric requirements. The wools are a little thinner and the cottons a little heavier; silks and rayons are semitropical. Southern California also is a leader in bathing suits and play clothes.

There are some problems, however, chief of which is distribution. California cannot get its clothes into production and on to the store shelves as fast as New York. Labor costs, too, are higher. Moreover, the California market emphasizes quality rather than price, and it originates styles rather than copies them.

Furniture Southern California has a young, rapidly growing, and important furniture industry. In fact, it has the only important such industry in the West. Los Angeles is the principal center, its advantages being progressive management, skill in design, workmanship and market analysis, along with an important market. California consumes about ten per cent of the furniture and house-furnishing retail sales of the entire country. Unlike the centers in the East and Middle West, furniture manufacturers here are not near their lumber, textile, or metal suppliers. California does have softwood and some hardwoods, but the bulk of the latter must be shipped in.

Los Angeles is not hampered by tradition, its designers being willing to experiment. The impact of Hollywood on much of America's thinking has enabled Los Angeles to become a style center in furniture precisely as it has in the clothing industry. Particularly is it pioneering in outdoor furniture, and the new style concept of ease and sprawling comfort is making itself felt even in the indoor type of furniture.

Other Manufacturing There are additional manufactures that are important. Of these, rubber and rubber tires, mining and oil-well equipment, calculating machines, chemicals, automobiles, and photographic equipment are prominent. In the manufacture of automobile tires, Los Angeles, with each of the "Big Four" maintaining large plants, stands second only to Akron, capital of this industry. As an automobile-assembly center, Los Angeles ranks high. The manufacture of photographic equipment here was a natural response to the prominence of the motion picture industry.

Resorts and Tourism

The Southern California Subregion, with its mild, sunny climate, is an American "Riviera." Southern California offers the tourist mountains, beaches, citrus groves, offshore subtropical islands, a large city, and Hollywood. These draw visitors from all parts of the continent and the world, and the Los Angeles Chamber of Commerce, with its various allied organizations, does a good job in advertising the attractions of the subregion.

At first Southern California attracted people largely during the mild winter season. Although summers are relatively cool near the beaches, the inner parts of the Los Angeles Basin often record high temperatures, which, according to the natives, are "unusual." The winter season is a festive occasion, with many pageants and entertainments, climaxed by the "Tournament of

Roses" and the famous Rose Bowl football game at Pasadena on New Year's day.

Generally speaking, the natural attractions of the subregion (mountains, beaches, islands) are the haunts of local residents on vacation, while the man-made attractions draw the out-of-state visitors. Disneyland, for example, has become a tourist goal that ranks with the Grand Canyon, Yellowstone Park, Niagara Falls, and the Empire State Building in popularity. Movie and television studios are always swarmed with visitors, and such specialized commercial spots as Knott's Berry Farm, Marineland, and Farmer's Market are nationally famous.

To provide for the legitimate tourist trade, Southern California has many large resort hotels in the mountains, along the coast, and on the offshore islands, and has so improved its highway system that all parts of the state are easily accessible by hard-surface roads. Railways and airways have contributed greatly to the development of the resort business by providing swift transportation from distant centers of the East. The Diesel-powered trains on the Santa Fe and the Union Pacific railroads make the trip from Chicago in less than 40 hours, and transcontinental jet planes place Los Angeles less than five hours from New York. The automobile tourists, however, come in greatest numbers.

Major Urban Problems

According to the 1960 census, the population of California is more highly urbanized (86.4 per cent) than that of any other state except New Jersey and Rhode Island. And this urbanization is particularly pronounced in the Southern California Subregion. Such population agglomeration results in numerous problems, especially in Los Angeles.

Smog The most infamous nuisance in Anglo-America is the Los Angeles smog. The almost unique physical site of the city,

sandwiched as it is between desert-backed mountains and a cool ocean, causes frequent development of an inversion lid over the Los Angeles Basin that inhibits vertical air movements and creates stagnant atmospheric conditions. As pollutants are scattered in the air from automobile exhausts, factory smokestacks, electricity generation, and even human lungs, the right combination of conditions can cause eye-watering, lung-searing, nostril-burning smog. Such conditions occur only occasionally, but are a plague on the city at such times. Much work has been done by the quasi-governmental Air Pollution Control District since 1947 to lessen the smog, but its eradication is as yet only a fond hope.

Water In spite of much talk to the contrary, Southern California does not face an immediate shortage of water; rather, it is a potential problem for the future. Intelligent planning has provided for water to be pumped from distant sources (the Owens Valley, 350 miles away and the Colorado River, 240 miles away) to augment local underground supplies. However, the long-run future for water supply is still uncertain.

Flood and Fire The relatively small amount of precipitation falls almost entirely in the winter. As it flows down the steep hill slopes into urban areas so extensive that they are inadequately supplied with storm drains, destructive floods and mud slides often result. During the rainless summers, on the other hand, forest and brush fires are ever imminent. The tangled chaparral, chamisal, and woodland vegetation of the abrupt hills and mountains that abut and intermingle with the urbanized zones is readily susceptible to burning. Only carefully enforced fire precautions, a network of fire breaks and fire roads, and efficient suppression crews are able to hold down the damage.

Local Transportation Going from one place to another in a sprawling urban area is a time-consuming and often vexing operation. Southern California city-dwellers mostly live in detached single-family homes, which results in only a low population density. Such a density cannot economically support useful mass-transit facilities, so California has no subways, few commuter trains, and inadequate local bus service. As a result, Californians are almost wholly dependent on the automobile for local transport. To ease the inevitable congestion of ordinary streets, expensive multilane freeways are relied upon to keep the traffic moving. This solution to the traffic problem, which seems to be the only feasible one under the circumstances, is hardly more than a holding operation, for the vehicles multiply faster than the freeway miles. Los Angeles has the highest automobile density of any city in the world,[4] one automobile per 2.4 persons.

The Central Valley

The Central Valley Subregion consists of a broad trough lying between the Sierra Nevada and the Coast Ranges and averaging about 50 miles in width and more than 400 miles in length (Figure 14-7). It is outstanding agriculturally, ranking as the largest single concentration of fruit farms and vineyards in the United States. It is also the largest continuous block of agricultural land in California.

The Natural Environment

Structurally, the Valley is synclinal, having been warped downward when the Sierra Nevada and the Coast Ranges were uplifted. The long period of erosion that followed

[4] Comparable figures for New York, Philadelphia, and Chicago, for example, are 6.1, 5.0, and 3.5, respectively. Automobile Manufacturers Association, *Automobile Facts and Figures, 1959-60* (Detroit: 1960), p. 22.

this uplift caused the trough to be filled by great quantities of sand, silt, and gravel washed down from the mountains. In places the alluvium has a known thickness of more than 2,000 feet. The Valley is divided into three drainage basins: the Sacramento Valley in the north, the San Joaquin in the middle section; and the Tulare Lake Basin, an area of interior drainage, in the extreme south. The Sacramento River flows south through the northern half of the Central Valley, and the San Joaquin flows north through the southern half. They converge near San Francisco Bay, emptying into the Pacific Ocean through the only large break in the Coast Range. Their delta comprises one of the state's leading truck-farming and horticultural areas.

Climatically, the area has mild, rainy winters and warm to hot summers. Local variations occur, however, where elevation produces a modification of the general climatic type. The climate is often called the "hot summer" mediterranean climate. Lying between the Coast Range and the Sierra Nevada, most parts suffer from a deficiency of rainfall. The precipitation decreases rapidly from more than 30 inches in the north to less than 6 inches in the extreme south. The maximum falls in winter. So far as temperature is concerned, the Valley is characterized by mild winters with a long growing season, and very hot summers; daytime temperatures ordinarily exceed 100° F.

The soils in the Central Valley consist of immature alluvium materials deposited by the torrential flood waters of the rivers. Continuous deposition of alluvium prevents most of the valley soils from attaining mature profiles. Nevertheless, it is the alluvial fans that serve as the foundation for productive agriculture.

In the southern part of the Valley near Tulare Lake, alkaline conditions make large areas unsuited to irrigation agriculture, although several thousand acres have been

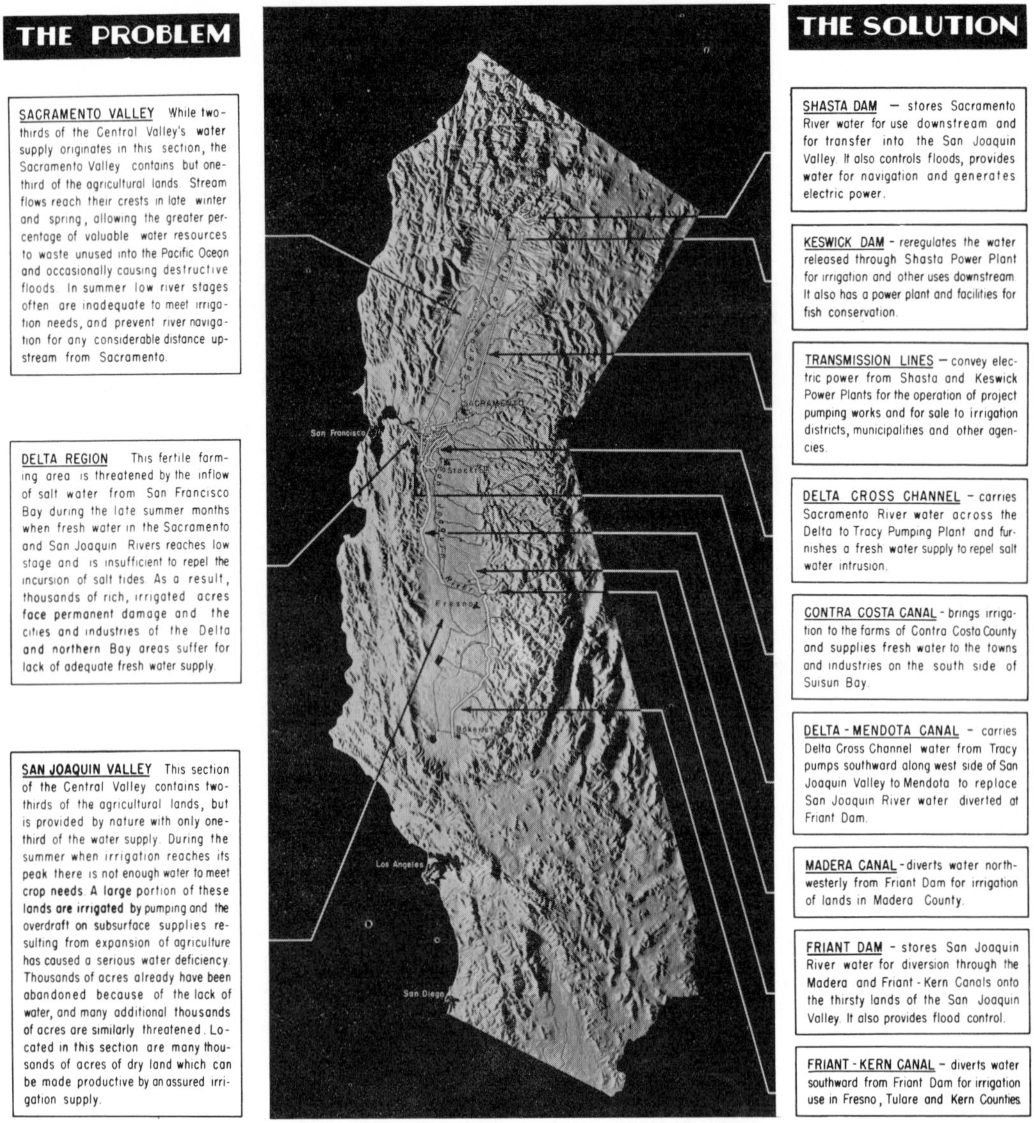

SACRAMENTO VALLEY   While two-thirds of the Central Valley's water supply originates in this section, the Sacramento Valley contains but one-third of the agricultural lands. Stream flows reach their crests in late winter and spring, allowing the greater percentage of valuable water resources to waste unused into the Pacific Ocean and occasionally causing destructive floods. In summer low river stages often are inadequate to meet irrigation needs, and prevent river navigation for any considerable distance upstream from Sacramento.

DELTA REGION   This fertile farming area is threatened by the inflow of salt water from San Francisco Bay during the late summer months when fresh water in the Sacramento and San Joaquin Rivers reaches low stage and is insufficient to repel the incursion of salt tides. As a result, thousands of rich, irrigated acres face permanent damage and the cities and industries of the Delta and northern Bay areas suffer for lack of adequate fresh water supply.

SAN JOAQUIN VALLEY   This section of the Central Valley contains two-thirds of the agricultural lands, but is provided by nature with only one-third of the water supply. During the summer when irrigation reaches its peak there is not enough water to meet crop needs. A large portion of these lands are irrigated by pumping and the overdraft on subsurface supplies resulting from expansion of agriculture has caused a serious water deficiency. Thousands of acres already have been abandoned because of the lack of water, and many additional thousands of acres are similarly threatened. Located in this section are many thousands of acres of dry land which can be made productive by an assured irrigation supply.

SHASTA DAM — stores Sacramento River water for use downstream and for transfer into the San Joaquin Valley. It also controls floods, provides water for navigation and generates electric power.

KESWICK DAM — reregulates the water released through Shasta Power Plant for irrigation and other uses downstream. It also has a power plant and facilities for fish conservation.

TRANSMISSION LINES — convey electric power from Shasta and Keswick Power Plants for the operation of project pumping works and for sale to irrigation districts, municipalities and other agencies.

DELTA CROSS CHANNEL — carries Sacramento River water across the Delta to Tracy Pumping Plant and furnishes a fresh water supply to repel salt water intrusion.

CONTRA COSTA CANAL - brings irrigation to the farms of Contra Costa County and supplies fresh water to the towns and industries on the south side of Suisun Bay.

DELTA - MENDOTA CANAL — carries Delta Cross Channel water from Tracy pumps southward along west side of San Joaquin Valley to Mendota to replace San Joaquin River water diverted at Friant Dam.

MADERA CANAL - diverts water northwesterly from Friant Dam for irrigation of lands in Madera County.

FRIANT DAM — stores San Joaquin River water for diversion through the Madera and Friant - Kern Canals onto the thirsty lands of the San Joaquin Valley. It also provides flood control.

FRIANT - KERN CANAL — diverts water southward from Friant Dam for irrigation use in Fresno, Tulare and Kern Counties.

Figure 14-7. The Central Valley of California. (Courtesy U.S. Bureau of Reclamation.)

reclaimed by an elaborate system of pumps and drainage ditches which impound the flood waters for irrigation during the dry season. Along the lower course of the Sacramento-San Joaquin Rivers, much land is water-logged and hence is unsuited to cultivation. On the whole, however, most of the Central Valley is covered with rich alluvium that provides excellent plant food for agriculture, and this, together with the abundance of irrigation water, makes these areas some of the most important farming sections of the entire continent.

Because of the low rainfall, nearly all of the Central Valley was originally grassland, with tall grasses and scattered oaks in the better-watered northern section and bunch grass and desert vegetation in the drier southern part. The largest area of open grassland in the state lies along the edge of the

Central Valley. Chaparral occupies considerable areas in the hills.

Settlement

Although a slow infiltration of English-speaking settlers into this subregion occurred during the first half of the nineteenth century, the total non-Spanish population was small. Remoteness from populous centers and the vast undeveloped landholdings of the Spaniards served to retard any rapid westward drift to California. The discovery of gold in 1848, however, touched off the spark that brought hordes of people from everywhere in a mad dash—particularly to this area.

The Gold Rush In January, 1848, shortly before the signing of the treaty closing the Mexican War, James W. Marshall discovered flakes of gold in the river gravels of one of the canyons of the Sierra Nevada. During the following summer, news of the discovery spread to the coast of California and to Oregon, and from both places hundreds of men rushed to the Sacramento area. The stampede caused San Francisco to be almost deserted, and for a time the local newspaper was suspended. Before winter the news of the great gold find had spread to the East and to northwest Europe, and before the end of 1848 the real rush had set in. During one month in the spring of 1850, 18,000 people were estimated to have gone overland to California. By the end of that year the state's population was 92,000; ten years later it had risen to 380,000. The "forty-niners" suffered untold hardships on their way to the "gold diggings," but nothing daunted them.

The Period Following the Gold Rush Gold mining continued important for some years after 1848, but the more easily worked stream gravels were soon exhausted, and the majority of individuals either had to find other occupations or move to new mining areas elsewhere in the West. The discovery of gold in the Rockies of Colorado and of silver in Nevada took a large number of miners eastward. Many of the people, however, who had moved to California realized its potential worth as an agricultural area and began to secure land from the old Spanish *ranchos* that were being broken up and sold. Remoteness from large centers of population made it impossible for these areas to produce farm products for the outside market, but they had a decided advantage for supplying California. Subdivision of the great ranches into small tracts brought many new home-seekers to California, particularly after the close of the Civil War, and soon the Central Valley became an outstanding wheat-producing area. With the completion of the first "transcontinental railroad" in 1869, providing a greater outlet for agricultural surpluses, the Valley blossomed forth as one of the great "bonanza" wheat-growing areas of the nation.

Agriculture

Agriculture was relatively unimportant for years after the Gold Rush. The reasons for this were that (1) most of the adventurous people who came to the mining region had little or no farming background or even interest; (2) there was little inclination to farm so long as hopes were good for making a "strike" in mining, (3) uncertainties of land titles arose from existent grants, and (4) parts of the area—for example, the lower Sacramento Valley—had large extents of swamp and overflowed land.

Even the climate was different. The rain came during the winter. So great a departure from the climate of the East and Middle West, according to the Commissioner of Agriculture, subjected "the culture of the soil to novel conditions, unsettling old traditions, and defying some of the most tenaciously held lessons of experience in the older parts of the country." No wonder agriculture was slow in getting a foothold in the Central Valley.

Offsetting the dry season of summer was the possibility of irrigation, especially on the east side of the valley, for many rivers flowed westward from the Sierra Nevada.

Wheat was the first great crop of the Valley. It could be planted in the winter and harvested in the dry summer and the grain could be transported economically to distant domestic and even to export markets. The crop was grown on large farms averaging 400 acres, though one ranch on the west bank of the Sacramento had 50,000 acres under cultivation in 1880. Barley also became an important winter crop. It was widely used as feed for draft animals and particularly for the pack trains.

Irrigation in the Central Valley   In the 1880's when irrigation began to be practiced in this subregion, much land that previously had been used for ranching or for growing wheat or other small grains was placed "under the ditch." Prior to that time the courts of California had upheld the doctrine of riparian rights for the waters of the Valley, which allowed the owners of land bordering streams to maintain the flow of water in those streams in undiminished volume. This doctrine, designed for a humid country, was unsuited to a land where the chief purpose of water was to be for irrigation, and it had the effect of granting a large supply of water to certain overflow lands that did not need it and of prohibiting the use of water on good irrigable lands not adjacent to streams. Within recent years, however, the courts have ruled that even riparian landowners are entitled to only a "reasonable use" of stream waters and that the surpluses may be diverted. Following the peak year of grain production in the Central Valley (1885), irrigation has increased steadily. The irrigated lands of the Valley represent more than 65 per cent of the total for California.

The Central Valley Project   Almost from the beginning of irrigation in the Central Valley, need was felt for some central control of irrigation waters so that the heavy winter precipitation on the Sierra Nevada could be better conserved for summer use. Some fifty active irrigation districts have distributed waters to more than two million acres of irrigated lands, and on some of the major streams, such as the Tuolumne, the Stanislaus, and the Merced, large storage reservoirs have been constructed, but still no unified project has been completed. In 1920, Robert B. Marshall worked out an elaborate plan for the coordinated exploitation of water resources of the Central Valley. Although the plan was rejected, it created interest in a Central Valley Project. The California legislature began an investigation, and plans were issued in 1923 and revised in 1925, 1927, and 1930. The plans were replaced by a final one presented by the state engineer, Edward Hyatt; this was ultimately adopted, with minor changes, by the state legislature.

The present Central Valley Project (Figure 14-7) has two main purposes: (1) the supplying of water to the dry southeastern San Joaquin Valley and (2) the prevention of salt-water encroachment in the delta area. Actually there is enough unused water to meet present needs in full and to provide for further growth. The shortage results from the failure to save flood waters. An annual average of about 20 million acre-feet of water flows unused into the Pacific Ocean from the streams of the Central Valley.

The big over-all problem is that two-thirds of the water but only one-third of the irrigable farm lands are in the Sacramento River Basin, whereas one-third of the water but two-thirds of the irrigable farm lands are in the San Joaquin River Basin.

The ultimate program of the Bureau of Reclamation is to utilize fully and efficiently all the water resources of Central Valley.

The master plan contemplates 48 dams and 20 large canals, powerhouses and other works, and would double the Central Valley's irrigated area.

Agricultural Pattern of the Valley Generally speaking, the crops grown in the Valley are suited to topographic, edaphic, irrigation, and drainage factors, rather than to latitude. Irrigation water comes from the Sierra Nevada, so the eastern side of the Valley is easier to irrigate and consequently is more productive. Extension of irrigation canals to carry pumped water to the western side of the Valley is being increased. Seepage from upper level irrigation has caused alkali accumulation in the "trough" (lowest part of the Valley) to such an extent that several hundred thousand acres have reverted from cultivation to grazing usage.

A traverse of the San Joaquin Valley from east to west would show the following land-use cross-section: (1) nonirrigated grain (wheat and barley) and cattle pastures in the eastern foothills; (2) oranges and lemons (irrigated) in the sheltered foothill basins; (3) irrigated deciduous fruits, nuts, grapes, vegetables, potatoes, and cotton on the upper slopes of the alluvial fans; (4) irrigated cotton, alfalfa, and dairy farms on the lower alluvial fan slopes; (5) irrigated rice, cotton, sugar beets, and asparagus, and nonirrigated pasture in the trough; (6) irrigated cotton, grain, and flax (Figure 14-8) or nonirrigated pasture and grain on the west side; (7) poor grazing in the dry western foothills.

Crops

Cotton Cotton production expanded rapidly after 1925 in the San Joaquin Valley, which is today one of the nation's outstanding cotton-growing areas. In addition, cotton is now the most important single crop in the State.

Figure 14-8. Deep-well irrigation in the San Joaquin Valley. This water is pumped from a 2,000-foot well on the dry western side of the Valley. The crop in the background is flax. (Photo courtesy Standard Oil Company of California.)

Most of California's cotton acreage is in the Central Valley, particularly in the middle and southern portions. So important has the crop become that it has changed the system of farming in many parts of the valley, since it has been more profitable than fruits, vegetables, and even dairy products. It has replaced much irrigated pasture formerly used for sheep. The major factors controlling the localization of cotton are the climate, the availability of irrigation water, and the value of competing crops. The long, hot, growing season, the freedom from rain during picking, and the flat land are additional favorable factors, as is the absence of the cotton boll weevil. Until 1951 the area was free of the pink bollworm.

The invasion of the Valley by the pink bollworm is the most serious insect threat so far experienced by California cotton grow-ers. Unlike the cotton boll weevil, the pink bollworm thrives under arid conditions.

This subregion grows exclusively an up-land type of cotton which was developed specifically for the San Joaquin Valley cli-mate and soil. It produces relatively long staples and yields heavily. Because of its superior quality (it has a uniform length of fiber, fewer kinks, and good spinning quali-ties) and the early recognition of the ad-vantages of specialization in one variety, legislation enacted at the request of the growers themselves makes it unlawful to grow any other variety in the counties from San Joaquin to Kern.

The crop is harvested both by hand and by mechanical pickers. Hand picking is cleaner but more expensive. So far, hand pickers have to follow up the machines. Since cotton must not be picked when wet, because it balls up and grades low, mechan-ical pickers start working a field only after the dew is off, and they stop before the dampness of evening commences.

Until recently nearly all the labor force was migrant. Now part of it is being settled at least for the four or five cotton months; then it moves into the fruit- and field-crop areas as the several crops come in season.

Grains and Other Field Crops ALFALFA, the chief hay crop of the subregion, accounts for more than 80 per cent of the production of all hay crops. It is grown mainly under irrigation. Because of the long growing sea-son, alfalfa is cut from three to six times annually. It is grown for hay, seed, alfalfa meal, and pasture, and is a principal legume grown for soil improvement. Its high nutri-tional value makes it the preferred rough-age for dairy cows. Its wide adaptability accounts for its widespread distribution throughout the area.

LADINO CLOVER is the basic legume in California's 600,000 acres of irrigated pas-ture. The crop is grown mostly in the Sac-ramento and northern San Joaquin valleys, where it thrives on the heavy clay or loam soils. It does well on shallow soil underlaid by a tight layer of clay or a hardpan, and so is a key factor in the development of irri-gated pasture. It is productive and palat-able, fast-growing and long-lived. It does well on soils too shallow for such deep-rooted crops as alfalfa, sugar beets, and tree fruits.

SUGAR BEETS [5] The first really successful sugar-beet factory in the Southwest was be-gun in 1879 at Alvarado; nine years later a second factory was built at Watsonville. California leads the nation in sugar-beet production, and the principal growing area, though by no means the only one, centers in the Sacramento and the northern and cen-tral San Joaquin valleys, including the delta. Beets are raised on thousands of farms, on many of which other crops cannot be grown to advantage because they are less tolerant of alkali.

The beets are grown under contract with sugar-refining companies of which there are three operating in the Valley. A single plant usually contracts for about 20,000 acres of beets. Assuming a yield of 20 tons to the acre, such a factory processes 400,000 tons of beets annually.

The beets are harvested in accordance with a company schedule and shipped to a designated factory by truck or rail or to a loading station for shipment to the factory. Beets are transported only about 30 miles because of their considerable weight and bulk in proportion to value and because of their perishability.

WHEAT, once the most important crop in the Valley, declined rapidly in importance between 1899 and 1909, partly because of the use of the better lands for more inten-

[5] Despite California's importance in sugar-beet production, only a few of the salient conditions are presented here because the crop has received adequate attention in previous chapters.

sive crops and partly because of the depletion of soil fertility from continuous cropping. High prices for wheat during World War I caused a revival in production, but today wheat occupies a relatively small acreage. The crop is both dry farmed and irrigated. California wheat is soft wheat and hence commands no premium price.

BARLEY grows in the same lands as wheat but is better adapted to the dry climate of the Central Valley. Areas of heaviest production are found in the northern part of the San Joaquin Valley and in the Sacramento Valley. In the latter, particularly, it is both dry-farmed and irrigated. Barley now greatly exceeds wheat in acreage, because it usually yields enough more per acre to offset the price advantage of wheat. Most of the crop is fed to animals, although about one-fourth is used for malting. Very little barley is exported.

RICE is grown on several hundred thousand acres, mostly in the Sacramento Valley, the northern segment of the Central Valley. The crop has been grown on a commercial basis since 1912. Factors conducive to production are a plentiful supply of relatively cheap water, heavy clay soils highly retentive of water, good drainage, and high summer temperatures. Additional factors are the long, warm growing season and the freedom from rains during harvest. The heavy soils are of limited value for other crops, hence the number of crops which can be rotated is small. These crops consist primarily of Ladino clover, which is well adapted to heavy, adobe soil, beans, barley, and wheat. A common rotation is rice, beans, wheat, beans, and rice.

Rice is seeded on the watered fields by airplane almost to the exclusion of drilling it on land, the reasons being that (1) it is a fast method, (2) slightly less seed is required, and (3) less attention need be devoted to the preparation of the seed bed (Figure 14-9).

The crop is irrigated and kept flooded until just before harvest (6 to 10 feet of water per acre is needed to bring the crop to fruition), water having the following functions: (1) it supplies the water to the plant for normal life processes; (2) it helps control weeds; and (3) it makes more uniform the temperatures affecting growth.

Rice growing in California is completely mechanized; leveling, plowing, discing, fertilizing, flooding, planting, spraying, draining, and harvesting all are done with expensive equipment. Thus, a Colusa County rice farmer, on the average, produces 300 acres of rice annually with $75,000 worth of equipment. Unlike most agricultural areas, there are few farmsteads to be found in California rice country; rice growing is no longer a family occupation— it has become an engineering enterprise. [6]

[6] Marschner, *Land Use and Its Patterns in the United States,* p. 204.

Figure 14-9. Seeding rice by airplane in the Central Valley. (Photo by John Black and Associates.)

Grapes Although grapes are grown widely over the state, the Central Valley, particularly the San Joaquin segment, ranks first in production. The grape's essential requirements are dry, hot summers, cool, wet winters (or irrigation for supplementing rainfall) and freedom from killing frosts.

California grapes are classified according to use as raisin, table, or wine grapes, and their geographical distribution based upon these uses is not identical. Some grapes are suitable for more than one purpose. Thus the Malaga is used as a table grape, for wine, and in some years for raisins; the Muscat is used for making both raisins and wine, and locally as a table grape; the Thompson (Sultanina), leading table and raisin variety, is regularly used for making wine.

The wide distribution of areas suitable for grapes for one use or another augurs well for the future of the industry. The availability and cost of labor, however, have become real problems. Several of the larger growers, accordingly, are violating Old-World tradition and are planting their vines widely enough apart to permit small powered cultivators to replace men with hoes in weeding and cultivating.

Citrus Fruits Some citrus, particularly oranges, is grown on the piedmont slopes of the Central Valley, and the area is becoming more important as urban sprawl envelops citrus groves in southern California. Navel and Valencia oranges are grown in the San Joaquin Valley in the Porterville and Lindsay districts. Since the navel is more tolerant of high summer temperatures and less susceptible to frost in winter than the Valencia, it is better suited to the Central Valley.

Deciduous Fruits and Nuts The Central Valley is one of the world's outstanding areas of deciduous tree-fruits and -nuts. The soils are deep and retentive of moisture, there is adequate water for irrigation,

the winter temperatures are sufficiently low to break the rest period of the trees, there is little danger from late spring frosts, and the growing season is long and hot. The crops belong to two climate zones: the *temperate*, where peaches, apricots, pears, and cherries are grown; and the *subtropical*, where figs, walnuts, and almonds are grown. Local differences in climate and soil greatly affect the distribution of these crops.

PEACHES, grown primarily in the Central Valley, are concentrated along the east side of the San Joaquin Valley in the vicinity of Fresno and Merced, where they are grown almost entirely under irrigation. In the Sacramento district, however, large peach orchards thrive without irrigation. Although California ranks first in the United States in the production of peaches, little of the crop is marketed fresh; most of it is canned and dried. The clingstone varieties are grown for canning, the freestone for canning, drying, and fresh consumption.

The long period of bright, sunny days, the low humidity, and the high summer temperatures in the Central Valley are excellent for peach growing. Diseases and pests are well controlled.

APRICOTS are grown in the Central Valley but are important only in selected areas. The tree is quite tolerant of soil conditions; its distribution, therefore, is controlled largely by climate. Since the tree tends to bloom early and since spring frosts may occur in the Valley, sites must be carefully selected. More than 90 per cent of the national crop is grown in California.

OLIVES California grows 99 per cent of the American crop of olives, and production is virtually confined to the Central Valley. In the Sacramento Valley, olive plantings are concentrated near Oroville, Corning, and Fair Oaks, and in the San Joaquin Valley in the Lindsay-Exeter district. In the San Joaquin Valley olive trees frequently serve as border plantings around citrus and deciduous fruit orchards, where they act as windbreaks, dust screens, and ornamental borders.

The olive is well suited to the Valley, for it can withstand much heat and aridity. It is susceptible, however, to damage by freezing temperatures. It can do well on soils too poor for other tree crops. For the most part the crop is irrigated. Fortunately for California, the olive is free from the insect infestations common to Mediterranean lands. This permits the olives to be picked ripe, and most of the crop is marketed in this form.

FIGS are widely distributed over the southern half of California, but commercial production is centered largely in the Central Valley, particularly in the San Joaquin segment. The fig tree needs a long, warm growing season, low humidity, and hot summers. Killing spring frosts and cold winters are detrimental.

NUT CROPS Both almonds and walnuts are commercially important in this subregion, but almonds are far more important. Almond production centers mainly in the Sacramento and northern San Joaquin Valleys, with 50 per cent of the bearing acreage in the former and 22 per cent in the latter. Successful culture is attuned to the long, warm growing season, absence of damaging spring frost, and the adequate supply of irrigation water. The great demand for shelled and salted almonds combined with a high tariff on imported nuts enables California to be a huge producer.

English walnuts rank just behind oranges and peaches as California's most valuable tree crop, [7] and the California crop is more than 90 per cent of the national total. In the last four decades the production center has shifted from Southern California to north-

central California, especially the northern part of the San Joaquin Valley.

Vegetables Asparagus, beans, tomatoes, and potatoes all are very important in the Central Valley; most other vegetables, however, are of only secondary importance.

ASPARAGUS is a major crop in the Delta of the Sacramento and San Joaquin Rivers; in fact, more than 90 per cent of the state's total acreage is here. Geographical conditions are particularly favorable in the Delta: the soils are a mixture of muck and alluvium, the temperatures are modified by the sea breezes through Carquinez Strait, and there is a plentiful supply of irrigation water.

FIELD BEANS production is outstanding from Merced County north to Tehama County. The extreme heat of the southern San Joaquin Valley rules out bean production there. The varieties grown are limas, pinks, blackeye, cranbury, Mexican red, red kidney, and bayo.

POTATOES, because of their low value per unit of weight and their perishability, should be grown relatively near their market. Since California now ranks first in population among the states of the Union, an appreciable market is at hand. Nevertheless, potatoes are among the least important of the state's row crops. The largest white-potato acreage is on the San Joaquin Delta. The crop is grown under large-scale methods. Kern County grows more than 75 per cent of the state's *early* potatoes. California specializes in early potatoes—those that can be marketed in May and June. The yield is more than twice the early-potato yield of any other state.

TOMATOES are a major crop in California, and the Central Valley is one of the principal growing areas. In the Valley, because of its long growing season, tomatoes mature before the really high temperatures begin. The crop is grown both for the fresh market and for canning.

[7] Kenneth Thompson, "Location and Relocation of a Tree Crop—English Walnuts in California," *Economic Geography,* Vol. 37 (April 1961), p. 134.

Industrialization of Agriculture

The open, relatively level floor of the Central Valley and the relative scarcity of farm labor both stimulate the wide employment of labor-saving machinery.

Because of the climate and the kinds of crops grown, however, the problems are not precisely like those in other agricultural areas. It is not surprising to learn, therefore, that Californians are noted for their versatility in solving peculiar crop problems through the use of special inventions. The combined harvester-thresher was being used on the big Central Valley farms as early as the 1880's. During World War II, when field labor was particularly scarce, a number of "dirt farmers" in the Central Valley developed machinery adapted to their own special products. One farmer developed a machine for shaking walnuts off the trees. Another device is the sloping catching-frames which are placed under the trees for collecting and delivering the fruit to field boxes. Vacuum and brush pickups even gather the nuts from the ground. Other contributions include a green-asparagus harvester, tomato-picking aids, a mechanical apricot-cutter, a hay-making machine which lifts hay to the wagons, a sugar-beet harvester, a hay-bale shredder, and a weed cutter. Pneumatic shears are used for pruning. Onions are harvested by machine. One machine sorts adobe lumps from beans. As noted earlier, airplanes now seed from the air nearly all of the California rice crop; they also fertilize and spray much of the rice.

Probably in no other part of Anglo-America has farming "progressed" from a way of life to an industrial enterprise to such an extent as it has in the Central Valley. The farm family is by no means a thing of the past, but increasingly it is being replaced by the farm corporation that controls huge acreages with carefully calculated large-scale efficiency. Sometimes the corporation owns its own machinery; some farms, for example, have as many as 50 mechanical cotton-pickers (cost: $10,000 each). In other instances the corporation owns nothing but the land, with the farm manager subcontracting the entire crop-growing operation—planting is done by one firm, cultivation by another, spraying by an airplane contractor, and harvesting by a crew of migratory workers. Thus Central Valley farming is a mixture of big business and agriculture. In most years, four of the six leading agricultural counties in the United States, as measured by value of farm products sold, are Central Valley counties.

Crop Processing

Because harvested fruits and vegetables may deteriorate rapidly, most processing of these items tends to be done near the fields where they are grown. Consequently, the Central Valley carries on a great deal of processing of various types of agricultural products—cotton ginning, cotton-oil processing, flour milling, beet-sugar refining, meat packing, rice milling, almond processing, the drying of raisins and other fruits, and wine making.

Sugar Refining California is the only state to refine both beet and cane sugar. It has already been pointed out that California ranks first in production among the 22 beet-growing states. A beet-sugar factory, in order to operate profitably, must process about 400,000 tons of beets annually, which means contracting for about 20,000 acres of beets. It must also have access to a large supply of good water—200,000 to 400,000 gallons per hour—at moderate cost. Each factory draws upon a restricted area of beet land and operates seasonally. Most of the factories are located in the northern part of the Central Valley.

Wine Making Grapes are grown in 47 of the 58 California counties, and 40 per cent of the crop enters the wine industry.

Many of the vineyards are enormous, the largest occupying some 5,000 acres. Almost 20,000 California farmers grow grapes. Grapes beget wineries, and hence maps of the two coincide remarkably well.

California, with 400 wineries located mostly in eight different areas, manufactures 90 per cent of the total commercial wine made in the United States.

Almost every known variety of grape and wine type finds a congenial *milieu* somewhere in the state. The temperature and rainfall maps largely tell the story of wine varieties and specialties, though altitude and soil types also play a role. These last two factors are quite variable, even among neighboring vineyards.

The Drying of Raisins The nation's raisin production is confined mainly to the San Joaquin Valley, and Fresno is synonymous with raisins. This area yields about half the world output. Annual production varies widely according to price and market; in some years 400,000 tons will be dried and in another 170,000 tons. Though some raisins are dehydrated artificially, probably 85 per cent are sun-dried. When the fruit has attained a sugar content of about 25 per cent some time during the latter half of August, the clusters of grapes are handpicked and spread on squares of heavy paper between the rows of vines, where they are allowed to dry for about 10 to 15 days. Four pounds of grapes dry into one pound of raisins. This is no time for rain, and normally none falls.

Canning and Freezing The canning of fruits and vegetables got its start more than a century ago in San Francisco. Since 1915 California has been the leading canned-foods producer among the states, with special emphasis on fruits. The state is now also the leader in production of frozen fruits and vegetables.

This industry is characterized by contract growing of the crops, horizontal integration, and vertical integration. Here is a significant enterprise in which the distinction of what is agriculture and what is industry grows increasingly less meaningful.

The major center of vegetable and fruit processing is the San Francisco Bay area. However, due to increased suburbanization and industrialization of that area, an increasing proportion of the canning and freezing now is done in the Central Valley, particularly at Stockton, Sacramento, Fresno, and Bakersfield.

Livestock

During the period of Spanish settlement, huge tracts of land were granted to the colonists for ranches. Although cattle ranching was the leading activity during the entire Spanish-Mexican period because of the abundance of native grasses and the mild climate, it was never especially profitable. With the increase in the demand for foodstuffs following the discovery of gold, the better lands in the Central Valley were plowed up and planted to cereals—particularly wheat. Hence cattle and sheep ranching were crowded onto the poorer hill lands of the coast or into the drier parts of the San Joaquin Valley.

Beef Cattle The distribution of beef cattle is fairly wide throughout the state, though the Central Valley is the leading area. The cattle are now marketed at lighter average weight than they were formerly, and feeding in the area is now well developed.

Dairy Cattle Widely distributed over the state, also, are dairy cattle, but here again the Central Valley is outstanding. The huge output of alfalfa serves as the principal roughage. The Holstein breed predominates. Most of the Valley milk is sold as whole milk or cream for manufacturing, though some market milk is sent to Valley cities, to those in the Bay Area, and to metropolitan Los Angeles.

Sheep In sheep, California ranks next to Texas and Wyoming, with approximately six per cent of the nation's total. Sheep, though widely distributed over the state, are most highly concentrated in the Central Valley and the North Coast which together have about 85 per cent of the state's total. The pattern of distribution changes very slightly from decade to decade. Sheep raising is prosecuted under both farm and range conditions, the former being most highly developed in the lower Sacramento Valley; here the flocks are maintained during summer and fall primarily on native pasture, volunteer grain fields, grain stubble, and beet tops. The foothills bordering the Valley provide winter grazing and lambing grounds for thousands of head of range ewes. As feed in the Valley dries up, many sheepmen in the Sacramento Valley and in parts of the San Joaquin Valley truck or ship their stock into the high pastures of the Sierra Nevada. Many sheep are moved into the Sacramento-San Joaquin Delta each fall for feeding.

Changes, however, are occurring in the sheep business: much land formerly devoted to sheep raising is now being used for crops because the latter are more profitable. Skilled sheep labor is both scarce and ex-pensive; grazing in the national forests has been reduced; and wool prices have fluctuated widely. Nevertheless, there is much land in the state that can be utilized more profitably by sheep than by anything else.

Petroleum and Natural Gas

The San Joaquin Valley petroleum district, like the region's other three, lies in the southern part of the state. The San Joaquin Valley district, comprising more than 25 fields (Figure 14-10), is by far the largest of California's oil-producing areas. It also ranks first in proved reserves, first in estimated ultimate production, second in past production, and third in average estimated ultimate production per acre. Although some of its fields are declining, there has been an extension of production in recent years to the south and west slopes of the Valley. Bakersfield is the producing center of the district.

California is one of the nation's four leading producers of natural gas. Though gas was first brought in at Stockton in 1864, it was not until 1937 that the business really became outstanding, with successful production at depths greater than 10,000 feet. Despite heavy production in the Stockton district, the Coalinga Field, and elsewhere

Figure 14-10. Oil derricks in the Midway-Sunset Field on the margin of the San Joaquin Valley. (Photo courtesy Spence Air Photos.)

within the region, large quantities are shipped in from Texas, New Mexico, and Alberta.

The Sierra Nevada

From some points of view the Sierra Nevada is the least important of the four subregions (Figure 14-1). Population is much smaller than elsewhere and economic opportunities are fewer. Mining, logging, grazing, and recreation are the leading occupations. Of these, mining is declining in importance. Transportation is a big problem, particularly in winter.

The Natural Environment

The Sierra Nevada is an immense mountain block 50 to 80 miles wide and 400 miles long. It was formed by a gigantic uplift which tilted the block westward. The eastern front is marked by a bold escarpment which rises 5,000 to 10,000 feet above the alluvial-filled basins of the Intermontane Region to the east, this escarpment marking one of the most definite geographical boundaries on the continent. The western slope, although more gentle, is deeply incised with river canyons and has been greatly eroded by glaciers, forming such magnificent canyons as those of the Yosemite and Tuolumne.

The summits of the Sierra Nevada have suffered severe glacial erosion and consist of a series of interlocking cirques. Complex faulting, mountain glaciation, and stream erosion account for most of the details of the mountain mass. Some of the block-faulted valleys contain lakes, the most noted of which is Lake Tahoe.

The Sierra Nevada, because of its great elevation and because it presents a formidable barrier to the rain-bearing winds from the Pacific Ocean, has its heaviest precipitation on the western slope, and this flows down into the Central Valley, providing it with water for irrigation; the eastern, rain-shadow side is comparatively dry. Although some rain falls throughout the summer, the maximum precipitation comes as snow during the winter season. The western slope receives the heaviest snowfall of any part of the United States, the average being more than 400 inches a year. Heavy snows tend to emphasize the barrier nature of the Sierra Nevada and have caused great expense to transportation lines operating across them.

On the western slopes of the Sierra Nevada, dense forests of conifers dominate the landscape. These include ponderosa pine, Douglas fir, lodgepole pine, sugar pine, and sequoia, and constitute some of the most magnificent forests of the continent. Higher up on the slopes the large trees give way to smaller dwarfed varieties and these ultimately give way on the highest summits to tundra vegetation.

As a result of some of man's practices such as destructive logging, accidental and willful fires, and excessive grazing, there is progressive deterioration from woodland of better type and greater value to woodland of less value, or to chaparral or sagebrush.

The Economy

Lumbering and the Forest-products Industries The middle portions of the Sierra Nevada are covered with dense stands of conifers, including western yellow pine and sugar pine. Hence California is an important lumber-producing state.

Logging and lumbering began with the development of mining. For a long time the chief uses for wood products were mine props, crossties for railroads, and construction timber for dwellings and other buildings in the mining camps. Logging operations in those days were extremely wasteful, and doubtless much more timber was destroyed, through fire and careless logging methods, than was actually utilized.

With the development of the national forests, much of the formerly cut-over and burned-over land was withdrawn from logging activities, though a large part still remains in the hands of major lumber companies. The establishment of the national forests in the Sierra Nevada was partly to re-establish forest stands for future lumbering industries, but chiefly to protect the watersheds of the numerous streams that provide waters for irrigation, domestic use, and power. These national forests also serve as important recreational centers for the entire region, and they provide summer pastures for a large range-livestock enterprise.

Since the snows in the mountains are extremely heavy, most logging activities are confined to the summer months. Logging camps, temporary settlements that are moved from season to season, are usually located in remote areas. When logs can be moved out of the forests, they are brought to such lumber towns as McCloud and Weed, where they are converted into lumber. California, particularly metropolitan Los Angeles with its tremendous demand, is deficient in lumber supply. Hardwoods for furniture and cabinet purposes must be brought in from other regions since the Sierra Nevada forests are mostly coniferous.

The forest-products industries of the Sierra Nevada are of much importance to the region, but they occupy a place of minor significance as compared with the great lumber-producing areas in the Pacific Northwest or the South.

Mining Mining made "California" a name known to almost everyone—really put the region "on the map." In recent years, however, mining has been largely overshadowed by agriculture, manufacturing, and tourism, despite the fact that the state continues to be rich in minerals.

Gold still is mined on a limited scale in the Sierra Nevada, but in value the yellow metal is now surpassed by several other minerals. Throughout the western side of the Sierra Nevada are reminders of better days, when an active mining economy dominated the subregion. Ghost and semighost towns are common, as are the remnants of mills, smelters, and cyanide tanks. This is particularly true of the Mother Lode country, between Mariposa and Placerville.

Grazing There are four life zones in California (Figure 14-11). Generalizing, it may be said that the Lower Sonoran in the Central Valley is confined to areas below 500 feet in altitude. It consists of scattered desert shrubs and a few species of annual and perennial grasses. The Upper Sonoran lies immediately above the Lower Sonoran at elevations up to 3,000 feet. It includes the foothill and valley lands where the precipitation is slightly greater and the temperature somewhat lower than in the zone below. Chaparral is common. Native and introduced annuals predominate. The Transition Zone, occupying a narrow elevational range between 3,000 and 5,000 feet just above the Upper Sonoran, contains the commercial timber of the subregion. Rainfall here is greater and temperatures lower than in the zone below. The Boreal, a relatively small zone,[8] lies above the Transition Zone at elevations above 5,000 feet. Here the snowfall is high and temperatures low. Grazing is limited to a short midsummer and late summer period. Sheep graze it most advantageously.

In order to obtain maximum utilization of the range, the typical practice is to graze the animals in the Lower Sonoran and lower reaches of the Upper Sonoran during winter and as late in spring as the forage remains succulent, and then move them into the Transition Zone and finally into the Boreal Zone in summer and early autumn. This

[8] The term "Boreal" is used here to include the Canadian, Hudsonian, and Arctic-Alpine Zones.

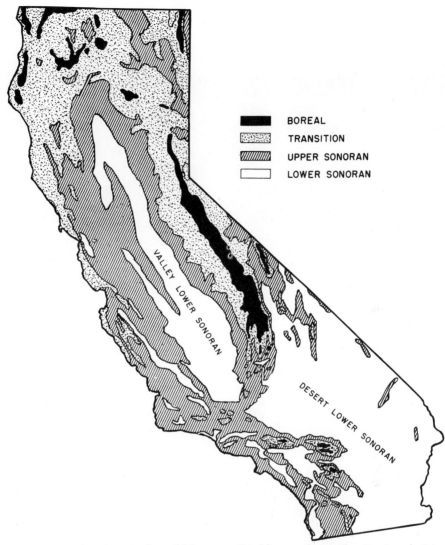

Figure 14-11. Biological life zones of California. (Map after Dr. Joseph Grinnell.)

transhumance is followed particularly by those stockmen who own or lease private lands in the high mountains or obtain grazing permits from the Forest Service to run stock in the national forests. Both cattle and sheep are raised in the mountains.

Recreation The great extent of the Sierra Nevada, 50 to 80 by 400 miles, their height, the deep canyons, waterfalls, lakes, fish-laden streams and lakes, forests, historical interests (ghost towns), and good

roads have made the mountains a great attraction for tourists and vacationists. In the Sierra Nevada are located three of the nation's most famous national parks: Sequoia, Kings Canyon, and Yosemite, noted for their magnificent groves of giant sequoia trees, spectacular glaciated valleys, waterfalls, and wildlife. Another particularly scenic area is Lake Tahoe, [9] which nestles

[9] The rapidly growing Nevada gambling and resort town of Stateline is on its southern shore.

Figure 14-12. Rampaging nature! The Southern Pacific's westbound streamliner *City of San Francisco* was stalled with 222 passengers for 80 hours in the heavy snowdrifts 15 miles west of Donner Summit in the Sierra Nevada. There were two weeks of almost continuous snowfall. Snow packed at average depths of 18 feet at Donner Summit. Drifts 20 to 30 feet deep were common. (Photo courtesy the *San Francisco Chronicle*.)

in a large pocket between the double crest of the Sierra Nevada.

Most visitors to the subregion come in summer; but there is some year-round use. Hunters, primarily seeking deer, come in the fall; skiers flock to such booming centers as Squaw Valley, Lake Tahoe, and Mammoth Mountain in winter; and fishermen are attracted in late spring.

Transportation

The nature of the terrain is such that transportation routes within the Sierra Nevada nearly all trend in a northeast-southwest direction, for this is the trend of the long western canyons that provide means of access. These canyon floors have relatively gentle gradients, but are narrow. In many cases there is not room for both road and railroad on the same side of the stream, so that they must exchange sides at the same spot. North-south transportation is virtually impossible in the main portion of the range, except by foot or horseback.

A few important rail lines cross the northern portion of the Sierra, as at Donner Pass, utilizing many tunnels to maintain an acceptable grade. Disruption of service by rock slides and snow avalanches, as well as by occasional furious blizzards, is to be ex-

pected every winter (Figure 14-12). There are elaborate protection devices, such as snow and rock sheds and fences, and warning devices, such as overhead wires that give an electric signal when broken by falling rock or sliding snow.

Roads are built into the subregion only at great cost, considerable difficulty, and with notable scarring effects on the land. Bridges, culverts, and tunnels are common. In many instances the valleys are so narrow as to require that the roads be built hundreds of feet up on the slopes. The "High Sierra" is so rugged that no road crosses it between Tioga Pass (in Yosemite National Park) and Walker Pass, a distance of over 160 miles.

The Central Coast

The Central Coast is a highly diversified and productive area. Farming, grazing, mining, logging, fishing, manufacturing—just about everything—is done somewhere in this subregion.

The area consists of the Coast Ranges and their valleys. Only the central portion, however, is considered here—that extending from northern Sonoma County, about 80 miles north of San Francisco, to San Luis

Obispo County, about 260 miles to the south (Figure 14-1).

The Natural Environment

The Coast Ranges lie west of the Central Valley and tend to run parallel with the coast. Their nearly even crests average 2,000 to 4,000 feet above sea level. Severe faulting throughout the ranges has resulted in numerous intervening valleys that have been eroded by small streams. The entire mountain mass is divided into fault blocks that are tilted in different directions. Along the coast, ancient shore terraces (in places as high as 1,500 feet above sea level) show that much of the area has been uplifted. More recently in geologic time, a moderate amount of localized sinking allowed the sea to break through some of the fault valleys of the outer coastal range and submerge the lower valleys of the streams. Golden Gate and San Francisco Bay were formed by this type of subsidence.

The coastline is generally steep and rocky. There are few bays or other indentations. Offshore currents are strong, and the combination of rugged land and active water is spectacular.

On the whole, the subregion is characterized by mild winters and warm to hot summers, with the maximum precipitation in winter. Great warmth and dryness characterize the interior portions in summer.

The Coast Ranges receive more moisture than the Central Valley and are somewhat cooler in summer, but, since few of the summits exceed 2,000 feet in elevation, they do not get the heavy precipitation of the Sierra Nevada. Certain portions, however, such as the Santa Cruz Mountains, receive very heavy rainfall.

Along the coast a distinctive variation of the Central California climate exists in what is known as the "Fog Belt"—an area characterized by mild winters and cool summers with a maximum of fog during the sum-

mer.[10] Because of the prevalence of fog, the summer maximum temperature occurs in August and September, but throughout the entire area cool summers are characteristic. Rainfall comes largely during the winter season.

The vegetation in this belt of foothill and valley country consists largely of grass, both native and introduced annuals. There is evidence supporting the claim that before grazing became extensive here, the plant population consisted largely of palatable perennial grasses. These apparently were transformed by overgrazing, droughts, and introduction of mediterranean plants.

In the "Fog Belt," the Coast Range supports considerable coniferous forest growth. Oak is quite common on the lower slopes (Figure 14-13), and in the rainier and fog-

[10] R. J. Russell, "Climates of California," *University of California Publications in Geography*, Vol. 2 (1926), p. 82.

Figure 14-13. Beef cattle on a hillside in the Santa Clara Valley. The vegetation is typical of the central coast ranges—grass and open oak forest. (Photo courtesy San Jose Chamber of Commerce.)

gier parts, such as in the vicinity of Santa Cruz, considerable numbers of the large redwoods appear; small groves occur locally elsewhere, also. North of San Francisco Bay, along the northwest coast, lies the world's greatest redwood forest, but that area falls within the North Pacific Coast Region (Chapter 16).

The soils are variable because of differences in parent material, climate, age, and location. Residual soils are found in the hills, transported soils in the valleys. The former, lying atop bedrock and usually not more than three or four feet deep, are little used except for fruit trees on occasional foothills. Irrigation is not feasible on most such slopes because of cost and physical difficulties, and the soils are too shallow for dry farming. For the most part, if put to agricultural use at all, they are used for pasturing range livestock; their carrying capacity averages one animal unit [11] to every 5 to 20 acres.

The soils, particularly in the Russian River, Santa Clara, Salinas, and Santa Maria Valleys, are fertile. If soils alone were involved, production could be greatly increased, but the big problem is water. There appear to be no large opportunities for development of irrigation here.

Agriculture

Conditions of natural environment vary so widely in this subregion that there is much specialization. Sonoma and Marin counties on the north are among California's leading dairy areas, producing fresh or market milk for the San Francisco Bay Area. Petaluma in Sonoma County is among the nation's leaders in commercial poultry raising, and the nearby Sebastopol area is

[11] An animal unit is a measure of livestock consumption of feed. It is the amount of forage required to maintain for a period of one year, 1 cow, steer, horse, or mule, or 5 hogs, or 7 sheep or goats, or 100 poultry.

famous for its fresh berries and apples. The Napa Valley farther east produces wine grapes, prunes, and other crops.

The valleys in the San Francisco Bay Area, particularly the Santa Clara, are the heart of prune, apricot, almond, pear, and walnut growing and even rank high in production of wine grapes, vegetables, and field crops (Figure 14-14). The same area is also one of the world's leading flower-growing areas. Among the more favorable factors are the high percentage of possible sunshine, the mild winters, and the low cost of heating greenhouses. The chief obstacles have been the salinity of the soils and the great distance from Eastern markets with resultant high shipping costs. Most of the flowers, which are sold in the East, are shipped by air.

The Pajaro Valley (in which Watsonville is located) is probably California's most famous late-apple growing area and it is important also for artichokes, strawberries, and other crops.

The Santa Maria and Santa Ynez Valleys to the south are large producers of vegetables and flower seeds.

Along the Pacific in this subregion are outstanding vegetable-growing areas—those yielding cool-climate varieties such as lettuce, artichokes, peas, and Brussels sprouts.

Three valleys in the subregion are discussed in some detail, as representative examples.

The Salinas Valley Largest in Central California is the Salinas Valley, the north end of which is nationally famous for carrots and lettuce; it also grows large acreages of white beans, sugar beets, and strawberries. In the hotter and drier southern end, field crops and livestock are important; here even beef cattle are being raised on high-value lands of irrigated pastures.

At present, lettuce is making the Salinas Valley known throughout the United States as the "Salad Bowl." Here, close to the Pa-

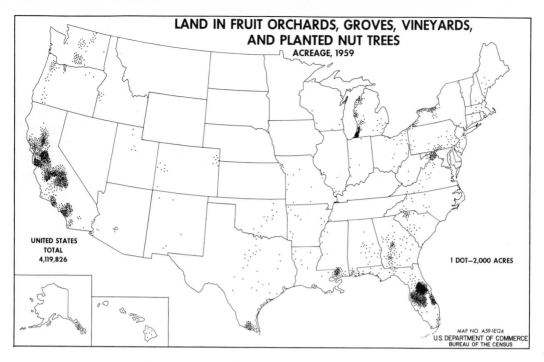

Figure 14-14. Land in tree crops and vineyards in the United States. The importance of central California is striking.

cific Ocean, with the proper proportion of warm sun to cool fog, on level terrain and in fertile soil, lettuce is grown commercially nine months of the year—April through most of December. To a certain extent it may be said that lettuce has been tailored to the valley rather than that geographical conditions here are ideal for the crop. This is not to say, however, that natural conditions are not highly propitious. The valley grows mostly spring and fall lettuce but also some summer lettuce. During the period from April to December, it produces about half of all the lettuce consumed in the country, with shipments running up to 300 cars per day (Figure 14-15). This valley normally grows about 70 to 80 per cent of the California interstate shipments. The Imperial

Figure 14-15. Harvesting lettuce in the Salinas Valley. (Photo courtesy the Southern Pacific Company.)

Valley, only other major California producer, grows only winter lettuce; during the rest of the year its climate is too hot for this crop. From time to time there is overproduction. Then in order to stabilize prices, large areas are plowed up.

All the lettuce is irrigated, the water supply coming from wells used to tap natural reservoirs. With three crops a year, water requirements are high—as much as six acre-feet.

The gross pattern of farming in the Salinas Valley shows vegetables near the coast, mixed farming in the interior areas, and grazing on the uplands.

The Santa Clara Valley The Santa Clara Valley embraces the southern arm of San Francisco Bay between the Coast Ranges—the Diablo Range on the east, the Santa Cruz on the west. Hollister is commonly considered to be at about the southern boundary of the valley.

Since San Francisco is very near and San Jose is in the valley, the utilization is industrial, commercial, and agricultural. In fact, this valley is one of the choicest agricultural areas in Anglo-America.

At first a frontier Spanish-Mexican livestock-ranging area, the Santa Clara Valley went through a wheat-growing stage when the crop was grown for gold miners. Now a fruit- and vegetable-growing stage prevails, and the valley ranks as a foremost horticultural area.

Fruit is grown intensively on the valley floor, but the surrounding ranges are much less intensively utilized. This is most noticeable in summer when the valley is green and the lower mountain slopes yellow-brown.

The valley bottom east of San Jose consists largely of prune orchards. In some places these are interrupted by vineyards, or by orchards of pears and apricots and even by fields of alfalfa, tomatoes and broccoli. Santa Clara ranks high in vegetable production, particularly tomatoes, and is one of the state's six leading tomato-growing counties. Additional crops are peas, spinach, cauliflower, and beans.

The reasons for concentration of horticulture in the Santa Clara Valley are the same as those for concentration of agriculture in the whole state—mild winters, long growing season, abundance of sunlight, and water for irrigation. Water is the critical problem in the Santa Clara Valley now.

Santa Clara County ranks first among all California counties in the production of prunes and apricots and it ranks near the top in that of pears. Most of the prunes are dried, but only about 20 per cent by the sun, the rest being mechanically dried. It is believed that dehydration will eventually become the accepted method of drying for all fruits except apricots and raisins, because it results in cleaner, higher-quality fruits at lower cost and with less labor. It also reduces the drying time. From 17 to 32 per cent of the apricots grown are canned, as is about half of the Bartlett pear crop. The largest and most specialized Bartlett pear-canning area in the United States is the Santa Clara Valley. Whereas other pear-growing areas seldom can more than 25 per cent of their Bartlett crop, the Santa Clara Valley cans nearly 50 per cent.

Since World War II, the population in Santa Clara Valley has increased greatly and much horticultural land is being taken out of agricultural use for suburban dwelling and industrial use. In the past several years, tens of thousands of acres of Class I and II land have been so converted. Many persons who work in San Francisco commute daily from as far south as San Jose, Los Gatos, and Santa Cruz because they want to avoid the fogs which, during summer, regularly hang over the central Bay Area but seldom penetrate the Santa Clara Valley. Many wealthy retired families live along or in the foothills of the Santa Cruz Range as far south as Los Gatos.

There is still considerable grazing in the foothills of and in the Coast Ranges themselves in this subregion. It is estimated that ranches totaling more than one-half million acres extend the length of the eastern foothills of the valley.

The population, agriculture, and industrial growth of the Santa Clara Valley in the final analysis will depend upon the water supply, which in turn will depend upon the measures taken by the occupying group to guarantee a future adequate and economical amount.

The Napa Valley Nestling between two of the parallel Coast Ranges north of San Francisco Bay is small, beautiful Napa Valley. Its deep alluvial valley soils are intensively utilized for tree crops, particularly prunes, and for vines.

Napa Valley is one of the famous wine districts that focuses on San Francisco. Here the temperatures are cooler than in those areas to the east and south. Most of the grapes are grown on hillsides without irrigation (Figure 14-16). The fruit grown here develops a higher acidity—a quality desired for making table wines. Many of its wineries are set in the valley among acres and acres of grape vines. Napa is famous for its red and white dry table wines and for its dessert wines.

Fishing

Commercial fishing off the central California coast is of moderate significance. The total catch landed at San Francisco and Monterey (the only fishing ports of note) is about equal to that landed at San Diego, and is less than one-third as much as the Los Angeles catch.

Fishing from San Francisco is oriented toward chinook salmon, to the north, and albacore tuna, to the south. Proceeds from these two species amount to over half of the total value of fish landed. Dungeness crabs are taken in considerable quantity; and the only two whaling stations in the United States operate in San Francisco Bay (annual catch: about 300 whales).

Fishermen from Monterey, home of famous "cannery row," concentrate on catching sardines. However, this fishing never has regained its earlier vigor, and only 3 or 4 of the 13 sardine canneries are currently in operation. Tuna and mackerel also are landed at Monterey.

Manufacturing

The San Francisco Bay area is one of California's two leading industrial areas, but it is greatly overshadowed by the other, Los Angeles. Only in canning and ship-

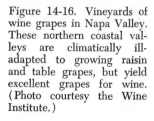

Figure 14-16. Vineyards of wine grapes in Napa Valley. These northern coastal valleys are climatically ill-adapted to growing raisin and table grapes, but yield excellent grapes for wine. (Photo courtesy the Wine Institute.)

building does it rank first, and shipbuilding is a "war baby" industry that booms only in time of conflict. However, the San Francisco Peninsula rapidly is becoming one of the nation's leading manufacturers of electronic equipment.

More than 100 major electronics producers have established facilities in the area, particularly around Palo Alto. Nearly all of them are concerned with research and development work, although they may engage in parts production or product assembly as well. The electronics producers generally are not lured by traditional industrial location factors, and the concentration in the Bay area emphasizes the "unorthodox" features of attraction.[12] The two principal location factors operative here are: (1) excellent university research laboratories, which supply much "brain power" to the industry, as well as providing facilities for further study by industry employees; and (2) the popularity of the area as a place to live for the engineers and technicians who make up the bulk of the employees. Em-

[12] C. Langdon White and Harold M. Forde, "The Unorthodox San Francisco Bay Area Electronics Industry," *Journal of Geography,* Vol. 59 (September 1960), pp. 251-58.

ployee recruitment is greatly simplified if the "good life" can be used as a lure.

Food processing is the principal type of manufacturing in the subregion as a whole, canning and freezing plants being supplied with fruits and vegetables from the productive Santa Clara Valley and from the delta lands of the Sacramento and San Joaquin Rivers. In addition to the canning, freezing, and drying of fruits and vegetables, there is considerable processing of such exotic products as cacao, coffee, copra, and cane sugar. Several large tin-plate, glass, and paper-container plants have located in the area to service the food processing industries.

Manufacturing plants are widely dispersed from San Francisco eastward to Antioch and southward to San Jose. Most of them are located along the main railways, which keep to the tidal shores of the Bay, where the land is level and cheap and where disposal of industrial waste is easy. Water for some purposes is also available in quantity. The majority of the largest plants, those employing 500 workers and more, are in the East Bay counties—Alameda and Contra Costa.

Among the outstanding industries in the

Figure 14-17. Oil refinery at Richmond in the Bay Area. (Photo courtesy Standard Oil Company of California.)

Figure 14-18. A portion of San Francisco. "Everybody's favorite city" is a major tourist attraction. Principal harbor docking and unloading facilities are shown. A portion of the San Francisco–Oakland Bay Bridge is in the foreground, and the Golden Gate Bridge connects the city with the Marin Peninsula in the background. The Pacific Ocean is at upper left. (Photo courtesy San Francisco Chamber of Commerce.)

Bay Area are oil refineries (Figure 14-17), chemical and munitions plants, a cane-sugar refinery (the only one on the West Coast), meat packing establishments, tanneries, steel mills, electronics plants, food-machinery factories, electrical-equipment plants, a helicopter plant, and cement, ceramics, fiberglass, chemical, and salt works.

The San Jose area is in the midst of a phenomenally rapid transition from an industrial economy based strictly on food processing toward one based on durable-goods manufacture. There has been outstanding development in the field of electronic and electrical-machinery production. The over-all industrial growth since 1950 rivals that of any area in Anglo-America.

Tourism

Tourism is a business of considerable importance in the subregion. There are two areas of major attraction: (1) San Francisco and (2) the coast.

San Francisco is a city of beauty and charm unexcelled in Anglo-America. Its hill-and-water site, its cosmopolitan air, and its many points of scenic and historic interest have given it an international reputation as a place to visit (Figure 14-18).

The central coast is stirringly beautiful, when not fog-bound, and is a favorite holiday area, particularly for Californians. Principal interest is focused on the Monterey Peninsula, where spectacular scenery, marine fauna (sea lions, sea otters, water birds), and a reputation for glamor (Monterey, Carmel, Big Sur, Pebble Beach) exist in close conjunction.

The Outlook

The future of this region, which includes all but the wettest and driest parts of California, seems bright. Blessed in climate—possibly the most highly publicized in the world—as well as in the bases for a thriving agriculture, with a rich heritage in forests, minerals, and scenic attractions, California has a population growth rate greater than that of any other state.[13] In fact, every cen-

[13] During the 1950's, California's population increased by 5,130,981, an increase overwhelming more than that of any other state. Florida was next with a growth of 2,180,255, followed by New York with 1,952,112 and Texas with 1,868,483.

sus since 1920 has shown California outstripping all other states in population growth. Probably better than any other state, it exemplifies that perpetual internal migration that makes the American people the most mobile in the world. This impressive and sustained trek seemingly will not be stayed.

Year after year, California ranks as the leading agricultural state, and many of its counties are in the vanguard in national standing. During World War II, it contributed one-eighth of the total necessary agricultural production. More and more the agriculture of this region will be devoted to the production of specialized fruit and truck crops and to dairy products. General farming will shrink to small proportions.

Subtropical California is the most highly urbanized region in Anglo-America; and this tendency is more likely to accelerate than to diminish. It is an urban growth that has a relatively solid base. Manufacturing and service industries are also expanding at an amazing rate.

For decades it has been predicted that the great economic desert separating California from the heartland of the nation would eventually stifle prosperity on the West Coast. However, no such eventuality has occurred, nor is it likely to. It is an incontrovertible fact that California is not self-sufficient in natural resources and that distance eastward to the next large market is great. However, the resources of the Far West are abundant, and the California mar-

TABLE 13

Selected Cities and Towns of the Subtropical Pacific Coast

City or Town	Urbanized Area	Political Center	City or Town	Urbanized Area	Political Center
Alameda	......	63,855	Ontario	......	46,617
Alhambra	......	54,807	Oxnard	......	40,265
Altadena	......	40,568	Palo Alto	......	52,287
Anaheim	......	104,184	Pasadena	......	116,407
Arcadia	......	41,005	Pico Rivera	......	49,150
Bakersfield	141,763	56,848	Pomona	186,547	67,157
Bellflower	......	45,909	Redondo Beach	......	46,986
Berkeley	......	111,268	Redwood City	......	46,290
Beverly Hills	......	30,817	Richmond	......	71,854
Buena Park	......	46,401	Riverside	......	84,332
Burbank	......	90,155	Sacramento	451,920	191,667
Chula Vista	......	42,034	San Bernardino	377,531	91,922
Compton	......	71,812	San Diego	836,175	573,224
Daly City	......	44,791	San Francisco	2,430,663	740,316
Downey	......	82,505	San Jose	602,805	204,196
Fremont	......	43,790	San Leandro	......	65,962
Fresno	213,444	133,929	San Mateo	......	69,870
Fullerton	......	56,180	Santa Ana	......	100,350
Garden Grove	......	84,238	Santa Barbara	72,740	58,768
Glendale	......	119,442	Santa Clara	......	58,880
Hayward	......	72,700	Santa Monica	......	83,249
Inglewood	......	63,390	South Gate	......	53,831
Lakewood	......	67,126	Stockton	141,604	86,321
Long Beach	......	344,168	Sunnyvale	......	52,898
Los Angeles	6,488,791	2,479,015	Torrance	......	100,991
Modesto	......	36,585	Vallejo	......	60,877
Norwalk	......	88,739	West Covina	......	50,645
Oakland	......	367,548			

ket is now large enough to be a potent factor in its own right.

Accordingly, it can be expected that population and urban growth will continue apace, that urban sprawl will envelop more and more land, and that settlement "spillover" will rapidly "colonize" the nearer margins of the Mojave and Imperial Deserts.[14]

The near future, then, is expected to show a continuation of gross current trends—California, the never-never land of American mythology, will continue to boom. In the long run, the outlook is less rosy. There must be a limit to frantic urban growth. Probably the potential urban and industrial water problem can be solved by desalinization of sea water, but smog, transportation difficulties, urban crowding, and the sheer mass of humanity may combine to destroy the "California way of life" and, with it, the principal reasons for a continued population boom.

Selected Bibliography

Baugh, Ruth E., "California: A Type Study of a State," *Education*, Vol. 69, September 1948, pp. 16-23.

Cole, Chester F., "California's Water Requirements," *Journal of Geography*, Vol. 59, September 1960, pp. 268-270.

Cunningham, William Glenn, *The Aircraft Industry: A Study in Industrial Location*. Los Angeles: L. L. Morrison, 1951.

Durrenberger, R. W., and W. G. Byron, *Patterns on the Land: Geographical, Historical, and Political Maps of California*. Los Angeles: Brewster Publishing Co., 1957.

[14] Antelope Valley, for example, just over the San Gabriel Mountains from Los Angeles, is a distinct part of the Mojave "high" desert from a physical standpoint, but its cultural development (in the southwest portion) is so intricately associated with Los Angeles that it probably should be included in the Subtropical Pacific Coast Region.

Edwards, Gordon, "The Rise of Orchardville," *Landscape*, Vol. 11, Autumn 1961, pp. 25-29.

Gregor, Howard F., "Spatial Disharmonies in California Population Growth," *Geographical Review*, Vol. 53, January 1963, pp. 100-122.

———, "The Plantation in California," *Professional Geographer*, Vol. 14, March 1962, pp. 1-4.

———, "Urban Pressure on California Land," *Land Economics*, Vol. 33, November 1957, pp. 311-325.

Griffin, P. F., and R. N. Young, *California, The New Empire State: a Regional Geography*. San Francisco: Fearon Publishing Co., 1957.

———, and Ronald L. Chatham, "Population: a Challenge to California's Changing Citrus Industry," *Economic Geography*, Vol. 34, July 1958, pp. 272-281.

Jenkins, O. P., *Geologic Guidebook Along Highway 49—Sierran Gold Belt, the Mother Lode Country*, Department of Natural Resources, Bulletin 141, San Francisco: 1948.

———, *Geologic Guidebook of the San Francisco Bay Counties*, Division of Mines, Bulletin 154. San Francisco: 1951.

Lantis, David W., and John W. Reith, "Los Angeles," *Focus*, Vol. 12, May 1962, 6 pp.

Nelson, Howard J., "The Spread of an Artificial Landscape over Southern California," *Annals of the Association of American Geographers*, Vol. 49, September 1959, pp. 80-100.

Taylor, Alice, "San Francisco," *Focus*, Vol. 9, March 1959, 6 pp.

Thompson, Warren S., *Growth and Changes in California's Population*. Los Angeles: Haynes Foundation, 1955.

White, C. Langdon, "Is the West Making the Grade in the Steel Industry?," *Business Research Series*, No. 8, Graduate School of Business, Stanford University, 1959.

———, and Harold M. Forde, "The Unorthodox San Francisco Bay Area Electronics Industry," *Journal of Geography*, Vol. 59, September 1960, pp. 251-258.

Zierer, Clifford M., ed., *California and the Southwest*. New York: John Wiley & Sons, 1956.

chapter fifteen

The Hawaiian
Islands

The smallest "region" of Anglo-America is Hawaii, lying some 2100 miles southwest of California in the Pacific Ocean. It is tied to the mainland by political affiliation and commercial dependence, which are strong enough to predominate over the volcanic base, tropical climate, Polynesian history, and Oriental population that have tended to set the islands apart from Anglo-America in the past.

Actually the Hawaiian archipelago is a 2,000-mile string of islands, islets, and reefs that extends westward across the Pacific from the island of Hawaii (at 155° West Longitude) to Kure (at 178° West Longitude). For practical purposes the term "Hawaiian Islands" normally is restricted to a group of two dozen islands that extends 400 miles from Hawaii to Niihau (Figure 15-1). The total land area of the Hawaiian Islands is approximately 6,500 square miles (slightly less than that of New Jersey),

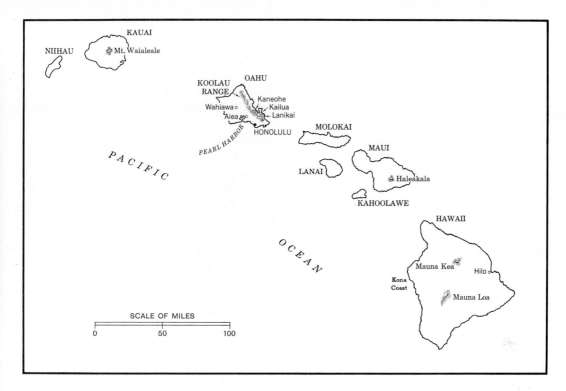

Figure 15-1. The Hawaiian Islands. A region of tropical farming, tourism, and military bases.

nearly all of which is made up of eight major islands, listed here in order of size: Hawaii (4,021 square miles), Maui, Oahu, Kauai, Molokai, Lanai, Niihau, and Kahoolawe (45 square miles). The area of Hawaii is nearly twice the total area of the other seven.

The Physical Setting

Origin and Structure of the Islands The islands represent isolated tops of a subterranean mountain range that have been built up so much by volcanic action as to protrude above sea level, where their surface has been modified by further vulcanism and by subaerial erosion. The volcanoes are of the quiescent shield type that develop by emission of lava rather than by explosive ejection of rock fragments. In essence, the larger islands are basaltic domes in various stages of dissection. The two highest peaks of the islands, Mauna Kea (elevation 13,784

feet) and Mauna Loa (elevation 13,679 feet), are sometimes described as the highest in the world from base to summit, for their bases are set some 18,000 feet below sea level on the floor of the Pacific.

Vulcanism has continued to the present; there are two major active volcanoes on "the Big Island" (Hawaii), and several smaller areas of geothermal activity. Periodic lava flows actually are expanding the area of the Big Island, forming new peninsulas on the southeast side.

Coralline limestone has been uplifted in a few places to form flattish coastal plains of modest size. In addition, there are submerged fringing coral reefs partially, but not completely, surrounding most of the islands. Coral sand frequently has been washed up to form beaches in bays that are sheltered between rocky lava headlands.

Surface Features The islands are all dominated by slopeland, and most are dis-

425

tinctly mountainous. Sheer cliffs, called *palis,* and rugged, steep-sided canyons provide the most abrupt changes in elevation. Flat land is scarce, even around the coastal fringes.

Hawaii is dominated by Mauna Kea and Mauna Loa, but it is traversed by other mountains that add to its rugged appearance. Famed Kilauea Crater, a secondary volcano on the southeastern flank of Mauna Loa, contains a fiery lake of molten lava. Elsewhere on the Big Island are other extinct volcanoes (Kohala and Hualalai), small plateaus, and bold cliffs. There are a few short rivers on the northern and eastern sides of the island, some of which drop into the sea as waterfalls over sheer cliffs.

Maui is composed of two volcanic complexes separated by a narrow lowland isthmus. The extinct volcano Haleakala (elevation 10,032 feet) towers over the eastern part of the island. Its crater is one of the largest in the world, with a circumference of about 25 miles and a depth of 3,000 feet. The West Maui Mountains are much lower, but are rugged.

Oahu comprises two mountain ranges separated by a rolling plain. The Waianae Mountains parallel the west coast, and the more extensive Koolau Range parallels the east coast. The Nuuanu Pali of the latter range is one of the most spectacular terrain features in Anglo-America, its sheer cliffs descending from cloud-shrouded peaks to a fertile coastal fringe. The lowland between the mountains is abruptly dissected by deeply-incised, steep-sided gorges in several places, and at its southern end is the embayment of Pearl Harbor, one of the largest and finest harbors in the North Pacific. Honolulu's two conspicuous natural landmarks, Diamond Head and Punchbowl, are the stumps of extinct volcanoes.

Kauai is thoroughly dominated by Mount Waialeale, which rises to 5,170 feet in the center of the island. Heavy rainfall results in numerous short rivers plunging coastward, often cutting deep canyons, of which Waimea Canyon is the most spectacular. The coastal fringes have little flat land, with the steep Na Pali of the northwest coast prohibiting the building of a complete circumferential roadway.

Kahoolawe, a barren, hilly island with a maximum elevation of nearly 1,500 feet, is uninhabited and used only as a military firing-range target. Lanai is also hilly. The long narrow island of Molokai consists of a rugged mountain mass on the east and a broad sandy plateau on the west. Niihau consists of a moderately high tableland in the center, with low plains at either end of the island.

Climate In its basic characteristics, the climate of the Hawaiian Islands is controlled by three factors: (1) its subtropical location in a vast ocean, which accounts for generally mild, equable temperatures and an abundance of available moisture; (2) the northeast trade winds, which blow almost continually across the islands during the summer, but are less pronounced, though persistent, during the winter; and (3) the terrain, whose height and orientation are the major determinants of temperature and rainfall variations.

The dominance of the trade winds throughout the region means that there are usually some clouds in the sky, the humidity is relatively high on the average, temperatures are mild to warm, there is some wind movement to hasten evaporation, and light showers of brief duration are to be expected with some frequency.

The most striking aspect of the climate is the variation in rainfall from place to place. In general, a windward (essentially northeast in this region) location receives considerably more precipitation than does a leeward one. As moisture-laden air rises over a topographic barrier, it expands and cools, and becomes incapable of retaining

Figure 15-2. Heavy rains sometime result in flood conditions. The Trade Winds carry a great deal of moisture, and sometimes drop a lot of it in one area. (Photo courtesy Soil Conservation Service, U.S. Department of Agriculture.)

all the moisture it contains. Rainfall results (Figure 15-2). As the same air descends the lee side of a mountain it contracts and becomes warmer, and can hold more moisture; thus rainfall is unlikely. Specifically, it can be seen that the higher mountains receive most rain on the northeast flanks at moderate elevations of 2,000 to 4,000 feet, while the lower mountains receive most rain along or near the crest line.[1] This difference is the result of the movement of the onshore trades, which blow *over* the lower mountains, but *around* the higher ones.

This windward-leeward relationship results in extraordinary rainfall variations within short horizontal distances. A weather station on the northeast slope of Mount Waialeale on Kauai (said to be the rainiest spot on earth) records an average of 476 inches of rain annually, while 15 miles away at Kaumakani the average is only 20 inches. Variations on the same order of magnitude occur on Oahu, Molokai, Maui, and Hawaii, as well. Only the three small and relatively low-lying islands do not have similar variations. Within the urbanized area of Honolulu it is possible to choose a building site with a 93-inch average rainfall, or one with a 25-inch average only 5 miles away.[2]

Temperatures are uniformly mild. Honolulu's January average of 72° F. is close to its July average of 78° F., and the highest temperature ever recorded in the city is only 88° F., in comparison to an absolute minimum of 57° F. Only in locales of great altitude do temperatures drop markedly below the mild range; for example, the Mauna peaks of the Big Island are sometimes snow-covered.

Soils Heavy rain and steep slopes have been the principal determinants of soil development. In general, the slopelands have only a thin cover of soil, while the flattish lands have deep soil development. Most of the mature soils are lateritic by nature, having been leached by percolating water. The average soil in agricultural areas is red in color, moderately fertile, and relatively permeable, so that irrigation is often necessary, even in places of considerable rainfall.

Biota Mild temperatures and abundant precipitation provide conditions for lush vegetation. The better-watered areas are noted for thick growth of tropical trees and shrubs. Most of the areas of thick forest,

[1] David I. Blumenstock, "Climate of Hawaii," *Climates of the States* (U.S. Weather Bureau Publication [Washington: Government Printing Office, 1961]), p. 8.

[2] Loyal Durand, Jr., "Hawaii," *Focus,* Vol. 9 (May 1959), .p. 2.

however, have been denuded by commercial logging or overgrazing. In areas of intermediate rainfall, the flora sometimes reflects more arid conditions, because the highly permeable volcanic soil permits water to percolate rapidly to great depths, frequently beyond the reach of plant roots. Xerophytic plants characterize such areas. The introduction of exotic plants has been particularly characteristic of this region, so that now a large proportion of the total vegetative cover represents earlier imports.

Animal life has always been limited on the islands. Native fauna was mostly restricted to insects, lizards, and birds. The most conspicuous wildlife today consists of feral livestock (livestock that has reverted to the wild). Tens of thousands of feral sheep, goats, and pigs roam the islands, and there are considerable numbers of feral cattle, dogs, and cats as well. These animals are guilty of much destruction of plants and other animals, and are a major nuisance in some areas, particularly on the Big Island. However, they provide an important recreational resource, for sport hunting. Other exotic species, such as mouflon, axis deer, and mongoose, are also present in some numbers.

Population

Early Inhabitants Nothing is known of the pre-Polynesian inhabitants of the Hawaiian Islands, except that they are reported to have been short in stature and peaceful by nature. Presumably they were either destroyed or assimilated by waves of Polynesian settlers, the first of which were said to have arrived from the western Pacific between 750 and 1000 A.D. After several hundred years of isolation, there was another great Polynesian immigration in the 14th and 15th centuries, followed by a second lengthy period of insular seclusion. These people have been known through recent history as Hawaiians, and are char-

acterized by bronze skin, large, dark eyes, heavy features, and dark brown or black hair. Although their social and community life was intricately complicated by restrictions and regulations, making a living was relatively simple. They had domesticated pigs and chickens, as well as a variety of cultivated food plants. Fruits and vegetables were common, but dietary staples were fish and poi (the cooked and pounded root of the taro plant).

European Penetration The islands were officially discovered by Captain James Cook of England in 1779; however, it is thought that a Spanish captain named Gaetano had been there more than two centuries previously, and still other seafarers may have touched the islands before Cook. It is clear, nevertheless, that Cook's visit "opened up" the "Sandwich Islands," as he called them, to the world. Before long the islands became important bartering, trading, and refreshment stops for merchant vessels of England, France, Spain, Russia, and the United States, and for whalers and pearlers of many nationalities. British influence was strong for many years, but few colonists were attracted. Missionaries from New England arrived during the 1820's, and these dedicated people became very influential by the 1840's. Moderate but increasing numbers of United States settlers migrated to the islands during the nineteenth century.

Oriental Influx Asiatics came and were brought to Hawaii in considerable numbers during the last half of the nineteenth century, usually in response to a need for cheap labor. The first Chinese were brought in to work on the sugar plantations in 1852. Japanese began to arrive in 1868, first as fishermen blown off course, and later as plantation workers. In spite of restrictions, Japanese immigration greatly exceeded that from any other country. The first Filipino sugar workers came in 1906, and many more were brought in during succeeding years. Other immigrants came from Korea, Samoa, other Pacific islands, and Portugal's Atlantic islands (Azores, Cape Verde).

The Contemporary Melting Pot The present population of the islands is much more complex and varied than that of any other region in Anglo-America (Figure 15-3). All ethnic groups have intermarried, particularly in recent decades. Pure Hawaiians are almost nonexistent today, composing less than five per cent of the total population. Part-Hawaiians are three times as numerous. Japanese have intermarried the least with other groups; only about 15 per cent of their marriages have been intermarriages. About one-third of the total population today is of Japanese extraction. Caucasians (called *Haole*) from mainland Anglo-America make up about 16 per cent of the total; Filipinos, 12 per cent; and Chinese and Portuguese, about 7 per cent each. One out of every 10 persons currently residing in the islands is an alien.

Economy

Economic opportunities have always been limited in the region because of its insular position and lack of natural resources. Although bauxite and titanium have been discovered, no mineral deposits have ever provided income of significance. Commercial fishing has been only partially successful. Logging of sandalwood was once very important, and formed the basis of a thriving trade with the Orient, but the stands of sandalwood have long since been depleted. Consequently, the basic economic activity of the region has nearly always been agriculture.

Although only one-tenth of the land is arable, the soil is generally productive, there is no danger of frost, and natural rainfall and abundant ground water provide sufficient moisture. The first foreign cash crop was tobacco, which flourished during the

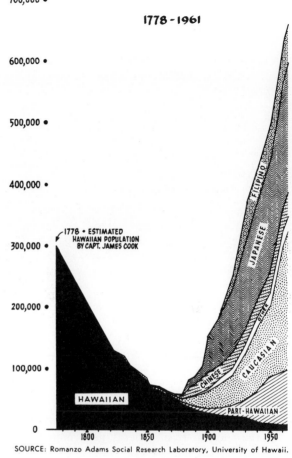

SOURCE: Romanzo Adams Social Research Laboratory, University of Hawaii.

Figure 15-3. The historic pattern of ethnic change in Hawaii. By permission of the Bureau of Business Research, Bank of Hawaii, *Hawaii: Planning for Island Growth*, p. 7 (Honolulu: 1961)

first half of the nineteenth century and then faded out. During the Gold Rush period in California, foodstuffs of various kinds were exported to the West Coast. This trade was significant to the Hawaiian economy for only about a decade, and then virtually ceased. The provisioning of whalers and other ships bolstered the production of local food crops from the 1820's till the 1870's, but that, too, declined. Eventually it became evident that the best hope for agriculture was to specialize in growing subtropical crops for the mainland market. Exports were badly needed, and there was not

429

Figure 15-4. An extensive pineapple "ranch." (Photo courtesy Del Monte Foods.)

enough land to grow all the needed foodstuffs anyway, so emphasis turned to plantation raising of specialty crops.

Sugar Since the 1870's, sugar has been the leading crop of the region, and today it generates twice as much income as any other crop (Figure 15-5), although in the region's over-all economy, this is second to the income from federal government expenditures.

Sugar cane was grown in Hawaii long before the first Europeans came, but the first successful plantation was not established until 1835, on Kauai. Irrigation came into use about two decades later. The scale of operations has always been large, primarily because of the inherited pattern of feudalistic landholdings.

There are now about 27 large sugar "ranches" or plantations, which produce some 90 per cent of the crop.[3] Mechanization is the order of the day, with hand harvesting, field railroad systems, and ratoon crops mostly a thing of the past. At harvest time, the cane is first defoliated by burning. Then bulldozers with sheer blades cut the cane and pile it in windrows. The cane is

[3] "Aloha Oe, Hawaii," *Monthly Review,* Federal Reserve Bank of San Francisco, August 1959, p. 106.

Figure 15-5. Loading harvested cane on a truck for transport to a sugar mill. (Photo courtesy Soil Conservation Service, U.S. Department of Agriculture.)

then transferred by cranes with double-jawed grabs to trucks, which take it to the mills (Figure 15-5). Besides the plantations, there are some 1900 small independent producers, mostly on the Big Island, who operate on a much smaller scale by contract through the plantations. Most of the refining (which is done in a refinery in California) and all of the marketing of the raw sugar is handled by a producers' cooperative, the California and Hawaiian Sugar Refining Corporation.

The region ordinarily supplies about 12 per cent of the sugar used in the United States, mostly in the western states. The principal cane-growing areas are on the north coast of the Big Island, in the lowland of Maui, in several places on Oahu,, and around the coastal margin of Kauai. On both sugar and pineapple plantations the majority of workers today are Filipinos.

Pineapple The pineapple presumably was introduced from Tahiti about 1800, but there was no real commercial production until about 1890. The industry became notable after Dole's development of improved varieties in 1903 and Ginaca's invention of a mechanical peeling, coring, and slicing machine 10 years later.

There are only about 14 plantations, and their large size facilitates mechanization. After the fields have been shaped and contoured by earth-moving equipment, other machines lay spaced strips of special mulch paper that retains moisture and retards weed growth. Holes are punched in the paper and slips planted through the holes. Spraying, fertilization, irrigation, and hormone application are accomplished by mobile equipment that swings booms 50 to 65 feet long over the field. The fruit is picked by hand and placed on boom conveyor belts that take the pines to trucks. These then distribute the fruit to the nine canneries. The industry employs about 10,000 people the year round, but more than twice

that many are needed during the summer harvest (Figure 15-4).

Pineapple is a major crop on all the islands except Big Island, Kahoolawe, and Niihau. There are normally one million plants growing at any given time, and more than 700 million cans of pineapple are packed annually. The industry has lacked stability in recent years. Unlike sugar, pineapple does not have a guaranteed market, and the industry is feeling the pinch of competition from Puerto Rico, Mexico, and the Far East. Before World War II, the region supplied about 80 per cent of total world production, but the proportion has been decreasing in recent years.

Other Crops Coffee is the third most valuable crop, but its importance has declined since peak production at the end of the nineteenth century. Almost all production is concentrated in a narrow strip along the Kona (southwest) coast of the Big Island. Most of the coffee farms are small holdings owned and operated by Japanese

Figure 15-6. Spreading coffee beans out to dry on the Kona Coast of Big Island. (Photo courtesy Soil Conservation Service, U.S. Department of Agriculture.)

Figure 15-7. Harvesting papayas. The workman cuts the stem of the fruit with a long knife and catches the papaya as it falls. (Photo courtesy Soil Conservation Service, U.S. Department of Agriculture.)

families. Various labor-saving devices (as harvesting ladder, platform drying room, coffee pulper, tractor) are used, but much labor is required (Figure 15-6). Total value of production is only about three per cent that of sugar cane. World overproduction has hurt the Hawaiian coffee industry badly, with the result that the Kona area has a depressed economy. Marketing emphasis is on capturing a larger share of the instant-coffee market for the strong Kona coffee.

Relatively small amounts of foodstuffs for local consumption are grown on the islands; the great bulk must be imported. Subtropical specialty crops, mostly grown on small farms, are of some importance. Ornamental shrubs and flowers rank fourth in value of all crops; they are mostly grown on Oahu and around Hilo on the Big Island. Next in significance are papayas (Figure 15-7) and bananas, followed by taro (a wet-field crop grown more or less like rice), macadamia nuts, alfalfa, and passion fruit.

Livestock Cattle, chickens, swine, and sheep are the principal forms of domestic livestock in the region. Cattle ranches occupy more than three-quarters of the agricultural land. Most ranches are large—one is reputed to be among the five largest in Anglo-America—and concentrate on the raising of beef cattle. Grain feeding is uncommon; and, although some hay is produced, generally the animals subsist on pasturage. Nearly all of the meat is consumed on the islands, but this satisfies less than two-thirds of the local demand for beef. Hides and skins are exported. Cattle ranches are most notable on the Big Island, but also occupy much of Maui and Molokai, and the entire island of Niihau is owned and operated as a single ranch.

There are a few sheep ranches, particularly on Hawaii. Dairy farms are concentrated on Oahu. Poultry and swine are raised on small holdings on all of the larger islands.

Fishing Although fish has been a major staple of the diet of the islanders since ancient times, commercial fishing rarely has been of great significance. The early Hawaiians had a professional class of fishermen; they also raised favorite varieties of food fish in ponds. Today, however, native fishing skills have practically disappeared.

Most commercial fishing in the region is carried on by people of Japanese extraction, often in sampans. There are only about 600 active fishermen. Most fishing is done from Oahu, although catches are landed at all six of the larger islands.

The tuna industry was progressing favorably and tuna exports had achieved the rank of third in value among total exports before World War II, but they no longer maintain that position. Tuna still is the major fish, making up about 60 per cent of the total catch. Most of it is canned locally, and some Japanese tuna is also imported for packing. The other principal fish caught are scad, snapper, and marlin. Generally speaking, the fishery resource is underexploited; however, labor difficulties, competition with mainland tuna packers, and problems in catching bait fish are inhibitory factors.

Salt-water fish ponds are moderately common on some of the islands. Mullet is by far the most common species raised in these ponds.

Tourism The most rapidly expanding sector of the Hawaiian economy is tourism. Beaches, climate, scenery, ceremonies, hospitality, and a trans-Pacific crossroads location are the major assets. These items are exploited by one of the most thorough and best-organized publicity efforts anywhere; the renown of a holiday in Hawaii is worldwide.

Much of the business life of the region is geared to the visitor. Companies that cater to sleeping, eating, entertainment, and transportation services are continually expanding their operations. The number of visitors to the islands increased by 500 per cent during the decade 1950-1960.[4] Most tourists come from mainland United States, and about 40 per cent are from California. However, the islands have become a major stopping point for international travelers as well. The great majority of all passenger ships and planes crossing the Pacific call at Honolulu.[5] It is unrivaled as the major terminal city within the entire Pacific Basin, excluding the marginal centers of California, Japan, and Australia. Summer is the busiest season, with June decidedly the peak month. A smaller secondary level occurs in December and January.

The Waikiki area of Honolulu is the unquestioned center of island tourism (Figure

[4] "Hawaii: Planning for Island Growth," Department of Business Research, Bank of Hawaii, Honolulu, 1961, p. 19.
[5] There are some direct-line routes from San Francisco, Seattle, and Vancouver to Japan, and a few flights directly from Los Angeles to Tahiti and the southwest Pacific, but these are relatively minor in comparison with the routes that pass through Honolulu.

15-8). It is a seething hive of hotels, restaurants, elegant shops, sparkling beaches, and fashionable sunburns. Most visitors, however, manage to see some other parts of the region as well. Two interisland air carriers offer frequent and convenient service among the six larger islands, and it is estimated that more than four-fifths of the visitors from mainland Anglo-America go to at least one other island in addition to Oahu.[6] The volcanic features of the Big Island and the exceptional scenic beauty of Kauai are the principal attractions among the "outer islands."

[6] Samuel P. Weaver, *Hawaii, U.S.A.* (New York: Pageant Press, Inc., 1959), p. 241.

Figure 15-8. The Waikiki area of Honolulu. This is the principal tourist center of Hawaii. Note the yacht harbor, the numerous luxury hotels, the extensive beach front, and the peak of Diamond Head in the background. (Photo courtesy Hawaii Visitors Bureau.)

Federal Government Expenditures The largest generator of wealth in the islands is the federal government. Because of the strategic value of its mid-Pacific location, Hawaii contains some of the nation's largest military bases. It is the headquarters for the U.S. Pacific Command, as well as the administrative center for the Pacific operations of each of the three individual services.

Approximately one out of every three members of the region's labor force is employed by the federal government, mostly in military establishments. The armed forces spend more than $400,000,000 annually, divided almost equally among military payroll, civilian payroll, and the purchase of goods and services.

Unfortunately for Hawaii, military spending is uncertain. An economy that is largely based on such uncertainty exists in a nervous state of health. The region's business welcomes governmental expenditures, but the acquired overdependence on them is to be regretted.

Political Geography

Throughout this region's early history the islands were politically fragmented. Various kings and chiefs ruled different islands and parts of islands, with a sporadic pattern of warfare and change. The uniting of the region under one ruler was accomplished by Kamehameha I, but it required 28 years of war, diplomacy, and treachery. He began the bloody civil war on the Big Island in 1782, and it lasted for nine years. Later he conquered Maui and Molokai, and overwhelmed Kalanikupule's army to seize control of Oahu. The other islands came under his rule by 1810.

Six kings and a queen successively carried on the monarchy after Kamehameha's death in 1819. The first constitution was promulgated during the reign of Kamehameha III, and the kingdom became a constitutional monarchy. Most of the influential Hawaiians became increasingly interested in some

sort of liaison with Britain, but a location near the United States and increased trade with California (sugar, rice, coffee) in the 1850's and 1860's, as well as the establishment of regular mail service with San Francisco, foreshadowed the manifest destiny of annexation by the United States. The monarchy declined after 1875, and Queen Liliuokalani was deposed in 1891.

An American immigrant served as President of the interim republic until annexation was completed in 1900. The two basic motives for annexation were, for Hawaii, to increase trade, especially in sugar, and, for the United States, to secure a major Pacific naval base. In spite of much agitation for statehood, the islands remained a territory for nearly six decades. In 1959 Hawaii was admitted as the fiftieth state.

Problems and Prospects

Land Ownership One of the most unusual aspects of Hawaiian geography is the system and pattern of land ownership. Approximately 42 per cent of the total land area is under government control. This is a much smaller proportion than obtains in many states west of the Mississippi; but, furthermore, another 46 per cent is held by a mere 60 estates, trusts, and other large owners. Thus, less than 12 per cent of the land is subject to general private ownership. Many plans have been advanced, particularly by the new state legislature, to enable individuals to obtain small parcels of land. As a result, the number of farms is increasing and the average farm size is decreasing, both in direct opposition to the trends on the mainland. More than half of the farms in Hawaii are now less than 10 acres in size. Homesteads have been proliferated on Molokai, Hawaii, and Oahu, but generally the land is in large estates. Traditionally, these estates do not pass freely to heirs; instead, trusts of various kinds are set up to administer them. This has resulted in "freezing" the ownership, and the land is leased in large blocks rather than being sold. One-third of the private land in the islands is owned by four major estates, and eight others control another one-seventh. Such a situation is not inherently unsavory, but the long-range effect may prove deleterious to economic growth, as well as to social and political conditions.

The problems engendered are particularly pronounced in urban areas. The example of the Royal Hawaiian Hotel in Waikiki illustrates the dilemma faced by prospective developers:

> The title to the land is in the Bernice P. Bishop Estate, which is the lessor, and the Sheraton Hotels as successor to the Matson Navigation Company, the owner of the buildings, is the lessee. The lease has less than sixteen years to run, at which time the lessee is faced with the loss of the buildings to the lessor, or the alternative of securing a new lease. If it is able to secure a new lease it will be subject to much higher rentals to cover the increase in the value of the buildings which it erected on the leasehold. The lessor will thus have gained during the rental period the rental paid by the lessee, the increase in value of the land which has been very great during the rental period, and the increase in value due to the erection of the valuable buildings. The result of such a condition is that the lessee cannot afford to erect buildings the life of which will exceed the term of the lease. This is evidenced by the newer constructions which show much less solid foundations if the land is leased.[7]

Land ownership may turn out to be one of the region's greatest problems.

Economic Oligarchy Another unusual characteristic of the business life of the region is the predominant position of a half dozen institutions in the economy. Large factoring companies were established in the nineteenth century to provide services to whalers. Later they shifted their concern to the development of sugar plantations. The factoring companies helped the plantations

secure needed mainland supplies, provided a variety of services, and made the sugar-marketing arrangements.

These agencies financed early ventures at big risks, and grew rapidly when profits were large. Although the number of factoring companies has decreased by consolidation, they have expanded their managerial, executive, and financial functions widely, and are now active in very diverse fields.

Unionism Because of its economic dependence on two main crops and its insular location some distance from the mainland, the region is particularly susceptible to pressure exerted by organized labor. Approximately one-fourth of the labor force belongs to organized unions, the largest and most influential by far being the International Longshoremen's and Worker's Union —I.L.W.U. This organization began its phenomenal rise to power during World War II, beginning with the pineapple industry, and spreading to several other phases of the economy. Today it is probably the most powerful organization of any kind in the islands. In the past, the economy has been severely strained by pineapple strikes, and a 1949 shipping strike almost throttled the region. Unbridled unionism, then, is another uncertain factor for regional prosperity.

Transportation Here, as for other islands far removed from mainland, the problem of transportation is always notable. The islands depend upon imports from the mainland, and the region's economy depends upon exports to the world. Furthermore, because the region consists of a group of islands, the physical matter of moving people and goods from one place to another within the region can be intricately complicated. Factories in Honolulu must have materials that originate on the other islands, and citizens of the "outer islands" need goods produced in or shipped through Honolulu.

Most tourists arrive by air; but the shipment of food and other commodities is handled by surface transport, which is slow and

[7] Reprinted by permission. Weaver, *Hawaii, U.S.A.*, p. 127.

expensive. Furthermore, it is subject to disruption by labor disputes, weather, and other factors. The problem of transportation is one of the immutable facts of life in the region.

The Outlook

Perhaps in no other region are the hazards and the potentials so clear-cut. From an economic standpoint, there is cause for concern, but also reason for optimism. The sugar industry is well established and protected by quotas, so it can be expected to undergo gradual expansion as the total national market grows, although it may decline on Oahu due to urban pressure for use of the land. The future for pineapples is much less certain, but quality merchandise and established merchandising should be able to withstand most foreign competition. There is much room for expansion in fishing, although the rate of growth is likely to be slow. Continued rapid development of tourism is the brightest hope for the future; the mobility of Americans seems to know no bounds, and the appeal of the islands appears to grow with time. If a distinct business recession were to engulf the mainland, of course, the tourist industry would be among the first to be hurt. Manufacturing shows fine prospects for growth, but primarily in the fields that are not basic to the total economy, i.e., those that supply goods for the Hawaiian market.

The cloudiest aspect of business has to do with government expenditures. Hawaii is essentially a garrison state with an economy that is largely artificial, and hence precarious. Decreased military spending in the near future is unlikely, but substantial reductions in the long run probably are to be expected.

From a social standpoint, Hawaii has been an American showcase for racial assimilation. Continued intermarriage will probably blur individual ethnic strains into a more widespread Hawaiian blend. The state's population should grow faster than the national average, due to a relatively high birth rate and continued immigration of people attracted by the prospect of island living. Greatly expanded urbanization is likely, particularly on Oahu, where Greater Honolulu, along with its extended suburbs of Lanikai-Kailua-Kaneohe, will spread north and south on both sides of the Koolau Range.

TABLE 14

Selected Cities and Towns of the Hawaiian Islands

City or Town	Urbanized Area	Political Center
Aiea	......	11,826
Hilo	......	25,966
Honolulu	351,336	294,194
Kailua-Lanikai	......	25,622
Kaneohe	......	14,414
Wahiawa	......	15,512

Selected Bibliography

"Aloha Oe, Hawaii," *Monthly Review*, Federal Reserve Bank of San Francisco, August 1959, pp. 102-110.

Coulter, John Wesley, *The Pacific Dependencies of the United States.* New York: The Macmillan Company, 1957.

Day, A. Grove, *Hawaii and Its People.* New York: Duell, Sloan, and Pearce, 1955.

Durand, Loyal, Jr., "Hawaii," *Focus*, Vol. 9, May 1959.

————, "The Dairy Industry of the Hawaiian Islands," *Economic Geography*, Vol. 35, July 1959, pp. 228-246.

Eiselen, Elizabeth, "Geographic Problems of Our Fiftieth State," *Journal of Geography*, Vol. 59, March 1960, pp. 132-135.

Jones, Stephen B., "The Weather Element in the Hawaiian Climate," *Annals of the Association of American Geographers*, Vol. 29, March 1939, pp. 29-57.

Pearcy, G. Etzel, "Hawaii's Territorial Sea," *The Professional Geographer*, Vol. 11, November 1959, pp. 2-6.

Philipp, Perry F., "Hawaii's Problems and Many Assets," *Land:* The 1958 Yearbook of Agriculture, pp. 440-448.

Weaver, Samuel P., *Hawaii, U.S.A.* New York: Pageant Press, 1959.

chapter sixteen

The North Pacific Coast

The North Pacific Coast Region occupies the northwest coastal fringe of Anglo-America between the crest of the Cascade Mountains in Oregon and Washington and the Coast Mountains of British Columbia and Alaska on the east, and the Pacific Ocean on the west. It is nowhere more than 150 miles wide, but it is more than 2,500 miles long (Figure 16-1), extending from northern California to Alaska's Aleutian Islands.

Despite its great latitudinal extent, condi-

tions throughout the region are somewhat similar as a result of the dominance of the temperate marine climate. Similarity is also evident in the rocky coast, and the moist, forest-covered slopes.

The Terrain

The entire region is dominated by mountains. These vary in height from the comparatively low coastal ranges of northern California, Oregon, and Washington to the

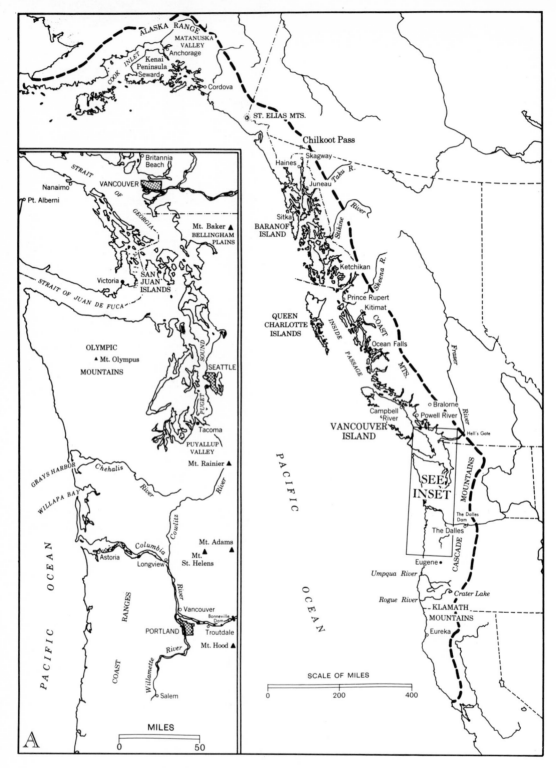

Figure 16-1. The North Pacific Coast. A region of lumbering, fishing, farming, manufacturing, commerce, and spectacular scenery.

438

higher ranges of the Cascade Mountains with their superb volcanic peaks and to the great alpine ranges of British Columbia and Alaska surmounted by Mount McKinley (elevation 20,300 feet), the highest peak on the North American continent.

The general pattern of topographical lineament consists of three very long features, northwest-southeast in trend, generally parallel to one another throughout the region. The westernmost zone comprises low but rugged mountains that become higher, more rugged and more severely glaciated toward the north. Just to the east is the longitudinal coastal trough that is prominent from Oregon to the Yukon. The eastern zone consists of complex mountain masses surmounted by spectacular volcanic peaks.

The coastal ranges within the United States portion of this region comprise a series of somewhat distinct mountain areas. They include the Coast Ranges of northern California, the Klamath Mountains which tie these ranges to the southern Cascades, the Coast Ranges of Oregon, the Olympic Mountains of Washington, and the mountains of Vancouver Island.

The California Coast Ranges, consisting of folded and faulted structures, have an even, though discontinuous, crest line. The entire mountain mass is divided into a series of blocks that are tilted in various directions. The streams that break through these ranges follow structural valleys. The mountains frequently project out into the ocean, forming bold rocky headlands.

The Klamath Mountains appear as a complex and steeply dissected plateau with summit level of 2,000 to 4,000 feet. The stream canyons that radiate from the Klamath show the influence of glaciation in their upper reaches.

The Oregon Coast Range, which extends northward from the Klamath almost to the mouth of the Columbia River, is dissected by the deeply entrenched Rogue and Ump-

qua Rivers and by several smaller streams that flow across this mountain mass to the Pacific Ocean. The gaps through the mountains facilitate travel between the coast and the interior valleys but do not seriously affect the barrier nature of the Coast Ranges so far as climate is concerned.

In Washington, the Olympic Mountains, with their somewhat uniform summit level, appear to be the remnant of an old erosion surface that has been greatly carved by glaciation. Mount Olympus (elevation 8,200 feet), the highest peak in the range, rises as a monadnock above the other peaks. Because of the extremely heavy snowfall in these mountains, some small glaciers still exist near their summits.

In Canada, this linear mountain system is continued in low but often steep ranges of Vancouver Island, the Queen Charlotte Islands, and the Alexander Archipelago. In the far northwest they become more massive to include the spectacular St. Elias Mountains and the Alaska Range.

Between the Cascades to the east and the Olympics and Oregon Coast Ranges to the west lies the structural trough of the Willamette Valley and Puget Sound. The trough was formed by the sinking of this land mass at the time the Cascades were elevated. In glacial times a large lobe of ice advanced down Puget Sound and was instrumental in forming that body of water. The Willamette Valley today is a broad alluvial plain 15 to 30 miles wide and 125 miles long, while the Puget Sound lowland is somewhat smaller in area, since a large part of it was submerged. North of Puget Sound, glacial erosion and submergence formed the "Inside Passage," which extends as a submerged waterway almost to the Yukon Territory.

The Cascade Range, extending from Lassen Peak in northern California to southern British Columbia, is divided into a southern and a northern section by the deep gorge of the Columbia River. The relief features of the southern part are due largely to up-building, while those of the northern part have been carved out of the uplift mass by streams and glaciers. One of the most interesting features of the southern Cascades is Crater Lake, which occupies the crater of an extinct volcano. Toward the northern end of this section, Mount Hood (elevation 11,225 feet), a nearly perfect volcanic cone, rises sharply above the general level of the Cascades. The Columbia River crosses the entire Cascade Range through a deep narrow gorge, indicating that the stream is antecedent, although its course may have been determined to some extent by faulting. All of the northern Cascades, composed largely of a huge granitic mass, have been severely eroded by glaciers, and within this area are numerous small active mountain glaciers today. Surmounting the mass of the Northern Cascades are five prominent extinct volcanoes, now snow- and ice-capped —Mount Adams, Mount St. Helens, Mount Rainier, Glacier Peak, and Mount Baker (Figure 16-2).

North of the international boundary, the ranges that correspond to the Cascades are known as the Coast Mountains. They average 100 miles in width, are nearly 900 miles in length, and have been eroded severely by mountain glaciers. Deep canyons of the Fraser, Skeena, Stikine, and Taku Rivers have cut across the range, forming features similar to the Columbia Gorge.

Northwest of the Mount Fairweather–Chilkoot Pass district, the Alaska Range and St. Elias Mountains extend westward and ultimately blend into one, constituting the Alaskan Peninsula. Beyond the Peninsula is the 1,300-mile extent of the fog-bound, essentially treeless, spectacularly volcanic Aleutian Islands. Between the Alaska Range and the coastal mountains lies the Susitna-Matanuska Valley, the only lowland area of any extent in this northern part of the region. The Alaska Range presents some of the most superb mountain scenery on the continent.

Climate

In an area so dominated by mountains, marked vertical differences of temperature are to be expected; however, uniformity of lowland temperatures is characteristic of the North Pacific Coast Region. Temperatures range from 38° to 67° F. in central Oregon and from 33° to 55° F. along the coast of Alaska. In some interior valleys,

Figure 16-2. Mount St. Helens, one of the major volcanic peaks of the Northern Cascades. Clear-cut logging areas are shown in the foreground. (Photo courtesy the Weyerhaeuser Company.)

however, such as the Matanuska, the average winter temperature drops to about 16° F. Practically all valleys of this region have a growing season of more than 100 days. The most distinctive feature of the region is the complete change in climatic conditions from winter to summer.

The seasonal distribution of precipitation is uniform throughout the region; it is frequently stormy from September to May and considerably less rainy in summer.

During the winter, gigantic cyclonic storm systems, which migrate eastward across the Pacific basin, bring simultaneous rains for 1,000 miles north and south along this coastal region. Mountainous terrain influences the areal distribution of precipitation, southwest slopes receiving copious rainfalls and northeast sides receiving scant ones. The southwest flank of the Olympic Mountains, saturated in winter, has an average annual rainfall of 150 inches, the maximum for the United States. In contrast, the northeast side of these mountains, only 75 miles away, has an annual rainfall of 16 inches, which, without the aid of irrigation, is too little to support even good pastures.

Modified by the terrain, the east-west precipitation pattern falls into four easily recognizable belts: (1) the coastal strip, with abundant rainfall and little snow; (2) the windward side of the coastal ranges, with excessive precipitation; (3) the leeward side of the coastal mountains and the interior trough, with only a moderate rainfall and rare snows; and (4) the western slope of the Cascades (in the United States) and Coast Mountains (in Canada), with nearly 100 inches of precipitation— mainly winter snows.

The winter season is cloudy, monotonously damp, and protected from chilling continental winds by a double barrier of mountains to the east. Summer, the dry season, is characterized by mild temperatures, light surface winds, coastal fogs, and

low clouds. Throughout the region the average number of clear days is less than 100. [1]

Vegetation and Soils

Except in some of the interior valleys, the heavy precipitation throughout this region makes it a land of forests. In the northern California Coast Ranges and in parts of the Klamath Mountains, the dominant tree is the redwood, and within this area may be found some of the most magnificent forests of the world. Along the coasts of Oregon and Washington and in the Cascade Mountains, the Douglas fir is dominant, constituting one of the major lumber trees of the continent. Other trees within this area are western hemlock, western red cedar, and Sitka spruce. In the Canadian section, Douglas fir is the most valuable species, followed by hemlock. In southeastern Alaska, the Sitka spruce is the leading tree. The forests of this region are almost exclusively coniferous.

A marked contrast in natural vegetation exists between the Willamette Valley of Oregon and the Puget Sound area of Washington. In the former, the barrier nature of the Coast Range tends to produce a light summer rainfall, while in the latter the rainfall is slightly heavier in summer because the gaps in the Coast Range allow more rain-bearing winds from the Pacific to enter the valley. The slightly cooler temperature of the Puget Sound Valley also causes it to be somewhat more humid. As a result, the native vegetation of the Willamette Valley was largely prairie grass, while that of the Puget Sound area was a dense stand of giant Douglas fir trees with limited expanses of prairie. This contrast in vegetation types profoundly influenced the settlement of the two areas. Much of the region consists of rough mountainous terrain. Pro-

[1] Douglas B. Carter, personal communication.

ductive soils are confined largely to the valleys and are not especially fertile. The Willamette Valley with its predominance of prairie soils is by far the most important agricultural section. The Fraser and Skagit deltas have alluvial soils of considerable fertility.

Occupance of the Region

In the United States portion of the North Pacific Coast, white settlers found numerous small groups of Indians in the river valleys and coastal areas who derived most of their livelihood from fishing and hunting. In Canada and Alaska, the Haida and Tlingit Indians represented a more advanced stage of culture, living along the shore of the Inside Passage and depending largely upon coastal waters for their food. They built large dugout canoes from native cedar trees, and became skilled woodcarvers, as shown by their totem poles, designed usually to show the genealogy of each family. In California, Oregon, and Washington, Indians are now insignificant in number, although some of them still carry on fishing activities or are seasonally employed in canneries, mills, and in the fruit harvest. In Canada and Alaska, however, they are still relatively numerous. In southeastern Alaska they constitute a sizable portion of the population and are employed in salmon fishing and canning.

Early Exploration   The voyages of Vitus Bering between 1728 and 1742 led to the advance of Russian trappers and fur-traders southward along the Alaskan coast. In 1774 the Spaniard Juan Perez sailed as far north as latitude 55°. Another important voyage was that of the English Captain Cook in 1778, who explored the coast between latitudes 43° and 60° N, and further complicated the claims to this strip of coast. In 1792 a New England trading vessel reached the mouth of the Columbia River and estab-

lished the fourth claim to the region. Thus by the end of the eighteenth century four nations, Spain, Russia, Great Britain, and the United States, had explored and claimed in whole or in part the Pacific Coast of North America from San Francisco Bay to western Alaska. Permanent Spanish settlements were never established north of San Francisco Bay, but by 1800 Russia was entrenched on Baranof Island in southeastern Alaska, and had its seat of colonial government at Sitka. Further settlements were made to the south, but agreements were signed with the United States and Great Britain in 1824 and 1825 limiting the Russians to territory north of the 54°40′ parallel. Spain abandoned her claim to all land north of the 42nd parallel. This left the Oregon country, between the Spanish settlements in California and the Russian settlements in Alaska, to the United States and Great Britain. British claims were based partly on the voyages of Captain Cook but more on the explorations of the Hudson's Bay Company, which had sent expeditions into the area via the Saskatchewan River, the Selkirk Rockies, and the Columbia River. The claims of the United States were based primarily upon the discovery of the mouth of the Columbia River by an American sea captain and later upon the explorations of Lewis and Clark, who reached the coast in 1805 via an overland route.

Later Settlements   Spain made no further attempts at colonization in the North Pacific, and Russia was content to establish additional settlements in southeastern Alaska north of the 54°40′ parallel. Great Britain and the United States, however, became active in the settlement of the disputed territory between Spanish and Russian America. Following the Lewis and Clark expedition, the American Fur Company in 1810 established a trading post at Astoria at the mouth of the Columbia, but this settlement was seized by agents of the

Hudson's Bay Company during the war of 1812. British forts on the lower Columbia dominated the area until 1818, when an agreement was reached for joint occupance by English and American traders.

At first, the only Americans who reached this far-off land were a few trappers and traders, but in the early 1830's New England colonists came overland via the Oregon Trail, and soon a mass migration began. The great trek along the Oregon Trail took place in the early 1840's. These pioneers, determined to establish a Pacific outlet for the United States, had as their "battle cry" the slogan "Fifty-four forty or fight." Most of them located in the prairie land of the Willamette Valley of Oregon, and by 1845 there were 8,000 Americans in the Oregon Country. In the settlement of the "Oregon Question" in 1846, the United States got the lands south of the 49th parallel, except for Vancouver Island, and Great Britain got the land between there and Russian America. However, the final status of the San Juan Islands, now a part of the State of Washington, was not decided until 1872.

Influence of the California Gold Rush Most of the early settlers were in the Willamette Valley, and some of the young men of that area were among the first to move southward to the California "gold diggings" when the discovery of gold became known. The Willamette Valley, being in an excellent position to provide grain and other foodstuffs for the mining communities at favorable prices, soon became the chief source of foodstuffs. The Oregon Donation Land Law of 1850 further attracted settlers by giving 640 acres to a married man and 320 acres to a single man if he would settle in the area by December of that year. Neither the Puget Sound area nor the coasts of Canada and Alaska profited from the Gold Rush, because at that time their potential agricultural lands had not been developed.

The Transfer of Alaska After furs became depleted in the 1840's, the Russians began to lose interest in their far-off American possession. Although they had leased or sold some of their posts to the Hudson's Bay Company (Wrangell in 1840), they were loath to sell Alaska to Great Britain because of the Crimean War, and therefore offered it to the United States. The purchase was made in 1867 for the sum of $7,200,000, or less than two cents per acre. Except for a few fur trappers, however, citizens of the United States showed little interest in this vast northern territory until the end of the century, when gold was discovered in the Klondike district of Canada and at Nome, Alaska.

The Coming of the Railroads to the Pacific Northwest The Puget Sound country was still remote from populous centers of the continent and, until the completion of the Northern Pacific Railroad in 1883, its only outlet for bulky commodities of grain and lumber was by ship around Cape Horn. Nevertheless, a number of small sawmills were erected in the area between 1840 and 1850 to export lumber to the Hawaiian Islands and later to supply the mining camps of California. In 1893 the Great Northern completed its line across the mountains to Puget Sound, and some time later the Chicago, Milwaukee, St. Paul and Pacific Railroad built into the region. Meanwhile the Union Pacific established direct connection with Portland, and the Southern Pacific linked Portland with San Francisco. These rail connections made possible the exploitation of the great forest resources, which became important about the beginning of the present century, and contributed also to the industrial development and urban growth of that part of the region.

Influence of the Klondike Gold Rush When gold was discovered in the Klondike in 1897 and at Nome in 1898, a stampede began that closely rivaled the California rush of 1849. The most direct route to the Klondike field was by ship through the Inside Passage from Seattle to Dyea and later Skagway, thence over Chilkoot Pass or White Pass to the headwaters of the Yukon River, and finally by river boat or raft about 500 miles downstream to Dawson—a long, hard, dangerous trip. When gold was found in the beach sands at Nome, the trip was made entirely by ship, but in each case Seattle profited by being the nearest port having railroad connections with the rest of the United States.

The Pacific Coast of Canada Settlements were established on Vancouver Island as early as 1843, but there was little activity in the British part of this region until the great Fraser River–Cariboo gold rush, which commenced in 1858. British Columbia became a Canadian province in 1871. Major economic development had to await the completion of the Canadian Pacific Railway to Vancouver in 1885, and later the building of the Grand Trunk Pacific (now the Canadian National) Railway to Prince Rupert in 1914. These two ports serve western Canada, but the former is by far the more important.

Ethnic Groups Between 1900 and 1920, more than 100,000 European immigrants— Scandinavians, Germans, Finns, Swiss, and Hollanders—came to the Puget Sound area and the lower Columbia River Valley. In addition to the Europeans, an equal number of Americans of European parentage came from the immigrant colonies established earlier in the Corn Belt, the Upper Lake States, and the northern Great Plains. Some immigrants were attracted to western Washington and Oregon by the climatic similarity of the area to northwestern Europe, but most of them migrated across the continent in search of new land and new opportunities.

Since the Willamette Valley had been occupied previously by native American settlers, the wave of north European migrants moved into the lowlands of western Washington. The Bellingham Plain, the Skagit Delta, and certain minor valleys west of the Cascades attracted Scandinavians, Germans, and Hollanders, noted for their dairying, poultry raising, and bulb growing. Lynden, near the Canadian border, is a compact Dutch settlement specializing in butter, poultry, and bulbs. The Tillamook area of western Oregon more than fifty years ago attracted Swiss dairymen who laid the basis for the most profitable cheese-making industry in western United States.

The fishing industry at Astoria is dominated by Finns and Norwegians, who own and operate the fleet. The Ballard district of Seattle, base of a large fishing fleet, a large mill, and most of the tug fleet, has the greatest concentration of Scandinavians in the North Pacific Coast Region. North of the Columbia River, Scandinavian groups constitute a larger percentage of the population than anywhere else in the United States except Minnesota. [2]

Agriculture

The North Pacific Coast is still largely in timber, relatively little of the land being suited to agriculture. Dairying, the dominant farming activity of the region, accounts for a large part of the agricultural land being in pasture, with hay and oats occupying more than half of the land in crops.

Since most of the region consists of high mountains, steep slopes, and heavily forested terrain, the many rich valleys of limited capacity are dwarfed by the immensity of the coastal mountain region. Some of the more important agricultural areas that contain most of the crop land are: (1) Umpqua and Rogue River Valleys of southwestern Oregon, (2) the Willamette Valley, (3) the Cowlitz and Chehalis valleys and

[2] Burton L. Anderson, personal communication.

the lowlands around Puget Sound in Washington, (4) the Bellingham Lowland, (5) the lower Fraser Valley of British Columbia, (6) southeastern Vancouver Island, and (7) the Matanuska Valley of Alaska. Of these, the Willamette Valley, having more than two million acres in crop lands, is by far the largest and best developed. The least developed of all is the recently colonized Matanuska Valley of Alaska.

Early Agricultural Development The Willamette Valley was settled rapidly after the acquisition of the Oregon country in 1846, though a large number of agricultural colonists had occupied the area prior to that date. The valley, protected to some extent from the rain-bearing winds from the Pacific Ocean, was a grassland which appealed to the early settlers. They recognized in the area a type of farming land similar to that which they had left in the Middle West, and soon, practically all of the prairie lands were pre-empted and planted in grains. The California Gold Rush, with its great demand for foodstuffs, encouraged the farmers of the valley to grow grains and other agricultural products. When railroads were built into this valley in the 1880's and 1890's, a wave of new settlers arrived, attracted by the generous offers of land. Since most of the Willamette Valley prairies had been occupied prior to the advent of the railroads, the new settlers had to make farms by cutting the forests. Many of them had cleared forest lands in the East, but the gigantic size of the trees and the difficulty of stump removal in the North Pacific Region discouraged them. However, nearly four million acres in the Oregon–Washington part of this region has been transformed into agricultural land by logging and subsequent clearing.

The Present Agricultural Situation Although some grain is still grown in the Willamette Valley, and to a lesser extent elsewhere, the agriculture of this region is of two dominant types, dairying and fruit production. Dairying is by far the most important livestock activity, although poultry production and the raising of beef cattle and sheep assume some importance. In the dairy industry, this region, especially the Puget Sound section, resembles New England, in that most of the fluid milk is designed for the large urban markets near by.

Fruit crops occupy a smaller acreage than pasture or grain but have a greater value than either. The Willamette Valley specializes in peaches, apples, prunes, berries, and cherries, as well as walnuts and filberts. Apples, most widely distributed of the group, are also grown in large quantities on the southeastern part of Vancouver Island. Prunes and cherries are largely confined to the Umpqua and Willamette valleys. Salem, in the Willamette Valley, is one of the largest cherry-canning centers in the United States. Strawberries, raspberries, blackberries, and loganberries are grown extensively throughout the region, but the major production is confined to the Willamette Valley.

The region is well suited to certain kinds of vegetables, particularly cabbage, kale, and mustard, but most of these are grown for local consumption. It is also an important producer of potatoes and hops. Local areas around Portland, in the Puyallup Valley, Bellingham Plain, and southeastern Vancouver Island have specialized in flower bulbs. The more northern agricultural areas of British Columbia and Alaska practice subsistence agriculture almost entirely.

Agriculture in Oregon and Washington The older settled parts of the Willamette Valley and the Puget Sound Lowlands present an agricultural picture of a mature cultural landscape such as can be found in few places in the West. In the Willamette Valley, one can drive for miles on excellent highways past fruit farms (prunes, cherries, berries) hop fields, small fields of

Figure 16-3. A spring scene in the Willamette Valley near Newburg. Fruit trees are blossoming and crops and pastures are experiencing early growth. (Photo courtesy Oregon State Highway Commission.)

wheat and oats, excellent pastures, and specialized fields that produce commercial grass seeds or mint (for the oil). The Willamette Valley, occupied by farmers of the third or fourth generation on the same farms, is the old, long-settled, prosperous heart of Oregon that grows most of the fruit, berry, vegetable, and grain crops of the North Pacific Coast Region. Dairying is the principal occupation, but diversified horticultural and general farms are also common (Figure 16-3). Various specialty crops are raised—this is perhaps the leading strawberry area in the nation, for example—but most everything that can be grown here can also be raised in eastern United States where markets are much larger.[3] Consequently, farming is much less intensive in the Willamette Valley than it might be if local markets could absorb more of the produce.

In the Puget Sound Lowlands, where considerable land is diked or drained, are the region's best dairy and pasture lands. Market gardening is an important agricultural activity that has increased in ratio with the growth of the large urban centers;

[3] Higbee, *American Agriculture: Geography, Resources, Conservation,* p. 163.

it should increase in importance. The vegetable acreage includes peas, beans, cabbage, cauliflower, spinach, sweet corn, rhubarb, and tomatoes as the chief crops. Vegetables are grown in this area for use in the local urban markets, but the surplus is shipped to other parts of the United States. The quick freezing of field peas has caused a marked expansion in pea acreage.

Of the numerous specialty crops grown within this subregion, three deserve special mention: (1) the hop industry of the Willamette Valley, (2) the bulb industry of the Puget Sound Lowlands, and (3) the pea industry of the Bellingham Plain.

At one time the Willamette Valley was the major producer of hops in the United States, but in recent years it has been surpassed by the Yakima Valley area on the eastern side of the Cascade Mountains. Yields in the Willamette Valley are lower than in the Yakima Valley, but the total area in hops is still large. The sprinkler type of irrigation used in the Willamette Valley, although the most effective method on rolling lands, aids the spread of mildew which is detrimental to the vines. Since the hop yards in this area are relatively small (25 to 50 acres) and are frequently only a phase of diversification on larger farms, mechanization of harvesting such as is practiced on the larger Yakima hop farms is not profitable; therefore, most of the hop cones are picked by hand.

Although large quantities of flowers are grown in the vicinity of Portland (Figure 16-4), and the extensive fields of gladiolus add materially to the scenic beauty of the area, the major commercial bulb industry is located in three areas of the Puget Sound Lowlands: (1) the Puyallup Valley, (2) the Bellingham Plain, and (3) the Fargo Lake area near Vancouver, Washington. Most of the bulb growers in these areas came directly from Holland or are of Dutch ancestry. These areas, with their mild, humid climate and favorable soils, and ready local markets in the large cities of the Northwest, provided the ideal setting for the bulb industry. Tulip and narcissus bulbs are dominant, and are used in the greenhouse forcing trade.

In the Pacific Northwest, peas constitute one of the leading specialty crops. Because of the perishable nature of threshed peas, canneries must be located in the producing areas. Within this region the first real production (1923) was at Friday Harbor in the San Juan Islands. Additional canneries were soon opened on the Washington mainland and on the coast of British Columbia, and the canning business became large. The usual yield of shelled peas is about one ton to the acre. Although they have only about one-third the food value of alfalfa, the pea vines are fed as silage to dairy cattle. In recent years freezing has tended to replace canning, and a few freezing plants in western Washington now handle the entire pack.

Agriculture in British Columbia Most of the agricultural areas of British Columbia are concentrated on the delta of the Fraser River or on southeastern Vancouver Island. In these areas general mixed farming and dairying are carried on; there are also many specialty crops—fruits, berries, vegetables, and flowering bulbs. The leading agricultural industry of the Lower Fraser Valley is the production of whole milk for the Vancouver market. Pasture occupies the largest proportion of the farm land. Vegetables and small fruits are raised on the lowland soils, while orchard fruits are confined to the upland areas.

Figure 16-4. A daffodil field near Salem, Oregon. (Photo courtesy Oregon State Highway Commission.)

Figure 16-5. The Matanuska Valley is the most important farming area in Alaska. Most of it was originally forested, so that land clearing has been necessary. (Photo courtesy the Alaskan Agricultural Experiment Station.)

The southeastern lowlands of Vancouver Island contain about 50,000 acres of cultivated land. These lands are not continuous, but are confined to deltas and to lake plains. Temperatures are similar to those of the Fraser Delta, but the rainfall is considerably lower. In addition to dairying, poultry raising, and the cultivation of fruits and vegetables, this area has specialized in the growing of spring flowers such as daffodils and narcissi for the eastern Canadian market. Since most of the coastal region of British Columbia is mountainous and incapable of being farmed, the remaining arable lands comprise less than 20,000 acres scattered in many small isolated valleys on the mainland and on some of the islands. Most of these areas produce mainly subsistence crops.

The Matanuska Valley of Alaska The Matanuska Valley, a fairly extensive, well-drained area of reasonably fertile silt-loam soils, lies at the head of Cook Inlet about 125 miles inland from Seward, Alaska. The area of the Valley which can be tilled is estimated at 48,000 acres, less than one-third of it cleared and under cultivation at present. Some settlement occurred in the Valley about 1910, and a few pioneer farmers of that period raised hay, grain, and root

crops with reasonable success. The United States Department of Agriculture established an experiment station at Matanuska as early as 1915, but no further government aid was given until 1935, when the Federal Emergency Relief Administration sent 895 colonists from Michigan, Wisconsin, and Minnesota who had been on relief. [4] Many of these farm families were unsuited for agricultural pioneering and in time were returned to the States.

The farms of the Valley, averaging about 40 acres (Figure 16-5), were cleared by tractors and other machinery. Two years after improvement, some of the lands produced as much as six tons of hay per acre. Other crops today include spring wheat and barley (raised for feed), peas, root crops, strawberries, and garden vegetables. These were sold primarily to the small urban market at Anchorage. A canning plant and a cooperative creamery located at Palmer provide an outlet for the surplus. About two-thirds of Alaska's cultivated acreage is in the valley, but difficulties are considerable. Dairying is the chief occupation. There is plenty of summer grazing land in the

[4] Kirk H. Stone, "Populating Alaska: The United States Phase," *Geographical Review*, Vol. 42 (1952), pp. 384-404.

valley and in the adjacent Talkeetna Mountains, but during the long winter, shelter and feed add heavily to farm costs.

With limited level land and a very short growing season, the agricultural possibilities of coastal Alaska can never be great.

Lumbering and the
Wood-Products Industries

The North Pacific Coast Region, with its temperate marine climate, contains possibly the most magnificent stand of timber in the world. The trees decrease in size from the giant redwoods of northwestern California and the large Douglas firs and Western red cedars of Oregon, Washington, and British Columbia, to the smaller varieties of spruce, hemlock, and fir along the coast of Alaska. Originally probably 95 per cent of the region was covered by these great forests.

Except for the lumbering operations in the California redwood forests and smaller logging and pulpwood cutting in the forests of the Alaskan section, the major lumbering and wood-products activities coincide with the Douglas fir forest subregion in Oregon, Washington, and Southern British Columbia.

The Douglas fir subregion is exceeded in acreage by nearly every other commercial forest area on the continent, but it surpasses any of them in saw-timber volume because of the large size of the trees and the density of their stand. Ease of logging and transportation in the Puget Sound area and along the lower course of the Columbia River attracted the lumberman as early as the middle of the nineteenth century. Today the old-growth Douglas fir forests are largely depleted and have been succeeded by dense stands of regrowth, including red alder as well as young firs. In the less accessible parts of the subregion, however, excellent stands of timber are still found, and

Figure 16-6. This mammoth Douglas fir began growing about 1,000 years ago. It has a diameter of nearly 16 feet, a height of 210 feet, and is estimated to contain 105,650 board feet of usable lumber. (Photo courtesy Crown Zellerbach Corporation.)

under sustained-yield management they could last for many years. Fires such as the one at Tillamook, Oregon, in 1933, which destroyed 380 square miles of forests, have taken a heavy toll. Every effort is being exerted to reduce the hazard, including prevention measures, both public and private, and better fire-fighting techniques. While this forest subregion contains a number of commercial trees, the Douglas fir outranks all others. Practically all the trees are conifers, the hardwoods occupying a place of minor importance.

The Douglas fir has a greater saw-timber volume than any other tree species on the continent (Figure 16-6), the size of the individual trees and the density of the stand being exceeded only by the sequoias and redwoods. Douglas fir attains its best development in western Oregon, Washington, and British Columbia, and constitutes more than 60 per cent of the saw-timber volume of this subregion. Sawlog-size trees range in diameter from 16 to more than 100 inches, and the average per-acre volume is about 60,000 board feet. Douglas fir is marketed throughout the world, the wood being widely used for structural timbers, flooring,

doors, factory lumber, piling, ties, and plywood.

Western hemlock ranks next to Douglas fir in importance and constitutes nearly a fifth of the total saw-timber volume of the subregion. The wood is light, straight-grained, and nonresinous. Because of the ease with which it can be worked, western hemlock is used extensively for paper pulp, common lumber, box-shook, and flooring.

Sitka spruce, although limited in extent within this subregion, is highly prized because of its special qualities, being light in weight, tough, nonresinous, and easy to work. The chief uses today for Sitka spruce include box-shook, ladder stock, basket and crate veneers, and paper pulp. Other species of significance include Western red cedar, white fir, and a variety of other firs, spruces, and pines that are locally notable.

Logging and Sawmill Operations The first sawmill in the Douglas fir subregion was erected by the Hudson's Bay Company in 1827 near Fort Vancouver on the Columbia River. Lumber was exported to Hawaii, and later, quantities were shipped to San Francisco and the California gold fields. Between 1850 and 1900, many sawmills

Figure 16-7. Felling a big tree. The logger's chain saw is cutting out an undercut wedge that will serve to direct the tree's fall. (Photo courtesy the Weyerhaeuser Company.)

Figure 16-8. Block-cut patches in an Oregon fir forest. (Photo courtesy the Weyerhaeuser Company.)

were established to supply the rapidly expanding world market.

The lumber industry of the continent has been migratory. As each timbered district was depleted, the industry was forced to move to a locality more remote from the consuming centers. When the lumber industry came from the Lake States and later from the South (Chapter 7) to the Pacific Northwest, it moved into the last timbered frontier. Today, this region and the South together produce most of the forest products of the continent. Not only does distance from market affect the industry in this region, but the gigantic size of the trees, particularly the Douglas fir, has forced the development of many new logging methods (Figure 16-7).

The method of logging used in this region and in some sections of the Northern Rocky Mountains differs from that used in all other parts of Anglo-America. Here, the "block-cut" method is used, in which every tree in a designated section of an area is removed, but none is removed from surrounding sections (Figure 16-8). Elsewhere, "selective cutting" is practiced, in which only certain trees in an area are selected and cut and the adjacent trees are left untouched.

Today the logging industry is highly mechanized. Giant Diesel-powered tractors or bulldozers "snake" the logs out of the forest. These are then hauled by large trucks or by rail to the sawmills, or to streams where they can be floated to the mills. In British Columbia, the common system of logging is the "sky-line," which utilizes two strong spar trees several hundred yards apart, with a cable fastened between them high above the ground. A traveling carriage runs along the cable or sky-line, and from it a steel rope is fastened to the logs. The logs, with one end elevated, are dragged to the head spar tree. By the use of sky-lines, logs can be taken from mountainous forests more cheaply than by any other method.

Some sawmills are located in remote forested areas, but the major ones are on deep water where logs can be rafted to the mill and the finished lumber can be exported. One of the most important tidewater mill centers in the region is Longview, Washington, on the Columbia River. Built by a major lumber company, it is an example of a planned wood-products city and port.

Since the opening of the Panama Canal in 1915, the North Pacific Coast Region has been favored by cheap water rates to the great consuming markets of the Atlantic Coast and to Northwestern Europe.

About 35 per cent of all the lumber sawed

in the United States and Canada comes from this region, although the pulpwood proportion is considerably less. While this production is scattered, it is most heavily concentrated along the lower Columbia Valley, in southwest Oregon, around Puget Sound, on the western and southwestern sides of the Olympic Peninsula, on the lower mainland coast of British Columbia, and in the central part of Vancouver Island. Lumber mills occupy extensive tracts along the lower Willamette and Columbia rivers, around Puget Sound, between Vancouver River and Powell River on the British Columbia mainland, and in the Port Alberni–Nanaimo section of Vancouver Island; huge

Figure 16-9. Deforestation and afforestation on a tree farm in Washington. As the diesel tractor pulls away the last of the harvested logs, an aerial-seeding helicopter prepares to drop seeds on the cleared patch. Approximately 25,000,000 seeds will be dropped on each square mile. (Photo courtesy the Weyerhaeuser Company.)

log booms (rafts) are common in the smaller inlets of Puget Sound and the Strait of Georgia.

Nearly three-quarters of the total area of "panhandle" Alaska is within the boundaries of Tongass National Forest—the nation's largest. This area contains most of the commercial timber of Alaska, a resource as yet little exploited, but with tremendous potential value.

Forest-Products Industries   The manufacture of pulp and paper is rapidly becoming a leading industry. Although a considerable quantity of pulp is exported, the paper mills of the subregion are consuming an ever-increasing quantity in the manufacture of kraft paper and newsprint. Hydroelectric power is sufficient for the development of a sizable paper industry, and there is a steady export to other domestic areas. The British Columbia section has a number of paper and pulp mills in the vicinities of Vancouver, Nanaimo, Port Alberni, Powell River, Campbell River, Ocean Falls, Kitimat, and Prince Rupert. Pulping is done in Alaska at Ketchikan, Sitka, and Juneau.

The veneer and plywood industry is also expanding, with eastern companies establishing new plants in the North Pacific Coast Region.

Forest Conservation

If careful logging practices are followed, if forest fires are reduced, and if reforestation is practiced in the cut-over lands, this forest region should continue to produce an important part of the continent's wood products, and the industries here should not suffer the decline that has characterized other forested regions. This is the last timbered frontier on the continent. It must be used wisely if woodworking industries are to continue to be important (Figure 16-9).

Tree Farms   Much of the cut-over land of western Oregon and Washington has regenerated a new Douglas fir cover 30 to 50 years old. Large tracts have been organized into tree farms dedicated to perpetual forest production. [5] Encouraged by low tax rates, these privately owned forests are carefully managed for maximum fire protection and regrowth. The tracts, which are located in the Coast Range and hilly portions of the Puget-Willamette trough, are already producing increasing volumes of pulp wood, poles, small timbers, and Christmas trees, by thinning of the stands.

A continued volume of high-grade lumber and plywood production which requires large logs is increasingly dependent on the public timber sales of the Forest Service and the Bureau of Land Management of the federal government. These agencies together with the National Park Service and the Bureau of Indian Affairs now control over 75 per cent of the remaining virgin forest in Oregon, Washington, and Alaska. Mature timber in selected national forest areas is auctioned off for removal by private firms. Similarly, most of the British Columbia timber is owned by the national or provincial governments. The sustained-yield program embraced in the British Columbia Forest-Management Act has far-reaching implications.

The Fishing Industry

The North Pacific Coast is one of the major fishing regions of the continent and ranks in total catch with the banks fisheries of the North Atlantic. Here, however, fish are not caught on banks or in the deeps, but are mostly taken in coastal waters or in the lower courses of streams; and they are packed in canneries nearby. Salmon is the major species caught, [6] although in recent years halibut and herring have increased in importance.

Salmon For a long time, salmon has been the chief food of the Indians living along the North Pacific Coast. The first attempt by white man to preserve salmon was made in 1834, and salmon were first canned in 1866 near the Columbia River. From these meager beginnings, the salmon fishing and canning industry has grown to become, today, one of the major activities of the region. Five species of salmon are caught in the coastal waters of this region. These are: (1) the chinook or king, (2) the sockeye or red, (3) the humpback or pink, (4) the silver or coho, and (5) the dog or chum salmon. The sockeye, although smaller than the king, is the most valuable, most sought, and most caught of the five species. The king ranks next, and pinks and chums are becoming more important each year. An interesting description of the life history of the Pacific salmon follows.

All species of Pacific salmon are anadromous, that is, the adults migrate from the ocean into fresh-water streams to spawn. They proceed up rivers, such as the Columbia, until they arrive at the same tributary where they themselves began life some years before. Very few stray to other streams. The female salmon deposits her eggs in a nest, or redd, which she digs in the gravel of the stream or shallow lake-shore waters. In the process of egg laying, the fertilized ova are covered with successive layers of gravel to a depth of several inches. The time required for the eggs to hatch depends on the temperature of the water. Newly hatched fish live in the gravel of the redd and gradually absorb the food in the abdominal yolk sac. At the end of this period, usually in the late winter or early spring, they struggle up through the gravel and begin to seek food. How long the young fish stay in fresh water varies considerably with the species, but

[5] A typical acreage may be divided into 70 sections, with one section being clear-cut each year, and immediately afforested. At the end of the seventieth year all sections will have been cut, and the first section, now supporting a mature even-aged stand, is ready for harvest again.

[6] Salmon is Canada's most valuable commercial fish; it ranks third (after shrimp and tuna) in the United States.

eventually they migrate downstream to the sea, where they remain from 1 to 3 years and grow rapidly. When they approach sexual maturity, they return to fresh water to spawn and thereby complete the cycle. All Pacific salmon die after spawning.[7]

METHODS OF FISHING The chief methods of catching salmon are by purse seines and gill nets; some commercial trolling is done. Indians still net salmon along some of the streams, but the total taken in that manner is not large. Floating and stationary traps, very important until 1959 in the Inside Passage, were outlawed by the Alaskan legislature in one of the first pieces of legislation enacted after Alaska became a state.

The total salmon catch has been declining in recent years, especially in United States waters.

DEPLETION AND CONSERVATION OF SALMON The chief cause of the depletion of the salmon-runs in the western streams is man himself. Destruction of the salmon has come through (1) overfishing in rivers and

[7] Clifford J. Burner, "Characteristics of Spawning Nests of Columbia River Salmon," *Fishery Bulletin 61*, Fish and Wildlife Service (Washington: Government Printing Office, 1951), p. 97.

oceans, (2) damming up streams, and (3) pollution of spawning grounds.

The construction of dams across the Columbia River has a continuing adverse effect on the industry. Fish ladders permit salmon to pass around low dams like the Bonneville (Figure 16-10), but high dams, such as Grand Coulee, are apparently impassable. The Fraser River in British Columbia, leading salmon stream of the Pacific Northwest, had a destructive landslide at Hell's Gate that partly blocked it in 1913, the very year that a large run was ascending. Most of the fish never reached the spawning grounds, and, as a result, salmon-runs in that stream have never been very large since. However, restocking, fishways, and other enlightened management schemes have restored the runs to a reasonable level in recent years.

The conflict of interests between advocates of hydroelectricity generation and salmon fishermen is probably the principal long-term cause of disharmony in the region. It is becoming increasingly clear that the two resources are virtually incompatible, and one can be developed only at the expense of the other. In the United States,

Figure 16-10. A fish ladder at Bonneville Dam. This ladder is more than 1300 feet long and allows salmon and other fish to bypass the dam by "jumping" up from pool to pool, each pool being about one foot higher than the one before. The dam is seen in the background, with the Columbia River boiling up through outlets. (Photo courtesy Oregon State Highway Commission.)

the dam-builders seem to have the upper hand; in Canada, the fishermen are more in control. Further conflict is assured in the future on both sides of the border. [8]

CANNING Canneries are located on tidewater, readily accessible to fishing boats and tenders and also convenient to ocean shipping for marketing the canned product. Many Alaskan canneries are isolated and in use only during the summer season; yet these small canneries, whose only access to the outside world is by steamer or airlift, account for more than half of the annual pack. A cannery location requires plenty of fish, a safe ship landing, and an abundance of pure fresh water. The cannery is usually built out on piles to assure deep water so that ships can approach and so that the fish refuse can be dumped into the water and be carried away with the tide. Some canneries employ as many as 300 workers in summer but maintain only a caretaker or two in winter. Canadian salmon canning is done mostly at Prince Rupert and Vancouver. The principal canneries outside Alaska and British Columbia are mainly around the shores of Puget Sound.

As soon as fishing boats or scows bring their catch to the cannery, the fish are unloaded mechanically into bins. Streams of fresh water are played on the fish to remove all dirt and slime. Next they go to the dressing machine, known as the "Iron Chink," which cuts off the head, tail, and fins, scoops out the entrails, and removes the scales. Formerly this was all done by hand. After being washed again and inspected, the salmon pass through a series of revolving gang knives, which slice the fish into proper sizes. Other machines fill and seal the cans, which are fed into the cookers. In

[8] For a more detailed presentation of this problem, see M. E. Marts and W. R. D. Sewell, "The Conflict Between Fish and Power Resources in the Pacific Northwest," *Annals of the Association of American Geographers,* Vol. 50 (March 1960), pp. 42-50.

the most modern canneries, practically every operation is done by machine. Tins from Seattle arrive at Alaskan canneries in a collapsed form requiring little space in the hold of the ship, and machines ream out and assemble the can.

The bulk of the canned salmon is marketed through Vancouver or Seattle to the large consuming centers of Anglo-America and abroad. Although most of the salmon are canned, large quantities are now being marketed fresh, salted, smoked, or "mild cured."

Other Fish While salmon are commercially the most important fish in North Pacific waters, large quantities of halibut, herring, pilchard, and tuna are also caught. In addition, a sizable shellfish industry (particularly oysters) has developed in recent years.

Halibut, by far the most important of the other commercial fish and one of the standard food fishes of America, is a large deep-sea flounder which weighs up to 200 pounds. Unlike salmon, halibut lives and spawns in deep waters. The eggs then rise to near the surface and drift with the currents. The small fish, when hatched, work toward the shallow waters near the shore. Halibut spawn more than once in their life cycle but do not enter fresh-water streams. They are caught in deep water either by baited hooks or by power-trawling. After many years of declining halibut catches, this American-Canadian fishery was strictly regulated on a quota basis, and has been stabilized at a productive level. In an average year, about one-third of the total catch is in Alaskan waters, one-third in British Columbia waters, and the remainder off Washington, Oregon, and California.

Halibut are marketed as fresh (frozen) fish, and the chief landing ports are Prince Rupert and Seattle. They are then sent by fast rail service to all parts of Anglo-America. Today many freezing plants on the

West Coast ship only the choicest parts of the fish eastward, thereby saving freight costs on the bones and other inedible parts. A recent demand for halibut liver oil, which is high in vitamins A and D, has caused the growth of a subsidiary industry that brings halibut fishermen an additional income.

Tuna, the newest of the commercial fish along the northwest coast, are caught with short rods from fishing boats, using lures or bait. Tuna are canned chiefly at Astoria, near the mouth of the Columbia River. The canning method differs from that for salmon; tuna must be cooked first, then packed in cans, and finally steamed in order to sterilize the pack.

Other edible fish caught in the offshore waters of this region include the herring, pilchard, Bering Sea codfish, sole, and other bottom fish. Astoria, Grays Harbor, Seattle, and Prince Rupert serve as the home ports for most of the fishing boats. A million-dollar oyster industry using modern cultivation methods has developed mainly in and around Willapa Bay. This bay, with its 100 square miles of shallow tidal flats, offers excellent conditions for growing the Pacific oyster. Eighty per cent of the oysters in the region come from the Willapa district, reaching the market either fresh or canned. The British Columbia oyster fishery is in the Strait of Georgia. It depends upon a yearly import of spat from Japan, as the native resources have long since been fished out.

Other important shellfish taken in Pacific Northwest waters are crabs (especially around the Queen Charlotte Islands) and shrimp. The most striking recent development in North Pacific shellfishing has been the greatly increased catches of king crabs in the Gulf of Alaska. These demersal giants weigh up to 25 pounds and may have a "claw spread" of six feet. They are scooped off the bottom by trawl, the meat is extracted and frozen on board ship, packaging is accomplished in tidewater plants in Alaska and Washington, and the frozen packages are marketed mostly in eastern United States.

Mining

Until the discovery of gold in the Klondike and in the beach sands at Nome—both areas outside this region—little interest was shown in minerals, as the mountains of the North Pacific Coast seemed poor in metallic wealth, and the dense vegetation discouraged systematic exploration. Even as late as 1880, some years after the United States purchased Alaska, the annual gold production of that territory amounted to only $20,000.

Various discoveries of gold, silver, lead, and copper have led to moderate flurries of mining activity in southern Alaska in the past, but practically all of the operations are of historical interest only. Ore output in this part of the region is negligible today.

One of the two principal coal fields being exploited in Alaska is in this region—the Matanuska field. Production is about 300,000 short tons per year, and most of the output goes to military installations near Anchorage.

Beginning in 1957, there was an oil boom on the Kenai Peninsula, not far from Anchorage. Output is still quite small, but the Swanson River Field is expected to have a billion-barrel potential, and represents the first notable commercial petroleum production in Alaska, except for the Barrow Naval Reserve area in the far north.

In the Canadian portion of the region there is moderate production of iron ore, copper, coal, and gold. About five per cent of the total Canadian yield of iron ore is produced from mines near Quinsam Lake on Vancouver Island and on nearby Texada Island. There are several copper mines, but the leading producer by far is at Britannia Beach, just north of Vancouver. Near Comox on Vancouver Island is a major producer of bituminous coking coal. At Bralorne on the Bridge River are two large gold mines.

Power Generation

Because of the mountainous terrain and heavy rainfall, the region has one of the greatest hydroelectric potentials of any part of Anglo-America, but most development has been fairly recent. Some large facilities were established to provide power to the Trail smelter several decades ago, but Grand Coulee Dam (in the Intermontane Region) and Bonneville Dam were the first major projects on the United States side of the border. Bonneville Dam occupies a Columbia River water gap in the Cascades a few miles east of Portland. The Dalles Dam, also in this region, is 50 miles upstream from Bonneville. Smaller hydroelectric facilities are scattered throughout the region, but British Columbia's Kitimat project ultimately will produce almost as much power as Grand Coulee Dam.

The entire region is one of abundant potential water power. However, particularly in the southern half, the power potential is not "firm"; i.e., there are marked seasonal fluctuations in stream flow which cause erratic power generation. Further, good dam sites are often some distance from population centers. Consequently, it is often more economical to develop thermal electric power in the midst of major markets by using fuel brought in from outside the region. This is now the trend in the North Pacific Coast Region. In British Columbia, for example, thermal electricity is being developed twice as fast as hydroelectricity (although hydro-power is still responsible for more than 90 per cent of the province's electricity generation). Oil, gas, and wood waste are the principal fuels employed.

Industrial and urban expansion will be hampered if electricity demand outstrips minimum annual supply.

Manufacturing

Aside from the food- and wood-processing industries already mentioned, manufacturing in the North Pacific Coast Region must of necessity be limited because of the lack of variety in raw materials, the limited local market, and great distances from other large markets. There are only a few concentrations of industry.

The Willamette Valley The only industrial center of note is metropolitan Portland. Wood-products industries are the most important type, though they are slowly decreasing in relative importance as other types of manufacturing expand. Food processing, particularly canning, ranks second, and pulp and paper manufacture is third. Woolen textiles are a specialized industry based on Oregon wool.

Along the lower course of the Columbia River are several large sawmills, pulp mills, and shipyards, as well as four aluminum plants. The latter, located here on the basis of electricity availability, are in The Dalles and Troutdale, Oregon, and in Vancouver and Longview, Washington.

The Puget Sound Area The principal industrial center of the North Pacific Coast Region is Seattle. Its typical factories process food and timber, but the outstanding industrial firm is Boeing Aircraft Company, whose gigantic enterprise normally employs some 20,000 workers. Considerable shipbuilding is done in Seattle, and across Puget Sound at Bremerton.

Thirty miles south of Seattle is Tacoma, whose large tideflat industrial area is dominated by wood-products industries. In addition, there are two huge metallurgical works—one of the world's largest copper smelters and an aluminum plant.

Coastal British Columbia Greater Vancouver is Canada's fourth largest industrial center. It is in the heart of an active logging and fishing area, its population is half the size of British Columbia's, and it is a major transportation crossroads. Sawmilling is the leading type of manufacturing, and other forms of wood processing (pulp, paper, veneer, plywood, planing mills) are notable. In addition, there is a moderate amount of shipbuilding, a growing petroleum refining industry (utilizing Prairie Province oil), and considerable processing of fish.

Secondary Canadian industrial centers are Victoria and Port Alberni. At Kitimat, on the far north coast, is the famous facility recently constructed by the Aluminum Company of Canada. In Canada's largest construction project since the building of the Canadian Pacific Railroad, the Nechako River was literally turned around and sent via a ten-mile tunnel through the Coast Mountains and over a 2,600-foot fall to Kemano, where an abundance of hydroelectricity is generated. This is transmitted 50 miles to Kitimat, where it is used to reduce the bauxite that is imported from Jamaica and British Guiana (Figure 16-11). Eventually Kitimat's smelter will be the world's largest, and the "new" town of Kitimat is well on the way to becoming the third largest urban center in British Columbia.

Resorts and Tourism

The North Pacific Coast is one of the continent's most scenic regions,[9] and is rapidly becoming one of its major playgrounds. Remoteness from large population centers, as

[9] The scenery, however, is frequently shrouded in fog, cloud, or mist.

well as the inaccessibility of many of the scenic spots, has retarded the development of resorts. Construction of new highways and, to a lesser extent, the extension of air and steamship service have greatly stimulated travel. The United States section is the best-developed, having three national parks, Olympic, Mt. Rainier, and Crater Lake, and several national monuments, state parks, and other recreational areas. The Canadian section and the Inside Passage of southeastern Alaska rank among the world's most scenic areas, with their spectacular mountains, glaciers, and fjords that are easily accessible by ocean and coastwise steamers. Along the coast of southern Alaska, however, is found the continent's most magnificent scenery, culminating in the majestic peak of Mt. McKinley, and set aside for the public in the Mt. McKinley National Park. Although most tourists come during the summer season, the recent development of winter sports in the Cascade Mountains of Oregon and Washington has greatly increased the year-round volume of business.

Transportation

Despite the mountainous terrain, most parts of the North Pacific Coast are well

Figure 16-11. The Kitimat aluminum-reduction works. Ships carrying ore dock at the ice-free harbor in the foreground, covered conveyor belts take the ore to circular storage bins, and eventually to the smelter in the background. (Photo courtesy Aluminium Company of Canada, Limited.)

served by railways, highways, airways, and seaways. Water transportation is still of major importance, as shown by the large ocean ports of Portland, Tacoma, Seattle, and Vancouver, which export great quantities of lumber and wood products. The British Columbia and Alaska sections are even more dependent upon water transportation, although Alaska is connected with the United States by a highway, and the British Columbia coast is served by the two Canadian transcontinental railways.

Railroads The southern part of the North Pacific Coast Region in Oregon, Washington, and British Columbia, is served by seven major transcontinental railroads, and a number of smaller feeder lines. The transcontinental lines are: (1) the Southern Pacific, from New Orleans via Los Angeles and San Francisco; (2) the Union Pacific from Salt Lake City and the East; (3) the Chicago, Milwaukee, St. Paul, and Pacific from Chicago; (4) the Northern Pacific from Minneapolis; (5) the Great Northern from Minneapolis; (6) the Canadian Pacific from Winnipeg and Montreal; and (7) the Canadian National from Winnipeg and Montreal. The five United States lines have their western termini at Portland or Seattle, while the two Canadian transcontinental roads use Vancouver and Prince Rupert as their Pacific ports. In Alaska, two short lines extend inland from the coast to connect (1) Skagway with Whitehorse and (2) Seward with Fairbanks. This latter railroad is owned by the United States government.

Highways Most of the highways in Oregon and Washington are excellent. These roads have been of great value in reaching remote areas not touched by railroads; not only have they served to get out large quantities of timber, but they have also stimulated the tourist trade by providing easy access to numerous wilderness areas of superb scenery.

Road mileage is very limited in the British Columbia portion of the region, except in the lower Fraser Valley and the southern half of Vancouver Island. Highway travel is even more restricted in southern Alaska, where only Cordova, Valdez, and the Kenai Peninsula—Anchorage area have connections to the interior. None of the cities and towns of the Panhandle has land-route connections with the rest of Anglo-America except Skagway (railroad to Whitehorse) and Haines (summer road to the Alaska Highway).

Water Transport Water transportation is very significant for the region. There are four outstanding ports—Vancouver, Seattle, Tacoma, and Portland. Vancouver has the third busiest harbor in Canada, after Montreal and Sept Isles, particularly shipping wheat, timber products, and petroleum products. It handles much traffic with Alaska that formerly went through Seattle. The other three mentioned are general cargo ports, with considerable emphasis on wood-products shipments.

Airways Most centers of the Pacific Northwest are served by airways, which also provide connections with Canadian territory and Alaska. New flying fields built in the Alaskan coastal districts during World War II are providing isolated areas with rapid transportation to the "outside." The Seattle-Tacoma International Airport is the major point of departure for trans-Pacific flights, either via Hawaii, or via Alaska and the Great Circle route, to Japan. Vancouver is also a major air hub, and traffic at Anchorage is increasing rapidly.

The Outlook

Today the leading occupations of the region are lumbering and allied wood-products industries; general agriculture (especially in the broad Willamette Valley); specialized agriculture (dairying, fruit growing, poultry farming, market gardening); fishing; mining

TABLE 15

Selected Cities and Towns of the North Pacific
Coast

City or Town	Urbanized Area	Political Center
Aberdeen	......	18,741
Anchorage	......	44,237
Astoria	......	11,239
Bellingham	......	34,688
Bremerton	......	28,922
Corvallis	......	20,669
Eugene	95,686	50,977
Eureka	......	28,137
Everett	......	40,304
Juneau	......	6,797
Ketchikan	......	6,483
Klamath Falls	......	16,949
Kodiak	......	2,628
Longview	......	23,349
Medford	......	24,425
Nanaimo	......	14,135
New Westminster	......	33,654
North Vancouver	......	23,656
Olympia	......	18,273
Port Alberni	......	11,560
Portland	651,685	372,676
Prince Rupert	......	11,987
Salem	......	49,142
Seattle	864,109	557,087
Sitka	......	3,237
Springfield	......	19,616
Tacoma	214,930	147,979
Vancouver, B.C.	790,165	384,522
Vancouver, Wash.	......	32,464
Victoria	154,152	54,941

in limited amount; and metallurgical industries, in growing array. Abundance of hydroelectric power tends to offset the lack of local mineral fuel, and pipelines have brought oil and gas to the region from Alberta and the Peace River country. Much of the terrain is still in forests—virgin or second growth. The Puget Sound area supports several large urban centers that have a combined population of more than a million people. The cities of this region are primarily trade centers with their future partly dependent upon coastwise and trans-Pacific commerce.

This is primarily a region of extractive industries. The natural resources which once seemed almost limitless—timber and fish—are now being more carefully managed, and all activities dependent upon them should, therefore, be able to continue indefinitely. Agriculture is limited in area, but through specialization and intensification has become increasingly more valuable to the regional economy. The outlook for increased forestry exploitation is promising; the fisheries future seems to be limited to about the present relatively low level of activity; mining potentialities are uncertain, but mineral extraction will probably be more important in the future than it is today. There will doubtless be a growing shift to steady thermal electricity generation, with the abundant but erratic water-power resources reserved as "back-up" or "peak period" facilities. Future expansion and prosperity in the region will be largely urban.

Aside from the agricultural, urban, and industrial areas, this region will remain primarily a wilderness dominated by a few extractive industries. Tourism, hunting, and sports fishing will play increasingly important roles in these areas.

Selected Bibliography

Barbour, George B., "Kitimat," *Geographical Journal*, Vol. 125, June 1959, pp. 217-222.

British Columbia Lands Service, *The Prince Rupert-Smithers Bulletin Area.* Victoria: The Queens Printer, 1959.

———, *The Vancouver Island Bulletin Area.* Victoria: The Queen's Printer, 1957.

Green, Carleton, *The Impact of the Aluminum Industry on the Economy of the Pacific Northwest* (a digest), Stanford Research Institute, June 1954.

Highsmith, Richard M., Jr., "Irrigation in the Willamette Valley," *Geographical Review*, Vol. 46, January 1956, pp. 98-110.

———, and A. M. Baron, "Oregon's Hood River Valley," *Journal of Geography*, Vol. 57, October 1958, pp. 353-360.

———, and John L. Beh, "Tillamook Burn: The Regeneration of a Forest," *The Scientific Monthly*, Vol. 57, 1952, pp. 139-148.

Highsmith, Richard M., Jr., and Elbert E. Miller, "Open Field Farming in Yakima Valley, Washington," *Economic Geography*, Vol. 28, 1952, pp. 74-87.

Kuchler, A. W., "The Broadleaf Deciduous Forests of the Pacific Northwest," *Annals of the Association of American Geographers*, Vol. 36, 1946, pp. 122-147.

MacKinnon, Dixon, "Man-Made Spawning Channels for Pacific Salmon," *Canadian Geographical Journal*, Vol. 63, July 1961, pp. 28-39.

Marts, M. E., and W. R. D. Sewell, "The Conflict Between Fish and Power Resources in the Pacific Northwest," *Annals of the Association of American Geographers*, Vol. 50, March 1960, pp. 42-50.

Matheison, R. S., "Economic Trade in the Alaskan Salmon Industry," *Australian Geographer*, Vol. 8, September 1960, pp. 17-24.

McGovern, P. D., "Industrial Development in the Vancouver Area," *Economic Geography*, Vol. 37, July 1961, pp. 189-206.

Miller, Elbert E., and Richard M. Highsmith, Jr., "The Hop Industry of the Pacific Coast," *Journal of Geography*, Vol. 49, 1950, pp. 63-77.

Minghi, Julian V., "The Conflict of Salmon Fishing Policies in the North Pacific," *Pacific Viewpoint*, Vol. 2, March 1961, pp. 59-84.

Rogers, George W., *Alaska in Transition: the Southeast Region*. Baltimore: Johns Hopkins Press, 1960.

Siddall, William R., "Seattle: Regional Capital of Alaska," *Annals of the Association of American Geographers*, Vol. 47, September 1957, pp. 277-284.

Van Cleef, Eugene, "Prince Rupert—an Error in Location," *Journal of Geography*, Vol. 58, February 1959, pp. 127-132.

chapter seventeen

The
Yukon-Kuskokwim
Basins

Almost continental in magnitude, the Yukon-Kuskokwim Region is one of the most sparsely populated, least known, and least developed areas in Anglo-America (Figure 17-1). It has suffered and has been largely neglected because of misconceptions and apathy on the part of the people in both Canada and the United States. Such disparaging epithets as "Icebergia," "Seward's Folly," "Uncle Sam's Icebox," and "Walrussia" contributed to give the Alaskan seg-

ment a bad reputation as a land of ice and snow, unfit for the habitation of any human beings other than a few miserable Indians and Eskimos. And, surprising as it may seem, this misconception is still widely prevalent.

The discovery of gold in the Klondike and the defense program enabled the region to be at least temporarily rediscovered.

Yet, in spite of neglect and ignorance, the Yukon-Kuskokwim Basins form one of Anglo-America's more colorful regions. There

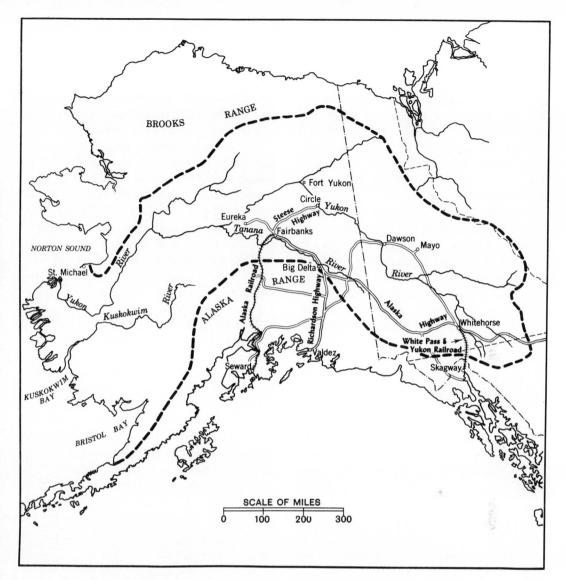

Figure 17-1. The Yukon-Kuskokwim Basins. A region of mining, hunting and fishing, trapping, subsistence farming, and military preparedness.

are few persons who do not thrill to the names of Dawson, Klondike, Whitehorse, and Fort Yukon. The popular writings of Jack London, Rex Beach, Joaquin Miller, and Robert W. Service, which deal with man's battles against a hostile nature, have become a part of America's folklore.

The Yukon-Kuskokwim Region, lying in the basins of the Yukon and Kuskokwim Rivers, extends from the Alaska Range on the south to the Brooks Range on the north,

and from the source of the Yukon in Canada to the Bering Sea. Because the Seward Peninsula lacks the Yukon Basin's extremes of temperature and supports no agriculture, it is considered a part of the Tundra rather than of this region.

The Physical Setting

Formerly considered a location that was extremely poor, unimportant, and definitely in a "back eddy," the Yukon Basin, as a result of proximity to the Soviet Union, is now considered strategic. The "polar concept" assumes that if another major war is touched off, the Arctic and subarctic regions will provide the pathways for the initial and perhaps the decisive blow. The development in the Yukon today owes its importance as much to the strategic factor as to the economic, if not more.

Climate   For the most part, the climate is decidedly continental, being characterized by extremes of temperature from summer to winter and by light precipitation. Summers are short and warm, winters long and cold. The average temperature of the three warmest months is about 57° F. Early June and late August are critical periods, for frost is likely, with resultant crop damage. The average January temperature is about −20° F. and the average for July is 60° F., an annual range of more than 80 degrees. Periods of extreme cold, however, seldom last long. The lowest temperature on record is −76° F., at Tanana, south of the Arctic Circle, and the highest is 100° F., at Fort Yukon, north of the Arctic Circle. The range of temperature is smaller near the Bering Sea, where winters are less cold and summers less hot. The growing season varies from 80 to 90 days, though the 18 to 19 hours of daylight in summer partly compensate for this short period and for the rather low heating power of the sun's rays.

The average annual precipitation varies from 10 to 12 inches, about three-fifths of it falling during the period May through September. About one-fifth falls as snow. Ordinarily only June and July are snowless. The snow cover, amounting to about 24 inches, is quite evenly distributed; there is little drifting because of the low velocity of surface winds. The rigors of winter have serious economic effects, the entire work cycle being determined by the weather.

Terrain   The terrain of the region near the main river consists mostly of dissected, rolling, flat-topped hills whose summits show marked uniformity of elevation over a wide area. Known as the Yukon Plateau, it has an average elevation of 2,000 to 3,000 feet and is rimmed by mountains on the southwest, east, and north. In the Yukon Valley from Whitehorse to Circle, mountains lie along the river banks or near them (Figure 17-2), so that only the narrow river terraces give any promise of possible cultivation. Near

Figure 17-2. The Yukon River in northwestern Canada. The town of Dawson occupies the river terrace in the foreground. (Photo courtesy Canadian Government Travel Bureau, Ottawa.)

Circle on the great bend in the Yukon are the marshy flats which continue downstream to Fort Hamlin. In the Tanana Valley area there are two main types of land—the terraces or bench lands and the bottom lands or flats. Each type has its distinctly different features of microclimate and consequent difference in crops.

For many miles along its lower course, the Yukon is virtually at sea level, and hence the land is marshy. An additional cause of poor drainage and hence of ponds, marshes, and lakes is the fact that the permanently frozen subsoil over much of the region prevents normal soak-in. In the 60-mile-wide Yukon Delta, the water is so shallow and the distributaries so numerous that seagoing vessels cannot enter.

Soil Since detailed soil studies have been made in but a few places, only broad generalizations regarding soils are possible.[1] Most of the soils in the Tanana Valley are water-sorted sediments and are cold and poorly drained. The poor drainage results from permafrost, or permanently frozen ground, which lies usually 12 to 36 inches below the surface under a natural vegetative cover of moss, thick turf, and peat. This cover prevents maximum penetration of heat into the soil by shading, by decreasing air circulation, by retaining moisture in and just above the soil, and by intercepting rain. The subsoil is completely frozen in places.

When cleared, this soil in the Fairbanks area develops into a gray-brown to dark yellowish-brown, fine sandy loam. The well-drained and relatively warm wind-laid deposits of the Fairbanks soil series make a satisfactory soil for agriculture. Unfortunately, the soil is given to erosion once the natural vegetation is removed.

Black soils especially are important, for they best absorb solar energy. Thus the summer temperature of black soils of the bottom land is higher than that of the grayish soils of the bench lands. Hence crops in such soils grow faster and mature in a shorter period, provided the permafrost line is not near the soil surface.

Permafrost In this region, permafrost occurs everywhere, but it is not continuous as in the Tundra Region to the north. Permafrost is in delicate equilibrium with several other elements of the natural environment; hence, if disturbed, the landscape becomes modified. Whether permafrost is a negative or a beneficial factor in agriculture depends on the particular local permafrost conditions and the climatic factors relating to heat exchange.

Natural Vegetation The natural vegetation consists largely of light forest growth of white spruce, cottonwood, balsam, poplar, and Alaska white birch on the bench lands and on the better-drained valley floors. The ground cover comprises dwarf heath shrubs, mountain cranberry, mosses, dwarf dogwood, and bluegrass. White spruce, with a shallow and flexible root system, is the tree species best suited to soils with permafrost. Black spruce, larch, and white birch have shallow but not as flexible root systems and are less frost-tolerant. Living roots cannot, of course, either penetrate or occupy permafrost.

In the Tanana Valley, black spruce, dwarf birch and dwarf willow, Labrador tea, and mountain cranberry grow on the cold, poorly drained lowlands. Everywhere the type of vegetation has strong indicator value as to soil and drainage conditions.

Vegetation in winter may be subjected to severe water loss through exposure to dry winds at the very time the roots are encased

[1] C. E. Kellogg and I. J. Nygard, *Report on Exploratory Investigations of Agricultural Problems of Alaska,* Department of Agriculture, Miscellaneous Publication No. 700 (Washington: Government Printing Office, 1949).

———, *Exploratory Study of the Principal Soil Groups of Alaska,* Department of Agriculture, Monograph No. 7. (Washington: Government Printing Office, 1951).

Figure 17-3. A herd of domesticated reindeer in a corral in central Alaska. (Photo courtesy Bureau of Indian Affairs.)

in frozen soil and hence cannot absorb water. Tree growth is slow, and trees seldom exceed six inches in diameter. Desiccating winds during the long, cold winter are believed to limit tree growth on frozen ground. It is for this reason that the tree line extends farthest north in sheltered valleys. Toward the northwest, the trees thin out and finally disappear in the tundra. Grass and tundra dominate the lower valleys near the Bering Sea.

Wildlife The animal most closely associated with this region (excluding the Bering Sea littoral) and the one most highly valued is the caribou. Migrations of caribou, which travel in large herds, are much like those of the bison on the American Great Plains before they were exterminated in the 1880's. Each summer the caribou travel north, crossing the Yukon between Selkirk and Circle, and return later to their winter quarters near the Alaska Mountains or between the St. Elias and Coast Ranges. Caribou meat furnishes the principal item in the diet of the natives, and the skin makes ideal clothing for the far north. Unfortunately, caribou are being depleted rapidly, though large numbers still persist.

Moose and black bear are plentiful. The marauding wolf, traveling alone or in pairs in summer but in packs in winter, kills thousands of caribou annually. Among the smaller animals are the marten, mink, marmot, ground squirrel, Arctic hare, and snowshoe rabbit—the last two changing color from brown in summer to white in winter.

There are three notable introduced species in the region. The Siberian reindeer, a domesticated relative of the native caribou, was first brought to Alaska in 1891 (Figure 17-3). Attempts to establish commercial herds among the Eskimos generally have failed, but the government maintains small Eskimo-oriented herds in this region at St. Michael, on Nunivak Island, and on the Pribilof Islands. Musk oxen, long since exterminated in Alaska, were reintroduced in the 1930's, and a flourishing herd now exists on Nunivak Island. Bison were introduced from Montana in 1928, and there are now increasing herds near Big Delta and in the upper Copper River country.

In summer, millions of ducks and geese make their nesting grounds on the Yukon Flats. Finally, there are the billions of gnats, black flies, and mosquitoes which thrive in this region of poor drainage and high summer temperatures. Travelers insist that the mosquito is the curse of the Yukon; that they can overcome with a fair degree of satisfaction all the other obstacles—the vast stretches of swamps, the isolation, and the bitter cold. The mosquito retards immigration and lowers the quality of work. Farmers and miners must wear head nets and canvas gloves during May, June, July, and August. So greatly do mosquitoes torment cattle that some farmers prepare smudges in their pastures to enable the animals to get relief.

Settlement

The Yukon and Kuskokwim Basins have never been colonized in the traditional way. The economic background of every white settlement has been the demand from distant areas for the furs and the gold which this region could supply. Obstacles to sedentary living are: (1) the long, bitterly cold winters; (2) the pestiferous insects; (3) the high-cost transportation, creating almost prohibitive prices; (4) the limited market for farm products; and (5) the isolation. This last is the most important. Can this difficulty ever be reduced? It is the starting point of all studies of the region. The problem involves the isolation not only of the region from the *ecumene* of the United States and Canada, but of the different settlements from one another.

The population of the region by white peoples has ebbed and flowed. Obviously the loss was great after the Gold Rush. Then a gain was recorded until the interlude of World War I brought a drop. In 1920 came a small increase which has persisted up to the present time. Alaska's rate of population growth in recent years has been great (75 per cent between 1950 and 1960, the third highest rate among the 50 states), but the actual increase in population is small (97,524 between 1950 and 1960; 35th among the states). However, the most rapid growth has been in southern Alaska, rather than in the Yukon-Kuskokwim Basins.[2]

[2] For example, the population of Fairbanks grew by 131 per cent during the 1950's, while that of Anchorage, which is more than three times as large as Fairbanks, was increasing by 293 per cent.

The density of population in this region is markedly less than in any other state.

Most of the people live close to lines of transportation—rivers, railroads, roads, and airfields. General accessibility is a prime requisite for permanence of settlement: lacking it, all other apparent advantages are useless.

Since the number of white women is considerably smaller than the number of white men, interbreeding occurs and, as a result, many Alaska natives are of mixed blood.

In the entire region, only Fairbanks, Dawson, and Whitehorse may be classed as significant permanent white settlements. A map showing the paucity of significant settlements is accordingly impressive. The discovery of gold brought the few centers into being, although mining is much less important now. Fairbanks has agricultural and military functions, and Whitehorse owes its existence to transportation advantages at the crossroads of north-south and east-west traffic.

There is considerable instability in the farm population. A large proportion of the present homesteaders will not successfully fulfill the homestead requirements and hence will lose the land. In the Fairbanks area, 90 per cent of the privately owned land has been thus relinquished.

Most settlers do not stay. To make a go of settlement in this region requires courage and capital. Courage alone is not enough: roughly $200 an acre is required for buying equipment and for building a house and for living until the land begins to produce. Many, victims of their own imagination, have failed because they came to the northland with a glamorous viewpoint about the frontier and with romantic notions about pioneering. They had probably seen too many motion pictures and television programs about the "Far North." Experience taught them the country was not the way they had imagined it. Others, of course, fail because of lack of capital and lack of courage.

The number of Indians and Eskimos is very small, for game does not exist in adequate numbers to sustain primitive man in appreciable numbers. In the entire Yukon Territory only 15 per cent of the population is Indian, and there are practically no Eskimos.

Eskimos In former times, the Eskimos of the lower Yukon and Kuskokwim Valleys lived wholly off the region, illustrating superbly man's capacity to adjust himself to nature. They now barter furs for flour, tea, sugar, canned goods, woolen clothing, and other products and are quite dependent upon the white man. While they are remarkable in transition, there is little chance they can endure in the white man's civilization which, in one generation, has swept them into a new world. They have little resistance to the contagious diseases that invariably go with the advance of civilization.

Indians Indians are widely but thinly distributed over the region. They are Athapaskans and Kutchins—regarded by some authorities as the last wanderers to cross Bering Strait from Asia. They are often on the move because of their unceasing quest for food. Seldom is it possible to obtain sufficient game in any one place to sustain them for more than a few weeks. Originally they knew nothing about agriculture, living entirely on the fish and game they caught and the berries they gathered. They preferred the meat of the caribou, whose skin they required for clothing.

Economic Pursuits

Mining The rich gold placers discovered in the Klondike brought a feverish stampede of about 80,000 persons to the region in 1898. Most of these knew nothing about this north country, but they were willing to exchange a few weeks, a few months, or perhaps even a few years of hardship and adventure for a fortune. The trail, nearly 600 miles long, was a bitter and hazardous one, leading over notorious and dangerous Chilkoot Pass and later the less difficult White Pass, Dead Horse Gulch, the rock desert, and the Miles Canyon Rapids. Unlike the American West, the Yukon had no "oases"—places where the weary might rest and refresh themselves. *But gold was there!* Production reached 10 million dollars in 1898 and 16 million in 1899. Relatively few individuals, however, found prospecting profitable, and by 1910 many of those still alive had returned to the United States.

More than a billion dollars' worth of minerals, three-fourths gold, has been removed from this region. Gold is taken both from placers and veins, though the Yukon is essentially one of gravel mining. The first miners separated gold from sand and gravel with a pan, rocker, or cradle. So slow were these methods, however, that a prospector could work only about two cubic yards a day. Then came the sluice box with its string of boxes into which gravel was shoveled and through which a stream of water was sent. Unfortunately, much of the gold lay in frozen ground which could not be worked until thawed. At first the ground was thawed with wood fires, then with steam engines. Today cold water is used. In this method, pierced pipes, spaced 16 to 32 feet apart, are driven deep into the ground and cold water forced through them. The water seeps to the surface and is used again. Sixty to 120 days are required to thaw the gravels with this method.

After the more accessible and richer gravels were worked and prospecting became less profitable, large-scale corporate enterprises purchased the better holdings. Much of the placer mining today is done by huge dredges, which cost several million dollars and can remove as many as 10,000 cubic yards of gravel per day.

THE YUKON-KUSKOKWIM BASINS

In the early 1960's, however, the last big dredge-mining company in Alaska sharply curtailed its operations because of the high cost of mining low-grade placer deposits. There are still a few active placer operations in the Dawson area of the Yukon Territory, which yield some two per cent of Canada's national gold output.

The mining of base metals is growing in importance. United Keno Hill Mines near Mayo, Canada's largest single source of silver, also produces considerable lead, zinc, and gold. With output largely from this one area, the Yukon Territory provides 20 per cent of the silver, 6 per cent of the lead, and 2 per cent of the zinc mined in Canada.

Coal of inferior quality is widespread, but the small population, lack of manufacturing, and limited railroad mileage keep production at a low figure. It is important locally, however, for transportation costs are high and the winters bitterly cold. Two-thirds of the coal mined in Alaska is from the Healy River Field not far from Fairbanks. Ladd and Eielson Air Force bases are the principal consumers of the coal.

Trapping and Fishing Before white men reached the Yukon country, the staple of the Indian diet was salmon. These were caught as they migrated upstream to the spawning ground. The catch was smoked and much of it cached above ground beyond the reach of dogs and wolves. The Eskimos killed walruses, seals, and whales and carried on some fishing.

With the coming of the white man, trapping became important. Following the purchase of Alaska by the United States, virtually all the Americans and probably most of the Russians who stayed on were employed in fur trading. They traded flour, sugar, tea, and other items to the Indians for peltries. Despite the fact that trapping and fishing continue to be the chief activities of the Indians who live in the region, the enterprise yields at best only a pre-carious living, for fur-bearing animals are not numerous and trapping is not really profitable. The methods followed are the traditional ones. In summer the Indians remain near the settlements along the principal streams. When the trapping season opens in autumn, they move into the interior.

This enterprise has declined to a secondary position in Alaska, and it has declined significantly in the Yukon Territory. With greater regulation on the part of the governments, and by keeping white men away from the areas surrounding native villages, the industry might be revived, for the natural habitat is not unfavorable. The long, cold winters give the animals thick coats.

Commercial salmon fishing is a major seasonal activity in the region. Salmon go up the Yukon and Kuskokwim Rivers to spawn,[3] and are heavily fished in Bristol and Kuskokwim Bays and in Norton Sound. Approximately one-fourth of the Alaskan salmon catch is from this region; fishing is done mostly with gill nets, but some is done with purse seines and haul seines. Competition from Japanese gill-net fishermen far at sea (the west 175th meridian is the provisional abstention line) apparently has caused a decline in the catch in recent years, but the total effect is difficult to assess.

The Pribilof Islands, northwest of Unalaska and southwest of Nunivak Island, are the sole breeding grounds of the Alaska fur seal. From the discovery of the Pribilofs in 1786 until the present, more than 8,000,000 fur seal pelts have been taken. The history of sealing there has been one of alternating periods of ruthless exploitation and of careful conservation. At present, under conditions controlled by international convention, between 50,000 and 100,000 fur seals are "harvested" on the Pribilofs each year.

[3] Some king salmon travel 1800 miles up the Yukon to spawn in the McClintock River, a journey reportedly unrivaled by other anadramous fish. See Wilson, ed., *North of 55°*, p. 112.

Forest Industries Forest industries were not important in the past, are unimportant now, and offer little promise for future development. The cold, long winters, short summers, and light precipitation conspire to keep the trees small. They might be used for pulpwood were there not so many other regions better located and with superior growing conditions.

Most of the cut is for fuel for river steamers and mining operations, or for domestic firewood and for sawmills at Fairbanks and a few other points. Everywhere the timber is for local consumption.

Agriculture Farming began in this region about 1900 for producing food for prospectors. Most of the first farmers were men who became disillusioned as gold miners and therefore turned to agriculture. Since transportation costs on all food items from the United States were high, a good profit could be made on their commodities in the mining camps, and in Dawson and Fairbanks.

Agriculture is unimportant now and will probably continue so into the remote future. This status results not only from the natural environmental conditions, which force man to utilize every ounce of ingenuity he can muster, but also from the small market and the great distance and poor transport facilities to markets. The region is definitely noncompetitive as a source of agricultural products for all but the small local market.

Farming is highly localized and its pattern is spotty. The Tanana Valley near Fairbanks is the principal area, and it has only about 4,000 acres under cultivation. About 70 per cent of the cleared land is on the higher terraces and bench lands; here grains and vegetables do best. The remaining 30 per cent is in the lowlands and is used principally for pasture and silage crops. Some good farm land is located along the Alaska Highway west of Whitehorse and between Selkirk and Dawson.

The crops are essentially the hardy type grains (oats, barley, rye, and wheat), root crops (potatoes, beets, radishes, carrots, and parsnips), and vegetables (peas, cabbages, and lettuce).

Vegetables were the first crops to be introduced into the region, and they continue to be the most important. About 90 per cent of the farmers are engaged in vegetable growing. The local demand for vegetables has always exceeded the supply. Potatoes are the leading vegetable crop.

Since the completion of the railroad from Seward to Fairbanks, grain has been imported. The Yukon area cannot compete, and the commercial production of wheat and barley has now virtually ceased. Today oats ranks first in importance among the grains. The crop is cut green for use as feed. Hay is not an important crop, because August, harvest time, is the wettest month and grass will not dry in the fields. Hence silage crops are grown.

The problems of agriculture are many. The climate is restrictive (95-day growing season at Fairbanks). Soils are generally shallow, lacking in fertility, and poorly drained. Farm labor is scarce and expensive. Markets are limited. Fertilizers (a distinct necessity) are costly. And it takes longer for a new farm to produce in Alaska than in the more southerly states.

> Cropland sites underlaid by permafrost, common in the Tanana Valley, are at first too wet for cropping, and may need to lie fallow up to five years after clearing, while the sun is drying and warming the uncovered topsoil.[4]

Recreation Some sportsmen and a few tourists visit the region, but the faunal and scenic attractions are limited in comparison with those in adjacent regions. The Klondike has historical fascination, and boat trips on the upper Yukon attract some

[4] Department of Commerce, *Alaska: Its Economy and Market Potential* (Washington: Government Printing Office, 1959), pp. 41-42.

interest, but in general the region lacks appeal for visitors. In addition, the isolation, difficulty of access, seasonal limitations (severe winter weather and abominable summer insects), and high cost of living are great hindrances to the development of tourism.

Even so, this is a frontier land that can be penetrated directly by road, rail, or airplane, so that a very modest but continually increasing number of "outsiders" visit the region each year.

Transportation

So large, isolated, and relatively unproductive is the Yukon-Kuskokwim Region that it has only six outlets: (1) the Yukon River and its several navigable tributaries, (2) the White Pass and Yukon Railway, (3) the Alaska Railroad, (4) the Richardson Highway, (5) the Alaska Highway, and (6) the airways.

Waterways The *Yukon,* chief highway of this tremendous land, is navigable for river boats to Whitehorse, a distance of about 2,200 miles, during some three months of the year. The *Tanana* is navigable to Fairbanks by small boats specially built to go against its swift current. The *Kuskokwim* is navigable for 650 miles during some four months. Unfortunately, the numerous distributaries of the delta and the badly shifting channel virtually preclude ocean-going vessels from entering the Yukon. All river transportation comes to a complete standstill during the winters. Freight traffic on Alaskan rivers is dwindling each year.

Railways The total mileage in the enormous area of Alaska and Canada's Yukon Territory is small,[5] but railways play a vital role. The *White Pass and Yukon Railway* was built in 1898 during the feverish boom days of the Klondike. It is 111 miles long

[5] Most of their mileage is in the North Pacific Coast Region (Chapter 16) and not in the Yukon-Kuskokwim Basins.

and extends from Skagway over White Pass to Whitehorse. Upon its completion, freight rates, which had fluctuated from 30 cents to a dollar per pound, dropped to just under five cents. The *Alaska Railroad,* extending 470 miles from Seward to Fairbanks, was built by the United States government to help develop and settle interior Alaska. It was completed in 1923. This route has greatly stimulated mining in its tributary area and, in turn, mining supplies the larger part of the traffic.

Probably no new railways will be built, certainly not at public expense. Even extensions should be made only after careful planning and after a definite need has been shown. Probably no railroad in this region can pay its own way year in and year out, though in some years the Alaska Railroad has made expenses.

Roads The small population, the enormous distances, and the prevalence of much swampy surface mean great expense in building and maintaining good roads. Hence this region is almost empty of roads. The *Richardson Highway,* extending 371 miles from Valdez on Prince William Sound to Fairbanks in the interior, was the chief means of access, especially in winter, prior to the building of the Alaska Railroad. It was a trail in 1907, became a wagon road in 1910, and was improved for automobile traffic during the 1920's. It rises from sea level to an elevation of 3,310 feet and then descends into the beautiful Tanana Valley. The *Steese Highway,* 160 miles long, is really a prolongation of the Richardson Highway from Fairbanks on the Tanana to Circle on the Yukon. Extending farther north than any other road in the region, it penetrates some of the outstanding and most highly mechanized gold-mining districts of Alaska. Recently constructed roads now connect Whitehorse with Dawson and Dawson with Mayo. Construction is under way on a highway to extend from Fairbanks to Nome. When it will be completed

Figure 17-4. A segment of the Alaska Highway. This road, built during World War II, is not purely a product of military emergency with no peacetime future. Each year it is more widely used. (Photo courtesy Bureau of Public Roads, U.S. Department of Commerce.)

is problematical, but the first section (Fairbanks to Eureka) is now open.

The *Alaska Highway*, extending 1,523 miles from Dawson Creek in British Columbia's Peace River country to Fairbanks, was built in 1942 as a wartime project by the United States. It opened up some previously untouched areas in Canada's northeastern British Columbia and southern Yukon as well as in Alaska—a corridor northward through the wilderness (Figure 17-4). It is a gravel-surfaced road, 26 feet wide, with moderate grades and curves and traverses an almost entirely unsettled area—one inaccessible to river transport. The highway was built when it was feared the Japanese might prevent use of the Inside Passage by the United States at a time when machinery, food, and all heavy freight moved to Alaska by vessel. It also connected a series of airports previously constructed by the Canadian government between Edmonton and Alaska. The portion within Alaska has been surfaced.

Airways Aviation has become the chief solution to the transportation problems of the Yukon Basin. The airplane is the cheapest means of long-distance travel and seems ideally suited to the small population scattered over this enormous region. Alaskans use planes as other Americans use automobiles and buses. This is apparent from the fact that the number of passenger miles flown there annually is 15 times that of mainland United States on a per capita basis. The air cargo business, per capita, is 100 times greater. In fact, it was not until aviation tapped the region that it was really opened up. Large-scale construction of railroads and roads cannot be undertaken by private enterprise. Only governments can sponsor nonprofitable lines. Moreover, the rivers are not navigable in winter. In the Yukon are most of the placer camps, but they are badly isolated, the operating season is short, and many workers leave camp when the freeze-up begins in autumn, returning only when work begins in spring. Accordingly, a rapid, economical means of transportation such as the airplane is of inestimable value. Prospectors can now fly to their destination, whereas in the old days they lost most of the season in traveling to and from their workings. Trips that used to require months by the old fur traders are now covered in a few hours by air. Vilhjalmur Stefansson asserts that an Eskimo can go from Fairbanks to Nome more cheaply by airplane than he can by his own dogsledge. The cost of food for himself and his dogs and of lodging during the trip is far greater than the price of an airplane ticket would be.[6]

The Outlook

This vast region is today supporting a population of less than 80,000. The whites are largely engaged in mining, transportation, and defense construction; the Indians and Eskimos, in fishing, trapping, and hunting, though increasing numbers of natives are being lured to construction jobs by high wages. Construction work has been the largest single contributor to Alaska's private economy for more than a decade.

The region appears to be essentially a reserve for the future, a region where only whites of the pioneer type—people willing to risk all to find something better—will venture. It is a paradox that Americans, who have been the greatest frontiersmen on earth, have thus far neglected Alaska. But a subsistence-farming existence without near neighbors and without roads, schools, churches, and motion-picture theaters does not attract today's average Anglo-American. Settlers avoid going to distant lands, especially ill-favored ones, unless they can appreciably improve their financial condition in a reasonably brief time.

Yet the people in this region are young and vigorous. The Yukon Territory has a smaller proportion of old people than any Canadian province, and Alaska has a smaller proportion than any of the other 49 states. This preponderance of young adults results in a high birth rate (the Yukon's is the highest in Canada, and Alaska's is the highest in the United States).

The population, however, is not a stable one. There is considerable seasonal fluctua-

tion in the population, with a summer peak and a winter ebb. Many people come into the region for temporary summer jobs and then go "outside" at the end of the season.

Gold mining, the dominant resource-based activity of the past, appears to be dying. Other minerals may be found, but how important mining will be will depend not only upon the presence of minerals but also upon how profitably they can be extracted and transported. Remoteness and uneconomical transport (except for products having high value per unit of weight or bulk) are the principal disadvantages of this region. The lone prospector has almost given way to the dredge, and most miners today are salaried employees of large syndicates.

The region is in the midst of an economic "boom" that has been in effect for two decades. Yet it is an artificially stimulated boom. Without heavy government expenditures for continued defense construction (expansion of military bases, Distant Early Warning line, Ballistic Missile Early Warning system, "White Alice" communication network), there would be much less money in circulation.

There is little resource base for economic expansion. Yet certainly the future of the Yukon-Kuskokwim Basins cannot be safely planned on a foundation of defense expenditures. The region must create and produce. But how—and what? The answer is not yet forthcoming.

[6] Vilhjalmur Stefansson, "The American Far North," *Foreign Affairs,* Vol. 17 (April 1939), p. 517.

TABLE 16

Selected Cities and Towns of the Yukon-Kuskokwim Basins

City or Town	Political Center
Bethel	1,258
Dawson	881
Fairbanks	13,311
Fort Yukon	701
Whitehorse	5,031

Selected Bibliography

The Alaska Book. Chicago: J. B. Ferguson Publishing Co., 1960.

Benninghoff, William S., "Interaction of Vegetation and Soil Frost Phenomena," *Arctic,* Vol. 5, 1952, pp. 34-44.

Bensin, Basil M., "Agroecological Analysis of the Crop Plants Root System in the Tanana Valley Region of Alaska," *Bulletin, Ecological Society of America,* Vol. 27, April 1946.

Bostock, H. S., "Physiography and Resources of the Northern Yukon," *Canadian Geographical Journal,* Vol. 63, October 1961, pp. 112-119.

Eiteman, Wilford J., and Alice Boardman Smuts, "Alaska, Land of Opportunity—Limited," *Economic Geography,* Vol. 27, 1951, pp. 33-42.

Gasser, G. W., "Agriculture in Alaska," *Arctic,* Vol. 1, 1948.

Gruening, Ernest, "The Political Ecology of Alaska," *Scientific Monthly,* Vol. 73, December 1951, pp. 376-386.

Miller, E. Willard, "Agricultural Development in Interior Alaska," *Scientific Monthly,* Vol. 73, October 1951, pp. 245-254.

Moore, Terris, "Alaska," *Focus,* Vol. 13, November 1962, pp. 1-6.

Péwé, T. L., "Permafrost and Geomorphology in the Lower Yukon River Valley," *Geological Society of America Bulletin,* Vol. 58, 1947.

Stern, Peter M., "Alaska," *Focus,* Vol. 4, September 1953, pp. 1-6.

Stone, Kirk H., "Populating Alaska: The United States Phase," *Geographical Review,* Vol. 42, 1952, pp. 384-404.

U.S. Department of Commerce, *Alaska: Its Economy and Market Potential.* Washington: Government Printing Office, 1958.

U.S. Department of the Interior, *Mid-Century Alaska.* Washington: Government Printing Office, 1959.

chapter eighteen

The Tundra

The Tundra,[1] one of the larger regions in

[1] Greenland, though Danish, is included as part of Anglo-America in this book because: (1) it is situated close to the Canadian Arctic Archipelago and is generally portrayed with North America on small- and medium-scale maps; (2) from the standpoint of physical geography the inhabited portions of Greenland are very similar to Ellesmere and Baffin Islands; (3) the native people of Greenland are either Eskimos or descendants of Eskimos; and (4) Greenland is tied strategically to Anglo-American defense by air bases, meteorological stations, and radar warning systems.

Anglo-America (Figure 18-1), is the most sparsely populated, the least productive economically, and certainly the least promising so far as man's future occupance is concerned. In few parts of the earth is nature more unyielding or more niggardly, and nowhere else are people's ways of living more closely attuned to the physical environment. Huge areas of land, some as large as western European countries, never have been explored by white men. The Tundra Region

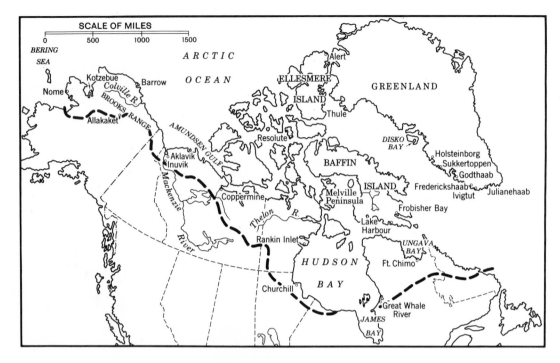

Figure 18-1. The Tundra. A region of hunting, trapping, fishing, and mining.

is primarily the land of the Eskimos; yet they have established themselves permanently only in small numbers.

Parts of this region have long been known to white men. Five centuries before Columbus reached the New World, Norsemen had visited the coast of Labrador. Eric the Red, who first colonized Greenland near the close of the tenth century, recognized the unattractive appearance of the landscape in giving Greenland its name, "for," he said, "that might attract men thither when the land has a fine name." [2] Thus, along with the hot dry deserts, the rainy tropics, and the lofty mountains, the tundra is one of the least desirable places for settlement. The few white inhabitants have gone to the Tundra Region to get furs, exploit minerals, convert the natives to Christianity, represent their respective governments, or to man defense

or weather stations. Cities and towns as we think of them in the United States are non-existent, though a dozen settlements in west Greenland would rate as large villages. In the more remote areas, a settlement nucleus may not include more than two or three families.

The Tundra Region includes the part of Anglo-America that extends from the Bering Sea on the west to the Atlantic Ocean on the east and from the Taiga on the south to the Arctic Sea on the north; it includes also the vast Arctic archipelagos north of the Canadian mainland and the island of Greenland. The region thus comprises parts of Alaska, parts of Canada, and Greenland.

There is considerable ignorance of the Tundra Region. More first-hand information has been gained about it in the past two decades than in the preceding two centuries. Probably the most important concept is that this is not a totally uniform area, but that there are many areas, and few if any statements apply to all of them.

[2] Isobel W. Hutchison, "Flowers and Farming in Greenland," *Scottish Geographical Magazine*, Vol. 46 (July 1930), p. 216.

There are permanently ice and snow covered areas, such as the northeastern part of the Canadian Arctic ... and the vast Greenland Ice Cap. There are areas where most of the snow disappears in the short summers and the *tundra* vegetation becomes visible, with its characteristic abundance of flowering plants. Some areas are rolling grasslands, others are moss- and lichen-covered, still others are bare rock outcrops. In some parts, the ground will thaw out to a depth of three or four feet, in others to only three or four inches. Beneath lies the permanently frozen earth called *permafrost*. There are also wide variations in the precipitation, but characteristically it is on the low side ... There are even wider variations in the length of the growing season.[3]

The tundra is not, as novelists would have it, a land of perpetual ice and snow. Winter temperatures are low, true, but they are higher than in the taiga to the south. Point Barrow has yet to record winter temperatures as low as those characterizing certain stations in North Dakota and Montana. Extremes become greater south of Point Barrow, since the country increases in altitude and is more remote from the ameliorating effects of the ocean. Thus the temperature range at Allakaket, 350 miles to the south, is much greater; whereas the lowest and highest temperatures at Point Barrow are −56° F. and 78° F. respectively, those at Allakaket are −79° F. and 90° F. However, everywhere in the Tundra Region winters are long and summers short, so although the temperature range at Point Barrow is the more limited, the growing season is only 17 days, whereas at Allakaket it is 54. There can be two to four months without snow. The growing season in the area north of the Brooks Range in Alaska is less than 40 days.

Air at low temperatures cannot absorb or retain much water vapor, so the precipitation is light, varying over most of the area

[3] "Resources of the Arctic," *Focus*, Vol. 2 (February 1952), p. 2.

from 5 to 12 inches, with the maximum in summer. The precipitation is mostly fine, dry snow or sleet. At Point Barrow, snow begins falling by the middle of August. In the Canadian Arctic, most of the snow falls in October and November.

Winds, especially in winter, are very strong and frequently howl day after day. They greatly affect the sensible temperature; thus, on a quiet day a temperature as low as −30° F. is not at all unpleasant if one is suitably clothed, but on a windy day a temperature of zero may be quite unbearable.

The periphery is greatly influenced by the ocean; thus the Polar Sea is 15 to 25 degrees warmer in winter and cooler in summer than lands to the south.

North of the Arctic Circle, the climatic phenomenon of greatest significance to human beings is the seasonal changes in the length of days and nights. The sun may remain continually above the horizon for more than 24 hours—even as long as five months at the northern extremity of Ellesmere Island, 83° N. latitude.

The strip of Labrador coast is much the same over a distance of 600 miles, latitude playing a minor part. The Labrador Current, carrying floes and bergs, causes the immediate coast to be barren and bleak. Where the altitude remains the same, vegetation increases with distance from the ocean. There is no such thing as our summer; frost may occur in every month.

The climate of the Arctic is especially worthy of note, because the source of much of the weather affecting southern Canada and the northern half of the United States is there. In winter, cold air masses from the Arctic Ocean move up the Mackenzie Valley toward Hudson Bay. These cold air masses come into conflict with warm air masses from the tropics, producing cyclonic storms which travel across Canada and the United States from west to east.

The Physical Setting

Terrain It is extremely difficult to generalize on the terrain of such an extensive region. The surface features of the polar lands include all varieties of relief, from low, swampy coastal plains to high ice plateaus and glaciated mountains. Vast lowlands, monotonously flat and poorly drained, are especially extensive. The most notable mountains include the Brooks Range in Alaska and various highlands on Ellesmere Island, Baffin Island, and coastal Labrador.

Most streams have tortuous courses, and estuaries characterize their coastal reaches. Near the coast many split into distributaries.

Innumerable lakes dot a large part of the mainland and the southern part of the Arctic Islands. Some of the lakes are small, some large. Greenland, coastal Labrador, and the eastern archipelago have fjorded coasts. Off many of the coasts lies a fringe of rounded islets—*skerries*.

Soils The tundra has few well-developed soils. Most of them are closely related to bog soils. Because of former glaciation, there is a considerable accumulation of morainic materials and rewashed glacial deposits. Much of the tundra lacks soils altogether except in the valleys.

Permafrost Where winters are longer than the periods of summer thaw, there are large areas of *permafrost*, which may be several hundred feet thick. A layer of top soil, which annually freezes and thaws to a depth varying from a few inches to several feet, lies above it. The depth to which the soil freezes and thaws depends upon exposure to sun and wind, the water content of the soil, the type of soil, the snow cover, and the type of vegetation.

Natural Vegetation The uninformed regard the Arctic as a cold and forbidding place perpetually covered with ice and snow, where no plant life can exist. Yet, actually as far north as land reaches grow numerous species of flowering plants besides lower forms of plant life, such as mosses, lichens, algae, and fungi.

Most of the Arctic region as here considered refers to that part of Anglo-America lying north of the tree line, the great coniferous forest belt. The line on the map separating the tundra from the forest symbolizes a zone within which the trees gradually become smaller and more scattered until they disappear altogether. It coincides rather closely with the 50° isotherm for the warmest month. This zone in most instances lies south of the Arctic Circle—reaching the 55th parallel on the west side of James Bay.

However, from area to area the boundaries between taiga and tundra differ, and the extent to which the taiga penetrates the tundra seems to depend more upon the velocity of the north winds than upon any other circumstance. That wind rather than absolute cold seems to influence the northward extension of tree growth appears to be proved by the fact that as far north as spruce grows it produces an abundance of seed, at least in normal seasons.[4] Temperature has some influence also, for in areas having higher summer temperatures, the forest encroaches upon the tundra. Thus in the valley of the Mackenzie the forest straggles to beyond the Arctic Circle—almost to the 70th parallel.

The really characteristic vegetation of this region then is tundra; here is a great variety of primitive plants and grasses, with lichens especially being evident (Figure 18-2). The plain west of Hudson Bay, the rolling upland south of Amundsen Gulf, and the lowland of central west Baffin Island are the most extensive areas of tundra vegetation. Here lichens are the dominant plants, forming the principal food supply of the caribou herds that migrate over the region.

The vegetation has great value in this re-

[4] E. A. Porsild, "Plant Life in the Arctic," *Canadian Geographical Journal*, March 1951, pp. 120-145.

Figure 18-2. Typical tundra scene on the northern part of Baffin Island. A portion of the margin of the Barnes Icecap is at left. (Photo courtesy the Geographical Branch of the Department of Mines and Technical Surveys of Canada.)

gion, because, directly or indirectly, it is the food of all the land animals. It is assimilated directly by the herbivores; and these are the prey of the carnivores.

Native Animal Life In no other region is the fauna so important to man. There has long been an intimate association between the abundance or scarcity of animal life and the welfare of the natives of the region. This close relationship is diminishing, but is still pronounced.

Aquatic mammals, of which there are many, have long been the mainstay of Eskimo livelihood. Several varieties of *seals* range throughout the region, and they are the most common quarry of Eskimo hunters. The *walrus* is a ponderous, slow-breeding (the female does not reproduce until the sixth year, and then only has one pup every other year) creature that is verging on extermination over much of its range. It must live in an area of strong currents that keep the sea ice moving all winter, for it does not gnaw a breathing hole through the ice as does the seal. The Atlantic walrus inhabits most of the eastern Arctic Ocean, as far west as Coppermine, with particular concentration around the Melville Peninsula; the Pacific walrus inhabits the Bering Sea; there is a 1,000-mile gap between the

ranges of the two. *Whales* of various species are much-sought by the Eskimos and Greenlanders, but by far the most common is the white whale or *beluga*. They occur in considerable numbers throughout the Arctic, mostly in salt water but often going up the larger rivers (they have been seen as far up the St. Lawrence as Quebec City). At maturity their length is between 10 and 15 feet. The *narwhal* is much less common, but is highly prized because of the ivory-like "horn" of the male. The *killer whale* normally is not hunted by natives, but is a significant predator for all aquatic life, including walrus and polar bear.

The *polar bear* ranges widely in the Arctic, living almost constantly on sea ice except for occasional land denning to give birth. They are sometimes found several tens of miles from the nearest land, and have been seen as far south as the Twin Islands in James Bay. Unlike other bears, which are omnivorous, polar bears are almost wholly carnivorous. There is considerable concern for their survival, partly because of natives' overuse, but especially because of hunting by air-borne "sportsmen" in such places as the international waters north of Point Barrow.

The outstanding land animal is the *bar-*

479

Figure 18-3. A small herd of caribou galloping across the tundra in northern Canada.

ren-ground caribou (Figure 18-3). During its migrations between tundra and taiga, it is a vital factor in the economy of thousands of Indians, Eskimos, and whites in the Arctic. The Keewatin herd (occupying the area west of Hudson Bay) is the principal herd, but its numbers have decreased from several million in the 1940's to a low point of about 200,000 in 1960; however, there are indications of an upward trend since then. Two other major herds (though much smaller than the Keewatin herd) exist on Baffin Island and in the vicinity of the Alaska-Yukon boundary. Smaller groups are found in many places.

The only other native ungulate of the tundra is the *musk ox*. There are some 2,000 on Ellesmere Island, with the greatest concentration around Hazen Lake in the north, in the shelter of a 10,000-foot mountain range that provides a protected area of much milder climate and better forage. Another 500 or so occupy the Thelon Valley in the Keewatin District, where there is another "oasis" of mildness. Smaller numbers are scattered in other parts of the Northwest Territories and northern Greenland.

Fur-bearers of note include the *Arctic fox*, a prolific breeder whose population seems to run in cycles; the *muskrat*, which

is particularly abundant and important in the Mackenzie delta; the *lemming*, a queer nocturnal burrowing rodent noted for its seemingly stupid migrations; the *Arctic wolf*, principal predator of the region; and the *Arctic hare*, whose population pattern follows wildly fluctuating cycles.

Fish life is abundant, if not particularly varied. Cod, herring, and Arctic char are important species.

Of the birds, the snow owl, ptarmigan, gyrfalcon, raven, and snow bunting are year-round inhabitants. Others, summer residents, arrive by the thousands to breed in the seclusion and security of the tundra. They are also attracted by the prolific insect life.

Because of the abundance of poorly drained land, insects find this region a paradise during the short summer season. Over much of the tundra there are ten times as many mosquitoes per square mile as there are in the Tropics.[5]

The People

In this vast region there are only about 70,000 inhabitants. Approximately 30 per cent of this total consists of Eskimos or

[5] War Department, *Arctic Manual*, TM, 1-240 (Washington: Government Printing Office, January 17, 1944), p. 104.

mixed-bloods in which the Eskimo strain is dominant; only about 1 per cent is Indian; about 7 per cent is white; and the remainder, nearly 60 per cent, is "Greenlander"—mixed-bloods of Eskimo and Danish extraction in Greenland. These people are widely scattered in small settlements; there are no towns of more than 5,000 population in the region.

The Eskimo The traditional inhabitants of the tundra are the Eskimos. These short, Mongoloid people are dispersed throughout Arctic America from northern Greenland to the islands of the Bering Sea and the coast of northeastern Siberia. Most occupy the Tundra Region, although a few thousand live in the Yukon-Kuskokwim deltas and associated offshore islands. Many dialects are spoken, but most are mutually intelligible. Actually, there are two "different" languages, one based in Greenland and one in southwestern Alaska.

In their native state the Eskimos have shown remarkable ingenuity in adapting themselves to an almost impossible environment. They live in one of the coldest and darkest parts of the world, and in one that is among the poorest in available fuel. Yet they have not only survived but have enjoyed life in self-sufficient family groups. Their entire livelihood was dependent originally upon fishing and hunting, whereas practically all Eurasian tundra people were herdsmen.

The coming of the white man to Eskimo country marked the beginning of the end for their "normal" way of life. European diseases, mid-latitude foods, liquor, rifles, motor boats, and a new set of mores were introduced; and the over-all result was more often bad than good.

The Eskimo today has drifted toward "civilization." Relatively few exist by subsistence hunting and fishing. More and more take temporary jobs on construction projects, in salmon canneries, and at other white outposts in the Arctic. The trading post, the DEW line station, the tuberculosis sanitarium, and the relief check are increasingly important in their way of life.

The Indian There are less than 1,000 Indians in the entire Tundra Region, and practically all are in Canada. Generally speaking, the tree line has served as the northern boundary of Indian occupance, just as it has served as the southern border of Inuit (Canadian Eskimo) settlement. In only four localities—Aklavik and Inuvik in the Mackenzie delta, Great Whale River on the eastern shore of Hudson Bay, and Fort Chimo at the southern end of Ungava Bay —do Indians and Eskimos live adjacently. The Indian livelihood in this region is based on hunting, trapping, fishing, and temporary construction work.

The Whites Norsemen under Eric the Red reached Greenland in 986 with 14 ships and about 400 people. A republic was maintained for the next 270 years. The descendants of these and other settlers survived as Europeans as late as 1520, and then disappeared as though the earth had swallowed them, leaving no authentic records. Apparently they merged with the Eskimo population, and were absorbed.

Whites living permanently in the region now number some 5,000, a total that is growing. Well over half are in Alaska, where Nome is the largest white settlement by far (approximately half of the town's population of 2,500 is white). Most of the whites who live in the region today man defense and weather installations, or are government officials, prospectors, fur traders, or missionaries.

The Greenlanders Only in Greenland has the Eskimo had a long history of contact with "outsiders." Most of the people of Greenland today—a total of some 30,000— officially are classified as Greenlanders, and are actually a Mongoloid-Caucasian cross between Eskimos and Danes. They live relatively sedentary lives; most have permanent homes. They are distributed around the coast, particularly on the southwestern side and secondarily on the northwest and southeast. There are virtually no inhabitants of the northern and northeastern coasts of Greenland.

The enlightened policy of the Danish government has protected the Greenlanders from both contact and exploitation by outsiders in recent decades. As a result, the population has increased in numbers, improved in health, and gained in wealth. The economy of Greenland is limited and employment is a problem, but in general the Greenlanders are better off than their modern Eskimo counterparts in Canada and Alaska.

Economic Activities

Fishing Fishing on a subsistence basis is important both in summer and in winter. The Eskimos use leisters, harpoons, hooks, and nets. The leister consists of a pointed middle prong and two elastic side prongs of antler, which are barbed to hold the fish. It is fitted to a long wooden shaft. Inland tribes on the "Barren Grounds" and in the Colville River area in Alaska employ the harpoon. With this method, the Eskimo, from a small snow hut, watches for the fish through a hole in the ice. The most important method of fishing through the ice is with a jig, an unbarbed iron hook set in the under edge of an oval bone sinker. Deep-sea fishing is carried on only in the outer regions—Alaska, and Greenland-Labrador, where cod and halibut are present in great numbers. Cod are caught with a jig, and halibut with a special kind of composite hook. However, much of the deep-sea fishing is commercial, modern methods being used. Only the commercial fishing off the Labrador coast and Greenland is considered in this chapter, since commercial fishing in Alaska was discussed in Chapter 16.

COAST OF LABRADOR Fishing is the only economic enterprise of note in this segment of the region, entire communities depending almost wholly upon it. Actually the people have but one idea, one interest—fish. This is natural where the sea is rich in plankton and fish and the land exceedingly poor in agricultural possibilities. Coastal Labrador lacks most of the qualities that make life easier in other parts of the world, and hence opportunities for making a living are indeed limited. If fish were not abundant, there would be no people.

Fishing is carried on only in summer, the season beginning in late June. A heavy catch is procured until winter abruptly terminates the season. Labradorians (*Liveyeres*) and a few thousand Newfoundlanders fish in these cold waters, the latter coming in boats of all sizes. Although the *Liveyeres* work hard, remoteness from markets retards their progress.

GREENLAND Commercial fishing on the south and west coasts became important in 1916 as a result of the decline in the number of seals in South Greenland and the increasing effect of the warm current off Greenland. This warming has caused many communities of seal hunters to shift their attention more wholeheartedly to fishing. As the seals shifted northward, cod moved in to replace them. The Danish Government rendered considerable aid to the fisheries: it established and supervised fishing stations; it aided in selling the fish; it sent experts to organize and conduct the industry along modern lines; and it procured for the native a more favorable income from his fish. Each of the larger towns (Holstenborg, Sukkertoppen, Godthaab, Frederikshaab, and Julianehaab) has a fish-canning or -freezing plant, and Greenland has changed from a closed country with respect to trade to one that is open to the world.

The principal fish caught are cod, Norway haddock, Atlantic salmon, caplin, and

Greenland shark. Especially flourishing at this time is cod fishing off the southwest coast of Greenland—a situation largely attributable to the warming up that the area has been experiencing possibly due to a northward extension of the Gulf Stream. Today the cod is at home in the waters of west Greenland as far as 73° N., whereas in 1900 it seldom was encountered beyond 64° N. Furthermore, comparable movements of herring, haddock, and halibut have occurred in the more open waters of the North Atlantic (Figure 18-4).

In 1948 two very large shrimp beds were found at Disko Bay. The shrimp are canned locally for export, mainly to the United States.

OTHER COMMERCIAL FISHING   The cooperative movement is beginning to gain a foothold among the Eskimos, particularly with regard to fishing. In Canada's eastern Arctic three Eskimo fishing cooperatives sell char, which is in great demand as a gourmet dish "down south."

A commercial whaling operation (for oil) at Churchill takes some 600 belugas each year.

Hunting   Hunting is still a very important means of livelihood for the natives of this region, except around the larger settlements.

In some areas (as in northern Greenland and Ellesmere Island) where winter conditions persist almost year-round, ice hunting for sea mammals is a specialty. In other areas (as the Colville River country of Alaska and parts of the Keewatin District in Canada) there are inland groups that specialize in caribou hunting. However, most native settlements are on the coast, and there are well-marked seasonal changes in hunting patterns. A typical "quarry rotation" might be seals in early fall, walrus in late fall, bear and fox in winter, seals in spring, fish and beluga in early summer, and caribou in late summer.

SEA HUNTING   Nowhere on earth are there more skillful sea hunters than the Eskimos. They know the intimate habits of all the sea animals. The most valuable animal of all is the seal. Kayaks and motorboats are used in sea hunting.

ICE HUNTING   This takes place only when the ice is firm. The quarry is seal, white whales, and polar bear. The meat of the seal supplies the Eskimos with their staple food item. The haired skin is used for clothing, and the dehaired skin for waterproof boots

Figure 18-4.   Fishing boats in the harbor at Faeringehavn, Greenland. (Photo copyright by Royal Danish Ministry of Foreign Affairs; courtesy of Danish Information Office.)

Figure 18-5. Two Eskimos hunting seals off Bylot Island in the Canadian Arctic. The harpooned seal is being pulled to the far side of the ice crack. (Photo courtesy National Film Board, Ottawa.)

and kayak covers. The oil is used for fuel. Formerly the seals were harpooned; now they are shot and then harpooned (Figure 18-5).

Walrus, which congregate on islands off the coasts in late summer and on newly formed sea ice in autumn, are hunted, but the meat is less popular with the Eskimos than is that of seals. Much of it is fed to dogs.

Polar bears are sought on moonlight nights in winter and in the dazzling sunlight of spring. The meat is used largely for dog feed, the fur for bedding and robes.[6]

LAND HUNTING Land hunting, though not so necessary as that on sea and ice, is, nevertheless, important. Caribou, hare, fox, and birds provide sleeping bags, stockings, furs, and birdskin underwear. The meat of these animals also adds variety to the Eskimo's diet.

A notable crisis has developed with re-

spect to caribou hunting, especially for the Keewatin herd. The rapid decline in numbers of this herd has already been mentioned. Causes of the decrease are many, including diseases, parasites, wolf predation, windchill, drowning, and inclement weather at calving time, but the leading mortality factor by far has been improvident overuse by natives (both Eskimos and Indians). The ready availability of modern guns and ammunition has led to orgies of overhunting as the migrating herds passed by. Education of natives to the problem and to other sources of food [7] has begun to make an impression, but the crisis is far from past.

Trapping The principal means of livelihood of the Canadian Eskimos is trapping. Fur traders have induced the Eskimo locally to trap for skins as well as for meat, clothing, and shelter. This has led to some overexploitation locally of certain animal resources. The main victim has been the white Arctic fox. This animal and the muskrat of the delta of the Mackenzie River are the two outstanding commercially exploitable fur-bearers. In a few parts of the region,

[6] In spite of their intimate association with the ocean, few Eskimos can swim. However, ability to maintain balance when jumping from ice floe to ice floe is an important capability. Thus one of the most popular Eskimo outdoor sports—*Nalukatok,* or blanket tossing—has a practical origin and application. In *Nalukatok,* each participant is tossed high from a blanket or walrus hide, and strives to land on his feet and continue bouncing. The winner is the one who can be bounced the most times before losing his balance.

[7] For example, a pair of Eskimo villages were moved from an inland location to the west shore of Hudson Bay to utilize the abundant beluga resource there.

outsiders are carrying on commercial trapping near native villages. Some trapping areas in Alaska have been so badly exploited by white men that the natives must migrate or starve. Whites are forbidden by law to trap in the Canadian tundra. The region is a preserve for Eskimos.

Commercial trapping makes the Eskimo subject to the white man's world, on which he depends both for necessities (traps) and luxuries (phonographs). Whereas formerly the Eskimo hunted caribou and seals for clothing and meat, he now frequently traps, getting his clothing and food from the trader. Sometimes unsuccessful or unskilled Eskimo trappers in Arctic Canada go on relief, trading goods being paid for by the government. In Greenland, the natives trade blubber and skins, which they really need for themselves, for coffee, dried peas, flour, rice, sugar, and tea—European foods for which they have acquired a taste. The Danes discourage such trade, however.

Grazing Throughout the tundra, as a result of the depletion of the native food supply by the whites, the respective governments are attempting to transform the natives from hunters into graziers.

Observing that Siberian Chukchee Eskimos kept reindeer as insurance against famine during the periodical depletion of wild life and sea food, two Americans purchased reindeer in Siberia and employed Lapp herders to instruct the Alaskan Eskimos, who were then apprenticed for four years in the care of reindeer. At the end of their apprenticeship, each owned a herd of approximately fifty. Actually the animals require little care, for they need no shelter and secure their own feed. They must be herded, however, to prevent straying and to protect them against predatory animals, particularly wolves.

So long as white men and Eskimos used the same ranges, there was serious overgrazing and there were numerous misunder-standings. Accordingly, the United States government purchased all the reindeer in Alaska owned by nonnatives and now prohibits ownership except by Eskimos.

About 1928 the Canadian government, noting that the supply of game for its Eskimos was fluctuating, and being favorably impressed by the American experiment in Alaska, contracted for the delivery of 3,000 reindeer from Alaska to the delta of the Mackenzie. It was believed that with these as a nucleus a considerable portion of northern Canada might be stocked in due time. The drive, estimated to take from 18 to 24 months for a distance of about 1,600 miles, actually required six years, and the distance covered was 2,500 miles.

The experiment near the Mackenzie River Delta has faced many difficulties, however, and the enterprise has not been a success. The Eskimo is reluctant to become a herder. He is at heart a hunter and the only labor in which he delights is the chase. Moreover, the reindeer herds are located in one of Canada's best muskrat-trapping grounds.

It should be realized that the entire tundra is not used for grazing reindeer. Nor is it all suitable. Much is rocky, a large proportion of the surface is covered with lakes, suitable forage is limited, and mosquitoes and flies also restrict the area available. Attempts to introduce reindeer into Labrador and Baffin Island have met with no success. In Greenland, about 260 reindeer were introduced into the Godthaab area in 1952, and, if successful, the experiment will be extended to other areas.

A small number of cattle have been kept since 1782 in Greenland, and sheep have been raised successfully since their introduction in 1906. In the Julianehaab area of southwestern Greenland are now many thousands of sheep. Sheep are sheltered in winter and are fed cured native grasses, willow, turnips, and dried fish.

Minerals and Mining Considerable mineral wealth is known to exist in this region, and possibly new strikes of sensational importance may be made in the future. Transportation difficulties, the curse of the tundra, have retarded commercial mining. Much of this region has never been prospected, and for huge areas there is only limited information. Aviation, more than anything else, is opening up the Canadian and Alaskan mineral fields; airplanes can reach the most remote districts in a day or two and can transport supplies to sections which prospectors previously considered too remote. The helicopter, too, is proving highly valuable for prospecting.

A map of commercial mining in Anglo-America shows only a small amount of activity in this region. It is known that there is considerable petroleum in northern Alaska. There the United States has set aside the Naval Petroleum Reserve, a tract of about 35,000 square miles. Coal also is widely distributed. In the Alaskan part of the region, more than a dozen beds of sub-bituminous and bituminous coal ranging from 4 to 20 feet in thickness are known, and coal-bearing rocks have been found through a belt of country 100 miles wide and 300 miles long. This coal supply should prove of inestimable value locally because of the absence of other fuel. Some gold, silver, antimony, tungsten, and asbestos have also been located in Alaska.

A mine at Rankin Inlet on the northwestern shore of Hudson Bay produces considerable nickel and copper.

Soft coal is mined and used in settlements in northeastern Baffin Island. There is also considerable coal on the west coast of Greenland, and, while the quality is not good, the mine at K'utdligssat produces enough to supply all Greenland.

In the Canadian tundra, iron ore is known to be present in several areas, particularly in the Labrador Trough southwest of Ungava Bay. The first mine most likely will be located about 20 miles inland from Hopes Advance Bay. The principal problem will be shipping, for ice restricts navigation in the bay some eight months each year.[8]

The only deposit of commercial cryolite in the world is being worked in southern Greenland at Ivigtut. The mine, a great quarry mostly below sea level, is one of the most northerly on earth. Its royalties provide the colony's chief revenue. Mining is carried on throughout the year. The mine is almost depleted now, however, and shipments from stock are expected to cease by about 1973.

Agriculture Since the Tundra Region has a short growing season, much of it only 40 days, and since the soils for the most part are shallow, acidic, and poorly drained, commercial agriculture is impossible. In certain highly favored localities in the Canadian Arctic, hardy vegetables are grown under glass. In coastal Labrador, cabbage, beets, and lettuce are also grown, seeds being started indoors while snow still covers the ground. In Greenland, root crops such as turnips, radishes, and potatoes are successfully grown as far north as 66° 15'. Umanak claims to have the most northerly garden in the world. Here broccoli and radishes, turnips and lettuce do fairly well.

In southeastern Greenland, there is considerable emphasis on cutting and curing hay from hardy grasses, for feeding the sheep during the long winters. A few crops are grown as well, particularly potatoes.

Villages, Settlements, and Trading Posts

A settlement (often called "village") in the Tundra Region usually means a cluster of a few igloos, tupeks, or houses. In Canada, a settlement may include a store or a Hudson's Bay Company post, a school

[8] Trevor Loyd and David C. Nutt, "Transportation of Ungava Iron Ore," *The Canadian Geographer,* No. 15 (1960), p. 31.

house, Anglican mission, radio station, weather station, and homes.

The characteristic abode of the Eskimos prior to the coming of the white man was the permanent village located at some spot on the coast or on a river bank of a coastal stream suitable for hunting and fishing. The major location factor was proximity to navigable water containing sea mammals. The sealing economy thus placed a premium on scattered small settlements. The fishing economy encourages a few large settlements; so does the need for education, health services, and similar benefits. The tendency in Greenland today is toward large settlements and the abolition of little hamlets.

The number of significant settlements is small. The famous gold rush town of *Nome* still suffers from isolation, but is the supply center for an extensive placer-mining district and for Bering Sea Eskimos. *Kotzebue* is a major Eskimo settlement. The strategic town of *Barrow* (air base and weather station; administrative center for the Naval Petroleum Reserve) has probably the largest Eskimo settlement in the Tundra. *Ak-*

lavik and *Inuvik* are the only really northern Canadian mainland communities of any size. The former was built on the basis of muskrat trapping, but has become an important communication and administrative center. The entire town was moved 33 miles in 1954-58 (from West Channel to East Channel of the Mackenzie) to secure a site unhampered by permafrost, flooding, and silt problems. Its normal population of less than 1,000 is doubled when Eskimo fishermen arrive in summer. Inuvik is a planned town and northern administrative center. *Churchill* has been a major summer grain-shipping port for years, and is becoming an important import point for the Prairie Provinces (Figure 18-6). *Lake Harbour* and *Frobisher Bay* on Baffin Island represent an older Eskimo settlement and a modern air base-oriented village, respectively.

In Greenland, there are three types of population centers: (1) "towns," which may contain up to 3,000 inhabitants (Figure 18-7); (2) trading centers, with a general store and a population of a few dozen to a few hundred persons; and (3) "settlements," usually a cluster of homes of a few

Figure 18-6. Grain ships and loading facilities at Churchill. (Photo by George Hunter; courtesy Manitoba Department of Industry and Commerce.)

Figure 18-7. A residential section of Godthaab, Greenland's capital. (Photo courtesy Danish Information Office.)

hunters and their families. Most of the population is located on the west coast; less than a half dozen agglomerations are on the east coast. The principal towns are *Godthaab* (the capital) (Figure 18-8), *Frederikshaab* and *Holsteinborg* (major fishing centers), and *Narssak* and *Christianshaab* (sites of packing plants for sheep and shrimp).

Transportation

One of the biggest hindrances to economic development in this region is transportation. Travel over most of the tundra is possible in summer only by canoe or pack dog and in winter by dogteam. Railroads and roads are almost nonexistent, for they are uneconomical in so thinly populated a region. Villages on the sea are accessible to small ocean-going vessels for a few weeks each year (the open season on the coast near Point Barrow, Alaska, is practically limited to the month of August). Only products of high value in proportion to bulk or weight such as furs and gold are worth transporting very far by sledge or canoe.

However, the airplane is breaking down the region's isolation. It has reduced travel time from weeks to hours. Areas formerly too remote for mining are now within easy reach. The airplane carries the miner, his equipment, and mining machinery, as well as mail, medical supplies, and food. It also establishes gasoline caches. Maps accurate

Figure 18-8. A view of Godthaab, showing the Seminary. (Photo copyright by Royal Danish Ministry of Foreign Affairs, courtesy of Danish Information Office.)

in minute detail are now being made from aerial photographs. Moreover, rather than waiting for the open-water shipping period of late summer, trappers are employing airplanes to bring out bales of prime furs during winter when the highest prices prevail. However, freight charges and passenger fares are high.

There are regularly scheduled commercial flights to Nome, Barrow, Aklavik, Coppermine, and Frobisher Bay; and charter flights can be made to almost any settlement in the Tundra.

What remoteness means can be appreciated by noting that the scattered settlements of the eastern Canadian Arctic have their hard and lonely routine broken only once a year when a government patrol boat brings supplies that must last for an entire year. The ship, which travels 10,000 miles during the short summer, remains at each point of call for only a few hours or at most a few days.

The Hudson Bay Railway, 510 miles long, extending from The Pas, Manitoba, to Churchill on Hudson Bay, passes through a flat country broken by lakes and rivers. The terrain offers few construction difficulties except where spongy soil requires heavy ballast. The deep harbor at Churchill is one of the few shelters for deep-sea vessels along the shallow west coast of Hudson Bay.

Strategic Significance

Anglo-America's Tundra Region, despite its sparse population and comparative lack of development, has assumed new importance since World War II. Sharing with the Soviet Union the major part of the polar world, the Tundra becomes Anglo-America's first line of defense against transpolar attack.

Three principal types of outposts have been established in the region—either by the United States, or by joint Canadian and United States action, or by the United States

with Danish permission and cooperation—as primary defense measures. (1) Radio and meteorological stations, as at Alert on the northeastern tip of Ellesmere Island or at Resolute on Cornwallis Island, are manned the year round, with extra crews in the summer. (2) Distant Early Warning line radar stations are strung across the entire width of the Tundra. (3) Large military air bases are established at such places as Frobisher Bay and Thule, with hundreds or thousands of personnel on continuous duty.

The Outlook

The region will continue as a land of great distances and few people, where nothing more than a scanty livelihood is obtainable by trapping, hunting, fishing, or grazing. Cities in the true sense will, as now, be nonexistent.

Trapping will continue to be important to the natives, but it is too dependent upon the vagaries of fashion, fluctuation of prices, and biological cycles to provide a steady means of livelihood for large numbers of people.

Can the natives be taught to herd reindeer, or possibly the musk ox? The four principal attempts with the former species have been far from successful, and the latter has never been domesticated to any practical extent.

It is probable that a continually increasing proportion of native income will be derived from part-time employment on construction jobs and from temporary assistance to weather observers, wildlife technicians, and other outsiders on temporary projects in the region.

There is a small but growing trend to take Eskimos "south" for training, and then return them to the Tundra with a new skill. This has been successful on a small scale with hard-rock miners at Rankin Inlet, with fur-dressers at Aklavik, and in a few other instances, and could be the beginning of formation of a nucleus of semiskilled labor that would not be dependent on construction work.

It is clear that most Eskimos and Indians of the Tundra will eventually have to make the transition to a "civilized" way of life, and no doubt the transition will be a difficult and painful one in many ways. They love the North and are adjusted to northern living, and so could become the backbone of northern development if they could acquire the best of the white man's ways without losing their identities. But with the perishing of the "old" way of life, employment opportunities must be made available or the native is likely to sink into a slough of apathy and degradation.

Restricted economic opportunities for the people will also be a stumbling block for the future of Greenland. Resources are limited and transportation costs are high. In spite of Denmark's high resolve, Greenland will probably remain an "underdeveloped" area for some time to come.

In Anglo-America the "underdeveloped" regions frequently have their economy bolstered by tourists and sportsmen. The transportation handicaps in the Tundra, however, which are greater than in any other region, are strong inhibiting factors. A few hunters fly into the region on expensive expeditions for polar bear or walrus, but this cannot be expected to expand much. A trickle of tourists visits Kotzebue to see Eskimos or to Frobisher Bay to see the "true Arctic" (there are three weekly flights from Montreal to Frobisher Bay, marking almost the only directly scheduled functional connection between the Tundra and an important population center), and this trickle should grow, but only gradually.

The significance of the region is destined to be as a buffer zone, at least for the near future. It is an area where eyes can be watchful and ears can be attuned across the

Pole, where a few valuable warning minutes can be gained, and where the very first dramas of a shooting war—if it comes—are likely to be enacted.

The Ice Cap

Greenland, the world's largest island, is a great plateau 1,800 miles long and 800 miles wide at its greatest breadth.[9] Four-fifths of it, or an area of 668,000 square miles, is an ice desert. This ice cap, with an average thickness of nearly 5,000 feet, discharges to the sea through narrow valley glaciers. Fjords characterize the plateau margin. Near both the eastern and western coasts are to be found fairly high mountains, but over much of this interior plateau the surface is flat, with few minor irregularities. Greenland experiences bitterly cold temperatures, and its winds are among the strongest in the world; the northern parts are dark for long periods in winter. The ice cap has no permanent inhabitants and is utterly lacking in utility, offering no prospects for the future.

TABLE 17

Selected Cities and Towns of the Tundra

City or Town	Political Center
Aklavik	599
Barrow	1,314
Churchill	3,932
Frederikshaab	1,817 *
Frobisher Bay	512
Godthaab	4,306 *
Holsteinborg	2,331 *
Inuvik	1,248
Julianehaab	2,407 *
Kotzebue	1,290
Narssak	1,524 *
Nome	2,316
Rankin Inlet	585
Sukkertoppen	2,676 *

* 1960 data from the *Danish Statistical Yearbook.*

[9] Recent research indicates that the ice may be underlaid by several separated land masses.

Selected Bibliography

Bergeron, Robert, "Ungava Bay—Ungava Peninsula," *Canadian Geographical Journal,* Vol. 57, July 1958, pp. 20-29.

Bird, J. Brian, "The Scenery of Central and Southern Arctic Canada," *The Canadian Geographer,* No. 15, 1960, pp. 1-11.

"Canada Counts Its Caribou," *National Geographic Magazine,* Vol. 102, August 1952, pp. 261-268.

Flint, R. F., "The Ice Age in the North American Arctic," *Arctic,* Vol. 5, 1952, pp. 140-151.

Hare, F. Kenneth, "The Labrador Frontier," *Geographical Review,* Vol. 42, 1952, pp. 405-424.

Lloyd, Trevor, "Ivigtut Cryolite and Modern Greenland," *The Canadian Geographer,* No. 3, 1953, pp. 39-52.

———, "Map of the Distribution of Eskimos and Native Greenlanders in North America," *The Canadian Geographer,* No. 13, 1959, pp. 41-42.

———, "Progress in West Greenland," *Journal of Geography,* Vol. 49, 1950, pp. 319-328.

———, and David C. Nutt, "Transportation of Ungava Iron Ore," *The Canadian Geographer,* No. 15, 1960, pp. 26-34.

Mackay, J. Ross, *The Anderson River Map-Area, N.W.T.,* Memoir 5. Ottawa: Geographical Branch, Department of Mines and Technical Surveys, 1958.

Miller, E. Willard, "The Hudson Bay Railway Route: a Geographical Reconnaissance," *Journal of Geography,* Vol. 57, April 1958, pp. 163-170.

Raitt, W. Lindsay, and A. Stewart Fraser, "A New East Greenland Community," *Scottish Geographical Magazine,* Vol. 74, April 1958, pp. 13-27.

"Report on the North," *Imperial Oil Review,* Vol. 44, October 1960.

"Resources of the Arctic," *Focus,* Vol. 2, February 15, 1952.

Ross, W. Gillies, "The Igloolik Eskimos," *Scottish Geographical Magazine,* Vol. 76, December 1960, pp. 156-163.

Sonnenfeld, Joseph, "Changes in an Eskimo Hunting Technology, an Introduction to Implement Geography," *Annals of the Association of American Geographers,* Vol. 50, June 1960, pp. 172-186.

Taylor, Andrew, "Our Polar Islands: The Queen Elizabeths," *Canadian Geographical Journal,* Vol. 52, 1956, pp. 232-351.

Tener, J. S., "The Present Status of the Barren-ground Caribou," *Canadian Geographical Journal,* Vol. 60, March 1960, pp. 98-105.

Therkilsen, Kjeld Rask, "Greenland Looks Ahead," *The Geographical Magazine,* Vol. 33, February 1961, pp. 545-555.

appendix a

The Physical
Background
of Anglo-America

Anglo-America lies entirely north of the Tropic of Cancer and largely south of the Arctic Circle, and thus is almost completely within the middle latitudes. The land mass also fronts on both the Atlantic and the Pacific Ocean and so is in a favored position to play a dominant role in world trade. In addition, its great size causes it to have a wide variety of land forms, climatic types, vegetation associations, and soils.

Because of its structural axes, North America is wedge-shaped, with its widest part to the north. In the center of the continent between the Appalachian Mountains and the Rocky Mountains lies an extensive plain that is drained to the south by the Mississippi River and its tributaries, to the northeast by the St. Lawrence, and to the north by the several streams that flow into the Arctic Ocean, such as the Nelson and the Mackenzie. East of the Appalachians is a fairly extensive coastal plain that is crossed by many short but economically and historically important streams such as the Potomac, the James, and the Roanoke. A similar condition exists along the Gulf Coast both east and west of the Mississippi drainage. In the western part of the continent the several basins and ranges that constitute the Cordilleran System so completely dominate the area that there are no extensive plains and few major streams—in fact, a considerable part of this area has interior drainage. On the Pacific slope are several

Figure A-1. The Physiographic Regions of Anglo-America: (1) Arctic Slope, (2) Laurentian Uplands, (3) Atlantic and Gulf Coastal Plain, (4) Appalachian Region, (5) Interior Plain, (6) Interior Uplands, (7) Rocky Mountains, (8) Intermontane Province, (9) Pacific Coast Region, and (10) Yukon Basin. (After Fenneman and Atwood.)

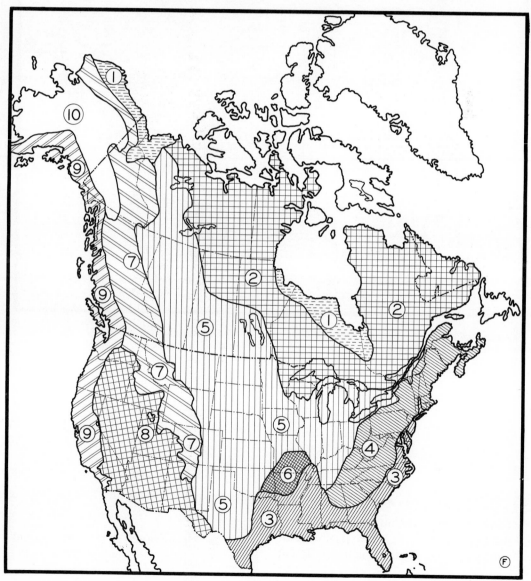

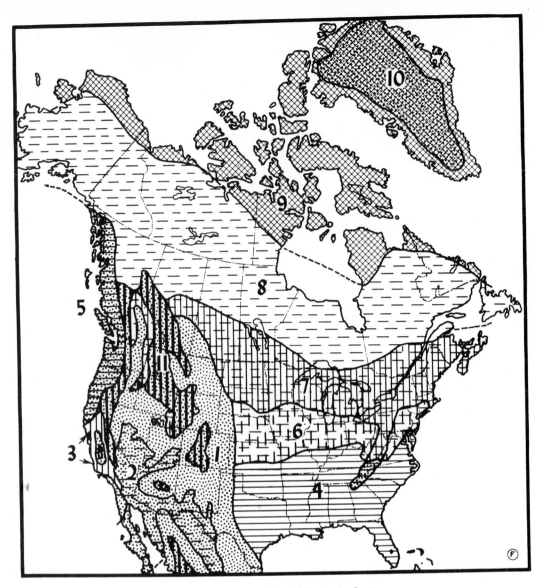

Figure A-2. Climatic Regions of Anglo-America: (1) Middle Latitude Steppe, (2) Middle Latitude Desert, (3) Mediterranean or Dry-Summer Subtropical, (4) Humid Subtropical, Warm Summers, (5) Marine West Coast, Cool Summers, (6) Humid Continental, Warm Summers, (7) Humid Continental, Cool Summers, (8) Subarctic, (9) Tundra, (10) Ice Cap, and (11) Undifferentiated Highlands. (After Trewartha.)

important coastal valleys that are drained by such streams as the Sacramento-San Joaquin, the Columbia, and the Fraser.

The Physiographic Regions

Anglo-America contains a number of major physiographic regions and subregions (Figure A-1), most of which are found within the United States, although a few appear only in Canada. The map here presented is based primarily upon the classification of regions as worked out by N. M. Fenneman[1] for the United States portion

[1] N. M. Fenneman, "Physiographic Divisions of the United States," *Annals of the Association of American Geographers*, Vol. 18 (1928), pp. 261-353.

and by W. N. Thayer [2] for the Canadian portion. Wallace W. Atwood [3] has published a map for the entire continent in his volume, *The Physiographic Provinces of North America,* to which the reader is referred for more detail regarding descriptions of the physiographic provinces.

Climate

The latitude of Anglo-America is an important factor in the seasonal distribution of pressure and winds. Since the whole area lies north of the Tropic of Cancer, it has no large tropical regions. Poleward, the continent extends beyond the Arctic Circle, but the major part lies within the middle latitudes and thus is dominated by the eastward movement of air masses, weather fronts, and storms.

There are almost as many classifications of climate as there are climatologists. While all classifications are fundamentally the same, their minor variations and complex nomenclatures may confuse the reader. Unfortunately, no standard classification, such as Fenneman's for physiographical regions, has been adopted for climates. The map in this book shows one of the most widely used classifications [4] (Figure A-2).

Natural Vegetation

Anglo-America's natural vegetation is divided into three classes—forests, grasslands, and shrublands (Figure A-3).

The *forests* are grouped into five zones: (1) the northern coniferous forests, or taiga; (2) the eastern mixed forests; (3) the southern pineries; (4) the Rocky Mountain forests; and (5) the Pacific Coast forests.

[2] W. N. Thayer, "The Northward Extension of the Physiographic Divisions of the United States," *Journal of Geology,* Vol. 26 (1918), pp. 161-85.
[3] Atwood, *The Physiographic Provinces of North America* (Boston: Ginn & Co., 1940).
[4] Vernor C. Finch, Glenn T. Trewartha, Arthur H. Robinson, and Edwin H. Hammond, *Elements of Geography,* 4th ed. (New York: McGraw-Hill Book Co., 1957), pp. 123-126.

The taiga (zone 1), composed mostly of coniferous trees growing under extremes of temperature in a region where the winters are very cold, occurs widely across Canada and in the northern part of the United States. Because of the longer growing season along the southern margin of this forest, large trees are found here. They have wide annual growth rings that are the result of rapid growth during the short but warm summer season. At the northern margin, the trees resemble those found at timber line on high mountains.

Three belts of forested land extend southward from the taiga. One prong follows the Appalachian Mountains and adjacent lowlands, another the Rocky Mountains, and a third the Pacific coastal ranges and the Sierra Nevada. Part of the easternmost prong (zone 2) consists of a tier of mixed forest just south of the taiga, an expansive area where hardwoods [5] composed the original vegetation, and a southern zone of mixed forest; and the other part (zone 3) is the extensive pine lands of the southeastern states. Borders between zones are indistinct, of course, for the characteristic tree species mingle considerably.

The Rocky Mountain prong (zone 4) is mostly mountain forest. In the Southern Rockies trees grow only in the uplands, but

[5] The terms "hardwoods" and "softwoods" are the most generally accepted popular names for the two classes of trees, the *Angiosperms* and the *Gymnosperms.* Most Angiosperms, such as oak, hickory, sugar maple, and black locust, are notably hard woods, and many Gymnosperms, such as pines and spruces are rather soft woods. But there are a number of outstanding exceptions. Basswood, poplar, aspen, and cottonwood, all classified as hardwoods, are in reality among the softest of woods. Longleaf pine, on the other hand, is about as hard as the average hardwood, although it is classified as a softwood. The most accurate popular descriptions for the two groups are "trees with broad leaves" for the Angiosperms, and "trees with needles or scale-like leaves" for the Gymnosperms (from Forest Products Laboratory, *Technical Note 187,* Madison, Wisconsin).

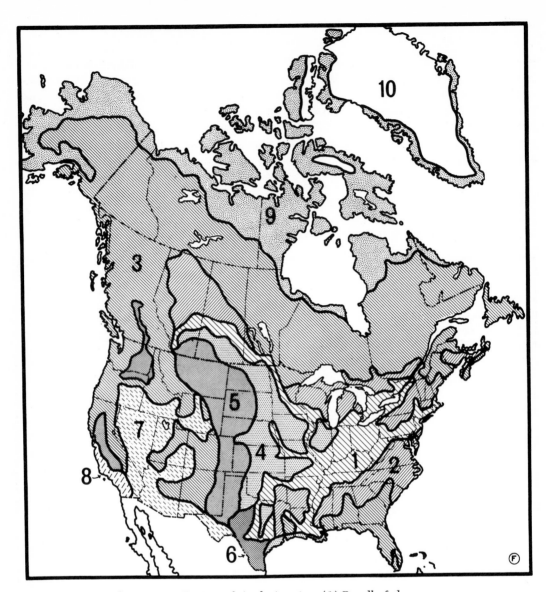

Figure A-3. Natural Vegetation Regions of Anglo-America. (1) Broadleaf deciduous forest, (2) Mixed broadleaf deciduous and needleleaf evergreen forest, (3) Needleleaf evergreen forest, (4) Medium-height grassland, (5) Low-height grassland, (6) Mixed grassland and mesquite, (7) Broadleaf evergreen shrubland, (8) Chaparral-manzanita association, (9) Tundra, and (10) Little or no vegetation. (After Kuchler.)

in the Northern Rockies some of the lowlands also are forested. In the Rocky Mountain forest, Engelmann and blue spruce are common, with western yellow pine covering the lower slopes. Aspen, the first tree to occupy an area after a fire, is one of the few deciduous trees. Because of rugged terrain, this forest has not been exploited to any great extent. Most of the stands are incorporated in national forests. Open spaces—parks—have grass and are used for grazing. Except for piñon and juniper on the higher ridges, and the somewhat extensive ponderosa pine forests of the Colorado Plateau, the area between the Rocky Mountains and the Sierra Nevada is lacking in trees.

The Pacific Coast prong (zone 5) is also mountain forest and consists primarily of softwoods. In Washington and Oregon, the Douglas fir is dominant, growing seven to eight feet in diameter and 200 feet in height.

In northern California and in the Sierra Nevada, the redwood and sequoia trees sometimes attain a diameter of 15 feet and a height of 300 feet.

Grasslands usually are found in areas where the rainfall is insufficient for trees, and most of them have never had any other

Figure A-4. Soil Regions of Anglo-America. (1) Tundra soils, (2) Podzols, (3) Gray-brown podzolic soils, (4) Red-and-yellow soils, (5) Prairie Soils, (6) Chernozems, (7) Chestnut-brown soils, (8) Dark-brown soils, (9) Gray-desert soils, and (10) Soils of mountainous areas. (After Marbut and others.)

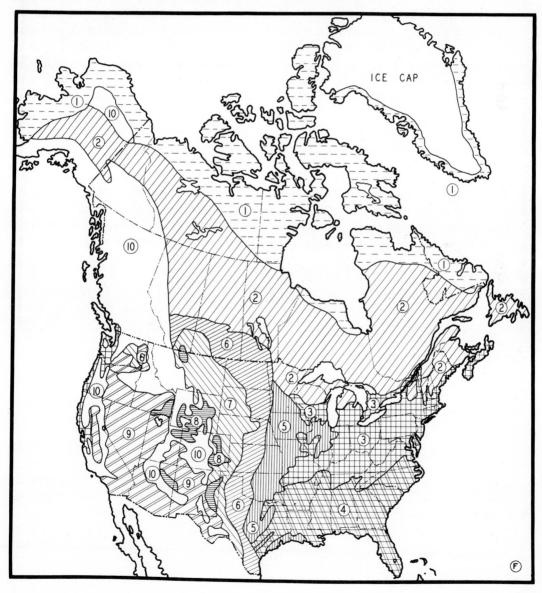

type of vegetation. Where grass is tall, the land is called "prairie"; where short, "steppe." Toward the drier margin the short grass vegetation grades into bunch grass. The *tundra* is clothed with a spongy mass of mosses and lichens—a special pseudo-grassland.

Shrublands vary considerably in their characteristics, but usually develop under an arid or semiarid climate. Their vegetative cover is usually a combination of bushes or stunted trees and sparse grasses. In southern and central Texas, mesquite is the dominant plant. In the area from Wyoming to Nevada, sagebrush provides the most extensive ground cover. In the southwest, cacti and other succulents are common. The chaparral-manzanita association of California includes some areas of grassland, and some of open oak woodland.

Soils

Soil [6] is more than merely the covering of the bedrock. A true soil must have remained in place long enough to develop a mature profile consisting of the A-, B-, and C-horizons. The topsoil (A-horizon) is composed largely of organic material (humus) contributed by the native vegetation, which also gives it color. The C-horizon, or parent material, is dependent largely upon the type of bedrock. The B-horizon is the distinguishing factor, for the division of soils into humid and arid groups is made on the basis of the minerals contained in the B-horizon. Characteristic minerals of the B-horizon are calcium carbonate and aluminum and iron compounds; the former is soluble, and the latter are insoluble. In humid soils, the calcium carbonate has been leached out to varying degrees. The most extensive leaching occurs in the most humid soils and these have a bright red color imparted by the iron (ferric oxide). In arid soils, the calcium is present and the iron is in the ferrous state. From the mineral composition of the B-horizon, arid soils are called *pedocals* and humid soils *pedalfers*.

Near the line of 20 inches of rainfall, or the hundredth meridian, is a transition between the humid east and the arid west. In the humid east, from north to south lie the belts of gray podzols, gray-brown podzolic soils, and red-and-yellow soils. The degree of leaching is progressively greater from north to south, because in the South, where the soil is not frozen in winter, leaching continues throughout the year. On the western margin of the pedalfers lie the prairie soils that form a transition between the pedalfers and the pedocals (Figure A-4).

In the West, the soil belts run predominantly north and south, as they result from decreasing precipitation toward the west. The easternmost soil of the pedocal group is the black *chernozem*. Next is the dark-brown soil, and finally the gray desert soil. In the Pacific Coast valleys, with their abundant rainfall, the soils are similar to those of the humid East. It is almost impossible to trace soil belts west of the Rockies. Large areas in the Rocky Mountains do not have true soils.

---

[6] For a more complete study of the soils of the United States, see Department of Agriculture, *Soils and Men*, 1938 Yearbook of Agriculture (Washington: Government Printing Office), pp. 1019-61.

appendix b

The Occupance
of Anglo-America

Until recently, little concrete evidence has been offered to support the view that man might have been present in Anglo-America during the glacial period. Discoveries in southwestern United States, however, suggest that man lived contemporaneously with such creatures as the imperator elephant and the Pleistocene horse—animals which became extinct in Anglo-America during the glacial period. The natives found by the early explorers from Europe and erroneously called "Indians" were newcomers to Anglo-America, having reached the Atlantic coast only a comparatively short time before they were discovered. In many cases they had not had time to make any permanent adaptation to their environment. It is usually assumed that the Indians came via the Bering Sea or the Aleutian Islands, and that the northeastern part of the continent was the last region reached by them. This may help to explain why the settle-

499

ments in the Southwest or in Mexico and Central America were more advanced than those of the Northeast. Other factors, however, that retarded the development of the Indians were paucity of protected habitats (except in southwestern United States), lack of domesticated animals other than the dog, and unfamiliarity with metals other than gold, silver, and copper.

Although the Indian was well adapted to his habitat, the land remained sparsely populated. When the white man arrived, America was comparatively empty. It is reliably estimated that New York City's population today is ten times that of all Anglo-America at the time of Columbus' arrival (1,500,000).

Many scholars believe the small Indian population to have been a result of their cultural stage (hunting and fishing), which allowed only two to eight persons per square mile. Others think incessant warfare, followed by unrest and famine and ineffectual political organization, might have been the cause. Still others make much of the conservative food habits whereby the Indians in their diet demanded a very high proportion of meat and fish. One authority thinks agriculture was of little importance in the East. On the other hand, there are those who believe that the majority of prehistoric aborigines, at least in that part of Anglo-America comprising the United States, were sedentary farmers and not roving hunters. They insist that the European never grasped the idea that there was not a typical Indian —that where the natural environment was favorable he accomplished much; where unfavorable, little. Had physical conditions been everywhere uniform, the distinctive cultures of different parts of the continent might not have developed.

The major Indian cultural groups found in Anglo-America include the Algonquin, the Iroquois, the Muskhogeans, the Caddoans, the Sioux, the Athapascans, and the Haida and Tlingits. In addition, there were numerous minor cultural groups of various degrees of development from the advanced civilizations of the Hopi and Zuñi to renegade tribes such as the cannibalistic Karankawans of the Texas Gulf Coast.

The Conflict Between the White Man and the Indian

White man subdued the Indian in a comparatively short time. One factor in this struggle was the contrast in cultural development. The European was using iron and steel, while even the most highly civilized natives were still in the Neolithic stage. The white man also had the horse and other domesticated animals, while the native had only the dog. When the white man came to the New World he had to combat few new diseases; on the other hand, he introduced several. Measles and smallpox killed the natives in great numbers and accounted in large measure for the victory of the white man. Furthermore, it seems evident that most tribes had been in Anglo-America only a comparatively short time and had not completely adapted themselves to the new environment when the Europeans came. From every point of view, the white man had the advantage.

The Indian made many contributions to agriculture. In the New World the most valuable discoveries were not gold but new foods. Among the food plants domesticated and developed by them and given directly or indirectly to the white man, corn or maize stands first. The Indian also contributed the white potato, tobacco, many kinds of beans, peanuts, pumpkins, squash, the sweet potato, tomatoes, and other foods.[1]

Many crops introduced from Europe grew well in Anglo-America. All cereals found favorable habitats. Only the Mediterranean

[1] For an interesting discussion of this topic, see Carl O. Sauer, *Agricultural Origins and Dispersals* (New York: American Geographical Society, 1952), pp. 40-61.

grape, which was accustomed to dry summers, failed in the eastern part of the New World, because the heavy summer rains encouraged the growth of a fungus. A native grape, the Concord, however, was successful. In southern California, the Spaniards had no difficulty in growing the Mediterranean grape, because there the climate was similar to that of its original habitat.

By fair means or foul, the white settlers killed off or pushed back the Indians. Today the remnants of most tribes in the United States live on reservations scattered throughout the West, and on a few reservations in the East.

Exploration and Early Settlement

In ancient times, European culture reached its highest development along the shores of the Mediterranean Sea. During the Middle Ages, the main cultural centers moved into Western Europe. However, several of the old Mediterranean cities, such as Venice, Genoa, Florence, and Constantinople (Istanbul), maintained their supremacy, their importance resulting from trade with the Orient. In the fourteenth century, Venice and Genoa became the main *entrepôt* ports for Oriental goods. When Constantinople was captured by the Ottoman Turks in 1452, trade routes to the East were closed. This caused the Italian cities to decline commercially.

The Portuguese, under the patronage of Prince Henry the Navigator, had explored the west coast of Africa even before the fall of Constantinople, and had rediscovered certain Atlantic islands. Columbus, a native of Genoa, sailing in the interest of Spain, crossed the Atlantic in 1492 and landed in the West Indies. Depending on an ancient Ptolemaic map, he underestimated the distance from Europe to Asia and at first thought he had reached India. Probably he realized his mistake on one of his three subsequent voyages. The quarrel between Portugal and Spain over their conflicting interests in the New World was settled by the Treaty of Tordesillas in 1494. Meanwhile, England sent out the Cabots, who discovered Newfoundland and the Gulf of St. Lawrence and claimed that territory for England. Later, Jacques Cartier, sailing under the flag of France, reached the Gaspé Peninsula.

About 1540, Cabeza de Vaca, after being shipwrecked on the Texas coast, wandered across the Southwest as far as Arizona, then turned southward down the west coast of Mexico. Coronado traveled through Arizona and New Mexico, Texas and Kansas, and then returned through the Southwest to Mexico. Having failed to discover the "fabulous" Seven Cities of Cibola, he considered the expedition a failure.

At about the same time, an expedition under Hernando DeSoto advanced northwestward from Florida and crossed the Mississippi River to the south of the present city of Memphis. DeSoto went as far west as the Ozarks, but upon returning from that area he died and was buried in the Mississippi. In spite of the extensive explorations of the South and Southwest, Spain made no definite claims to the area, because her explorers found no gold. Thereafter, her interests were concentrated largely in Mexico and South America.

It was not until the close of the sixteenth and the beginning of the seventeenth century that France and England made any further attempts to acquire colonies in North America.

The French came to Canada, dominated the St. Lawrence Valley, then the Great Lakes area, and ultimately claimed all lands drained by the Mississippi River and its tributaries. The English, reaching Anglo-America later, settled only on the east coast and in the West Indies. Each country ignored the claims of the others, all the grants to the English colonies reading "thence westward to the Pacific." The Finns and Swedes, who had settled in Delaware, were absorbed by the Dutch, who in turn were incorporated into the English colony.

The Negro Slave

Soon after the first white settlers occupied the land of Tidewater Virginia, there arose the problem of labor for clearing the forests, cultivating the soil, and harvesting the crops. Since land was free, no white man would consider working for another when he could have his own land; and the Indian of the Atlantic Coast could not be enslaved. At first, indentured servants—white men sent from England who temporarily sold their services for the price of ship passage to the New World—met the labor requirements. These, however, did not prove satisfactory, because they were not numerous enough to supply the demand and because it was difficult to keep them as slaves once they reached the frontier. To help solve the labor problem, Negro slaves were imported from Africa.

The first Negro slaves in the English Colonies were landed by a Dutch privateer at Jamestown in 1619. They were sold to the colonial government, which in turn sold them to planters along the James River. It was not until 1630 that a second cargo of Negroes was sold in the Virginia settlements. From 1635 on, a small number was imported nearly every year, partly from England and New Netherlands, but mostly from the West Indies. Despite the shortage of labor, Negroes were not popular at first, and even in 1690 there were only 5,000 in the tobacco colonies. However at the end of the seventeenth century the English Government restricted kidnaping and attempted to check the sending of convicts to America. As a result direct slave trade with Guinea developed, and slaveholding began in earnest. It is estimated that there were 400,000 slaves in the Colonies in 1760 and that three-fourths of them were in the southern Colo-

nies. The slaves made up about two-fifths of the entire southern population . . .[2]

Later, when cotton became the important crop of the Old South after the invention of the gin, Negro slave labor seemed essential for clearing new lands and for planting and picking the crop. Had it not been for this large supply of labor during the eighteenth and early nineteenth centuries, it is doubtful whether the Cotton Belt could have expanded so rapidly or whether the Old South could have attained its high ante-bellum cultural stage. By 1808, when further importation of African slaves was prohibited, nearly 20,000 were being brought into the United States each year. They were never employed successfully as laborers in the northeastern industrial states, and even in the Middle Atlantic States of Maryland and Virginia they were of doubtful value. Only in hot, humid areas of the deep South, where Europeans experienced difficulty in performing physical labor, could Negro slaves be employed profitably. Because slaves were unprofitable in the North, that section of the country demanded abolition, while the Cotton Belt states became more convinced than ever that slavery was essential. The result was armed conflict between the two factions, and the ultimate emancipation of the Negro. Since that time, the Negro problem both in the South and in the North has been a subject of much study and discussion.

Conflicts for Control of Anglo-America

By the early part of the seventeenth century, the English were entrenched along the Atlantic coast from Nova Scotia almost to Florida; the French dominated the Great Lakes and the Mississippi Valley; and the

[2] Everett E. Edwards, "American Agriculture—The First 300 Years," *Yearbook of Agriculture, 1940* (Washington: Government Printing Office, 1940), pp. 180-81.

Spanish held Florida, Texas, New Mexico, and all lands westward to the Pacific.

The main base of Russian America was on Baranof Island at Sitka, Alaska. No one disputed the Russian possession of the region around the Aleutian Islands, but in southeastern Alaska there were conflicting claims. The Spanish had sent out an expedition from Mexico, and claimed the coast as far north as 62° North Latitude. James Cook explored the Alaskan coast and claimed much of it for Great Britain. American clipper ships had traded up the West Coast, discovering the mouth of the Columbia River and the lands of the Northwest. Spain and Russia withdrew from the quarrel about the southern part of the area, leaving it to the United States and England. Spain relinquished her claims to the United States in the Treaty of 1819,[3] when Florida was purchased. In the early part of the nineteenth century, Russia ceased to make any further advances in the territory.

The Territorial Growth of the United States and the Westward Movement

In the space of fifty years, 1803-1853, the United States attained its present continental size, acquiring much of the territory by purchase (Figure B-1). Following the Revolutionary War and the creation of the United States as a new nation on the North American Continent, the first land annexed was Louisiana in 1803. This territory had a complicated history. France had ceded Louisiana to Spain at the close of the French and Indian War to prevent it from falling into the hands of England. Spain, in accepting Louisiana, hoped to block the advance of the English colonists. She soon realized, however, that the advance of the new American republic could not be stopped, and hence returned Louisiana to France so that France could act as a barrier between

[3] The treaty finally was ratified by Spain and the United States in 1821.

the young United States and Spanish Texas.

Spain was dismayed when France immediately sold the territory to the neighbor she dreaded most. American pioneers in the Ohio Valley had been demanding better treatment at New Orleans, their natural water outlet, and had begun to insist upon the purchase of that port by the United States. Some trans-Alleghenian people even threatened secession, because their economic interests were linked more closely with the port at the mouth of the Mississippi River than with any of the American ports on the Atlantic Seaboard. President Jefferson, realizing the seriousness of the situation, opened negotiations with France for the purchase of New Orleans, and ultimately secured the entire Louisiana Territory for 15 million dollars. Although Congress had not authorized this purchase, Jefferson concluded the transaction because he recognized the importance of this tract of land to the growing United States. Immediately he sent out an expedition under Lewis and Clark to explore the new territory. They ascended the Missouri River to its headwaters, crossed the Rocky Mountains, and descended the Snake and Columbia Rivers to the Pacific Coast. Organized expeditions were soon followed by trappers in the 1830's and 1840's. At this time the Great Plains were merely transit lands; no one was interested in occupying them, or made any attempt to settle them.

Spain, having lost most of her colonial possessions in the New World, and realizing her inability to stop the territorial advance of the United States, sold Florida in 1821 to the new nation.

By 1820, settlers were moving westward rapidly (Figure B-2). Meanwhile, Mexico, having separated from Spain, controlled a broad area extending from Texas westward to the Pacific and as far north as the present northern boundary of California. Realizing that Texas should be occupied immediately,

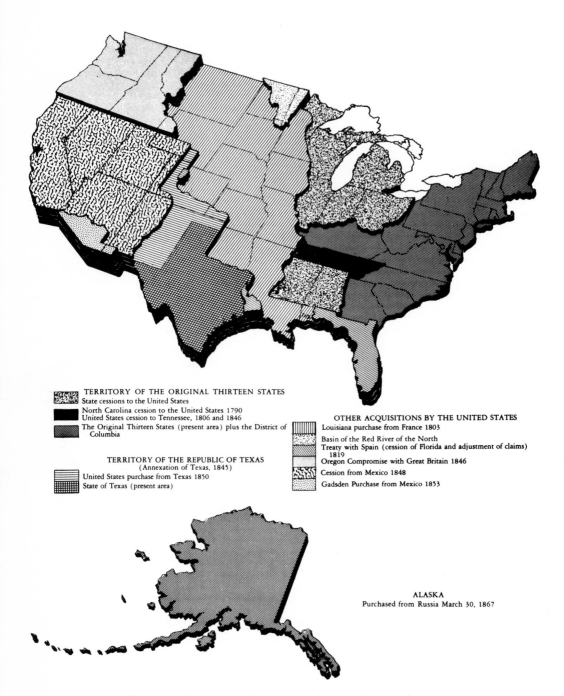

TERRITORY OF THE ORIGINAL THIRTEEN STATES
State cessions to the United States

North Carolina cession to the United States 1790
United States cession to Tennessee, 1806 and 1846

The Original Thirteen States (present area) plus the District of Columbia

TERRITORY OF THE REPUBLIC OF TEXAS
(Annexation of Texas, 1845)

United States purchase from Texas 1850

State of Texas (present area)

OTHER ACQUISITIONS BY THE UNITED STATES
Louisiana purchase from France 1803

Basin of the Red River of the North

Treaty with Spain (cession of Florida and adjustment of claims) 1819

Oregon Compromise with Great Britain 1846

Cession from Mexico 1848

Gadsden Purchase from Mexico 1853

ALASKA
Purchased from Russia March 30, 1867

Figure B-1. Territorial Growth of the United States. (Courtesy the Bureau of Land Management.)

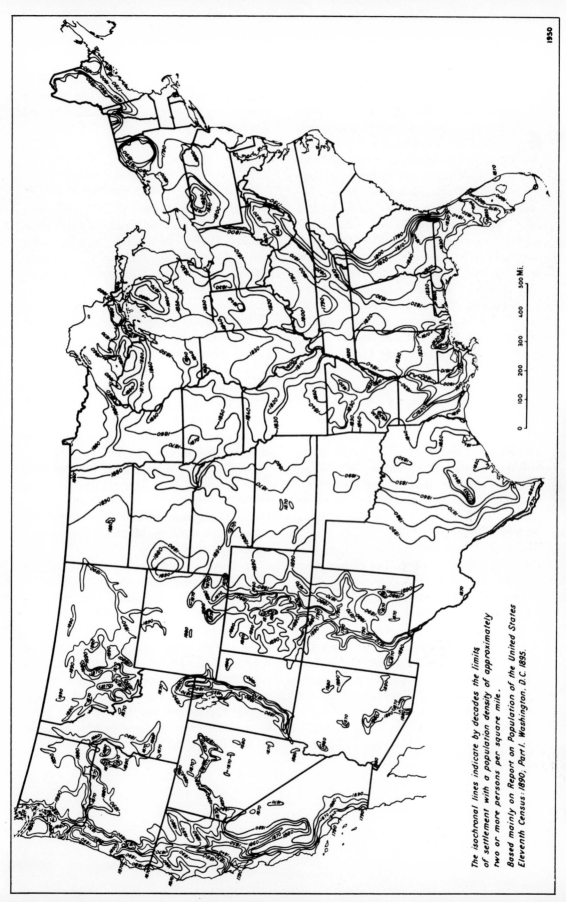

1950

The isochronal lines indicate by decades the limits
of settlement with a population density of approximately
two or more persons per square mile.

Based mainly on Report on Population of the United States
Eleventh Census: 1890, Part I. Washington, D.C. 1895.

Figure B-2. Expansion of Settlement in the United States, 1790-1890. (USDA Map.)

Mexico threw open the land to American settlers, giving them several times more land for homesteading than the United States later offered to its land-hungry population. Mexico soon saw the mistake of permitting Americans to homestead in Texas and tried to discourage further settlement by making it unpleasant for those already there, thus precipitating the Texas War for Independence. After operating as an independent republic for nearly a decade, Texas was annexed by the United States. In the Mexican War which followed, the United States was victorious. Mexico then ceded to the United States all territory in dispute, established the Rio Grande as the southern boundary of Texas, and sold her the southwestern territories including California. In 1853, the Gadsden Purchase was negotiated to extend the boundary of the United States south of the Gila River.

In Oregon, the claims of the United States and England conflicted. The former demanded the territory as far north as the southern boundary of Alaska, 54° 40′, on the basis of exploration by fur traders and by Lewis and Clark. England claimed the entire region because her trappers had descended the Fraser and Columbia Rivers. The United States dispatched settlers over the Oregon Trail to clinch her claims. England also joined the race. The two countries compromised, however, on the 49th parallel, which had already been agreed upon as the boundary, from the Lake of the Woods to the Rocky Mountains. This boundary was projected across the mountains without regard to relief. The only exception in the use of that parallel is Vancouver Island in British Columbia.

The purchase of Alaska from Russia in 1867 completed the acquisition of territory by the United States on the mainland of Anglo-America. The Hawaiian Islands were annexed by request in 1898, and achieved statehood in 1959.

The Formation of the Dominion of Canada

At the close of the French and Indian War, Canada became a part of the British Empire. Unlike the English colonies to the south, Canada remained loyal to Britain. The War of 1812 was largely a war between the United States and British Canada. At its close, the two countries agreed to abolish all fortifications along their common border and to maintain no navies on the Great Lakes. Since then, only customs houses mark the boundary between these two great nations on the longest unguarded international boundary in the world.

As England extended her domain to the Pacific Ocean, need was felt for some type of home government. In 1867, the Dominion of Canada was organized. This included all of British North America north of the United States except Newfoundland and its colony, Labrador. In 1949, Newfoundland became a province of the Dominion of Canada.

In recent years Canada has attained virtual independence from the British Empire. It is an autonomous state—a rich and powerful unit in the Commonwealth of Nations. With Anglo-America occupied and developed by two of the major English-speaking nations of the World, the United States of America and the Dominion of Canada, it seems certain that they will be drawn more closely together in the future. Their problems are largely the same in time of peace as well as in time of war.

Index

Index

Atwood, Wallace W., 70, 316, 495
Automobile assembly, Southern California, 397
Automotive Industry, 12, 51-53
Avalon Peninsula, 250
Avocados:
    Humid Subtropical Coast, 195
    Southern California, 390

B

Bailey, R. Y., 118
Baltimore, 124, 128
Banks fishing, 84-85
Barre, Vermont, 90
Barrow, Alaska, 487
Barrows, Harlan H., 220
Basin and Range Province, 340-42
Basing point system, 42
Baton Rouge, 204, 209
Bauxite:
    Arkansas, 180
    Hawaii, 429
    Humid Subtropical Coast, 207
Bay of Fundy, 76
Baytown, Texas, 208
Beaches, forming of, Hawaiian Islands, 425
Beale, Calvin L., 5
Beaumont, Texas, 209
Beaver, 254, 256, 257
Bedford-Bloomington, Indiana, 240
Beets, 195
Bell Island, Newfoundland, 92, 249
Berkshire Hills, 69
"Big Muddy," 227
"Big Steel," 30
Bingham, Utah, 367
Biological life zones of California, map, 413
Birmingham, Alabama, 152-53
Bisbee, Arizona, 369
Bishop, Texas, 206, 207
Black Belt:
    agriculture, 165-66
    livestock, 175
    soil, 162-63
Black Hills, South Dakota:
    mining, 309, 310
    resorts, 313
Black Prairie:
    agriculture, 166-67
    soil, 162-63
Black Warrior River, 152-53
Blueberries, 80
Blue Grass area, 217, 219, 223
Blue Grass Basin, 233
Blue Mountain area, 353-54

Blue Ridge–Great Smoky Mountains:
    agriculture, 140-41
    environment, 133
    manufacturing, 152-53
    recreation, 156
    resorts, 156
    settlement, 137
Blue Ridge Parkway, 156
Blumenstock, David I., 427
Bogue, Donald J., 5
Boll weevil, 164
Bonneville Dam, 457
"Boreal," 412
Boston, 38
Boston and Albany Railway, 12
Boundary claims, U.S. and Canada, 506
Bowman, Isaiah, 6
Braceros, 170
Bradley, Virginia, 203
Bradford cattle, 113-14
Brebner, J. B., 73
Bridger, Jim, 349
British Columbia, manufacturing, 457-58
British Columbia Forest-Management Act, 453
Brown, Ralph H., 137
Brush, W. D., 269
Bryce Canyon National Park, 375
Buchans, Mines, 250
Buffalo, 287, 289
Buffalo, New York, 30-31, 44, 45, 240
Bureau of Indian Affairs, forest conservation, 453
Bureau of Land Management, 364, 453
Bureau of Reclamation, 227, 303
Burin Peninsula, Newfoundland, 250
Burlingame, Roger, 52
Burner, Clifford J., 454
Butte-Anaconda District, Montana, 324-25

C

Cabbages, Humid Subtropical Coast, 195
Cabeza de Vaca, 501
Cabrillo, 385
California (See also Southern California):
    biological life zones, map, 413
    Gold Rush, 443, 445
    population growth, 384
    precipitation, map, 383
Camel caravan, 373
Canada, formation of, 506

Canadian National Railway, 250, 266
Canadian Pacific Railway, 289
Canadian Rockies, summer tourism, 333-34
Canadians, French (See French Canadians)
Canadian Shield, 46-47, 214, 251, 252, 253
Canids, 254
Cape Breton, coal, 89
Cape Canaveral, Florida, 210
Cape Cod, 79-80, 95
Cape Cod Canal, 95
Caraquet, New Brunswick, 86
Cariboo Gold Rush, 444
Caribou, 479-80
Carlsbad Caverns, 313
Carmel, California, 421
Carrots, Humid Subtropical Coast, 195
Carter, Douglas B., 441
Cascade Range, 439-40
Catawba River, 121
Cattle, beef, 113-14
    Agricultural Interior, 220, 221, 235
    Brahman, 198, 199
    Central Valley, 409
    crossbreeding, 198, 199
    crossbreeding, Imperial Valley, 357
    distribution of, map, 237
    Great Plains, 289, 290, 306-8
    Greenland, 485
    Hawaii, 432
    Humid Subtropical Coast, 190
    Intermontane Basins and Plateaus, 350, 365-66
    introduction of, Great Plains, 287
    overgrazing, 305
    Rocky Mountains, 328
    Santa Gertrudis, 198-99
    shipping to market, Great Plains, 308
    typical ranch, Great Plains, 307-8
    working on the range, Great Plains, 308
    Zebu, 198
Cattle, dairy:
    Agricultural Interior, 236-38
    Central Valley, 409
Celanese Corporation of America, 206, 207
Celery, Humid Subtropical Coast, 195
Celotex, 192
Central Coast:
    agriculture, 416-19